W9-BZA-469

7TH EDITION

CRIMINAL BEHAVIOR

A PSYCHOSOCIAL APPROACH

Curt R. Bartol
Anne M. Bartol

PEARSON
Prentice
Hall

Upper Saddle River, New Jersey 07458

Library of Congress Cataloging-in-Publication Data

Bartol, Curt R., 1940-
   Criminal behavior : a psychosocial approach.—7th ed. / Curt R. Bartol,
Anne M. Bartol.
      p. cm.
   Includes bibliographical references and indexes.
   ISBN 0-13-185049-0
   1. Criminal psychology. 2. Criminal behavior—United States. I. Bartol,
Anne M. II. Title.

   HV6080.B37 2005
   364.3—dc22

                                                        2004014139

Executive Editor: Frank Mortimer, Jr.
Assistant Editor: Korrine Dorsey
**Director of Manufacturing
   and Production:** Bruce Johnson
Managing Editor: Mary Carnis
Design Director: Cheryl Asherman
Production Liaison: Brian Hyland
Production Management: Susan Free,
   The GTS Companies, York, PA Campus

Manufacturing Buyer: Cathleen Petersen
Design Coordinator: Miguel Ortiz
Cover Design: de Phino Graphic Design
Cover Illustration: Getty Images/Photodisc Blue
Interior Design: Carol Sawyer, Rose Design
Copy Editor: Edith De Lay
Printer/Binder: Phoenix Book Tech

Copyright © 2005 by Pearson Education, Inc., Upper Saddle River, New Jersey 07458.
Pearson Prentice Hall. All rights reserved. Printed in the United States of America. This publication is protected by Copyright and permission should be obtained from the publisher prior to any prohibited reproduction, storage in a retrieval system, or transmission in any form or by any means, electronic, mechanical, photocopying, recording, or likewise. For information regarding permission(s), write to: Rights and Permissions Department.

Pearson Prentice Hall™ is a trademark of Pearson Education, Inc.
Pearson® is a registered trademark of Pearson plc
Prentice Hall® is a registered trademark of Pearson Education, Inc.

Pearson Education LTD.
Pearson Education Singapore, Pte. Ltd
Pearson Education, Canada, Ltd
Pearson Education–Japan

Pearson Education Australia PTY, Limited
Pearson Education North Asia Ltd
Pearson Educación de Mexico, S.A. de C.V.
Pearson Education Malaysia, Pte. Ltd.

10 9 8 7 6 5 4 3 2
ISBN 0-13-185049-0

To Madeleine
. . . because of everything you are and everything you will be

CONTENTS

Chapter 3

Origins of Criminal Behavior: Biological Factors   81

Chapter 4

The Psychopath: A Focus on Biopsychological Factors   118

CHAPTER 5

ORIGINS OF CRIMINAL BEHAVIOR: LEARNING AND SITUATIONAL FACTORS   162

CHAPTER 8

HOMICIDE, ASSAULT, AND FAMILY VIOLENCE   281

CHAPTER 9

CRIMINAL HOMICIDE: A CLOSER LOOK   326

Chapter 10

Sexual Offenses 368

Chapter 11

Economic Crime, Public Order Crime, and Other Crime 421

CHAPTER 12

DRUGS AND CRIME   479

CHAPTER 13

CORRECTIONAL PSYCHOLOGY   524

PREFACE

Criminal Behavior: A Psychosocial Approach is a textbook about crime from a psychological perspective. More specifically, this text portrays the criminal offender as embedded in and continually influenced by multiple systems within the psychosocial environment. One focus of this book is that meaningful theory, well-executed research, and skillful application of knowledge to the "crime problem" require an understanding of the many levels of events that influence a person's life course—from the individual to the individual's family, peers, schools, neighborhoods, community, culture, and society as a whole. Like earlier editions, the seventh edition views criminal offenders as existing on a continuum, ranging from serious, repetitive offenders who begin their criminal careers at a very early age to occasional offenders who offend at some point during their life course, usually during adolescence. The book reviews the contemporary research, theory, and practice concerning the psychology of crime as comprehensively and accurately as possible. The behavioral, emotional, and cognitive aspects of crime are examined, from the perspective of both the offender and the victim. The book also reviews current research that focuses on the cognitive aspects of criminal offenders, delving into their perceptions, reasoning, beliefs, decision making, and attitudes. The causes, classification, prediction, prevention, intervention, and treatment of criminal behavior are also examined.

The organization and structure of the text remain basically the same as in earlier editions. The organization of the text runs from the broad, theoretical aspects of crime to specific offense categories. Developmental and biopsychological positions are presented in the early chapters, whereas social learning and cognitive aspects come later. Nonetheless, many changes were made to reflect legislative and judicial trends, student interests, and rapidly expanding research and theory on the psychology of crime.

This edition includes completely rewritten chapters on mental disorders (Chapter 6), the psychopath (Chapter 4), and correctional psychology (Chapter 13). The chapter on drugs and crime (Chapter 12) has been extensively updated to include ever-changing trends in drug abuse and evolving survey research on that abuse. After the events of September 11, 2001, sections on international and domestic terrorism (including bioterrorism) were added to Chapters 1 and 9. The section Criminal profiling, on (Chapter 9) has been greatly expanded, rewritten, updated, and reorganized. Also added are sections on sniper attacks (Chapter 8), developmental risk factors for juvenile delinquency (Chapter 2), moral disengagement (Chapter 5), reactive and proactive forms of aggression (Chapter 7), same-sex domestic violence (Chapter 8), and missing, abducted, runaway, and thrown-away children (Chapter 8). The sections on the effects of mass media on aggression (Chapter 7), crime and physical anomalies (Chapter 3), gender differences in aggression, infanticide (Chapter 8), and robbery (Chapter 11) have been greatly expanded. Crime data and statistics have been updated and expanded throughout the text, and the number of tables, figures, and pedagogical aids has increased from that in the previous edition.

This text is designed to be a core text in undergraduate and graduate courses in criminal behavior, criminology, the psychology of crime, crime and delinquency, and forensic psychology. The book is heavily research-based and provides a readable summary of contemporary research in all areas of crime. Most of the research is presented within a theoretical context and thematic structure to give an organized flow to the coverage of the many topics. The book's major goal is to encourage an appreciation of the many complex issues surrounding criminal behavior and to avoid oversimplified, prejudicial, dogmatic conclusions about the "crime problem." If, after studying the text with an open mind, the reader puts it down seeking additional information, and if the reader has developed an avid interest in discovering better answers, then this text will have served its purpose well.

The material contained in this book has been classroom-tested for over 30 years. During those years, many students have made substantial contributions to the readability of the text and made numerous suggestions for the inclusion of topics of greatest interest from the student perspective.

ACKNOWLEDGMENTS

When the first edition of this book was published in 1980, the author was optimistic that it would be well received, due in good part to the expertise of the editorial and marketing folk at Prentice-Hall. Since then, various editors and staff have skillfully led *Criminal Behavior* through six subsequent editions. Special recognition is due Sharon Chambliss, the book's guardian angel over many years, but our deep gratitude goes to our publisher and all of its representatives.

This seventh edition was made possible with the competent assistance of Production Editor Korrine Dorsey, Project Manager Susan Free, Product Information Coordinator Patrice Tobin, and Marketing Coordinator Adam Kloza. Our copyeditor, Edith De Lay, whom we will remember fondly as "e," was—to put it simply—terrific.

Several reviewers of earlier editions suggested changes that have been incorporated here. The reviewers were Gai Berlage, Iona College, New Rochelle, NY; Audra Kallimanis, Mount Olive College, Mount Olive, NC; and William Kelly, Auburn University, Auburn, AL.

We are also grateful to those undergraduate and graduate psychology students at Castleton State College who have read versions of the chapters critically and suggested improvements. Over the past few years, four different classes of bright and personable graduate students have commented on sections of the book. Some have provided direct research assistance. Jen Trager, now a doctoral student in criminal justice, prepared an instructor's manual for the sixth edition as well as many of the summary tables that remain in this new edition. Meghan Hunt and Jillian Harrigan found new resources, filed interminably, and prepared figures and tables. Shelly Macumber, Erica O'Toole, Michael Bonner, Melissa Burbank, and Jeffrey Sandler all helped with tasks as varied as commenting on previous editions, answering phones, organizing correspondence, and house sitting.

As always, we are grateful for the support of family and friends, most particularly Gina and Jim, Ian and Soraya. With patience and a good dose of wacky humor, they tolerate the inconveniences that occur when we face deadlines on "the book." Above all, though, they have given us the two very best excuses for taking breaks from the writing routine, Kai Arman Bartol and Madeleine Riley Cook. Here's to love.

CHAPTER 1

INTRODUCTION TO CRIMINAL BEHAVIOR

Crime is commonly defined as conduct or failure to act, in violation of the law forbidding or commanding it, for which a range of possible penalties exists upon conviction. Criminal behavior, then, is behavior in violation of the criminal code. To be convicted of crime, a person must have acted intentionally and without justification or excuse. Although there is a very narrow range of offenses that do not require this criminal intent (called strict liability offenses), the vast majority of crime requires it. Obviously, this legal definition encompasses a great variety of acts, ranging from murder to petty offenses.

Crime intrigues people. Sometimes it attracts us; sometimes it repels us; occasionally it does both at once. It can amuse, as when we hear about capers and practical jokes that presumably do not harm anyone. It can frighten, if we believe that what happened to one victim might happen to us. Crime can also anger, as when a beloved community member is brutally killed. Violent crime, in particular, draws attention; consider the rampant excitement and fear in a neighborhood or small town when news of a local murder hits the street.

Although interest in crime has always been high, understanding why it occurs and what to do about it has always been a problem. Public officials, politicians, "experts," and many people in the general public continue to offer

1

simple and incomplete solutions for obliterating crime: more police officers on the streets, closed-circuit television, street lights, sturdy locks, karate classes, stiff penalties, speedy imprisonment, and capital punishment. Researchers often offer abstract interpretations and suggestions that have limited effects on crime rates. As in most areas of human behavior, there is no shortage of experts, but there are few effective solutions.

Our inability to prevent crime is partly because we have trouble understanding criminal behavior, a complex phenomenon. Because crime is complex, explanations of crime require complicated, involved answers. Psychological research indicates that most people have limited tolerance for complexity and ambiguity. People apparently want simple, straightforward answers, no matter how complex the issue. Parents become impatient when psychologists answer questions about child rearing by saying, "It depends"—on the situation, on the parents' reactions to it, on any number of possible variables. This preference for simplicity helps to explain the popularity of do-it-yourself, 100-easy-ways-to-a-better-life books. Let it be said from the outset: This is not *Criminal Behavior for Dummies*.

This text presents criminal behavior as a vastly complex, poorly understood phenomenon. Readers looking for simple solutions will have to either reorient their thinking, set the text aside, or read it in dismay. There is no all-encompassing psychological explanation for crime, any more than there is a sociological, anthropological, psychiatric, economic, or historical one. In fact, it is unlikely that sociology, psychology, or any other discipline can formulate basic "truths" about crime without help from other disciplines and areas of research. Criminology needs all the interdisciplinary help it can get to explain and control criminal behavior. An integration of the data, theories, and general viewpoints of each discipline is crucial. However, to review accurately and adequately the plethora of studies and theories from each relevant discipline is far beyond the scope of this text. Our focus is the psychological perspective, although other viewpoints are also described.

The psychology of crime is really a subdivision of the general field of forensic psychology, and forensic psychology itself is one of the forensic sciences. The term *forensic* refers generally to anything pertaining to the law or the courts of justice, and it encompasses both criminal and civil law. Consequently, *forensic science* is the scientific study of issues, incidents, and evidence in relation to legal principles and cases. Examples of forensic science include forensic engineering, forensic linguistics (language), forensic medicine, forensic pathology, forensic psychiatry, and forensic psychology. Another commonly encountered term is *forensic laboratory*. Forensic laboratories are usually maintained or sponsored by governmental agencies specifically to examine physical evidence in criminal and civil matters and are expected to provide testimony on the physical evidence in a court of law. Forensic laboratories, for example, may be asked to examine latent fingerprints, firearms, explosives and fire debris, toxic materials, and other pertinent evidence found at or near the crime scene and then may be expected to provide expert testimony to the court.

Forensic psychology refers broadly to the production and application of psychological knowledge to the civil and criminal justice systems. It includes such areas as police psychology, the psychology of crime and delinquency (the main subject matter of this text), correctional psychology (including institutional and community corrections), psychology and law, victim services, and the delivery and evaluation of intervention and treatment programs for juvenile and adult offenders. Forensic psychology is a rapidly emerging field of both academic study and professional application.

The primary aim of this text is to review and integrate recent scholarship and research in the psychology of crime, compare it with traditional approaches, and offer a theoretical framework for the study of crime. We cannot begin to do this task without first calling attention to philosophical questions that underlie any study of human behavior.

PERSPECTIVES ON HUMAN NATURE IN THEORIES OF CRIME

All psychological theories of crime—and many sociological ones as well—have underlying assumptions about or perspectives on human nature. Three major ones can be identified (see **Table 1–1**). The **conformity perspective** views humans as creatures of conformity who want to do the "right" thing. To a large extent, this assumption represents the foundation of the humanistic perspectives in psychology. Human beings are basically "good" people trying to live to their fullest potential.

An excellent example of the conformity perspective in criminology is the **strain theory** of Robert K. Merton. Merton's strain theory argues that humans are fundamentally conforming beings who are strongly influenced by the values and attitudes of the society in which they live. In short, most members of a given society desire what the other members of the society desire. The "right" thing, therefore, is what a society or a group within a society says is the "right" thing. American society, according to strain theorists, advocates that the accumulation of wealth or status is all-important and represents the

TABLE 1–1 Perspectives on Human Nature

PERSPECTIVES ON BEHAVIOR	THEORY EXAMPLE	HUMANS ARE . . .
Conformity perspective	Strain theory (Merton)	Basically good; strongly influenced by the values and attitudes of society
Nonconformist perspective	Social control theory (Hirschi) Biological theories of crime	Basically undisciplined; individual's ties to social order are weak; innate tendencies must be controlled by society
Learning perspective	Differential association theory (Sutherland) Social learning theory (Rotter, Bandura)	Born neutral; behavior is learned through social interactions with other people

symbols that all members should strive for. Strain theorists contend that humans, being fundamentally conformists, readily buy into these notions. However, access and the means for reaching these well-advertised goals are not equally available to everyone. Some have the education, social network, personal contacts, and family influence to attain these goals. The socially and economically disadvantaged, however, do not have the opportunities, the education, or the necessary social network for attaining material wealth and economic or political power. Thus, the strain theory predicts that crime and delinquency occur when there is a perceived discrepancy between the materialistic values and goals cherished and held in high esteem by a society and the availability of the legitimate means for reaching these goals. Under these conditions, a strain between the goals of wealth and power and the means for reaching them develops. Groups and individuals experiencing a high level of this strain are forced to decide whether to violate norms and laws to attain some of this sought-after wealth or power or to give up on the American dream and go through the motions, withdraw, or rebel. In more recent years, strain theorists have emphasized that crimes of the rich and powerful also can be explained by strain theory. Even though these individuals have greater access to the legitimate means of reaching goals, they have a continuing need to accumulate even greater wealth and power and maintain their privileged status in society (Messner & Rosenfeld, 1994).

The second perspective—the **nonconformist perspective**—assumes that human beings are basically undisciplined creatures who, without the constraints of the rules and regulations of a given society, would flout society's conventions and commit crime indiscriminately. This perspective sees humans as fundamentally "unruly" and deviant if allowed to do what they feel like doing. Good illustrations of this perspective are found in biological and neurobiological theories, discussed in Chapters 3 and 4, and in Travis Hirschi's **social control theory**, discussed in several chapters. Social control theory contends that crime and delinquency occur when an individual's ties to the conventional order or normative standards are weak or largely nonexistent. In other words, the socialization that normally holds one's basic human nature in check is incomplete or faulty. This position perceives human nature as fundamentally "bad" or "antisocial," an innate tendency that must be controlled by society.

The third perspective—the **learning perspective**—sees humans as being born neutral (neither inherently conforming nor unruly). This perspective argues that humans learn virtually all their behavior, beliefs, and tendencies from the social environment. The learning perspective is exemplified most comprehensively by **social learning theory**, a main topic in Chapter 5, and Edwin H. Sutherland's **differential association theory**. According to differential association theory, criminal behavior is learned, as is all social behavior, through social interactions with other people. It is not the result of emotional disturbance, mental illness, or innate qualities of "goodness" or "badness." Rather, people learn to be criminal as a result of messages or "definitions" they get from others. Consequently, an excess of messages favorable to law violation over unfavorable messages promotes criminal activity. The conventional wisdom that bad company promotes bad behavior, therefore, finds validity in differential association theory. On the other hand, definitions favorable to law violation also may be obtained from associations with law-abiding individuals. Consider the comment, "Everybody cheats a little on taxes."

PERSPECTIVES IN CRIMINOLOGY

Criminology is the multidisciplinary study of crime. Many disciplines are involved in the collection of knowledge about criminal action, including psychology, sociology, psychiatry, anthropology, biology, neurology, political science, and economics. Over the years, the study of crime has been dominated by three disciplines—sociology, psychology, and psychiatry—but other disciplines or subdisciplines are becoming more actively involved. For example, criminal anthropology—a subdiscipline of sociology—is rapidly emerging as an active participant (Rafter, 1992).

Although our main concern in this text is with *psychological principles*, concepts, theory, and research relevant to criminal behavior, considerable attention is given to the research knowledge of the other disciplines, particularly sociology and psychiatry. Again, criminology needs all the help it can get in its struggle to understand, explain, and prevent criminal behavior.

It is not easy to make sharp demarcations between disciplines, because they overlap considerably in focus. For example, what distinguishes a given theory as sociological, psychological, or psychiatric is sometimes simply the stated professional affiliation of its proponent. The reader should also realize that condensing any major discipline into a few pages hardly does it justice. To obtain a more adequate overview, the interested reader should consult texts and articles within those disciplines.

Sociological Criminology

Sociological criminology has a rich tradition in examining the relationships of demographic and group variables to crime. Variables such as age, race, gender, socioeconomic status, interpersonal relationships, and ethnic-cultural affiliation have been shown to have significant relationships with certain categories and patterns of crimes (see **Table 1–2**). Sociological criminology, for example, has allowed us to conclude that young, African American males from disadvantaged backgrounds are disproportionately overrepresented as perpetrators and victims of homicide. The many reasons for this overrepresentation are reflected in the various perspectives and research findings that are covered in the book. Sociological criminology also probes the situational or environmental factors that are most conducive to criminal action, such as the time, place, kind of weapons used, and circumstances surrounding the crime.

TABLE 1–2 Major Perspectives in Criminology

PERSPECTIVE	INFLUENCE	FOCUS
Sociological criminology	Sociology	Examines relationships of demographic and group variables to crime; focuses on groups and society as a whole and how they influence criminal activity
Psychological criminology	Psychology	Focuses on individual criminal behavior; the science of the behavior and mental processes of the criminal
Psychiatric criminology	Psychiatry	The contemporary perspective examines the interplay between psychobiological determinants of behavior and the social environment; traditional perspective looks for the unconscious and biological determinants of criminal behavior

A major contribution of sociological criminology, however, is the attention it directs to topics that reflect unequal power distribution in society. This often takes the form of examining how crime is defined and how laws are enforced. It also addresses the underlying social conditions that may affect crime rates and encourage criminal behavior, such as inequities in educational and employment opportunities. Conflict theories in sociology are particularly influential in questioning how crime is defined and who is subject to punishment and in attempting to draw attention to the crimes of the rich and powerful.

Psychological Criminology

Psychology is the science of behavior and mental processes. **Psychological criminology**, then, is the science of the behavior and mental processes of the criminal. Whereas sociological criminology focuses on groups and society as a whole and how they influence criminal activity, psychological criminology focuses on individual criminal behavior—how it is acquired, evoked, maintained, and modified (Table 1–2). Both social and personality influences on criminal behavior are considered, along with the mental processes that mediate that behavior. Personality refers to all the biological influences, psychological traits, and cognitive features of the human being that psychologists have identified as important in the mediation and control of behavior. Recently, psychological criminology has shifted its focus to the cognitive aspects of offending. **Cognitions** refer to the attitudes, beliefs, values and thoughts that a person holds about the environment, interrelations, and him- or herself. Psychological criminology also examines and evaluates prevention, intervention, and treatment strategies that have been tried in reducing criminal behavior. However, sociological criminology does this as well.

In the past, psychologists assumed that they could best understand human behavior by searching for stable, consistent personality **dispositions** or **traits** that exerted widely generalized effects on behavior. A trait or disposition is a relatively stable and enduring tendency to behave in a particular way, and it distinguishes one person from another. For example, one person may be extroverted and have a consistent tendency to socialize and meet others, whereas another may be shy and introverted and demonstrate a tendency to socialize with only very close friends. Trait theories hold that people show consistent behavior across time and place and that these behaviors characterize personality. Many psychologists studying crime, therefore, assumed they should search for the personality traits or variables underlying criminal behavior. They paid little attention to the person's environment or situation. Presumably, once personality variables were identified, it would be possible to determine and predict which individual was most likely to engage in criminal behavior.

As you will learn, the search for any single personality type of the murderer, rapist, or burglar has not been fruitful. Contemporary psychology today has moved away from a trait approach to a more cognitive-based approach. Psychologists who provide law enforcement agencies with profiles of the rapist still at large, based solely on personality variables, are at best engaging in unvalidated clinical judgment and unsubstantiated hunches. However, psychologists can offer statistical probability about some demographic and behavioral patterns of certain offenders. For example, they might determine, roughly, that a rapist is probably young, white, unemployed, from the area, and so forth. They might also offer possible motives for the attack, based on research findings and accompanied by the necessary caveats. This "profile" information, however, is based on the collected knowledge from all sectors of criminology, including psychology, sociology, anthropology, psychiatry, political science, history, and economics. The mission of this book is to provide this interdisciplinary knowledge.

Thus, although trait psychology standing alone has lost favor, some aspects of this approach have survived, primarily in the profiling endeavor. **Criminal profiling** refers to the process of identifying personality traits, behavioral tendencies, geographical location, and demographic variables of an offender based on characteristics of the crime (Bartol & Bartol, 2004a, 2004b). To a very large extent, the profiling process is dictated by a database collected on previous offenders who have committed similar offenses. Currently, profiling is at least 90% an art based on speculation and only 10% science. It should be emphasized early in this text that criminal profiling is not restricted to serial murder or serial sexual assaults but has considerable value when applied successfully to property crimes, including arson, burglary, shoplifting, and robbery. Criminal profiling is covered in more detail in Chapter 9.

Reconstruction of the personality profile and cognitive features (especially intentions) of deceased individuals has gained increasing popularity over the past two decades. This postmortem (after death) psychological analysis is technically called **reconstructive psychological evaluation** or **equivocal death analysis** (Poythress, Otto, Darkes, & Starr, 1993). However, the more common term—and the one we use in this text—is **psychological autopsy**

(Brent, 1989; Ebert, 1987; Selkin, 1987). The psychological autopsy differs from criminal profiling in two important ways: (1) the profile is constructed on a dead person, and (2) the identity of the person is already known.

The psychological autopsy was first used to help authorities certify the cause of deaths that were initially ambiguous or uncertain as to the *manner* of how the person died (Shneidman, 1994). The term manner is emphasized in this context because it has special significance in death investigations. Manner refers to the *specific circumstances* in which death results. There are five specific circumstances in which death may occur: natural, accidental, suicide, homicide, and undetermined (La Fon, 2002). Today, the term psychological autopsy is usually reserved for investigative attempts to discover what may have been in the mind of the deceased person leading up to and at the time of death, especially if the death seems to be suicide. In most instances, the psychological autopsy is conducted by a trained psychologist, who, through interviews of family members, co-workers and friends, and a variety of psychological assessment measures, tries to reconstruct the cognitive processes of the deceased before the death. Note the emphasis on cognitive processes rather than on psychological traits. The vast majority of psychological autopsies are done in the United States, usually in civil or criminal litigation (D. Canter, 1999). In many civil cases relating to suicide, the psychologist is asked to reconstruct the possible reasons for a suicide to help establish legal culpability on the part of other persons or organizations (Bartol & Bartol, 2004a). For example, an organization may be held responsible if it can be established that its procedures, lack of health services, or workload led to stress levels that resulted in the eventual suicide of one of its workers.

Psychiatric Criminology

The terms *psychology* and *psychiatry* are often confused by the layperson and even by professionals and scholars in other disciplines. Psychiatric concepts and theories are often believed to be accepted tenets in the field of psychology. The two professions often see things quite differently and approach explanations of criminal behavior along a different course. Part of this difference is due to the dissimilarity in the education requirements for the two professions. Unlike psychologists, who have earned the degree Ph.D. (Doctor of Philosophy), Psy.D. (Doctor of Psychology), or, in some cases, Ed.D. (Doctor of Education), and who often complete specialized training in research and some area of psychology, psychiatrists first earn a medical degree (M.D.; or a D.O., Doctor of Osteopathy) and complete a medical internship, as other physicians do. Then, during a two- or three-year residency program, they receive specific training in psychiatry, often focusing on the diagnosis and treatment of individuals in forensic settings. Understandably, this medical training encourages a biochemical and neurological approach to the explanation of human behavior, and this is often reflected in the psychiatric theories of criminal behavior.

Many psychologists receive a one-year internship focusing on clinical training, which is often followed by a one- to three-year postdoctoral program focusing on both research and practice. In a majority of cases, the psychologist completes these training steps before practicing professionally. The emphasis of this training is usually far more on the cognitive (thought processes) and learned behavior of human action and less on the biochemical or neurological influences.

Traditionally, psychologists have not been permitted by law to prescribe medication to patients. However, this distinction between the two professions is beginning to disappear. On March 6, 2002, New Mexico became the first state in the United States to allow psychologists to prescribe psychoactive drugs (drugs designed to treat psychological problems). Several other states currently have pending legislation on prescription privileges for psychologists, and it is likely that in the years to come, properly trained psychologists will be able to prescribe psychoactive drugs in nearly all—if not all—the states.

American **psychiatric criminology**, sometimes called **forensic psychiatry**, has *traditionally* followed the Freudian, psychoanalytic, or psychodynamic tradition. The father of the psychoanalytical theory of human behavior was the physician–neurologist Sigmund Freud (1856–1939), whose followers are called Freudians. Many contemporary psychoanalysts subscribe to a modified version of the orthodox Freudian position and are therefore called neo-Freudians. Still other psychoanalysts follow the tenets of Alfred Adler (1870–1937) and Carl Jung (1875–1961), who broke away from Freud and formed schools of their own.

Collectively, all psychoanalytic positions form the psychodynamic school, which explains behavior in terms of motives and drives. This perspective views human nature as innately antisocial. That is, humans are biologically driven to get what they want when they want it unless they are held in check by internal (conscience) and external (society) forces. Without an organized society with rules and laws, humans (especially men, because of their biology) would aggress, plunder, steal, and even kill at will.

The psychoanalytic position assumes that we must delve into the abyss of human personality to find unconscious determinants of human behavior, including criminal behavior (Table 1–2). Consider the following comments by two psychiatrists. "The criminal rarely knows completely the reasons for his conduct" (Abrahamsen, 1952, p. 21). "Every criminal is such by reason of unconscious forces within him . . ." (Roche, 1958, p. 25). Psychoanalytic and psychodynamic theories acknowledge that behavior varies across situations. However, they conclude that there are enduring and generalized underlying dynamic or motivational dispositions that account for this diversity. "Surface" behaviors indirectly signal or symbolize dynamic, underlying attributes. Psychological defenses distort and disguise the "true" meaning of external or observed behaviors. The trained clinician, therefore, must interpret the significance of these external behaviors, because the actor is not aware of their purpose.

The Freudian, psychoanalytic, and psychodynamic positions strongly endorse the view that the prime determinant of human behavior lies within the person and that after the first few years of life the environment plays a very minor role. Consequently, criminal behavior is believed to spring from within, primarily dictated by the biological urges of the unconscious. The environment, culture, or society cannot be held responsible for crime rates; biopsychological needs and urges within the individual are the culprits.

It would be unfair, however, to simply classify contemporary psychiatric criminology as heavily Freudian or psychoanalytical. Contemporary psychiatric criminology is far more diverse, increasingly research based, and considerably less steeped in the traditional belief that criminals are acting out their uncontrolled animalistic, unconscious, or biological urges. Therefore, *traditional* psychiatric criminology is distinguished from *contemporary* psychiatric criminology throughout the text. The traditional psychiatric view represents the biological unconscious urges that drive humans, whereas the contemporary psychiatric view of crime represents the diverse and rich knowledge gained through research and clinical experience. Whenever possible, we rely on the more contemporary view of psychiatric criminology in this text.

DEFINITION OF CRIMINAL BEHAVIOR

In a text of this nature, one initial task must be to define criminal behavior and determine the object of our study. It is not easy to do this, since we are confronted with definitional as well as methodological dilemmas. Not only must we decide how to define crime and the criminal, but also we must struggle with the many statistical problems associated with crime reporting and interpretation.

As defined earlier in the chapter, criminal behavior is intentional behavior that violates a criminal code, intentional in that it did not occur accidentally or without justification or excuse. Because crime encompasses so many types of behavior, should we restrict ourselves to a legal definition and study only those individuals who have been convicted of behaviors legally defined as crime? Or should we include individuals who indulge in antisocial behaviors but have not been detected by the criminal justice system? Perhaps our study should include persons predisposed to be criminal, if such persons can be identified. As a review of criminology textbooks and literature attests, there is no universal agreement as to what group or groups should be targeted for study.

If we abide strictly by the legal definition of crime (see the first paragraph of this chapter) and base research and discussion only on those people who have committed crimes, do we consider only those who have been convicted and incarcerated or are serving a sentence in the community, or do we include those who have probably broken the criminal law but are not convicted? Even by conservative estimates, 16% to 18% of the total U.S. population have arrest records for nontraffic offenses (U.S. Department of Justice,

1988). Although some of these individuals are "truly criminal," an undetermined number of others were arrested but were not truly guilty. Furthermore, how can we include individuals who violate the law but escape detection or those who come to the attention of law enforcement officials but are never arrested?

Trying to study criminal behavior on the basis of incidence presents other problems for social scientists. The incidence of crime is usually measured in one of three ways:

1. Official police reports of reported crime and arrests, such as those tabulated and forwarded to the FBI for publication in its annual national statistical report on crime, the Uniform Crime Reports (UCR)
2. Self-report studies, whereby members of a sample population are asked what offenses they have committed and how often
3. National or regional victimization studies, which sample a population of households or businesses, asking respondents how often they have been victims of specified crimes

FBI REPORTING SYSTEMS

Uniform Crime Reporting System

The Federal Bureau of Investigation's **Uniform Crime Reporting** (UCR) Program, compiled since 1930, is the most cited source of U.S. crime statistics. The UCR Program publishes an annual document containing accounts of crimes known to police and arrest information received on a voluntary basis from local and state law enforcement agencies throughout the United States. The UCR data are available at the FBI Web site (*www.fbi.gov*). Interestingly, federal law enforcement agencies do not report through the traditional UCR Program, although a newly revised reporting system has been implemented that requires federal agencies to report. This new system, called the *National Incident-Based Reporting System*, is described shortly.

The first UCR data were published with fewer than a thousand agencies reporting. The 2002 UCR data collection was based on over 17,000 city, county, and state law enforcement agencies, representing about 95% of the U.S. population (Federal Bureau of Investigation, 2003). The UCR Program is the only major data source permitting a comparison of national data broken down by age, sex, race, and offense. A *Supplementary Homicide Report* contains data on victim and offender demographics, the offender–victim relationship, the weapon used, and the circumstances surrounding the homicide. Additionally, the FBI provides special reports on hate crimes, campus crimes, and law enforcement officers killed in the line of duty. Special reports have also been prepared on bank robbery, sniper attacks from 1982 to 2001, and the events of 9/11.

The UCR divides data in a number of ways, including by age, gender, and race of person arrested and by city and region of the country where the crime was committed. Crimes are also categorized according to seriousness. Serious crimes are called **index crimes** (or **Part I crimes**), nonserious crimes are **nonindex crimes** (or **Part II crimes**). However, this distinction can be misleading. For instance, larceny-theft, which includes shoplifting, is categorized as an index crime, whereas fraud and drug offenses are classified as nonindex crimes. Examples of nonindex crimes include vandalism, carrying weapons, and buying, receiving, and possessing stolen property. **Table 1–3** contains definitions of both index and nonindex crimes reported in the UCR. These definitions are not necessarily legally precise but are primarily broad classifications created by the FBI for statistical reporting purposes. **Figure 1–1** shows the proportion of the entire index that each of the eight index crimes represents.

In order to be recorded in the UCR, a crime must, at a minimum, meet the following requirements:

- Be perceived by the victim or by someone else
- Be defined as a crime by the victim or the observer
- In some way become known to a law enforcement agency as a crime
- Be defined by that law enforcement agency as a crime
- Be accurately recorded by the law enforcement agency
- Be reported to the FBI compilation center

FIGURE 1–1   Percentage Distribution of Index Crimes, 2002

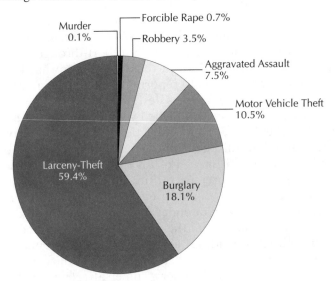

Source: Federal Bureau of Investigation (2003, p. 11).

TABLE 1–3 Definitions of Index Crimes and Nonindex Crimes in Uniform Crime Reports

INDEX CRIME

Murder and nonnegligent manslaughter	The willful (nonnegligent) killing of one human being by another
Forcible rape	The carnal knowledge of a female forcibly and against her will. Included are assaults and attempts to commit rape by force or threat of force. Statutory rape (without force) and other sex offenses are excluded.
Robbery	The taking or attempting to take anything of value from the care, custody, or control of a person or persons by force or threat of force or violence and/or by putting the victim in fear
Aggravated assault	An unlawful attack by one person on another for the purpose of inflicting severe or aggravated bodily injury. This type of assault is usually accompanied by the use of a weapon or by means likely to produce death or great bodily harm. Attempts to inflict injury are included.
Burglary	The unlawful entry of a structure to commit a felony or theft. There are three classifications: forcible entry, unlawful entry where no force is used, and attempted forcible entry.
Larceny-theft	The unlawful taking, carrying, leading, or riding away of property from the possession or constructive possession of another. It includes crimes such as shoplifting, pocket picking, purse snatching, thefts from motor vehicles, thefts of motor vehicle parts and accessories, and bicycle thefts.
Motor vehicle theft	The theft or attempted theft of a motor vehicle, including the stealing of automobiles, trucks, buses, motorcycles, motorscooters, and snowmobiles
Arson	Any willful or malicious burning or attempt to burn, with or without intent to defraud, a dwelling house, public building, motor vehicle or aircraft, or personal property of another

COMMON NONINDEX CRIMES

Other assaults (simple)	Assaults and attempted assaults in which no weapon is used and that do not result in serious or aggravated injury to victim
Forgery and counterfeiting	Making, altering, uttering, or possessing, with intent to defraud, anything false in the semblance of that which is true
Fraud	Fraudulent conversion and obtaining money or property by false pretenses
Embezzlement	Misappropriation or misapplication of money or property entrusted to one's care, custody, or control
Stolen property: Buying, receiving, possessing	Buying, receiving, and possessing stolen property, including attempts
Offenses against the family and children	Nonsupport, neglect, desertion, or abuse of family and children
Drug abuse violations	State and/or local offenses relating to the unlawful possession, sale, use, growing, and manufacturing of drugs
Sex offenses (except forcible rape, prostitution, and commercialized vice)	Statutory rape and offenses against chastity, common decency, and morals
Gambling	Promoting, permitting, or engaging in illegal gambling
Vandalism	Willful or malicious destruction, injury, disfigurement, or defacement of any public or private property, real or personal, without consent of the owner or persons having custody or control

Source: Adapted from FBI (1997).

It should be emphasized, though, that the UCR provides *crime report data* on only the eight index, or Part I, crimes. *Arrest data* are provided for both index and nonindex crimes. For example, both the report of a burglary (an index crime) and the arrest of one or more individuals for burglary would be recorded in the UCR reports. If a victim reports a simple assault (a nonindex crime), that would not be recorded; however, *arrests* of individuals for simple assault would be. This is a critically important distinction, because the crime rate—the percentage of crimes known to police per 100,000 population—is therefore presented only for index crimes. The violent crime rate is based on four index violent crimes (murder, forcible rape, robbery, and aggravated assault), and the nonviolent or property crime rate is based on three index property crimes (burglary, larceny-theft, and motor vehicle theft). Because of limited reporting of arson offenses by law enforcement, arson data are not included in the property crime rate.

Crime has decreased significantly in recent years. When looking at five- and ten-year trends, the 2001 total crime index figure represents a 10% decrease from the 1997 figure and an 18% decline from the 1992 level (Federal Bureau of Investigation, 2002). In 2001, the estimated total number of index offenses known to police was approximately 11.8 million.

It should be emphasized that the events of September 11, 2001, are not included in the UCR Program's offense rate, trend, or clearance data for that year. The events of that day were so unusual and the number of deaths so high (approximately 3,047 victims), that inclusion of the data would have skewed data analysis for 2001 as well as years to come. The FBI did, though, issue a special report that accompanied the typical homicide reports for that year.

The crime index *rate* (the number of index offenses known to police per 100,000 U.S. residents) continues to decrease. The crime index rate per 100,000 inhabitants in 2002 was 4,118.5, reflecting a 1.1% decrease from the 2001 rate, a 10.9% decline from the 1998 rate, and a 24.9% rate decline from the 1993 rate (Federal Bureau of Investigation, 2003). In 2002, violent crime accounted for about 12% and property crimes accounted for about 88% of the total crime index. As we noted above, these rates refer to very specific crimes and do not include crimes listed as Part II offenses.

On a regular yearly basis, the property crime of larceny-theft, which usually comprises approximately 60% of the total crime index, is the most frequently occurring of all index crimes (see Fig. 1–1). The violent crime of murder occurs the least frequently of all index crimes, accounting for only 0.1% of the total crime index.

An estimated monetary value of $16.6 billion in stolen property was reported in 2002 (Federal Bureau of Investigation, 2003). Among individual property crime, the 2002 estimated dollar losses were $3.3 billion for burglary, $4.9 billion for larceny-theft, and $8.4 billion for motor vehicle theft. Approximately one-third of all stolen property is eventually recovered. Property types with the greatest percentage of recoveries are motor vehicles, clothing and furs, livestock, and consumable goods.

The UCR also reports the **clearance rate** of all index crimes. The clearance rate refers to the *proportion* of reported crimes that have been solved through arrests or through exceptional means (such as the death of a suspect). The FBI (Federal Bureau of Investigation, 2000, p. 201) considers a crime cleared "when at least one person is arrested, charged with the commission of an offense, and turned over to the court for prosecution." When these or exceptional means criteria are met, "the reporting law enforcement agency clears or solves that particular offense for UCR purposes." For persons under age 18, "a clearance by arrest is recorded when an offender under 18 years of age is cited to appear in juvenile court or before other juvenile authorities, even though nonphysical arrest may have occurred" (p. 201). Nationwide, the average crime index clearance rate is about 20% (Federal Bureau of Investigation, 2003). The clearance rate in 2002 was 46.8% for violent crimes and 16.5% for property crimes, excluding arson (Federal Bureau of Investigation, 2003). The clearance rate was highest for murder (64.0%) and lowest for burglary (13.0%) (see **Table 1–4**). It should be noted that a clearance rate is not the same as a conviction rate; because the UCR represents only police data, what occurs later in the criminal process (e.g., the prosecutor's dropping of charges or the acquittal of a criminal defendant) is not taken into consideration.

UCR data are not without problems. One of the most frequently mentioned shortcomings is the *hierarchy rule*, which stipulates that, when a number of offenses have been committed during a series, only the more serious offense should be reported. For example, if an offender robs a bank, viciously assaults a bystander, steals a car, and murders the bank security officer, only the murder will be reported in the UCR data.

The compilation center also relies on the accuracy and compliance of local and state agencies to report crime statistics. The data also do not consider early discretionary decision making by law enforcement officers, such as a decision not to "found" a crime when it is reported by a member of the public or a decision not to arrest an individual. In addition, the index category emphasizes street crime, to the neglect of the equally serious "white-collar" crime, which includes a wide variety of offenses such as corporate, political, and professional crimes.

TABLE 1–4   2002 Clearance Rates for Index Crimes

Arson	17%
Aggravated assault	57%
Burglary	13%
Forcible rape	45%
Larceny-theft	18%
Motor vehicle theft	14%
Murder	64%
Robbery	26%

Source: Federal Bureau of Investigation (2003).

FIGURE 1–2   Property Crime Index Arrests per 100,000

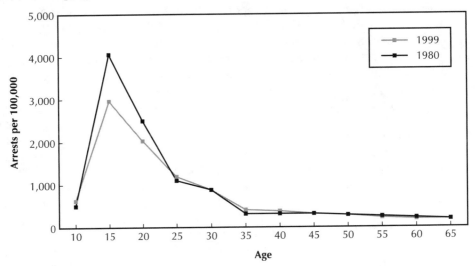

Source: Snyder (2000, p. 7).

Official crime statistics, like those of the UCR Program, are generally believed to underestimate most criminal offenses and are routinely criticized for errors and omissions. The overall number of criminal offenses that go undetected or are unknown by law enforcement agencies, known as the **dark figure**, is difficult to estimate, but data from an early victimization survey conducted by the U.S. Census Bureau suggest that, of every 100 offenses committed, 72 are never recorded in the official statistics (Skogan, 1977). However, Skogan also notes that most unreported violations appear to be minor property offenses rather than more serious crimes.

Figure 1–2, based on 1980 and 1999 UCR data, shows that arrest rates for serious property crimes peak at around age 17 or 18, just before the age range at which many courts begin prosecuting offenders as adults. With increasing age, and particularly after age 20, property crime arrests decline. On the other hand, arrests for violent crime gradually peak and show a gradual decline with age. **Figures 1–2** and **1–3** show the different trends in arrests for property crimes and violent crimes as the age of the offender increases. The figures also compare 1980 with 1999 arrest data for these trends, illustrating the significant decrease in property crimes and slight decrease in violent crimes in 1999.

National Incident-Based Reporting System

During the late 1970s, the law enforcement community called for the expanded use of the UCR and more detailed information on crime than the statistics being offered. In response, the UCR reporting system was evaluated under

FIGURE 1–3   Violent Crime Index Arrests per 100,000

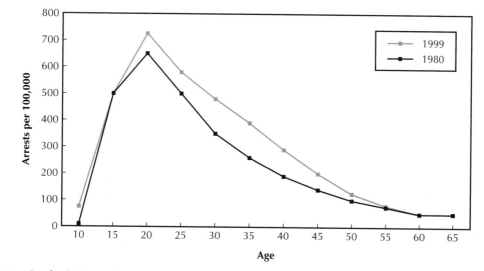

Source: Snyder (2000, p. 6).

federal contract by ABT Associates of Cambridge, Massachusetts. Recommendations of the research firm are reported in *A Blueprint for the Future of the Uniform Crime Reporting System* (Abt Associates, 1985). These recommendations formed the basis of the *National Incident-Based Reporting System* (NIBRS) under the Uniform Federal Crime Reporting Act passed by the U.S. Congress in 1988 (Public Law No. 100-690, 102 Stat. 4181). In this act, Congress required all federal law enforcement agencies, including those agencies within the Department of Defense, to collect and report data to the FBI on two categories of offenses: Group A, which includes 46 serious offense categories, such as arson, assault, homicide, fraud, embezzlement, larceny-theft, and sex offenses; and Group B, which includes 11 less serious offenses, such as passing bad checks, driving under the influence of alcohol, engaging in disorderly conduct, drunkenness, nonviolent family offenses, and liquor law violations (see **Table 1–5** for a list of Group A offenses).

In the *Group A Incident Report* information, a crime is viewed along with all its aspects. For example, the report of a crime includes information about the victim, weapon, location of the crime, alcohol/drug influence, type of criminal activity, relationship of victim to alleged offender, and residences of victims and arrestees (if someone was arrested) and a description of the property and its value. Presumably, this added information will become an indispensable tool for law enforcement agencies and researchers because it will provide them with detailed data about when and where specific types of crime take place, what forms they take, and the characteristics of their victims and

TABLE 1–5 National Incident-Based Reporting System (NIBRS) Group A Offenses

Arson	*Homicide offenses*
Assault offenses	Murder/nonnegligent manslaughter
Aggravated assault	Negligent manslaughter
Simple assault	Justifiable homicide
Intimidation	*Kidnapping/abduction*
Bribery	*Larceny-theft offenses*
Burglary/breaking and entering	Pocket picking
Counterfeiting/forgery	Purse snatching
Destruction/damage/vandalism of property	Shoplifting
Drug/narcotic Offenses	Theft from building
Drug/narcotic violations	Theft from coin-operated machines
Drug/equipment violations	Theft from motor vehicle
Embezzlement	Theft of motor vehicle parts/accessories
Extortion/blackmail	Motor vehicle theft
Fraud offenses	Pornography/obscene materials
False pretenses/swindle/confidence game	*Prostitution offenses*
Credit card/ATM fraud	Prostitution
Impersonation	Assisting or promoting prostitution
Welfare fraud	*Robbery*
Wire fraud	*Sex offenses, forcible*
Gambling offenses	Forcible rape
Betting/wagering	Forcible sodomy
Operating/promoting/assisting gambling	Sexual assault with an object
Gambling equipment violations	Forcible fondling
Sports tampering	*Sex offenses, nonforcible*
	Stolen property offenses
	Weapon law violations

Source: The National Center for the Analysis of Violent Crime, Annual Report, 1992 (Quantico, VA: FBI Academy, 1992), p. 22.

perpetrators. Like the nonindex crimes in the UCR, the crimes in Group B include only information about the arrestee and the circumstances of the arrest.

States were also invited to participate in the project. State and federal agencies participating in the NIBRS use automated systems to report information on Group A and Group B offenses to the FBI on a monthly basis. Ultimately, this new approach is intended to be a paperless (electronic) reporting system. However, the new system is expected to take several years to implement completely. Progress has been somewhat slow, but even so, data analyses based on Group A crimes are beginning to appear in the criminology literature and are mentioned periodically throughout this text. Eventually, the NIBRS is expected to replace the FBI's traditional UCR, which simply provides summary crime statistics.

The anticipated benefits of the NIBRS are primarily through the more precise information it should provide to researchers and investigators about when and where crime takes place, its form, and the characteristics of its victims and offenders. Another primary objective of the NIBRS is to get a better handle on the nature and extent of crimes involving illicit drugs.

Two additional crime categories now followed by the FBI but not *traditionally* included in the UCR system or the NIBRS reports are hate crimes and terrorism. We now turn our attention to these two very important criminal categories.

Hate Crimes

In 1989, Congress issued a mandate that the FBI collect data on "hate" or bias crimes. Known as the **Hate Crime Statistics Act**, it requires data collection on violent attacks, intimidation, arson, or property damage that are directed at a person or group of persons because of race, religion, sexual orientation, or ethnicity. The FBI defines a hate crime as "a criminal offense committed against a person, property, or society which is motivated, in whole or in part, by the offender's bias against race, religion, disability, sexual orientation, or ethnicity/national origin" (Federal Bureau of Investigation, 2002, p. 59).

In September 1994, the *Violent Crime Control and Law Enforcement Act* amended the *Hate Crime Statistics Act* to add disabilities, both physical and mental, to the hate crimes category. The disability bias data collection began in January 1997. Also, in 1994, Congress passed the *Hate Crimes Sentencing Enhancement Act*, which provides for longer sentences when the offense is determined to be a hate crime.

The *Church Arson Prevention Act*, signed into law in 1996, amended the Hate Crime Statistics Act by extending the type of data collected. The alarming increase in arson of churches prompted the passage of the *Church Arson Prevention Act*. Between October 1991 and May 1996, 110 incidents of church arson were reported to federal authorities, with 33 of them occurring during the early part of 1996. Although the burnings included synagogues, mosques, and church congregations, more than half involved African American places of worship located in the southeastern United States. In an effort to further extend hate crime statutory provisions, Congress passed the *Hate Crime Prevention Act of 1999*, which allows the federal government more authority to investigate and prosecute hate crime suspects who allegedly committed their crime because of perceived sexual orientation, gender, or disability of the victim.

In addition to the above federal laws, over 40 states and the District of Columbia have hate or bias crime statutes (Bartol & Bartol, 2004a; Wessler & Moss, 2001). Almost all state jurisdictions that have these laws cover bias based on race, religion, ethnicity, and national origin, but significantly fewer states have statutes that cover bias based on gender, disability, or sexual orientation. Nearly all the state and federal statutes provide an enhancement of penalties once a person has been convicted of a bias or hate crime (Bartol & Bartol, 2004a).

In accordance with the Hate Crime Statistics Act, hate crime data are collected for 11 traditional offense categories and are divided into two major classifications: (1) crimes against persons and (2) crimes against property. Crimes against persons include murder and nonnegligent manslaughter, forcible rape, aggravated assault, simple assault, and intimidation. Crimes against property include robbery, burglary, larceny-theft, motor vehicle theft, arson, and de-struction/damage/vandalism of property. The data are submitted to the UCR by city, county, and state law enforcement agencies by various means, such as hard copy, floppy disk, and magnetic tape.

A victim of a hate crime may be either a person, a business, an institution, or society as a whole. In 2002, approximately two of every three hate crimes (67.5%) were crimes against persons, with intimidation being the most fre-quently reported (52.1%) (Federal Bureau of Investigation, 2003). Thirty-two percent were hate crimes against property (with vandalism predominating), and 0.6% were classified as crimes against society. Recent available data (2002) indicate that a majority of hate crimes are motivated by racial bias (48.8%), followed by ethnic/national origin bias (14.8%), religious bias (19.1%), sexual orientation bias (16.7%), and disability bias (0.6%) (Federal Bureau of Investi-gation, 2003). Interestingly, in the Spring of 2004, anecdotal accounts of in-creasing incidents of bias crimes against gays and lesbians began to surface in the media. This appears to be a backlash against the movement to recognize gay marriage in the United States. It remains to be seen whether these anec-dotal accounts will be reflected in the official FBI reports covering that year.

A vivid example of a hate crime occurred in early June 1998 in Jasper, Texas. James Byrd, Jr., a 49-year-old African American, was walking home from a family party when he was offered a ride by three white men, all of them known white supremacists. The men drove Byrd to a remote dirt road where they beat him severely. Then they chained Byrd to their pickup truck by the ankles and dragged him along the road, tearing his body to pieces. Police found Byrd's head, neck, right arm, torso, shoes, wallet, and other personal items scattered along the route. A mile-long trail of blood on the road marked the gruesome scene. Another high-profile hate crime was the 1998 murder of Matthew Shepard, a gay college student who was kidnapped, beaten, tied to a fencepost, and left to die. Shepard was found and hospitalized in a comatose state and died shortly thereafter.

We introduce the topic of hate crime early in the book to highlight it as a significant problem in contemporary society. Psychological theory and re-search have much to contribute toward the understanding of the factors that allow or facilitate hate crimes.

Terrorism

Terrorism is defined in the Code of Federal Regulations as "the unlawful use of force or violence against persons or property to intimidate or coerce a government, the civilian population, or any segment thereof, in furtherance of political or social objectives." Terrorism may be either domestic or interna-tional, depending on the origin, base, and objectives of the terrorist organiza-tion (U.S. Department of Justice, 2000a). *Domestic terrorism* refers to groups or an individual based and operating entirely within the United States or Puerto Rico without foreign direction. *International terrorism* refers to violent acts or acts dangerous to human life that are a violation of the criminal laws of the United States or any state and under the direction of a foreign government, group, organization, or person. The most vivid example of international terrorism is represented by the events that occurred on September 11, 2001, when an international terrorist group called al-Qaeda hijacked four commercial airliners and flew two of the aircraft into the twin towers of the World Trade Center in New York City and one into the Pentagon building located in Arlington County, Virginia. The fourth plane, presumably heading for the White House, crashed into a field in Somerset County, Pennsylvania, after heroic passengers conspired to overwhelm the hijackers and prevent them from remaining on their course toward Washington. The number of deaths totaled 3,047, including the 19 terrorist hijackers. As noted earlier, the extensive homicide (mass murder) statistics of September 11 were not part of the traditional UCR publication because they were significantly different from the day-to-day crimes committed in the United States (Federal Bureau of Investigation, 2002).

A well-known example of domestic terrorism occurred on April 17, 1995. A truck bomb destroyed the Alfred P. Murrah Federal Building in Oklahoma City, killing 167 (19 were children) and injuring 684 persons. Timothy McVeigh, a U.S. citizen and former soldier, was convicted and eventually executed for this crime. His coconspirator, Terry Nichols, pled guilty to avoid the federal death penalty. He is presently on trial in state court in Oklahoma and remains at risk of being sentenced to death. The Oklahoma City attack remains the deadliest domestic terrorist incident ever committed on U.S. soil. Further illustrations of domestic terrorism include the so-called "Army of God" that claimed responsibility for bombings of abortion clinics and an alternative lifestyle nightclub in Atlanta.

Although persons worldwide are victims of international terrorism, the U.S. Department of Justice tracks the terrorism aimed at U.S. property or citizens located in a foreign country. Examples of this terrorism include groups in Colombia who target American interests and who have kidnapped seven U.S. citizens and have carried out multiple bombings against oil pipelines used by American companies (U.S. Department of Justice, 2000a). Another example involves the American embassies in Nairobi, Kenya, and Dar es Salaam, Tanzania—in August 1998 both embassies were bombed almost simultaneously. The truck bombings killed 224, including 12 American citizens, and injured over 4,500 located in or near the embassies.

The number of victims killed or injured by terrorists differs widely from year to year. In addition to the domestic and international classifications, there are several other ways to classify terrorism. The FBI classifies terrorists according to political leanings. For example, *right-wing terrorists* are extremist groups that generally adhere to an antigovernment or racist ideology and often engage in a variety of hate crimes and violence. Recent stimuli that have encouraged right-wing militia groups or individuals to become active include gun-control legislation, the United Nations involvement in international affairs, and clashes between dissidents and law enforcement. Examples include the Unabomber, who sent mail bombs to individuals involved with technology, killing three and seriously injuring 23 over a 17-year period. The intention of the Unabomber was to stop the Industrial Revolution and technological progress in American society. Another example of right-wing extremists is the bombers of the Alfred P. Murrah Federal Building in Oklahoma City, referred to previously.

Another FBI classification relates to *radical environmental groups*, such as the Earth Liberation Front (ELF). The ELF organization received particular attention during the late 1990s by destroying homes, earth-moving equipment, powerlines, computer systems, and buildings that they believed damaged the earth's ecology. The organization's primary mission is to "speed up the collapse of industry, to scare the rich, and to undermine the foundations of the state." *Special interest extremists*, particularly violent antiabortion advocates, continue to be a problem in the United States.

During the past several decades, *nuclear/biological/chemical* (abbreviated NBC) forms of terrorism have become prominent. The thought of being exposed to an invisible or undetectable agent can be more frightening to the general public than the prospect of physical injury or death caused by conventional weapons. The use of sarin, a deadly nerve agent, in the subway system of Tokyo, Japan, in 1995 provided a horrifying example. The attacks were carried out by the doomsday cult *Aum Shinri Kyo* (Supreme Truth Sect); they resulted in the deaths of 11 people and injured more than 5,000. It is estimated that about 375 pounds of sarin is enough to kill more than 50,000 persons. The threat of NBC is more realistic today because terrorists are able to take advantage of the greater availability of information and weapons technology.

Bioterrorism involves the use of bacteria, viruses, germs, and other agents such as anthrax, bubonic plague, and smallpox (Marsella, 2004). A recent example of domestic bioterrorism is represented by the anthrax attacks that occurred in the United States less than a month after 9/11. The bioterrorist(s) sent the anthrax by letter to various persons in the eastern United States, including the Washington offices of Senators Patrick Leahy and Tom Daschle and the New York office of CBS anchor Dan Rather. Anthrax is an acute infectious disease caused by the spore-forming bacterium *Bacillus anthracis*. Although anthrax is most commonly found in hoofed mammals, it can also infect humans. Symptoms of the disease vary depending on how the disease is contracted but usually occur within seven days after exposure. The serious forms of human anthrax are inhalation anthrax, cutaneous (skin) anthrax, and intestinal (ingestion) anthrax. Inhalation (pulmonary) anthrax starts with inhalation of anthrax spores and has a mortality rate of about 95%, even with treatment. Cutaneous anthrax starts with the spore colonizing the skin through an abrasion, cut, or wound. The mortality rate of the cutaneous anthrax ranges from 20% to 25% without treatment and is less than 1% with treatment. Intestinal anthrax, which is usually contracted by eating contaminated meat, has a morality rate of 95%, even when treated.

The bioterrorist or bioterrorists (at this writing the author of the anthrax letters is unknown and the case is still under investigation) sent letters containing both inhalation and cutaneous anthrax to the victims. The anthrax spores were mixed with a light powder in the folds of the letters. The first known case of an anthrax letter attack killed a photo editor of a tabloid in Boca Raton, Florida, in October 2001. In total, the bioterrorist letters resulted in at least five deaths due to inhalation anthrax infections, and another eight cases of nonfatal cutaneous anthrax infections were reported during 2001. Bioterrorism, if delivered under the right conditions and by using a highly infectious biological agent, could be devastating to a society.

Other forms of terrorism include nuclear terrorism, such as the use of nuclear bombs or dirty bombs that make use of radioactive material, and chemical terrorism, such as the use of sarin gas as occurred with the *Aum Shinri Kyo* cult in Japan (Marsella, 2004). Terrorism is an area of obvious concern today, and this section has only provided a brief overview of statistical and informational aspects. There are many kinds of, and motivations for, terrorism, ranging from criminal terrorism to state-sponsored terrorism, the discussion of which would take us far afield of the mission of this text. However, some of the psychosocial aspects of terrorism are covered in more detail in Chapter 9.

The above section has focused on the official sources of gathering data on crime, specifically those sponsored by the FBI in its Uniform Crime Reporting system and in the NIBRS. We turn now to a discussion of other approaches to measuring crime, along with illustrations of the types of crime that are studied.

SELF-REPORT STUDIES

Many researchers believe that self-report (SR) studies provide a more accurate estimate of actual offenses than do UCR statistics, which are based on data provided by law enforcement, even though respondents may inflate or deflate reports of their own criminal activity. In a dated but revealing SR survey (Wallerstein & Wyle, 1947), 1,698 persons were asked to indicate on a list of 49 criminal offenses which, if any, they had committed. The list included felonies and misdemeanors but excluded traffic violations. Ninety-one percent of the nearly 1,700 respondents admitted that they had committed one or more offenses for which they might have received jail or prison sentences. The average number of offenses for each person was 18. None in the sample had served an actual prison sentence. This study suggests that most people have broken the criminal law at some point in their lives.

In another classic study by Short and Nye (1957), 3,000 high school students, with a guarantee of anonymity, were administered questionnaires about their unlawful actions. Results confirmed the high incidence of unlawful behavior such as reported in the Wallerstein and Wyle study. Additionally, the study demonstrated that the unlawful conduct was evenly distributed across all socioeconomic classes. Even if the offenses were not serious ones, if these

SR studies are representative, violations of the law are common across all levels of society, at least among young people. The Wallerstein and Wyle study did not address the issue of social class.

Most SR investigations focus on delinquency rather than adult offending. When SR studies are done with adults, they are primarily adults who are incarcerated, although there are exceptions. In a study of employee theft, for example, researchers found that about one-third of employees who returned surveys admitted to stealing from their employers (Hollinger, 1986). An SR survey of income tax evasion found 10% of the respondents admitting to cheating on their taxes (Tittle, 1980).

SR data are gathered through either interviews (personal or telephone) or questionnaires. In most SR measures, subjects are asked to indicate whether they have engaged in any of the listed illegal activities and, if so, how often. Nettler (1984), in his review of the SR research, concluded the following:

- Almost everyone, by his or her own admission, has violated some criminal law.
- The amount of "hidden crime" (the dark figure) is enormous.
- Most of the infractions are minor.

The last point is an important one because it is the basis for much of the criticism directed at SR studies. Most of the offenses included in a majority of SR questionnaires are relatively minor ones—so minor that they are likely to distort one's impressions of criminal offending unless the content of the questions is known. For example, the questionnaire used by Short and Nye was a 23-item delinquency scale that included such questions as whether one has ever defied his or her parents' authority (to their face). Other items included whether one had ever skipped school without a legitimate excuse, taken little things (worth less than $2), bought or drank beer, wine, or liquor, had sexual relations with persons of the opposite sex or the same sex, run away from home, or gone hunting or fishing without a license. Note that some of the above items (e.g., skipping school and running away) relate to offenses that are against the law only for juveniles, called "status offenses." More "serious" violations listed were fist fights, gang fights, taking a car for a drive without the owner's (including parents') knowledge, use of narcotic drugs, theft (over $50), and vandalism.

Recent SR studies, responding to the criticisms of earlier investigations, have directed their questions at more serious criminal activities. Still, we must be careful about drawing far-reaching conclusions based on the information from SR research unless the nature of the questions is known, as well as who was asked, why, and how. At this point, however, SR studies do suggest that minor criminal activity is extensive and widespread, at least among youth. Furthermore, SR studies continually show that the number of individuals involved in serious crimes is relatively small, but those few who do engage in serious criminal activity commit many crimes. Moreover, persistent, repetitive offenders do not specialize in any one crime (such as larceny) but show considerable versatility in criminal involvement, committing a wide variety of offenses, violent as well as nonviolent. We discuss this behavioral pattern in more detail in the next chapter.

Drug Abuse Self-Report Surveys

Several nationwide SR surveys collect data on drug abuse in the United States. The major surveys are the National Household Survey on Drug Abuse (NHSDA), the Monitoring the Future Study (MFS), and the Arrestees Drug Abuse Monitoring (ADAM) Program.

The *National Household Survey on Drug Abuse* (NHSDA) is an ongoing survey of the noninstitutionalized population of the United States, 12 years of age or older. The survey has been conducted by the federal government since 1971 and is the primary source of statistical information on the use of illegal drugs in the United States. It is designed to estimate the rates of drug use, the number of users, and other aspects related to illicit drugs, alcohol, and tobacco products. The survey collects data by administering questionnaires to a representative sample of the population at their places of residence across all 50 states and the District of Columbia. The sample includes residents of households, noninstitutional group quarters (e.g., shelters, rooming houses, dormitories), and civilians living on military bases. Beginning in 1999, the NHSDA interview has been carried out using a computer-assisted interviewing methodology. Computers are used for both personal interviewing conducted by the interviewer and audio computer-assisted self-interviewing. Nationally, nearly 69,000 persons were interviewed in 2001.

The *Monitoring the Future Study* (MFS) is a nationwide survey of high school students in the United States conducted at the Institute for Social Research at the University of Michigan and sponsored by research grants from the National Institute of Drug Abuse. Each year since 1991 a total of 50,000 8th-, 10th-, and 12th-grade students have been surveyed. The MFS also conducts a follow-up survey of each graduating class for a number of years after their initial participation. The mission of the MFS is to predict future trends of drug abuse based on current youth drug use. We describe these surveys and their informative results in more detail in Chapter 12.

The *Arrestees Drug Abuse Monitoring* (ADAM) Program collects data from adult males and females who are arrested in 33 metropolitan areas (or sites) in the United States. In addition, data are collected from male and female juvenile detainees in nine metropolitan areas. The ADAM program uses both urinalysis and self-report data to identify the level of recent drug use by the arrestees and juvenile detainees. The urinalysis provides a validity check on the openness of the arrestees in providing information about their drug abuse. The urine tests are provided for 11 drugs and SR information is collected for 15 drugs. The ADAM project offers invaluable insight into drug use of offenders nationwide.

VICTIMIZATION SURVEYS

Additional sources of data on criminal offending are victimization surveys. The main source of victimization data on crime is the *National Crime Victimization Survey* (NCVS), originally called the National Crime Survey (NCS). Workers for the Bureau of the Census interview—in person or by phone— a large national sample of households (approximately 42,000) representing more than 76,000 persons over the age of 12. The same households are interviewed every six months for a period of three years, and during each session they are asked about crime they have experienced over the past six months. Crimes committed against children below age 12 are not counted for privacy reasons and because the designers of the survey believe that younger respondents, compared to adults, are not as likely to provide accurate information. In addition, because young children may be victims of crime within their own households, the topic would be too sensitive to broach. The NCVS provides the largest national forum for victims to describe the impact of crime and characteristics of offenders.

The original impetus for the NCVS came from the President's Commission on Law Enforcement and the Administration of Justice in 1966. The commission wanted to supplement the UCR because of the widespread dissatisfaction with and distrust of the accuracy of this source. After considerable experimentation and a variety of pilot projects to test methods and their feasibility, the NCVS (then called the NCS) was fully implemented in July 1973. Although the survey has generally been regarded as an effective instrument for measuring crime victimization, the National Academy of Sciences concluded that the survey's methodology and scope could be improved. Consequently, the NCVS has undergone several changes and improvements since it was begun in 1973. The most recent significant changes in the NCVS occurred in 1992 when a redesigned interview method was put into place to improve survey methods and collect previously unreported data. This redesign and other ongoing developments of the NCVS have significantly changed the way in which the survey gathers data and information on victimization. The effects of these methodological changes on data are described in a report published by the Bureau of Justice Statistics (1997) entitled "Effects of the Redesign on Victimization Estimates."

The survey is currently designed to measure the extent to which households and individuals are victims of rape and other sexual assault, robbery, aggravated assault, simple assault, household burglary, motor vehicle theft, and personal theft. It also provides many details about the victims (such as age, race, sex, marital status, education, income, and whether the victim and the offender are related to each other) and about the crimes themselves. Specifically, the NCVS interviewer wants to know the following:

- Exactly what happened
- When and where the offense occurred
- Whether any injury or loss was suffered

- Whether the crime was reported to the police and, if not, why
- The victim's perception of the offender's gender, race, and age

According to the NCVS, residents age 12 or older experienced approximately 23 million crimes during 2002 (Rennison & Rand, 2003). Of that total, 17.5 million (76%) were property crimes (burglary, motor vehicle theft, and household theft), and 5.3 million (23%) were violent crimes (rape or sexual assault, robbery, aggravated assault, and simple assault). Approximately 180,000 (1%) were personal thefts (pocket picking and purse snatching).

If we examine the *rates* (victimization rate per 1,000 persons age 12 or older), we find that the NCVS data reveal that victimization in 2002 reached the lowest per capita rates in nearly 30 years (Rennison & Rand, 2003). For example, violent victimization rates fell 54% in the past 10 years, from 50 to 23 victimizations per 1,000 persons 12 years of age and older. The *number* of violent victimizations fell from 10.5 million in 1993 to 5.3 million in 2002. The property crime victimization rate fell 50%, from 319 crimes per 1,000 households to 159 per 1,000. In fact, the rate of every major violent and property crime declined from 1993 through 2002. Specifically, rape/sexual assault declined 56%; robbery, 63%; aggravated assault, 64%; simple assault, 47%; motor vehicle theft, 53%; household burglary, 52%; and property theft, 49%.

The NCVS data consistently show demographic differences in victimization rates. Males and blacks are victims of violent crime at rates higher than those of whites and persons of other races (Rennison & Rand, 2003). Persons ages 12 to 24 sustained violent victimization at rates higher than individuals of all other ages. The 16 to 19 age group is especially vulnerable. Persons ages 16 to 19 experienced overall violence, rape/sexual assault, and assault at rates higher than those for persons in other age categories. Persons in households with an annual income under $7,500 were more likely to be victims of overall violence than members of households with higher incomes. And persons who had never married were victims of violent crime at rates higher than those for married, widowed, or divorced/separated persons.

Relationship patterns are important in understanding the victimization rates also, particularly violent victimization. Females were most often victimized by someone they knew, whereas males were more likely to be victimized by a stranger in 2002 (Rennison & Rand, 2003). More specifically, female victims reported that 40% of the offenders were friends or acquaintances, 20% were intimates, and 7% some other relative. Thirty-one percent of the offenders were strangers. Male victims indicated that 37% of the offenders were friends or acquaintances, 3% were intimates, and 4% were described as some other relative. Strangers committed 56% of the violence against males. Robbery was the crime most likely to be committed by a stranger for both male and female victims.

Every year, about 1 million violent crimes are committed against persons by their current or former spouses, boyfriends, or girlfriends (Rennison & Welchans, 2000), a crime designated **intimate partner violence**. Intimate partner violence is committed primarily against women. Women are victims in about 85% of reported intimate partner violence; 22% of *all* violent crime committed against women is intimate partner violence. Women between 20 and 24 years of age are most likely to be victimized by an intimate partner (21 per 1,000 women). Black women are subject to intimate partner violence at a rate 35% higher than that for white women and approximately 2.5 times higher than the rate for women of other races. About two-thirds of the victims of intimate partner violence said they were *physically attacked*, and about one-third reported being victims of threats or attempted violence. Approximately one-half of all victims of intimate partner violence (both male and female victims) reported the violence to law enforcement authorities.

The NCVS, similarly to all national surveys, has its problems in accurately portraying victimization data. As described earlier in this section, the NCVS samples households and, therefore, does not usually include the experiences of homeless individuals or those living in institutional settings such as homeless or battered persons' shelters (Rennison & Welchans, 2000). Consequently, the extent of intimate partner violence experienced by the homeless or those persons residing in shelters remains largely unknown. For example, a survey conducted by the U.S. Conference of Mayors (1998) indicated that intimate partner violence was the primary cause of homelessness for women. Another study suggested that as many as 50% of homeless women and children became homeless after fleeing abuse (Zorsa, 1991).

Victimization surveys are considered a good source of information about crime incidents, independent of data collected by law enforcement agencies throughout the country. Often, the offending trends reported through NCVS data procedures differ substantially from those found in police data (Ohlin & Tonry, 1989).

Throughout the course of this text we refer to victimization studies to get a better grasp on criminal activity as well as to learn how crime affects victims. In many instances, however, we use surveys conducted by researchers independent of the NCVS. One excellent and meaningful survey sponsored by the National Institute of Justice in collaboration with the Centers for Disease Control and Prevention involved an examination of the extent and nature of stalking in American society. The survey, known as the National Violence Against Women Survey, was conducted by the Center for Policy Research (Tjaden, 1997).

Stalking: A Contemporary Example of Victimization Data

Stalking is defined as "a course of conduct directed at a specific person that involves repeated physical or visual proximity, nonconsensual communication, or verbal, written, or implied threats sufficient to cause fear in a reasonable person" (Tjaden, 1997, p. 2). Systematic information on stalking in the United States is limited, despite the attention it receives from the media and the legislatures (Tjaden, 1997). Most of the previous research has focused on the stalking of famous persons, entertainment personalities, or politicians, known as "celebrity stalking." However, a substantial increase in the stalking of "noncelebrities" over the past decade has generated numerous media accounts of stalking victims and the passage of antistalking laws in all 50 states and the District of Columbia (Tjaden & Thoennes, 1998a). Legal definitions of stalking vary widely from state to state. Whereas most states define stalking in their statutes as the willful, malicious, and repeated following and harassing of another person, some include such activities as lying-in-wait, surveillance, nonconsensual communication, telephone harassment, and vandalism (Tjaden & Thoennes, 1998a). Some states specify that at least two stalking events must occur before the conduct can be considered illegal.

In 1990, California became the first state to enact antistalking legislation. The impetus for this legislation was not the stalking/homicide of television actress Rebecca Schaeffer, as commonly believed, but had its roots in domestic violence (Lemon, 1994). A California municipal court judge initiated the development and passage of the antistalking law following his frustration over existing law that failed to protect four Orange County women who were killed in different incidents despite the issuance of restraining orders against their assailants. Since 1990, stalking statutes have spread rapidly to all states.

In an attempt to fill in the large gap in our knowledge about stalking, the Center for Policy Research conducted a comprehensive victimization survey of 8,000 women and 8,000 men 18 years of age or older on issues relating to violence (Tjaden & Thoennes, 1997). The survey revealed that 8% of women and 2% of men reported they had been stalked at some point in their lives (Tjaden, 1997). Overall, the survey indicated that approximately 1.4 million Americans are victims of stalkers every year, a surprisingly large number. In most cases, the stalking lasted less than one year, but some people were stalked for over five years. It is estimated that 1 of every 12 women and 1 of every 45 men in the United States has been stalked during his or her lifetime (Tjaden & Thoennes, 1998a).

The survey found that the motives of most stalkers were to control, intimidate, or frighten their victims. This observation was made by both male and female victims. Eighty-seven percent of the time the stalker was male, and 80% of the time the victim was female. In most stalking incidents, the victims (particularly women) knew their stalker. About half of the female victims were stalked by current or former marital or cohabiting partners, and a majority of these women (80%) had been physically assaulted by that partner either during the relationship, during the stalking episode, or during both. In about one-third of the cases, stalkers vandalized the victim's property, and about 10% of the time the stalker killed or threatened to kill the victim's pet. In nearly half of the cases, the stalker made overt threats to the victim. The survey dispels the myth that most stalkers are psychotic or delusional. Only 7% of the victims perceived their stalkers as "crazy" or abusers of drugs or alcohol.

Half of all victims reported the stalking to the police, and about one-quarter of the female victims obtained a restraining order. Not surprisingly, 70% of all restraining orders were violated by the assailant. About one-quarter of victims in cases where a restraining order was violated pursued prosecution. When prosecution was pursued, most cases resulted in conviction of the stalker and well over half received jail time. Although most of the stalking stopped within two years, the emotional and social effects of being stalked continued for many victims long after the incident. About one-third of the stalking victims sought psychological treatment because of the emotional and social trauma that resulted from the stalking episodes.

Meloy (1998) asserts that stalkers rarely cause serious physical injury to their victims, threaten them with weapons, or use weapons. Even so, the psychological trauma is often substantial. In a survey of 145 stalking victims (120 females, 25 males), Doris Hall (1998) reports that the experience of being stalked for months or even years is akin to psychological terrorism. A majority of the victims said their entire lives changed as a result of being stalked. "Many move or quit jobs, some change their names, others have gone underground, leaving friends and family in order to escape the terror" (p. 134). Some change their physical appearance or wear disguises. Others become exceedingly suspicious of the motives of others, often leading lonely and isolated lives. Many victims constantly worry that the stalker will find them and that the entire experience will start all over again.

Researchers have identified four very broad categories of stalking: (1) simple obsession stalking, (2) love obsession stalking, (3) erotomania stalking, and (4) vengeance stalking (Beatty, 2001). *Simple obsession stalking* accounts for the majority of stalking (about 60%) and often represents extensions of previous patterns of domestic violence and psychological abuse. The stalker in these case scenarios usually seeks power and control after a failed relationship with the victim. Simple obsession stalking is perhaps the most dangerous to the victim, because it is often motivated by the stalker's conclusion that "If I can't have you, nobody will." In *love obsession stalking*, the stalker and victim are casual acquaintances or complete strangers. Stalkers in this category are characterized by low self-esteem and tend to select victims they perceive to have certain qualities they believe will raise their self-esteem. Essentially they seek a love relationship with the object of their obsession, contrary to the wishes of their victim. For example, John Hinckley was convinced he would win the heart of actor Jodi Foster by shooting President Ronald Reagan.

Erotomania stalking is considered delusional, and the stalker is often plagued by serious mental disorders. These stalkers usually target public figures or celebrities in their misguided attempts to gain self-esteem and status. For example, talk show host David Letterman was stalked over a number of years by a woman who believed she was his wife. The woman frequently trespassed on Letterman's property, hid in his home, and even stole his car to go grocery shopping. Tragically, the delusional woman eventually took her own life. Fortunately, erotomania stalking appears to be relatively rare and normally the stalker is not violent. *Vengeance stalkers* are quite different from the other three because they do not seek a personal relationship with their targets (Beatty, 2001). Instead, vengeance stalkers try to elicit a particular response of change of behavior from the victims. For example, a stalker who wishes to torment someone responsible for a perceived injustice or violation of his or her rights might follow the "guilty party" day and night until feeling fairly compensated.

What terminates stalking? Some stalkers stop their activity toward the current victim when they find a new "love" interest. About 18% of the victims in the Center for Policy Research Survey indicated that the stalking stopped when their assailant got a new spouse, partner, or boyfriend/girlfriend. Informal law enforcement interventions also seem to help. Fifteen percent said the stalking ceased when the assailant received a warning from the police. More formal interventions such as arrest, conviction, and restraining orders do not appear to be very effective. When it comes to persistent, frightening stalking that creates risks to personal safety, the survey suggests that the most effective method may be to relocate as far away from the offender as possible, providing no information on the new location to the stalker.

Cyberstalking

A form of stalking that has emerged in recent years is **cyberstalking**, the use of the Internet or other forms of online communications to threaten or engage in unwanted advances toward another. Although online harassment and threats may take many forms, cyberstalking is in many ways similar to off-line stalking. In most instances the stalkers wish to establish relationships with the victims, and often they are males seeking females. In many cases, the cyberstalker and the victim had a prior relationship, and the cyberstalking begins when the victim attempts to break off the relationship (U.S. Department of Justice, 1999). Ultimately, much cyberstalking is designed to control the victim, usually through threats and harassment.

"Because e-mail is used daily by what some experts say are as many as 35 million people, and it is estimated that there are approximately 200,000 stalkers in the United States, the Internet is a perfect forum with which to terrorize their victims" (Jenson, 1996, p. 1). "Chat rooms" and e-mail have provided far-reaching and unregulated opportunities for cyberstalkers to harass unsuspecting victims, especially women. In addition, there is an enormous amount of personal information available through the Internet, and a cyberstalker can easily and quickly locate private information about a target. Unfortunately, victims of cyberstalking cannot be adequately protected due to the lack of enforceable laws to prosecute and deter this behavior (Jenson, 1996). And there are substantial obstacles to using criminal and civil law to thwart the persistent cyberstalker, bringing into question whether it is possible to regulate this type of behavior at all. Most stalking laws require that the perpetrator make a credible threat of violence against the victim (U.S. Department of Justice, 1999).

Meloy (1998) points out that the Internet provides a means of stalking that lacks the usual social constraints. "Only written words are used, and other avenues of sensory perception are eliminated; one cannot see, hear, touch, smell, or emotionally sense the other person" (p. 11). The lack of face-to-face interaction with their victims and the overall anonymity encourages some individuals who would not ordinarily behave in such a fashion to act out their fantasies. An example of cyberstalking is provided by Jenson (1996), who describes a South Carolina woman who was stalked by an unknown cyberstalker for several years via e-mail. Not only had the stalker threatened her life, but also he threatened to rape her daughter. In addition, the stalker posted the woman's home address on e-mail for 35 million people to see.

The Internet does provide an extremely inviting avenue for cyberstalkers, which may have substantial ramifications in the future. To date, however, very little systematic research has been conducted to examine the prevalence and incidence of cyberstalking, the personal characteristics of cyberstalkers, effective deterrents to cyberstalking, or even the psychological consequences of being cyberstalked.

The National Center for Victims of Crime (NCVC, 2000) has several recommendations for victims of cyberstalking. Please check the NCVC Web site (listed in the References) for suggestions on how to handle cyberstalking.

THE FOCUS OF THE BOOK

A major challenge faced by the authors in preparing this book has been striking the balance between antisocial behavior and criminal behavior or between antisocial individuals and legally defined criminals. Some scholars have argued (e.g., Sellin, 1970; Tappan, 1947)—and the law agrees—that one who engages in undetected criminal activity is not a criminal in the strictest or operational sense, because a criminal is by definition one who has been detected, arrested, *and* convicted. However, from a psychological point of view, we encounter problems when we limit ourselves to studying persons legally defined as criminals or behavior legally defined as crime. Legal classifications are determined by that which society, at some point in time, considers socially harmful. It may or may not also be considered morally wrong. Therefore, because each society has a different and changing set of values, what may be judged a criminal act in one society may not meet the criteria in another, or even in the same society at a later time. Many states in the United States differ significantly in their criminal codes and are continually revising them. Chemical (drug) possession, prostitution, and dissemination of obscene material are examples of activities that generate ever-changing statutes and, if not changing statutes, selective enforcement.

Members of every society (and consequently every society's legal system) perceive and process violators of the criminal code with some disparity, so that the offender's background, social status, personality, motivation, sex, age, race, and legal counsel, as well as the circumstances surrounding the offense, may all affect the criminal justice process. It is highly likely that individuals who have been arrested, convicted, and punished represent a distinctly different sample from those who participate in illegal activity but avoid detection, conviction, or punishment.

Approximately one-fifth of those arrested get to the trial stage, according to Sarbin (1979), who describes the legal process of becoming a criminal. First, the agents of social control (usually the police) label the individual as a suspect. Next, the agents may decide that the suspect should be arrested. Third, the arrested party may be charged with a crime, at which point he or she becomes a defendant. Fourth, the defendant may be tried and convicted, at which point he or she becomes an offender (a felon or a misdemeanant, depending upon the seriousness of the crime). Finally, the offender may be incarcerated in a correctional facility and be labeled a convict, inmate, prisoner, or criminal. Alternately, the offender may be placed on probation, effectively serving a sentence in the community. At each step in the process there is a funneling effect that shows that fewer and fewer individuals reach each subsequent step in the criminal justice process. This funneling process is prominently displayed in numerous criminal justice texts to illustrate how the system operates. It is applied in civil law as well. H. Hart and Sacks (1958) called it the "great pyramid of legal order," and Galanter (1974) called it the "legal iceberg." Hundreds of thousands of individuals get filtered out, for a variety of reasons.

One reason is the error and subjectivity that cannot realistically be removed from determinations of guilt or innocence or from determinations of fault in civil cases. Another is the human decision-making process. In criminal cases, for example, it has been demonstrated that the characteristics of the victim may influence how much punishment is assigned to the offender. Landy and Aronson (1969) report evidence that if the victim is a respectable citizen (i.e., successful and altruistic), the offender will receive a stiffer sentence than if the case involves an "unrespectable" victim (i.e., despicable and dishonest). C. Jones and Aronson (1973) found that defendants who raped a married woman or virgin were more likely to receive longer sentences than defendants who raped a divorced woman. It has also been found that the more serious a traffic accident, the greater the tendency for jurors to believe that the principals involved were at fault (Walster, 1966). Although these were early experiments in social psychology, later studies also confirmed that subjective factors have considerable influence on jury decision making (Bartol & Bartol, 2004a). In addition, discrepancies in sentencing have led to widespread demands for determinate sentencing, where the punishment is carefully calibrated to the offense and there is less room for discretion on the part of sentencing judges.

The aforementioned studies support Lerner's hypothesis (1970, 1980) that people need to believe that they live in a just world where the undeserving are appropriately deprived or punished. This **just world hypothesis** predicts, for example, that some victims of rape, assault, or homicide are assumed by many people to have gotten what they deserved or asked for. The implications of this hypothesis in relation to juries' determinations of guilt and judges' decisions as to whether to place a person on probation or sentence the person to prison are obvious.

It is generally acknowledged, therefore, that incarcerated individuals are not representative of the "true" criminal population. And as we have long suspected but only recently documented with the increasing availability of DNA evidence, persons incarcerated are not even necessarily true criminals. Yet, with rare exceptions, researchers studying the "criminal mind" use as subjects only those individuals who have reached the final stage of the legal process: inmates in correctional institutions. Consequently, if we discuss only legally determined criminals, we will be neglecting a considerable segment of the population that actually breaks the law. To some extent, we have little choice but to do just that. Because this book is based on research, the kinds and amounts of available empirical data dictate to a great extent what will be covered.

In addition, if we discuss only behavior that is legally defined as crime, we omit a segment of behavior that is clearly relevant to our concerns. For example, a vast body of psychological research deals with topics like aggression, sexual arousal, and moral development. Because of their implications for the eventual development of behavior that is legally defined as crime, we cover these areas in the text. One major aspect of psychological criminology that the reader will discover while reading this text is that the psychological study of crime takes three approaches to defining crime. One approach defines crime along the lines of a psychiatric diagnosis, as outlined in the *Diagnostic and Statistical Manual of Mental Disorders* (DSM-IV). This approach studies the relationship between crime and diagnoses such as antisocial personality disorder, conduct disorder, and psychopathy, and is discussed more fully in the next chapter, on juvenile delinquency, as well as in Chapter 4. The second approach defines crime as violations of the law, as discussed in this chapter. This approach appears repeatedly throughout the remainder of the book when we cover specific offense categories. The third psychological approach to the "crime problem" is to study the development and maintenance of aggressive and hostile behavior in children and adults, a topic covered more fully in Chapters 5 and 7.

The great majority of crime in the United States is neither serious nor violent. The great majority of offenders are not serious, chronic offenders. Psychological criminology, however, is most concerned about the minority. Therefore, the main focus of the book is the persistent, repetitive *offender*—or the persistent, repetitive antisocial *behavior*—whether detected or undetected by the criminal justice system. In other words, in this text we concentrate on the individual who has frequently committed serious crimes or antisocial acts over an extended period of time (at least several years). On the other hand, we also give attention to the rare individual who engages in one incomprehensible crime or in a series of heinous crimes over a short period of time.

CHAPTER 2

JUVENILE DELINQUENCY: DEVELOPMENTAL FACTORS

Juveniles may well be the most maligned age group in our society. Myths abound about their contribution to crime and the extent of damage for which they are responsible. During the last quarter of the twentieth century, it was common to read accounts of skyrocketing juvenile crime, young superpredators in our midst, declining morality in youth, and the woeful state of family life, which was seen as a major contributor to juvenile vandalism, drug use, thievery, and violence. To some extent these accounts were supported by statistics, particularly during the 1980s and early 1990s. However, fears were also fueled by atypical illustrations of juvenile crime, such as a particularly heinous account of a murder committed by a juvenile or those associated with a number of school shootings.

As we note in this chapter, although there is reason to be concerned about juvenile crime, the facts are not quite as alarming as they often appear to be from media accounts. Juvenile crime is troubling, but it is not intractable. Since the mid-1990s, we have seen a decrease in crime committed by youths across most crime categories, including both property and violent crime. Drug use, though, has seen significant increases. Youths charged with drug law violations, for example, increased 169% between 1990 and 1999 (National Center for Juvenile Justice, 2003). Juveniles as a group are responsible for a small percentage of arrests compared to adults, although they are arrested disproportionately compared with other age groups. Moreover, the typical juvenile is far more likely to be the victim than the perpetrator of a violent crime. Nevertheless, a significant number of juveniles do victimize one another, drug use persists, and the problem of youth violence has not disappeared. We review the data later in the chapter. Thus, though we have made strides in understanding the factors leading to these behaviors and developing strategies for prevention and treatment, much work remains to be done.

This chapter begins with a brief historical account of the development of a separate juvenile justice system in the United States. This is followed by a discussion of the nature and extent of juvenile crime and of the social and psychological factors associated with delinquency, particularly serious delinquency. The chapter ends with material on the prevention of delinquency, including research on promising programs designed to control it.

A BRIEF HISTORY OF JUVENILE JUSTICE

For over 100 years, juveniles and adults have been processed through courts in a separate fashion. Juvenile justice was officially ushered into the United States on the last day of the 1899 session of the Illinois legislature, when that body passed the seminal **Juvenile Court Act**. This comprehensive child welfare law defined a delinquent as a child under the age of 16 who violated a state law or any village or city ordinance. It also established this country's first juvenile court and regulated juvenile institutions within the state. The philosophy underlying the law was that juvenile offenders should not be given the same punitive treatment as adults but, rather, be given individual attention for their own protection as well as that of society (Chute, 1949). In addition, the law included provisions for dealing with dependent and neglected children.

Although other states had adopted various procedures and regulations relevant to their wayward and neglected youth, the Illinois Act was the first comprehensive attempt at codification. It rapidly became the model for juvenile justice, and by 1911, 22 states had adopted similar measures. By 1925, all but two states had established juvenile courts (Tappan, 1949). Today, they exist in some form in every state, either separately or as part of a family court system.

Most programs directed at preventing or treating juvenile delinquency in the early twentieth century were created and managed by psychiatrists, psychologists, or social workers. Not surprisingly, they called for individual counseling and psychotherapy for youthful offenders, usually by a social caseworker or a clinical practitioner. Illinois was also a pioneer in this area; the first clinic established to provide psychiatric diagnoses to juvenile courts, the Juvenile Psychopathic Institute, opened its doors in Chicago in 1909. Shortly thereafter, the Judge Harvey H. Baker Child Guidance Clinic was established in Boston (Chute, 1949).

In 1930, however, a monumental project was undertaken—again in Chicago—by sociologists proposing a different approach to the prevention of juvenile offenses. Called the Chicago Area Project, it paved the way for a re-assessment of existing treatment and prevention programs for delinquents. It also represented the first systematic challenge by sociologists to the domination of psychologists and psychiatrists in both private and public juvenile programs (Schlossman & Sedlak, 1983).

The Project, which lasted 30 years, has been amply described, lauded, and criticized in the sociological and criminal justice literature. Essentially, it immersed researchers, practitioners, and volunteers into urban communities with higher than average rates of delinquency. They obtained oral histories and accounts of juvenile activities, organized recreational programs, offered "curbstone counseling," and mediated with police and juvenile courts on behalf of community youth. The Project deemphasized the individualized casework approach and drew attention to the role of the community as an agent of informal social control to prevent delinquency. Readers interested in more detail about the Project might refer to Schlossman and Sedlak's (1983) instructive history and assessment.

Approximately 20 years ago, Lloyd Ohlin (1983) traced three major shifts in federal policy regarding youth offending, beginning in the 1960s. He attributed the first shift to the Chicago Area Project and others like it. In the early 1960s, Ohlin noted, federal policymakers drew on community organization strategies to foster community responsibility for juvenile misbehavior and funded a variety of social programs toward that end. The programs in general were not successful, however, partly due to naiveté and partly due to the massive social changes in society that were occurring during the 1960s. "We are much more aware today that juvenile justice depends on the successful operation of a broad formal and informal network of social relationships that guide youth development" (Ohlin, 1983, p. 464). Ohlin noted that "the growing gap between expectation and achievable results fostered disillusionment, alienation, social unrest, and ultimately, abandonment of the programs themselves" (p. 464). He also suggested, however, that we can learn valuable lessons from the failure of those early community programs.

The second shift in social policy was spearheaded by a series of presidential commissions studying the broad problems of crime and violence. In 1967 the first of these commissions, the President's Commission on Law Enforcement and Administration of Justice, set the tone. Its primary task was to recommend ways to identify and control delinquents and status offenders. The Commission recommended six major strategies: (1) decriminalization of status offenses (such as running away from home); (2) diversion of youth from court procedures into public and private treatment programs; (3) extension of due process rights to juveniles in the same spirit in which they had been extended to adult offenders; (4) deinstitutionalization, whereby delinquents would be cared for in group homes or small treatment centers instead of the traditional large institutions, reform schools, or training schools; (5) diversification of services; and (6) decentralization of control of juvenile proceedings and care. The spirit of the Commission's recommendations was reflected in the landmark federal law, the *Juvenile Justice and Delinquency Prevention Act* (JJDPA) passed in 1974. At the same time, Congress created the Office of Juvenile Justice and Delinquency Prevention (OJJDP), a federal agency that conducts and sponsors research on juvenile issues, provides grants to states to study and implement changes in their juvenile justice systems, and generally serves as a watchdog over a wide range of practices affecting juveniles across the country.

As Ohlin (1983) noted, the mid-1970s also saw the beginning of a nationwide shift toward a law-and-order commitment. Apparently in response to a rapidly growing fear of crime and serious juvenile delinquency, the public began to demand quicker punishments and mandatory sentencing procedures, first for adults and eventually for juveniles. Ohlin noted that this new focus reflected in part a strong conservative reaction to the liberal policies advocated by the National Crime Commissions of the 1960s.

This law-and-order approach continued through the 1980s and 1990s, and it was often accompanied by broad legislative reform. For example, although all states have long had mechanisms for transferring some juveniles to criminal courts, in the 1990s the possibility of a transfer for a juvenile increased dramatically. Over the five-year period of 1992 to 1997, 45 states expanded the laws making it possible to try juveniles in criminal courts (Snyder, Sickmund, & Poe-Yamagata, 2000). Most of these not only lowered the age at which youths may be tried as adult offenders for serious violent offenses like rape or murder, but also expanded the range of crimes for which juveniles can be tried as adults. Furthermore, by the end of 1997, 28 states excluded juveniles of certain ages charged with certain offenses from juvenile court jurisdiction. Pennsylvania, for example, enacted a law excluding juveniles 15 or older from juvenile court if they are charged with a specified violent crime, allegedly committed with a deadly weapon, or have previously been adjudicated for the same crime.

Researchers are still exploring the results of these statutory changes. Although the percentage of cases transferred to criminal courts by judges (judicial waiver) has remained small and stable—approximately 1% to 1.6% (National Center for Juvenile Justice, 2003; Stahl et al., 1999), it is believed that prosecutors and state legislatures have widened the pool of juveniles whose cases are heard in criminal courts. In other words, many juvenile cases are heard in criminal courts by means of a prosecutor's "direct file" decision or by statutory law, and they do not require a judge's decision. The numbers and types of cases waived vary widely by jurisdiction, however, as documented in a recent study (Snyder et al., 2000). Nevertheless, some common variables seem to be at work in transfer decisions. For example, Snyder et al. found that the use of weapons, injury to the victim, the juvenile's age, and the juvenile's history of offending all affected the transfer decision.

Transferring youth to criminal courts often has unintended consequences. According to a recent study involving data from Pennsylvania (D. L. Myers, 2000), juveniles tried in criminal courts received harsher sentences than their juvenile court counterparts, a fact that would not necessarily disturb those who advocate transfer. However, transferred juveniles also were more likely to reoffend while awaiting trial, because—like adults—they were released on bail while waiting further proceedings. Had they not been transferred, many of these youths would have been detained pending their delinquency hearing and/or adjudicated more quickly.

Additionally, those juveniles who were transferred, convicted, and incarcerated were released while they were in their late teens or early twenties, often without having received adequate rehabilitative services. Myers maintains that the juvenile system offers better treatment than is offered during these short stays in jails and prisons.

Despite increases in transfer provisions, the great majority of youths charged with crime nationwide—over 90%—are processed in the juvenile courts. Nevertheless, even these juveniles have been given the message that they will be held accountable for their offenses. Sometimes this has come in the form of dispositions that were more punitive than rehabilitative, such as juvenile boot camps, which grew rapidly in popularity during the 1990s but have now lost favor among juvenile justice professionals in many states. However, juveniles are also held accountable in programs that require them to surmount increasingly difficult challenges, such as wilderness experiences, or in programs that require them to confront the harm they inflicted, such as victim–offender reconciliation programs. Many advocates for juveniles have argued that society can hold juveniles accountable without being excessively punitive and while still providing them with support and meaningful rehabilitative programs. The tough-on-crime approach, therefore, is competing with growing recognition that a multifaceted approach to the problem of juvenile crime is needed. Communities are being encouraged to work alongside juvenile justice professionals to develop resources to prevent offending as well as to intercede when children are at risk of engaging in delinquent behavior.

In recent years we have also seen increasing attention directed to the legal rights of juveniles, a topic that should be acknowledged but is peripheral to the subject of this text. More relevant to the text is another area engendering current research, the decision-making abilities of juveniles from a developmental perspective (Grisso & Schwartz, 2000). A growing body of psychological research investigates the extent to which juveniles with varying degrees of developmental abilities are capable of making decisions in their own best interests and should be held responsible for their offenses.

Finally, it must be mentioned that the 100th anniversary of the first juvenile court provided a stimulus for "taking stock" of the juvenile justice system. As often happens with significant birthdays and anniversaries, the milestone prompted numerous discussions and questions revolving around the effectiveness of the system, its strengths and weaknesses, and the prognosis for its future survival. Whereas some scholars advocate abolition of the system or drastic change in its operations, others hold out more hope for a separate system that persists in adopting a rehabilitative approach to juveniles.

DEFINITION OF JUVENILE DELINQUENCY

Juvenile delinquency is an imprecise, nebulous, social, clinical, and legal label for a wide variety of law- and norm-violating behavior. At first glance, a simple **legal definition** seems to suffice: *Delinquency is behavior against the criminal code committed by an individual who has not reached adulthood*. But the term delinquency has numerous definitions and meanings beyond this one-sentence definition. In some states the legal definition also includes status offending, which is not behavior against the criminal code but behavior prohibited only for juveniles. For example, running away, violating curfew laws, and truancy all qualify as **status offenses**.

Social and psychological definitions of delinquency may overlap considerably, just as each overlaps with legal definitions. Social delinquency consists of a wide variety of youthful behaviors considered inappropriate, such as aggressive behavior, truancy, petty theft, vandalism, and drug abuse. The behavior may or may not have come to the attention of the police. It is not unusual for "social delinquents" to be referred to community social service agencies or to juvenile courts, but they never legally become delinquents until and unless they are found in a hearing to have committed the crime for which they are charged. For example, a juvenile court intake officer may place juveniles on "informal probation," giving them a second chance to be supervised in the community rather than formally referred to juvenile court, where they face the possibility of being adjudicated delinquent.

Psychological definitions of delinquency include conduct disorder and antisocial behavior. **Conduct disorder** (CD) is a diagnostic term used to represent a group of behaviors characterized by *habitual* misbehavior, such as stealing, setting fires, running away from home, skipping school, destroying property, fighting, being cruel to animals and people, and frequently telling lies. Like the social delinquent, the psychological delinquent may or may not have been arrested for these behaviors. Some of them, in fact, are not even against the criminal law. The term *conduct disorder* is more fully described in the *American Psychiatric Association's Diagnostic and Statistical Manual,* fourth edition (APA, 1994), commonly referred to as the DSM-IV. The DSM-IV—now in a slightly revised edition referred to as the DSM-IV-TR (2000)—divides CDs into two categories, depending on the onset of the misbehaviors. If the misconduct begins in childhood (before age 10), it is called CD: childhood-onset type. If the misconduct begins in adolescence, it is called CD: adolescent-onset type.

The clinical term **antisocial behavior** is usually reserved for more serious habitual misbehavior, especially a behavioral pattern that involves direct and harmful actions against others. It is to be distinguished, however, from the term *antisocial personality disorder*, a diagnostic label reserved primarily for adults who display conduct disorders as children or adolescents and continue serious offending well into adulthood. We discuss antisocial personality disorders in more detail in Chapter 6.

Returning to the legal definition, a juvenile delinquent is one who commits an act defined by law as illegal and who is adjudicated delinquent by an appropriate court. This would occur after a juvenile has pled guilty or after a prosecutor has met the burden of proving all elements of the crime beyond a reasonable doubt. The legal definition is usually restricted to persons under age 16, but states vary in their age distinctions. Under federal law, juveniles may be prosecuted as adults at age 15. A handful of states give criminal courts, rather than juvenile courts, automatic jurisdiction over juveniles at age 16. However, all states allow juveniles to be tried as adults in criminal courts under certain conditions and for certain offenses, and as noted earlier, the pool of juveniles eligible for transfer is increasing. In a highly publicized case in early January 2001, 12-year-old Lionel Tate was convicted of killing a 4-year-old girl while wrestling and was sentenced to life without parole. However, in December 2003 a judge granted him a new trial. He later pled guilty and was placed on probation. The lowest age specified in statutes for processing in criminal courts is 10; when no minimum age is specified, even children under age 10 have appeared in criminal court.

Juvenile courts are part of the civil court system and differ significantly from criminal courts in both terminology and procedure. For example, prosecutors in juvenile courts file petitions of delinquency rather than criminal complaints; judges conduct hearings, not trials; if found to have committed the act, the juvenile becomes a delinquent, not an offender. In general, juvenile court proceedings are not open to the public. However, juveniles are still protected by many due process safeguards associated with criminal trials, such as written notice of charges, legal representation, the right to confront and cross-examine witnesses, and protection against self-incrimination. It should be noted, however, that a study of delinquency hearings in six jurisdictions (Feld, 1988) found that fewer than one-half of juveniles were represented by attorneys at their delinquency hearings. More recent studies indicate that rates of representation are increasing, but the actual figures vary widely by jurisdiction (Grisso & Schwartz, 2000). Juveniles are not constitutionally entitled to a trial by jury, but a state may provide its juveniles with a jury trial if it so wishes. When juveniles are tried in criminal courts, the trial by jury is guaranteed, although, like adults, they are entitled to waive the jury and opt for a bench trial instead, in which the presiding judge makes the decision as to the offender's guilt or innocence.

Once a juvenile is adjudicated delinquent, a wide range of rehabilitation options is available, both in the community and in public and private residential facilities (see **Figure 2–1**). As for adults, the most common sanction for juveniles is probation or supervision in the community. To the extent possible, the juvenile system tries to provide rehabilitative programs to the juvenile while he or she remains at home or, alternately, in a group- or foster-home setting. Secure, residential treatment facilities—the equivalent of adult jails or prisons—are usually considered the last alternative when other placements have failed. Juveniles who have committed serious crimes, however, may be placed immediately in a secure, residential setting.

FIGURE 2–1   A Simplified View of Caseflow through the Juvenile Justice System

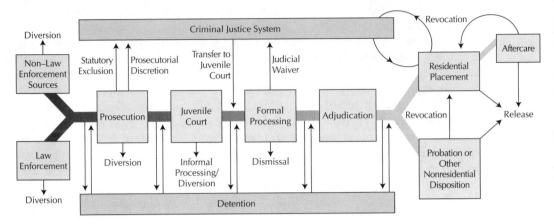

Note: Procedures vary among jurisdictions.

As noted earlier, the 100th anniversary of the first juvenile court prompted considerable examination of the juvenile system, even including proposals for its abolition. Scholars have proposed numerous philosophical, structural, and procedural changes to better balance the interests of society, the child, and the parent (e.g., American Bar Association, 1979; Grisso & Schwartz, 2000). Although there is considerable disagreement among policymakers and scholars as to how the system should be improved, there are hopeful signs on the horizon. The end of the twentieth century saw strong leadership from a variety of national organizations, including the Office of Juvenile Justice and Delinquency Prevention (OJJDP), which continues in its role as an effective advocate in a range of juvenile issues. A number of nongovernmental research and advocacy organizations, such as the Annie E. Casey Foundation and Amnesty International, also fund research on critical juvenile issues and serve as "watchdogs" for the rights of juveniles. Social scientists—such as those associated with the MacArthur Research Network—are conducting important research on the extent to which juveniles understand their legal rights and the extent to which they can make decisions in their own best interest.

It is not our purpose here to deal with the problems of the juvenile justice system at any length or to evaluate the recommendations for change. Their existence only serves as a backdrop for our main topic, which is the behavior of youths adjudicated delinquent and how serious criminal behavior in youths is acquired and maintained. Additionally, we are concerned about the social and the psychological delinquents who may not come to the attention of the formal justice system, but who are still a considerable threat to their own well-being as well as to the safety of the community. Our main focus throughout this chapter is on the chronic, repetitive offender who moves from adolescence to adulthood in a continuing cycle of offending and reoffending.

THE NATURE AND EXTENT OF JUVENILE OFFENDING

The nature and extent of delinquent behavior—both what is reported and what is unreported to law enforcement agencies—are essentially an unknown area (Krisberg, 1995; Krisberg & Schwartz, 1983), even more so than adult crime. We simply do not have complete data on the national incidence of juvenile delinquency, broadly defined. We do have some statistics collected by law enforcement agencies (e.g., through the UCR reporting system), the courts, and facilities for delinquents. The government regularly publishes reports on juvenile court statistics and on children in custody in both detention and treatment facilities (see **Figure 2–2**). Nevertheless, as for adult crime, there is a huge

FIGURE 2–2   Case Processing Overview for Juveniles, 1999

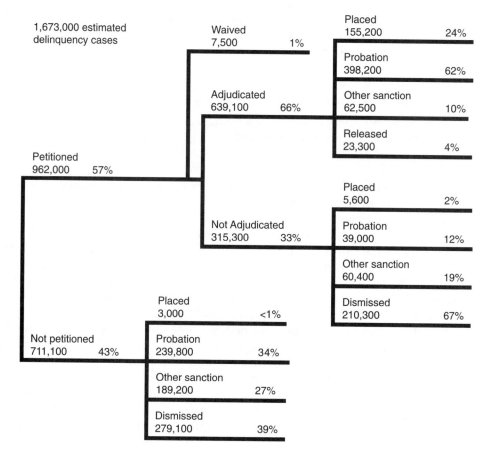

Note: Cases are categorized by their most severe or restrictive sanction. Category data may not add up to totals because of rounding.

Source: National Center for Juvenile Justice (2003, p. 38).

TABLE 2–1   The Nature of Juvenile Offending

UNLAWFUL ACTS	DEFINITION
Unlawful acts against persons	Violent crimes, similar to those crimes committed by adults, such as aggravated assault, robbery, sexual assault
Unlawful acts against property	Property crimes, similar to those crimes committed by adults, such as burglary, larceny theft, vandalism
Drug offenses	Possession, distribution, and/or manufacture of drugs
Public order offenses	Nuisance crimes against society, such as noise violations
Status offenses	Acts only juveniles can commit, such as violation of curfew, running away, school truancy

dark figure. As Barry Krisberg (1992, p. 2) notes, "Put simply, the amount of crime committed by juveniles is unknown and perhaps unknowable."

Usually, unlawful acts committed by delinquents are placed into five major categories (see **Table 2–1**).

1. Unlawful acts against persons
2. Unlawful acts against property
3. Drug offenses
4. Offenses against the public order
5. Status offenses

The most recently available juvenile court statistics (National Center for Juvenile Justice, 2003) indicate that an estimated 1.7 million delinquency cases were handled by courts with juvenile jurisdiction in 1999. More than half of all delinquency cases involve a youth younger than age 16. In addition, nearly one-quarter (24%) of all delinquency cases handled in 1999 involved a female juvenile, compared to 19% in 1990. Most referrals to juvenile court are for crimes against property (42%), followed by offenses against the public order (23%) and crimes against persons (23%), then drug offenses (11%) (National Center for Juvenile Justice, 2003). The first four categories in the above list are comparable in definition to crimes committed by adults and are discussed shortly. Before we turn to these criminal acts, it is important to digress briefly on the troubling case of status offending.

Status offenses are acts that only juveniles can commit and that can be adjudicated only by a juvenile court. As discussed earlier, typical status offenses range from misbehavior, such as violations of curfew, running away from home, and truancy, to offenses that are interpreted very subjectively, such as unruliness, unmanageability, or incorrigibility. However, only four status offenses are tabulated by the National Center for Juvenile Justice (2003): running away, truancy, ungovernability (also known as incorrigibility or being beyond the control of one's parents), and underage liquor law violations (e.g., a minor in possession of alcohol, underage drinking). Although a number of other behaviors are often considered status offenses (e.g., curfew violations, tobacco offenses), they are usually not discussed in governmental reports.

The juvenile system has historically supported differential treatment of male and female status offenders. Adolescent girls, for example, have often been detained for incorrigibility or running away from home, when the same behavior in adolescent boys was ignored or tolerated. Until recently, about three times as many girls were detained for status offenses as boys (U.S. Department of Justice, 1988). In recent years, as a result of suits brought on behalf of juveniles, many courts have put authorities on notice that this discriminatory approach is unwarranted. Even so, recent figures indicate that girls are still more likely than boys to be arrested as runaways (National Center for Juvenile Justice, 2003; Snyder, 2000) (see **Figure 2–3**).

It has been argued that, because status offenses lend themselves to so much subjectivity, they should be removed from the purview of all state juvenile courts (American Bar Association, 1979). Some states have clearly moved in this direction. On the other hand, although most states do not label status offenders "delinquents," they do allow their detention and/or supervision because

Figure 2–3   Proportion of Males and Females in Petitioned Status Offense Cases

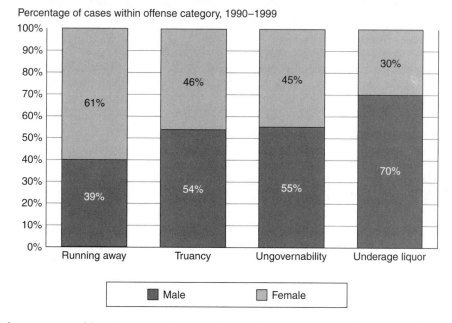

Note: The proportion of females was greater in petitioned status offense cases than in delinquency cases. Females accounted for 61% of petitioned runaway cases. In no other offense category (status or delinquency) was the female share of cases greater than the male share.
Source: National Center for Juvenile Justice (2003, p. 53).

they are presumed to be in need of protection either from their own rash behavior or the behavior of others. The statutes allowing this are usually referred to as PINS or CHINS laws (person or child in need of supervision). Under these laws, runaways or incorrigible youngsters are subject to juvenile or family court jurisdiction, often at the instigation of their parents, even though they may not have committed an act comparable to a crime. These statutes also allow juvenile or family courts to address the needs of neglected and dependent children.

Nevertheless, status offenders should not be kept in secure facilities. The JJDPA (1974) mandated that states receiving federal funds must make progress toward "deinstitutionalizing" all status offenders (both boys and girls). According to the JJDPA (1998), the great majority of states were in full or substantial compliance with this mandate by the mid-1990s. However, some states have found alternative, creative ways of confining status offenders. Costello (2003) reports the following four tactics: (1) refer or commit them to secure mental health facilities; (2) allege a delinquent act rather than a status offense (e.g., trespass rather than runaway); (3) develop "semisecure" facilities that technically are not secure but operate as secure; and (4) hold status offenders in contempt for violating court orders, thereby "bootstrapping" them into delinquency. Thus, although the JJDPA mandate may be honored on paper, the spirit of the mandate is often violated. In sum, large numbers of status offenders continue to be taken into custody by police. Additionally, status offenders continue to be removed from their homes and placed in nonsecure residential settings.

In this chapter, although status offending and minor delinquent crime are considered, our focus is on violent offending and more serious property offending. We are particularly interested in the developmental trajectories that lead to serious delinquency. In recent years, developmental psychologists have conducted extensive research on this topic, as we note shortly.

Data on Serious Juvenile Offending

Serious or habitual juvenile offenders rarely restrict their behaviors to one type of offense category. We have learned from a variety of data sources that the range of their antisocial conduct covers both property and violent offenses. Youth crime data are collected from (1) official records of police arrests, such as the FBI's UCR (see, e.g., **Figure 2–4**); (2) reports of victimization, such as the *National Crime Victimization Survey* (NCVS); (3) self-reports of delinquent involvement, whereby national samples of youth are asked to complete questionnaires about their own behavior, such as in the *National Youth Survey* (Elliott, Ageton, & Huizinga, 1980); (4) juvenile court processing, as reported by the *National Center for Juvenile Justice* (NCJJ); (5) juvenile corrections, as reported in the *Census of Juveniles in Residential Treatment* (OJJDP, 2000); and—though to a limited extent—(6) juvenile probation and aftercare statistics. (Aftercare is the equivalent of parole in the adult system.)

FIGURE 2–4   Percentage of Total Arrests (Adults and Juveniles) Involving Juveniles, 2002

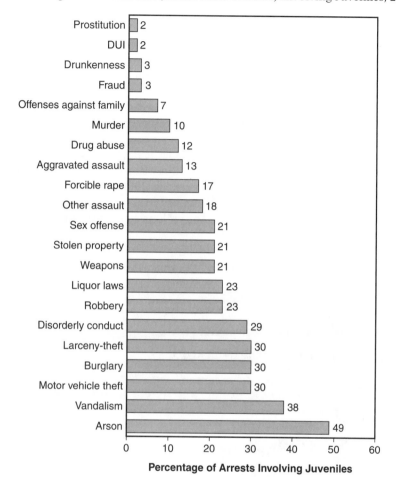

Source: Federal Bureau of Investigation (2003).

The last three sources of information have the major disadvantage of greatly underestimating the number of actual offenses and offenders. A very high proportion—perhaps the majority—of cases is either undetected, is handled informally, is referred to court diversion programs, or is dismissed before reaching the courts. In other words, because of parental involvement, negotiations, and compromises, many juveniles do not require adjudication.

Public opinion surveys have periodically revealed that many people believe serious youth crime is increasing at a steady and alarming rate (Krisberg, 1992). As we saw earlier, in the 1990s states across the country adopted legislation aimed at getting tough on juvenile crime, and even the juvenile justice system itself began to adopt programs focused on accountability. To some extent, these shifts were in response to increasing rates of offending among the young. Between 1989 and 1994, the arrest rates for juveniles increased significantly, approximately 20% across most crimes. The increase in violent crimes was particularly significant, however. In 1980, juveniles were known to be the offender in 8% of all homicides. In 1994, they were known to be the offender in 16% of all homicides, a significant increase (Sickmund et al., 1997).

The most recent juvenile crime figures are more promising, however. Juvenile crime, particularly violent crime, peaked in 1994 and has been decreasing steadily since then. According to the UCR data, between 1994 and 2000, the juvenile arrest rate for violent crime index offenses fell 41% (Snyder, 2002). In fact, the juvenile violent crime arrest rate in 2000 was the lowest since 1985. In 2002, juveniles were the known offenders in 5.4% of all homicides and represented 14.8% of all those arrested for violent crimes (see **Figure 2–5**) (Snyder,

FIGURE 2–5   Proportions of Juvenile Arrests and Clearance Rates

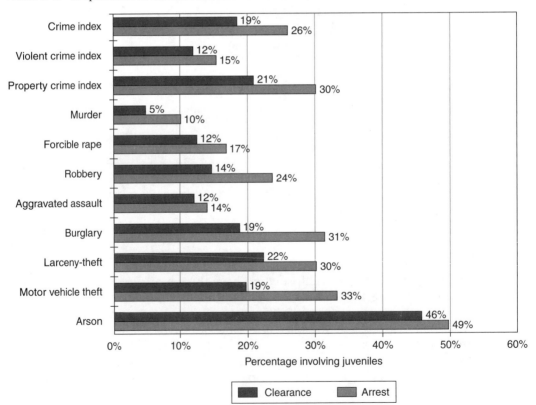

Source: Snyder (2003, p. 2).

2003). After more than a decade of increases, homicides by juveniles have been steadily decreasing since 1993. Between 1993 and 2000, the juvenile murder arrest rate fell 74%, to its lowest level since the 1960s (Snyder, 2002).

Between 1994 and 2000, the juvenile property crime index offense arrest rate dropped 37%, to its lowest level since the 1960s (Snyder, 2002). "Specifically, juvenile burglary arrest rates declined throughout the 1980s and 1990s, the juvenile larceny-theft arrest rate was at its lowest level in 20 years, and juvenile motor vehicle theft and arson arrest rates were near their 20-year lows" (p. 5). On the other hand, between 1990 and 2000, the juvenile proportion of all arrests for drug abuse violations increased from 8% to 13%. And juvenile arrests for curfew and loitering violations increased 81% between 1991 and 2000. Demographically, 28% of curfew arrests in 2000 involved juveniles under age 15 and 31% involved females. In addition, 28% of arrests for running away from home involved females, and 39% involved juveniles under age 15.

How does violent juvenile crime compare with the incidence and rate of property offenses—burglary, larceny-theft, and motor vehicle theft? According to the 2002 UCR data, the four violent index categories (murder and voluntary manslaughter, forcible rape, robbery, and aggravated assault) represent slightly over 4% of all juvenile arrests (see **Table 2–2**). The nonviolent index offenses (larceny-theft, motor vehicle theft, burglary, and arson), represent an additional 22% of all juvenile arrests. Thus, approximately three-fourths of all juvenile arrests are for the 21 nonindex offenses that include simple assaults, vandalism, drug abuse violations, disorderly conduct, and curfew and loitering violations.

The racial composition of the juvenile population in 2000 was 79% white, 16% black, 4% Asian/Pacific Islander, and 1% American Indian (Snyder, 2002). Most Latinos (an ethnic designation and not a race) were classified as white. Black juveniles, however, were overrepresented in arrests for violent

TABLE 2–2   Juvenile Arrests for Index Crimes, 2002

OFFENSE CHARGED	TOTAL UNDER AGE 18	TOTAL UNDER AGE 10
Total index crimes	1,624,192	19,904
Violent crimes	66,508	826
Murder	973	0
Forcible rape	3,361	42
Robbery	17,893	85
Aggravated assault	44,281	699
Property crime	349,099	5,308
Burglary	61,843	1,153
Larceny-theft	248,861	3,535
Motor vehicle theft	32,544	65
Arson	5,851	552

Source: Federal Bureau of Investigation (2003).

crimes and, to a lesser extent, property crimes. "Of all juvenile arrests for violent crimes, 55% involved white youth, 42% involved black youth, 2% involved Asian youth, and 1% involved American Indian youth. For property crime arrests, the proportions were 69% white youth, 27% black youth, 2% Asian youth, and 1% American Indian youth" (Snyder, 2002, p. 10).

In 2000, 20% of the youths arrested were handled by arresting law enforcement agencies themselves, while 71% were referred to juvenile court (Snyder, 2002). Seven percent were referred directly to criminal court, while approximately 2% were referred to either a child welfare agency or some other law enforcement agency. Thus, we see that the proportion of arrests sent to juvenile court has increased somewhat over the past decade, with 64% of the juveniles being referred to juvenile court in 1990, compared to the 71% referred in 2000. Between 1990 and 1999, the number of delinquency cases processed by juvenile courts nationwide increased by 27% (National Center for Juvenile Justice, 2003).

SCHOOL CRIME

During the last quarter of the twentieth century, much public attention was directed at the problem of school crime. Anecdotal and media accounts of children being victimized at school by other children prompted researchers to study the issue in an attempt to document the magnitude of the problem. In 1974, Congress funded a three-year study to assess the nature and extent of crime, violence and disruption in the nation's schools. The National Institute of Education, which conducted the study, released its findings in 1977, and the Safe School Study (NIE, 1977) remains the most comprehensive study available, although its findings are dated. For an assessment of the findings of that study, interested readers are referred to Richard Lawrence's (1998) book, *School Crime and Juvenile Justice*, as well as to a reexamination of the findings of the study by Gottfredson and Gottfredson (1985). Briefly, Gottfredson and Gottfredson concluded that community factors, frequently out of the control of school administrators, were highly correlated with victimization of both students and teachers.

The National Center for Education Statistics publishes school crime data in the *Indicators of School Crime and Safety;* the most recent copy, at this writing, is dated 2003. Other significant school crime studies are conducted periodically as supplements to the NCVS. Thus far, these have been done in 1989, 1995, and 1999. A representative sample of students between 12 and 19 years of age attending both public and private high schools is included. The most recent NCVS data on school violence indicate that it is down since the time the surveys were begun. This is consistent with the latest National Center for Education Statistics report (2003), which indicates the following.

- Between 1995 and 2001, the percentage of students who reported being victims of crime at school decreased from 10 to 6.

- Victims of theft decreased from 7% to 4%.
- Victims of violence decreased from 3% to 2%.

The report also indicates that there was no detectable increase or decrease over time in

- the percentage of students threatened or injured with a weapon,
- the percentage of teachers physically attacked by a student,
- hate-related graffiti, or
- marijuana use, alcohol use, and drug distribution at school.

In one category, bullying, the report detects an increase. Specifically, in 2001, 8% of students reported that they had been bullied at school, up from 5% in 1999.

Although the above trends suggest that school crime is not getting worse, the raw numbers and the prevalence remain sobering. For example, in 1999–2000, an estimated 1.5 million violent incidents occured in public elementary and secondary schools, and there were an estimated 218,000 thefts. Seventy-one percent of public schools experienced one or more violent incidents, and 20% experienced one or more serious violent incidents (e.g., rape, physical attack, or fight with a weapon).

Even so, in addressing what we have learned from surveys of school crime, Lawrence (1998) seeks to put the problem in perspective. He notes that, on average, 99% of students are free from violent school crime in a month's time. Furthermore, "There is no strong evidence that serious crime in schools is an extensive problem or that the problem has increased significantly; serious physical injuries or financial loss are rare in schools, although minor victimizations and verbal threats do occur regularly" (p. 29). He notes also that, with the exception of some urban schools in some high-crime areas, students and teachers are safer in most schools than they are in other locations in the community.

Nevertheless, in an effort to maximize the safety of students and teachers, federal, state, and private funds have been made available to schools to develop a plethora of programs designed to guard school premises and/or to resolve conflicts among students. In some communities, police officers are assigned to patrol schools and school grounds. In the 1990s, teen courts and peer mediation centers were established, sometimes on school premises, to educate youth about the justice system, engage them in solving their own problems, and hold each other accountable for unacceptable behavior.

The topic of school crime took on a more chilling urgency in the late 1990s, however, when a rash of school shootings made headlines. Communities across the United States that had previously had a low profile—West Paducah, Kentucky; Jonesboro, Arkansas; Pearl, Mississippi; Springfield, Oregon—suddenly became notorious. The most infamous case was the mass murder of 12 students and one teacher at Columbine High School in Littleton,

Colorado, in April 1999. The two teenage boys who did the shooting apparently committed suicide during the incident. Twenty more students were injured. Although there had been a number of school shootings prior to Columbine (there were at least 10 school shootings between 1996 and 1999), the Columbine shooting prompted a great deal of alarm and concern nationwide. In addition, the media and some experts were quick to make gross generalizations about the school violence problem. O'Toole (2000, p. 4) lists the usual wrong or unverified impressions of school shooters often promoted by the news media. Among them are the following:

- School violence is an epidemic.
- All school shooters are alike.
- The school shooter is always a loner.
- School shootings are exclusively motivated by revenge.
- Easy access to weapons is the most significant factor.
- Unusual or aberrant behaviors, interests, or hobbies are hallmarks of the student destined to become violent.

Despite the media attention given to Columbine and other schools, it is important to keep school crime, including violence, in perspective. Note that the school shootings previously described occurred during a time when juvenile violent crime on the whole was going down; thus, although the shootings were terrifying, they were not representative of the juvenile crime picture. Furthermore, although the media understandably report incidents of children having guns on school premises, there is no documentation that this is a widespread problem. Although it is important to be alert to possible dangers facing school-aged children and the adults who work with them in the schools, the reality is that the risk of victimization is lower in that environment than in private homes or the community at large.

THE SERIOUS DELINQUENT

Both self-report studies and official data indicate that only a small percentage of the juvenile population engages in serious delinquent behavior, whether it is defined legally, socially, or psychologically. Nevertheless, those who do often escape detection. An early self-report study (Weis & Sederstrom, 1981) indicated that only about 3% to 15% of serious offenses ever result in "police contact." Likewise, Elliott, Dunford, and Huizinga (1987) suggest that serious, repetitive juvenile offenders escaped detection 86% of the time over a five-year period. These figures further suggest that the incidence of offending may be substantially underestimated by official arrest data. In other words, a small percentage of youth is committing a substantial amount of offenses that do not come to the attention of police. Research also suggests that this group of youths—when they do enter the justice system—tend to be high in *recidivism*, or repeat offending (Bartol & Bartol, 1998). In addition, frequent offenders do not specialize in any one particular kind of offending, such as theft or larceny. Instead, they tend to be involved in a wide variety of offenses, ranging from minor property crimes to highly violent ones. Longitudinal research also indicates that repetitive offenders as a group were unusually troublesome in school, earned poor grades, and had inadequate or poor social skills. Furthermore, these troublesome behaviors often began at an early age, and the more serious the offender, the earlier these childhood patterns appeared. With these observations in mind, we now turn our attention to a topic directly relevant to the psychosocial nature of this text, namely, the social and psychological factors that appear to be correlated with persistent delinquent behavior among young people.

SOCIAL RISK FACTORS

Poverty and Social Class

Social class and general effects of poverty have been a central focus in research studies of crime and delinquency for over a century. Most pre-1960 sociological theories of delinquency considered it a crucial element in explanations of crime and delinquency. These theories predicted an inverse or negative relationship between **social class** and offending: The lower the social class, the greater the likelihood of involvement in delinquent or criminal behavior. During the mid-1950s and early 1960s, researchers began to wonder if the social class or poverty connection to offending was really all that strong. Much of this doubt stemmed from the findings of self-report studies that suggested that juvenile offending was as prevalent among middle-class youth as it was among lower-class youth. In addition, many criminologists during this time period were uncomfortable about targeting economically disadvantaged populations and suggesting that they were at fault for the delinquency problem.

There is little doubt, however, that poverty has a strong connection to persistent, violent offending, as measured by official, victimization, and self-report data. Accumulating research evidence strongly indicates that poverty is one of the most robust predictors of adolescent violence for both males and females (Hammond & Yung, 1994; H. Hill et al., 1994; Sampson & Wilson, 1993). We must be extremely careful both in interpreting these data and in making decisions about how to prevent future offending, however. Furthermore, it should be emphasized that this strong connection holds whether we are referring to victims or offenders. Children and youth living under dire economic conditions are more likely to be victims as well as offenders. Preschool children living in a low-income family characterized by poor housing and unemployment are at especially high risk to become delinquent and/or to become victimized (Dodge, 1993a; Farrington, 1991). Poverty in this context refers to a situation in which the basic resources to maintain an average standard of living within a specific geographical region are lacking. This typically includes the absence of sufficient income to meet the basic necessities of life.

The exact nature of the relationship between poverty and violence is not well understood. For example, poverty is often accompanied not only by inequities in resources, but also by discrimination, racism, family disruption, unsafe living conditions, joblessness, social isolation, and limited social support systems (H. Hill et al., 1994; Sampson & Lauritsen, 1994). Youth living under poverty conditions are more likely to attend inadequate schools, to drop out of school, to be unemployed, to carry a firearm, to be victimized, and to be a witness to a variety of violent events. Furthermore, having a low income affects people differently. For instance, the values of different ethnic and cultural groups provide a cultural context wherein poverty is perceived differently (Guerra et al., 1995). Some subgroups in society may perceive material deprivation as more acceptable if everyone else within that cultural context is in the "same boat."

Poverty influences the family in many ways, not the least of which is the impact on parents' behavior toward children. For instance, the stress caused by poverty in urban settings is believed to diminish parents' capacity for supportive and consistent parenting (Hammond & Yung, 1994). This situation may lead to coercive and highly aggressive methods of child control. Coercive methods of child control are more direct, immediate, and easy to administer. They require less time and energy to administer compared to parenting that emphasizes sensitivity, interpersonal skills, and patient understanding. It is much easier to slap a child than it is to explain and use more thoughtful parenting strategies. Furthermore, parenting that uses aggressive and violent tactics often provides models and a violent context that promote the cycle of violence in the next generation. Living in disadvantaged environments may also lead to the belief that economic survival and social status depend greatly on being aggressive and violent to others.

Important caveats must be offered in any discussion of serious delinquency and economic status, however. First, the strong correlation between low socioeconomic class and delinquency does not mean that poverty causes or inevitably leads to serious delinquency. The great majority of poor children and adults are law-abiding citizens, and children and adults from families of high economic status do engage in serious delinquency and crime. Both self-report and victimization data indicate that sexual assault, serious drug use, theft, and fraud are perpetrated by juveniles across all social classes. Second, in many communities children from the lower socioeconomic class are targeted by law enforcement practices more than children of the middle and upper classes are. They are more likely to be taken into custody by police, referred to juvenile courts, and adjudicated delinquent. Thus, they appear in the official government statistics that serve as our measures of crime. In addition, these children of the poor are taken into a system that often makes it more likely that they will continue in a pattern of delinquent behavior or adult crime, particularly when they are institutionalized. Children of the middle and upper classes, by contrast, are more likely to be handled informally, provided with legal assistance, or placed by their parents in private facilities for the treatment of their problem behavior (Chesney-Lind & Shelden, 1998; Schwartz, 1989).

Peer Experiences

Adolescents live in two separate worlds: one for the family and the other for friends (Berndt, 1979). Adolescents often seek advice from family in matters of finance, education, and career plans, but in making decisions about their social lives—dress, drinking, dating, drugs, recreational activities—adolescents overwhelmingly want to be attuned to the opinions of their peers (Sebald, 1986).

Consistently, the research literature finds peer association to be one of the strongest and most consistent single predictors of delinquency (Loeber & Dishion, 1983; Pepler & Slaby, 1994). Those adolescents who report having delinquent friends are more likely to report delinquent offending themselves. The relationship is so robust that some treatment programs for serious delinquents make it a priority to create new, healthier peer associations (e.g., Henggeler, 1994).

The relationship between peers and drug use seems especially strong. For example, Richard Johnson and his associates (R. E. Johnson, Marcos, & Bahr, 1987) found that peers have considerable influence on both the frequency and the type of drug used. They conclude, "It is not so much that adolescents use drugs because drug use of the friends makes drug use seem right or safe; rather, they apparently use drugs *simply because their friends do*" (p. 336).

However, peer influence is a complicated process. It is highly unlikely that peer influence by itself provides a complete picture of the development of serious delinquency and crime. Serious delinquency is the end product of many influences, including peers, family, and the social environment in general. Furthermore, there is no evidence in the research literature that association with delinquent peers precedes or even encourages offending (Farrington, 1987). In other words, the adolescent may have been prone to frequent antisocial behavior prior to the association with delinquent friends. Therefore, we cannot assert that delinquent peers cause other peers who associate with them to become delinquent, but serious delinquents do tend to hang around with delinquent peers, although their delinquent behavior was often apparent before their peer association. For example, the research is strong that aggressive children are rejected by peers (Dodge & Pettit, 2003; Pepler & Slaby, 1994). These rejected children seek out and associate with other rejected children who share similar values and goals (Cairns & Cairns, 1991; Cairns et al., 1988).

Recent research by Kenneth Dodge and associates (Dodge & Pettit, 2003) clearly indicates that the amount of exposure a child has to aggressive peers in day care or preschool is predictive of later child aggressive behavior, most likely because of modeling effects. In addition, being liked or disliked by the peer group in elementary school appears to influence the developmental trajectory for getting along with others later in life (Rubin, Bukowski, & Parker, 1998). Being disliked or rejected by peers not only encourages aggression but discourages the development of social and interpersonal skills. Recent research has found that social rejection by peers in the elementary school grades leads to a high probability of delinquent and antisocial behavior in high school and young adulthood (Dodge & Pettit, 2003). "Those children who were rejected for at least two or three years by second grade had a 50% change of displaying clinically significant conduct problems later in adolescence, in contrast with just 9% chance for those children who managed to avoid early peer rejection" (p. 353).

Preschool and School Experiences

Children who spend large amounts of time in unsupervised afterschool care in the early elementary school years are also at elevated risk for delinquency (Pettit, Laird, Bates, & Dodge, 1997). In addition, these children, because they are unsupervised, are more likely to associate with other unsupervised or delinquency-prone peers.

Early school failure is also linked to antisocial development and delinquency (Dodge & Pettit, 2003). "Meta-analyses suggest that retention in kindergarten and in the early grades has long-term detrimental effects on behavior outcomes in spite of immediate academic benefits" (p. 353). Furthermore, peers appear more likely to view children "who stay back" more negatively, potentially leading to further peer rejection and ridicule.

Family Background

It is estimated that over 12 million American families with children are maintained by only one parent (U.S. Bureau of the Census, 2001). Early studies based on official data found that delinquents were more likely than nondelinquents to come from homes where parents were divorced or separated (Eaton & Polk, 1961; Glueck & Glueck, 1950; T. Monahan, 1957; Rodman & Grams, 1967). This led to conclusions that the single-parent home—or the "broken home," as it was called—could be blamed for much delinquency. Beginning in the 1970s, when self-report data indicated that delinquent behavior was widespread, criminologists began to question these conclusions. Today, the topic of the single-parent home is still found in the delinquency literature. However, researchers are more likely to examine accompanying factors such as the quality of the parent–child relationship, the family's economic status, and the degree of emotional support provided to the family by other adults, such as extended family members or community agents.

A wide variety of circumstances can lead to a single-parent home. The home may have started that way, as when an unmarried woman gives birth to or adopts a child. In addition, two-parent homes may be "broken" by a wide variety of circumstances—death, desertion, divorce, and separation. Such separations do not affect all families the same way. Furthermore, there is evidence that children from single-parent homes that are relatively conflict-free are less likely to be delinquent than children from conflict-ridden "intact" homes (Gove & Crutchfield, 1982). The composition of the home also must be considered. That is, who is living in the home—grandparents, stepparent, relatives, or friends? The "nontraditional" family has become a fixture in today's society. Many researchers define family as individuals related by blood or by legal arrangements (i.e., marriages, adoptions, legal guardianships, civil unions). Others point out that individuals who live together in long-term committed relationships—either as friends or as sexual partners—and who may be caring for their own or other people's children, are also family.

While the relationship between single-parent homes and delinquency continues to be commonly reported, we are far from explaining it—and it may be pointless to try. If the single-parent home is a risk factor, it is probably influenced by other interacting variables. Rather than concentrating on the *structure* of the family, a focus on the *process* is far more desirable. As Flynn (1983, p. 13) asserts, "One point is indisputably clear in the literature: A stable, secure, and mutually supportive family is exceedingly important in delinquency prevention."

Parental Disciplinary Practices

Gerald Patterson (1982, 1986) concluded years ago that the parents or caretakers of delinquency-prone children support their use of antisocial behavior by inadvertently reinforcing such behaviors and by failing to reinforce prosocial ones. Within these families, continual aversive exchanges were observed between parents and the aggressive children, suggesting that these children may be both the architects and the victims of aggressive interactions (Pepler & Slaby, 1994). Such dynamics can, of course, be found in all types of families and from all socioeconomic classes. Again, the process is the more critical variable. Studies such as the above prompted the development of parent-education or parent-training programs, intended to provide parents with more effective strategies for dealing with the antisocial behaviors of their children. Critics note that such programs are largely ineffective because families who would benefit from them are often faced with a multitude of challenges that are not addressed simply by teaching the parents how to interact with their children. "Indeed, families characterized by multiple risk factors associated with child/adolescent behavior problems (e.g., marital distress, socioeconomic disadvantage, social isolation, single parenthood, parental depression) tend to show fewer and shorter gains following [parent-education] treatment" (T. Brown, Borduin, & Henggeler, 2001, p. 448).

Factors such as inconsistent parental disciplinary practices (J. McCord, 1979) and harsh, physical punishment by parents are also strongly correlated with delinquency (Straus, 1991). Inconsistent or physically harsh discipline in the home may result in more delinquency than consistent and reasoning forms of discipline. Early studies found that delinquents repeatedly complained that their parents were unfair and nonobjective in administering discipline (Glueck & Glueck, 1950; McCord, McCord, & Zola, 1959), a complaint voiced much less frequently by nondelinquents.

From a psychological perspective, we can easily see why inconsistent discipline is a problem. Inconsistent discipline yields inconsistent dispensation of reinforcement. If a five-year-old boy punches or kicks his four-year-old neighbor, he may be ignored by his parent on one occasion and chastised for being too aggressive the next. It is likely, also, that his socially desirable behaviors—such as sharing a toy—will not be strengthened in the home environment. In addition, punishment contingent on the whim and mood of a parent rather than on any specific behavior on the part of the child contributes to an extremely unpleasant and unpredictable environment. In one of the very few studies examining the parenting practices of families living in the inner city, Gorman-Smith et al. (1996) found that some aspects of family relationship characteristics and parenting practices are consistently linked to violent delinquency, regardless of ethnic or socioeconomic characteristics. Three of the most influential factors are poor parental monitoring of the child's activities, poor discipline, and a lack of family cohesion.

Physical punishments—like slapping, hitting, and punching—are, of course, also problematic. They provide a pattern to be modeled when youngsters are themselves frustrated and disenchanted. Murray Straus (1991) concluded that although harsh physical punishment produces some conformity in children during the short term, over time it tends to increase the probability of violent delinquency and crime. Straus further discovered that parents who believe in physical punishment not only hit the children more often but are more likely to go beyond a slap or spanking and seriously assault the child. For example, they may resort to punching and kicking, which carry greater risk of injury to the child and which qualify as child abuse. Research by Leonard D. Eron and his colleagues (Eron, Huesmann, & Zelli, 1991) reveals that this cycle of violence and aggression remains in aggressive-prone families for at least three generations.

It is important to remember that the relationship between parental disciplinary tactics and delinquency does not occur in isolation. Straus (1991) reports that in several studies he conducted, 90% of the parents surveyed used some kind of physical punishment with their three- and four-year-olds. If there were a simple, direct relationship between parents' use of physical punishment and violence, the violence rates would be far higher than they are now. However, the physical punishment found by Straus was predominantly a slap on the bottom or on the hand, intended to prevent the child from continuing a negative behavior, such as shoving a playmate. Although many parents believe children should never be slapped—there are alternative methods of encouraging prosocial behavior—the Straus research suggests that a great majority may use such disciplinary approaches.

A lack of parent–child involvement and parental rejection have also been found to be strong predictors of serious delinquency (Farrington, 1991). S. E. Brown (1984) cites evidence that emotional abuse and neglect may play an even more critical role in the development of delinquency than physical punishment. Emotional abuse includes such behaviors as frequently screaming at the child, calling the child insulting names, excessively criticizing, or generally ignoring the child. Neglect usually refers to a gross lack of proper supervision and physical care.

The lack of warmth between parent and child appears to be a very strong factor that contributes to child antisocial outcomes and delinquency (Dodge & Pettit, 2003). "Maternal [and we might add paternal] warmth contributes to positive long-term outcomes either through its modeling effects or by setting a comfortable context in which other parent teaching efforts might prove successful" (p. 353). Dishion and Bullock (2002) have referred to the "nurturance hypothesis," where considerate attention, emotional investment, and positive behavioral management by parents, when combined, can lead to a socially competent and psychologically healthy child who is likely to be resistant to antisocial influences.

After reviewing the research literature, Loeber and Dishion (1983) also discovered that a combination of family factors could increase the power of prediction of delinquency and crime. Combinations of several family factors—such as family size, quality of parental supervision, parental drinking habits, employment history, and criminality—are more impressive than any single factor, particularly with reference to male delinquency. Loeber and Dishion concluded that children from large families that are characterized by employment problems, disorganization and instability, inadequate supervision, conflict and disharmony, and poor parent–child relationships are at much greater risk of becoming delinquent than children from families without these features.

PSYCHOLOGICAL RISK FACTORS

DEVELOPMENTAL FACTORS

Over the past three decades, the psychological study of crime has shifted away from accepting personality traits as sole or even major determinants of criminal and delinquent behavior toward a more interactive cognitive and developmental focus. There is good evidence that serious, persistent delinquency patterns begin in early childhood. Learning experiences begin early and build on themselves. Researchers have noted differences in impulsiveness, social skills, and feelings for others between children who ultimately became serious delinquents and nondelinquents as early as in their first few school years. Even at an early age, children who have learned to be aggressive or belligerent are unpopular and are excluded from peer groups (Hartup, 1983; Olweus, 1978; Patterson, 1982). In fact, Coie, Underwood, and Lochman (1991) contend that aggressiveness is the single most important reason for a child to be rejected by peers.

As a group, highly aggressive, troublesome children demonstrate social and interpersonal skills that are below average for their age. Those children who continue offending into adolescence and young adulthood are troublesome in school, beginning as early as the first grade (Farrington, 1987), and perform below average in most school achievement tasks (D. Kelly, 1980; Schafer & Polk, 1967). Low achievement, low vocabulary, and poor verbal reasoning have been found to correlate significantly with later delinquency (Farrington, 1979).

Stealing is another early predictor of delinquency. In fact, in a literature review by Loeber and Dishion (1983), habitual stealing—as reported by parents and teachers—emerged as one of the strongest predictors of later delinquency. Furthermore, youngsters who engaged in stealing, even at the elementary school level, also tended to be simultaneously demonstrating other problem behaviors such as lying, truancy, and running away. Frequent dishonesty appears to be another behavioral pattern that predicts quite early a tendency toward repetitive offending (Farrington, 1979; Loeber & Dishion, 1983).

Research and theory on developmental paths leading to delinquency has expanded considerably over the last decade. Originally, this approach saw two developmental paths, identified by psychologist Terrie Moffitt (1993a, 1993b) and her colleagues. On one path they placed the child who begins a lifelong trajectory of delinquency and crime at a very early age, probably around three or even younger. Moffitt (1993a, p. 679) observes, "Across the life course, these individuals exhibit changing manifestations of antisocial behavior: biting and hitting at age four, shoplifting and truancy at age ten, selling drugs and stealing cars at age sixteen, robbery and rape at age twenty-two, and fraud and child abuse at age thirty." These individuals, whom Moffitt calls **life course–persistent** (LCP) offenders, continue their antisocial ways across all kinds of conditions and situations. Moffitt reports that many of these LCP offenders exhibit neurological problems during their childhoods, such as difficult temperaments as infants, attention deficit disorders, and **hyperactivity** as children, and learning problems during their later school years. Judgment and problem-solving deficiencies are often apparent when the children reach adulthood. LCP offenders generally commit a wide assortment of aggressive and violent crimes over their lifetimes.

LCPs as children miss opportunities to acquire and practice prosocial and interpersonal skills at each stage of development. This is partly because they are rejected and avoided by their childhood peers and partly because their parents, teachers, and caretakers become frustrated and give up on them (Coie, Belding, & Underwood, 1988; Coie, Dodge, & Kupersmith, 1990; Moffitt,

1993a). According to Moffitt (1993a, p. 684), ". . . if social and academic skills are not mastered in childhood, it is very difficult to later recover from lost opportunities." Furthermore, as noted previously, disadvantaged homes, inadequate schools, and violent neighborhoods are factors that are very likely to exacerbate the ongoing and developing antisocial behavioral pattern.

The great majority of "delinquents" are those individuals who follow a second developmental path: They begin offending during their adolescent years and stop offending somewhere around their 18th birthday. Moffitt labels these individuals **adolescent-limited** (AL) offenders. Their developmental histories do not demonstrate the early and persistent antisocial problems that members of the LCP group manifest (see **Table 2–3**) However, the frequency—and, in some cases, the violence level—of offending during the teen years may be as high as that of the LCP youth. In effect, the teenage offending patterns of the ALs and the LCPs may be highly similar (Moffitt et al., 1996). "The two types cannot be discriminated on most indicators of antisocial and problem behavior in adolescence; boys on the LCP and AL paths are similar on parent, self-, and official records of offending, peer delinquency, substance abuse, unsafe sex, and dangerous driving" (p. 400). That is, a professional could not easily identify the group classification (AL or LCP) simply by examining juvenile arrest records, self-reports, or information provided by parents during the teen years.

The AL delinquent is most likely, during the teen years, to be involved in offenses that symbolize adult privilege and demonstrate autonomy from parental control. Examples include vandalism, drug and alcohol offenses, theft, and status offenses such as running away or truancy. In addition, AL delinquents are likely to engage in crimes that are profitable or rewarding, but they also have the ability to abandon these actions when prosocial styles become more rewarding. For example, the onset of young adulthood brings on opportunities not attainable during the teen years, such as leaving high school for college, obtaining a full-time job, and entering a relationship with a prosocial person.

TABLE 2–3   Summary of Comparisons between Life Course–Persistent (LCP) and Adolescent-Limited (AL) Offenders

	LCP	AL
Crime or antisocial behavior, begins	Early (perhaps as early as age 3)	Later (usually during the early adolescent years)
Criminal behavior	Continues throughout the offender's life	Usually stops after early adulthood
Types of criminal behaviors	Assorted	Assorted
Developmental background	Often shows neurological problems, ADHD, conduct problems	Usually normal and without neurological problems
Academic skills	Usually below average	Usually average to above average
Interpersonal and social skills	Usually below average	Usually average to above average

AL delinquents are quick to learn that they have something to lose if they continue offending into adulthood. During childhood, in contrast to the LCP child, the AL youngster has learned to get along with others. It should also be emphasized that "the theory of AL antisocial behavior regards it as an adaptation response to modern teens' social context, not the product of a cumulative history of pathological maldevelopment" (Moffitt & Caspi, 2001, p. 370). They normally have a satisfactory repertoire of academic, social, and interpersonal skills that enable them to "get ahead." Therefore, the developmental histories and personal dispositions of the AL youths allow them the option of exploring new life pathways, an opportunity not usually afforded the LCP youths. In short, Moffitt's theory hypothesizes that most young persons who become AL offenders are able to desist from crime when they age into maturity, turning gradually to a more conventional lifestyle (Moffitt & Caspi, 2001).

However, in a more recent follow-up study, Moffitt, Caspi, Harrington, and Milne (2002) discovered that many ALs, at age 26, were still in trouble. "Although AL men fared better overall than LCP men, they fared poorly relative to the 'unclassified' men (who represented males with no remarkable delinquency history" (p. 199). The researchers found that AL men accounted for twice their share of the property and drug convictions during adulthood compared to men without a delinquency history. It seemed as though some AL men relied on crime to supplement their incomes. The researchers further stated that "the very name 'adolescence-limited' reveals that this much offending by AL men at age 26 was not anticipated by our theory" (p. 200). The researchers, in an effort to explain the discrepancy, speculated that perhaps adulthood in contemporary society may begin after 25 years of age. Therefore, this new developmental stage, called "emerging adulthood," prolongs the crime-promoting conditions of adolescence. "This stage is characterized by roleless floundering, in which young people neither perceive themselves to be adults, nor choose to occupy any adult roles historically favored by people in their 20s (e.g., parenthood, marriage)" (p. 200).

Furthermore, the theory has been developed primarily on the developmental trajectories of males. Do females demonstrate a similar pattern? Moffitt and Caspi (2001) report evidence that the developmental typology fits both genders. However, males are far more likely to follow the LCP form of antisocial behavior (approximately 10 to 1), whereas the gender difference is negligible for the AL form (approximately 1.5 to 1). These findings appear to be consistent with other studies (Kratzer & Hodgins, 1999; Mazerolle et al., 2000). In other words, the vast majority of female delinquents usually fit the AL pattern. In addition, the childhood backgrounds of females who do show the AL pattern are normal—like those of males—and do not demonstrate psychopathological indicators and neuropsychological problems so commonly reported in the childhoods of LCPs.

Other researchers using a developmental perspective have identified more than two trajectories. For example, Daniel Nagin and Kenneth Land (1993) were able to identify four developmental paths in British boys: the never-convicteds, the ALs, the high-level chronics (HLCs), and the low-level chronics (LLCs). The offending paths of the ALs followed the typical contour: Offending began late, reached a peak at age 16, and then showed a precipitous decline to zero by age 21 (Nagin, Farrington, & Moffitt, 1995). The LLC curve showed a rise through early adolescence, reached a plateau, and remained at the same level well past age 18. The HLC group (essentially the same as Moffitt's LCP) showed an early and frequent antisocial and offending pattern that continued through adolescence at a high rate and remained high well into adulthood. A very common feature of the chronic offender is a behavioral pattern characteristic of attention deficit disorder. It should be emphasized, however, that persons who have been diagnosed with attention deficit disorder are not necessarily chronic offenders. On the other hand, chronic juvenile offenders tend to be diagnosed with attention deficit hyperactivity disorder at some point during their development.

Shaw, Gilliom, Ingoldsby, and Nagin (2003) also found four trajectories that led to school-age conduct problems in children ranging in age from two to eight years. Their longitudinal study of 284 low-income boys identified the following developmental trajectories: persistent problem, high-level desister, moderate-level desister, and persistent low. The factors that differentiated the boys with high and low conduct problems in early childhood were the child's own fearlessness and elevated symptoms of depression in the mother. The boys who persisted in problem behaviors in the middle childhood years were more likely to be high in fearlessness and to have experienced maternal rejection. These factors were significant even when researchers controlled for the mother's education, her age, and the child's IQ. The vast majority of the children, however, showed a gradual decline in conduct problems from age 2 to age 8. Only a small group—5.6% of the total sample—demonstrated a high rate of problem behavior throughout the six-year-span. The children and the parent/child interactions were observed both in a laboratory and in a home setting.

It should be noted that the characteristics identified as significant—fearlessness, maternal depression, and maternal rejection—had been identified in previous studies as being positively related to conduct problems in children. It is also important to point out that the researchers used as their sample a population of low-income families who used a Women, Infants, and Children (WIC) program in a metropolitan area. While 65% of the mothers were married or living with a partner at the time of the first assessment, researchers studied only the mother–child dyad. Furthermore, they included only boys in the research, presumably because the conduct problems of physical aggression they studied tend to be more typical of boys. Shaw et al. made note of these limitations of their study and indicated that it would be important to extend it to other social classes as well as to girls.

In discussing the implications of their study, Shaw and colleagues (2003) noted that parent training is not enough to meet the needs of children who persist in demonstrating overt antisocial behavior. The characteristic of the child—fearlessness in approaching provocative stimuli—appears to be an important component in the child's conduct problems. Finally, similarly to the critics of parent training alone, the researchers highlighted the multiple challenges faced by families living in economically aversive situations. "Interventions are recommend that are multisystemic . . . geared to the developmental challenges and transitions of early childhood . . . and tailored to the issues that compromise individual parents' abilities to provide safe and caring environments for their offspring" (p. 15).

A more extensive study combined data sets of research from six sites in the United States and Canada (Broidy et al., 2003) and included information on girls as well as boys. The research conclusions—that early childhood physical aggression predicted adolescent aggression—applied only to boys, however. Despite the fact that most girls—like most boys—were not physically aggressive in childhood, some girls, like some boys, were. However, girls' involvement in delinquency was extremely difficult to predict, compared with boys' involvement. Specifically, boys who were physically aggressive and displayed non–physically aggressive conduct problems in childhood were likely to engage in delinquency—both violent and nonviolent—during adolescence. Interestingly, this research also found that hyperactivity did not independently predict delinquency, once conduct problems were controlled. We discuss hyperactivity in more detail below.

Hyperactivity and Attention Deficit Disorders

The term *hyperactive syndrome* (also called minimal brain dysfunction, hyperkinesis, attention deficit disorder, or currently **attention deficit hyperactivity disorder [ADHD]**) includes a heterogeneity of behaviors. The central three are (1) inattention (does not seem to listen or is easily distracted), (2) impulsivity (acts before thinking, shifts quickly from one activity to another), and (3) excessive motor activity (cannot sit still, fidgets, runs about, is talkative and noisy).

ADHD is the leading psychological diagnosis for American children (Cowley, 1993). Educators note that ADHD children have difficulty staying on task, remaining cognitively organized, sustaining academic achievement in the school setting, and maintaining control over their behavior. Satterfield (1987) notes that, whereas most childhood disorders are temporary and are not predictive of psychopathology in later life, hyperactive syndrome presents a different story. "The hyperactive child presents a remarkably immutable syndrome that forecasts an ominous picture of the future. The clinical picture often worsens as the child grows older, with resulting adolescent problems of academic failure and serious antisocial behavior" (p. 146). Although the common belief is that one eventually outgrows hyperactivity, the evidence is that the key symptomatic features of hyperactivity persist into adulthood (Klinteberg, Magnusson, & Schalling, 1989; Thorley, 1984). It is estimated that over 10 million Americans are affected by the disorder, three-quarters of them males (Cowley, 1993), but the estimates range widely for school-age children, from

1% to 20% (Developmental Disabilities Branch, 2000). Basically, to date, no systematic nationwide research has been conducted to identify the extent, seriousness, or nature of ADHD.

ADHD is a puzzling problem, the cause of which is largely unknown. Some scientists contend that ADHD children are born with a biological predisposition toward hyperactivity; others maintain that some children are exposed to environmental factors that damage the nervous system. Rolf Loeber (1990) demonstrated how exposure to toxic substances during the preschool years often retards children's neurological development or otherwise influences it in a negative way, often resulting in symptoms of ADHD. For example, children exposed to low levels of lead toxicity (from paint) are more hyperactive and impulsive, and are easily distracted and frustrated. They also show discernible problems in following simple instructions. The causal factors of ADHD are probably multiple and extremely difficult to identify.

Some researchers have observed that ADHD children do not possess effective strategies and cognitive organization with which to deal with the daily demands of school. These children often have particular difficulty in understanding and using abstract concepts. ADHD children also seem to lack cognitively organized ways for dealing with new knowledge.

Although many behaviors have been identified as accompanying ADHD, the overriding theme is that ADHD children are perceived as annoying and aversive to those around them. Although ADHD children are continually seeking and prolonging interpersonal contacts, they eventually manage to irritate and frustrate those people with whom they interact (Henker & Whalen, 1989). They are often rejected by peers, especially if they are perceived as aggressive (Henker & Whalen, 1989). This pattern of peer rejection appears to continue throughout the developmental years (Reid, 1993).

As research on ADHD accumulates, it is becoming increasingly apparent that ADHD is not so much a disorder of activity as it is a *disorder of interpersonal relationships*. Even those ADHD children who are not aggressive and who manage to control some of their "hyperactivity" still have problems with their social interactions. They lack friendship and intimacy (Henker & Whalen, 1989). Terrie Moffitt (1993b; Moffitt & Silva, 1988) observes that a very large number of ADHD children self-report delinquent behaviors by early adolescence. She also found that children between five and seven years of age who demonstrate the characteristics of both ADHD and delinquent behavior not only have special difficulty with social relationships but also have a high probability of consistent serious antisocial behavior into delinquency and beyond (Moffitt, 1990b). Experts argue that the most common problem associated with ADHD is delinquency and substance abuse. The data strongly suggest that youth with symptoms of both ADHD and delinquent behavior are at very high risk for developing lengthy and serious criminal careers (Moffitt, 1990b; Satterfield, Swanson, Schell, & Lee, 1994). David Farrington (1991), in his well-cited research, also found that violent offenders often have a history of hyperactivity, impulsivity, and attention deficit problems.

Nevertheless, as indicated above, more recent research is suggesting that hyperactivity is *not* a good predictor of delinquency when conduct problems are controlled for. Broidy et al. (2003), in their multisite study, found that hyperactivity was not predictive of either violent or nonviolent delinquency in the absence of such conduct problems as physical aggression and nonphysically aggressive problem behaviors.

The most common method of treatment for ADHD is stimulant medication (methylphenidate; more commonly known by trade names like Adderall and Ritalin). The FDA also has approved nonstimulant medication (atomoxetine) in the form of Strattera. However, although medication helps some children, with many others it has limited success and numerous side effects, some of them severe. This is the case particularly with stimulant medication. Counseling and psychotherapy are often used, often in conjunction with medication, but they, too, have had very limited success with this puzzling phenomenon, particularly over the long term. ADHD children generally demonstrate multiple problems that can be best treated through treatment strategies that include all the factors impinging on the child at any given time. These treatment approaches are called *multisystemic* and are dealt with more fully in Chapter 13.

Conduct Disorders

ADHD frequently co-occurs with a diagnostic category called "conduct disorders" (Offord, Boyle, & Racine, 1991; Reid, 1993), but as suggested above, the two should be considered separate entities. As mentioned previously, the diagnosis conduct disorder (CD) represents a cluster of behaviors characterized by persistent misbehavior. Examples of this misbehavior include stealing, fire setting, running away from home, skipping school, destroying property, fighting, frequently telling lies, and cruelty to animals and people. According to the DSM-IV (American Psychiatric Association, 1994), the central feature of CD is the *repetitive* and *persistent* pattern of behavior that violates the basic rights of others.

As demonstrated in the developmental trajectory studies discussed above, behavioral indicators of a CD can be observed in the context of interactions with parents well before school entry (Reid, 1993). For instance, children who are aggressive, difficult to manage, and noncompliant in the home at age 3 often continue to have similar problems when entering school. Furthermore, these behaviors show remarkable continuity through adolescence and into adulthood. CD children frequently have significant problems with school assignments, a behavioral pattern that often results in their being mislabeled with a "learning disability." It is important to note that genuinely learning-disabled students are not necessarily conduct disordered, however. In other words, the two designations may overlap, but each is also a distinct categorization. Aggressive CDs are at high risk for strong rejection by their peers

(Reid, 1993). This rejection generally lasts throughout the school years and is very difficult to change (Reid, 1993). As described earlier, children who are consistently socially rejected by peers miss critical opportunities to develop normal interpersonal and social skills. Lacking effective interpersonal skills, these youth are forced to get their needs met through more aggressive means, including threats and intimidation.

As noted earlier in the chapter, the DSM-IV identifies two subtypes of CDs based on the onset of the repetition and persistence of the misbehavior: the *childhood-onset type* and the *adolescent-onset type*. According to the DSM-IV, the childhood-onset type occurs when the pattern begins prior to age 10. The adolescent-onset type, on the other hand, is characterized by the absence of any pattern before age 10. The DSM-IV also notes that if the CD pattern begins before age 10, the prognosis is not good, compared with a more favorable prognosis for a later onset. The DSM-IV is consistent with LCP and AL antisocial behavioral patterns reported by Moffitt, Reid, and others.

There is some recent research suggesting that individual maladjustment and family influences are more highly associated with childhood-onset CDs, whereas ethnic minority status and exposure to deviant peers is more highly associated with adolescent-onset CDs (McCabe et al., 2001). The researchers also found that those children who exhibit childhood-onset CDs, are more likely to commit more serious or aggressive offenses than adolescent-onset CDs, although the results were not as strong as the first finding.

An estimated 6% to 16% of the male population is believed to have behavioral features of CD. The prevalence in girls ranges from 4% to 9.2% (Cohen, Cohen, & Brook, 1993; Zoccoulillo, 1993). A study by Anna Bardone and her colleagues (Bardone, Moffitt, & Caspi, 1996) found that CD patterns in girls are a strong predictor of a lifetime of problems, including poor interpersonal relations with partners/spouses and peers, criminal activity, early pregnancy without supportive partners, and frequent job loss and firings. Similar to CD boys, CD girls appear destined for a life of interpersonal conflict with the social environment.

Contrary to statements found in many crime and delinquency textbooks, few contemporary psychologists believe that delinquent offenders, as a whole, are emotionally disturbed or psychologically maladjusted youths in need of conventional psychotherapy. This is not to say that the possibility of emotional disturbance should not be considered. Some juveniles—particularly those serious delinquents who are held in institutional settings—do have emotional disorders that call for psychotherapy. Nevertheless, mainstream psychology views most delinquency, including the conduct associated with frequent offenders, as a learned behavior, acquired and maintained like all other human behavior. Most psychologists consider behavior a function of the environment (social) interacting with individual (psychological) factors. Thus, intervention strategies aimed at preventing further antisocial behavior must take into consideration the very wide range of factors that may influence it.

INTELLIGENCE AND DELINQUENCY

For some time, criminologists (and many psychologists) have been eager to label the relationship between intelligence and delinquency invalid and spurious. Even to mention the connection may prompt a derisive reaction. Years ago, Hirschi and Hindelang (1977, p. 572) wrote, "Today, textbooks in crime and delinquency ignore IQ or impatiently explain to the reader that IQ is no longer taken seriously by knowledgeable students simply because no differences worth considering have been revealed by research." According to Hirschi and Hindelang, these textbooks were wrong, because the delinquency literature consistently reported that delinquents do, as a group, score lower on standard intelligence tests than nondelinquents. The essential point that Hirschi and Hindelang made was that the inverse relationship between IQ scores and delinquency continues to be documented by the research, for whatever reason. Why this difference exists should be at the heart of the controversy.

In their 1977 article, Hirschi and Hindelang hypothesized that an indirect causal relationship exists between IQ and delinquency. By "indirect" they meant that a low IQ leads to poor performance and negative attitudes toward school, which in turn leads to delinquency. A high IQ, on the other hand, leads to good performance and positive attitudes toward school, which in turn leads to the internal acceptance of conventional values and conformity (nondelinquency). Therefore, Hirschi and Hindelang saw school performance and attitudes as "intervening variables" that mediate between IQ and delinquency.

Hirschi and Hindelang apparently assumed, as do many people that IQ truly reflects intelligence. The term IQ is an abbreviation of the intelligence quotient derived from a numerical score on a so-called "intelligence" test and originated out of what is now called the **psychometric approach**. The word psychometric means "mental measurement." Traditionally, the psychometric approach has searched for individual differences in persons through the use of psychological tests, including intelligence tests, scholastic aptitude tests (e.g., SAT), school achievement tests, personality inventories, and other specific abilities tests. The various tests are used for many purposes, such as selection, diagnosis, and evaluation. The psychometric approach continues to be widely used by practicing psychologists and mental health professionals. However, the term **psychometric intelligence** (PI) is increasingly being preferred to the traditional term "IQ" (Neisser et al., 1996).

Satisfactory performance on a vast majority of intelligence tests depends greatly on language acquisition and verbal development. Usually, a person must have considerable experience using and defining words—particularly English words. The examinee must be able to make conventional connections and see distinctions between verbal concepts. The examinee must also know the facts that the test designer deems important to know within mainstream culture. At the very least, almost all intelligence tests measure some aspect of academic skills that are taught in school or that predict success in school.

A vast majority of psychologists today would agree that PI scores are strongly influenced by social, educational, and cultural experiences. In short, all intelligence tests are culturally biased.

More important, PI scores and the concept of intelligence should not be confused. The term PI merely refers to a standardized score from a test. *Intelligence, on the other hand, is a broad, all-encompassing ability that defies any straightforward or simple definition.* It means many things to different people. Intelligence includes ability ranging from musical talent to logical mathematical skills. The term may also include wisdom, intuition, judgment, and even humor. It is, therefore, extremely important to make a distinction between PI and intelligence. While delinquents, as a group, do score lower on intelligence tests, this observation should not be construed as documenting that delinquents are less intelligent than nondelinquents. For example, Brazilian street children are masters at doing the math required for survival in their street business even though they have failed mathematics in school (Carraher, Carraher, & Schliemann, 1985; Neisser et al., 1996). Likewise, institutionalized delinquents often display artistic skills and a sense of humor that are not tapped by traditional PI scores.

The relationship between PI test scores and school performance is strong and consistent. "Wherever it has been studied, children with high scores on tests of intelligence tend to learn more of what is taught in school than their lower-scoring peers" (Neisser et al., 1996, p. 82). Schools help develop certain intellectual skills and attitudes. Quality schools generally have positive effects on PI. Preschool programs (e.g., Headstart) show significant positive effects on children during their early school years, and recent research shows that these gains do not fade when the program is over, provided there is periodic intervention during the child's middle school years (Zigler, 1994).

There is also a relationship between PI and years of education and, to a lesser extent, between social status and income. Interestingly, researchers have found that there has been a steady worldwide rise in PI scores over the years. In what is know as the "Flynn effect" (after James Flynn, who first noticed the increase), youth in technologically advanced countries have shown a gain of about three PI points per decade (Flynn, 1999; Kanaya, Scullin, & Ceci, 2003). In the United States, however, although psychometric intelligence scores have increased, scores on scholastic aptitude tests (such as the SAT) have decreased or remained the same.

Average PI scores do vary between ethnic groups. For example, many studies using different tests and samples typically show African Americans scoring significantly lower than whites (Neisser et al., 1996). Studies show, however, that this psychometric gap has been consistently closing since 1980 (Vincent, 1991). Asian Americans and whites, on average, score about the same on PI tests; Native Americans score slightly lower than other groups on verbal skills, but this slight difference may be the result of chronic middle-ear infections common among Native American children (McShane & Plas, 1984a, 1984b). Latinos, who make up the second-largest and fastest-growing minority group in the United States, typically score somewhere between African Americans and non-Latino whites. It is unclear what these reported differences mean, but there is no evidence to support the view that ethnic differences in psychometric intelligence are due to genetics or biological factors. Although genetics may play a role in *individual* differences in psychometric intelligence, there is little evidence for ethnic *group* differences.

Group differences in PI are most likely due to a combination of factors, dominated by cultural and social influences. According to Boykin (1986, 1994), for instance, the African-American culture is not quite in synchronization with the values and expectations of the American school system. To varying degrees, the black culture "includes an emphasis on such aspects of experience as spirituality, harmony, movement, verve, affect, expressive individualism, communalism, orality, and a socially defined time perspective" (Neisser et al., 1996, p. 95). If schools do not recognize and celebrate these positive aspects, African-American children may feel left out of the mainstream. According to Boykin, black children often find their cultural background in conflict with the culture of the school system, and consequently they become alienated from both the process and the products of that educational system. Equally problematic, however, is the fact that many black children attend inner-city schools, where the quality of education and services is below par. It is not surprising, then, that performance on standardized tests would reflect this inequity.

Other factors—such as poor nutrition, inadequate prenatal care, lack of adequate child-care facilities, and inaccessibility to occupational and training opportunities—also play critical but largely unknown roles in psychometric intelligence. PI scores are crude indexes of mainstream language skills that are heavily influenced by experience. In general, rich and varied experiences increase PI scores, and limited experience decreases them (Garbarino & Asp, 1981; Neisser et al., 1996). School experiences, if positive, may increase language skills; if negative, they may stagnate, or even decrease, language skills. PI scores are also strongly influenced by the type of test used, its content, the many characteristics of testing situations, and the training and skill of the examiner.

Still, even with these many variations, the inverse relationship between PI scores and the tendency toward delinquency is consistently reported (e.g., Binder, 1988; Quay, 1987; J. White, Moffitt, & Silva, 1989). As PI scores go down, the probability of misconduct increases, and vice versa. Children with low PI scores are at a higher risk for delinquent behavior, and as Anne Crocker and Sheilagh Hodgins (1997, p. 434) wrote, "To our knowledge, no study has failed to confirm this relation." The relationship is particularly strong for verbal PI scores (Culberton, Feral, & Gabby, 1989; Kandel et al., 1988). Furthermore, as noted by Crocker and Hodgins (1997), the relationship between low PI scores and delinquency appears to be independent of socioeconomic status, race, and detection by the police (Moffitt, 1990b; Lynam, Moffitt, & Stouthamer-Loeber, 1993). Moreover, it should be emphasized that this relationship is not specific to delinquency; the relationship is equally robust for adult offenders.

Very low PI scores—those that indicate mental disability—are of particular concern. Recent estimates indicate that at least 4% of the U.S. prison population qualify as being mentally retarded (Ashford, Sales, & Reid, 2001). Jails are believed to hold an even higher percentage. Crocker and Hodgins (1997) examined the criminality of mentally deficient men and women in a Swedish birth cohort composed of over 15,000 subjects. The subjects were followed from birth to age 30. Subjects who were placed in special classes for the mentally retarded (at both the elementary and the high school levels) were compared with normal subjects. Subjects considered mentally retarded were more likely to have been convicted for criminal offenses, including violent ones, than normal subjects. Crocker and Hodgins also found that, similar to mentally normal subjects, conduct problems in childhood (before age 12) were predictive of adult antisocial behavior in mentally deficient groups of both males and females.

What does the relationship between PI scores and delinquency and crime mean exactly? It probably means that delinquents *as a group*, particularly serious delinquents, have had limited experiences in mainstream society, faulty parenting, and poor school experiences, but it does not necessarily mean that they are less intelligent. Related to the PI question is the issue of learning disabilities. There is considerable empirical evidence that juvenile delinquents have a far greater incidence of learning disabilities than nondelinquents (N. Brier, 1989; Lombardo & Lombardo, 1991; Scaret & Wilgosh, 1989). While learning disabilities clearly exist, it is believed that they are overdiagnosed or misdiagnosed in many children, who then acquire a label that may follow them through the educational system. Like the PI question, it is very unclear what the relationship between delinquency and learning disability truly means.

GENDER AND JUVENILE OFFENDING

As a general rule, boys far outnumber girls in most types of offending, but most particularly in violent offending. Victimization data, self-report data, and official data (both police records and court statistics) all support this gender gap. In addition, the reported ratios of males to females for most crimes remained basically the same for decades, apparently regardless of cultural or societal changes. In fact, males were so overrepresented in violent crimes (approximately a nine-to-one ratio) that some theorists suggested that hormonal and biological factors were the most logical explanation for these gender differences (J. Wilson & Herrnstein, 1985).

The most recent data on juvenile arrests suggest, however, that the gender gap may be closing for some offenses. Between 1990 and 1999, arrests of juvenile females generally increased more (or decreased less) than juvenile male arrests in most categories (Snyder, 2000). In 1999, girls accounted for 17% of the juvenile arrests for index violent crimes, which approaches a six-to-one male–female ratio; they also accounted for 22% of arrests for aggravated assault and 30% of arrests for simple assault. The male–female arrest rates were closest for embezzlement (48% female), prostitution (54%), and running away (59%). If the gap is closing, factors other than biological ones must account for gender differences.

Research by developmental psychologists has shed considerable light on the gender difference in juvenile offending. There is growing recognition that biology is not a significant factor in explaining the gender differences in offending, including violent offending (D. Adams, 1992; Pepler & Slaby, 1994). Research by Eleanor Maccoby (1986), for example, indicates that girls and boys learn different types of prosocial behavior, with girls being more accommodating than boys. The current work of cognitive psychologists suggests that there may be socialized and cultural differences in the way boys and girls perceive their worlds. Social learning theorists have long held that girls are "socialized" differently from boys, or taught not to be aggressive. Anne Campbell (1993, p. 19) is representative of much of the current thinking when she notes that boys and girls are born with the potential to be equally aggressive, but girls are socialized not to be overtly aggressive, whereas boys are encouraged to be aggressive. The slight change in the ratio of violent offending, coupled with the overall decrease in juvenile violent crime discussed earlier in the chapter, suggests that the socialization of girls and boys is becoming more comparable. On the one hand, girls today are likely receiving the same aggression-supporting messages as boys (e.g., from media) and, also, have fewer restrictions on their behavior than they have had in the past. On the other hand, both genders are being encouraged to make good decisions and look for socially acceptable ways of channeling aggressive tendencies.

There still remain important differences in the offending of girls and boys, however. Girls are consistently taken into custody by police for status offending (particularly running away and curfew violations) more often than are boys. Additionally, they are arrested more often for shoplifting, despite the fact that boys self-report as much shoplifting behavior. It appears, also, that the value of the items stolen by girls is less than the value of those stolen by boys (Chesney-Lind & Sheldon, 1998). Finally, the connection between juvenile running-away and prostitution is a sobering one. Recent arrest figures indicate that the figures are about equal for girls and boys (54% female, 46% male; Snyder, 2000). Nevertheless, girls are believed to be far more likely than boys to run away because of victimization in the home and ultimately to take up prostitution to survive. In fact, a history of violent victimization, in or outside the home, seems to haunt both juvenile and adult female offenders (Acoca & Austin, 1996). According to one study (Acoca & Dedel, 1998), 92% of juvenile female offenders reported that they had been subjected to some form of emotional, physical, and/or sexual abuse. Twenty-five percent reported they had been shot or stabbed one or more times.

As many commentators have noted, we know far too little about girls' crime, the reasons it is committed, and the social and developmental factors that precipitate it (Broidy et al., 2003; Chesney-Lind & Shelden, 1998). In the 1990s, the OJJDP launched a major effort to fund more research and effective prevention programs directed at girls, a population whose needs are too often overlooked by both formal and informal agencies. Additionally, numerous private advocacy agencies are beginning to address their needs and offer supportive community-based programs (Community Research Associates, 1998).

It remains to be seen whether the gender gap in offending will close even more, increase, or remain stable in the years ahead. In addition to psychosocial development, numerous societal factors affect the patterns of offending for both juveniles and adults. These include the economy, community disorganization, the actions of police, the quality of schools, the resources available to courts and to correctional agencies, and the adequacy of health and social services, to name but a few. We can say with a high degree of confidence, though, that cultural and psychosocial factors, rather than biological and genetic, play a major role in determining gender differences in offending.

PREVENTION AND TREATMENT OF JUVENILE OFFENDING

The number of intervention, prevention, and treatment programs that have been attempted for children at risk and juvenile offenders runs into the thousands. The great majority of these programs are not formally evaluated, however, and of those that are, few have been demonstrated to be highly effective at reducing delinquency. This lack of success is especially clear in programs that try to change serious delinquent offenders or LCP offenders (Borduin et al., 1995; Moffitt, 1993a). Restrictive interventions for serious juvenile offenders, such as residential treatment programs, have been especially ineffective and extremely expensive, although there are rays of hope in even these settings. The average cost of holding a juvenile in a treatment facility for just one year is close to $34,000, and some estimates go as high as $64,000 (Coordinating Council on Juvenile Justice and Delinquency Prevention, 1996). Juvenile justice professionals typically use residential treatment only as a last resort, however, and only when less restrictive community alternatives have been attempted. The preferred option is a system of graduated sanctions designed to fit both the offense and the individual offender (Howell, 1998).

In discussing the response to juvenile offending, it is helpful to examine the topic from a public health model, which divides prevention strategies into three sometimes overlapping categories: (1) primary prevention, (2) secondary prevention, and (3) tertiary, or treatment-based, prevention (**Figure 2–6**). **Primary prevention** is designed to prevent behavior before it emerges or before a pattern of that behavior occurs. Usually primary prevention programs are established early in the developmental sequence of the child, preferably before the age of seven or eight. These programs are usually found within the

FIGURE 2–6   Prevention Strategies

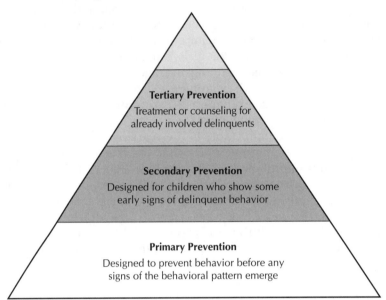

school system where there are large groups of young children, all of whom are exposed to the intervention. Examples include Project Headstart (Zigler, 1994), the Perry Preschool Project (Berrueta-Clement, Schweinhart, Barnett, & Weikart, 1987), and the many school-based prevention programs directed at first and second graders (Tolan & Guerra, 1994). However, primary prevention programs also occur for children in later school years as well as for adolescents.

A primary prevention program that has received good research results is mentoring, in which a child or youth is paired with an adult supportive figure (Sherman et al., 1998). "Big Brother" and "Big Sister" programs are good illustrations of the mentoring approach. Although mentoring is also done with already involved youth (secondary prevention), it is most typically associated with a primary prevention approach. Another primary prevention strategy— one that is even more likely to be offered to whole groups of children—is the conflict resolution curriculum taught in many schools today in an effort to prevent violent and aggressive behavior both within and outside of school. The model for such a curriculum is the Resolving Conflict Creatively Program, which was developed collaboratively by Educators for Social Responsibility Metropolitan Area and the New York City Board of Education (Aber, Brown, & Jones, 2003). The program has been implemented in New York City public schools as well as in a number of states across the country. In a recent review, Aber et al. (2003) found that children from the first to the sixth grades demonstrated positive changes in social and emotional development, as well as reductions in aggressive and violent tendencies, when their teachers taught a high number of lessons in conflict resolution. The positive effects of the program were apparent in both boys and girls of varying races, ethnicities, and socioeconomic classes.

Secondary prevention programs are designed for children who show some early signs of aggressive, antisocial, or law-violating behavior but have not yet been formally classified as delinquent. In some cases these children or their families have been referred to social service agencies or family or juvenile courts, but they have not been adjudicated delinquent. The basic assumption of secondary programs is that early detection and early intervention will prevent the child from engaging in more serious criminal actions later on. A well-known example of this preventive strategy is juvenile diversion, a process that steers juveniles away (diverts) from official court proceedings, offering them a second chance. Diversion is typically restricted to first-time offenders who allegedly committed nonviolent offenses, including those associated with substance abuse. The diversion *process* is accompanied by a wide range of diversion *programs* with goals that include the reduction of recidivism among these first-time offenders.

As an overall approach to crime prevention, diversion is extremely difficult to evaluate, primarily because the programs offered vary so widely. In addition, the programs are operated under different auspices, including private groups, probation departments, social services, and the juvenile courts. Some programs associated with diversion have begun to accumulate impressive research support, however. One such program is "youth courts" (often called "peer courts" or "teen courts"), which have been established in numerous communities. These courts, which may also operate independently of diversion, usually involve juveniles serving in a variety of capacities, including as jurors, judges, and attorneys. The courts are lauded for informing youth about the justice process as well as providing a therapeutic rather than a punitive approach to juvenile offending (Butts, Hoffman, & Buck, 2000; Shiff & Wexler, 1996). The OJJDP has been sponsoring ongoing research on the development and success of youth courts.

Other promising secondary prevention programs include gang monitoring by teams of community workers, probation officers, and law enforcement officers. This multiagency approach to reducing gang crime and violence typically involves primary as well as secondary prevention measures. Referred to as the "Spergel Model" in honor of Charles Spergel, the sociologist who developed it, this approach mobilizes community leaders and residents, reaches out to gang-involved youth, and provides academic, economic, and social opportunities for youth (OJJDP, 1999). Suppressing gang activities and holding gang leaders responsible for their behavior are other aspects of this promising approach, which is receiving ongoing evaluation by researchers at the University of Chicago.

The third, or **tertiary prevention**, strategy is often described by researchers and practitioners as "treatment" or "counseling" for already involved delinquents. The distinction between secondary and tertiary prevention is often blurred, however. This is because both approaches require the identification of at-risk children for the intervention services and often provide the same services. For our purposes, we use the term tertiary prevention for those programs designed to reduce serious and well-established delinquent or criminal behavior. In most cases, tertiary prevention or treatment strategies for serious delinquents are carried out in residential (institutional) settings but, unfortunately, with limited success. On the whole, community treatment models—even those for serious delinquents—show more impressive, positive results (e.g., Henggeler, 1994).

In an analysis of 200 evaluations of juvenile programs, Lipsey and Wilson (1998) found hope even in institutional treatment with serious offenders. Specifically, institutional programs that were administered by mental health personnel rather than correctional personnel had a greater likelihood of success. In addition, the age of the program, the quality of the service delivery, and the amount of services provided all helped reduce recidivism. Research is also clear that punitive approaches with juveniles are notoriously ineffective at reducing recidivism. According to psychologist Paul Gendreau and his associates (e.g., Gendreau, 1996; Gendreau & Goggin, 1996), the best-performing punitive option reduced recidivism only 6%, whereas the best treatment program reduced it 25%.

With respect to treatment programs for children at risk and noninstitutionalized delinquents, several factors seem to point to success. First, successful programs begin early in the child's development (even before or during the first grade). Second, they work with or within the many changing environments the child faces each day. Third, they focus on the family. Let's examine each critical point more closely.

There is clear evidence to indicate that the earlier the signs of antisocial or delinquent behavior, the more serious or violent the antisocial behavior will be later (Tolan & Thomas, 1995). As noted earlier in the chapter, Terrie Moffitt (1993b; Moffitt et al., 1996) found cogent evidence that the LCP delinquent shows discernible signs of antisocial behavior as early as age 3. Furthermore, the LCP offender who enters adolescence fully engaged in delinquent behavior is usually highly resistant to change. Consequently, effective prevention must begin early, preferably before entry into the first grade but at least by the middle childhood years. Reviewing the literature on developmental trajectories toward violence, Aber et al. (2003) noted that at the approximate age of eight to nine, children seem to display a notable shift in the social and cognitive processes that facilitate prosocial or antisocial behavior. Although girls were at a somewhat lower risk of aggression than boys at these ages, by the time they reached the age of 12 they had risk factors almost equivalent to boys. Interestingly, they surpassed boys on such factors as hostile attribution bias and aggressive fantasies.

Researchers have long indicated that risk factors for aggressive behavior and violence are more salient when accompanied by dire living conditions. For example, Nancy Guerra and her colleagues (1995) observed that aggressive and antisocial behavior may begin to develop much earlier in children living in the most economically deprived urban neighborhoods, suggesting that intervention and prevention programs must begin even earlier for some children. Furthermore, this observation appears to hold for both boys and girls (Tolan & Thomas, 1995). Consequently, preschool programs, such as Project Headstart and the Perry Preschool Project, hold enormous potential for the reduction of crime. Preliminary investigations have demonstrated that these programs can be effective and that their long-term effects are encouraging (Berrueta-Clement et al., 1987; Mulvey, Arthur, & Reppucci, 1993; Sherman et al., 1998).

There is little doubt that living conditions in the poorest inner-city neighborhoods are extremely harsh and the daily onslaught of violence, substance abuse, child abuse, and economic hopelessness are highly disruptive to a child's normal development. For the child exposed to an adverse family life, inadequate living standards, and little opportunity to develop even the rudiments of social and interpersonal skills for dealing effectively with others, the damage is a challenge to repair. Clearly, the longer a child is exposed to these adverse conditions, the more difficult it will be to modify his or her life course away from serious delinquency and adult crime.

That said, there are wide differences among families and children living in dire economic straits, just as there are among the more economically privileged, so we must be careful not to assume that any child is heading for a life of crime. We must also keep in mind that primary prevention strategies such as conflict resolution curriculum have demonstrated benefits for all socioeconomic classes. From a social policy perspective, once children have entered school, it is more acceptable to aim our primary prevention programs at all children rather than targeting and labeling some for special intervention based on their living situations.

Secondary and tertiary prevention programs that have demonstrated long-term success have used multifaceted approaches focusing on treating children through their broad social environment, with particular sensitivity to the family's cultural background and heritage. There is little doubt that intervention programs that neglect gender, ethnicity, socioeconomic status, and other demographic characteristics are destined to fail. In other words, a program designed to treat boys will not necessarily be effective for girls. A program that enrolls Asian American or Latino children and ignores their cultural heritage is unlikely to produce positive results. The same can be said about a program for socioeconomically disadvantaged youth that does not recognize and address the social obstacles placed in their paths.

Research has continually shown that the most successful interventions concentrate on the family—if the family can be preserved—while recognizing the other powerful influences outside the family. Scott Henggeler and his colleagues (Henggeler & Borduin, 1990; Henggeler, Melton, & Smith, 1992; Scherer, Brondino, Henggeler, Melton, & Hanley, 1994) have designed a promising treatment approach for serious juvenile offenders—**multisystemic therapy** (MST).

It focuses on the family while being responsive to the many other contexts surrounding it, such as the social services system, the neighborhood, and the school. While peer influences are important during development, using peers to change deviant behavior has been largely unsuccessful (Chamberlain, 1996; Dishion & Andrews, 1995). In some instances, the use of peer groups in treatment settings may actually increase deviant and criminal behavior. Therefore, an important component of MST is to help the juvenile shift from his or her deviant peers to a social network of prosocial peers.

Effective intervention also targets the known risk factors that occur along the child's developmental path. Before birth, successful intervention begins with ensuring prenatal health care and maternal nutrition, together with the elimination of toxic materials in the environment. Intervention must also include reduction of intrafamilial violence and the elimination of parental abuse of alcohol and other drugs. For children born into disadvantaged families living in inner cities, serious efforts must be directed at reducing the extreme economic deprivation that exists. However, all children—regardless of their socioeconomic status—are susceptible to the effects of media violence, racism, sex discrimination, homophobia, and other social problems that can share a part of the blame for crime. Thus, on a broader, societal scale, intervention demands a multifaceted approach.

SUMMARY AND CONCLUSIONS

Scientists can now point with confidence to a large list of risk factors associated with juvenile delinquency and criminal behavior. No single variable is particularly at fault. In this chapter we began to examine some of the risk factors associated with crime and delinquency, including peer and family influences, social class, exposure to violence, and individual differences in cognitive skills.

Youth whose families are included in the lower socioeconomic strata of society are disproportionately represented in both arrest and juvenile court statistics. This pattern continues, but not as strongly, in self-report research. Therefore, the social class variable must be considered within the context of the many influences that impinge on young lives existing within adverse economic environments. Features often associated with lower socioeconomic class—discrimination, inadequate schools, unsafe living conditions, joblessness, social isolation, and opportunities to learn law-violating behaviors from peers—all play roles in the formation of crime and delinquency.

Delinquency is clearly not limited to youths from the lower class, however. Self-report data suggest that social class differences become smaller when youths are asked to report their own offending. The law-violating behavior of youths from the middle and upper classes often elicits different responses from the law enforcement community, parents, and juvenile courts, so these more privileged youth are less likely to appear in official statistics.

We have examined the potential roles played by conduct disorders, ADHD, intelligence, and gender. We have seen that the backgrounds of persistent offenders are littered with numerous impediments to normal development. Moreover, there is a growing body of evidence that people who experience a series of failures and who lack personal efficacy tend to view many aspects of their environments as fraught with danger (Bandura, 1989). Lacking interpersonal skills and personal efficacy, and living in a social environment that fails to provide suitable opportunity to develop competence, many youths resort to a mean, bitter, "I don't care" approach to life. These seemingly embittered youths begin to contaminate all their social environments with this antisocial approach, and the social environments react similarly in an ongoing, bidirectional interaction. It is important to emphasize, though, that this presenting attitude may be false bravado, a way to avoid saying "I'm scared" rather than "I don't care."

Of course, not all youths react this way to a series of social and personal disasters. Some, helped partly by temperament and perhaps even more by opportunities and positive experiences, acquire interpersonal competencies, academic skills, and effective strategies to avoid a pattern of persistent offending as a way of life.

Social environments and peer groups are important in the development of internal standards, but people do not automatically model actions. They extract and process their own standards from the multiplicity of actions and reactions of individuals around them. From all of this divergent information, people develop personal standards against which they measure and evaluate their own conduct. For example, violence is not triggered simply by individual characteristics of temperament, biological predispositions, or personality factors. Nor is violence necessarily triggered by observations of violent behaviors in others. It is more likely to be a function of the way in which an individual "perceives . . . events, makes meaning of them, anticipates others' reactions, and chooses to act on these events" (Eron & Slaby, 1994, p. 10). We will learn later in the text that only a *minority* of highly aggressive and violent offenders began their criminal careers during adulthood; most displayed overt aggressive tendencies during childhood. Typically, even from the preschool years, highly aggressive or violent individuals have been found to show habits of thought that reflect lower levels of social problem-solving skills and higher endorsement of beliefs that support the use of violence. This is why programs that attempt to teach effective, alternative conflict-resolution strategies show promise.

The evidence is clear that prevention and intervention must begin early. Such early intervention is especially critical for children growing up in inner-city neighborhoods where risk factors for delinquency are more prevalent. When children reach school age, though, it is important to direct primary prevention at all children rather than to isolate certain groups. Research strongly indicates that intervention becomes more difficult and encounters more intransigent behavior patterns from teenagers who exhibit antisocial behavior from an early age. The life course–persistent offender, who enters adolescence fully engaged in delinquent or antisocial behavior, is usually highly resistant to change. The adolescence-limited offender, on the other hand, is far more likely to be responsive to intervention and treatment strategies during the teen years. Adolescence-limited offenders are also more likely to show spontaneous recovery from their delinquency patterns as they embark on a more responsible, "adult" life course.

Recent research indicates that there are multiple developmental paths, rather than the two-path theory originally proposed by Moffitt. Regardless of the number of paths, it will be obvious throughout the remainder of the text that theories emphasizing cognitive processes (i.e., beliefs, values, thoughts) are favored in contemporary psychological explanations of crime and delinquency. Our beliefs, values, images of ourselves, and philosophies are the primary guides of our behavior. They are reference points for justifying our conduct to ourselves and to others. Most people try to live according to their internal standards and respond to others according to their perspectives of human nature. If our friends, models, and heroes perceive life and the human condition in a certain way, we may well do the same. If cruelty, insensitivity to others, and a selfish orientation is the norm, this may be reflected both in our approach to life and in our perceptions of criminal behavior. Moreover, if we believe that "Everyone does it," we have neutralized the stigma attached to the conduct. Youth is a time when we begin to formulate basic philosophies of life. In most instances, delinquency seems to be an expression of the values the juvenile either has adopted or is testing as a result of being exposed to them through significant models in the environment.

CHAPTER 3

Origins of Criminal Behavior: Biological Factors

Many—perhaps most—contemporary criminologists would agree with the following statement: "Genetics may play a role in criminality, but it is only an insignificant one. There is little doubt that environment is the principal determinant and cause of criminal behavior." Greed, desire for power, high unemployment, poverty, poor education, faulty parenting, over-population, and group values that deviate from society's norms are often considered the major culprits in producing crime. Heredity-based physiological components are scoffed at, and their possible role as causal agents in criminality is often dismissed.

Why? Perhaps because accepting heredity as a factor in criminal behavior implies that criminal acts are unavoidable, inevitable consequences of the "bad seed," "bad blood," or "mark of Cain." Heredity is destiny. Little can be done to prevent the ill-fated person from becoming a criminal. Most behavioral scientists—and many social scientists—recognize, however, that behavioral traits result from an *interaction* of hereditary and environmental factors. We no longer ask whether behavior is due to heredity or environment; we agree that both are involved in a complex way. However, researchers usually focus on one or the other for intensive study. In this chapter, we discuss the work of psychologists who study heredity and biopsychology as factors in the genesis of criminal behavior.

Biopsychologists (psychologists who study the biological aspects of behavior) try to determine which genetic and neurophysiological variables play a part in criminal behavior, how important they are, and what can be done to modify them. In recent years, molecular biology has focused on specific genes as foundations for certain patterns of behavior. Further, "a central precept of molecular biology is that all the information needed to construct a mammalian body, whether human or mouse, is contained in the approximately 100,000 genes of mammalian DNA and that a set of master genes activates the DNA necessary to produce the appropriate proteins for development and behavior (Cacioppo, Berntson, Sheridan, & McClintock, 2000, p. 833). Biopsychologists do not believe that genetic or neurophysiological components are the sole or even the primary causal agents of human behavior. Most would say that understanding the social environment is as important as understanding the biological one. For example, one group of biopsychologists asserts: "Our thesis . . . is that the social world, as well as the organization and operation of the brain, shapes and modulates genetic and biological processes, and accordingly, knowledge of biological and social domains is necessary to develop comprehensive theories in either domain" (p. 833). In this chapter, we concentrate on the biological relationships to criminal behavior while, at the same time, continually appreciating the enormous influence of the social environment on the neurological and biological processes. We introduce the contemporary work in biopsychology as it relates to antisocial behavior and assess the results after we have taken a brief look at the early history of biopsychological research pertaining to crime.

The chapter first explores the biopsychological aspects of crime, including physical aspects and body shapes, and then moves on to one of the major theories and research areas in the psychology of crime, Eysenck's theory of personality. Eysenck's theory is covered in detail because it offers a compelling view of how personality, biological factors, and the social environment work together in developing criminal behavioral patterns.

THE BORN CRIMINAL

A pioneer researcher on the relationship among crime, genetics, and personality was Cesare Lombroso (1836–1909), the Italian physician and self-termed criminal anthropologist. Lombroso's original and basic premise, published in *L'Uomo Delinquente* [*Criminal Man*] in 1876, was that some people are born with strong, innate predispositions to behave antisocially. He was greatly influenced by the views that Charles Darwin expounded in *The Descent of Man*, especially the notion that some people are genetically closer to their primitive ancestry than others (Savitz, 1972). The criminal, Lombroso believed, represented a separate species that had not yet evolved sufficiently toward the more "advanced" *Homo sapiens*. This species was genetically somewhere between modern humans and their primitive origins in physical and psychological makeup. He called this evolutionarily retarded species *Homo delinquens* and considered those individuals mutations or natural accidents living among civilized humans.

Lombroso collected extensive data on the physical measurements of Italian prisoners and Italian military personnel (noncriminals). He concluded that the criminal was distinguished by certain physical anomalies: an asymmetrical skull, flattened nose, large ears, fat lips, enormous jaws, high cheekbones, and Mongolian eye characteristics (Ferrero, 1972). Moreover, *Homo delinquens*, also derisively called the "born criminal," had an affinity for tattoos, "cruel games," and orgies and had a peculiar primitive slang, all believed to be behavioral throwbacks to savage, undeveloped human or subhuman species. Lombroso maintained that the born criminal's artworks were often faithful reproductions of the first crude artistic attempts of primitive people. The implications were that this primitive creature, who instinctively demonstrated behaviors useful in the wild in millennia past, could not adjust socially and morally to the demands of modern times.

L'Uomo Delinquente went through several revisions, and by 1897 it had grown to three volumes totaling 1,903 pages. With each edition Lombroso modified his theory from the dogmatic one of 1876 to a more flexible but still basically genetic version. For example, early Lombrosian theory asserted that all criminals met the physical dimensions and psychological characteristics outlined. Later, possibly responding to criticism, Lombroso concluded that the born criminal actually accounted for only about one-third of the criminal population (Ferrero, 1972). The other two-thirds comprised a wide assortment of criminal types. Lombroso also suggested at that point that environmental factors were significant in the development of certain types of crime (Wolfgang, 1972). In 1911, Gina Lombroso summarized her father's last work and translated it into English. It was titled *Crime: Its Causes and Remedies*.

After considerable experience dealing with offenders, Cesare Lombroso moved away from his conviction that all criminals were innately antisocial but concluded that there are various types of offenders. Accordingly, offenders who were not born criminals fell into one of six categories. *Habitual* or *professional criminals* violated the law systematically and engaged in crime as a trade or occupation. The degrading influence of prisons (which Lombroso called "criminal universities"), including daily contact with other hard-core prisoners, played a significant role in the development of this offender. The second type was the - *juridical criminal*, who violated the law not because of any "natural depravity" but simply from lack of prudence, care, or forethought—the impulsive type. *Criminals of passion* violated the law because of their "intense love, honor, noble ambition, or patriotism." They may have murdered to defend their honor, their loved ones, or their country. *Criminaloids* had "weak natures" and were highly susceptible to good and bad example. They had innate characteristics very similar to those of born criminals, but the environment was an important determinant of their criminal action. *Born criminals*, by contrast, were dictated by strong biological predispositions to crime. Lombroso also recognized the *morally insane*, who is probably similar to the psychopath, and the *hysteric criminal* type, who is similar to the anxious, nervous individual.

Born criminals, the biologically predisposed, exhibited a lack of guilt or remorse for any wrongdoing (although they often alleged repentance) and a peculiar inability to learn the distinction between good and evil. Lombroso reported that they did not develop close friendships and were likely to betray companions and accomplices. They displayed "exaggerated notions of their own importance," were impulsive and cruel, and had a high tolerance for pain.

Lombroso at first considered the female offender to be very similar to the male offender, both psychologically and in physical appearance (Wolfgang, 1972). Singling out prostitution as representative of female crime, he saw it as an *atavism* (a throwback to primitive times) and suggested that most prostitutes were born criminals who lacked a "mother sense." He later modified this view. On second thought, the born criminal woman did not clearly exhibit the same physical anomalies as the born criminal male. Psychologically, however, she was more terrible and cruel than any man, almost monsterlike (Wolfgang, 1972). Lombroso based this on his belief that women in general have many traits in common with children, such as revenge, jealousy, and an inclination toward "vengeances of a refined cruelty."

Lombroso had a devoted following, which became known as the *Italian school of criminology*. His outrageous pronouncements often embarrassed other criminologists, however, and they sought ways to refute him. In 1913, Charles Goring (1913/1972) published an influential monograph reporting the results of a study comparing the physical measurements of 3,000 English convicts to those of an equal number of nonconvicts. He did not find the significant physical differences reported by Lombroso. Goring's research, however, was plagued by numerous methodological flaws, as were Lombroso's own investigations. Nevertheless, it proved devastating to the Lombrosian position. Armed with Goring's findings and eager to put the genetics and crime issue to rest, many criminologists quickly wrote the born criminal's obituary.

Although opinion varies about the value of Lombroso's contributions, there is little doubt that he had considerable impact on research directed at the relationship between genetics and the criminal personality. The late Stephen Shafer (1976, pp. 41–42), for example, suggested that Cesare Lombroso could easily be called the father of modern criminology because his theories have stimulated research and empirical investigations on the criminal's personality as well as the social environment. Abrahamsen (1960) argued that Lombroso paved the way for examining the criminal personality. And Wolfgang (1972, p. 287) stated, "The clinical, psychological, and psychiatric analyses of today that report data on personality traits . . . are similar to, but much more refined and sophisticated than many of the findings reported by Lombroso."

PHYSIQUE AND CRIME

Theorists have linked physical characteristics with personality ever since Hippocrates outlined a typology of physiques and tried to relate them to personality. He also introduced the concept of humors, or body fluids, which presumably influenced personality (C. Hall & Lindzey, 1970). The belief that fixed aspects of physical appearance are indicative of the qualities of a person is known as *physiognomy,* a field of study especially popular during the early nineteenth century (Collins, 1999). Cesare Lombroso carried on the tradition of physiognomy in the late nineteenth century. The modern path of physiognomy or constitutional psychology was set by the German psychiatrist Emil Kretschmer (1925), who distinguished four types of body structures and tried to connect them to specific mental disorders. He called one physique the *pyknic* and noted that it was characterized by a short, fat stature. The second type, exhibiting height and very thin features, was the *leptosomatic* or *aesthenic*. The muscular, vigorous physique was called the *athletic type*. The fourth, the *dysplastic*, represented an incongruous mixture of different physiques in different parts of the body, making it appear "rare, surprising and ugly" (C. Hall & Lindzey, 1970).

More pertinent to our discussion of crime is the theory of William H. Sheldon (Sheldon, Hartl, & McDermott, 1949; Sheldon & Stevens, 1942), who developed a similar but superior classification of body type in the United States and related physique to delinquency. Sheldon's method is called **somatotyping**. After extensively collecting and documenting physical measurements, Sheldon found he could delineate three basic body builds: the **endomorphic** (fat and soft), **ectomorphic** (thin and fragile), and **mesomorphic** (muscular and hard) (see **Figure 3–1**). The reader with some background in embryology will recognize that the terms refer to layers of the embryo. The endodermal embryonic layer develops primarily into the digestive viscera, and thus individuals who are plump (endomorphs) are tied to the digestive system. The mesodermal layer of the embryo develops into muscle; therefore, the tough, muscular body, well equipped for strenuous activity, is labeled the mesomorph. The ectodermal layer is developmentally responsible for the nervous system. Ectomorphs have a large brain and central nervous system compared to the rest of their body, which is usually tall and thin.

We should emphasize that Sheldon avoided making sharp distinctions between body types or somatotypes. People were scored on the basis of three 7-point scales corresponding to the three somatotypes, with a 7 indicating that they were exclusively that body type. This was a rare occurrence, however. For example, a "pure" mesomorph would have a somatotype of 1–7–1, with the 1s denoting the absence of any characteristic of that particular body build. A 3–2–5 person would be primarily ectomorphic (5) but have some features of endomorphs (3) and mesomorphs (2). The average body build would be assigned a 4–4–4 index, indicating constitutional balance (see Figure 3–1).

Figure 3–1   Sheldon's Somatotypes in Relation to Physique and Temperament

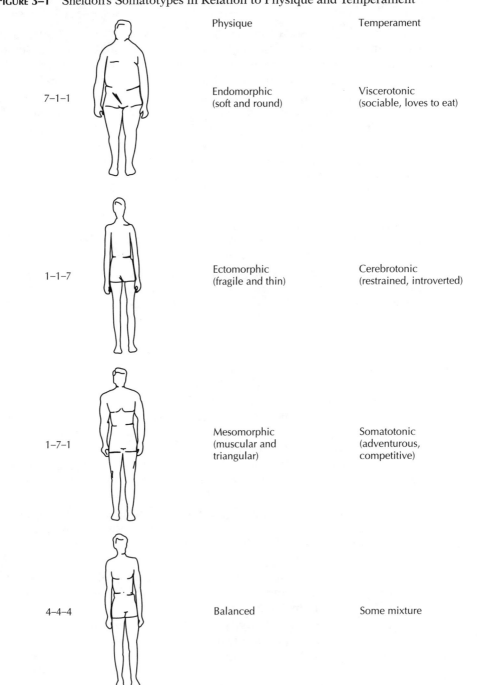

	Physique	Temperament
7–1–1	Endomorphic (soft and round)	Viscerotonic (sociable, loves to eat)
1–1–7	Ectomorphic (fragile and thin)	Cerebrotonic (restrained, introverted)
1–7–1	Mesomorphic (muscular and triangular)	Somatotonic (adventurous, competitive)
4–4–4	Balanced	Some mixture

Sheldon found a strong **correlation** between personality (or temperament) and somatotype—in other words, he linked certain personality types with certain body types. One personality loves comfort, food, affection, and people. This type is usually even-tempered and easy to get along with. Sheldon labeled this disposition *viscerotonia*, and as you might have guessed, he connected it closely to the basic endomorph. A second personality type ordinarily needs vigorous physical activity, risk taking, and adventure. A person with this temperament, according to Sheldon, is more likely to be indifferent to pain and is aggressive, callous, even ruthless in relationships with others. This cluster of personality traits was called *somatotonia* and was linked with the mesomorph. *Cerebrotonia* labels the person who is inhibited, reserved, self-conscious, and afraid of people; it correlates highly with the ectomorphic body build.

Sheldon began to test his theory in 1939 by exploring the relationship between delinquency and physique. His first study involved nearly 400 boys in a residential rehabilitation home. Biographical sketches—family background, medical history, mental and educational performance, and delinquent behavior—were collected for each boy, and they were all assigned somatotype ratings. Sheldon studied his delinquents for eight years, comparing them to a group of male college students. He found that the college men generally clustered around the "average" somatotype of 4–4–4. Delinquents, on the other hand, tended to be heavily mesomorphic, but there were also signs of endomorphy. Ectomorphs were rare in the delinquent group. On the basis of his study, Sheldon concluded that there were definite somatotypic and temperamental differences between delinquent and nondelinquent males.

Subsequent investigations (primarily on males) provided additional, although not very strong, support for Sheldon's findings. Glueck and Glueck (1950, 1956) found that mesomorphs were proportionately overrepresented in the delinquent population (60%, with 30% endomorphs). In general, their findings established that delinquent boys were larger and stronger than nondelinquent boys. In another study, Cortes and Gatti (1972) reported that delinquent subjects (100 boys adjudicated delinquent by the courts) were much more mesomorphic than nondelinquents (100 male high school seniors). Fifty-seven percent of their delinquent group could be easily classified as mesomorphic, compared to 19% of the nondelinquents. These percentages roughly correspond to those cited by Glueck and Glueck (1950) in their study of 500 youths. Hartl, Monnelly, and Elderkin (1982) claimed that, in their 30-year follow-up of Sheldon's original group, the relationship between mesomorphs and antisocial behavior still held.

More sophisticated research yielded different results. McCandless, Persons, and Roberts (1972) found physique unrelated to either self-reported delinquency or the seriousness of the criminal offenses. Wadsworth (1979), using data from the British National Survey, reported that delinquents, especially those who committed serious offenses, were generally smaller in stature and appeared to reach puberty later than their nondelinquent peers. While no somatotyping was done, the results suggest that the delinquents were not mesomorphs, since mesomorphs reportedly reach puberty before the other body types (Rutter & Giller, 1984). Finally, in their longitudinal study of working-class boys in London, West and Farrington (1973) reported little association between delinquency and either height–weight ratios or physical strength.

Wilson and Herrnstein (1985, p. 90), in their influential but controversial book, *Crime and Human Nature*, concluded that the evidence on the relationship between physique and crime "leaves no doubt that constitutional traits correlate with criminal behavior." Some of the evidence does suggest a relationship between body build and crime, but there is also a significant amount of evidence that indicates that there may be no relationship. Thus, the research is equivocal and far from conclusive. While it may make logical sense to argue that the mesomorph's physique, because it is so muscular and strong, is well suited for involvement in aggressive or antisocial acts, much more sophisticated and well-executed research needs to be conducted before we can get a better understanding of the physique–crime connection. In a recent study, Sampson and Laub (1997) found evidence that mesomorphy is a poor predictor of adult arrests for any crime, including violence. Thus, while mesomorphy seems to be related to official delinquency, it does not seem to be related to criminal offending during adulthood.

Attractiveness

Some researchers have studied physical features, such as facial characteristics, and related them to body build, criminal activity, or treatment by the criminal justice system. As we learned in the beginning of the chapter, some advocates of physiognomy argue that physical features, such as the spacing of the eyes, shape of the forehead, and body stature and shape, are related to honesty, intelligence, and even criminal conduct. Others contend that facial and general physical attractiveness are also related to temperament and certain enduring personality traits. But it is not clear whether the physical attributes directly influence the development of personality characteristics, whether they elicit responses from the social environment that encourage the development of certain personality characteristics, or whether there is some complicated interaction between the physical characteristics and the environment.

One of the most robust findings in the research literature is that physical attractiveness presents a significant advantage for both children and adults across a wide range of situations and experiences (Langlois et al., 2000). For example, attractive children and adults are *judged* more positively than unattractive children and adults, even by those who know them well; attractive children and adults are *treated* more positively than unattractive child and adults, even by those who know them well; and attractive children and adults exhibit more positive behaviors and traits than unattractive children and adults (Langlois et al., 2000). In general, attractive individuals are more successful, have better social skills, and are more mentally healthy than unattractive persons (Langlois et al., 2000). And these observations hold for both genders. It is reasonable to suppose, therefore, that attractiveness may show some connection to criminal behavior.

Unfortunately, the amount of research devoted to the attractiveness–crime connection is very sparse and limited methodologically. Cavior and Howard (1973), concentrating on facial features, found that both African-American and white delinquents were rated significantly less attractive than nondelinquents. Moreover, correctional personnel often comment that inmates, as a group, have "uglier" faces than the general population, but very little research has been directed at verifying these observations.

Facial unattractiveness, promoting rejection by peers and unfavorable treatment from the social environment, may play a role in the development of crime and/or increase the probability of being adjudicated delinquent by the courts. Research has found that attractive children are favored by adults and other children. In fact, attractive children are less negatively evaluated than less attractive children, even when they have committed identical antisocial acts (Dion, 1972; Dion, Berscheid, & Walster, 1972). In one study using a simulated jury, good-looking defendants were treated more gently and were considered less dangerous than a comparable group of unattractive defendants (Sigall & Ostrove, 1978).

The thesis that physical unattractiveness might have something to do with criminal behavior has been applied to rehabilitation. In the mid-1970s, corrective surgery was offered to inmates with facial deformities at Rikers Island, as part of a pilot project testing the value of plastic surgery as a rehabilitative measure (Kurtzberg, Mandell, Lewin, Lipton, & Shuster, 1978). The surgery was to be performed just prior to release. After extensive medical and psychological screening, 425 inmates were divided into four groups. Depending on his group, the inmate received either surgery, counseling, both, or neither (the control group).

The results, though complex, showed some support for the benefits of a new image. The offenders who seemed to benefit most from the intervention were nonaddicts who received surgery; they were substantially less likely to engage in crime during a one-year follow-up period than a comparable group of offenders who received no surgery. Interestingly, the group that received counseling alone committed more detected crime during the follow-up period than even the group that had neither counseling nor surgery. Although the study's results are not clear-cut, they do suggest that physical improvements also improve offender self-image and the likelihood of acceptance by others. Possibly individuals with an improved appearance has less need to defend or prove their worth through crime or to react aggressively to slights or challenges. And, possibly, the slights and challenges are fewer in number.

Based on a nationwide survey, Thompson (1990) estimates that 5,000 to 6,000 inmates in the United States undergo some type of cosmetic or reconstructive surgery each year. Moreover, in his review of the research literature, Thompson found that six of the nine studies examining recidivism rates after cosmetic or reconstructive surgery concluded that reoffending was significantly reduced following the surgical treatment. However, since there are a number of methodological problems in all these studies, other interpretations and conclusions of the data are possible. It is also unclear whether corrective surgery reduces recidivism over the long haul or merely delays a return to jail or prison.

In a more recent study, Zebrowitz and colleagues (Zebrowitz, Andreoletti, Collins, Lee, & Blumenthal, 1998) examined the influence of "babyfaceness" on the behavioral patterns and personalities of boys, including their involvement in delinquency and adult crime. The researchers point out that considerable research has shown that most people believe that babyfaced people are likely to have childlike traits—such as submissiveness and dependency—and are more likely to be warm, affectionate, honest, weak, and naive. Although this babyfaced stereotype has been well documented, the question of the accuracy of the stereotype is another matter. In one study, Zebrowitz, Collins, and Dutta (1998) reported that, in contradiction to the stereotype, middle-class babyfaced adolescent boys were far more assertive and hostile than their mature-faced peers. In a second study, Zebrowitz, Andreoletti, et al. (1998) discovered that babyfaced boys from lower–socioeconomic status (SES) families were more likely to be delinquent and commit significantly more crimes than their mature-faced peers, refuting the stereotype of babyfaced boys as warm, submissive, and physically weak. Delinquency and crime data were compiled from the criminal history data of each delinquent from birth to age 17. The criminal history data were drawn from the Crime Causation Study archived at the Henry A. Murray Research Center, Radcliffe College, Cambridge, Massachusetts. The researchers also found that babyfaced boys from higher-SES backgrounds tended to confirm the traditional stereotype, showing less likelihood of being delinquent than their mature-faced peers. The researchers hypothesized that the effect of a babyface on delinquent status and crime frequency in lower-SES boys may have been derived from their desire to promote the reputation that they are tough. In other words, the boys may have compensated for the expectation that they would exhibit unassertivenss, dependency, and weakness by behaving contrary to these undesirable expectations.

Minor Physical Anomalies

Throughout the past three decades there has been sporadic interest in the relationship between certain physical attributes and temperament. Specifically, some researchers have focused on **minor physical anomalies** (MPAs)—such as asymmetrical ears, soft and pliable ears, curved fifth fingers, ocular hypertelorism (widely spaced eyes), multiple hair whorls, webbed toes, furrowed tongue—and learning disabilities, hyperactivity, schizophrenia, aggressiveness, and clumsiness. MPAs were first described by Down in 1866 and have been related to a variety of neurodevelopmental disorders, including schizophrenia, autism, ADHD, and learning disabilities (Gangestad & Yeo, 1994). MPAs appear to result from disrupted or slowed process during prenatal development (Gangestad & Yeo, 1994).

These MPAs seem to correlate (albeit weakly) with some temperamental and behavioral attributes in children. For example, high numbers of MPAs are found in active, aggressive, and impulsive preschool boys (Paulhus & Martin, 1986) and in boys demonstrating conduct disorders (Halverson & Victor, 1976; Pine, Shaffer, Schonfeld, & Davies, 1997). MPAs are generally not noticed either by people who have them or by others. They are discernible only to trained observers and do not significantly interfere with attractiveness. The occurrence of MPAs is hypothesized to be associated with teratogenic factors (factors that produce physical defects in the developing embryo) operating within the first trimester of pregnancy.

The assumption is that the same teratogenic factors that produce minor physical abnormalities also affect the central nervous system in a way that contributes to behavioral problems and developmental deviations. Presumably, hyperactivity, impulsiveness, restlessness, and inattentiveness are all potential reflections of central nervous system defects that go hand-in-hand with MPAs. While the hypothesis connecting MPAs with a propensity toward delinquent or criminal behavior is intriguing, very little research has attempted to test the hypothesis directly. In a study by Mednick and Kandel (1988), an experienced pediatrician assessed MPAs in 129 12-year-old boys, and then the researchers followed the boys' development until they were 21 years old. The researchers discovered that MPAs were related to violent offending, but only if the boys were from unstable, nonintact homes. Boys from stable homes did not show the relationship. Furthermore, Mednick and Kandel did not find an MPA relationship for property crimes, only violent crimes. In another study, Brennan, Mednick, and Kandel (1993) found that subjects who had delivery complications at birth and a high number of MPAs were more likely to be adult violent offenders than individuals who had only one of those conditions or neither of them. These results suggest that disruptions in the normal development of the nervous system may render the individual at some risk to engage in violent behavior.

In order to measure MPAs, a checklist was devised by Waldrop and his colleagues (Waldrop & Halverson, 1971; Waldrop, Halverson, & Shetterly, 1989). Examiners record the presence and degree of anomalies and an aggregate MPA score (usually the number of MPAs observed) is used in the data analysis.

A related physical anomaly is called "fluctuating asymmetry" (FA), which, together with MPAs, constitutes a developmental instability (DI) index (Yeo, Gangestad, Thoma, Shaw, & Repa, 1997). FAs are individual variations in bilateral symmetry in physical features that—in the general population—are symmetrical (Yeo et al., 1997). An example of an FA is a discernible difference in ear length. In the general population, the left and right ears are usually equal in size, whereas a person with an FA may show a slighter longer left ear or right ear. A similar example is differences in foot size, with one foot measurably different from the other foot. Several studies have found that both FA and MPAs are elevated in a variety of neurodevelopmental disorders (Yeo &

Gangestad, 1993), *suggesting* that DI measures may be related to conduct disorders or antisocial behavior. Yeo et al. (1997), using a sample of undergraduate college students, discovered the DI index was related to cognitive functioning and other brain processes. To our knowledge, however, there have been no studies that have directly examined the relationship between the DI index and criminal behavior. Clearly, much more research is needed in this intriguing area before even tentative conclusions can be drawn.

TWIN STUDIES

One way to determine the role of genetics in criminality is to compare the incidence and type of criminal convictions among identical and fraternal twins. Fraternal twins (also called dizygotic twins) develop from two different eggs fertilized by two different sperm, and are no more genetically alike than ordinary siblings. Identical twins (monozygotic twins) develop from a single egg (fertilized by a single sperm) that splits in two, forming two embryos. Identical twins are always the same sex, share the same genes, and are usually remarkably similar in appearance and behavior. However, approximately two-thirds of monozygotic twins are monochorionic (share the same chorion), and one-third of the monozygotic pair is dichorionic (two different chorions) (Rhee & Waldman, 2002). The chorion is the outer membrane enclosing the embryo. Therefore, some identical twins develop in slightly different prenatal environments, which may contribute to individual differences that may emerge as the twins develop into maturity. In fact, several studies have found that monochorionic, monozygotic twins are more similar in personality and cognitive ability than dichorionic, monozygotic twins (Rhee & Waldman, 2002). Theoretically, however, by comparing fraternal twins and identical twins, researchers should be able to identify the relative contributions of genes compared to environmental factors in the development of personality, cognitive ability, and behavior in general.

Two important concepts need to be recognized before a good understanding of twin studies can be achieved: *shared environments* and *nonshared environments*. Shared or common environments include prenatal and life experiences affecting both twins in the same way. For example, twins raised by the same biological parents share a common hereditary and home environment. Shared environments in this sense are apt to promote high trait or behavioral similarity between twin pairs, especially for identical twins. Nonshared environments, on the other hand, include living experiences that are different for each twin, such as being raised in a different home environment. Therefore, in order to determine the relative influence of genes on behavior, compared to the environment, shared and nonshared aspects must be considered.

For example, twin research indicates that, for a variety of traits, the magnitude of genetic and nonshared environmental influences increases as a person gets older, whereas the magnitude of shared environmental influences decreases (Loehlin, 1992; Plomin, 1986; Rhee & Waldman, 2002). That is, as the child begins to spend more time outside the family circle, especially when he or she becomes a young adult, the influence of the shared environment (family) tends to wane, whereas the influence of genetics and nonshared environments (e.g., peers) becomes more discernible. For example, Rhee and Waldman (2002) describe a longitudinal study by Matheny (1989) that revealed that the temperaments (e.g., emotional tone, fearfulness, approach or avoidance toward others) became more similar for identical pairs than for fraternal pairs as they grew older. Thus, we might expect that the developmental age of the subjects in any twin study may play an important role in determining the influences of genetics compared to the environment. We return to this point shortly.

Some investigators suggest that identical twins are so physically alike that they probably elicit similar social responses from their environment (shared environment), more so than fraternal twins. In this sense, they are more likely to develop similar personalities. There may be merit to this viewpoint, but research does not yet support it. Rather, some research has found that identical twins reared apart are more alike in some personality attributes than are identical twins reared in the same home environment (Canter, 1973; Shields, 1962). When reared together, identical twins may make a conscious effort to accentuate their individual identities, whereas when reared apart they may have less need to be different.

Concordance, a key concept in twin study research, is the genetics term for the degree to which related pairs of subjects both show a particular behavior or condition. It is usually expressed as percentages. Assume that we want to determine the concordance of intelligence among 20 pairs of identical twins and 20 pairs of fraternals. If we find that 10 pairs of the identical twins have approximately the same IQ score, but only 5 pairs of the fraternals obtain the same score, our concordance is 50% for identicals and 25% for fraternals. The concordance for identicals would be twice that of fraternals, suggesting that hereditary factors play an important role in intelligence. If, however, the two concordances were about the same, we would conclude that genetics is irrelevant, at least as represented in our sample and measured by our methods.

Numerous early twin studies using this concordance method have indicated that heredity may be a powerful determinant of intelligence, schizophrenia, depression, neurotic disorders, alcoholism, and criminal behavior (Claridge, 1973; Hetherington & Parke, 1975; McClearn & DeFries, 1973; Rosenthal, 1970, 1971). The first such study relative to criminality was reported by the Munich physician Johannes Lange (1929) in his book *Crime as Destiny* (Christiansen, 1977; Rosenthal, 1971). The title reflects Lange's Lombrosian conviction that criminal conduct is a predetermined fate dictated by heredity. He found a criminality concordance of 77% for 13 pairs of adult identical twins and only 12% for 17 pairs of adult fraternal twins. Auguste Marcel Legras (1932) then found a 100% criminal concordance for five pairs of identicals. Note that both of these studies used small samples. Subsequent studies, using more sophisticated designs and methods of twin identification and sampling, continued to find a substantially higher criminal concordance for identical twins compared to fraternals. The levels were not as high as those reported by either Lange or Legras, however. **Table 3–1** summarizes relevant investigations of criminal concordance. Although these tabulated investigations differed in method and definitions of criminality, the combined concordance levels demonstrate that, where criminal behavior is concerned, identical twins seem to be better matched than fraternal twins.

Hans Eysenck reviewed other twin studies, found similar concordances, and concluded: "Thus concordance is found over four times as frequently in identicals as in fraternals, a finding which seems to put beyond any doubt that heredity plays an extremely important part in the genesis of criminal behaviour" (H. Eysenck, 1973, p. 167). Rosenthal, however, injects a word of caution, stressing the many pitfalls of the concordance twin method and the ramifications of using different legal definitions of criminality. Nevertheless, he allows, ". . . It is clearly not possible to rule out the potential fact that genetic factors may indeed be the primary source of the higher concordance rate in MZ (identical) as compared to DZ (fraternal) twins" (Rosenthal, 1975, p. 10).

Eysenck further complicates the issue by suggesting that twin studies may actually have deflated the true concordance rate, since it is likely that identical

TABLE 3–1   Summary of Twin-Criminality Studies Showing Pairs and Concordance Rates

	IDENTICAL TWINS			FRATERNAL TWINS		
RESEARCHER(S)	NO OF PAIRS	PAIRS CONCORDANT	PERCENTAGE	NO. OF PAIRS	PAIRS CONCORDANT	PERCENTAGE
Lange (1929)	13	10	77	17	2	12
Legras (1932)	4	4	100	5	0	0
Rosanoff (1934)	37	25	68	60	6	10
Kranz (1936)	31	20	65	43	20	53
Stumpfl (1936)	18	11	61	19	7	37
Borgstrom (1939)	4	3	75	5	2	40
Rosanoff et al. (1941)	45	35	78	27	6	18
Yoshimasu (1961)	28	17	61	18	2	11
Yoshimasu (1965)	28	14	50	26	0	0
Hayashi (1967)	15	11	73	5	3	60
Dalgaard & Kringlen (1976)	31	8	26	54	8	15
Christiansen (1977)						
Males	71	25	35	120	15	13
Females	14	2	21	27	2	8
Total	339	185	55	426	73	17

twins were often confused with fraternal twins, especially in the earlier studies. If the twins are of the same sex, it is difficult to distinguish identicals from fraternals from appearance alone. Today, blood type, fingerprints (which are highly similar but not identical), and various genetically determined serum proteins allow differentiation. Since these methods were not available to earlier investigators, Eysenck contends that mixups may have confounded the results. However, the concordance rates may just as easily have been inflated as deflated.

As Table 3–1 shows, twin studies have not invariably found high criminal concordance rates in favor of identical twins. One study by Dalgaard and Kringlen (1976) found no significant difference between identicals and fraternals. The Dalgaard–Kringlen sample included all the registered male twins born in Norway between 1921 and 1930. However, 32% of the sample was deleted from the analysis for various reasons, which might have affected the results. Also, the label "criminal" was applied to traffic violations, military offenses, and treason during World War II, as well as to all actions against the penal code. This was a broader definition than was used in most twin studies. The late Karl O. Christiansen, who devoted much of his research work to twin studies, could not explain the lack of significant differences reported by Dalgaard and Kringlen. He advocated an additional study to determine whether "some special conditions exist in Norway that would dampen the expression of genetic factors . . ." (Christiansen, 1977, p. 82).

Overall, despite procedural and definitional problems and except for the Dalgaard–Kringlen data, the studies examining concordance rates among twins have consistently indicated higher concordance for identical twins. More recent research, however, indicates that these higher concordance rates may hold only for adult nonviolent offending and not for juvenile offending (Blackburn, 1993). In a careful review of the literature, Adrian Raine (1993, p. 79) concludes, "Summary statistics from 13 twin analyses show that 51.5% of MZ twins are concordant for crime compared to 20.6% for DZ twins, indicating substantial evidence for genetic influences on crime."

The twin data clearly suggest that it might be wise to consider heredity a significant component in criminality. However, it should also be emphasized that the research cited above favors the heritability of nonviolent crime but not violent crime (Dodge & Pettit, 2003; Raine, 1993). Most early concordance research either did not define criminal behavior clearly or used nonviolent criminal behavior largely to the exclusion of violent criminal behavior. In addition, "[A]lthough specific genes . . . may have special relevance for the development of conduct problems, the genetic base for most problem behaviors likely reflects combinations of genes that are expressed in different ways at different points of life" (Dodge & Pettit, 2003, p. 351). Thus, some combination of genes does appear to render certain children at risk for developing delinquent or antisocial behavior, but environmental factors play prominent roles in the formation of that behavior also (Dodge & Pettit, 2003; Rhee & Waldman, 2002).

ADOPTION STUDIES

Another method used to identify crucial variables in the interaction between heredity and environment is the adoption study, which helps identify environments most conducive to criminality. There have been exceedingly few such investigations, however, and those few have been fraught with methodological problems.

One of the first adoption studies was carried out in Denmark by Schulsinger (1972), who explored the incidence of psychopathy in the biological relatives of adopted adults. Schulsinger compared 57 adopted adults whom he labeled psychopathic to a control group of 57 nonpsychopathic adopted adults. The two groups were matched for sex, age, social class, and age of transfer to the adopting family. The study's direct implications for criminal behavior are questionable, because Schulsinger defined psychopathy by his own loose criteria. Individuals who were impulse-ridden and who exhibited acting-out behavior qualified. As we will see in Chapter 4, these descriptions do not necessarily connote either psychopathy or criminality.

Schulsinger found that 3.9% of the biological relatives of psychopathic adoptees could also be classified as psychopathic, whereas only 1.4% of the control group's biological relatives could. The results just failed to reach statistical significance, indicating that we should be very cautious about accepting their implications. It is interesting, though, that psychopathy—even given its loose definition—was about two and a half times more frequent in the family backgrounds of acting-out adoptees.

Crowe (1974) conducted a better-designed study, a follow-up of 52 persons relinquished for early adoption by female offenders. Ninety percent of the biological mothers were felons at the time of the adoptive placement, the most common offenses being forgery and passing bad checks. Twenty-five of the adoptees were female, and all were white. Another 52 adoptees with no evidence of criminal family background were selected as a control group and matched for sex, race, and age at the time of adoption.

For the follow-up phase of the study, Crowe selected 37 index and 37 control subjects who had by then reached age 18. (Index subjects in research are those subjects who are of major concern.) Seven of the index adoptees had arrest records: As adults, all seven had at least one conviction, four had multiple arrests, two had multiple convictions, and three were felons. Of the 37 matching controls, 2 had adult arrest records and only 1 of these had been convicted. Each subject's personality was diagnosed by three clinicians based on test results and data gathered in an interview; no family background was included. The clinicians made their diagnoses independently of one another and without knowing the subject's group. Six of the adoptees born of female offenders were labeled "antisocial personality"; one control-group subject was labeled "probable antisocial personality."

Crowe found a positive correlation between the tendency of the index group to be antisocial and two other variables: the child's age at the time of adoptive placement and the length of time the child had spent in temporary care (orphanages and foster homes) prior to that placement. The older the child of an offender upon adoptive placement and the longer the temporary placement, the more likely the child would grow up antisocial. The control-group members were not affected by these conditions. This suggests either that the two adoptee groups responded differently to similar environmental conditions or that the adoption agency placed the offspring of female offenders in less desirable homes—and there was no indication that this selective placement had occurred.

Hutchings and Mednick (1975) also conducted a study examining the effects of genetics and environment. They reasoned that if there is a genetic basis for criminality, then there should be a significant relationship between the criminal tendencies of biological parents and those of their children who were adopted by someone else. In 1971, using Copenhagen adoption files, Hutchings and Mednick identified 1,145 male adoptees, who were by then 30 to 44 years old. They were matched with an equal number of nonadoptee controls on sex, age, occupational status of fathers, and residence. The researchers learned that 185 adoptees (16.2%) had criminal records, compared to 105 nonadoptees (8.9%). A check on the biological fathers of the adoptees revealed that they were nearly three times more likely to be involved in criminal activity than were either the adoptees' adoptive fathers or the fathers of the nonadopted controls. Furthermore, there was a significant relationship between the criminality of the sons and that of the fathers. Where the biological father had a criminal record and the adoptive father had none, a significant number of adoptees still became criminal (22%); but where the biological father had no record and the adoptive father had a criminal record, the number of adoptees who pursued criminal activities was lower (11.5%). If both the biological and the adoptive fathers were criminal, the chances that the adoptee would also be criminal were much greater than if only one man was criminal. Hutchings and Mednick concluded that genetic factors continue to exert strong influences in the tendency toward criminality, even though environmental factors also play important roles.

One serious limitation of the Hutchings–Mednick data, as well as of any adoption study, is that agencies often try to match the adopted child with the adoptive family on the basis of the child's biological and socioeconomic background. The Crowe study involving the children of offenders found no evidence of this, but the Danish agency used in the Hutchings–Mednick investigation confirmed that this was done. To their credit, the researchers not only recognized this problem, but also admonished that extrapolations to American society should be made cautiously, since Danish society is more homogeneous in cultural values and race.

The most comprehensive adoption study to date was conducted by Mednick, Gabrielli, and Hutchings (1984, 1987). These researchers compared the court convictions of 14,427 adoptees (adopted between 1927 and 1947) in a small European country with the conviction records of their biological and adoptive parents. The study showed a significant relationship between the conviction history of the adoptees (for both males and females) and that of their biological parents. Specifically, if either biological parent had been convicted of a crime, the risk of criminality in the adoptee (the biological child) increased significantly. This relationship was especially strong for male adoptees who were chronic or persistent offenders. As we might expect, chronic offenders accounted for a disproportionate share of the total offending for the entire cohort. Interestingly, there was no evidence that the type of crime committed by the biological parent had any relation to the type of crime committed by the biological child. Both the biological parent and the biological child tended to engage in crime but selected different kinds of crime. There was also no indication that the adopted children knew about the criminality of their biological parents. The researchers concluded that some factor transmitted by criminal parents increased the probability that their children would engage in criminal behavior. Elsewhere, Gabrielli and Mednick (1983, p. 63) commented, "It is reasonable . . . to conclude that some people inherit biological characteristics which permit them to be antisocial more readily than others."

In summary, twin and adoption studies suggest that genetic components may contribute moderately to a tendency to become criminal, especially pertaining to nonviolent crime, but they have also found that environment is highly important (Blackburn, 1993; Ellis, 1982; Raine, 1993). The available data so far indicate that some people may be born with a biological predisposition to behavior that runs counter to social values and norms and that environmental factors may either inhibit or facilitate it.

In addition to genetic factors, *in utero* experiences may also play a role in the predisposition toward criminal behavior. For example, exposure to a toxic or diseased prenatal environment may predispose children to problem behavior. "Fetuses exposed to opiates or methadone are at heightened risk for conduct problems 10 to 13 years later, as are fetuses exposed to alcohol, marijuana, and cigarette by-products during pregnancy" (Dodge & Pettit, 2003, p. 351). Also, before and after birth, lead poisoning found in old paint can lead to long-term conduct problems in adolescence and young adulthood (Dodge & Pettit, 2003). As noted by Kenneth Dodge and Gregory Pettit (p. 351), "Thus, because of genes or in utero experiences, some children are born with a hyperpersistent behavior facilitation system, an underactive behavioral inhibition system, autonomic nervous system hyperreactivity, cognitive problems in sustaining attention to cues, low cerebrospinal fluid concentrations of serotonin metabolites . . . which affect delay of gratification, or a difficult style of temperament. All of these factors predispose young children to adolescent conduct problems." Whether the children grow up to become persistent, chronic offenders appears to depend largely on how their social environments respond to these neurobiological problems. Life experiences that involve harsh treatment, social rejection, and failure place children at high risk to engage in antisocial and criminal behavior throughout their lives.

One comprehensive theory that describes the interactions of neurobiological factors and the social environment is represented by the personality theory of British psychologist Hans J. Eysenck. We now turn our attention to this interesting perspective.

EYSENCK'S THEORY OF PERSONALITY AND CRIME

The late Hans J. Eysenck (Eysenck & Gudjonsson, 1989) was convinced that sociological theory had little to offer toward the understanding and treatment of crime. "In many ways we disagree with various sociological theories that have become so popular since World War II but which, we believe, are fundamentally erroneous and counter to fact" (p. 1). Instead, Eysenck argued that psychological knowledge provides the key answers and strategies for the prevention of criminal behavior. "We believe that psychology is a fundamental discipline which underlies any advances we may make in the prevention of crime, and the treatment of criminals" (p. ix). Not only will psychology lead the way toward the solution of crime, Eysenck told us, but the neurological underpinnings of personality are one of the prime determinants of antisocial and criminal behavior.

Hans Eysenck (1977) proposed that criminal behavior is the result of an *interaction* between certain environmental conditions and features of the nervous system. He believed that a comprehensive theory of criminality must allow for an examination of the neurophysiological makeup and the unique socialization history of each individual. Statements that crime is caused by social conditions such as poverty, poor education, and unemployment are as inaccurate as hereditary and biological explanations. Crime cannot be understood in terms of heredity alone, but it also cannot be understood in terms of environment alone (H. Eysenck, 1973, p. 171). Eysenck also suggested that different combinations of environmental, neurobiological, and personality factors give rise to different types of crime (S. Eysenck & Eysenck, 1970). This position implies that different personalities are more susceptible to certain crimes than others, an issue we return to shortly.

Unlike most contemporary theories of crime, Eysenck's theory places heavy emphasis on genetic predispositions toward antisocial and criminal conduct. Eysenck (1996, p. 146) asserted, "Genetic causes play an important part in antisocial and criminal behaviour. This simple fact is no longer in doubt." It is important to note at the outset that he was not suggesting that individuals are born criminal but, rather, that some people are born with nervous system characteristics that are significantly different from those of the general population and that affect their ability to conform to social expectancies and rules. "It is not crime itself or criminality that is innate; it is certain peculiarities of the central and autonomic nervous system that react with the environment, with upbringing, and many other environment factors to increase the probability that a given person would act in a certain antisocial manner" (H. Eysenck & Gudjonsson, 1989, p. 7). Eysenck isolated features of the central and autonomic nervous systems to account for a substantial

TABLE 3–2   Summary Table of Eysenck's Theory

PERSONALITY TRAIT	NEUROBIOLOGICAL INFLUENCE	HIGH SCORES	LOW SCORES
Extraversion	RAS, CNS	Stimulation seeking	Stimulation avoidance
Neuroticism	Autonomic NS	Nervous, unstable	Stable, calm
Psychoticism	Excessive androgen	Tough-minded	Tender-minded

Note: RAS, reticular activating system; CNS, central nervous system; NS, nervous system.

portion of the differences found in personality in general. The way each individual's nervous system functions may be as unique as his or her personality characteristics. Carrying this one step further, we could posit that some nervous systems are more likely to engage in criminal activity because of their reactivity, sensitivity, and excitability.

Based on a series of empirical studies and statistical analyses, Eysenck argued that there are four higher-order factors of personality—one higher-order factor for ability called "g" (general intelligence), and three higher-order factors for temperament, called **extraversion**, **neuroticism**, and **psychoticism** (**Table 3–2**). Eysenck believed that the ability factor is an important factor in the cause of criminality but is less important than the temperament factors. He wrote, "We may conclude that intelligence is a factor in the causation of criminality but that its contribution is probably smaller than one might have thought at first" (H. Eysenck & Gudjonsson, 1989, p. 50).

Most of the research on crime and personality has focused on extraversion and neuroticism, which are essentially the core concepts of Eysenckian theory. Eysenck did not identify psychoticism until he found a need to account for behaviors not fully explained by extraversion or neuroticism.

Eysenck visualized each of the three temperament or personality factors on a continuum, with the neuroticism and extraversion lines at right angles and intersecting. Psychoticism is on a separate continuum. Most people fall in the intermediate or midpoint area of each, and people are rarely at either extreme. (See **Figure 3–2**: Most people fall within the square.) The extraversion dimension runs from the extreme pole extraversion to the extreme pole introversion, with the middle range called **ambiversion**. Thus, depending on where a person falls on this dimension, that person may be an extravert, introvert, or ambivert. The neuroticism continuum runs from the polar ends of neuroticism to stability, with no middle label. Psychoticism runs from tough-mindedness (high psychoticism) to tender-mindedness (low psychoticism), also with no label for the middle majority. The extraversion dimension is believed to reflect basic functions of the central nervous system, which consists of the brain and spinal cord, while neuroticism represents functions of the peripheral nervous system (nerve pathways outside the central nervous system). As yet, neither Eysenck nor other researchers have postulated a nervous system mechanism for psychoticism.

FIGURE 3–2   Illustration of Eysenck's Personality Dimensions for Neuroticism and Extraversion

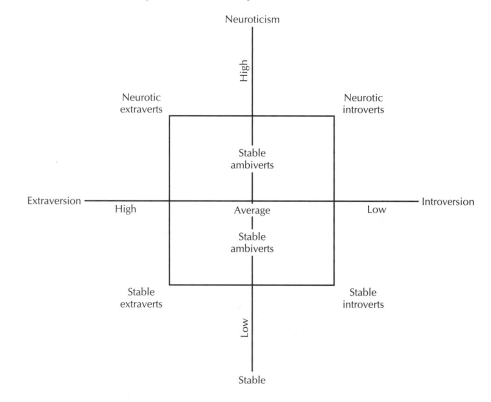

Eysenck developed several self-report questionnaires to measure these personality variables, the best-known being the British Maudsley Personality Inventory and its American editions, the Eysenck Personality Inventory and the Eysenck Personality Questionnaire (EPQ). More recently, the Eysenck Personality Questionnaire—Revised (EPQ-R) has been published. The questionnaires have stimulated extensive research to explore both their validity and Eysenck's concept of personality. Overall, worldwide research has supported the general theory, but when it is applied to criminality, the support begins to crumble. We review some of this research later in the chapter, after examining more closely the basic concepts behind each dimension.

Extraversion

Behavioral Characteristics and Incidence.   Usually, two of every three people will score in the "average" range on the extraversion dimension, thus disqualifying them from studies based on extraversion and introversion. Roughly 16% of the population are extraverts, another 16% introverts, and the remainder (68%) ambiverts.

According to Eysenck, the typical extravert is sociable, impulsive, and optimistic and has high needs for excitement and for a varied, changing environment. Extraverts tend to lose their temper quickly, become aggressive easily, and be unreliable. They like to have people around, enjoy parties, and are usually very talkative. The typical introvert, on the other hand, is reserved, quiet, and cautious. He or she keeps feelings under close control and generally tries to avoid excitement, change, and most social activities. Introverts tend to be reliable and unaggressive and to place great value on ethical standards (H. Eysenck & Rachman, 1965). Ambiverts exhibit some features of both extraversion and introversion, but not to the same degree or consistency as extraverts and introverts.

Think of the extraversion dimension as a continuum representing a progressive need for stimulation, which can be defined as the impact stimuli have on areas of the brain. The impact is analogous to the taste of food. Some people have a relatively consistent tendency to prefer spicy, hot foods (e.g., Szechuan cuisine) that have more impact on their taste centers, while others more often choose bland foods (e.g., macaroni and cheese) because they do not desire the high taste impact. Some people prefer and actively seek out more stimulation or stimulus impact from other areas of their lives as well—they like rousing music, perpetual bustle, hallucinogenic drugs. Eysenck maintained that people at the extraversion end of the dimension require high levels of stimulation from their environment because of their biological makeup.

If you conceptualize the dimension this way, you may find that the popular term "extrovert" (note the spelling) takes on added meaning. Extroverts are sociable creatures who like to be around people and to be immersed in activity because of the stimulation this provides them. It is important to note, though, that our everyday usage of the nouns *extrovert* and *introvert* are not identical to Eysenck's polar classifications.

Because extraverts have higher needs for excitement and stimulation to break the daily boredom, they are also most likely to run counter to the law. They tend to be impulsive, fun-loving, thrill-seeking people who are willing to take chances and stick their necks out. They enjoy pranks and practical jokes and find challenge in opportunities to do the unconventional or even to engage in antisocial behavior. In an interesting study involving Brazilian offenders, Labato (2000) found that extraverts are more likely to use dramatic, powerful firearms when committing crime, whereas introverts have a strong tendency to use less dramatic weapons, such as knives. Some features of the extraverted nervous system not only encourage stimulation seeking but also inhibit the acquisition and internalization of society's rules, as we will see shortly.

Physiological Bases of Extraversion–Introversion.   Eysenck (1967) hypothesized that people differ along the extraversion–introversion axis because of genetic differences in certain mechanisms in their central nervous system, particularly the tiny but complex network of neurons located in the central

Figure 3–3 Location of the Reticular Activating System (RAS) Relative to Other Brain Structures

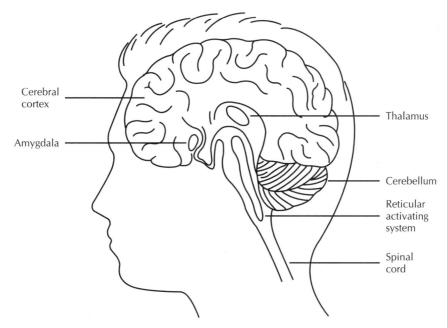

part of the brain stem called the reticular activating system (RAS) (see **Figure 3–3**). The RAS, which we discuss in detail in Chapter 4, is believed to act as a sentinel that awakens and keeps alert the portion of the brain called the cerebral cortex. All higher-level functions, like thinking, memory, and decision making, occur in the cerebral cortex (French, 1957). The RAS arouses the cerebral cortex and keeps it alert to incoming stimuli. Nerve pathways communicating information to the cerebral cortex branch off into collateral pathways traveling to the RAS. In effect, these collaterals "tell" the RAS to alert the brain to incoming information.

Eysenck postulated that both extraverts and introverts inherit an RAS that handles cortical arousal in a unique way, differently from the RAS of the general population. The extravert's RAS does not seem to generate cortical excitation or arousal effectively. In fact, it appears to reduce the impact of stimulation and the arousal properties of stimuli before they can reach the cortex. The introvert, on the other hand, apparently has inherited an RAS that amplifies stimulation input, keeping cortical arousal at relatively high levels. So we have the extravert, who is cortically underaroused, seeking additional stimulation to achieve an optimally aroused cortex, and the introvert, who is cortically overaroused, trying to avoid stimulation. The ambivert, who obtains an intermediate level of arousal, is generally content with moderate amounts of stimulation.

In Chapter 4 we also discuss the concept of optimal level of stimulation or cortical arousal. One motivation behind human behavior is the desire to achieve a just-right level of stimulation and cortical arousal. Too much stimulation becomes aversive and even painful, while too little results in boredom and eventual sleep. It is assumed that the extravert, because of the dampening effect of the RAS, needs higher levels of stimulation to maintain that just-right or optimal level of cortical arousal. The introvert, because of the amplifying effect of the RAS, desires relatively lower levels of stimulation. This explains the typical extravert's attraction to spicy foods, loud music, and vividly colored objects, and the introvert's preference for bland foods, soft music, and cool or dark-colored objects.

The extravert's stimulation needs are well documented (see H. Eysenck, 1967, 1981). As mentioned previously, the greater tendency of extraverts to seek sensation is presumably more likely to put them in conflict with the law. Eysenck suggested that most people involved in criminal activity are cortically underaroused and have a strong drive to obtain stimulation or sensation from their environment. They are thus drawn to risk taking, joy riding, and illegal activities that have high stimulation value. Put quite simply, according to Eysenck's theory most criminals are extraverts.

Before leaving the section on extraversion, let's digress for a moment on the effects of alcohol on cortical arousal. Alcohol is a general central nervous system depressant. It lowers cortical arousal to the point that one may pass out or fall asleep. Extraverts without alcohol are already "half in the bag," and with alcohol they are even less alert. For introverts, however, alcohol has the effect of lowering a normally high cortical arousal to a point where they become more extraverted, behaviorally and physiologically. Thus, the usually quiet, reserved person may become boisterous or perform a soft shoe routine on the coffee table after a few drinks. The drunk introvert now has an extraverted arousal level and seeks more stimulation.

Eysenck supposed that the active, aroused cortex is a better inhibitor of activity than the poorly aroused one. Therefore, high cortical arousal leads to inhibition, while low cortical arousal allows subcortical regions of the central nervous system to function without restraint. Alcohol lowers the alertness of the cortex, which presumably lessens its censorship over the primitive, subcortical regions of the nervous system. This facilitates inappropriate, antisocial behaviors usually held in check by the cortex. Thus, according to the Eysenckian perspective, under the influence of alcohol, introverts will do things they normally would not do. On the other hand, even relatively small quantities of alcohol influence the extravert, who already functions at a low level of cortical arousal, toward even more uninhibited behavior. The correlation between alcohol and crime is a strong one and is discussed in greater detail in Chapter 12.

By now, you should have a basic understanding of one of Eysenck's personality dimensions. We now move on to consider the second dimension, which is equally important.

Neuroticism

Like extraversion, neuroticism is a significant variable in the relationship between personality and crime. Sometimes called emotionality, this dimension reflects an innate biological predisposition to react physiologically to stressful events. Basically, neuroticism deals with the intensity of emotional reactions. It is believed to occur in the general population at the same frequencies as extraversion, with 16% of the population falling above and below one standard deviation from the mean.

A person high on the neuroticism scale reacts intensely and lastingly to stress. In fact, even under low-stress conditions, the person is likely to be moody, touchy, sensitive to slights, and anxious and likely to complain of various physical ailments like headaches, backaches, and digestive problems. He or she tends to overreact to stress and has difficulty returning to a normal, calm state. People high in emotionality also have a strong propensity to develop neurotic features such as phobias and obsessions. Their opposites, persons at the other end of the continuum, display emotionally stable, calm, and even-tempered behavior. They tend to keep their wits about them under stress and intense excitement and to select appropriate reactions to emergencies. Researchers testing Eysenckian theory refer to high-emotionality individuals as neurotics and their counter opposites as stables.

Neurophysiological Bases of Neuroticism–Stability.   Whereas the extraversion–introversion dimension is linked to the central nervous system, the neuroticism–stability continuum relates to the autonomic nervous system, which can be divided into the sympathetic and parasympathetic nervous systems (see **Figure 3–4**). The *sympathetic system* activates the body for emergencies by increasing heart rate, respiration flow, blood flow, pupil dilation, and perspiration. The *parasympathetic system* counterbalances the sympathetic; it brings the body back to its normal arousal state. According to Eysenck, differences in emotionality are due to variances in the sensitivity of these subdivisions, which are both under the control of the so-called visceral brain or limbic system. In addition to a complicated array of neuronal circuitry, the *limbic system* includes the neurological structures known as the hippocampus, amygdala, cingulum, and hypothalamus. The hypothalamus appears to exert the greatest amount of control over the autonomic nervous system and thus represents the central mechanism in emotionality.

Neurotics are believed to have unusually sensitive limbic systems, so they achieve emotionality quickly, and for longer periods of time. (The term *neurotic* as used here should not be confused with the neurotic classification of mental disorders, which is discussed in Chapter 6.) Theoretically, it may be that their sympathetic system is activated quickly while their parasympathetic system is slow in counterbalancing this. Stables, low in emotionality, may possess an underactive sympathetic system and an overactive parasympathetic system.

FIGURE 3–4 Illustration of the Sympathetic and Parasympathetic Subdivisions of the Autonomic Nervous System

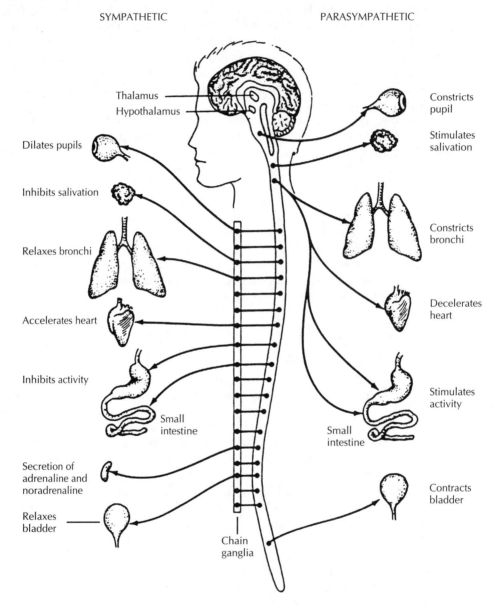

Although autonomic activation appears to produce a generalized arousal state in everyone, there is good reason to believe that each person reacts to the stress in unique ways. Some of us tense the muscles in our neck, forehead, or back; others breathe more heavily; for others, the heart pumps faster. This tendency for response specificity may account for the various forms of neurotic behaviors displayed by humans reacting to stress. Some complain of headaches; others, of digestive problems or backaches. (Obviously, we are not suggesting that all backache sufferers are neurotics.)

Eysenck assumed that the person high on emotionality is more likely to engage in criminal activity than the person low on that dimension. He based this assumption on the consistent research finding that emotionality can serve as a drive, pushing an individual to resort to habitual ways of behaving. Under high emotionality (high drive) a person is more vulnerable to his or her habits—good or bad. Thus, if the individual has acquired antisocial habits, he or she will be more driven to commit them under high-drive than low-drive conditions. Neuroticism, therefore, encourages whatever mindless or habitual behaviors the person has acquired. Furthermore, because habits are usually not as well ingrained in the young as they are in the old, we would expect neuroticism to be an important factor with respect to adult criminals, less so with adolescents, and least so with young children (H. Eysenck, 1983).

The two dimensions we have looked at thus far are usually combined in classifying an individual's personality. That is, based on Eysenck's personality inventories, a person will be a neurotic introvert, a stable extravert, a neurotic ambivert, and so forth. If we accept Eysenck's views up to this point, we should agree that the neurotic extravert is the most likely of the possible personality types to be involved in criminal behavior.

Psychoticism

No neurophysiological mechanism has been established to explain the characteristics of psychoticism, Eysenck's most recently formulated dimension. Eysenck (1996) does suggest, however, that high levels of the male hormone testosterone combined with low levels of the enzyme monoamine oxidase and the neurotransmitter serotonin may play a significant role in the formation of psychoticism.

Psychoticism seems to be highly similar to primary psychopathy, which we discuss in Chapter 4. Behaviorally, psychoticism is characterized by cold cruelty, social insensitivity, unemotionality, disregard for danger, troublesome behavior, dislike of others, and an attraction to the unusual. "Psychotics" are hostile toward others and enjoy duping or ridiculing them. It is important that we distinguish between Eysenck's psychotics and persons who are psychotic in the clinical sense of being out of touch with reality. Although the latter label is losing favor among clinicians, it appears frequently enough in the literature to warrant making the distinction. Psychosis as a classification of mental disorder and abnormality is dealt with in Chapter 6.

Eysenck's psychoticism dimension has not received the research attention that extraversion and neuroticism have. However, he hypothesizes that, like extraversion and neuroticism, psychoticism will prove to be a striking characteristic of the criminal population. He suggests that psychoticism will be especially prominent in hard-core, habitual offenders convicted of crimes of violence

(H. Eysenck, 1983). Furthermore, unlike neuroticism, it apparently is important at all stages of development, from childhood through adolescence to adulthood.

Thus far we have only defined Eysenck's dimensions, and in the case of neuroticism and extraversion, we have isolated the physiological mechanisms that control them. None of this explains, however, why neurotics, extraverts, and psychotics are more likely to be criminal. The reason has to do with some very basic psychological principles to which we now turn our attention.

Crime and Conditionability

A basic premise of this text is that criminal behavior is learned. Traditionally, psychologists have delineated three major types of learning: **classical** or **Pavlovian conditioning**, **instrumental learning** or **operant conditioning**, and **social learning**. It is important now to examine these processes more carefully if we are to approach an understanding of why some people engage in crime.

The reader with a background in introductory psychology will recall Ivan Pavlov's famous experiments with dogs that learned to salivate at the sound of a bell. Pavlov discovered that pairing a neutral stimulus (in this case a bell) with a significant stimulus (for example, food) would result in the dogs' eventually learning to associate the sound of the bell with that of food. How do we know the dogs learned to make that association? Because they salivated at the mere sound of the bell, a response they usually reserved for food. The process of learning to respond to a formerly neutral stimulus (bell) that has been paired with another stimulus that already elicits a response (salivation) is basically *classical* or *Pavlovian conditioning*. In classical conditioning, animals (or persons) have no control over the situation, even over what happens to themselves. The animal is "forced" to take the consequences. The bell will ring and food will appear shortly afterward, regardless of what the animal does. In anticipation, and without any effort on its part, the animal salivates. This learning occurs not because of any reward or gain, but merely because of the association between the bell and the food.

In *instrumental learning* (or *operant conditioning*), the process is quite different. The learner must do something to the environment in order to obtain a reward or, in some cases, to avoid punishment. Instrumental learning is based on learning the consequences of behaving a certain way: If you do something, there is some probability that a certain rewarding event (or at least an avoidance of punishment) will occur. A child may learn, for example, that one parent will give her a piece of candy to quell a temper tantrum; the other parent will not yield. The child will eventually learn to use temper tantrums when Dad is around, but not to use them in front of Mom (or vice versa).

One important aspect of instrumental learning should be stressed: There must be a goal driving the animal or person to operate on the environment. That is, the individual must have a purpose or expectation for his or her behavior, and must expect a reward for the response. A reward or reinforcement is the event that increases the likelihood of a response. Classical conditioning, by contrast, results from an association between stimuli and takes place without reward.

Social learning is more complex than either classical conditioning or instrumental learning, because it involves learning from watching others and organizing social experiences in the brain. Since Eysenck did not deal directly with social learning principles, we reserve this topic for Chapter 5.

Eysenck (1977) turns the question of criminal behavior around from the usual, "Why do people become criminal?" to "Why don't more people engage in criminal behavior?" To answer this with the adage "Crime doesn't pay" is nonsense, since there is evidence that for much of the criminal population, crime does pay. After all, one of the chief motivators of behavior may be the desire to gain reward and pleasure (referred to as hedonism). "It would seem . . . that a person may, with a fair degree of safety, indulge in a career of crime without having to fear the consequences very much" (H. Eysenck, 1964, p. 102). According to Eysenck, those detected, convicted, and incarcerated often represent that portion of the criminal population who are of lower intelligence, poorly taught, unable to afford an influential attorney, or simply unlucky. So, if instrumental learning is a major factor, there should be substantially more crime, because people would more often than not be rewarded for operating criminally on their environment. Moreover, when punishment does occur, it is so long in coming that it cannot reasonably be considered a deterrent. Eysenck suggests, in fact, that delayed and sometimes arbitrary punishment may actually encourage criminal activity.

To explain why more people do not become criminal, Eysenck contends that classical conditioning has a stronger effect on most people than instrumental learning. That is, most people behave themselves because they have been classically conditioned during childhood about the rules of society. That guiding light, superego, conscience, or whatever it is that makes us feel uncomfortable before, during, and after a socially and morally disapproved act is, according to Eysenck, a *conditioned reflex*. He notes that in most families children are reprimanded or punished for behavior that is against the social mores. Immediately after engaging in a socially or morally frowned-on act, say, punching a friend, a child finds that punishment quickly follows.

Let's return to Pavlov's dog experiments for a moment and substitute a painful shock for the food. Immediately following the sound of the bell, the dog receives a severe electrical shock (punishment) through the grids in the floor of the cage. After a number of trials (bell followed by shock) the dog, rather than salivating at the bell, begins to shake in fear. The animal has been classically conditioned to fear the sound of the bell, even when shock no longer follows it. The dog now associates shock with the bell rather than food.

Eysenck asserts that basically the same sequence occurs in childhood— inappropriate behavior followed by reprimand. For example, child punches another child, mother reprimands. Following a few repetitions of this sequence, the thought of punching stimulates fear of the consequences. In essence, "by punishing antisocial behavior numerous times, parents, teachers, and others concerned with the upbringing of the child, including his or her peers, perform the role of the Pavlovian experimenter" (H. Eysenck, 1983, p. 60). The child associates punching with punishment, and this bonding between the behavior and the aversive consequences should deter him or her from performing the act. Moreover, the closer the individual comes to performing the act, the stronger the association (fear) becomes.

Most people, Eysenck believes, do not participate in criminal activity (he prefers the term antisocial behavior) because, after a series of trials, they have made strong connections between deviant behavior and aversive consequences. On the other hand, those persons who have not made adequate connections, either because of poor conditionability (e.g., extraverts) or because the opportunity to do so was not presented (socialization), are more likely to display deviant or criminal behavior. According to Eysenck, these people do not anticipate aversive events strongly enough to be deterred, since the association has not been sufficiently developed.

Pavlov observed that dogs differ widely in their conditionability to the sound of a bell and theorized that these differences come from properties of their nervous systems. Eysenck also made this observation, commenting that "German Shepherds are very law abiding: They are easily conditioned and are well known to animal fanciers and shepherds for this property. Basenjis, however, are natural psychopaths, difficult or almost impossible to condition, disobedient and antisocial" (H. Eysenck, 1983, p. 61). Eysenck advanced the same observation concerning humans: Extraverts condition less readily than introverts due to biological differences in their nervous systems. Introverts condition better and therefore are less likely to engage in behavior contrary to society's laws and mores.

The principles of conditioning have been firmly established in the field of psychology as a valid explanation for many forms of behavior. The conditioning process appears to be a powerful force in the socialization of children, particularly in the suppressing of undesirable behaviors. There is every reason to believe that it may be a critical process in determining who becomes involved in deviant or criminal behavior. However, there is also evidence that conditioning can serve as an instigator of such behavior. As we will see in later chapters, the association between pleasurable events and specific behavior is also an extremely powerful motivator of criminal activity.

According to Eysenck, the conditioned conscience has two effects on behavior: It may prevent us from indulging in forbidden activities or it may make us feel guilty after we commit them. The conditioned conscience inhibits us from engaging in antisocial activities by its association with prior adverse consequences. In addition, once we have committed the act we tend to feel uncomfortable about our transgressions. Eysenck (1983) supposed the difference rests in the timing of the aversive consequences. Reprimanding a child before or during an act would produce different effects than reprimanding a child after the act. The former situation would result in feelings of discomfort before the act (or while committing it), whereas the latter would produce discomfort (guilt) after the act.

What part does neuroticism or emotionality play? As noted earlier, Eysenck predicted that neuroticism functions as a drive strongly encouraging the performance of behavior previously acquired during childhood. That is, neuroticism amplifies existing habits in a person's repertoire of responses. If a neurotic extravert has not been properly conditioned to avoid stealing and has engaged in frequent, successful stealing in the past, neuroticism will function as a strong force or drive toward the old habit—stealing. In other words, behavior (inappropriate or appropriate) = prior conditioning or learned habits x (intensified by) emotionality.

According to Eysenck (1983, p. 65), "The general growth in permissiveness in homes, schools, and courts has led to a significant reduction in the number of conditioning contingencies to which children are exposed. It would follow as a direct consequence that they would grow up with a much weaker conscience, and consequently that many more children would be led to engage in criminal and antisocial activities." In essence, Eysenck was asserting that increases in crime observed in the 1970s and 1980s could be traced directly to conditions within the home or schools that were not conducive to the development of a conditioned conscience toward avoiding antisocial conduct.

The Evidence for Eysenck's Theory

Now that we have scrutinized Eysenck's theory of criminality, the relevant question becomes, "Can we find research to support it?" Eysenck's theory of criminality predicts that criminals, as a group, will demonstrate lower levels of cortical arousal (extraversion), demonstrate higher levels of autonomic (sympathetic) arousal (neuroticism), and be more tough-minded (psychoticism). In short, he postulates that criminals will score high on the E (extraversion), N (neuroticism), and P (psychoticism) scales of the Eysenck Personality Questionnaire (EPQ) and that these dimensions are more than merely correlated with crime; they are causally related to it.

In some cases the research supports Eysenck's hypothesis, but many studies also refute the hypothesis. Although some research seems to damage the theory, these results do not necessarily mean that Eysenck is wrong. Research findings that fail to support parts of a theory suggest that the theory might be modified to account for the new data, provided the experiments were carefully conducted. The theory as a whole may still be promising and useful.

Passingham (1972) reviewed all literature on Eysenck's theory prior to 1972 and found flaws in the basic experimental design of most of the experiments. He noted that few of the studies used adequate controls to compare criminal and noncriminal populations. A control group, of course, should be matched as closely as possible to the experimental group, with all relevant variables (e.g., socioeconomic class, economic and cultural background, and intelligence) the same. Without an adequate control group, meaningful comparisons and valid conclusions are impossible. For example, suppose we designed a study to determine whether the personalities of criminals are significantly different from those of noncriminals, and suppose we used college students as a control group. If we found a significant difference, we could only conclude that the criminals differ from college students. But a college sample very probably differs from a criminal sample on a number of significant variables, such as socioeconomic class. Since college students are generally middle-class or higher, and since criminals studied in the research usually are not, the results might reflect a difference between social classes, not necessarily between criminal and noncriminal personalities. The college group, therefore, is not an adequate control group.

Passingham also found that most researchers explaining Eysenck's theory did not delineate subgroups of offenders. They merely selected a heterogeneous sample of prisoners, administered questionnaires, and made comparisons and conclusions based on responses from a control group, often poorly selected. Prisoners are prisoners for a constellation of reasons and offenses. Eysenck recognized this when he commented (1971, p. 289) that "not all crimes are likely to be equally highly correlated with extraversion, and some types of criminals, such as the recidivist 'old lag,' lacking entirely in the social skills needed to make a success of living outside an institution, may in fact show introverted tendencies." In fact, many murderers and sex offenders do show strong introverted patterns. It is imperative, therefore, that researchers study categories of offenders to determine whether certain personalities are linked to certain offenses. A later review by Farrington et al. (1982) indicated that some of the aforementioned problems were corrected, but many still remain.

In general, Eysenck's prediction that the criminal and antisocial populations should score significantly higher on the extraversion scale has not been consistently supported (Allsopp, 1976; Farrington, et al., 1982; Feldman, 1977; Passingham, 1972). The results are especially inconsistent for adult male offenders and for delinquents of both sexes. While some studies (e.g., Buikhuisen & Hemmel, 1972; J. Price, 1968) report high extraversion scores for these two groups, other investigations cite evidence that they score lower than the general population (e.g., Cochrane, 1974; Hoghughi & Forrest, 1970). Some researchers found no difference between prisoners and delinquents compared to control groups (e.g., P. Burgess, 1972; Little, 1963). Other studies found significantly higher E scores for violent offenders compared to other types of offenders (Gossop & Kristjansson, 1977). Studies separating the extraversion characteristics that reflect impulsiveness from those that reflect sociability found that adult male prisoners score higher on impulsiveness than do male noncriminals, but score lower than noncriminals on sociability. This may reflect the irrelevance of the sociability questions for incarcerated prisoners, since sociability tendencies may be dampened in a correctional facility.

Berman and Paisey (1984) examined the relationship between antisocial behavior and personality in American male juvenile delinquents. Subjects were divided into two groups: 30 juvenile males found guilty of assault or confrontation with a victim—called the assaultive group—and 30 juvenile males found guilty of offenses involving property without confrontation with a victim—called the nonassaultive group. These male juveniles were being held at the Dade County Juvenile Detention Center (Miami, Florida) awaiting disposition. All were English-speaking whites. The assaultive group, compared to the nonassaultive group, scored significantly higher on all three of the Eysenckian personality dimensions, P, E, and N, particularly on P.

In Spain, Silva, Martorell, and Clemente (1986) compared the Junior EPQ scores of 42 delinquent males confined in a reformatory to those of 102 non-delinquent males. They found that P and N scores were significantly higher in the delinquent group. However, contrary to what Eysenck predicted, E scores were significantly higher in the nondelinquent group. In London, Lane (1987) compared "60 pupils with convictions" with "60 pupils without convictions." The criminal group scored substantially higher on the P scale, whereas the noncriminal group scored higher on the N scale. There were no differences between the groups on the E scale. Lane asserted somewhat discouragingly, "Extraversion . . . for so long the central feature of the theory on conduct disorder and criminality, fails to hold up consistently" (p. 805). Moreover, N scores were consistently in the opposite direction than that which Eysenck predicted, with the noncriminal group scoring higher than the criminal group. Lane concludes, "A way of resolving these variations may be to take the argument outside the narrower conditioning model and place it within a broader multifactorial and interactive concept which links individual differences with behavioural and sociological analyses" (p. 806).

The aforementioned studies used official data, comparing EPQ scores of delinquents with those of nondelinquents or the scores of one group of delinquents with another group. Some studies have not used officially recognized offenders but have tapped the incidence of offending in the general population through self-report questionnaires. The most popular self-report scale in Great Britain is the Antisocial Behavior Scale, originally developed by H. B. Gibson (1967) and later revised by Allsopp and Feldman (1976). However, research using the Antisocial Behavior Scale has not been supportive of Eysenck's theory of criminality either. Jamison (1980), using 1,282 secondary school children (ages 13 to 16) in and around London, found a robust correlation between self-reported antisocial conduct and the P scale but a negligible or weak relationship with N and E, respectively. Powell and Stewart (1983), also using British subjects from the secondary and junior schools, found that self-reported antisocial behavior was strongly related to P scale scores, weakly to E scale scores, and negligibly to N scale scores. Similar results have been reported by Rushton and Chrisjohn (1981) for Canadian college students.

The research results examining the relationship between neuroticism and criminal or antisocial conduct are clear: It is not supported. Moreover, the relationship between extraversion and antisocial conduct is only weakly supported, but the relationship between psychoticism and crime appears to be moderately supported. The failure of E scale findings to strongly support

Eysenck's hypothesis may reflect a weakness in his argument that most criminals are poor conditioners. While many may have "faulty consciences," the
poor conditioning perspective seems too limited. It might be more accurate to
suggest that some criminals have offended because of poor conditionability,
others because they perceived antisocial behavior as one of the few avenues
available to them for gaining something, and still others for a combination of
both reasons or other reasons. Most inmates are not in prison because of a
failure to associate social transgressions with feelings of guilt and anxiety.
Rather, they are incarcerated for a variety of offenses, prompted by a variety
of motives, and associated with a variety of social situations. Because the E
scale, which reflects conditionability, is not sensitive enough to account for
this, more prisoner subgroup research is needed.

Bartol and Holanchock (1979) administered the EPQ to 398 inmates at a
maximum-security prison in New York state. Sixty-two percent were African
American, 30% Hispanic, and about 7% white. The sample was divided into
six offender groups according to conviction history: homicide, aggravated assault and attempted murder, rape and sexual assault, robbery, burglary, and
drug offenses. When the inmate had committed offenses in more than one
category, he was classified according to the most serious. A control group
comprised persons who were in waiting rooms at various state employment
agencies in predominantly African-American and Hispanic areas of New York
City. We found 187 males who agreed to fill out the EPQ; from all indications,
this control group matched the criminal group in age, race, socioeconomic
class, and employment history.

All six criminal groups scored lower than the control group on the E scale,
but there were significant differences among the criminal subgroups. Sex offenders were the most introverted, followed by burglars. Robbery offenders
were the most extraverted.

While demonstrating the ability of the EPQ to distinguish among offenders in this particular sample, the aforementioned study does not support
Eysenck's position on extraversion. Although there appeared to be many reasons for this lack of support, a dominant one was cultural. Prisoners in our
study were generally from the African-American or Latino/Hispanic regions of
New York City, and many had been convicted of violent crimes. Eysenck studied predominantly European white prisoners convicted primarily of property
crimes. This observation stresses the importance of considering cultural factors when studying heterogeneous criminal populations.

Farrington et al. (1982) found little support for the Eysenckian theory of
criminality in their review of the literature, which included their own investigation of antisocial individuals in London and Montreal. "Our conclusion is
that, at the present time, it seems unlikely that the Eysenck theory, the
Eysenck scales, or the Eysenck items are of much use in the explanation of
delinquency" (p. 196).

We should not discard the Eysenckian theory this blithely, however.
Enough studies find some support for it to warrant speculation and research

on why the results are equivocal. Are they due to cultural differences, sampling differences in either offender or control populations, or the wording of questions on the personality inventory? Also, the P scale has been somewhat supported by research using both convicted delinquents and self-reported offenders. This finding suggests that people who engage in antisocial or criminal conduct tend to be insensitive, aggressive, impulsive, tough-minded individuals who are highly self-centered. Obviously, more research should be directed at this personality dimension.

Although Eysenck's theory is in a state of flux, we have given it a considerable amount of attention here for three reasons. First, the theory is one of the few comprehensive statements about the role of genetics in antisocial behavior. We still have much to learn from this attempt, and perhaps some modifications will strengthen its explanatory potential. Second, Eysenck's theory recognizes the interaction of the environment—specifically via classical conditioning—with characteristics of the nervous system. Of particular importance is the attention Eysenck gives to individual differences in the nervous system as a biological basis for personality in general (Nebylitsyn & Gray, 1972). Criminology cannot afford to discount the existence of biological factors in antisocial behavior, even if these factors account for the behavior of only a small percentage of the population. At this point, however, it appears that Eysenck's emphasis on classical conditioning as a primary explanation of criminality and his tendency to ignore other forms of learning and mediational (cognitive) processes may be the theory's most damaging weaknesses. In addition, Gordon Trasler (1987) notes that even the concept of conditionability is fraught with difficulties and encourages much debate among contemporary psychologists. There is even considerable debate about what the term means, and the empirical evidence examining the concept remains elusive and conflicting. Finally, Eysenck's theory is unique because it represents one of the few attempts by a psychologist to formulate a general, universal theory of criminal behavior.

SUMMARY AND CONCLUSIONS

Realizing that crime, like all human behavior, results from an interaction among heredity, neurophysiology, and environment, we have looked in this chapter at the research on the genetic and biological makeup of persons who become criminal. The pioneer in genetic–biological criminology, Cesare Lombroso, asserted that there is a "born criminal," physically distinct from the general population and predisposed to act antisocially. Lombroso's theory was periodically revised, but the final version retained the notion of innate criminal tendencies, at least in some offenders. Lombrosian theory was soon put to rest, but it prompted other theorists to posit that there might be more to crime causation than social and environmental factors alone.

Later theorists studied the relationship of body build (Kretschmer) or body type (Sheldon) to crime. Their studies and later studies supported a correlation with crime, but questionable methodology often made it impossible to determine whether a causal relationship existed. To what extent genetically determined physical characteristics may influence criminal behavior remains unknown.

The genetic factor has also been explored in twin and adoption studies. To date, there have been over a hundred twin and adoption studies of antisocial behavior (Rhee & Waldman, 2002). Yet it is difficult to draw firm conclusions concerning the magnitude of genetic and environmental influences on antisocial behavior on the basis of current research. Some empirical studies, however, have found a high concordance rate between identical twins engaged in crime, lending some credence to genetic predisposition. These studies have shown that even when separated at birth, identical twins tend to be similar in their pursuit of criminal careers. However, researchers continually have difficulty separating the social environment (shared or nonshared) from the nature–nurture equation, and it is becoming increasing clear that the social and biological approaches to understanding human behavior are complementary rather than antagonistic (Cacioppo et al., 2000). There have been relatively few adoption studies conducted, primarily because of the inaccessibility of records. Researchers in this area who say their research supports the genetic viewpoint admonish that the social environment can either stimulate or inhibit any inborn tendency toward criminality.

Eysenck proposed an interaction theory of crime, seeing it as the result of environmental conditions (primarily classical conditioning) working on inherited features of the nervous system. The essence of Eysenckian theory is that individuals with certain types of nervous systems (introverts) condition better, or learn the mores of society much more readily, than individuals with other types (extraverts and ambiverts). In other words, introverts link transgressions with disapproval much sooner than others do. Some people would say introverts have a stronger conscience and experience more fear prior to their transgressions and more guilt after committing them. However, as we note in Chapter 10, this quick associative or conditioning ability also means that introverts are more likely to acquire sexually deviant behavior.

Eysenck hypothesized that neuroticism or emotionality intensifies existing habits, which in some cases may be antisocial ones. Individuals with high emotionality may be more driven toward antisocial habits than individuals with low emotionality. Psychoticism, a dimension that has received less research attention, appears to correlate with features of the psychopath and frequent offenders.

It is obvious that the Eysenckian position needs revision and refinement. As it now stands, the theory has flaws that could be damaging to its construct validity. One glaring weakness is its reliance on classical conditioning to the exclusion of mediational (cognitive) factors and social learning. Despite these problems, Eysenck's work represents a broad, testable theory of criminality that continues to stimulate research. More importantly for our purposes, the theory integrates nicely the biopsychological perspective with the social environmental perspective in the formation of antisocial behavior.

One thing needs to be emphasized here. Assigning a major role in the causation of criminal behavior to diverse neurological deficits and nervous system functioning is overly simplistic. While biopsychological and neurophysiological factors may play some role in the formation of criminal behavior, it is far more likely that crime—especially violent behavior—develops as a result of a series of complicated interactions with significant others in the social environment. Nevertheless, a considerable body of contemporary research explores the relationship between "violence and the brain." This research is discussed in detail in Chapter 7.

CHAPTER 4

THE PSYCHOPATH: A FOCUS ON BIOPSYCHOLOGICAL FACTORS

P sychopathy has become the central focus of research in psychological criminology, particularly as it relates to adult criminal behavior. Most recently, juvenile psychopathy has become the subject of considerable debate, with a number of researchers questioning its validity and implications. The term **psychopath** is currently used to describe a person who demonstrates a discernible cluster of psychological, interpersonal, and neuro-physiological features that distinguish him or her from the general population. As we will see in this chapter, the psychopath is not identical to the person with an antisocial personality disorder, but some researchers and clinicians continue to confuse the two terms (Gacono, Nieberding, Owen, Rubel, & Bodholdt, 2001). Because psychopathy is such an important topic in criminal psychology, we devote an entire chapter to describing the research and clinical characteristics of this interesting behavior.

HISTORICAL BACKGROUND

Throughout its history, the term *psychopath* has been a controversial label used to summarize a wide variety of attitudinal, emotional, and behavioral features. In the early 19th century, the French psychiatrist Philip Pinel felt a need to distinguish the person who habitually exhibited asocial and antisocial actions (not necessarily criminal) but did not exhibit signs of mental illness as it was then understood. He coined the term *manie sans délire* (mania without frenzy) to describe this behavior disorder, which included such features as cruelty, irresponsibility, and immorality (Rotenberg & Diamond, 1971). In 1837 the British psychiatrist J. C. Pritchard renamed the clinically strange group of disorders "moral insanity," presuming that they manifested a "derangement" and a failure to abide by society's expectations of religious, ethical, and cultural conduct. To Pritchard, this was evidence of a mental disease. His term was accepted and used by both the public and the medical profession for over half a century. In 1888, however, the German psychiatrist J. Koch decided that moral insanity had unwarranted negative connotations, and he proposed another designation, "psychopathic inferiority." Our modern conception of the psychopath is derived directly from Koch's label.

Psychopathic inferiority encompassed numerous behaviors, some of which are still linked with the psychopathic personality as we recognize it today, but many of which are associated instead with neurotic or personality disorders. The early psychiatrists believed that this disorder was constitutional, likely inbred by a genetic strain that produced a basic flaw in one's personality. There were implications, which in some respects continue today, that psychopaths were evil, human vessels of the devil, bent on destroying the moral fabric of society—"the devil made them do it."

Emil Kraepelin, who had an affinity for classification schemes, delineated seven categories of psychopathy in his *Clinical Psychiatry: A Textbook for Physicians* in 1913. The seven subtypes were the excitable, the unstable, the impulsive, the eccentric, the liars and swindlers, the antisocial, and the quarrelsome. All represented constitutional predispositions. Not to be outdone, Kahn (1931) suggested 16 trait-syndromes for the psychopath. In 1930, G. E. Partridge considered psychopathy an exclusively social, rather than mental, maladjustment and proposed the term *sociopath* to replace psychopath (Pennington, 1966).

To stem the proliferation of symptoms and labels and to check the resulting ambiguity, the American Psychiatric Association in 1952 dropped psychopath from its *Diagnostic and Statistical Manual* (DSM) and officially adopted **sociopath**, or, more specifically, "sociopathic personality disturbance, antisocial reaction." (The DSM is discussed again in Chapter 6.) Some contemporary researchers and clinicians use the terms psychopath and sociopath interchangeably. The purist, however, considers the sociopath a habitual criminal offender who has not been properly socialized. The psychopath may or may not be criminal and, presumably, manifests specific empirically verifiable behaviors and biological predispositions that differ from those of the general population. Currently, the term sociopath is often used by criminologists to refer to the repetitive offender who does not respond appropriately to treatment, rehabilitation, or incarceration.

In 1968, the American Psychiatric Association changed the label sociopath to *personality disorder, antisocial*. The DSM-III (APA, 1980), DSM-III-R (APA, 1987), and DSM-IV (APA, 1994, p. 645) continued to use the term **antisocial personality disorder** to refer specifically to an individual who exhibits "a pervasive pattern of disregard for, and violation of, the rights of others that begins in childhood or early adolescence and continues into adulthood." In other words, antisocial personality disorder is closely allied with persistent criminality. For example, approximately 80% of the incarcerated male offenders in Canadian federal prisons met the DSM-III-R criteria for antisocial personality disorder (Correctional Service of Canada, 1990; Hare, Forth, & Stachan, 1992). Other researchers have suggested slightly more conservative estimates, ranging between 30% and 50%, but they note that it is not unusual to reach more than the 50% mark in some facilities (Gacono et al., 2001). However, antisocial personality disorder is not the same as psychopathy, despite the fact that its description in the most recent editions of the DSM (DSM-IV and DSM-IV-TR) very closely parallels definitions of psychopathy.

Psychologist Robert Hare (1970), one of the world's leading experts on psychopathy, proposed a useful scheme to outline three categories of psychopaths: the primary, the secondary or neurotic, and the dyssocial. Only the **primary psychopath** is a "true" psychopath. The primary or "true" psychopath has certain identifiable psychological, emotional, cognitive, and biological differences that distinguish him or her from the general or criminal population. We discuss these differences in some detail throughout the chapter. The other two categories meld a heterogeneous group of antisocial individuals who comprise a large segment of the criminal population. **Secondary psychopaths** commit antisocial or violent acts because of severe emotional problems or inner conflicts. They are sometimes called acting-out neurotics, neurotic delinquents, symptomatic psychopaths, or simply emotionally disturbed offenders. The popular entertainment media often refer to these persons as "psychopathic killers" or use some other attention-getting terminology designed to conjure bloodthirsty disturbed persons indiscriminately killing everyone they meet. The third group, **dyssocial psychopaths**, displays aggressive, antisocial behavior they have *learned* from their subculture, like their gangs or families. In both cases, the label psychopath is misleading, because the behaviors and backgrounds have little if any similarity to those of primary psychopaths. Yet both secondary and dyssocial psychopaths are often incorrectly called psychopaths because of their high recidivism rates.

As noted above, the term antisocial personality disorder describes a pervasive pattern of disregarding the rights of others. Antisocial personalities are further described as those persons who "fail to conform to social norms with respect to lawful behaviors. They may repeatedly perform acts that are grounds for arrest, such as destroying property, harassing others, stealing or pursuing illegal occupations" (American Psychiatric Association, 1994,

p. 646). Also, as noted above, the descriptions of the psychiatric term antisocial personality disorder follow very closely the descriptions of the psychological term psychopathy. However, the definition of antisocial personality disorder is more narrow than that of primary psychopathy because it restricts its definition to behavioral indicators. Hare's definition of primary psychopathy includes both emotional and cognitive aspects. Nevertheless, with each new publication of the DSM, the characteristics used to describe the antisocial personality are increasingly similar to Hare's primary psychopathy in behavioral terms. It is easy to understand why clinicians often confuse the terms.

This text adopts Hare's scheme, considering "primary psychopath" an empirically and clinically useful designation. It is distinguished from secondary or neurotic psychopath in its behavioral, cognitive, and neurophysiological features. From this point on, when we refer to the psychopath, we mean the primary psychopath. He or she is unique: neither neurotic, psychotic, nor emotionally disturbed, as commonly believed. Primary psychopaths are usually not volcanically explosive, violent, or extremely destructive. They are more apt to be outgoing, charming, and verbally proficient. They may be criminals—in fact, in general they run in perpetual opposition to the law—but many are not. The term **criminal psychopath** is used here to identify those primary psychopaths who engage in repetitive antisocial or criminal behavior. In Chapter 6, we discuss antisocial personality disorder in more detail.

Examples of Psychopaths

The late Ferdinand Waldo Demara, Jr., the "Great Impostor," who forged documents and tried dozens of occupations without stopping to obtain a high school education, is a good example of a primary psychopath. A brief description of some of his exploits may help put the psychopath in perspective. (See Critchton, 1959, for a more complete version.)

Demara frequently came into contact with the law, primarily because he persisted in adopting fake identities. He once obtained the credentials of a Dr. French, who held a Ph.D. in psychology from Harvard. Demara was in the U.S. Navy at the time, awaiting a commission on the basis of other forged documents, but when he realized he was in danger of exposure via a routine security check, he decided he would prefer the Dr. French identity. He dramatized a successful suicide by leaving his clothing on the end of a pier with a note stating, "This is the only way out." Navy officials accepted his "death," and Demara became Dr. French. With his impressive credentials in hand, he obtained a Dean of Philosophy position at a Canadian college, successfully taught a variety of psychology courses, and assumed administrative responsibilities.

He developed a friendship with a physician, Joseph Cyr, and learned the basics of medicine from their long conversations. He eventually borrowed and duplicated Cyr's vital documents—birth, baptism, and confirmation certificates, school records, medical license—and obtained a commission in the Royal Canadian Navy as Dr. Cyr. He read extensively to nurture his growing knowledge of medicine.

During the Korean War, Demara/Cyr was assigned to a destroyer headed for the combat zone. The ship met a small Korean junk carrying many seriously wounded men, who were brought onboard for emergency medical care. Three men were in such critical condition that only emergency surgery could save their lives. Although Demara had never seen an operation performed, he hurriedly reviewed his textbooks. With unskilled hands, he operated through the night. By dawn, he had not only saved the lives of the three men, but had also successfully treated 16 others.

Demara/Cyr's deeds were broadcast over the ship's radio and disseminated, along with his photo, by the press. The real Dr. Cyr, shocked to see Demara's visage over his own respected name, immediately exposed him. Demara was discharged from the Canadian Navy, which, to save itself from additional embarrassment, allowed him to leave without prosecution. Demara's biography represents an example of a psychopath who did not engage in life-long violent crime.

Many psychopaths do commit violent crimes, though, some of them heinous and brutal. Neville Heath—charming, handsome, and intelligent—brutally and sadistically murdered two young English women (Critchley, 1951; P. Hill, 1960). Like Demara, Heath had an extraordinary career, much of it in the armed forces. Unlike Demara, his brushes with the law were very serious and occasionally ended in imprisonment. He was commissioned and dishonorably discharged on three separate occasions, once each in the British Royal Air Force, the Royal Armed Service Corps, and the South African Air Force. He flew in a fighter squadron in the RAF until he was court-martialed for car theft at age 19. He then committed a series of thefts and burglaries and was sentenced to Borstal Prison. Pardoned in 1939, he joined the Royal Armed Service Corps but was dismissed for forgery. On his way home to England, he jumped ship and eventually managed to obtain a commission in the South African Air Force until his past caught up with him. When not in trouble, Heath was regarded as a daring, confident, and highly charming officer—and a rake. After the third court-martial, he developed a taste for sadistic murder.

You may be able to identify other examples of psychopaths at their worst. The notorious Charles Manson, who in the 1960s exhibited an uncanny ability to attract a devout cluster of unresisting followers, is one probable example. The fictional Hannibal Lechter, whose sadistic offenses and deadly charm have captivated screen audiences, is another.

Throughout the remainder of this chapter we examine in more detail the behavioral patterns, the cognitive processes, the interpersonal features, the neuropsychological characteristics, and the general background of the psychopath.

BEHAVIORAL DESCRIPTIONS

One pioneering authority on the behavioral characteristics of the psychopath was Hervey Cleckley, a well-known psychiatrist from Augusta, Georgia, who died in 1984 at the age of 79. A large part of Cleckley's professional recognition came as a result of the nonfiction book, *The Three Faces of Eve*, which he coauthored with Corbett Thigpen. The book, which is about the phenomenon of "multiple personality," was made into a very popular 1957 movie with the same title. However, his major professional contribution to the field of psychiatry can be found in his often-quoted text, *The Mask of Sanity* (first published in 1941). The book describes in clear and empirically useful terms the major behaviors demonstrated by the full-fledged or primary psychopath, as distinct from the other psychopathic types referred to previously.

Superficial charm and average to above-average intelligence are two of the psychopath's main features, according to Cleckley, and they are both especially apparent during initial contacts. Many psychopaths usually impress others as friendly, outgoing, likable, and alert. They often appear well-educated and knowledgeable, and they display many interests. They are verbally skillful and can talk themselves out of trouble. In fact, their vocabulary is often so extensive that they can talk at length about anything (Hare, 1991). However, systematic study of their conversation reveals that they often jump "from one topic to another and that much of their speech is empty of real substance, tending to be filled with stock phrases, repetitions of the same ideas, word approximations, abstract terms and jargon used in a superficial or inappropriate fashion, logically inconsistent statements and phrases, and half-formed sentences" (p. 57). As Hare (1996, p. 46) notes, "In some respects, it is as if psychopaths lack a central organizer to plan and keep track of what they think and say." However, since psychopaths are so charming and manipulative, these language shortcomings are not readily apparent.

Psychometric studies (studies that use standard psychological tests as measures) indicate that psychopaths usually score higher on intelligence tests than the general population (Hare, 1970, 1996), particularly on individually administered tests. In fact, Hare wryly comments, the psychopaths who were the sample for his studies were probably the least intelligent of their ilk, since they were not quite bright enough to avoid being convicted for their offenses. (Hare has conducted much of his research on imprisoned psychopaths.) Recent research (e.g., Ishikawa, Raine, Lenez, Bihrle, & Lacasse, 2001) has found that a useful dichotomy of criminal psychopaths may be to divide them into "successful" psychopaths (those who have committed crimes but avoided arrest and conviction for offenses) and "unsuccessful" psychopaths (those who have been convicted and imprisoned). We return to this dichotomy later in the chapter.

Psychopaths usually do not exhibit mental disorders, either mild or severe. Most lack any symptoms of excessive worry and anxiety, psychotic thinking, delusions, severe depressions, or hallucinations. Even under high-pressure conditions they remain cool and calm, as did Ian Fleming's fictitious James Bond, probably a prime example. Feasibly, the doomed psychopath might enjoy a steak dinner (*au poivre*) with gusto just before being executed. The infamous multiple murderer Herman W. Mudget, alias H. H. Holmes, retired at his normal hour the evening before his execution, fell asleep easily, slept soundly, and woke up completely refreshed. "I never slept better in my life," he told his cell guard. He ordered and ate a substantial breakfast an hour before he was scheduled to be hanged. Until the moment of death, he remained remarkably calm and amiable, displaying no signs of depression or fear (Franke, 1975).

Not everyone agrees with the view that psychopaths do not suffer from some mental disorder. Some clinicians argue that psychopathy and schizophrenia are part of the same spectrum of disorders (Hare, 1996). Some forensic clinicians maintain that they occasionally see a mentally disordered offender who qualifies as both a psychopath and a schizophrenic (Hare, 1996). There is some evidence to suggest that it is not uncommon to find psychopaths who seem mentally disordered in maximum-security psychiatric units for highly violent or dangerous patients.

Other principal traits of the psychopath are selfishness and an inability to love or give affection to others. According to Cleckley, egocentricity is *always* present in the psychopath and is essentially unmodifiable. The psychopath's inability to feel genuine, meaningful affection for another is absolute. Psychopaths may be likable, but they are seldom able to keep close friends, and they have great difficulty understanding love in others. They may be highly skillful at pretending deep affection, and they may effectively mimic appropriate emotions, but true loyalty, warmth, and compassion are foreign to them. Psychopaths are distinguished by flat emotional reaction and affect. And since psychopaths have so little need to receive or give love, psychopaths, as a group, have relatively little contact with their families, and many change their residences frequently (Hare, 1991). In addition, they do not usually respond to acts of kindness. They show capacity only for superficial appreciation. Paradoxically, they may do small favors and appear considerate toward someone one day and appropriate her life savings the next.

Psychopaths have a remarkable disregard for truth and are often called "pathological liars." They seem to have no internalized moral or ethical sense and cannot understand the purpose of being honest, especially if dishonesty will bring some personal gain. They have a cunning ability to appear straightforward, honest, and sincere, but their claims to sincerity are without substance.

Psychopaths are unreliable, irresponsible, and unpredictable, regardless of the importance of the occasion or the consequences of their impulsive actions. Impulsivity appears to be a central or cardinal feature of psychopathy (Hart & Dempster, 1997). This pattern of impulsive actions is cyclical, however. Psychopaths may, for months on end, be responsible citizens, faithful spouses, and reliable employees. They may experience great successes, be promoted, and gain honors, as did Demara and Heath. Skillfully as they have attained these socially desirable goals, they have an uncanny knack of suddenly unraveling their lives. They become irresponsible and may pass bad checks, sabotage the company computer, go on a drunken spree, or steal the boss's car. They also tend to have a "bad temper" that flares quickly and leads to arguments and attacks. Psychopaths may later say they are sorry and plead for another chance—and most will probably get it. Invariably, if the psychopath is a young adult, the irresponsible behavior will return.

Even small amounts of alcohol prompt most psychopaths to become vulgar, domineering, loud, and boisterous and to engage in practical jokes and pranks. Cleckley noted that they choose pranks that have no appeal for most individuals and that seem bizarre, inappropriate, and cruel. They lack genuine humor and, not surprisingly, the ability to laugh at themselves.

Cleckley (1976) described a potentially promising, brilliant physician in his early forties who was loved by his patients and had managed to develop a thriving practice during his "upswing" periods. His negative, psychopathic behaviors, however, were colossal blunders:

> This man's history shows a great succession of purposeless follies dating from early manhood. He lost several valuable hospital appointments by lying out sodden or by bursting in on serious occasions with nonsensical uproar. He was once forced to relinquish a promising private practice because of the scandal and indignation which followed an escapade in a brothel where he had often lain out disconsolately for days at a time.
>
> Accompanied by a friend who was also feeling some influence of drink he swaggered into his favorite retreat and bellowed confidently for women. Congenially disposed in one room, the party of four called for highballs. For an hour or more only the crash of glasses, scattered oaths, and occasional thuds were heard. Then suddenly an earnest, piercing scream brought the proprietress and her servants racing into the chamber. One of the prostitutes lay prostrate, clasping a towel to her breast, yelling in agony. Through her wails and sobs she accused the subject of this report of having, in his injudicious blunderings, bitten off her nipple. An examination by those present showed that this unhappy dismemberment had, in fact, taken place. Although both men had at the moment been in bed with her, the entertainer had no doubt as to which one had done her the injury.
>
> Feeling ran strong for a while, but, by paying a large sum as recompense for the professional disability and personal damage he had inflicted, the doctor avoided open prosecution. Before a settlement had been made, the guilty man attempted to persuade his companion to assume responsibility for the deed. It would be less serious for the other man, he argued, since his own prominence and professional standing made him a more vulnerable target for damaging courtroom dramatics and for slander. His companion, however, declined this opportunity for self-sacrifice with great firmness. (pp. 206–207)

Although often above average in intelligence, psychopaths appear to be incapable of learning to avoid failure and situations that are potentially damaging to themselves. Some theorists suggest that the self-destructive, self-defeating deeds and attitudes reflect a need to be punished to mitigate the guilt they subconsciously experience or, more simply, that they are driven by a masochistic purpose. Evidence refuting these explanations is offered later in this chapter.

When psychopaths drift into criminal activity, impulsivity will usually prevent them from performing like professional criminals. Psychopaths are more likely to participate in capers and hastily planned frolics or in spontaneous, serious crimes for immediate satisfaction. The professional criminal has purpose and a plan of action; the psychopath is impulsive and lacks long-range goals.

A cardinal fault of psychopaths is their absolute lack of remorse or guilt for anything they do, regardless of the severity or immorality of their actions and irrespective of their traumatic effects on others. Since they do not anticipate personal consequences, psychopaths may engage in destructive or antisocial behavior—such as forgery, theft, rape, brawls, and fraud—by taking absurd risks, and for insignificant personal gain. When caught, they express no genuine remorse. They may readily admit culpability and take considerable pleasure in the shock these admissions produce in others. Whether they have bashed in someone's head, ruined a car, or tortured a child, psychopaths may well remark that they did it "for the hell of it."

Psychopaths have little capacity to see themselves as others perceive them. Instead of accepting the facts that would normally lead to insight, they project and externalize blame onto the community and family for their misfortunes. Interestingly, educated psychopaths have been known to speak fluently about the psychopathic personality, quoting the literature extensively and discussing research findings, but they cannot look into their own troublesome antics or mount a reasonable attack on their actions. They articulate their regrets for having done something, but the words are devoid of emotional meaning, a characteristic Cleckley calls **semantic aphasia**. Johns and Quay (1962) remarked that psychopaths "know the words but not the music." Similarly, Grant (1977) notes that the psychopath knows only the book meaning of words, not the living meaning. Hare (1996, p. 45) concludes, "In short, psychopaths appear to be semantically and affectively shallow individuals."

Finally, an important behavioral distinction underlying much of Cleckley's description is what Quay (1965) refers to as the psychopath's profound and pathological stimulation seeking. According to Quay, the actions of the psychopath are motivated by an excessive *neuropsychological* need for thrills and excitement. It is not unusual to see psychopaths drawn to such interests as race car driving, skydiving, and motorcycle stunts. We examine this alleged need for stimulation in the pages that follow.

In recent years, it has become useful for research purposes to focus on psychopaths who repeatedly commit crimes, collectively called criminal psychopaths. Concentrating on psychopaths who are violent or chronic offenders provides invaluable information about their backgrounds, learning history, and behavioral patterns. Such research also might offer key strategies for how to deal with and potentially treat this challenging group of individuals.

THE CRIMINAL PSYCHOPATH

Probably no topic has caught the attention of psychologists interested in the development of habitual criminal behavior more in recent years than the topic of criminal psychopathy. Again, we must emphasize that many psychopaths have no history of serious antisocial behavior and that persistent, serious offenders are not necessarily psychopaths. For our purposes here the term *criminal psychopath* is reserved for those psychopaths who demonstrate a wide range of *persistent* antisocial behavior. As a group, they tend to be "dominant, manipulative individuals characterized by an impulsive, risk-taking and antisocial life-style, who obtain their greatest thrill from diverse sexual gratification and target diverse victims over time" (Porter et al., 2000, p. 220). As further noted by Stephen Porter and his colleagues (p. 227): "Given its relation to crime and violence, psychopathy is arguably one of the most important psychological constructs in the criminal justice system."

Prevalence of Criminal Psychopathy

Robert Hare (1998) believes that the distribution of psychopaths in the general population is about 1%, whereas in the adult prison population it is between 15% and 25%. Some researchers (e.g., Simourd & Hoge, 2000) contend, however, that these estimates may be inflated. Simourd and Hoge (2000) concluded that only 11% of their inmate population could be identified as criminal psychopaths. The sample in the Simourd–Hoge study consisted of 321 inmates serving a current sentence for violent offending. More than half of them had been convicted of a previous violent offense, and almost all of them had extensive criminal careers. Percentage estimates of criminal psychopathy within any given population must be tempered by the type of facility, as well as the cultural, ethnic, age mix, and criminal history, of the targeted population. Interestingly, the American Psychiatric Association (1994) estimates that the overall prevalence of antisocial personality disorder in the community at large is about 3% in males and about 1% in females. In clinical samples (those receiving therapy for various disorders), the prevalence estimates vary between 3% and 30%, depending on the characteristics of the sample surveyed. Keep in mind, though, that antisocial personality disorder is *not* identical to psychopathy.

Offending Patterns of Criminal Psychopaths

Gretton et al. (2001, p. 428) emphasize that criminal psychopaths generally "lack a normal sense of ethics and morality, live by their own rules, are prone to use cold-blooded, instrumental intimidation and violence to satisfy their wants and needs, and generally are contemptuous of social norms and the rights of others." In many cases, this persistent offending is extremely violent in nature. Hare (1996, p. 38) posits, "The ease with which psychopaths engage in . . . dispassionate violence has very real significance for society in general and for law enforcement personnel in particular." Hare refers to a report by the Federal Bureau of Investigation (1992) that found that nearly half of the law enforcement officers who died in the line of duty were killed by individuals who closely matched the personality profile of the psychopath. In addition, the offenses of psychopathic sex offenders are likely to be more violent, brutal, unemotional, and sadistic than those of other sex offenders (Hare, Clark, Grann, & Thornton, 2000; Porter, Birt, & Boer, 2001; Woodworth & Porter, 2002). In addition, psychopathic sex offenders appear to be more motivated by thrill seeking and excitement rather than simply sexual arousal (Porter, Woodworth, Earle, Drugge, & Boer, 2003). Psychopaths as a group also appear to be significantly more sadistic than violent nonpsychopaths (Holt, Meloy, & Stack, 1999), and commit more diverse and severe forms of sexual homicides (Firestone, Bradford, Greenberg, & Larose, 1998; Porter et al., 2003). Porter and his colleagues (2003) found that in a sample of the male offenders incarcerated in two Canadian federal prisons for homicide, nearly half could be classified as sexual homicide offenders. (In order to be classified as a sexual homicide, there had to be physical evidence of sexual activity with the victim before, during, or after the homicide). Serial murders described as unusually sadistic and brutal also tend to have many psychopathic features (Hare et al., 2000; Stone, 1998). Collectively, the research suggests that psychopaths may be more likely than other offenders to derive pleasure from both the nonsexual and the sexual suffering of others (Porter et al., 2003).

Many of the murders and aggravated assaults committed by nonpsychopaths occurred during domestic disputes or extreme emotional arousal. This pattern of violence is rarely observed for criminal psychopaths (Hare et al., 1991; Williamson, Hare, & Wong, 1987). Criminal psychopaths frequently engage in violence as a form of revenge or retribution or in a state of intoxication. Many of the attacks of nonpsychopaths are toward women they know well, whereas many of the attacks of criminal psychopaths are directed toward male strangers. Hare et al. (1991, p. 395) point out that the violence committed by criminal psychopaths was callous and cold-blooded, "without the affective coloring that accompanied the violence of nonpsychopaths." Research also indicates that rapists who have psychopathic characteristics are more likely to have "nonsexual" motivations for their crimes, such as anger, vindictiveness, sadism, and opportunism (Hart & Dempster, 1997).

PSYCHOLOGICAL MEASURES OF PSYCHOPATHY

Currently, the most research-based instrument for measuring criminal psychopathy is the 22-item **Psychopathy Checklist (PCL)** (Hare, 1980) and its 20-item revision **(PCL-R)** (Hare, 1991). More recently, the PCL-R has been published in a second edition, which includes new information on its applicability in forensic and research settings. The second edition also has been expanded for use with offenders in other countries and includes updated normative and validation data on male and female offenders. A 12-item short-form version has also been developed, the **Psychopathy Checklist: Screening Version (PCL:SV)** (Hart, Cox, & Hare, 1995; Hart, Hare, & Forth, 1993). Other additions are the **Psychopathy Checklist: Youth Version (PCL:YV)** and the **P-Scan: Research Version**. The P-Scan is a screening instrument that serves as a quick screen for psychopathic features and as a source of working hypotheses to deal with managing suspects, offenders, or clients. It was developed for use in law enforcement, probation, corrections, civil and forensic facilities, and other areas in which it would be useful to have some information about the possible presence of psychopathic features in a particular person. Of course, the P-Scan needs much more research before it can be used as a valid instrument in practice. All five checklists are conceptually and—with the exception of the P-Scan—psychometrically similar.

The PCL scales are largely based on Cleckley's (1976) conception of psychopathy (see **Table 4–1**) but are specifically designed to identify psychopaths in male prison, forensic, or psychiatric populations. Since the PCL-R is currently the most frequently used instrument as both a research and a clinical instrument, it is the center of attention for the remainder of this section. The PCL:YV is beginning to be researched more extensively and is covered in more detail in the section Juvenile Psychopathy (below).

The PCL-R evaluates the emotional, interpersonal, behavioral, and social deviance facets of criminal psychopathy from various sources, including self-reports, behavioral observations, and collateral sources, such as parents, family members, friends, and arrest and court records, which can help to establish

TABLE 4–1 Psychopathic Behaviors Identified by Hare and Cleckley

HARE'S PCL CHECKLIST	CLECKLEY'S PRIMARY PSYCHOPATHY CRITERIA
Glibness/superficial charm	Superficial charm and good intelligence
Grandiose sense of self-worth	Pathological egocentricity
Pathological lying	Untruthfulness and insincerity
Conning/manipulative	Manipulative
Lack of remorse or guilt	Lack of remorse or guilt
Shallow affect	General poverty of affective reactions
Callous, lack of empathy	Unresponsiveness in interpersonal relations
Failure to accept responsibility for actions	Unreliability
Promiscuous sexual behavior	Impersonal sex life
Lack of realistic, long-term goals	Failure to follow any life plan
Poor behavioral controls	Impulsive
High need for stimulation/prone to boredom	Inadequately motivated antisocial behavior
Irresponsibility	Poor judgment
	Absence of delusions or nervous symptoms
	Suicide very rare

the credibility of self-reports (Hare, 1996; Hare, Hart, & Harpur, 1991). In addition, item ratings from the PCL-R, for instance, require some integration of information across multiple domains, including behavior at work or school, behavior toward family, friends, and sexual partners, and criminal behavior (Kosson, Suchy, Mayer, & Libby, 2002). Typically, highly trained examiners use all this information to score each item on a 0-to-2 scale, depending on the extent to which an individual has the disposition described by each item on the checklist (0 = consistently absent; 1 = inconsistent; 2 = consistently present). Scoring is quite complex, however, and requires substantial time, extensive training, and access to a considerable amount of background information on the individual. A score of 30 or above usually qualifies a person as a primary psychopath (Hare, 1996). In some research and clinical settings cutoff scores ranging from 25 to 33 are often used (Simourd & Hoge, 2000). Hare (1991) recommends that persons with scores between 21 and 29 be classified as "middle" subjects, who show many of the features of psychopathy but do not fit all the criteria. Subjects scoring below 21 are considered "nonpsychopaths."

The research has strongly supported the reliability and validity of the PCL-R for distinguishing criminal psychopaths from criminal nonpsychopaths and for helping correctional and forensic psychologists involved in risk assessments of offenders (Hare, Forth, & Stachan, 1992; Hare, 1996). In addition, the instrument provides researchers and mental health professionals with a universal measurement for the assessment of psychopathy that facilitates international and cross-cultural communication concerning theory, research, and eventual clinical practice (Hare et al., 2000). Currently, the PCL-R is increasingly being used as a clinical instrument for the diagnosis of psychopathy across the globe, although it appears to be most useful in identifying psychopathy among white North American males (Hare et al., 2000). Interestingly, Scott Lilienfeld and his colleagues (Lilienfeld, Gershon, Duke, Marion, & de Waal, 1999) have developed a psychopathy scale for chimpanzees, called the Chimpanzee Psychopathy Measure. Preliminary data indicate that the scale appears to be a reliable measure of psychopathic-like behavior in chimpanzees. According to the researchers, the psychopathic behavior of chimps includes excessive displays of sexual activity, daring behaviors, teasing, silent bluff displays, and temper tantrums. These data underscore the potential neuropsychological basis for psychopathy in humans.

Core Factors of Psychopathy

It is important to note that the research on the PCL-R strongly indicates that psychopathy is multidimensional in nature. When expert ratings of psychopathy on the PCL-R were submitted to a **factor analysis** (a statistical method that identifies different dimensions), at least two behavioral dimensions or factors emerged (Hare, 1991; Harpur, Hakstian, & Hare, 1988; Hart et al., 1993). Factor 1 refers to the interpersonal and emotional components of the disorder and consists of items measuring remorselessness, callousness, and selfish use and manipulation of others. In this sense, the psychopath feels no compunctions about using people largely to meet his or her own needs or desires. Factor 2, on the other hand, is most closely associated with a socially deviant lifestyle, as characterized by poor planning, impulsiveness, an excessive need for stimulation, proneness to boredom, and a lack of realistic goals. Some researchers have found that Factor 1 appears to represent planned predatory violence, while Factor 2 correlates with spontaneous and disinhibited violence (Hart & Dempster, 1997). Factor 1 is also linked to resistance and inability to profit from psychotherapy and treatment programs (Seto & Barbaree, 1999). Factor 2 appears to be related to socioeconomic status, educational attainment, and cultural/ethnic background, whereas Factor 1 may be linked to biopsychological influences (Cooke & Michie, 1997). Research also suggests that Factor 1 *may* be a stronger indicator of psychopathy than Factor 2 (Cooke, Michie, Hart, & Hare, 1999). In addition, while it is quite clear that Factor 1 does a better job of identifying psychopathy in general, there is some evidence that Factor 2 does a better job of predicting general recidivism and violent recidivism (Walters, 2003).

More recent research with both children and adults, however, reveals that there may be *three* (and possibly more) behavioral dimensions at the core of psychopathy beyond the original two (Cooke & Michie, 2001; Frick, Bodin, & Barry, 2000; Kosson, Suchy et al., 2002). David Cooke and Christine Michie (2001), for example, found from their factor analysis of PCL-R data that psychopathy probably consists of at least three basic factors: (1) arrogant and deceitful interpersonal style, (2) impulsive and irresponsible behavioral style (highly similar to the original factor 2), and (3) inadequate emotional (affective) reactions. Factors 1 and 3 are essentially subdivisions of the original Factor 1 reported in earlier studies. The term "inadequate reactions" refers to the lack of sincere positive emotions toward others and the demonstration of callousness and lack of empathy. The terms *arrogant* and *deceitful interpersonal style*, on the other hand, refer to the glibness, superficial charm, and grandiose sense of self-worth that is so characteristic of the psychopath.

There is also some preliminary research indicating that the PCL-R may be measuring some factors that are unique to female psychopaths (Salekin, Rogers, & Sewell, 1997; Salekin, Rogers, Ustad, & Sewell, 1998; Vitale & Newman, 2001). We return to this point shortly, under The Female Psychopath.

RECIDIVISM

Research studies indicate that the recidivism rate (criminal reoffending) of psychopaths is very high. According to Porter et al. (2000), research suggests that psychopaths reoffend faster, violate parole sooner, and commit more violence while incarcerated than nonpsychopaths. In one study (Serin, Peters, & Barbaree, 1990), the number of failures of male offenders released on unescorted temporary absence programs (furloughs) was investigated. The failure rate for psychopaths was 37.5%, while none of the nonpsychopaths failed. The failure rate during parole was also examined. While 7% of nonpsychopaths violated parole conditions, 33% of psychopaths violated their conditions. In another study, Serin and Amos (1995) followed 299 male offenders for eight years after their release from a federal prison. Sixty-five percent of the psychopaths were convicted of another crime within three years, compared to a reconviction rate of 25% for nonpsychopaths. Quinsey, Rice, and Harris (1995) found that within six years of release from prison, more than 80% of the psychopaths convicted as sex offenders had violently re-offended, compared to a 20% reoffending rate for nonpsychopathic sex offenders. Richards, Casey, and Lucente (2003) found that the PCL-R and the PCL:SVA measures of persistent offending history, in conjunction with high scores on the PCL-R, are probably two of the best predictors of violent recidivism available anywhere. In fact, the PCL-R is a strong predictor of recidivism even when the offender's criminal history is not known to the examiner (Hemphill & Hare, in press; Hemphill, Hare, & Wong, 1998).

High recidivism rates are also characteristic of psychopathic adolescent male offenders. (Shortly, though, we discuss the controversy over whether juvenile psychopathy even exists.) According to Gretton et al. (2001), these offenders are more likely than other adolescent offenders to escape from custody, violate the conditions of probation, and commit nonviolent and violent offenses over a 5-year follow-up period. The high recidivism rates among adult and juvenile offenders have prompted some researchers to conclude that there is "nothing the behavioral sciences can offer for treating those with psychopathy" (Gacono, Nieberding, Owen, Rubel, & Bodholdt, 1997, p. 119). This is partly because psychopaths tend to "be unmotivated to alter their problematic behavior and often lack insight into the nature and extent of their psychopathology" (Skeem, Edens, & Colwell, 2003, p. 26).

TREATMENT AND REHABILITATION STRATEGIES

What kind of treatment is available for those adult male offenders who qualify as psychopaths? Hare (1996, p. 41) asserts, "There is no known treatment for psychopathy." Indeed, based on the research examining the effectiveness of various treatment programs, there does not appear to be any effective treatment program for adult psychopaths in the criminal justice system today. Hare (1996, p. 41) admonishes, though: "This does not necessarily mean that the egocentric and callous attitudes and behaviors of psychopaths are immutable, only that there are no methodologically sound treatments or 'resocialization' programs that have been shown to work with psychopaths." Other researchers take a decidedly different perspective and believe that untreatability statements concerning the psychopath are unwarranted (Salekin, 2002; Skeem, Monahan, & Mulvey, 2001; Skeem, Poythress, Edens, Lilienfeld, & Cale, 2002; S. Wong,

2000). For example, Spain, Douglas, Poythress, and Epstein (2004) report that some types of treatment may be more effective with juvenile psychopaths than with adult psychopaths. There is also some evidence that adult psychopaths who receive larger "doses" of treatment are less likely to demonstrate subsequent violent behavior than those who receive less treatment (Skeem, Edens, & Colwell, 2003). It should be mentioned that a vast majority of the research has focused on recidivism rates of male psychopathic offenders, and very little is known about the recidivism rates of female psychopathic offenders.

It is usually difficult to properly evaluate the effectiveness of programs designed to treat psychopaths because of their ability to manipulate the system. For example, many psychopaths volunteer for various prison treatment programs, show "remarkable improvement," and present themselves as model prisoners. They are skillful at convincing therapists, counselors, and parole boards that they have changed for the better. Upon release, however, there is a high probability that they will reoffend. In fact, there is some evidence to suggest that psychopaths who participate in therapy are more likely to engage in violent crime following the treatment than psychopaths who did not receive treatment. Rice, Harris, and Cormier (1992) investigated the effectiveness of an intensive therapeutic community program offered in a maximum-security facility. The study was retrospective in that the researchers examined records and files 10 years after the program was completed. The results showed that psychopaths who participated in the therapeutic community exhibited higher rates of violent recidivism than did psychopaths who did not. The results were the reverse for nonpsychopaths: Nonpsychopaths who received treatment were less likely to reoffend than nonpsychopaths who did not receive treatment.

Some critics of this study have remarked that the therapeutic community referred to was highly atypical of treatment programs in correctional facilities and has limited generalizability. Furthermore, the researchers themselves cautioned that the psychopaths used in the study were an especially serious group of offenders. Eighty-five percent had a history of violent crimes. Whether less serious psychopathic offenders will show similar results is unknown. The researchers conclude, "The combined results suggest that a therapeutic community is not the treatment of choice for psychopaths, particularly those with extensive criminal histories" (Rice, Harris, & Cormier, 1992, p. 408). Hare (1996) suggests that group therapy and insight-oriented treatment programs— both of which were features of the program reviewed above—may help the psychopath develop better ways of manipulating and deceiving others.

THE FEMALE PSYCHOPATH

Very little research has been conducted so far on psychopathy in women, including female offenders. In general, research suggests that there are significantly fewer female than male psychopaths, both in the general population and among persons convicted of crime. Based on PCL-R data, Salekin et al.

(1997) reported that the prevalence rate of psychopathy for female offenders in a jail setting was 15.5%, compared to the 25% to 30% prevalence rate estimated for incarcerated male offenders. Salekin and colleagues (1998) also found that 12.9% of their sample of 78 female inmates qualified as psychopaths. In another investigation involving 528 adult women incarcerated in state prisons in Wisconsin, Vitale, Smith, Brinkley, and Newman (2002) reported that 9% of their participants could be classified as psychopaths.

Hare's PCL and PCL-R have been developed almost exclusively on male criminal psychopaths. Some earlier studies using the PCL-R suggest that female criminal psychopaths may exhibit different behavioral traits than male criminal psychopaths (Hare, 1991; Vitale et al., 2002). Although the data are far from conclusive, female psychopaths, compared to male psychopaths, appear to demonstrate a lack of realistic long-terms goals and show a greater tendency to be sexually promiscuous (Salekin et al., 1997). In addition, they may not express the same emotional processing abnormalities as male psychopaths (Sutton, Vitale, & Newman, 2002).

There is also evidence that female psychopaths are less aggressive and violent than male psychopaths (Mulder, Wells, Joyce, & Bushnell, 1994). Female psychopaths may also recidivate less often than male psychopaths (Salekin et al., 1998). The evidence suggests, in fact, that psychopathic female inmates may have recidivism rates that are no different from the recidivism rates reported for nonpsychopathic female inmates (Salekin et al., 1998).

In an early study, Robins (1966) found that female psychopaths followed the same behavioral patterns as male psychopaths, except that they were more frequently involved in sexual misconduct. In her sample, 79% of the females displayed abnormally high sexual activity and "excessive" interest in sexual matters. This finding is common in other female psychopath research. However, in the absence of other behavioral descriptors, it suggests that the psychopath label associated with some of these studies may have been attached indiscriminately to women who were believed to engage inappropriately in sexual activity.

In summary, earlier research on possible gender differences in psychopathy was complicated by a tendency to equate sexual activity in women with abnormal stimulation-seeking behavior. When "excessive" or "aberrant" sexual activity is separated from other behaviors, female psychopaths appear to have characteristics largely similar to those of male counterparts.

Salekin et al. (1997) believe there are at least two behavioral categories of female psychopaths. One category appears to be characterized by a lack of empathy or guilt, interpersonal deception, sensation seeking, and proneness to boredom. The second group appears to be characterized by early behavioral problems, promiscuous sexual behavior, and adult antisocial (not violent) behavior. In recent years, we have seen a renewed interest in studying the female psychopath. It appears, therefore, that further investigations into gender differences of core factors may result in a more refined description of both male and female psychopaths.

RACIAL/ETHNIC DIFFERENCES

Kosson, Smith, and Newman (1990) pointed out that a majority of psychopathic measures that have been developed used primarily white inmates as subjects. In their research, they discovered that psychopathy, as measured by Hare's PCL, does exist in African-American male inmates in a pattern that approximates the behavioral traits of white male inmates. However, Kosson et al. found one important difference. African-American criminal psychopaths seem to be less impulsive than white criminal psychopaths. This finding raises some questions as to whether the PCL is entirely appropriate for use with African-American inmates. On the other hand, Jennifer Vitale et al. (2002), using the PCL-R, found no significant racial differences in the scores and distributions of female psychopaths. More specifically, Vitale et al. report that 10% of the 248 incarcerated Caucasian women who participated in their study reached the cutoff scores of 30 or higher on the PCL-R, compared to 9% of the 280 incarcerated African-American women who had similar scores. Jennifer Skeem, John Edens, and Lori Colwell (2003), based on their analysis of existing studies, conclude that the differences between blacks and whites are minimal. Questions remain, however, as to the potential differences among other minority or ethnic groups, such as Latinos, Native Americans, and Asians/Pacific Islanders.

Some researchers have raised the intriguing and troubling issue of whether the stigmatizing diagnosis of psychopathy is likely to be used in a biased manner across minority or disadvantaged groups (Edens, Petrila, & Buffington-Vollum, 2001; Skeem, Edens, & Colwell, 2003 Skeem, Edens, Sanford, & Colwell, 2003). In essence, the consequence of being diagnosed a psychopath is becoming more serious (Skeem, Edens, Sanford, & Colwell, 2003). For example, Skeem, Edens, Sanford, and Colwell (2003) note that Canada and the United Kingdom use the diagnosis of psychopathy to support indeterminate detention for certain classes of offenders. Furthermore, "there is evidence that psychopathy increasingly is being used as an aggravating factor in the sentencing phase of US death penalty cases, where it has been argued that the presence of these personality traits renders a defendant a 'continuing threat to society'" (Skeem, Edens, Sanford, & Colwell, 2003, p. 17). Edens, Petrila, and Buffinton-Vollum (2001) suggest that perhaps the PCL-R should be excluded from capital sentencing until more solid research on its ability to predict future dangerousness in minority and disadvantaged individuals is established.

JUVENILE PSYCHOPATHY

As we have seen, one of the serious shortcomings of the extensive research conducted on psychopathy is that it has focused almost exclusively on white, adult males residing in North America (Frick et al., 2000). Consequently, research on juvenile (adolescent and child) psychopathy is sparse. However, there has been a rapid surge in research interest in the topic in recent years. Attempts to apply the label "psychopathy" to juvenile populations "raise several conceptual, methodological, and practical concerns related to clinical/forensic practice and juvenile/criminal justice policy" (Edens, Skeem, Cruise, & Cauffman, 2001, p. 54). Some debate has focused on whether psychopathy can or should be applied to juveniles at all. Can features of adult psychopathy be found in children and adolescents in the first place? Others are concerned that—even if psychopathy can be identified in adolescents—the label may have too many negative connotations. More specifically, the label implies that the prognosis for treatment is poor, a high rate of offending and recidivism can be expected, and the intrinsic and biological basis of the disorder means that little can be done outside of biological interventions. This encourages those working in the juvenile justice system to give up on juveniles so labeled. A third debate contends that psychopathy assessments of youths must achieve a high level of confidence before they can be employed in the criminal justice system (Seagrave & Grisso, 2002).

Several instruments for measuring preadult psychopathy have been developed in recent years, including the *Psychopathy Screening Device* (PSD; Frick, O'Brien, Wootton, & McBurnett, 1994), the *Childhood Psychopathy Scale* (CPS; Lynam, 1997), the *Psychopathy Content Scale* (PCS; Murrie & Cornell, 2000, 2002) and the *Psychopathy Checklist: Youth Version* (PCL:YV; Forth, Kosson, & Hare, 1997). All four instruments are currently being used primarily as research measures rather than as clinical–diagnostic measures and as Seagrave and Grisso (2002) point out, may eventually have important implications for prevention of future serious delinquency. Consequently, they may soon become extensively used in forensic clinical practice. According to Seagrave and Grisso (2002), "It is not overstated to imagine that juvenile psychopathy measures will become one of the most frequently used instruments in forensic assessments of delinquency cases of any kind within a few years after they are made generally available to forensic clinical examiners" (p. 220).

The PCL:YV, designed for assessing psychopathy in adolescents ages 13 or older, is a modified version of the *Psychopathy Checklist—Revised* (PCL-R). Basically, the instrument attempts to assess psychopathy across the youth's life span, with an emphasis on school adjustment and peer and family relations. Similarly to the adult PCL-R, the PCL:YV requires a lengthy standardized, semistructured clinical interview and a review of documents by a well-trained psychologist. Scores of 0 (consistently absent), 1 (inconsistent), or 2 (consistently present) are obtained for each of 20 behavioral dimensions of psychopathy. The instrument—like the PCL-R—generates a total score and two factor scores. Factor 1 reflects an interpersonal/affective dimension and includes items that measure glibness/superficial charm, grandiosity, manipulativeness, dishonesty, and callousness. Factor 2 reflects behavioral or lifestyle features such as impulsiveness, irresponsibility, early behavioral problems, and lack of goals. Recent research (Corrado, Vincent, Hart, & Cohen, 2004) indicates that the PCL-YV significantly predicts general and violent recidivism among adolescent boys. In addition, this research suggests that the predictive power of the youth version stems primarily from the impulsive, stimulation-seeking traits found in Factor 2. However, critics of these scales have argued that many of the above features represent normal adolescent development, mistaken in this context for psychopathy.

The PSD is a behavior rating scale in which some of the items on the PCL-R were rewritten for use with children (Frick et al., 2000). Currently, the PSD comes in three versions: (1) a teacher version, (2) a parent version, and (3) a self-report version. Using the teacher and parent versions of the PSD, Frick et al. (1994) found (through a factor analysis) that juvenile psychopathy may be made be up of two major dimensions. One dimension was labeled callous–unemotional, and the other impulsivity–conduct problems. Later, however, Frick et al. (2000) found evidence (again, through a factor analysis) to support a *three*-dimensional core for childhood psychopathy. Two of the factors (callous–unemotional and impulsivity) were similar to the core dimensions found for adults in Frick and colleagues' earlier study. However, the construct of impulsivity seems to be much more complex in children than in adults and the researchers discovered that the construct may be subdivided into impulsivity and narcissism (grandiose sense of self-worth). Again, though, these may simply be normal features of adolescence.

In fact, one of the major problems of identifying juvenile psychopaths is that psychopathy—if it exists in this age group—may be very difficult to measure reliably because of the transient and constantly changing developmental patterns across the lifespan. For example, psychopathic symptoms in childhood may look very different from those exhibited in adulthood (Hart, Watt, & Vincent, 2002). That is, some of the behavioral patterns of children and adolescents may be similar to those of psychopaths for a variety of reasons but may not really be signs of psychopathy. Children in an abusive home often demonstrate an abnormally restricted range of emotions that are similar to the emotional characteristics of psychopathy. Actually, they are the child's way of coping in a very stressful home environment (Seagrave & Grisso, 2002). Furthermore, "Some adolescent behavior may . . . appear psychopathic by way of poor anger control, lack of goals, and poor judgment, but is actually influenced by parallel developmental tasks encountered by most adolescents" (p. 229). Going against the rules is part of many adolescents' attempts to gain autonomy from adult dominance, such as found in adolescent-limited offending.

Edens and his colleagues (2001) also point out that some of the items on the various psychological measures of psychopathy (especially the PCL-R and the PCL:YV) are inappropriate for use with adolescents. For example, some items focus on such things as lack of goals and irresponsibility. If these features are not present, then the adolescent might receive scores in the psychopathy direction. However, adolescents generally have not crystallized their life goals and responsibilities to any great extent and consequently such items "seem less applicable as definitive markers of psychopathy for adolescence than for adults" (p. 58). We must be careful, then, not to generalize what we know about the adult psychopath to a juvenile who has been given the same label. Johnstone and Cooke (2004) admonish that it may be far too early to talk about psychopathic disorder in children. Instead, they suggest it is perhaps more appropriate to use a term like "psychopathic-like traits" when referring to childhood populations.

Nevertheless, many researchers are persisting in their attempts to identify juvenile psychopaths and measure psychopathic tendencies. In a study examining the prevalence rate of psychopathy among children, Skilling, Quinsey, and Craig (2001) found that 4.3% of a sample of over 1,000 boys in grades 4 to 8 could be classified as psychopathic on every measure employed in the study. However, the incidence of psychopathy among juvenile offenders remains equivocal. Campbell, Porter, and Santor (2004) found that only 9% of their sample of incarcerated adolescent offenders could be classified as psychopaths. The authors note, though, that their sample was primarily nonviolent in nature, with only 15% having a history of violent offending. On the other hand, Dåderman and Kristiansson (2003) found that 59% of their sample of violent adolescents with severe Conduct Disorders qualified as psychopaths. Similarly, Brandt, Kennedy, Patrick, and Curtain (1997), using a sample of incarcerated adolescents with persistent violent offending histories, reported that they could identify 37% of the sample as psychopathic. It is clear, therefore, that the sample used in a study, as well as the measuring instrument itself, will strongly influence the numbers of identifiable psychopathic traits within a given group of adolescents.

Lynam (1997) designed the CPS on the premise that adult psychopaths present a very different population pool than juvenile psychopaths. Adult criminal psychopaths often have been psychologically scarred by years of drug and alcohol abuse, physical fighting, lost opportunities, and multiple incarcerations (Lynam, 1997). Lynam reports results suggesting that psychopathy begins in childhood and can be measured reliably in children ages 12 and 13. He found that psychopathic children, like their adult counterparts, were the most aggressive, severe, frequent, and impulsive offenders, a characteristic that was stable across time. Moreover, he discovered that the CPS was a better predictor of serious delinquency than socioeconomic status, previous delinquency, IQ, or impulsivity.

The Psychopathy Content Scale (PCS) was developed from the Millon Adolescent Clinical Inventory (MACI), a personality inventory designed for use in clinical and correctional settings (Murrie, Cornell, Kaplan, McConville, & Levy-Elkon, 2004). The PCS, a self-report inventory, borrows 20 items from the MACI that relate to psychopathy-like behaviors. Although the instrument shows promise, research so far indicates that it is not as useful as the PCL:YV in identifying psychopathic-like behaviors in juveniles (Murrie et al., 2004). Several other instruments for measuring or identifying juvenile psychopathy are being developed and researched, such as the Youth Psychopathic features

Inventory (Andershed, Kerr, Stattin, & Levander, 2002; Poythress, Dembo, Wareham, & Greenbaum, in press; Skeem & Cauffman, 2003) and the Antisocial Process Screening Device (Frick & Hare, 2001).

Research so far does indicate that there is *some* validity in measures of juvenile psychopathy (Edens et al., 2001; Kosson, Cyterski, Steverwald, Neuman, & Walker-Matthes, 2002; Murrie & Cornell, 2002), but a vast majority of the researchers also believe that much more research needs to be done on this concept (see, generally, Johnstone & Cooke, 2004). Edens et al. (2001) admonish that the extant research remains unclear as to whether juvenile psychopathy is related to persistent violence in adulthood or whether juvenile psychopathy is untreatable, as commonly supposed for adult psychopathy. "It is imperative that we learn more about the stability, nature, and manifestations of psychopathy during the adolescent years, and develop and refine age-appropriate risk assessment tools based on this knowledge" (p. 77).

PSYCHOPHYSIOLOGICAL DIFFERENCES

Basic Neurophysiological Concepts and Terminology

Contemporary research favors the view that psychopathic behavior results from a complex interaction between neuropsychological and learning or socialization factors. Although the research on psychopaths in recent years has focused on the psychometric characteristics of psychopaths, neuropsychological factors remain a crucial component in the understanding of psychopathic behavior. Neuropsychological indicators (called markers) have been repeatedly found in psychopaths, as reflected in brain-wave patterns, electrodermal (skin conductance) measures, cardiovascular, and other nervous system indices (Fishbein, 2001). It is important, therefore, to become familiar with additional neuropsychological vocabulary and basic structures of the nervous system, some of which appeared in Chapter 3. The concepts presented here also lay the foundation for topics in later chapters (e.g., Chapter 7, on aggression and violence; Chapter 10, on sexual offenses; and Chapter 12, on drugs).

The human nervous system can be divided into two major parts, on the basis of either structure or function. The structural division—the way it is arranged physically—is perhaps the clearest distinction. The central nervous system (CNS) and the peripheral nervous system (PNS) are the two principal parts. The CNS comprises the brain and spinal cord, and the PNS comprises all nerve cells (called neurons) and nerve pathways located outside the CNS (see **Table 4–2**). In other words, those nerves that leave the spinal cord and brain stem and travel to specific sites in the body belong to the PNS. This includes all the nerves connecting the muscles, skin, heart, glands, and senses to the CNS.

The basic function of the PNS is to bring all the outside information to the CNS, where it is processed. Once the CNS has processed information, it relays

TABLE 4–2   Divisions of the Human Nervous System

I. Central nervous system (CNS)
   A. Brain
   B. Spinal cord
II. Peripheral nervous system (PNS)
   A. Skeletal nervous system (communicates with voluntary muscles)
   B. Autonomic nervous system
      1. Parasympathetic nervous system (relaxes and deactivates after emergencies)
      2. Sympathetic nervous system (activates for emergencies)

the interpretation back to the PNS if action is necessary. When you place your finger on a hot object, the PNS relays this raw datum (it is not yet pain) to the CNS, which interprets the datum as the sensation of pain and, in return, relays a command to the PNS to withdraw the finger. The PNS cannot interpret; it only transmits information to the CNS and carries communications back. In the following pages, we consider the significance of each of these systems to the diagnosis of psychopathy.

Central Nervous System Differences

Structurally, the CNS consists of the brain and spinal cord. Interpretation, thoughts, memories, and images all occur in the cerebral cortex (the highest center of the brain). It is the processing center for stimulation and sensations received from the outside world and the body via the PNS. The cerebral cortex, which is the outer surface of the human brain, contains more than 100 billion nerve cells (called *neurons*) (Hockenbury & Hockenbury, 2004; Scientific American, 1999). Each neuron has a complicated communication link to numerous other neurons, creating an extremely complex and poorly understood communications network. Although the physical structures of the brain do not directly concern us, the electrical and arousal properties of the cortex are relevant in understanding the electroencephalograms (brain-wave patterns) and psychological characteristics of the psychopath.

Brain-Wave Patterns.   Electrical activity in the CNS became the subject of serious study in the late 1920s, when the German psychiatrist Hans Berger developed sophisticated equipment enabling him to record oscillatory electrical potentials on the scalps of human subjects. The electrical oscillations recorded from the cortex are electroencephalograms (EEGs); the device that records them is the electroencephalograph. Because of the oscillatory characteristics of the EEGs, they are referred to as brain waves. Berger's technique allowed the study of electrical properties of the brain without discomfort to the subject. His work was not immediately recognized, and it was not until the early 1940s that his discovery accelerated investigations of the brain. Considerable EEG research continues to be conducted today, primarily because the procedure is relatively nonintrusive and inexpensive and can provide information about cortical processes that are difficult to obtain from the highly sophisticated neuroimaging scans used today (Monastra et al., 1999).

Berger (1929) discovered that when EEG recordings were made on a relaxed adult, usually with eyes closed, the electrical activity generally oscillated between 8 and 12 cycles per second (cps). He called this brain-wave pattern, which appeared with some consistency under relaxed conditions, *alpha rhythms*. Nevertheless, he did not know what brain function he was recording. To this day, investigators remain uncertain of the exact meaning of brain rhythms, despite rapid technological advances in recording hardware. Many believe that brain waves represent the synchronous, almost-symphonic firing of billions of neurons, the purpose of which remains unknown. We do know, as did Berger, that the EEG is an ever-changing reflection of the cortex's arousal levels and is sensitive to various changes in both the external and the internal (mood and thought) environments. By studying alpha rhythms, researchers have learned the characteristics of the cortex during sleep, drug ingestion, development, and malfunction, such as epileptic seizures. EEG patterns have also provided us with partial hints about the way the psychopath's cortex functions. Some of the cortical functions of the psychopath appear to be significantly different from those of the nonpsychopath.

Subsequent to Berger's findings, researchers delineated several other cortical rhythms. The *delta rhythm* spans 0.5 to 3 cps, is high voltage, and indicates that the cortex is at its lowest stage of activity and arousal. The *theta rhythm* has 4 to 7 cps, is lower voltage than the delta rhythm, and represents a stage slightly higher in cortical arousal. Together, delta and theta are often referred to as slow-wave activity, because of their relatively low frequency or oscillation rates. Alpha rhythms, which have 8 to 12 cps, represent a higher level of cortical arousal than slow-wave activity and are the "normal" rhythm for the relaxed adult. Individuals who have a greater amount of slow-wave activity may not process information as efficiently or effectively (Fishbein, 2001). Fast-wave *beta rhythms* have 13 to 30 cps, are low voltage, and reflect active cognitive processes, thinking, or general arousal states. Beta rhythms are sometimes referred to as desynchronic of alpha, since they occur under conditions that block the occurrence of alpha rhythms. For example, if an EEG recording is being made while a person is relaxed with eyes closed and someone suddenly calls out the person's name, there will be an immediate blocking of alpha, with resultant beta rhythms. For our purpose, it is important to remember that beta reflects high states of cortical activity and arousal.

EEGs seem to change with age. The delta and theta rhythms that predominate in childhood give way to alpha and beta in normal adulthood, except during sleep, when the delta and theta patterns return. Throughout infancy, childhood, and adolescence, the brain rhythms also become progressively more regular, and the cortex increases its potential for higher states of arousal. At birth, brain rhythms are irregular and often nonexistent. During the first year, delta begins to occur with some regularity on both sides of the brain (Fois, 1961). After the first year, the theta rhythm dominates the EEG pattern, eventually giving way to alpha rhythms, which begin to dominate at about age 10. The alpha gradually becomes regular and usually "matures" at about age 14. Beta rhythms develop at about age 16. The rhythms in the developing human are particularly susceptible to psychological stress and other factors in the environment. Highly irregular theta rhythms, for example, accompany older children's temper tantrums. They become more regular when the child lies down and calms down. The stages of sleep are also delineated on the basis of brain rhythms, the lighter stages characterized by theta patterns and the deeper stage by deltas. Other things being equal, the more aroused and alert the cortex, the higher the frequency and the lower the voltage of the brain waves.

Adrian Raine (1993) points out that there have been hundreds of studies examining the EEGs of criminals, delinquents, psychopaths, and violent offenders. Further, Raine notes that a large number of studies (e.g., Milstein, 1988; Volavka, 1987) have found a variety of EEG abnormalities in certain criminal populations, especially those populations who engage in *repetitive violent offending*. On the other hand, most of the research has major methodological flaws that make firm conclusions unwarranted. We now turn our attention to some of the EEG research on psychopathy.

EEG Research on Psychopaths

When researchers discovered that brain waves could be monitored, they began to hypothesize individual differences in those patterns and to devise experiments to test those hypotheses. In a pioneer study during World War II, D. Hill and Watterson (1942) investigated the EEG patterns of 151 male British military personnel who were not adjusting to military service and were believed to be psychopathic. The investigators divided the men into three classifications: aggressive, mixed, and inadequate psychopaths. The groups actually represented heterogeneous clusters of personality disorders and obviously failed in many respects to meet Cleckley's or Hare's criteria as we have presented them Table 4–1. One group, however, the aggressive psychopaths, closely resembled Hare's criminal psychopath. Men in this group had a history of "violence to others regardless of the consequences, repeated destruction of property, or a combination of such kinds of aggressive impulsive behavior" (Hill & Watterson, 1942, p. 47). The results indicated that 65% of the aggressive psychopaths demonstrated abnormal EEGs, compared to 15% of a group of "normals" used as controls. Most abnormal EEGs were of a slow-wave variety—delta and theta; the control group exhibited the usual adult alpha and beta patterns.

This study prompted many other EEG studies using individuals with various kinds of behavior disorders, including psychopathy. Subsequent studies of psychopaths have consistently revealed significantly higher incidences of EEG abnormality of a slow-wave variety (e.g., Craft, 1966; Hare, 1970). In a series of studies conducted by Knott, Platt, Ashby, and Gottlieb (1953), between 49% and 58% of 700 psychopaths had EEG abnormalities, mostly of a slow-wave variety. It should be noted that between 10% and 15% of the general population show abnormal EEGs, with "abnormal" being defined in a number of ways. Additional studies by Arthur and Cahoon (1964) and Ehrlich and Keogh (1956) also found that well over half of the psychopaths measured had abnormal EEGs, with most reflecting slow-wave patterns. It should be noted, however, that many of the EEG studies failed to employ a strict criteria of psychopathy (Raine, 1993), and therefore, some of the research findings may be based on a hodgepodge of criminal populations.

Assuming that many of the EEG studies did use primary psychopaths, it is unclear why many psychopaths display slow-wave activity (immature brain-wave patterns). As noted, it is not even clear what cortical functions the EEG represents. Do EEG abnormalities generate psychopathic behavior, or does psychopathic behavior cause EEG abnormality? The answer is not known. It could be that neither causes the other. It is interesting to note that slow-wave activity may serve as a powerful basis for differentiating persons with ADHD from those who do not have this disorder (Monastra et al., 1999). For example, Chabot and Serfontein (1996) were able to correctly identify approximately 95% of non-ADHD and 93% of ADHD children on the basis of slow-wave activity as measured by EEGs. Several other EEG studies have found similar results (see Monastra et al., 1999).

Hare (1970) suggests that slow-wave activity represents delayed brain maturation. Since some evidence indicates that EEG patterns of many psychopaths resemble those of children, it is arguable that the brain and cortical functioning of the psychopath is immature and childlike. Hare refers to this as the **maturation retardation hypothesis**, also known as the *maturation lag hypothesis*. It is appealing because the behavioral patterns of the psychopath—self-centeredness, impulsivity, inability to delay gratification, and inordinate stimulation seeking—resemble the behaviors of children.

There is also evidence that, with increasing age, the immature EEG patterns of some psychopaths develop into mature ones and that there is a corresponding change toward more socially approved behavior (Gibbens, Pond, & Stafford-Clark, 1955). Robins (1966) found support for this observation, discovering that the change was most likely to occur between the ages of 30 and 40. It may be that the psychopath's cortex matures later in life than that of the normal adult. It should be emphasized, however, that the EEG evidence to date is sketchy and fragmented, and considerably more data are necessary before the maturation retardation hypothesis deserves widespread support.

In several cross-sectional and longitudinal studies of the criminal histories of male psychopaths and nonpsychopaths, Hare and his colleagues (Hare, 1986; Hare & Jutai, 1983; Hare, McPherson, & Forth, 1988; Harpur & Hare, 1994) did find that the criminal activities of the criminal psychopath decrease at around age 40. The decrease is more dramatic for nonviolent crimes than for violent ones, however (Hare et al., 1992). Hare et al. (1988) further observe that the psychopath's dramatic decline in prison time and conviction rate after age 40 is often preceded by an equally dramatic increase in these variables between the ages of 25 and 30. The reasons for these discernible shifts remain unknown and are largely left to speculation. One popular hypothesis is "burnout"—that is, the frequent wear-and-tear of convictions and prison time eventually takes its toll on the antisocial activities of the criminal psychopath. Hare, however, finds the burnout hypothesis highly unlikely because the psychopath is relatively free of stress, tensions, anxieties, and conflicts that typically lead to emotional burnout. Of course, another favorite hypothesis is maturational lag, described earlier. Other hypotheses include learned strategies for remaining out of prison, or the cognitive realization that the future is bleak without changes in lifestyle. After all, even the criminal psychopath may eventually learn after a series of aversive consequences of antisocial behavior. In sum, the available evidence does suggest a reduction in offending (although not necessarily a complete termination of offending) at around age 40 for most male criminal psychopaths, but the reasons for this career shift remain unknown. Hare (Hare et al., 1992) cautions that although some psychopaths become less criminal with age, they often remain disagreeable people right into old age. They continue to demonstrate the same egocentric, manipulative, and callous traits characteristic of the psychopath well past age 40 (Hare, 1996). Moreover, not all psychopaths show a dramatic decrease in gross criminal behavior at middle age but many remain criminally active well beyond age 40.

Positive Spikes. In the late 1950s and early 1960s, some researchers (e.g., Kurland, Yeager, & Arthur, 1963; Niedermeyer, 1963) noticed that a brain rhythm of a different variety occurred during sleep in many psychopaths and highly aggressive individuals. Against a background of the usual slow-wave activity found in sleep, spontaneous bursts of brain waves with frequencies of 6 to 14 cps appeared in certain locations of the cortex (especially in the temporal lobe) in 66% of the aggressive subjects. These individuals had a history of uncontrollable and violent episodes of destructive urges, usually triggered by small, trivial slights. The aggressive explosions often resulted in extensive damage to property and injury or death to others. The brain-wave bursts are called *positive spikes*, and they have also been found to occur in the brain waves of psychopaths during awakened states. Researchers observe that, following the aggressive episodes, the individual expresses no guilt but is fully aware of the aggressive or even violent behavior (Hare, 1970).

In sum, contemporary research focusing on CNS characteristics reveals indications of inordinate amounts of abnormal brain-wave patterns, mostly of a childlike nature, in the EEGs of psychopaths. The data suggest that the psychopathic CNS is immature and perhaps does not develop fully until around age 40 or later. There are also data to suggest that highly aggressive criminal psychopaths may demonstrate other abnormal brain-wave patterns, such as positive spikes. We should be cautious, however, in coming to firm conclusions about the complex relationships between brain-wave activity and psychopathy. Research conducted three or more decades ago may have used a less precise definition of psychopathy in assigning categories.

Hemisphere Asymmetry and Deficiency

The human brain can be divided anatomically into two cerebral hemispheres—right and left. These two cerebral hemispheres seem to coexist in some sort of reciprocally balancing relationship in cortical functioning and information processing. For most individuals, the right hemisphere specializes in nonverbal functions, whereas the left specializes in verbal or language functions. Furthermore, the left hemisphere processes information in an analytical, sequential fashion. Language, for example, requires sequential cognition and the left hemisphere seems to be the best equipped for this operation. The right hemisphere, on the other hand, seems to process information holistically and more globally. For example, the right hemisphere is involved in the recognition of faces, a complicated process requiring the processing of information all at once or simultaneously. Thus, the right and left hemispheres are two functionally differentiated information processing systems.

In addition to information processing, research is now finding that these two cerebral hemispheres also make different contributions to human emotions (Jacobs & Snyder, 1996; Tomarken, Davidson, Wheeler, & Doss, 1992). The right hemisphere appears to be particularly important in the understanding and communication of emotion (Kosson, Suchy et al., 2002; Wheeler, Davidson, & Tomarken, 1993). The left seems to be closely tied to self-inhibiting processes, in contrast to the right, which appears to be more spontaneous and impulsive (Tucker, 1981). Furthermore, there must be a balance of contribution from each hemisphere for normal judgment and appropriate self-control (Tucker, 1981) and self-regulation of emotion (Tomarken et al., 1992). These control and judgment processes are especially prevalent in the frontal lobes (front sections of the brain).

Hare (1998; Hare & Connolly, 1987; Hare & McPherson, 1984) hypothesizes that criminal psychopaths manifest an abnormal or unusual balance between the two hemispheres, both in language processing and in emotional or arousal states. Hare notes that criminal psychopaths are often strikingly inconsistent in their verbalized thoughts, feelings, and intentions. Criminal psychopaths seem to be highly peculiar in the organization of certain perceptual and cognitive processes. Their left hemisphere seems, in some ways, to be deficient in linguistic processing because they do not rely on the verbal sequential operations to the extent that a majority of individuals do. Hare (1998) also hypothesizes that as the language task increases in complexity, nonpsychopathic persons rely more and more on the left hemisphere to process the information, while psychopaths rely more on the right hemisphere. Recent research supports this hypothesis (A. Lorenz & Newman, 2002).

There is also some research indicating that psychopaths are less accurate than nonpsychopaths at reading emotional expressions portrayed by faces. More specifically, psychopaths appear to be less accurate than nonpsychopaths in facial emotional recognition under conditions designed to promote reliance on left-hemisphere processing (Kosson, Suchy et al., 2002). These data are in support of the *left-hemisphere activation hypothesis* (Kosson, 1998), which states that psychopaths exhibit deficits on a variety of tasks that require activation of the left hemisphere.

Since language plays a very important role in the self-regulation of behavior, one of the contributing factors in the extremely impulsive, episodic behavior of psychopaths may reside in some deficiency in their use of internal language. This characteristic was pointed out some time ago by Flor-Henry (1973; Flor-Henry & Yeudall, 1973), who was convinced that psychopathy is closely linked to left-hemispheric language dysfunction. There has been some research to suggest that the right hemisphere of psychopaths may be deficient as well (Herpertz & Sass, 2000). Research by Day and Wong (1996) and Silberman and Weingartner (1986), for example, suggests that many psychopaths have impairments in the right hemisphere that prevent them from experiencing emotions as strongly as the normal population. Other researchers have found evidence that psychopaths exhibit an **emotional paradox**. "That is, psychopaths demonstrate normal appraisal of emotional cues and situations in the abstract (i.e., verbal discussion), but they are deficient in using emotional cues to guide their judgments and behavior in the process of living" (A. Lorenz & Newman, 2002, p. 91). In other words, psychopaths seem to be able to talk about emotional cues but lack the ability to use them effectively in the real world. This deficiency seems to be due to processing problems located in the left hemisphere (Bernstein, Newman, Wallace, & Luh, 2000; Lorenz & Newman, 2002).

Nachshon (1983; Nachshon & Denno, 1987) points out that many studies have found that a disproportionate percentage of violent, repetitive offenders has left hemispheric dysfunction. Researchers in Germany found similar results (Pillmann et al., 1999). Moreover, several researchers have argued that left-handedness may be an indicator of left-hemispheric dysfunction and have predicted that left-handedness will be overrepresented in the criminal or psychopathic population. Fitzhugh (1973) reported that about one-third of a group of juvenile delinquents were left-handed, while Andrew (1978) found that about one of five adult male offenders preferred their left hand. However, in a later study, Andrew (1980) reported that the left-handers seemed to be less violent than right-handed offenders. On the other hand, Nachshon and Denno (1987), in their investigation of 1,066 black male children—whose mothers participated in the Philadelphia Collaborative Perinatal Project— found that nonoffenders (based on official statistics) showed a significantly higher incidence of left-handedness than offenders. Thus, the research results are far from conclusive. Researchers have used different samples, have not been very definitive about their sample composition, and have used a variety of procedures and methods in obtaining and analyzing the data. Much more needs to be done before we can entertain any conclusions about left versus right preferences or left- versus right-hemispheric functioning in criminal or psychopathic populations.

Frontal Lobe Neuropsychological Studies

Some studies suggest that psychopaths may suffer from frontal lobe problems or dysfunctions. The frontal lobe refers to that section of the cerebral cortex we commonly call the forehead. The frontal lobes (there are two) are believed to be responsible for the "higher-level" cognitive functions of abstraction, decision making, cognitive flexibility, foresight, the regulation of impulses, and the control of appropriate behavior (Ishikawa et al., 2001). In other words, the frontal lobes perform the "executive functions" of the human brain.

Gorenstein (1982) and J. P. Newman, Patterson, and Kosson (1987) report findings indicating that psychopaths may have some defects in frontal lobe processing. On the other hand, research by Hare (1984), Hoffman, Hall, and Bartsch (1987), and Sutker and Allain (1983) failed to support the frontal lobe hypothesis. These equivocal results prompted Ishikawa et al. (2001, p. 423) to assert: "Clearly, research on the frontal dysfunction hypothesis in psychopaths is far from conclusive." However, a recent meta-analysis of the extant research on the topic by Morgan and Lilienfeld (2000) *suggests* that psychopaths, as a group, do show executive function deficits, which may result in faulty impulse control, judgment, and planning under certain conditions.

Cathy Widom (1978; Widom & Newman, 1985) points out that the mixed research results may stem from differences in the population of psychopaths being tested. Specifically, Widom (1978) found that psychopaths recruited from newspaper advertisements did not demonstrate the same level of frontal lobe deficits as incarcerated psychopaths. Widom speculated that "successful psychopaths" (community-based psychopaths who escaped conviction of their offenses and who answered the ad) probably had better functioning frontal lobes for controlling their behavior than the "unsuccessful" institutionalized psychopaths. Consistent with Widom's results, Ishikawa et al. (2001) discovered that successful psychopaths do not show the same psychophysiological or neuropsychological deficits as unsuccessful psychopaths. Overall, the researchers found that successful psychopaths exhibited stronger and better organized executive functions than either the unsuccessful psychopaths or the controls used in the study. Interestingly, the *unsuccessful* psychopaths did show most of the neuropsychological or neuropsychological characteristics reported in the previous studies conducted over the past 30 years.

At this point, the evidence suggests that the frontal lobes may play an important role in explaining some of the observed behavioral differences between psychopaths and nonpsychopaths. Furthermore, frontal lobe dysfunction may not be simply limited to psychopaths, but may be a feature that is characteristic of many other types of offenders (Raine, 1993).

Stimulation Seeking

Herbert Quay (1965) suggested that much of the psychopath's behavior represents an extreme form of stimulation seeking. He hypothesized that psychopaths do not receive the full impact of sensations from the environment and thus are always craving more. Therefore, in order to get the optimal amount of stimulation necessary to keep the underaroused cerebral cortex satisfied, they must engage more frequently in various forms of excitement than the normal person.

Several early studies have supported Quay's hypothesis. For example, Wiesen (1965) found that psychopaths worked harder for visual (colored lights) and auditory (music on a radio) stimulation than did a group of nonpsychopaths. In a second experiment that provided continued bombardment with lights and music, Wiesen also demonstrated that nonpsychopaths worked harder than psychopaths to obtain three seconds of silence and relative darkness.

Skrzpek (1969) delineated psychopaths and "neurotic delinquents" on the basis of a behavior rating list for psychopathy and neuroticism developed by Quay (1964). He found that conditions that increased "cortical arousal" (e.g., where the subject was required to make difficult auditory discriminations) decreased preference for visual complexity in both the psychopathic and the neurotic groups but was most pronounced in the latter. On the other hand, a brief period of stimulus deprivation (presumably low cortical arousal) increased preference for complexity in both groups, but a significantly greater increase was shown by the psychopaths.

In an attempt to test Quay's hypothesis that deficient responsivity of the nervous system might account for pathological stimulation seeking, Whitehill, DeMyer-Gapin, and Scott (1976) conducted an experiment using 103 boring slides of "concrete facades of a modern college campus building." As subjects, the researchers used 55 institutionalized "disturbed" preadolescent boys. The professional staff at the institution rated eight boys psychopathic (antisocial) and eight neurotic. A group of seven "normal" noninstitutionalized adolescent boys, matched with the index subjects for age, were used as controls. The average age was 11.5 years. Results showed that the psychopathic and normal boys looked at the slides significantly less than the neurotic group. More importantly, the psychopathic preadolescents showed a significant decrease in viewing time earlier than the other groups, suggesting that they became bored more quickly than the other groups. Whitehall et al. concluded that the data support the pathological stimulation-seeking hypothesis and favored a physiological ingredient in the formulation of psychopathy. In another project, Orris (1969) found that, compared to nonpsychopaths, psychopathic boys performed more poorly on a boring task requiring continuous attention and that they engaged more in boredom-relieving activities like singing or talking to themselves.

Optimal Arousal of the Cerebral Cortex

A number of theorists have postulated (e.g., Berlyne, 1960; Fiske & Maddi, 1961; Hebb, 1955) that organisms seek to maintain preferred or optimal levels of stimulation, with stimulation referring to the amount of sensation and/or information processed by the cortex. In effect, their theories argue for an inverted U-shaped function, with intermediate levels of stimulation most preferred and the extremes least preferred (see **Figure 4–1**). Insufficient amounts of stimulation lead to boredom, which can be reduced by an increase in stimulation-seeking behavior. On the other hand, exceptionally high levels of stimulation are also aversive and may promote behavior designed to avoid stimulation in an effort to bring the stimulus input to a more pleasurable level.

Cortical arousal appears to have a direct relationship with the amount of stimulation received by the cortex. Low stimulation produces a relatively low level of cortical arousal, whereas high levels of stimulation initiate high cortical arousal. To fall asleep, we must lower the cortex's arousal level by minimizing external and internal stimulation (noises, lights, thoughts). If we do not wish to fall asleep, but our cortical arousal is low (e.g., during a boring

FIGURE 4–1   Optimal Levels of Stimulation for Ambiverts, Introverts, and Extraverts

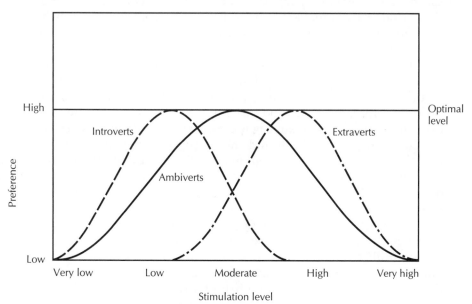

Note: Introverts reach their optimal level sooner than ambiverts or extraverts do.

lecture), we seek excitement to increase the arousal level. On the other hand, if stimulation becomes excessive, such as via a blaring radio or the pandemonium of rush-hour traffic, we are distressed if unable to control the stimulus input. Some psychologists argue that much behavior can be explained as an attempt by the person to maintain optimal or just-right levels of stimulation— levels that are the most comfortable and pleasurable to the individual.

It is generally agreed that there are individual differences in the quality and quantity of stimulation necessary for each person to reach the hypothetic optimum. Some of this individual difference may be attributed to certain physiological structures, particularly those found in the brain stem. Hans Eysenck (1967), you will recall, hypothesized that personality differences are largely due to differential needs for stimulation, which are dictated by functional properties of the reticular formation.

The reticular formation can be conveniently divided into several anatomical areas. Chief among these is the reticular activating system (RAS), a tiny but complex nerve network located in the central portion of the brain stem. The RAS underlies our attentiveness to the world and acts as a sentinel that activates the cortex and keeps it alert. Sensory signals or inputs from all parts of the body must travel through the brain stem on their way to the processing center, the cortex. Inside the brain stem, they branch into two major pathways. One major pathway goes through a relay station known as the thalamus; the other travels through the RAS, which, in turn, alerts the cortex to incoming information being routed through the thalamic pathway. The RAS-generated arousal is nonspecific in that it energizes the entire cortex, not any specific area. Therefore, any particular stimulation or sensation, from the outside world or from inside the body, has both a coded message (which travels through the thalamus) and a nonspecific arousing effect (which travels through the RAS).

The RAS can also decrease cortical arousal. If certain incoming stimuli are no longer significant or relevant, the cortex "tells" the RAS to filter out that particular group of stimuli. That process is called adaptation or **habituation**. Therefore, repetitive and insignificant stimuli are prevented by the RAS from unnecessarily bombarding the cortex with meaningless detail.

Contemporary research and theory suggests that the psychopath has a pathological need for excitement and thrills because of some deficiency in or excessive habituation property of the RAS. We emphasize the word "suggest" because, while the research seems consistent in demonstrating that psychopaths appear to have a strong need for stimulation, research has not clearly identified what neurophysiological mechanisms are involved. However, mainstream theory concerning the neurophysiological processes are as follows. Either the RAS does not activate the cortex sufficiently to receive the full impact of the incoming information or it adapts too quickly, thereby shutting down the cortex's activation before it receives complete information. Either way, the psychopath is unable to reach optimal arousal levels with the same amount of stimulation that normals find adequately arousing. So the psychopath engages in behaviors that society refers to as thrill seeking, chancy, antisocial, or inappropriate in order to reach satisfying optimal cortical arousal.

The general concept of arousal has been used interchangeably with cortical arousal throughout this chapter. In discussing psychopathy, many investigators refer to other forms of arousal, like autonomic (anxiety) or behavior arousal. Basically, these terms mean the same thing. Many states of activation or arousal involve overlapping systems (Korman, 1974). Thus, although there may be slightly different processes and mechanisms involved in different states of arousal, all must involve the heightened arousal levels of the cortex.

In an interesting experiment, Chesno and Kilmann (1975) tested the arousal hypothesis of psychopathy by manipulating stimulation variables (aversive white noise and shock) and personality variables (psychopaths, neurotics, and normals). Ninety male offenders incarcerated in a maximum-security penitentiary were selected for the experiment by various criteria. Psychopaths were classified according to Cleckley's criteria. The procedure involved an avoidance learning task, with electric shock being administered for certain incorrect choices by the subject. During the avoidance learning task, each subject received either 35, 65, or 95 decibels of white noise through earphones. (White noise is an auditory stimulus that sounds like a hissing radiator.)

If the arousal hypothesis is correct, the underaroused psychopath under low levels of stimulation should require some form of increased stimulation. Since errors in avoidance learning led to electric shock, psychopaths would be most likely to commit errors and benefit by the stimulation provided by the electric shock. Accordingly, as external stimulation increases (higher levels of white noise), the psychopath should have a decreased need for stimulation and, therefore, should learn to avoid the shock more effectively. The results of the study supported the hypothesis. Psychopaths made significantly more avoidance errors than the other groups as the stimulation decreased, which suggests that they prefer punishment to boredom. The finding may explain the well-known inability of psychopaths to benefit from punishment in situations low in stimulation, like prisons or even classrooms. It might even be that imprisoned psychopaths would "learn better" if the conditions under which they were incarcerated were more stimulating.

Therefore, psychopaths apparently do not learn to avoid aversive circumstances because of underarousal. However, if their arousal is increased, their avoidance learning should correspondingly increase. Furthermore, there is evidence that if incentives (e.g., money or other rewards) are used, avoidance learning in psychopaths also increases. In summarizing the research on this topic, Newman and his colleagues (J. Newman, Patterson, Howland, & Nichols, 1990; J. Newman & Kosson, 1986; J. Newman, 1987) have studied how rewards or incentives change the avoidance learning patterns of psychopaths. Their research suggests that, with adequate incentives, psychopaths become highly motivated to learn certain tasks and requirements. In fact, psychopaths under incentive conditions may learn better than nonpsychopaths.

Raine (1993, p. 228) writes: "Psychopaths do indeed learn poorly when the reinforcer is physical or social punishment, but they do appear to learn well when (1) their arousal is increased, or (2) they are sufficiently motivated by financial incentives."

Peripheral Nervous System Research

The PNS is subdivided into a *skeletal division*, comprising the motor nerves that innervate the skeletal muscles involved in body movement, and an autonomic division, which controls heart rate, gland secretion, and smooth muscle activity. Smooth muscles are those muscles found in the blood vessels and gastrointestinal system; they look smooth under a microscope in comparison to the skeletal muscles, which look striped or textured.

The autonomic segment of the PNS is extremely relevant to our discussion of the psychopath, because here, too, research has consistently uncovered a significant difference between the psychopath's and the general population's reactivity or responsiveness to stimuli. The autonomic division is especially important, because it activates emotional behavior and responsivity to stress and tension. It can be subdivided into the *sympathetic* and *parasympathetic systems* (see Figure 3–4).

The sympathetic system is responsible for activating or arousing the individual for fight or flight before (or during) fearful or emergency situations. As you will recall, the psychopath displays a James Bond–like coolness, even in stressful situations. We might explain this in one of two ways. Either the sympathetic nervous system does not react sufficiently to stressful stimuli or the parasympathetic system springs into action in the psychopath more rapidly than in nonpsychopaths. There is research support for both of these positions.

Before discussing the psychopath's autonomic nervous system in more detail, we should note the principles and techniques of measuring autonomic activity. Emotional arousal, which is largely under the control of the autonomic nervous system, can be measured by monitoring the system's activity, such as heart rate, blood pressure or volume, and respiration rate. The most commonly used physiological indicator of emotional arousal, however, is the *skin conductance response*, also known as the *galvanic skin response*. Since skin conductance response is the label most advocated by contemporary researchers (Lykken & Venables, 1971), it is used throughout this chapter.

The skin conductance response is simply a measurement of the resistance of the skin to conducting electrical current. Although a number of factors in the skin influence its resistance, perspiration seems to play a major role. Perspiration corresponds very closely to changes in emotional states and has, therefore, been found to be a highly sensitive indicator of even slight changes in the autonomic nervous system. Other things being equal, as emotional arousal increases, perspiration rate increases proportionately. Small changes in perspiration can be picked up and amplified by recording devices, known as polygraphs or physiographs. An increase in perspiration lowers skin resistance to electrical conductance. In other words, skin conductance increases as emotional arousal (anxiety, fear, and so on) increases.

We noted earlier that psychopaths lack the capacity to respond emotionally to stressful or fearful situations. Essentially, they give the impression of being anxiety-free, carefree, and cool, and they display a devil-may-care attitude. We would expect, therefore, that compared to the normal population, the psychopath has a comparatively underactive, underaroused autonomic nervous system. What has the research literature revealed? Consistently, investigators have reported low skin conductance arousal in psychopaths (Fishbein, 2001). "Deficits in measures of SC [skin conductance] arousal are believed to be associated with low autonomic arousal levels which are, in turn, related to low emotionality, poor conditionability, lack of empathy and remorse, and ability to lie easily" (p. 51). We now turn our attention to the division of the nervous system most responsible for skin conductance arousal.

Autonomic Nervous System Research

In a pioneering study, Lykken (1957) hypothesized that since anxiety reduction is an essential ingredient in learning to avoid painful or stressful situations, and since the psychopath is presumed to be anxiety-free, then the psychopath should have special difficulty learning to avoid unpleasant things. Recall that two characteristic features of psychopaths are their inability to learn from unpleasant experiences and their very high recidivism. Lykken carefully delineated his research groups according to Cleckley's criteria. His psychopaths (both males and females) were drawn from several penal institutions in Minnesota and were classified as either primary or neurotic psychopaths. College students comprised a third group of normals.

Lykken designed an electronic maze that subjects were expected to learn as well as possible in 20 trials. There were 20 choice points in the maze, each with four alternatives, with only one being the correct choice. Although three alternatives were incorrect, only one of these would give the subject a rather painful electric shock. Lykken was primarily interested in discovering how quickly subjects learned to avoid the shock, a process called **avoidance learning**. He reasoned that avoidance learning would be rewarded by the reduction of anxiety on encountering the correct choice point, but since psychopaths are presumably deficient in anxiety, their performance should be significantly worse than that of normals. The hypothesis was supported.

Prior to the maze portion of the experiment, Lykken measured the skin conductance changes of each subject while he or she tried to sit quietly for 30 to 40 minutes. During this time, the subjects would periodically hear a buzzer and occasionally receive a slight, brief electric shock several seconds after the buzzer. Eventually, the buzzer became associated with the shock. In normal individuals, the sound of the buzzer itself produced an anxiety response in anticipation of the electric shock (classical conditioning) and was reflected by a substantial increase in skin conductance response. Psychopaths, however, were considerably less responsive to this stress. Furthermore, psychopaths were incapable of learning to avoid the painful electric shocks, while the normals learned significantly better.

Lykken's data indicate that psychopaths do in fact have an underresponsive autonomic nervous system and, as a result, do not learn to avoid aversive situations as well as most other people. More recent research continues to support these findings (Gottman, 2001; Ogloff & Wong, 1990). Does this provide at least a partial explanation for why psychopaths continue to get into trouble with the law, despite the threat of imprisonment?

Schachter and Latane (1964) followed up on Lykken's work by using similar apparatus and basic procedures, with the exception of one major revision. Each subject was run through the maze twice, once with an injection of a harmless saline solution and once with an injection of adrenaline, a hormone that stimulates physiological arousal. Subjects were prisoners selected on the basis of two criteria: how closely they approximated Cleckley's primary psychopath and how incorrigible they were, as measured by the number of offenses and time in prison. Prisoners high on both criteria were psychopaths; prisoners relatively low on both were nonpsychopaths.

Injections of adrenaline dramatically improved the performance of the psychopath in the avoidance learning task. In fact, with adrenaline injections, the psychopaths learned to avoid shocks more quickly than did normal prisoners with similar injections. On the other hand, when psychopaths had saline injections, they were as deficient in avoidance learning as Lykken's psychopaths.

Since anxiety is presumed to be a major deterrent to antisocial impulses, the manipulation of arousal or anxiety states by drugs may suggest policy implications for the effective treatment of convicted psychopaths. Specific drugs apparently have the potential to increase the emotional level of psychopaths to a point equivalent to the level of the general population.

Subsequent research by Hare (1965a, 1965b) found that primary psychopaths have significantly lower skin conductance when resting than do nonpsychopaths. Other researchers have reported similar results (Herpertz & Sass, 2000). In a major study, Hare (1968) divided 51 inmates at the British Columbia Penitentiary into three groups—primary psychopaths, secondary psychopaths, and nonpsychopaths—and studied them under various conditions, while constantly monitoring their autonomic functioning. The experimental conditions also permitted the observation of a complex physiological response known as the *orienting response*.

The orienting response is a nonspecific, highly complicated cortical and sensory response to strange, unexpected changes in the environment. The response may take the form of a turning of the head, a dilation of the eye, or a decrease in heart rate. It is made in an effort to determine what the change is. Pavlov referred to the orienting response as the "what-is-it" reflex. It is an automatic, reflexive accompaniment to any perceptible change, and it can be measured by various physiological indices. The orienting response produces, among other things, an increase in the analytical powers of the senses and the cortex.

Hare found not only that psychopaths exhibit very little autonomic activity (skin conductance and heart rate), but also that they had smaller orienting responses than did nonpsychopaths. His data suggest that psychopaths are less sensitive and alert to their environment, particularly to new and unusual events.

Hare later reported intriguing data relating to the heart or cardiac activity of the psychopath. The aforementioned conclusions were based on skin conductance data. When cardiovascular variables are considered, however, some apparent anomalies appear. While skin conductance is consistently low, cardiac activity (heart rate) in the psychopath is often as high as that found in the nonpsychopathic population (Hare & Quinn, 1971). Hare (1976) comments, "The psychopaths appeared to be poor electrodermal [skin conductance] conditioners but good cardiovascular ones" (p. 135). That is, although psychopaths do not learn to react to stimuli as measured by skin variables, it appears that they learn to react autonomically as well as nonpsychopaths when the heart rate is measured. Hare suggests that the psychopath might be more adaptive to stress when "psychophysiological defense mechanisms" are brought into play, thereby reducing the impact of stressful stimuli.

Hare and his colleagues designed experiments in which the heart rate could be monitored throughout the experimental session. In one experiment, a tone preceded an electric shock by about 10 seconds (Hare & Craigen, 1974). In anticipation of the shock, psychopaths exhibited a rapid acceleration of heartbeat, followed by a rapid deceleration of heart rate immediately before the onset of the noxious stimulus (a "normal" reaction is a gradual but steady increase in heart rate until the shock). However, their skin conductance remained significantly lower than that of nonpsychopaths. Therefore, psychopaths appear to be superior conditioners when cardiac activity is measured, indicating that they do indeed either learn or inherit autonomic adaptability to noxious stimuli. Hare suggests that this accelerative heart response is adaptive and helps the psychopath tune out or modulate the emotional impact of noxious stimuli. This, he speculates, may be the reason that skin conductance responses are relatively low in the psychopath.

Lykken (1955) also conducted experiments testing the performance of psychopaths on polygraph equipment. If psychopaths are generally underaroused, we would expect that lie detectors would be unable to differentiate their deceptive from their truthful responses, since polygraphs rely on physiological reactivity to questions. Also, psychopaths should have no trouble being deceptive, since they are typically adept at manipulating and deceiving others. Lykken's research confirmed these expectancies. Psychopaths emitted similar skin conductance responses, regardless of whether they were lying or telling the truth. Nonpsychopaths displayed significant differences in reactivity; their lie ratios, reflected by skin conductance, were higher than those of psychopaths. Because of the artificial atmosphere of the laboratory compared to real-life situations, particularly stressful ones, Lykken admonished against uncritical acceptance of his findings until further testing.

Few studies have since directly examined the relationship between psychopathy and lie detection. However, Raskin and Hare (1978) did reexamine the Lykken study, using more sophisticated equipment and better standardization for lie detection. Using 24 psychopathic prisoners and 24 nonpsychopathic prisoners, they found that both groups were equally easily detected lying about a situation involving a $20 mock theft. This contradictory finding underscores the fact that fine-tuning is still needed if we are to understand the neurophysiological characteristics of the psychopath.

There is evidence, for example, that sufficiently aroused or motivated psychopaths will give physiological responses to interesting events that equal the responses of nonpsychopaths (Hare, 1968). On the other hand, when it comes to highly stressful, serious occasions, psychopaths appear to have incomparable skill at attenuating guilt or aversive reactions (Lykken, 1978). The simulated crime scene in the Raskin–Hare experiment not only was relatively unstressful, but also may have been regarded by the psychopath as an interesting "game." The acid test for the lie detection hypothesis will rest with carefully designed experiments in real-life, highly stressful situations. The present data do not justify firm conclusions. Christopher Patrick and his colleagues (Patrick, Bradley, & Lang, 1993) conducted a study designed to test in what ways the startle reflex action in psychopaths differs from that in the normal population. An example of a startle response is the eye blink reflex in response to a puff of air. These researchers note that psychophysiological research on the psychopath has relied almost exclusively on skin conductance and cardiovascular measures. The researchers found that criminal psychopaths (measured by Hare's PCL-R) exhibited much lower startled responses under aversive conditions than nonpsychopaths did. Their findings confirm previous research showing that criminal psychopaths show smaller autonomic responses under aversive conditions than do other nonpsychopathic offenders. Hare (1993, 1996) postulates that psychopaths suffer from a general "hypoemotionality." That is, it appears that psychopaths fail to experience the full impact of any kind of emotion—positive or negative. The psychopath may be born with this hypoemotionality, and that may account for their lack of remorse throughout their lifetimes.

In summary, the research reviewed thus far allows us to make four tentative conclusions about the autonomic functioning of the psychopath. First, psychopaths appear to be both autonomically and cortically underaroused, both under rest conditions and under some specific stress conditions. They are much more physiologically "drowsy" than nonpsychopaths. Second, because they lack the necessary emotional equipment, psychopaths appear to be deficient in avoidance learning, which might account partially for their very high recidivism rates. Third, some data suggest that if emotional arousal can be induced, such as by adrenaline, psychopaths can learn from past experiences and avoid normally painful or aversive situations, such as prison, embarrassment, or social censure. And fourth, with adequate incentives, such as monetary rewards, psychopaths can learn from past experiences and avoid aversive consequences as well as anyone.

Adrian Raine (1993), in his excellent review of the relevant research, finds that many of these psychophysiological indicators discussed for psychopaths may be characteristic of repetitive violent offenders in general. In fact, with reference to resting heart rate levels in *noninstitutionalized offenders*, he concludes, "This is probably the best replicated and most robust biological finding on antisocial behavior reported to date" (p. 190).

We noted earlier that psychopaths are often profoundly affected by alcohol, even in small amounts. Alcohol is a general CNS depressant, decreasing arousal levels in the nervous system. Research indicates that underaroused psychopaths are already half-asleep and "half in the bag"; alcohol has the general effect of "bagging" them completely. Therefore, we would expect that the psychopath not only would get intoxicated more rapidly than the nonpsychopath of comparable weight, but also would probably pass out sooner. We would also expect the psychopath to have few sleep difficulties. Steven Smith and Joseph Newman (1990) found that a higher percentage of criminal psychopaths have been polydrug users compared to criminal nonpsychopaths. In addition, criminal psychopaths were particularly heavy alcohol abusers, and alcohol may have played a very significant role in prompting their extensive antisocial behavior.

Recent research has shown that adult psychopaths usually exhibit significant antisocial behavior in their childhoods (Seagrave & Grisso, 2002). It is reasonable, therefore, to expect researchers to begin searching the developmental trajectory of psychopathy in order to identify tomorrow's psychopaths. The next section examines what we currently know about the childhood of the psychopath. In light of our earlier discussion of juvenile psychopathy, though, we must be careful not to assume that adult psychopaths were necessarily psychopathic as juveniles.

THE CHILDHOOD OF THE PSYCHOPATH

We have discussed the behavioral descriptions and biopsychological components of psychopaths. Now, how did they get that way? Criminal behavior and other behavior problems are often assumed to be rooted in the home, usually in homes with conflict, inadequate discipline, or poor models. From our discussion of the biopsychological components of psychopaths, however, it is obvious that the answer is not that simple. Psychopathy seems to be a result of a highly complex interaction of biopsychological, social, and learning factors.

Cleckley (1976) was not convinced that any common precursors exist in the family backgrounds of psychopaths, even though relatively homogeneous classifications of psychopathy do exist. However, even if we accept that neurophysiological factors may be causal factors in the development of psychopathy, this does not mean they are hereditary. In fact, there is little evidence to support a strong genetic influence on psychopathy. It is possible, though, that psychopaths are born with a biological predisposition to develop the disorder, independent of any genetic factors. In line with the Eysenckian view, it could be that psychopaths have a nervous system that interferes with rapid conditioning and association between transgression and punishment. Because of this defect, the psychopath fails to anticipate punishment and, hence, feels no guilt (no conscience). As an alternative to the defect argument, it is possible that certain aspects of the psychopath's nervous system simply have not matured. Another possibility is that genetics, toxicity (e.g., lead paint) in utero, birth difficulties, temperament, and other early developmental factors may affect certain processes in the nervous system, rendering some children vulnerable to develop conduct problems and psychopathic characteristics. These early contexts are especially prevalent for disadvantaged children. In addition, it should be emphasized that social factors play a major role in affecting these predispositions. "For example, a problematic temperamental predisposition at 6 months of age *and* low socioeconomic status at birth *and* early life experiences of physical abuse *and* peer rejection in early elementary school combine to predict clinically significant conduct-problem outcomes . . . in adolescence" (Dodge & Pettit, 2003, p. 354).

It is surprising that so little research has been directed at social and family factors in the development of psychopathy, especially when we consider how much research attention has been directed at biological factors and psychometric measures. One of the first studies on the childhood experiences of psychopaths was conducted by L. A. Marshall and Cooke (1999). They found, using the PCL-R to define psychopathy, that psychopaths are more likely to have experienced both family (e.g., parental antipathy, indifference, abuse, and neglect) and societal difficulties (e.g., negative social and school experiences) than nonpsychopaths are. Other recent research has consistently identified poor parental monitoring and discipline methods as related to psychopathy and violent offending in adults (Tolan, Gorman-Smith, & Henry, 2003).

Interestingly, though, Hare and his colleagues (1992) find no support for the hypothesis that psychopaths come from a "poor" or "inadequate" family life. Hare does not dispute the research that finds that a "poor," abusive family life is associated with the early emergence of criminal behavior in nonpsychopaths, but when it comes to psychopaths, the inadequate or dysfunctional family link is weak or nonexistent.

Psychopathic characteristics—if not psychopathy itself—can be identified early in an individual's development. In a longitudinal study conducted by Robins (1966), clinical records verified that 95% of adult psychopaths investigated had demonstrated psychopathic behaviors in childhood. After an extensive review of the literature, Quay (1972) notes that psychopathic behaviors in adults are probably labeled "conduct disorders" or "excessive aggressiveness" in childhood. Childhood behaviors that elicit those labels include extreme disobedience, disruptiveness, fighting, temper tantrums, irresponsibility, and attention seeking. ADHD is also a common feature. Again, though, it is premature to label someone with those characteristics a child or juvenile psychopath, because the characteristics may be attributed to a range of other causes.

Recent research finds support for a relationship between ADHD and criminal psychopathy (Loeber & Stouthamer-Loeber, 1998). Rolf Loeber and Magda Stouthamer-Loeber (1998, p. 246) point out that ADHD appears to do three things in development of repetitive aggressive and violent behavior: (1) It is associated with poor cognitive and academic functioning; (2) it is implicated in the maintenance of oppositional (antisocial) behavior; and (3) it activates an early, accelerated development of aggressive behaviors, conduct problems, and substance abuse. It appears likely, then, that *some* childhood ADHD is a precursor of *some* adult psychopathy, a finding that underscores the neurophysiological factors in psychopathy. In general, however, with the exception of the work on ADHD, few studies have been directed at the neurophysiological components of potential psychopaths during early childhood.

A fruitful avenue for exploring the childhood of the psychopath—especially the criminal psychopath—would be close examination of the life course–persistent (LCP) offender described by developmental theorists, particularly Terrie Moffitt and her colleagues. The reader will recall that this theory was explored in Chapter 2 in some detail. Developmental theory postulates that LCP offenders manifest antisocial behavior across all kinds of conditions and situations in their childhoods. Neurologically, LCPs demonstrate a variety of minor neuropsychological disorders, such as difficult temperaments as infants, attention deficit disorders or hyperactivity as children, and learning and language problems as adolescents. Socially, LCPs are rejected by their peers during their preteen years and are annoying to adults. Emotionally, they exhibit virtually no empathy or concern for others, show very little bonding to family, and often are sadistic and manipulative. They are highly impulsive and lack insight. As they develop, LCPs commit a wide assortment of aggressive and violent crimes across life spans. A careful reading of LCPs developmental histories often shows a striking resemblance to the symptomology of criminal psychopaths. Recall, though, that theorists—including Moffitt—are suggesting that there may be more than two developmental paths. This is still very much an example of research in process.

SUMMARY AND CONCLUSIONS

The primary psychopath should be distinguished from people who may be classified as psychotic, neurotic, or emotionally disturbed. The primary psychopath should also be distinguished from the sociopath, who is similar in many ways. However, the term sociopath usually refers to a person who *habitually* violates the law and who does not seem to learn from past experience. Another common term—antisocial personality disorder—also is distinct from the term psychopath, even though these two terms are often confused by clinicians and researchers. This is understandable, because the diagnostic category Antisocial Personality Disorder, as defined in the latest editions of the DSM, has many parallels to Robert Hare's concept of criminal psychopathy.

The psychopath as discussed here may or may not run afoul of the law. In addition, psychopaths demonstrate a variety of behavioral and neurophysiological characteristics that differentiate them from other groups of individuals. Hare has proposed the term *criminal psychopath* to describe those persistent and repetitive offenders of the law. In this sense, the criminal psychopath, the sociopath, and the person with antisocial personality disorder are similar in their offending patterns.

Psychopaths most often function in society as charming, daring, witty, intelligent individuals, high on charisma but low on emotional reaction and affect. They appear to lack moral standards or the ability to manifest genuine sensitivity toward others. If criminals, they become the despair of law enforcement officials because their crimes appear to be without discernible or rational motives. Even worse, they show no remorse and little ability to be rehabilitated.

We reviewed much of the neurophysiological research suggesting that the psychopath is different from the rest of the population on a number of physiological measures. Psychopaths seem to be underaroused, both autonomically and cortically, a finding that may account for their difficulty in learning the rules of society. However, there is some evidence to suggest that, with adequate incentives, psychopaths may learn societal expectations very well. Recalling our discussion of Eysenck's theory in Chapter 3, it is clear that psychopaths would be stable extraverts with high psychoticism. Psychopaths, like extraverts, apparently are not aroused enough to profit as easily from the classical conditioning that perhaps sets most of us on the straight and narrow path in childhood. If, in addition to this physiological lack, psychopaths' family situations leave them without appropriate models, then they are doubly cursed.

Many psychopaths also apparently have abnormal brain-wave patterns, mostly of a slow-wave, childlike variety, which suggests that their nervous systems are immature, at least until middle age. There are indications of more than the usual amounts of positive spikes, which are brain-wave bursts that correlate with aggressive episodes and impulsivity. Research has failed to discover, however, whether these abnormalities engender psychopathic behavior, or vice versa. There is also little evidence to support a strong hereditary influence, although we should not overlook the possibility that psychopaths may be born with a biological predisposition to the disorder.

Studies on the childhood of psychopaths strongly suggest that they may have been ADHD children, causing chaos for parents and teachers. It would be folly to maintain, though, that the ADHD child of today is the psychopath of tomorrow. Perhaps because they are physiologically underaroused, psychopaths do not respond as well to admonishments, threats, or actual punishment as do their nonpsychopathic peers. They do not learn society's expectations and the rules of right and wrong, possibly because anxiety-inducing disciplinary procedures are not that anxiety-producing for them. In many respects, the criminal psychopath follows a developmental path highly similar to the LCP offender described in developmental theory, outlined in Chapter 2.

There are still numerous gaps in our knowledge of the psychopath, one being in the area of gender differences. Research on female psychopaths is scant. Some research suggests that behavioral characteristics for females are generally similar to those of male psychopaths, with slightly more emphasis among females on sexual acting-out behavior. This probably reflects a cultural bias, however, since women have been traditionally chastised more than men for behavior deemed inappropriate according to sexual mores. However, research on female criminal psychopaths using Hare's Psychopathy Checklist—Revised (PCL-R) implies that their behavioral patterns may be somewhat different from those of male criminal psychopaths.

A highly controversial area relating to psychopathy is the measurement and existence of juvenile psychopathy. Some researchers are very actively involved in developing scales to assess this construct and in comparing features of juvenile and adult psychopaths. Other researchers prefer to focus on psychopathic "characteristics" in juveniles that may or may not mean that they are themselves psychopathic. Many juveniles, for example, are impulsive, seek stimulation, and appear to be noncaring; these features are often part of the normal turmoil of adolescent development. While it is worthwhile to study these characteristics, we must not rush to judgment and assume they are indicative of psychopathy. Others are even more cautious, suggesting that the concept itself simply is not valid when applied to juveniles. However, representatives of each of the above groups have expressed concern that juvenile psychopathy will be misdiagnosed, condemning juveniles to a label that is frequently associated with defeat: Psychopaths do not feel remorse, therefore cannot be helped.

Contemporary research on psychopathy is robust and shows few signs of abating. By now it is quite clear that Hare's primary psychopath—as measured by the PCL—has many unique features that include a distinctive cognitive and emotional style, physiological indicators, and perhaps a childhood marked by parental deficiency and conduct problems. These features combine to render the psychopath highly resistant to treatment. This is particularly frustrating to clinicians working with criminal psychopaths, many of whom know how to play the clinical games that will make it appear that they have changed their behavior.

·······················▶

CHAPTER 5

ORIGINS OF CRIMINAL BEHAVIOR: LEARNING AND SITUATIONAL FACTORS

People do not come into situations empty-headed. They have an infinite store of living experiences and an extensive repertoire of strategies for reacting to events. Up to this point, we have not acknowledged these strategies, concentrating instead on heredity and neurophysiology and the significant roles they may play in the development of criminal behavior. To some extent, in the previous chapter on the psychopath, we covered such childhood influences as parenting and the availability of appropriate models. However, the physiological features were key to understanding the development of psychopathy.

Biological/physiological factors appear to account in part for individual differences in susceptibility to classical conditioning. Since the capacity to be conditioned strongly affects fear of reprisal, it contributes to the inhibition of socially undesirable criminal behavior. However, classical conditioning presumes that the human being is an automaton. That is, classical conditioning assumes that humans act in a monotonous routine manner without active intelligence. Pair a neutral stimulus with a closely following painful event and the alert, intact robot will eventually, and automatically, connect the stimulus with the pain. This sequence is probably a very powerful factor in many behaviors, but certainly not in all or even most. Conditioning is only one of several factors involved in the acquisition of criminal behavior.

To understand criminal behavior, it is crucial that we regard all individuals— whether or not they violate the rules of society—as active problem solvers who perceive, interpret, and respond uniquely to their environments. For the moment, consider unlawful behavior as subjectively adaptable rather than deviant. In this sense, unlawful conduct is a response pattern that a person has found to be effective, or thinks will be effective, in certain circumstances.

Violent crimes like aggravated assault and homicide are sometimes called "irrational," "uncontrollable," "explosive," or "motiveless" and, therefore, are believed to resist or defy analysis (e.g., President's Commission on Law Enforcement and Administration of Justice, 1967). Later in this text, however, we will find that different types of violence can be placed into different theoretical frameworks. The decision to act violently may be a quick one, but the violent behavior is usually not irrational or uncontrollable. Even behavior that can be attributed to a severe mental disorder may be adaptive, though it may not be legally culpable.

Engaging in criminal behavior might be one person's way of adapting or surviving under physically, socially, or psychologically dire conditions. Another person might decide that violence is necessary to defend honor, protect self, or reach a personal goal. In either case, the person is choosing what he or she believes is the best alternative for that particular situation (although real choice may be illusory in the case of the person who is severely mentally disordered). It is not, of course, necessarily the alternative that others would choose, or what society condones. What, besides susceptibility to classical conditioning, accounts for the difference? In a very general sense, learning— both operant (or instrumental) and social learning—is an extremely important component in the equation. In the following pages we expand the concept of conditioning to include these two distinct forms of learning, which play a major role in the acquisition and maintenance of criminal behavior. Later, we introduce situational factors that appear to affect the learning process. Since each of these topics springs from the school of psychological thought called behaviorism, we begin our discussion there.

BEHAVIORISM

Behaviorism officially began in 1913 with the publication of a landmark paper by John B. Watson (1878–1958), "Psychology as the Behaviorist Views It." The paper, which appeared in *Psychological Review*, is considered the first definitive statement on behaviorism, and Watson is thus acknowledged as the school's founder. However, Watson was by no means the first to discuss the basic elements of behaviorism. Its roots can be traced back at least to Aristotle

(Diserens, 1925). Watson's behaviorism represents a recurring phase in the cyclical history of psychology. A psychology of consciousness or mind is followed by a psychology of action and behavior (behaviorism), from which a psychology of mind and consciousness reemerges. Today, psychology is moving once again toward a psychology of mind, especially cognitive processes. For the moment, let's return to Watsonian behaviorism, which has heavily influenced psychological interpretations of criminal behavior.

Watson frequently declared that psychology was the science of behavior. He believed that psychologists should eliminate the "mind" and all of its related vague concepts from scientific consideration because they could not be observed or measured. He was convinced that the fundamental goal of psychology was to understand, predict, and control human behavior, and that only a rigidly scientific approach could accomplish this.

Greatly influenced by Ivan Pavlov's famous research on classical conditioning, Watson thought that psychology should focus exclusively on the interplay between stimulus and response. A stimulus is an object or event that elicits behavior. A response is the elicited behavior. Watson was convinced that all behavior—both animal and human—was controlled by the external environment in a way similar to that described by Pavlov in his initial study—stimulus produces response (sometimes called S–R psychology). Therefore, for Watson, classical (or Pavlovian) conditioning was the key to understanding, predicting, and controlling behavior, and its practical applicability was unlimited.

The chief spokesperson for behaviorism for several decades was B. F. Skinner (1904–1990), who was the most influential psychologist in the United States in the twentieth century. The Skinnerian perspective especially dominated the application of behavior modification or behavior therapy in the correctional system and at many institutions for the mentally handicapped or disturbed. Some contemporary theories about criminal behavior (e.g., Akers, 1985, 2000) try to integrate Skinnerian behaviorism with sociological perspectives. It is worthwhile, therefore, to spend some time sketching the Skinnerian approach to human behavior in general before assessing its impact on the study of criminal behavior.

Like Watson, Skinner believed that the primary goal of psychology is the prediction and control of behavior. And like Watson, he believed that environmental or external stimuli are the primary—if not the sole—determinants of all behavior, both human and animal. The environmental stimuli become **independent variables**, and the behaviors they elicit the **dependent variables**. In the behavioral sciences, a variable is any entity that can be measured. A behavior (or response) is called "dependent" because it is under the control of (or dependent on) one or more independent variables. The consistent relationships between independent and dependent variables (stimulus and response) are scientific laws. Thus, according to Skinner, the aim of behavioristic psychology is to uncover these laws, making possible the prediction and control of human behavior.

Unlike Watson, Skinner did not deny the existence and sometimes useful-ness of private mental events or internal stimuli. He emphasized, however, that these stimuli are not needed by a science of behavior, since the products of mental activity can be explained in ways that do not require allusion to unob-served mental states. Specifically, mental activity can be explained by observ-ing what a person does, and it is what a person does that counts. Watson, remember, insisted that consciousness and mind simply do not exist. Thought, to Watson, was little more than tiny movements of the speech apparatus.

At this point, we must emphasize the need to distinguish between behav-iorism as a *perspective on human nature* and behaviorism as a *method of science*. As a method of science, behaviorism posits that knowledge about human behavior can be best advanced if scientists use referents that have a physical basis and can be *publicly observed* by others. Since private events that happen inside our heads cannot be seen by others, they cannot be subjected to the rules of science. According to Skinner, behavioral science data must be comparable to be verified or disconfirmed. Otherwise, psychology would re-main a philosophical exercise steeped in armchair speculation and untestable opinions. Self-proclaimed experts could continue to assert that shoplifting is an addiction, just like alcoholism, without being taken to task about the valid-ity of their statements. Only a well-executed, systematic study in which the terms *shoplifting* and *addiction* are clearly spelled out and rigorously tested will advance our knowledge about the accuracy of the shoplifting–addiction connection. Therefore, every psychological experiment, every sentence writ-ten into a psychological report, should be anchored to something that we can all observe or that is testable by another professional. Rather than merely say-ing that someone is anxious or angry, we must identify the precise behaviors that prompt us to make these interpretations. This offers a basis for others, in-cluding the person being observed, to agree or disagree with us. "You're twitching in your chair. You must be bored." "No, I'm not! It's the woolen un-derwear my aunt sent from Vermont."

Concerning behaviorism as a perspective of human nature, Skinner—and a majority of psychologists with a strong behavioristic leaning—embraced the view that humans differ only in degree from their animal ancestry. The behav-ior of humans follows the same basic natural laws as that of all animals. Like Darwin, Skinner saw no radical differences between humans and animals. Even human language and conceptual thinking are nondistinctive. Verbal behavior "is a very special kind of behavior, but there is nothing by way of processes involved that would distinguish it from non-verbal behavior and hence [verbal behavior] would not distinguish man from the [other] animals" (Skinner, 1964, p. 156). To Skinner, therefore, research on subhumans like monkeys, rats, and pigeons has great value; if carefully done, it will reveal lawful relationships between all organisms and their environments.

By recognizing how behaviorism views human nature, we are better able to understand the basic framework behaviorism employs in studying and explaining criminal behavior. It also helps us understand the fundamental recommendations advocated by this perspective for reducing or changing criminal behavior, such as might be found in the management policy of certain correctional facilities.

Clearly, Skinner was also a strong **situationist**. All behavior is at the mercy of stimuli in the environment, and individuals have virtually no control or self-determination. Independent thinking and free will are myths. Animals and humans alike react, like complicated robots, to their environments. The environmental stimuli and the range of reactions are complex and infinite, but with careful research, this complexity is not unmanageable. Complex human behavior can be broken down into more simple behavior, a procedure sometimes referred to as **reductionism**. In other words, complicated behavior can be best understood by examining the simplest stimulus–response chains of behavior. This point brings us to the issue of operant conditioning.

Skinner accepted the basic tenets of classical conditioning but asserted that we need an additional type of conditioning to account more fully for all forms of behavior. Ivan Pavlov conducted a series of experiments on classical conditioning with hungry dogs at the turn of the twentieth century. The dogs did not operate on their environments to receive rewards; the event (food) occurred regardless of what they did. Skinner called this "responding conditioning" and contrasted it with a situation in which a subject does something that affects the situation. In other words, subjects behave in such a way that reinforcement is forthcoming. To uncover this operant conditioning principle, Skinner established an association between *behavior* and its *consequences*. He trained pigeons (apparently less troublesome and less expensive than dogs) to peck at keys or push levers for food. The pecking and pushing are operations on the environment. Operant conditioning, then, is learning either to make or to withhold a particular response because of its consequences. The operation should not be construed to imply self-determination, however. It is simply a reaction to stimuli in order to receive a certain consequence or reward. In this sense, the behavior that emerges from operant conditioning—although not automatic—is no more indicative of free will than is the behavior that emerges from classical conditioning.

The learning that comes about through operant conditioning was described before Skinner's time, but he is credited with drawing contemporary attention to it. In the early nineteenth century, for example, the philosopher Jeremy Bentham observed that human conduct was controlled by the seeking of pleasure and the avoidance of pain. In essence, this is what is meant by operant learning. It assumes that people do things solely to receive rewards and avoid punishment. The rewards may be physical (e.g., material goods, money), psychological (e.g., feelings of importance or control over one's fate), or social (e.g., improved status, acceptance).

Skinner called rewards **reinforcement**, defining that term as anything that increases the probability of future responding. Furthermore, reinforcement may be either positive or negative. In **positive reinforcement**, we gain something we desire as a consequence of certain behavior. In **negative**

reinforcement, we avoid an unpleasant event or stimulus as a consequence of certain behavior. For example, if as a child you were able to avoid the unpleasantness of certain school days by feigning illness, your malingering was negatively reinforced. Therefore, you were more likely to engage in it again at a future date, in similar circumstances—high school dress-up day, class discussion day in a difficult college course, or the day the district supervisor was scheduled to visit the office. Thus, both positive and negative reinforcement can increase the likelihood of future behavior.

Negative reinforcement is to be distinguished from punishment and extinction. In **punishment**, an organism receives noxious or painful stimuli as consequences of behavior. In **extinction**, a person or animal receives neither reinforcement nor punishment. Skinner argued that punishment is a less effective way to eliminate behavior, because it merely suppresses it temporarily. At a later time, under the right conditions, the response is very likely to reoccur. Extinction is far more effective, because once the organism learns that a behavior brings no reinforcement, the behavior will be dropped from the repertoire of possible responses for that set of circumstances.

According to Nietzel (1979), C. R. Jeffrey (1965) was one of the first criminologists to suggest that criminal behavior was learned according to principles of Skinnerian operant conditioning. Shortly afterward, Burgess and Akers (1966) agreed with this and further hypothesized that criminal behavior was both acquired and maintained through operant conditioning. But, as Nietzel points out, most of the direct evidence for this claim comes from experiments with animals. Evidence that the same occurs in humans is scarce and replete with possible alternate interpretations. Nevertheless, neither Jeffrey nor Burgess and Akers relied exclusively on Skinnerian theory. Rather, they combined sociologist Edwin Sutherland's principles of social learning with operant conditioning, particularly the reinforcement aspect, to suggest explanations for criminal behavior (F. Williams & McShane, 2004). We return to Sutherland's theory shortly.

The premise that operant conditioning is the basis for the origin of criminal behavior is deceptively simple: Criminal behavior is learned and strengthened because of the reinforcements it brings. According to Skinner, human beings are born neutral—neither good nor bad. Culture, society, and the environment shape behavior. Therefore, behavior will be labeled good, bad, or indifferent, as society chooses. What is judged "good" behavior in one society or culture may be labeled "bad" in another. Members of one group in a society may believe that it is "bad" for a child to masturbate or to pretend that a block of wood is a toy truck and "good" to hit the child to stop these behaviors. To others, the behavior of the adults who hit the child is "bad." Depending on the severity of the punishment, it may also be aggravated assault.

Skinner was convinced that searches for individual dispositions or personalities that lead to criminal conduct are fruitless, because people are ultimately determined by the environment in which they live. He does not completely discount the role of genetics in the formation of behavior, but he sees it as a very minor one; the dominant player is operant conditioning. According to Skinner and his followers, if we wish to eliminate crime, we must change society through behavioral engineering based on a *scientific* conception of man. Having agreed on rules and regulations (having defined what behaviors constitute antisocial or criminal offenses), we must design a society in which members learn very early that positive reinforcement will not occur if they transgress against these rules and regulations but will occur if they abide by them.

This is a tall order, since the reinforcements for behavior are not always obvious and may actually be highly complex. Property crimes like shoplifting and burglary, or violent crimes like robbery, appear to be motivated in many cases by a desire for physical rewards. However, they may also be prompted by a desire for social and psychological reinforcements, such as increased status among peers, self-esteem, feelings of competence, or simply for the thrill of it. It is a safe bet that much criminal behavior is undertaken for reinforcement purposes, positive or negative. The problem then becomes, How do we identify those reinforcements and how do we prevent them from happening or, at least, minimize their value?

Contemporary psychology still embraces a behavioristic orientation toward the *scientific* study of behavior but has grown cool toward the Skinnerian perspective of human nature. All behaviorists are not Skinnerians. Many find Skinner's brand of behaviorism too limiting (e.g., Bandura, 1983, 1986). While they agree that a stimulus can elicit a reflexive response (classical conditioning) and that a behavior produces consequences that influence subsequent responding (operant conditioning), they are also convinced that additional factors must be introduced to explain human behavior. **Cognitive learning** is also extremely important, for example. Cognitive learning involves the formation of concepts, schemas, theories, attitudes, beliefs, and other mental or abstract versions of the world. Cognitive psychologists, for example, would argue that mental processes are as crucial—if not more so—in understanding criminal action as behavior itself.

This brings us to the topic of mental states and brain-mediational processes, which Skinner urged us to shun. In recent years, many psychologists have been examining the roles played by self-reinforcement, anticipatory reinforcement, vicarious reinforcement, and all the symbolic processes that occur within the human brain. To avoid confusion, we must now begin to distinguish Skinnerian behaviorism from other forms, including social behaviorism (social learning) and differential association–reinforcement.

SOCIAL LEARNING

Early learning theorists worked in the laboratory, using animals as their primary subjects. Pavlov's, Watson's, and Skinner's theories, for example, were based on careful, painstaking observations and experiments with animals. The learning principles gleaned from their work were generalized to a wide variety of human behaviors. In many cases, this was a valid process. Few psychologists would dispute the contention that the concept of reinforcement is one of the most soundly established principles in psychology today.

However, behaviorists also suggested that, since all human behavior is learned, it can also be changed, using the same principles by which it was acquired. This generated a plethora of behavior therapies or behavior modification techniques. Use learning principles to establish conditions that change or maintain targeted behaviors and Voilà! Therapeutic success! The apparent simplicity of the procedures and methods was especially appealing to many clinicians and other professionals working in the criminal justice system, and behavior modification packages sometimes guaranteed to modify criminal behavior were rushed to correctional institutions, including facilities for juveniles. Prisoners (and juveniles) would be rewarded for good behavior with such incentives as cigarettes, canteen privileges, or an extra shower.

But oversimplification is dangerous when we deal with human complexity. Human beings do respond to reinforcement and punishment, and behavior therapy based on learning principles can change certain elements of behavior. Moreover, humans can be classically conditioned, although there are individual differences in their susceptibility. When we lose sight of the person and overemphasize the environmental or external determinants of behavior, however, we may be overlooking a critical level of explanation. Remember that human beings are, in large part, active problem solvers who perceive, encode, interpret, and make decisions on the basis of what the environment has to offer. Thus, internal factors, as well as external ones, may play significant roles in behavior. This is the essence of **social learning theory**, which suggests that to understand criminal behavior we must examine perceptions, thoughts, expectancies, competencies, and values. Each person has his or her own version of the world and lives by that version.

To explain human behavior, social learning theorists place great emphasis on cognitive variables, which are the internal processes we commonly call thinking and remembering. Classical and operant conditioning ignore what transpires between the time the organism perceives a stimulus and the time it responds or reacts. Skinnerian behaviorists claim, "If we can account for the facts by using observable behavior, why worry about the labyrinths of internal processes?" Social behaviorists, however, counter that this perspective offers an incomplete picture of human behavior.

The term *social learning* reflects the theory's strong assumption that we learn primarily by observing and listening to people around us—the social environment. In fact, social learning theorists believe that the social environment is the most important factor in the *acquisition* of most human behavior. They do accept the necessity of reinforcement for the *maintenance* of behavior, however. Criminal behavior, for example, may initially be acquired through association and through observation, but whether or not it is maintained will depend primarily on reinforcement (operant conditioning). For example, if a boy sees someone he admires (i.e., a role model) successfully pilfering from the local sporting goods store, the boy may try some pilfering of his own. Whether he continues that behavior, however, will depend on the personal reinforcement or value it assumes. If no reinforcement is forthcoming (he fails to pocket a baseball because someone else walked into the store or he finds that the gym shorts he stole do not fit), then the behavior will probably drop out of his response repertoire (extinction). If the behavior brings aversive results (punishment), this will inhibit or suppress future similar behavior, but probably not indefinitely.

Several clusters of psychologists are enrolled in the social learning school of thought. Additionally, the discipline of sociology has its own social learning school. We focus first on the work of two prominent representatives, psychologists Julian Rotter and Albert Bandura, since they seem to have the most to offer to the study of criminal behavior from the social learning perspective.

Expectancy Theory

Julian Rotter is best known for drawing attention to the importance of expectations (cognitions) about the consequences (outcomes) of behavior, including the reinforcement that will be gained from it. In other words, before doing anything, we ask, "What has happened to me before in this situation, and what will I gain this time?" According to Rotter, whether a specific pattern of behavior occurs will depend on our expectancies and how much we value the outcomes. To predict whether someone will behave a certain way, we must estimate that person's expectancies and the importance he or she places on the rewards gained by the behavior. Often, the person will develop "generalized expectancies" that are stable and consistent across relatively similar situations (Mischel, 1976). **Expectancy theory**, therefore, argues that a person's performance level is based on that person's expectation that behaving in a particular way will lead to a given outcome.

The hypothesis that people enter situations with generalized expectancies about the outcomes of their behavior is an important one for students of crime. Applying Rotter's theory to criminal behavior, we would say that when people engage in unlawful conduct, they expect to gain something in the form of status, power, security, affection, material goods, or living conditions. The violent person, for example, may elect to behave that way in the belief that something will be gained; the serial murderer might believe that God has sent him on a mission to eliminate all "loose" women; the woman who poisons an abusive husband looks for an improvement in her life situation. Simply to label a violent person impulsive, crazy, or lacking in ego control fails to include other essential ingredients in the act. Although self-regulation and moral development are involved—concepts we discuss in later chapters—people who act unlawfully perceive and interpret the situation and select what they consider to be the most effective behavior in the circumstances. Usually, when people act violently, they do so because that approach has been used successfully in the past (at least they believe it has been successful). Less frequently, they have simply observed someone else gain by employing a violent approach, and they try it for themselves. This brings us to Bandura's imitational model of social learning.

Imitational Aspects of Social Learning

An individual may acquire ways of doing something simply by watching others do it; direct reinforcement is not necessary. Bandura (1973b) introduced this idea, which he called **observational learning** or **modeling**, to the social learning process. Bandura contends that much of our behavior is initially acquired by watching others, who are called models. For example, a child may learn how to shoot a gun by imitating television characters. He or she then rehearses and fine-tunes this behavioral pattern by practicing with toy guns. The behavior is likely to be maintained if peers also play with guns and reinforce one another for doing so. Even if the children have not pulled the triggers on real guns, they have acquired a close approximation of shooting someone by observing others do it. It is likely that just about every adult and older child in the United States knows how to shoot a gun, even if they have never actually done so: "You aim and pull the trigger." Of course, shooting safely and accurately is much more complicated, but the rudimentary know-how has been acquired through **imitational learning** (also called modeling or observational learning). The behavioral pattern exists in our repertoires, even if we have never received direct reinforcement for acquiring it.

According to Bandura, the more significant and respected the models, the greater their impact on our behavior. Relevant models include parents, teachers, siblings, friends, and peers, as well as symbolic models like literary characters or television or movie personages. Rock stars and athletes are modeled by many young people, which is one reason we are exposed to so many public figures touting everything from cosmetics to a drug-free life to beer. Interestingly, the commercial and public service advertisements often miss the point. In observational learning, it is not so much what the model says as what the model does that is effective. If football stars actually avoided the use of drugs in their daily lives, their messages to youth might be more effective. Conversely, the messages that young people do get from sports and entertainment figures encourage, rather than discourage, criminal behavior. Media accounts of stars allegedly engaging in domestic violence, rape, child molestation, assault, illegal gambling, and tax evasion suggest that such behavior is normative rather than to be avoided.

The observed behavior of the model is also more likely to be imitated if the observer sees the model receive a reward. It is less likely to be imitated if the model is punished. Thus, according to social learning principles, convictions of sports and entertainment figures charged with the crimes mentioned above would suggest that the behaviors will not be imitated. Bandura believes—much like Rotter—that once a person decides to use a newly acquired behavior, whether he or she performs or maintains it will depend on the situation and the expectancies for potential gain. This potential gain may come from outside (the praise of others, financial gain) or it may come from within (self-reinforcement for a job the individual perceives as well-done).

Much of Bandura's research was directed at the learning of aggressive and violent behavior. We return to his theory, therefore, in Chapter 7. At this point, however, be aware that a substantial body of experimental findings gives impressive support to his views. For example, preschool children who watched a film of an adult assaulting an inflated plastic rubber doll were significantly more likely to imitate that behavior than were a comparable group who viewed more passive behavior (Bandura & Huston, 1961; Bandura, Ross, & Ross, 1963). Many studies employing variations of this basic procedure report similar results, strengthening the hypothesis that observing aggression leads to hostility in both children and adults (G. C. Walters & Grusec, 1977). In recent years, this research has been extended to viewing media violence and playing violent video games (Dodge & Pettit, 2003). While the research in these areas is not totally conclusive, the growing evidence is that people who observe aggressive acts not only imitate the observed behavior but also become generally more hostile and aggressive themselves (Bryant & Zillmann, 2002; Huesmann, Moise-Titus, Podolski, & Eron, 2003).

To some extent, social learning, as it is discussed by Rotter and Bandura, humanizes the Skinnerian viewpoint, since it provides clues about what transpires inside the human brain (or mind). It draws our attention to the cognitive, mediational aspects of behavior, while classical and operant conditioning focus exclusively on the environment. Social learning theorists use environment in the social sense, which includes the internal as well as the external environment. Skinnerians prefer to limit relevant stimuli to external surroundings.

Differential Association–Reinforcement Theory

Ronald Akers (1977, 1985; Burgess & Akers, 1966) proposes a social learning theory of deviance that tries to integrate the core ingredients of Skinnerian behaviorism, the social learning theory as outlined by Bandura, and the differential association theory of criminologist Edwin H. Sutherland (1947). Akers calls his theory **differential association–reinforcement**. Briefly, the theory states that people learn to commit deviant acts through interpersonal interactions with their social environment.

To understand differential association–reinforcement theory, we must grasp Sutherland's differential association theory, which dominated the field of sociological criminology for over four decades. It was first set forth in the third edition (1939) of Sutherland's *Principles of Criminology* and restated in 1947. Although Sutherland died in 1950, the theory was left intact in Donald R. Cressey's subsequent revisions of the original text (Sutherland & Cressey, 1978; Sutherland, Cressey, & Luckenbill, 1992).

Sutherland believed that criminal or deviant behavior is learned the same way that all behavior is learned. The crucial factors are with whom a person associates, for how long, how frequently, how personally meaningful the associations, and how early they occur in the person's development. According to Sutherland, in our intimate personal groups we all learn definitions, or normative meanings (messages or values), favorable or unfavorable to law violation. A person becomes delinquent or criminal "because of an excess of definitions favorable to violation of law over definitions unfavorable to violation of law. This is the principle of differential association" (Sutherland & Cressey, 1974, pp. 80–81).

Note that criminal behavior does not invariably develop out of association or contacts with "bad companions" or a criminal element. The messages, not the contacts themselves, are crucial. Furthermore, deviant messages or values must outweigh conventional ones. Therefore, Sutherland also believed that criminal behavior may develop even if association with criminal groups is minimal. For example, law-abiding groups—such as parents—may communicate subtly or bluntly that it is all right to cheat or that everyone is basically dishonest. This is an extremely important point that is reiterated when we discuss moral development. Nevertheless, contemporary reviews of differential association theory emphasize that the associations with deviant peer groups have a major effect on illegal behavior (F. Williams & McShane, 2004). What is not known is which came first: the behavior or the associations (F. Williams & McShane, 2004).

Sutherland's theory is probably popular among social scientists because, as one writer put it, "it attempts a logical, systematic formulation of the chain of interrelations that makes crime reasonable and understandable as normal, learned behavior without having to resort to assumptions of biological or psychological deviance" (Vold, 1958, p. 192). The theory also can be applied to the crimes of the rich and powerful as well as the crimes of the economically disadvantaged. In fact, Sutherland was most interested in applying it to white-collar crime, a term he coined. However, the theory is also ambiguous; because of this, it did not draw much empirical research at first (see Gibbons, 1977, pp. 221–228). How are a person's contacts to be measured and weighed? Also, as Cressey (Sutherland & Cressey, 1974) admits, the theory does not specify what kinds of learning are important (e.g., operant, classical, modeling). Nor does it adequately consider individual differences in the learning process. Among some sociologists, however, differential association theory remains popular and continues to attract research interest (F. Williams & McShane, 2004).

Akers (1985) tries to correct some of the problems with differential association theory by reformulating it to dovetail with Skinnerian and social learning principles. He proposes that most deviant behavior is learned according to principles outlined in Skinner's operant conditioning, with classical conditioning playing a secondary role. Furthermore, the strength of deviant behavior is a direct function of the amount, frequency, and probability of reinforcement the individual has experienced by performing that behavior in the past. The reinforcement may be positive or negative, in the Skinnerian meanings of the terms.

Crucial to the Akers position is the role played by *social* and *nonsocial reinforcement*, the former being the more important. "Most of the learning relevant to deviant behavior is the result of social interactions or exchanges in which the words, responses, presence, and behavior of other persons make reinforcers available, and provide the setting for reinforcement" (Akers, 1985, p. 45). It is also important to note that most of these social reinforcements are symbolic and verbal rewards for participating or for agreeing with group norms and expectations. For example, doing something in accordance with group or subcultural norms is rewarded with "Way to go," "Great job," "Good going," a pat on the back, or a friendly grin. Nonsocial reinforcement refers primarily to physiological factors or material acquisition that may be relevant for some crimes, such as drug-related offenses or burglary.

Deviant behavior, then, is most likely to develop as a result of social reinforcements given by significant others, usually within one's peer group. The group first adopts its own *normative definitions* of what conduct is good or bad, right or wrong, justified or unjustified. These normative definitions become internal, cognitive guides to what is appropriate and will most likely be reinforced by the group. In this sense, normative definitions operate as **discriminative stimuli**—social signals transmitted by subcultural or peer groups to indicate whether certain kinds of behavior will be rewarded or punished within a particular social context.

According to Akers, two classes of discriminative stimuli operate in promoting deviant behavior. First, positive discriminative stimuli are the signals (verbal or nonverbal) that communicate that certain behaviors are encouraged by the subgroup. Not surprisingly, they follow the principle of positive reinforcement: The individual engaging in them gains social rewards from the group. The second type of social cue, *neutralizing* or *justifying discriminative stimuli*, neutralizes the warnings communicated by society at large that certain behaviors are inappropriate or unlawful. According to Akers (1977), they "make the behavior, which others condemn and which the person himself may initially define as bad, seem all right, justified, excusable, necessary, the lesser of two evils, or not 'really' deviant after all" (p. 521). Statements like "Everyone has a price," "I can't help myself," "Everyone else does it," or "She deserved it" reflect the influence of neutralizing stimuli.

The more people define their behavior as positive or at least justified, the more likely they are to engage in it. If deviant activity (as defined by society at large) has been reinforced more than conforming behavior (also defined by society), and if it has been justified, it is likely that deviant behavior will be maintained. In essence, our behavior is guided by the norms we have internalized and for which we expect to be continually socially reinforced by significant others.

Akers accepts the validity of Bandura's modeling as a necessary factor in the initial acquisition of deviant behavior. But its continuation will depend greatly on the frequency and personal significance of *social reinforcement*, which comes from association with others.

Akers's social learning theory has received its share of criticism. Some scholars consider it tautological or circular: Behavior occurs because it is reinforced, but it is reinforced because it occurs. Kornhauser (1978) asserted that there was no empirical support for the theory. During the 1980s and 1990s, though, Akers himself—along with research colleagues—published a number of studies supportive of his theory, particularly as it related to drug use (e.g., Akers & Cochran, 1985; Akers & Lee, 1996; Krohn, Akers, Radosevich, & Lanza-Kaduce, 1982). Like Sutherland's differential association theory, Akers' approach retains respectability within sociological criminology.

FRUSTRATION-INDUCED CRIMINALITY

Several learning investigators (e.g., Amsel, 1958; J. Brown & Farber, 1951) have noted that when organisms—including humans—are prevented from responding in a way that had previously produced rewards, their behavior often becomes more energetic and vigorous. Animals bite, scratch, snarl, and become irritable; humans may snarl and become irritable and rambunctious (and may also bite and scratch). Researchers assume that these aroused responses result from an aversive internal state of arousal that they call *frustration.*

Thus, when behavior directed at a specific goal is blocked, arousal increases and the individual experiences a drive to reduce it. Behavior is energized, but more significantly, the responses that lead to a reduction in the arousal may be strengthened or reinforced. This suggests that people who employ violence to reduce frustration will, under extreme frustration, become more vigorous than usual, possibly even resorting to homicide. It also suggests that violent behavior directed at reducing frustration will be reinforced, since it reduces unpleasant arousal by altering the precipitating event or stimuli.

Leonard Berkowitz (1962) conducted numerous studies relating frustration to criminality. He divided criminal personalities into two main classifications: the **socialized offender** and the **individual offender**. You have already met socialized offenders. We have discussed them throughout this chapter as products of learning, conditioning, and modeling. They offend because they have learned to, or are expected to, as a result of their interactions with the social environment. The individual offender, by contrast, is the product of a long, possibly intense series of frustrations resulting from unmet needs. According to Berkowitz (1962), both modeling and frustration are involved in the development of criminal behavior, but one set of life experiences favors a particular criminal style. "Most lawbreakers may have been exposed to some combination of frustrations and aggressively antisocial models, with the thwartings being particularly important in the development of 'individual' offenders and the antisocial models being more influential in the formulation of the 'socialized' criminals" (p. 303).

Berkowitz (1969) adds an important dimension to frustration, suggesting that it is particularly intense if an individual has high expectancy of reaching a goal. People who anticipate reaching a goal, and who feel they have some personal control over their lives, are more likely to react strongly to interference than those who feel hopeless. In the first case, delay or blockage may generate intense anger and even a violent response, if the frustrated individual believes that type of response will eliminate the interference. The power of frustration may well have been what Maslow (1954) was referring to when he stated that crime and delinquency represent a legitimate revolt against exploitation, injustice, and unfairness. The frustration hypothesis also fits neatly into theories offered by radical or conflict criminologists. Individuals who feel suppressed by the power elite and feel they have a right to reap society's benefits may well experience intense frustration at continuing domination.

The frustration-induced theory helps to explain the behavior of looters during unexpected events like floods, fires, urban riots, and electrical blackouts. For example, between April 30 and May 3, 1993, businesses in Los Angeles were burned and looted largely, but not exclusively, by African Americans who were frustrated by a jury's acquittal of four white L.A. police officers in the March 1991 beating of African-American motorist Rodney G. King. Fifty-eight people were killed in the four days of rioting, and damage was estimated to be at least $1 billion. People of all ages and racial or ethnic backgrounds were stealing everything from food and alcohol to firearms and stereos. The rioting triggered smaller uprisings in several other cities, including San Francisco, Atlanta, Seattle, Las Vegas, and Miami. Authorities concluded that the riots were brought on by frustrations with economic, social, and political inequalities found in many sectors of American society, including the court system. The L.A. riot was similar to the August 1965 uprising in the Watts section of Los Angeles, when 34 were killed and 1,000 were injured. The riot was prompted by deeply felt frustrations with the same perceived inequalities in American society. Since 1965, there have been at least eight violent riots in major cities brought on by frustrations with the expanding inequalities found in America.

The frustration-induced theory suggests that individuals who commit larceny in these situations have materialistic goals (e.g., their fair share of middle-class goods) that they have not yet attained. Society blocked the goals, and the individuals became impatient and frustrated. When the opportunity to loot arises, they are there to take it. Demographic profiles of the 2,706 adults arrested and charged with looting during the New York City blackout of 1977 support this theory. The defendants had stronger community ties and higher incomes than the average defendant in the criminal justice system (*The New York Times*, August 14, 1977). Only about 10% were on welfare; approximately half were gainfully employed. Sixty-five percent of those arrested were African American and 30% were Hispanic. These data indicate that the defendants were, in general, eager to eliminate further delays in meeting their expectancy for a better life.

On the other hand, a good argument could be made for a modeling or social learning explanation. The data may represent nothing more than the naive response of a group of violators who modeled seemingly rewarding behavior but lacked the streetwise knowledge to escape detection. The more sophisticated groups, perhaps more representative of larceny suspects as a group, may have looted early and fled. The others, imitating the early groups, were still looting when the police arrived.

Berkowitz hypothesizes that the more intense and frequent the thwartings or frustrations in a person's life, the more susceptible and sensitive the person is to subsequent frustration. Thus, the individual who frequently strikes out at society in unlawful or deviant ways may have encountered numerous severe frustrations, especially during early development, but has not given up hope. In support of this argument, Berkowitz cites the research findings on delinquency (e.g., Bandura & Walters, 1959; Glueck & Glueck, 1950; McCord et al., 1959), revealing that delinquent children, compared to nondelinquents, have been considerably more deprived and frustrated during their lifetime.

Berkowitz also suggests that parental neglect or failure to meet the child's needs for dependency and affection is an internal frustrating circumstance that germinates distrust of all others within the child's social environment. This generalized distrust is carried into the streets and school, and the youngster may exhibit a "chip on the shoulder." The frustration of not having dependency needs met prevents the child from establishing emotional attachments to other people. The individual may thus become resentful, angry, and hostile toward other people in general. Current psychological approaches to delinquency would not disagree but would place far less blame on the parent. They are more likely to recognize the restrictions that parents face as a result of social problems like racism and economic inequality. In addition, contemporary psychologists recognize the influences of other social systems in the juvenile's life, including peers and the educational system.

SITUATIONAL INSTIGATORS AND REGULATORS OF CRIMINAL BEHAVIOR

Most contemporary theories and research support the view that human behavior results from a mutual interaction between personality and situational variables. However, several behavioral and social scientists (e.g., Alison, Bennett, Ormerod, & Mokros, 2002; Gibbons, 1977; Mischel, 1990) complain that much crime research and theory neglects situational variables in favor of dispositional factors. They contend that criminality in many cases may simply reflect being in the wrong place at the wrong time with the wrong people. For example, Gibbons (1977) comments, "In many cases, criminality may be a response to nothing more temporal than the provocations and attractions bound up in the immediate circumstances out of which deviant acts arise" (p. 229). Skinner, of course, exemplifies the position that behavior is controlled by environmental contingencies and events.

Haney (1983) discusses **fundamental attribution error**, which refers to a common human tendency to discount the influence of the situation and explain behavior by referring to the personality of the actor instead. Fundamental attribution error is a concept that applies to making attributions about others, not ourselves. For example, when correctional counselors were asked why inmates had committed the crimes that put them in prison, the counselors cited almost exclusively dispositional or personality factors (such as laziness or meanness) rather than environmental factors, such as upbringing, poverty, or social factors (Saulnier & Perlman, 1981). The inmates, on the other hand, said that the factors they believed landed them in prison were largely external in nature, such as poverty, poor employment opportunities, and physical and sexual abuse. When it comes to ourselves, we engage in **self-serving biases**, in which we tend to attribute good things about ourselves to dispositional factors and bad things to events and forces outside ourselves. For example, when we do well on an exam, we tend to attribute the cause to our intelligence and study habits. On the other hand, when we do poorly, we tend to attribute the cause to a poorly designed or unfair exam.

Haney believes that personality or internal states account very little for how we act. He contends that the important determining influence is the situation in which we find ourselves. In essence, Haney is arguing that, given the appropriate circumstances, anyone might engage in culpable criminal behavior—that we all have our price.

Situations are rarely static. Our behavior influences them to some extent, and they in turn influence our behavior. This reciprocal interaction between person and environment is one reason students of crime are beginning to pay more attention to victimology—victims often influence the course of criminal actions, including violent ones. **Victimology** is the scientific study of the causes, circumstances, individual characteristics, and social context of becoming a victim of a crime. Although victimologists are very careful not to blame victims for the crimes perpetrated against them, they do note that certain actions can facilitate, precipitate, and sometimes even provoke others to commit crime (Karmen, 2001). We discuss this further in Chapter 7. At this point we turn our attention to two situational factors that seem to play a particularly important role in antisocial behavior: authority and deindividuation.

Authority as an Instigator of Criminal Behavior

Sometimes people behave in a certain way because someone with power told them they must, even though the actions do not "set right" with their own principles. Kelman and Hamilton (1989) refer to this phenomenon as "crimes of obedience." "A crime of obedience is an act performed in response to orders from authority that is considered illegal or immoral by the larger community" (p. 46). The classic example of the influence of authority is the military order to kill indiscriminately or to commit some other atrocity, such as Lieutenant William Calley's carrying out the massacre of villagers at My Lai in the Vietnam War. An example of crimes of obedience in a political/bureaucratic context is the Watergate scandal, in which, on June 17, 1972, a group of men under the auspices of the White House burglarized and tried to "bug" the

Democratic National Headquarters in the Watergate apartment complex. Crimes of obedience appear to be widespread in the corporate world, an issue we deal with in more detail in Chapter 11.

In an attempt to delineate some of the variables involved in obedience to authority, Stanley Milgram (1977) designed a series of experiments, using as subjects persons who volunteered (for money) in response to a newspaper ad. The experiments, which eventually received intensive public scrutiny and are now cited in nearly every introductory psychology textbook, studied the amount of electrical shock people were willing to administer to others when ordered to do so by an apparent authority figure.

The subjects were adult males, ages 20 to 50, who represented a cross section of the socioeconomic classes. They were told that the researchers were studying the effects of punishment on memory. The experiment required a "teacher" and a "victim." Unknown to the volunteers, the victim was part of the experiment, a confederate who had been trained to act in a certain manner as part of the experimental design. In a rigged coin toss, the naive subject (the volunteer) always became the teacher, and the confederate the victim. The victim–learner was taken to an adjacent room and strapped into an "electric chair" in the presence of the "naive" teacher.

Next, the teacher was led back to a room where he saw a simulated shock generator—a frightening apparatus with 30 toggle switches presumably capable of delivering 30 levels of electric shock to the learner in the adjacent room. Each level was marked in volts, ranging from 15 to 450, and accompanied by a switch. In addition, labels indicated "slight shock," "danger: severe shock," and beyond, to the "XXX" level. Each time the learner gave an incorrect answer to a learning task, the teacher was instructed to administer a stronger level of shock. The victim, who did not of course receive any shock at all, purposefully gave incorrect answers; he had also been trained to scream in agony, plead with the subject to stop, and pound on the wall when the higher levels of shock were administered.

Milgram wanted to discover how far people would go under the orders of an apparent authority figure (the experimenter). He may have found more than he bargained for. Almost two-thirds of the subjects obeyed the experimenter and administered the maximum shock levels. In subsequent experiments, using similar experimental conditions but different subjects (including both males and females), Milgram continued to find similar results. Interestingly, when Milgram originally asked mental health experts to predict the outcome of this experiment, the majority of them thought that only a pathological few would obey the experimenter's commands to incrementally increase the shock to dangerous levels (Tsang, 2002). The experts apparently discounted the enormous pressures that the experiment placed on subjects and committed the fundamental attribution error, assuming that "the obedient person who obeys evil commands is sadistic and ill" (p. 27).

Many of Milgram's subjects, while obeying the experimenter's instructions, demonstrated considerable tension and discomfort. Some stuttered, bit their lips, twisted their hands, laughed nervously, sweated profusely, or dug their fingernails into their flesh, especially after the victim began pounding the wall in protest (Milgram, 1963). After the experiment, some reported that they wanted to stop punishing the victim but continued to do so because the experimenter would not let them stop. Milgram (1977, p. 118) concluded, "The individual, upon entering the laboratory, becomes integrated into a situation that carries its own momentum."

In subsequent studies, Milgram modified the procedure to include women and to determine more precisely what conditions inhibited or promoted this extreme obedience. For example, he varied the psychological and physical distance between the subject and the victim. To increase the psychological distance between the two, Milgram eliminated the cries of the victim that had been programmed into the original experiment. In another experiment, to minimize the physical and psychological distance between them, the subject sat next to the victim.

In general, Milgram found that the subjects obeyed the experimenter less as physical, visual, and auditory contact with the victim increased. However, the nearer the *experimenter* got to the "teacher," the more likely the teacher was to obey. Milgram found no evidence of significant personality or gender differences in the studies as far as shocking behavior was concerned, but he did find that female teachers were more distressed about their task than their male counterparts were.

The psychological and physical distance variable suggests some interesting implications. If we were to analogize between Milgram's studies and violent actions, we would expect that the more impersonal the weapon or situation (psychological and physical distance), the greater the likelihood for destruction and serious violence. Certainly, killing someone with a firearm at a distance and killing someone point-blank are two different tasks. And both methods differ from choking someone to death with one's bare hands. It would appear that the firearm offers a more impersonal and possibly easier way to eliminate someone and, thus, is more likely to lead to violent behavior. Admittedly, this suggestion makes some quantum jumps from a psychological experiment in an artificial setting, but it is a point worth considering when we discuss the relationship between weapons and violence in Chapter 8.

In assessing the profound influence of commands from an authority figure, we should also pay close attention to the reactions of the subjects in Milgram's study. Individual differences were noted in the way the subjects reacted to the situation, but not in their actual willingness to shock. Although some subjects refused to continue with the experiment when they believed that they were hurting the victim, most (about 65%) administered the full range of shock levels. Most also displayed anxiety and conflict.

Milgram noted a curious dissociation between word and action. Many subjects said they could not go on but, nevertheless, they did. Some justified their action by concluding that the experimenter would not permit any harm to come to the victim. "He must know what he is doing." Other subjects expressed different interpretations and expectancies, such as the belief that the scientific knowledge gained in the experiment justified the method. It is interesting to note that people who have not undergone the ordeal are quite convinced that they would be members of the defiant group who refused to deliver the extreme levels of shock. Later studies conducted both in the United States and abroad confirmed Milgram's findings, however (Penrod, 1983).

Milgram (1974) hypothesized that the subject's obedient behavior could be explained by a shift in the perceived role played by the subject. He referred to this shift in role as an "agentic state," in which "a person sees himself as an agent for carrying out another's wishes" (p. 133). In other words, subjects believe that they are no longer acting on their own accord but for another authorized agent. Tsang (2002, p. 28) notes that Bandura (1999) also theorizes "that many individuals in an obedient situation have a shift in attention from their responsibility as moral agents to their duty as obedient subordinates." Similar points of view have been expressed by Blumenthal (1999) and Kelman and Hamilton (1989).

Milgram suggested that our culture may not provide adequate models for disobedience to authority. Likewise, Kelman and Hamilton (1989) argued that it was important for schools to provide *all* children with opportunities to develop leadership skills and encourage them to be critical thinkers and to question authority in an effective manner. Milgram admonished (1977, p. 120) that his studies raise the possibility that human nature, or, more specifically, the kind of character produced in American democratic society, cannot be counted on to insulate its citizens from brutality and inhumane treatment at the direction of malevolent authority. A substantial proportion of people does what they are told to do, irrespective of the context of the act and without limitations of conscience, so long as they perceive that the command comes from a legitimate authority.

Milgram's theory may account to some extent for immoral or despicable acts committed under the influence of authority. Moreover, Milgram, convinced that situational factors normally override individual factors, would probably find personality or the morality of the individual fundamentally irrelevant in the explanation of the behavior. Other theorists, however, would argue that it is precisely personality or moral development that accounts for resistance to authority. Kelman and Hamilton (1989) would argue that the behavior in high-authority situations most likely is a result of an interaction between personality characteristics and the roles played. Philip Zimbardo (1970, 1973; Haney & Zimbardo, 1998), on the other hand, believes he has demonstrated the overwhelming power of roles in the famous Stanford Prison Experiment and, more broadly, in his concept of deindividuation, to which we now turn our attention.

Deindividuation

Deindividuation theory is based on the classic crowd theory of Gustave Le Bon. The theory, formulated in Le Bon's book *The Crowd: A Study of the Popular Mind* (1885/1995) was introduced into mainstream social psychology by

Festinger, Pepitone, and Newcomb in 1952 (Postmes & Spears, 1998). Deindividuation, according to Festinger et al. (1952), refers to the observation that in crowds or groups, many people lose their sense of individuality and remove self-imposed controls and internalized moral restraints over behavior. Thus, deindividuation is "closely associated with the feeling of not being scrutinized or accountable when submerged in the group" (Postmes & Spears, 1998, p. 240). Philip Zimbardo (1970) extended and further developed deindividuation theory in a number of well-known research projects. For Zimbardo, deindividuation involved feelings of reduced self-observation, and he sought to identify the things that could induce that state (Postmes & Spears, 1998).

Deindividuation, Zimbardo hypothesized, usually follows a complex chain of events. First, the presence of many other persons encourages feelings of anonymity. Then the individual feels he or she loses identity and becomes part of the group. Under these conditions, the individual can no longer be singled out and held responsible for behavior. Apparently this feeling then generates a "loss of self-awareness, reduced concern over evaluations from others, and a narrowed focus of attention" (Baron & Byrne, 1977, pp. 581–582). When combined, these processes lower restraints against antisocial criminal behavior and appear to be basic ingredients in mass violence. However, they also may be at work in nonviolent offenses, such as looting.

In one early experiment, Zimbardo (1970) purchased two used cars and left one abandoned on a street in Manhattan, New York, and the other on a street in Palo Alto, California (population of about 55,000 in the late 1960s). Zimbardo's deindividuation hypothesis predicted that, due to the large population of New York, people would more likely lose their identity and feel less responsible for their actions. Consequently, New Yorkers would be more likely to loot the abandoned vehicle. This is exactly what happened. Within 26 hours, the New York car was stripped of battery, radiator, air cleaner, radio antenna, windshield wipers, side chrome, all four hubcaps, a set of jumper cables, a can of car wax, a gas can, and the only tire worth taking. Interestingly, the looting was not done by delinquents or members of a criminal subculture; all the looters were well-dressed, middle-class whites. On several occasions the looting was done by entire families: children and parents together in a family enterprise.

On the other hand, the car in Palo Alto was untouched during the seven days it was left abandoned. At one point during a rainstorm, a passerby actually lowered the hood to prevent the motor from getting wet. Why such a dramatic difference?

Zimbardo suggests that the anonymity of the New York residents worked in combination with situational cues implying that they could get by without repercussions. Zimbardo's hypothesis contends that in high-population areas, who cares what you are doing as long as you are not bothering others or damaging a concerned party's property? Passersby in New York even stopped and chatted with the looters. In Palo Alto, people could be more easily identified. Moreover, a person engaging in this kind of behavior would expect to be the target of social disapproval or gossip.

Deindividuation is a commonly used concept to explain various expressions of collective behavior such as violent crowds, mindless hooligans, and the lynch mob as well as social atrocities such as genocide (Postmes & Spears, 1998). As we saw from the above car experiment, deindividuation is not necessarily associated with crowds, however. Nor is a massive population required. The effect may be achieved by a disguise, a mask, or a uniform also worn by others, or it may be achieved by darkness (Zimbardo, 1970). Research data suggest that people may be more abusive, aggressive, and violent when their identity is hidden. This phenomenon *might* explain why, throughout history, war paints, masks, and costumes have been donned by warriors preparing for battle (R. Watson, 1973). Even contemporary soldiers, guerrillas, and military advisers are deindividuated by their uniforms. Deindividuation also helps explain the apparent ease with which members of groups such as the Ku Klux Klan regress from being apparently respectable citizens by day to violent, hooded terrorizers by night. Again, however, it is too simplistic to assume that no dispositional or other factors are at work.

The disguise aspect of deindividuation was vividly illustrated in another sobering Zimbardo experiment (1973) known as the Stanford Prison Experiment. Zimbardo and his colleagues simulated a prison environment in the basement of the psychology building at Stanford University, with all the physical and psychological trappings of an actual prison: bars, prison uniforms, identification numbers, uniformed guards, and other features that encouraged identity slippage. (Critics of the experiment have noted, though, that the simulation lacked authenticity in a number of ways, including the sacklike uniforms and stocking caps worn by the "prisoners" and the mirrored sunglasses worn by the "guards" [R. Johnson, 1996].) Student volunteers were screened through clinical interviews and psychological tests to ensure that they were emotionally stable and mature. According to Zimbardo, the subjects finally selected were "normal," intelligent college students from middle-class homes throughout the United States and Canada. They were paid $15 a day for participating.

The experiment required two roles, guard and prisoner, which were assigned by random coin toss. The randomization assured that there were no significant differences between the two groups. The "prisoners" were unexpectedly "arrested" and brought to the simulated prison in a police car. There they were handcuffed, searched, fingerprinted, booked, stripped, "deloused," given a number, and issued a prison uniform. Each prisoner was then placed in a six- × nine-foot cell with two other inmates.

The guards wore standard uniforms and mirrored sunglasses to encourage deindividuation, but as noted above, they were not representative of the attire worn by "real" correctional officers. In addition, they carried symbols of power: a night stick, keys to the cells, whistles, and handcuffs. Before the prisoners could do even routine things (e.g., write a letter, smoke a cigarette), they had to obtain permission. Guards drew up their own formal rules for maintaining law and order in the prison (16 rules in all) and were free to improvise new ones.

Within six days, both guards and prisoners had completely absorbed their roles:

Three prisoners had to be released during the first four days because of hysterical crying, confusion in thinking, and severe depression. Many others begged to be paroled, willing to forfeit the money they had earned for participating in the experiment.

About a third of the guards abused their power and were brutal and demeaning. Other subjects did their jobs as tough but fair correctional guards, but none of these supported the prisoners by urging the brutal guards to ease off. The realism of the prison was apparently striking. "The consultant for our prison . . . an ex-convict with sixteen years of imprisonment in California's jails, would get so depressed and furious each time he visited our prison, because of its psychological similarity to his experiences, that he would have to leave." (Zimbardo, 1973, p. 164)

The situation became such that Zimbardo decided to terminate the experiment during the sixth day, instead of proceeding through the planned two weeks. The experiment prompted him to conclude, "Many people, perhaps the majority, can be made to do almost anything when put into psychologically compelling situations—regardless of their morals, ethics, values, attitudes, beliefs, or personal convictions" (Zimbardo, 1973, p. 164). Much the same conclusion had been reached by Milgram with respect to the influence of authority figures. Although the Stanford Prison Experiment underscores the crucial importance of situational variables in determining behavior, there were still significant individual differences in the way the subjects responded to the conditions. For example, only one-third of the guards became brutally enthralled with their power. Rather than making far-reaching conclusions on the basis of how a total of 21 subjects (both guards and prisoners) responded, it would be much more fruitful to give some attention to individual variables. For example, it would have been helpful to examine the values, expectancies, competencies, and moral development of the participants, in combination with the situational factors. What developmental factors most likely predisposed individuals to act the way they did, and exactly how did they perceive the situation? What did they expect to gain by their behavior? We return to the deindividuation issue when we discuss mass violence in Chapter 8 and offer other perspectives of what happens to people caught up in the excitement of the crowd.

Moral Disengagement

Bandura (1990, 1991) has proposed the **theory of moral disengagement** to explain why people do immoral or heinous acts against their own moral judgment when ordered to so by some higher authority or under high social pressure. According to Bandura, individuals, through social learning, internalize moral principles that bring self-worth when they are maintained and self-condemnation when they are violated. Consequently, it is not simply the power of the situation that determines individuals' actions. Additionally, individuals' moral principles and the ease with which they can become detached from them strongly influence the extent to which they will follow immoral or illegal orders. Bandura further supposes that before persons can engage in behaviors that violate their moral principles, they have to *disengage* their own moral sanctions to avoid self-condemnation. Specifically, "effective moral disengagement . . . frees one from the restraints of self-censure experienced as anticipative guilt for detrimental conduct" (Bandura, Caprara, Barbaranelli, Pastorelli, & Regalia, 2001, p. 127). For example, Bandura, Barbaranelli, Caprara, and Pastorelli (1996) found that delinquents used various methods of moral disengagement, relying most heavily on moral justification and dehumanization of victims. The delinquents could justify certain antisocial behavior by relying on habitual and various forms of moral disengagement from the social standards of conduct. Dehumanization refers to the process of maintaining beliefs that strip people of human qualities or invest them with demonic or bestial qualities (Bandura et al., 2001). "The victims are then seen as subhuman, without the same feelings or hopes as the perpetrators, and thus one can rationalize that normal moral principles do not apply" (Tsang, 2002, p. 41). Dehumanization is covered in more detail in Chapter 9.

In a more recent study, Bandura and associates (2001) discovered that male adolescents, compared to female adolescents, were "more prone to disengage moral self-sanctions from detrimental conduct, were quicker to rouse themselves to anger through hostile rumination, and were less prosocially oriented" (p. 131). These results, the researchers conclude, lend support to the influence of social learning as a major determinant of the frequently reported gender differences in detrimental or immoral conduct. "Girls are substantially more consoling, sharing, helpful, and affectionately demonstrative" (p. 131). Boys, on the other hand, tend to be far less likely to engage peers in discussions of their negative feelings and hostility toward others. Bandura's studies underscore the importance of considering the situation *and* the personal attributes of the person in understanding why people do what they do.

SUMMARY AND CONCLUSIONS

We have reviewed Skinnerian behaviorism, the social learning theories of Rotter and Bandura, the social learning theories of Sutherland and Akers, the Berkowitz frustration theory, and Zimbardo's concept of deindividuation in this chapter. Each emphasizes to varying degrees the importance of learning in the development and maintenance of criminal behavior.

Our perspective of human nature influences what factors we consider paramount in the acquisition of criminal behavior, such as learning factors or the biological determinants discussed in Chapters 3 and 4. Until now, we have focused on the possible origins of criminal behavior: biological factors, classical conditioning, operant conditioning, and observational learning. We have also introduced some of the external reinforcements involved in the maintenance and regulation of criminal behavior. They include tangible rewards as well as social and psychological ones. Collectively, external reinforcements that bring us material, social, or psychological gain are called positive reinforcements. Behaviors that enable us to avoid unpleasant circumstances are negatively reinforced.

Also included in the regulation of behavior is vicarious reinforcement, which consists of both observed reward and observed punishment. When we observe others (models) receiving rewards or punishments for certain behavior, we tend to alter our behavior correspondingly. Models are extremely important in the acquisition and regulation of criminal behavior. They are reference points for what we should and can do in a particular set of circumstances. Therefore, models may act as inhibitors or facilitators of behavior. People internalize the actions and philosophies of significant models, thereby making them part of their own behavioral repertoire and cognitive structure.

In addition to models, situational factors can be important contributors to criminal behavior. We focused in the chapter on the influence of authority figures and the environmental factors involved in the process of deindividuation. People sometimes engage in illegal or violent conduct because they are told or ordered to do so. Some psychologists have searched for individual differences that might predict the extent to which a person will or will not obey an order perceived to be immoral or illegal. In other instances, one's personal sense of identity appears to be lost in the excitement of the crowd. Under these deindividualized conditions, some people—again, not all—may do things they normally would not do. We return to these topics in Chapters 7 and 8.

CHAPTER 6

CRIME AND MENTAL DISORDER

It is a popular misconception that brutal, violent, and apparently senseless crimes are usually committed by people who are mentally ill or "sick." Someone who walks into a business establishment and randomly shoots its customers and employees must be mentally ill. Likewise, someone who sexually assaults, tortures, and kills a four-year-old child has to be sick. How else could these people do this? An alternate explanation focuses on the subhuman perspective: If not sick, they are less than human. Closely related is the view that these individuals are basically evil. Although the latter approaches are gaining ground, perhaps reflecting public impatience with perceived insanity loopholes in the law, there is still wide public subscription to a presumption of mental illness, particularly in the case of outrageous, inexplicable crimes.

The media have been instrumental in developing the connection between mental disorder and crime, particularly serious violent crime. Along with greed and revenge, mental illness is a basic motivation for criminality in the vast majority of crimes on television and other entertainment media (Surette, 1999). John Monahan (1992) cites an early survey (Gerbner, Gross, Morgan, & Signorielli, 1981) showing that on prime-time American television, 73% of all individuals characterized as mentally disordered also displayed some violent behavior. In a later analysis (Shain & Phillips, 1991), 86% of all print stories dealing with former mental patients focused on the violence of the patients, especially if the topics dealt with serial or mass murder.

The tendency to make the connection between crime and mental disorder is not new, nor is it limited to the media. Throughout the history of civilization, there has been a strong tendency to forge this link (Monahan, 1981). Most societies and their legal systems have been confused about and often frightened by mental disorder. In fact, the first mental hospital in the American colonies was established after Benjamin Franklin argued forcefully that the mentally ill were prone to violence and should be confined, involuntarily if need be, to protect society (Monahan & Geis, 1976).

Those who subscribe to the view that the mentally disordered are a threat assume that these individuals do not play by the rules of society, are unpredictable, and cannot control their own actions. Since they are apt to do anything at any given time, these "crazy people" are potentially dangerous. It should be emphasized, however, that the perception that mental disorder inevitably or even frequently leads to violence is not universal. Surveys suggest that only about one-quarter of the U.S. adult population strongly subscribe to such a view (Monahan, 1992). This more realistic appraisal is at least partly due to the efforts of advocates for the mentally ill, who have waged and supported public information campaigns aimed at disseminating truth and alleviating fear. However, while most people may not believe the mentally ill as a group are dangerous, many do believe that senseless or incomprehensible violent acts are the work of someone who must be "crazy" or "sick." Thus, to some members of the public, mentally ill people are dangerous; to others, people who commit bizarre crimes are mentally ill. Still others would subscribe to both views.

DEFINING MENTAL ILLNESS

Before we can examine the validity of the above beliefs, we must define our terms. *Mental illness* is a disorder of the mind that is judged by experts to interfere substantially with a person's ability to cope with life on a daily basis. It presumably deprives the person of freedom of choice, but it is important to note that there are degrees to this deprivation. In other words, even a seriously disordered individual has some decision-making ability. Mental illness is manifested in behavior that deviates notably from normal conduct. However, the word *illness* encourages us to look for etiology, symptoms, and cures and to rely heavily on the medical profession both to diagnose and to treat. It also encourages us to excuse the behavior of persons plagued with the "sickness." The term *mental disorder*, however, need not imply that a person is sick, to be pitied, or even necessarily less responsible for his or her actions. Therefore, although *mental illness* is still used in the psychological, psychiatric, and legal literature, as well as in both civil and criminal law, we prefer the less restrictive *mental disorder*.

Another term that must be distinguished is *mental retardation*, professionally known as developmental disability. This is a cognitive deficiency—measured by "IQ tests"—that cannot be cured. However, many mentally retarded individuals can be provided training and support services to lead productive and independent lives. Even so, mentally retarded individuals are sometimes charged with (primarily minor) offenses that result in their arrest, detention in jail, and serving time. Dual diagnoses of mental retardation and substance abuse have been observed in a significant number of these individuals (Day & Berney, 2001). Misperceptions about the mentally retarded are perhaps not as strong as misperceptions about the mentally disordered, but they represent a population whose needs may go unrecognized by the criminal justice system. Thus, while this chapter focuses primarily on issues related to the mentally disordered, we also give attention to unique problems faced by the developmentally disabled.

Mental disorders are manifested in a variety of behaviors, ranging in severity from dangerous, harmful acts to conduct that is essentially innocuous. Morse (1978) prefers the term "crazy behavior," which he characterizes as behavior that is obviously strange and unusual *and cannot be logically explained*. The person who walks onto the hotel elevator at the lobby level and faces the rear, staring blankly at the elevator's rear wall, while others are facing the front, is exhibiting strange behavior. However, if the elevator subsequently opens at the "back" door, there is a logical explanation: The person is a hotel guest or employee who is familiar with the elevator's setup. In the absence of such an explanation, the behavior becomes disconcerting to the other passengers and, if only mildly, "crazy." In this instance, some clinicians—again in the absence of a logical explanation—might see the behavior as symptomatic of an anxiety disorder or a dissociative disorder, depending on other aspects of the individual's behavior. However, the behavior, as described above, is not dangerous. On the other hand, a person who walks into a hotel lobby in a highly agitated state, brandishing a knife and stating that the hotel employees were all trained by Satan and must die for their sins, is exhibiting both "crazy" and dangerous behavior. There is obviously a crucial distinction between the above scenarios.

The DSM-IV

The concept of mental disorder, therefore, connotes a very wide range of bizarre, dramatic, harmful, or mildly unusual behaviors whose classifications are published in the ***Diagnostic and Statistical Manual of Mental Disorders (DSM)***. Compiled by committees appointed by the American Psychiatric Association (APA), the DSM—now in its fourth edition (DSM-IV; APA, 1994)—is the guidebook for clinicians seeking to define and diagnose specific mental disorders. It is used by virtually every mental health professional in the United States to guide diagnosis and to justify third-party reimbursement for treatment. The current version lists approximately 400 mental disorders (Comer, 2004). Interestingly, approximately half of the people in the United States will qualify for a DSM diagnosis at some point in their lifetimes (Comer, 2004). Diagnoses based on the DSM also are provided to courts in a wide range of forensic settings, including evaluations of competence to stand trial, mental state at the time of an offense, sentencing, and assessments of harm suffered by both victims of crime and plaintiffs in civil suits.

The DSM is reviewed and revised periodically to conform to the contemporary, mainstream thinking of psychiatrists and other mental health professionals. According to a recent edition (DSM-IV, 1994, p. xxi), a mental disorder

> is conceptualized as a clinically significant behavioral or psychological syndrome or pattern that occurs in an individual and that is associated with present distress (e.g., a painful symptom) or disability (i.e., impairment in one or more important areas of functioning) or with a significantly increased risk of suffering death, pain, disability, or an important loss of freedom. In addition, this syndrome or pattern must not be merely an expectable and culturally sanctioned response to a particular event, for example, the death of a loved one. Whatever its original cause, it must currently be considered a manifestation of a behavioral, psychological, or biological dysfunction in the individual.

As noted by Wakefield (1992), there are two basic principles that guide the DSM-IV definition for mental disorder. The first is that the mental condition must have negative consequences for the person. That is, the person must be experiencing some pain, distress, discomfort, or disability. The second principle rests on the assumption that a mental disorder is a dysfunction of some internal process within the person—that is, for some reason, something is wrong. This principle differentiates the disorder from the *normal or expected* internal processes that result from a trauma or tragedy of daily living, such as the loss of a loved one.

It is worthwhile to review some of the changes that have occurred in the DSM over the years. The DSM-III—the manual published in 1980—differed substantially in content from the DSM-I, published in 1952, and the DSM-II, published in 1968. For example, homosexuality—which the psychiatric profession recognized in 1973 was not a mental disorder—disappeared from the 1980 edition. Additionally, the DSM-III added post–traumatic stress disorder (PTSD) in recognition of the psychological suffering experienced by individuals who had experienced a highly traumatic life experience (e.g., war, rape, physical abuse, or a terrorist bombing).

The DSM-III-R, published in 1987, made additional changes, as did the DSM-IV, published in 1994. This latest edition was developed in an effort to maximize empirical input and to minimize subjectivity and bias. A slightly revised version of the DSM-IV called the DSM-IV-TR (TR stands for text revision) was published in 2000 and is the most recent edition available. The fifth edition of the DSM is expected to be released in approximately 2008.

For our purposes, three major changes from the early to the later editions are important: (1) a shift in focus from the *causes* of mental disorders to their behavioral indicators, (2) a reclassification of what were formerly called **neuroses**, and (3) an expansion of the subcategories of **psychosis**. We discuss each of these changes below.

The early DSMs were steeped in psychoanalytic, psychodynamic traditions and etiology. Categories were based on assumed psychodynamic causes, such as the influence of the id, Freud's conception of the unconscious personality. The DSM-III and DSM-III-R tried to eliminate theory and etiology and concentrate on description and classification, although it is debatable to what extent that was accomplished (Charney, 1980; Schacht, 1985; Wakefield, 1992). Since the 1980 version, if there is substantial research or clinical agreement on the causes of a disorder, this information is included; otherwise, there is generally no speculation. Instead, clinicians are offered more detailed, concrete bases for making diagnoses. Each category is described extensively, and its observable behaviors are carefully outlined.

The second major difference is reflected in the committee's decision to drop the label *neurosis*, because there was little agreement about its meaning. Neurosis has been replaced by three separate major categories: (1) **anxiety disorders**, which include phobias, generalized anxiety disorders, and obsessive compulsive disorders; (2) **somatoform disorders**, which include somatization and conversion disorders; and (3) **dissociative disorders**, including amnesias, fugues, PTSD, and multiple personality, now referred to as dissociative identity disorder (DID). Somatoform disorders refer to a pathological concern of individuals with the appearance, health, or functioning of their bodies, usually in the absence of any existing medical condition. Commonly, they have been called "hypochondrias." Since neurosis has been traditionally used to encompass all these categories, the committee recommended that they could still be subsumed under the term **neurotic disorders**. It is preferable, however, to use the distinct categories—anxiety, somatoform, and dissociative disorders.

When we refer to "crazy behavior," we are usually not talking about neurotic disorders, particularly the first two categories mentioned above. Although anxiety and somatoform disorders may be enduring and recurrent, they are also regarded as relatively mild. Generally, these disorders do not result in major problems or discomfort to others in society; only the person affected usually feels the discomfort. In essence, the disorder is an emotional reaction that distresses the individual (and perhaps indirectly those closest to him or her) and that the individual finds unacceptable. However, the person maintains contact with reality, and the behavior typically does not violate strongly held social norms. For example, although agoraphobia (an abnormal fear of open spaces) is a mental disorder (a type of anxiety disorder) from a clinical point of view, it is not the type of "crazy behavior" that concerns the public. Furthermore, anxiety and somatoform disorders are rarely associated with violent, frightening actions; they do not usually play a role in discussions of responsibility for criminal behavior.

On the other hand, the dissociative disorders—e.g., amnesia, fugue states, PTSD, and DID (formerly multiple personality disorder)—can be more troubling. Although it would be a mistake to presume that persons diagnosed with these disorders are dangerous, when some of these individuals have been accused of crimes they have presented the disorders as excusing conditions for criminal conduct, as we discuss later in the chapter. In the recent, sensational film *Identity*, DID saved an individual from execution. In reality, though, such defenses rarely succeed.

A third change in later editions of the DSM revolves around the subcategories of psychosis. In DSM-II, psychosis was a major section comprising schizophrenia, paranoid states, and major affective disorders (severe depression). Psychosis as a separate category does not appear in subsequent editions. Instead, schizophrenic disorders, paranoid disorders, affective or mood disorders (depression), and "psychotic disorders not elsewhere classified" appear as separate major categories. For our purposes, when we discuss research conducted before this change, we retain the labels "psychosis" and "psychotic behavior," which should be viewed as generic terms that can encompass any one of the four disorders just cited. Otherwise, we use the more recent terminology.

Although many other changes characterize the later versions of the DSM, the aforementioned are of greatest concern to us here. Changes in other categories, such as psychosexual disorders, are alluded to as they pertain to the topics being discussed in this text.

We now turn to the specific disorders identified in the DSM that are most likely to be associated with criminal conduct. It must be stressed, however, that (1) persons with these disorders are not "crime-prone;" and (2) even if individuals are diagnosed with these disorders, they still can be held responsible for criminal conduct.

For the present, the four categories of mental disorders most relevant are (1) schizophrenic disorders, (2) paranoid disorders, (3) mood disorders (serious depression), and (4) the personality disorder called "antisocial personality disorder." Note that the first two fall into what was previously called the "psychotic" category. The third was considered in that psychotic category only if serious enough, such as bipolar depression. The fourth is a separate category under the general label "personality disorders." These four disorders are relevant because they are most likely to be associated with violent, serious criminal, or antisocial behavior and are most often cited to support an insanity defense to criminal charges. We review each of these disorders and then assess their relevance to criminal behavior. However, toward the end of the chapter, we discuss less common disorders that, when cited in courts, attract considerable media attention.

Schizophrenic Disorders

Schizophrenia is the mental disorder that people most often associate with "crazy behavior," since it frequently manifests itself in highly bizarre actions. It is a mental disorder that continues to be extremely complex and poorly understood (Andreasen & Carpenter, 1993). The disorder generally begins early in life, often leads to social and economic impairment, and leaves traces on its victims for the rest of their lives (Andreasen & Carpenter, 1993). Behavioral manifestations of schizophrenia are varied, but there are some common characteristics.

Severe breakdowns in thought patterns, emotions, and perceptions are common. Spells of extreme social withdrawal from others are also typical. The thoughts and cognitive functioning of persons with schizophrenia become disorganized and fail to correspond to reality, and their speech will reflect this. The most common example is a loosening of associations, in which ideas shift between totally unrelated and only obliquely related subjects. Thought becomes fragmented and bizarre, and delusions—false beliefs about the world—are common.

The person with schizophrenia is typically inappropriate in emotion or affect (e.g., indiscriminate giggling or crying) or reflects emotional flatness, where very little—if any—emotional reaction is exhibited. The voice is monotonous; the face, immobile and expressionless. The major disturbances in perception are various forms of hallucinations, which involve sensing or perceiving things or events that others do not. The most common hallucinations are auditory, with the individual hearing voices or sounds that no one else in the vicinity hears.

The DSM-IV outlines five characteristic symptoms of schizophrenia, at least two of which must be manifested before a diagnosis can be entertained: (1) delusions, (2) hallucinations, (3) disorganized speech, (4) grossly disorganized behavior, and (5) inappropriate affect. Furthermore, the social interactions, self-care, and/or occupational life of the individual must show signs of being markedly below the level achieved prior to the onset. In addition, there must be continuous signs of the disturbance for at least six months.

The DSM-IV also recognizes five subtypes of schizophrenia: (1) disorganized, (2) catatonic, (3) paranoid, (4) undifferentiated, and (5) residual. Following is a brief summary of the essential features of each subtype.

1. *Disorganized type:* Inappropriate affect (flat, incongruous, or silly emotional responses) and marked incoherence and disorganization in thought patterns. Associated features include grimaces, strange mannerisms, complaints of nonexistent physical ailments, extreme social withdrawal, and other oddities of behavior.

2. *Catatonic type:* Severe disturbances in muscular and voluntary movement. Extended periods of mutism are common. Parrotlike and senseless repetition of a word or phrase just spoken by another person is also common. Prominent grimacing is another frequent characteristic. The catatonic may assume a bizarre posture for long periods of time (usually several hours) and then fly into an overactive, agitated state of screaming and throwing things.

3. *Paranoid type:* Characterized by delusions and hallucinations (usually auditory hallucinations). A person with paranoid schizophrenia may be

convinced that the world is inhabited by extraterrestrials who are plot-ting to take over the world. Another may hear voices commanding him to rid the world of red-haired individuals. Of all the schizophrenic types, the paranoid is the most frequently represented in criminal behavior.

4. *Undifferentiated type:* This type shows psychotic symptoms that cannot be classified into any of the foregoing categories. People with this type display active psychotic features, such as hallucinations, delusions, in-coherent speech, and confused and disorganized behavior, but do not meet the specifications of the other types.

5. *Residual type:* These individuals have had at least one episode of schizo-phrenia, and there is evidence that some of the symptoms are continu-ing. For example, the person may still display blunted emotions or illogical thinking, but no other symptoms.

The DSM-IV identifies a sixth category, *schizophreniform disorder*, a be-havioral pattern that shows at least two indicators of delusions, hallucina-tions, disorganized speech, grossly disorganized behavior, and emotional inappropriateness. It is a temporary disorder and underscores the difficulty in classifying schizophrenic disorders in general. In order to qualify for schizo-phreniform disorder, the symptoms must persist for at least one month but less than six months. If the symptoms continue for more than six months, the clinician is encouraged to classify the disorder into one of the five longer-lasting types.

Delusional Disorders

The **delusional disorders** (also called **paranoid disorders**) are characterized by the presence of one or more *nonbizarre* delusions that persist for at least one month. The judgment of whether the delusion's systems are bizarre or nonbizarre is especially important in deciding between a delusional disorder and schizophrenia. In delusional disorder, the delusions are reasonably be-lievable and not completely far-fetched. An example of a nonbizarre delusion is the belief that a neighbor is spying and attempting to poison one's dog, when there is no evidence to that effect: Even so, neighbors sometimes spy and sometimes do try to poison dogs. A bizarre delusion—more characteristic of schizophrenia—is the belief that the neighbor has disguised herself as a mosquito and is hovering outside one's window.

Delusional disorders often accompany other disorders like schizophrenia, organic mental disorder, paranoid personality disorder, and depressions. How-ever, the essential feature of all delusional disorders is the delusional system, which most often includes persecutory beliefs about being spied on, cheated, conspired against, followed, drugged, maliciously maligned, harassed, or ob-structed. Generally, anger, resentment, and sometimes violence accompany these false persecutory beliefs. Suspiciousness, either generalized or directed at one or more persons, is also common. The DSM-IV (APA, 1994) recognizes seven types of delusional disorders, but the persecutory type is the one most closely associated with criminal conduct, especially violent criminal conduct. Thus, individuals who believe they are being followed by someone intending to do them harm may try to kill or otherwise harm their "persecutor."

Depressive Disorders

The disorders described in this section have a variety of names and diagnostic labels, such as affective disorders, mood disorders, and bipolar depressive disorders. The most common label is **major depressive disorder**. The symptoms include an *extremely* depressed state that lasts for at least two weeks and is accompanied by a generalized slowing-down of mental and physical activity, gloom, despair, feelings of worthlessness, and perhaps frequent thoughts of suicide. Everyone has up and down periods but these mood changes are extreme, and the depression is deep and usually long-lasting. Persons with major depression describe themselves as down, discouraged, and hopeless. A less common form of depression is bipolar depression, in which there are both periods of depression and periods of excessive euphoria called *mania*.

The role of depression in the development of criminal behavior is just beginning to be explored. Preliminary data indicate that depression may be strongly associated with delinquency, especially in teenage girls (Kovacs, 1996; Obiedallah & Earls, 1999; Teplin, 2000). Depression seems to render teenagers—both boys and girls—indifferent to their own personal safety and the consequences of their actions. They just don't care what happens to them, which may increase the likelihood of gravitating toward delinquency. When depressed, people lose interest in life and the activities going on around them, isolating them further from social life and school or work.

Depression also very likely plays a significant role in mass murders, workplace violence, and "suicide-by-cop" incidents, in which a person sets up a situation wherein police are essentially forced to shoot. These incidents are discussed in greater detail in Chapter 9.

Antisocial Personality Disorder

The DSM-III and the DSM-III-R criteria for **antisocial personality disorder** (APD) have been among the most frequently criticized because of their vagueness and lack of empirical anchoring (Widiger, Frances, Pincus, Davis, & First, 1991). The DSM-IV and DSM-IV-TR, however, have tried to address these problems by incorporating more empirically based attributes into the criteria. As mentioned in Chapter 4, many of the new criteria closely follow the Robert Hare definition of the criminal psychopath.

The essential feature of a person with an APD is a history of continuous behavior in which the rights of others are violated. The individual must be at least 18 years of age and must have a history of some symptoms of conduct disorder before age 15. Recall that a diagnosis of Conduct Disorder is reserved for children and adolescents. Before a person can be diagnosed with APD, a pervasive pattern of disregard for and violation of the rights of others must be indicated by at least three of the following behavioral patterns.

1. Failure to conform to social norms or the criminal law, as reflected by frequent performance of acts that are grounds for arrests
2. Irritability and unusual aggressiveness, as indicated by repeated physical fights or assaults
3. Consistent irresponsibility, as reflected in a poor work history or failure to honor financial obligations
4. Impulsivity or a failure to plan ahead (characteristic at all ages)
5. Deceitfulness, as reflected in frequent lying, use of aliases, or conning others for personal profit or pleasure
6. Reckless disregard for the safety of others or self
7. Lack of remorse or guilt for wrongdoings, as indicated by indifference to or rationalization of having hurt, mistreated, or stolen from another

Additional symptoms, as outlined in the DSM-IV, include stealing, fighting, truancy, and resisting authority—typical childhood symptoms. Antisocial personalities (ASPs) lack empathy and tend to be callous, cynical, and contemptuous of the feelings, rights, and sufferings of others. Furthermore, they frequently exhibit precocious and aggressive sexual behavior, excessive drinking, and use of illicit drugs. There is a markedly impaired capacity to maintain lasting, close, warm, and responsible relationships with family, friends, or sexual partners.

On average, ASPs fail to become independent, self-supporting adults. They spend most of their lives in institutions (usually correctional facilities) or remain highly dependent on their families. Other accompanying features include restlessness, an inability to tolerate boredom, and a belief that the world is hostile. ASPs often complain of tension and depression, but they do not usually meet the criteria for a diagnosis of depression. They are often impulsive and unable to plan ahead.

APD occurs more frequently in males than in females. It is estimated that about 3% of the American male population and about 1% of the American female population fall into this category (DSM-IV; APA, 1994). Furthermore, the disorder is more common in lower-socioeconomic populations, partly because it is connected with impaired earning capacity and partly because of the greater likelihood of being raised in an economically disadvantaged, single-parent household with limited adequate role models and resources. Finally, the DSM-IV concludes that the disorder runs in families, possibly due to a genetic link that predisposes the child to antisocial behavioral patterns. Other perspectives would emphasize that family members share the disorder—not because of a genetic link—but because they also share the economic and social background that facilitates it.

Research dating from the 1970s has indicated that ASP is a common diagnosis of criminal defendants and offenders. In an early study, Henn and his colleagues conducted an extensive series of investigations on all defendants referred by a St. Louis, Missouri, court for psychiatric assessment over a 10-year period (Henn, Herjanic, & Vanderpearl, 1976a). Focusing on a sample of 1,195 defendants accused of a variety of crimes and referred for psychiatric assessment, Henn learned that the most frequent diagnosis was personality disorder, accounting for nearly 40% of all the diagnoses. Two-thirds of those classified as personality disorders were specifically designated ASP. The second most frequent diagnosis was schizophrenia (which also included those labeled probable schizophrenia), comprising 17% of the total. The other diagnostic labels (based on the DSM-I and -II) were evenly distributed and of low frequency.

Henn also found frequent references to alcoholism, primarily as a secondary diagnosis, in the diagnostic reports. Alcoholism cut across all diagnostic categories, with the notable exception of schizophrenia, for which only a few cases were reported. The combination of alcoholism and drug addiction as a secondary diagnosis was common in persons labeled ASP. These findings support those reported by Guze (1976), who found the diagnosis of alcoholism prevalent among offenders with a diagnosis of APD.

The pervasiveness of this diagnosis continues today. APD is very frequently offered as a diagnosis in criminal courts and in corrections, sometimes serving as a catch-all category. Researchers have noted that when courts press for a diagnosis, many clinicians will oblige by concluding that an individual qualifies for APD (Melton et al., 1997). In correctional facilities, rates of inmates considered APD range from 30% to 50%, and it is not unusual to find the diagnosis in over 50% of the population (Gacono et al., 2001). APD is such a common diagnosis applied to persons both accused and convicted of criminal offenses that some jurisdictions specifically exclude it from the list of mental disorders that can support an insanity defense.

The validity of APD as a meaningful concept has been debated. Blackburn (1988) contends that there is no single type of abnormal personality that is prone to chronic rule violation. Furthermore, he believes the diagnostic label "antisocial personality disorder" remains a mythical entity that fails to be meaningful for theory development, research, clinical communication, or prediction. Such a concept is little more than a moral judgment masquerading as a clinical diagnosis. Given the lack of demonstrable scientific evidence of clinical utility of the concept, it should be discarded (Blackburn, 1988, p. 511). Others have observed that there remains widespread confusion about the distinction between APD and psychopathy, with many clinicians viewing them as synonymous (Gacono et al., 2001). As noted earlier, the DSM-IV now describes APD in such a way that it is virtually indistinguishable from Hare's concept of psychopathy, described in Chapter 4.

MENTAL DISORDERS AND VIOLENCE

While the mental disorders described above may be associated with a variety of criminal offenses, it is the crimes of violence that are most disturbing. The depressed individual may embezzle funds in an effort to obtain a way out of his dire economic situation. The individual with a delusional disorder may break into a building to seek shelter from those who persecute him. The person with an APD may perpetrate a series of economic scams on unsuspecting victims. Publicity is most likely to accompany criminal behavior when it is violent, however, and the public is most fearful of these offenses, despite the fact that we are far more likely to be victims of economic crimes than violent crimes.

Long-term inpatient care or hospitalization of the mentally disordered is a practice that has largely disappeared. Consequently, the mentally disordered have become a more visible presence within the community. When problems arise, it is often the responsibility of law enforcement officials to handle the situation. This is not because the mentally disordered are dangerous. Rather, it is because they are often without shelter, may be disruptive, and may commit minor offenses, such as trespassing and petty theft. In the 1980s, it was widely acknowledged that jails—and sometimes prisons—were becoming repositories for individuals who could no longer be kept in mental institutions for lengthy periods (Teplin, 1984).

Early research literature consistently supported the position that mentally disordered individuals—even the severely mentally disordered—are no more likely to commit serious crimes against others than members of the general population are (Brodsky, 1973, 1977; Henn, Herjanic, & Vanderpearl, 1976a; Monahan, 1981; Rabkin, 1979). However, more recent research (Klassen & O'Connor, 1988, 1990; Monahan, 1992) finds that this cannot be said of a certain subset of the mentally disordered population. Specifically, male mentally disordered patients, *who have a history of at least one violent incident*, have a high probability of being violent within a year after release from the hospital. Furthermore, schizophrenia seems to be the disorder most closely connected to violence (Blackburn, 1993).

Some research also suggests that *currently* mentally disordered patients are involved in violent behavior far more often than the nondisordered members of the general population (Swanson & Holzer, 1991; Swanson, Holzer, Ganju, & Jono, 1990). This difference persists even when demographic and social factors are taken into account (Monahan, 1992). John Monahan (1992) stresses two things about the research showing a connection between mental disorders and violence. First, the relationship refers only to people *currently* experiencing a *serious* mental disorder. People who have experienced a serious mental disorder in the past and are not showing symptoms currently are not prone to engage in violent behavior. Second, it is still a fact that a great majority (over 90%) of the currently mentally disordered are not violent. Media portrayals of common psychotic killers driven berserk by bloodthirsty delusions are sensational, frightening, and perhaps entertaining, but in reality the phenomenon is rare. Finally, it must be emphasized not only that the mental disorder–violence link relates to the seriously mentally disordered (e.g., paranoid schizophrenics), but also that the relationship is stronger for individuals who also have a history of violent behavior.

Furthermore, it is possible, as some clinicians believe, that the more bizarre violent offenses are committed by the mentally disordered, particularly those categorized as schizophrenic or paranoid. Moreover, the more extreme violence of schizophrenics is typically directed toward family members or acquaintances, and bizarre self-mutilation is more likely than mutilatory murders (Blackburn, 1993). However, Ronald Blackburn (1993, p. 274) admonishes, "Although there appears to be an increased risk in schizophrenia, particularly in paranoid schizophrenia, it must be reiterated that only a small minority of patients in this category are violent, and that the disorder itself is rarely sufficient to account for violent acts in instances where they occur."

Individuals experiencing affective (mood) psychoses are less likely to be violent. When affective psychoses are associated with violence they are usually manifested in women within the context of extended suicide, in which the offender kills herself as well as others in her environment, including her immediate family (Blackburn, 1993). However, as noted in Chapter 9, mass murders in public settings are often committed by men who likely suffered from affective psychoses.

Some of the most current research on the potential violence of the mentally disordered has been conducted by the MacArthur Research Network (Monahan et al., 2001; Steadman et al., 1998). Researchers followed over 1,000 patients discharged from civil psychiatric hospitals in an effort to determine the extent to which they demonstrated aggressive behavior over a one-year period. The patients also had been measured on a wide range of "risk factors"—134 in all—while they were hospitalized. These included such factors as violent fantasies, history of abuse as a child, frequency of parents fighting with each other, and number of negative and positive persons in the social network, to name but a few. The data allowed the MacArthur researchers to develop a risk assessment instrument, the Multiple Iterative Classification Tree, which they believe can help clinicians identify low-, average-, and high-risk individuals. It is worth noting that about half of the discharged patients in this study were in the low-risk group, while the remaining patients were about evenly divided between the average- and the high-risk groups. However, no single risk factor was a significant predictor of violence. As Monahan et al., 2001 stated, ". . . The propensity for violence is the result of the accumulation of risk factors, no one of which is either necessary or sufficient for a person to behave aggressively toward others" (p. 142).

In sum, then, the research on the mentally disordered and violence allows us to conclude the following:

- Past mental disorder alone, even serious mental disorder, is not a good predictor of violence.
- Most persons who are currently mentally disordered are not violent.

- Violence is associated with current serious mental disorder, particularly when a history of violent behavior is also present.
- While researchers have developed some instruments to assess the likelihood that a person will engage in violence, no one factor serves as a strong predictor; violent behavior seems to be a result of an accumulation of risk factors, unique to each individual.

Bonta, Law, and Hanson (1998) argue that psychopathology or mental disorder—past or current—is not a major predictor of criminal conduct and violence in *offenders*—those who have been convicted of crime. Based on an extensive review of the recent research literature, Bonta and his colleagues concluded that offenders with mental disorders were no more criminally prone or violent than offenders without mental disorders. In fact, offenders with mental disorders were less likely to recidivate than nondisordered offenders. Consequently, Bonta and his colleagues concluded that while mental disorders may help predict violent behavior in some offenders, most of the time other factors—such as criminal history, substance or alcohol abuse, and family problems—are more useful in predicting violent behavior.

Police and the Mentally Disordered

During the last quarter of the twentieth century, researchers focused a good deal of attention on interactions between law enforcement officials and the mentally disordered. An early literature review of the criminal behavior of discharged mental patients is instructive (Rabkin, 1979). Rabkin found that a significant number of studies documented a higher arrest rate for discharged mental patients than for the general population, especially for assaultive behavior. Rabkin suggested two explanations for the disproportionate arrest rates. First, a small subset of patients who had criminal records prior to hospital admission continued their antisocial ways soon after discharge from the mental institution. These habitual offenders significantly inflated the arrest rates for all mental patients. In fact, those discharged patients *without* prior criminal records were substantially below the arrest rates for the general population. Second, most criminal offenses after discharge were committed by individuals who had been diagnosed with alcoholism, substance addiction, or APD, all of which appear consistently in the research. Alcoholism and substance addiction are in the fringe areas of traditional diagnoses because they do not represent what are considered serious or typical mental disorders. With respect to APD, as noted above, it was often used when clinicians could find no other way to label a person acting antisocially. When these three categories were omitted, Rabkin found that the arrest rates among the discharged patients, without a criminal history, were comparable to those reported in the general population. "When patients with arrest histories, primary diagnoses of substance abuse, and personality disorders are considered separately, the remainder of the patient group appears to be considerably less dangerous than are those members of the general public who are not mentally ill" (p. 26).

Research has also documented that police may be more apt to arrest the mentally disordered (Teplin, 1984). Trained graduate students in psychology observed 1,382 police–citizen encounters (involving 2,555 citizens) and evaluated the mental status of the citizens according to specific criteria (a symptom checklist that listed the major characteristics of severe mental disorders). The police determined that 506 citizens qualified as suspects, and they arrested 148. The graduate students classified 30 of the 506 suspects and 14 of the 148 suspects arrested as exhibiting definite symptoms of mental disorders. Therefore, the police arrested 20% more individuals with symptoms than without symptoms. Considering that many disordered individuals tend to have annoying symptoms, such as verbal abuse, belligerence, and disrespect, the slightly higher probability of arrest is hardly surprising. To some extent, police also may have taken some of these individuals into custody in order to provide them with shelter. However, police officers failed to recognize the behavior as representing a mental disorder in a large number of cases, believing the individuals were simply being disrespectful and asking for trouble.

In the 20 years since Teplin's now-classic study, significant changes have occurred nationwide relative to law enforcement's handling of mentally disordered individuals. First, police academies are more likely to offer some training in both recognizing and dealing with mental disorders. In some communities, police have taken the initiative to appoint specially trained liaison officers to work with the disordered (Smith, 2002). Second, communities across the nation are establishing specialized courts—mental health courts—that provide diversionary options to jailing and prosecuting the mentally disordered—and the mentally retarded—who are charged with nonviolent offenses or even minor violent crimes, such as simple assault. Rather than being held in jail, they are offered shelter and treatment or training services. Mental health courts are of recent origin and need continuing evaluation before we can conclude that they are effective. However, they offer a promising alternative to the short-term cycles of arrest, jail, court, release, and rearrest that characterize the lives of some mentally disordered individuals.

Mental Disorders Among the Incarcerated

Mental disorders in those incarcerated in prison and jail are sometimes cited as evidence of a link between crime and abnormal behavior. The incidence and nature of disorders among these populations are difficult to determine, however. Research reveals, for example, that the rates of serious mental disorders among prison inmates vary widely, ranging from 5% to 16% psychotic (Teplin, 1990). Among a sample of adult male jail detainees in Cook County (Chicago), Teplin (1990) found that 9.5% had experienced a severe mental disorder (schizophrenia, mania, or major depression) at some point in their lives, compared to 4.4% of males in the U.S. general population. Robins and Regier (1991) found that 6.7% of prisoners had suffered from schizophrenia at some point in their lives, compared to 1.4% of the U.S. population. In the New York correctional system, it is estimated that about 8% of the inmates have "severe" mental disorders and another 16% have "significant" mental disorders (Steadman et al., 1987). However, it is unclear whether the mental disorders were present prior to incarceration or developed as a result of being incarcerated. In addition, it is often not clear from the research what percentage of the disordered have been diagnosed with APD, the catch-all category discussed above.

More recent data suggest that the numbers may be increasing. A Bureau of Justice Statistics survey (1999), estimated that 238,000 mentally disordered offenders were incarcerated in U.S. prisons and jails in 1998. Overall, 16% of all state prison and local jail inmates and 7% of federal prisoners reported that they had a mental disorder or had stayed overnight in a mental hospital or treatment program (see **Table 6–1**). It is obvious that prison conditions can have deleterious effects on mental states. Therefore, an individual may become mentally disordered after being institutionalized, which may be reflected in these statistics. We assess the potential deleterious effects of imprisonment more fully in Chapter 13. However, considerable evidence indicates that many inmates or prisoners were showing signs of mental disorders prior to incarceration (Bureau of Justice Assistance, 2000).

Young offenders—including juveniles—may be more likely than adults to be diagnosed with mental disorder. Linda Teplin (2000) found that two-thirds of juveniles in a sample of more than 1,800 youths held in Chicago's Cook County Juvenile Temporary Detention Center tested positive for at least one drug, and two-thirds were diagnosed with at least one mental disorder. A considerable portion of the mental disorders in these juveniles consisted of

TABLE 6–1   Percentages of State Prisoners Considered Mentally Disordered and the Offenses That Led to Their Incarceration, 1998

OFFENSE	MENTALLY DISORDERED INMATES (%)	OTHER INMATES (%)
Violent	52.9	46.1
Murder	13.2	11.4
Sexual assault	12.4	7.9
Robbery	13.0	14.4
Assault	10.9	9.0
Property	24.4	21.5
Drug	12.8	22.2
Public order	9.9	9.8
Criminal history		
No	18.8	21.2
Yes	81.2	78.8

Source: Bureau of Justice Statistics (1999).

major depressions, especially among female juveniles. The Teplin study, known as the Northwestern Juvenile Project, strongly suggests that many mentally disordered juveniles are also abusing drugs and alcohol quite extensively at the time of their arrest.

In sum, although the statistical information is somewhat limited, few experts disagree that a significant number of mentally disordered individuals enter and remain within the criminal justice system. The next section focuses on the mentally disordered once they reach the criminal courts and once they are jailed or imprisoned. Key questions asked are the extent to which they are able to participate in court proceedings and whether they can be held criminally responsible for the offenses with which they have been charged. In other words, does their mental disorder hinder their ability to help their lawyers, and is their mental disorder an *excusing condition?* Once the mentally disordered are convicted, questions arise about the treatment they should receive and the risk that they will commit more crime if they are released. For some, decisions about their transfer from prisons to mental health facilities must be made. We discuss each of these issues with the exception of treatment in the following section. Treatment is covered in Chapter 13.

MENTALLY DISORDERED DEFENDANTS AND OFFENDERS

Four categories of individuals are included: (1) defendants found *incompetent to stand trial*; (2) individuals found *not guilty by reason of insanity*; (3) *mentally disordered sex offenders*; and (4) mentally disordered inmates, including those administratively transferred from a prison to a mental hospital ("transfers"). The first three categories have been adjudicated by the courts, and most have been committed involuntarily to a security section of a mental hospital (or hospital prison), presumably for psychotherapeutic reasons. Occasionally, the mentally disordered are allowed to remain in the community but are subjected to a regimen of outpatient therapeutic services.

Incompetent to Stand Trial

Some persons charged with a crime are considered so intellectually and/or psychologically impaired that—were they to be tried—they would be present in body but not in mind. The U.S. Supreme Court has determined that the trial of such an individual violates the Constitution. Specifically, defendants are competent to stand trial if they have "sufficient present ability to consult with their lawyer with a reasonable degree of rational understanding . . . and a rational as well as factual understanding of the proceedings . . ." (*Dusky v. U.S.*, 1960, p. 402). To protect the rights of the individual and to preserve the dignity of the court process, the law states that a person who is incompetent must not be tried.

The competency issue does not relate just to the actual trial, however. In fact, some scholars now prefer to use the term **adjudicative competence** rather than competence to stand trial (e.g., Bonnie & Grisso, 2000; Mumley, Tillbrook, & Grisso, 2003; Nicholson & Norwood, 2000). The former term relates to the ability to participate in a wide variety of court proceedings and court-related activities, including plea bargaining, preliminary hearings, and other pretrial hearings related to one's case. It also encompasses two distinct concepts: (1) the competence to proceed (which implies understanding the purpose of the proceedings and being able to help one's attorney) and (2) decisional competence (which implies the ability to comprehend the significance of various decisions to be made) (Mumley et al., 2003). If a criminal defendant is found **incompetent to stand trial** (IST), the court has essentially determined that he or she cannot understand the process that is occurring or effectively participate in it.

The competency issue can be raised at any time during the actual proceedings. For example, a defendant may be competent up to and into the beginning phases of a trial, but during a long and protracted trial he or she may become incompetent. A defendant also may be competent before and during trial but may be ruled incompetent at the time of sentencing.

Evaluations for competency to stand trial represent the most common referral for criminally related forensic assessments (Cruise & Rogers, 1998). Most typically, defendants referred for competency evaluation have a history of psychiatric care or institutionalization or exhibited signs of mental disorder at arrest or while detained in jail. Data indicate that approximately 25,000 criminal defendants nationwide, or about 1 in 15, are evaluated each year by state and federal courts for their competency to stand trial (Cruise & Rogers, 1998; Nicholson & Kugler, 1991). About four of every five of these evaluated defendants are found competent (Grisso, 1986; Nicholson & Kugler, 1991; Roesch, Zapf, Golding, & Skeem, 1999).

Interestingly, mental health clinicians have been criticized extensively in the literature for the poor quality of their assessments, even sometimes confusing competence with criminal responsibility (Skeem & Golding, 1998). In recent years, the quality of the assessments has improved, though examiners are still faulted for not making sufficient use of the competence assessment tools developed by researchers or providing adequate explanations to judges in their reports (Nicholson & Norwood, 2000).

It is important to emphasize the distinction between incompetence to stand trial and insanity, the legal concept discussed below. Although they may be related, the two concepts are distinct and should be assessed separately—although this is not always done. Criminal responsibility, which is at the core of the insanity defense, and competency to stand trial refer to a defendant's mental state/capacity at *two different points in time*. If a defendant pleads not guilty by reason of insanity, the law asks, "What was the defendant's state of mind at the time the offense was committed?" In competency considerations, the question becomes, "What is the defendant's state of mind at the present time, or at the time of the pretrial proceedings or trial?" An individual who was seriously mentally disordered at the time of an offense and whose criminal responsibility is questionable may have enough mental stability by the time of the trial to be competent to stand trial. On the other hand, a person may be of sound mind during the unlawful act but may later become disordered or disoriented and be determined incompetent to stand trial.

If found IST—a decision that must be made by the presiding judge—the defendant is typically sent to a mental institution or, less frequently, to an outpatient therapeutic program, until rendered competent. For those defendants who are restored to competency, some research suggests that the average time needed for restoration is about three months (Hoge et al., 1996). In a recent survey of mental health program directors across the United States, Miller (2003) found that outpatient treatment to restore competency was rare. Outpatient *evaluations* of competency were on the rise, however.

Until the 1970s, the typical procedure for evaluating competency required that defendants be confined within a maximum-security institution for a lengthy psychiatric–psychological evaluation (usually 60 to 90 days). Following evaluation, the defendant was granted a hearing on the matter of competency. If the court found the defendant unable to understand the charges or the judicial proceedings, or to help counsel in his or her defense, then the defendant would automatically be committed to a secure hospital for an indefinite period of time—until competent. Theoretically, this indefinite time period could extend—and sometimes did—into a lifetime of involuntary commitment.

In 1972, in *Jackson v. Indiana*, the Supreme Court declared that such an indefinite confinement violated the Constitution. While the Court allowed the confinement, it specified that if no progress was made toward competence, the individual must be released or must be recommitted under civil, not criminal statutes. Today, individuals found IST with little likelihood of being restored to competency often have their cases dismissed. However, in many jurisdictions, the prosecutor still retains the option of reinstituting charges if the person regains competency at some later time. While this is unlikely to happen, it satisfies the public's need for accountability, particularly if the crime was a serious one.

In recent years, ISTs have asserted additional constitutional rights in connection with their status, including the right to the "least restrictive or drastic alternative," specifically the right to be treated in a community setting rather than in an institution. As noted above, though, recent research suggests that community treatment is not the typical approach (Miller, 2003). In addition, because treatment is often offered in the form of psychoactive drugs, some defendants ruled IST have argued that they should not be forced to take these drugs. Psychoactive drugs are "those drugs that exert their primary effect on the brain, thus altering mood or behavior, or that are used in the treatment of mental disorders" (Julien, 1992, p. xii). Although these drugs have been improved considerably over the past two decades, many have side effects—including in some cases debilitating side effects—and are resisted by many patients.

In the latest Supreme Court ruling on this matter (*Sell v. U.S.*, 2003), the Court ruled that, in a case that did not involve violence, courts must be wary of ordering such medication against a defendant's will. Sell, a former dentist charged with insurance fraud, had been found incompetent and was hospitalized for treatment. He had a history of mental disorder and had prior hospitalizations, during which he had received psychoactive drugs. Psychiatrists again prescribed psychoactive drugs in an effort to render him competent to stand trial, but Sell refused to take them. Both a trial judge and a federal court of appeals ruled against him, but the U.S. Supreme Court did not agree. The Court noted that the trial court had not adequately weighed the advantages and disadvantages of the drugs, and it sent the case back to the court to do just that. However, for serious, violent crimes, where the government has a strong interest in bringing a defendant to trial, the Court has been less sympathetic to the defendant, refusing to hear an appeal of an order for involuntary medication (*U.S. v. Weston*, cert. denied). Rusty Weston is the individual charged with the lethal shooting of two Capitol police officers in 1998 and the nonlethal shooting of two other individuals. In light of the nature of the crimes, Weston's long history of serious mental illness, and the government's strong interest in bringing him to trial, courts have ruled in favor of the involuntary medication. Even so, the lower court in Weston's case had given careful consideration to the advantages and disadvantages of ordering the medication.

Research on persons found IST indicates that they are highly similar in background characteristics. Most have limited social and occupational skills and a history of criminal charges and psychiatric hospitalizations (W. Williams & Miller, 1981). Compared to the general population, ISTs are disproportionately unmarried, African American, and poorly educated (less than ninth-grade education) (Steadman, 1979). More recent research has continued to support these earlier findings (Nicholson & Kugler, 1991; Roesch, et al., 1999). However, these differences do not hold when we compare persons referred for evaluations and ultimately found competent to those referred and ultimately found incompetent. Competent and incompetent defendants do not differ significantly on demographic variables such as race, gender, and marital status (Nicholson & Kugler, 1991; Riley, 1998; Rosenfeld & Ritchie, 1998). They do differ, not surprisingly, on clinical variables. Thus, persons found incompetent are more likely to be diagnosed with a psychotic disorder or organic mental disorder (Warren, Rosenfeld, Fitch, & Hawk, 1997) or schizophrenia and affective disorders (Hoge et al., 1997).

The offense charged seems to play some part in the ultimate competency decision, but the research in this area is quite mixed. A meta-analysis by Nicholson and Kugler (1991) indicated that individuals adjudicated IST are much more likely than other criminal defendants to be charged with violent offenses. However, Warren et al. (1997) found that public order offenses were more likely to yield a finding of incompetence than were serious charges like homicide and sex offenses. Rosenfeld and Ritchie (1998) found that misdemeanor defendants were more likely to be found incompetent than felony defendants. Mumley et al.

(2003) surmise that these differences may be due to the clinical diagnosis; in other words, persons with more severe diagnoses may be charged with less serious offenses. IST defendants are often diagnosed psychotic or with other serious mental disorders. Nicholson and Kugler (1991) conclude: "Defendants who manifested disorientation and impaired memory, poor judgment, thought and communication disturbances, hallucinations, delusions, and bizarre, unmanageable behavior were considered unfit to proceed to trial more often than defendants who did not exhibit such symptoms" (p. 364).

In recent years, far more attention has been given to the issue of mentally retarded individuals and adjudicative competence. As Mumley et al. (2003) noted, "Unlike psychotic defendants, persons with mental retardation often do not show obvious signs of poor understanding or reasoning, so that attorneys may be less capable of identifying those who are in need of AC (adjudicative competence) evaluation" (p. 343). Consequently, we have little information on the extent to which mentally retarded defendants are referred for competency evaluation, and virtually no information on the proportion of IST defendants who are mentally retarded. However, researchers are developing instruments and guidelines for the assessment of competence in mentally retarded individuals (e.g., Coles, Freitas, & Tweed, 1996; S. Smith & Hudson, 1995).

The Mentally Disordered and Criminal Responsibility

The best known of the mentally disordered groups discussed here, due to widespread publicity, are those found **not guilty by reason of insanity** (NGRI). Insanity is a legal term, not a psychiatric or psychological one; for our purposes, it should be used only in the context of a criminal offense. Insanity refers to a person's *state of mind at the time an offense was committed.* When an individual is found not guilty by reason of insanity, a judge or jury have determined that the person was so mentally disordered at the time of the crime that he or she should not be held responsible. The law assumes that mental disorder *can* rob an individual of free will or the ability to make appropriate choices. Note that insanity should not be *equated* with mental disorder, even serious mental disorder. That is, a mentally disordered person can still be found responsible for committing a criminal offense. Likewise, an individual who is mentally retarded can still be held criminally responsible.

Insanity defenses, especially if they relate to a violent crime and are successful, receive extensive media coverage and commentary. When John Hinckley, charged with an attempt on the life of President Reagan, was found NGRI by a federal jury, there was widespread public indignation accompanied by numerous demands for repeal of the insanity defense in both federal and state law. Since the Hinckley acquittal by reason of insanity in June 1982, at least 34 states have made some kind of alteration to their insanity statutes (Steadman et al., 1993). Moreover, in response to the public outcry against the Hinckley acquittal, the U.S. Congress passed the *Insanity Defense Act of 1984,* which is discussed below. Virtually all of these legal changes made it more difficult for defendants who wished to plead NGRI.

It is important to note that the number of insanity defenses raised in the United States is believed to be very small compared to the total number of criminal cases. Furthermore, despite the outcry after the Hinckley verdict, insanity defenses are rarely successful. Unfortunately, there are no *systematic, nationwide* data on how often the insanity defense is actually used (McGinley & Paswark, 1989). County, state, and federal levels of government rarely share information about these issues (Steadman et al., 1993). Steadman and his colleagues write, "County level information on insanity pleas, for example, is rarely, if ever, aggregated to the state level, meaning almost nothing is known about the earliest stages of the insanity defense process" (p. 3). However, there are some very good estimates based on studies conducted by independent and governmental researchers. These researchers estimate that insanity defenses are used in only 1% of all U.S. felony criminal cases (Callahan, Steadman, McGreevy, & Robbins, 1991; Golding, Skeem, Roesch, & Zapf, 1999).

Data on acquittals suggest that the defense is typically not successful. In an eight-state study of 9,000 defendants who pleaded NGRI, Callahan et al. (1991) found a 22% to 25% success rate. Other studies have reported wide statewide differences, with a high of 44% in Colorado and a low of 2% in Wyoming (McGinley & Paswark, 1989). Cirincione and Jacobs (1999) found a mean of only 33.4 insanity acquittals per year across 35 states over the period 1974–1995. More importantly, acquittals seem to be closely tied to the diagnosis given to the defendant and, to some extent, to the crime charged (Cochrane, Grisso, & Frederick, 2001; Warren et al., 1997). Cochrane et al. found that federal defendants with diagnoses of psychotic disorders, affective disorders, and mental retardation had higher rates of acquittal than those diagnosed with other disorders. Personality disorders were negatively correlated with a finding of insanity. Recall that many states specifically exclude APD as a mental disorder to support an insanity defense. Warren et al. (1997) found that defendants charged with violent crimes against others had the highest acquittal rates, while sex offenders were significantly more likely to be *convicted*. Nevertheless, the research literature strongly indicates that the clinical diagnosis, more than the offense, seems to be the critical factor. This also explains the low acquittal of sex offenders, because these offenders are often not considered by clinicians to be mentally disordered.

In the United States, acquittals are far more difficult to obtain from juries (jury trials) than from judges (bench trials), a pattern that underscores the pervasive negative attitude the American public has toward the insanity defense. For instance, in their eight-state study, Callahan et al. (1991) found that only 7% of the acquittals were handed down by juries. In another study, Boehnert (1989) found that 96% of defendants found NGRI had gone before a judge. Thus, it seems wise for defendants who plan to use the insanity defense to have a bench trial (where the judge decides) rather than a jury trial. On the other hand, recent research suggests that, if jurors are informed of the consequences of an NGRI verdict—specifically that the defendant will likely be hospitalized for treatment—they may be more likely to acquit the defendant (Wheatman & Shaffer, 2001).

Callahan et al. (1991) found that successful NGRI defendants, compared to unsuccessful defendants, tended to be older, female, better educated, and single. They also had a history of hospitalization and were considered extremely disturbed. Furthermore, 15% of the acquitted defendants had not themselves raised the insanity defense, indicating that they were so disordered that an insanity verdict was essentially imposed on them. The tragic case of Andrea Yates, the Texas woman who drowned her five children in a bathtub in 2001, is inconsistent with several of the above criteria, however. Yates had some college education and a history of serious mental disorder, including postpartum psychosis, and hospitalization. Despite evidence of disorder— which even the prosecutor acknowledged—Yates was convicted and sent to prison. On the other hand, in April 2004, also in Texas, 39-year-old Deanna Laney was found NGRI of the bludgeoning deaths of her six- and eight-year-old sons. A third boy, a two-year-old, was severely assaulted but survived. A jury determined she was mentally ill and did not know the difference between right and wrong.

Defense attorneys generally do not recommend that their clients plead NGRI unless they are charged with a serious offense and the evidence against them is overwhelming. Nevertheless, it is a mistake to think that defendants charged with misdemeanor offenses do not raise this defense; it is sometimes used to obtain treatment for mentally disordered individuals who might not otherwise be eligible for institutionalization. However, when the possible penalty is capital punishment or life imprisonment without parole, an insanity defense becomes more palatable to the defense. In many jurisdictions, however, insanity acquittees are immediately confined to a mental institution, where they are kept for as long as needed to produce substantial improvement in their condition. In fact, research shows that persons found NGRI on average spend at least as much time in mental institutions or treatment facilities as they would have spent in prison if convicted (Golding et al., 1999). Moreover, the individual can be required to bear the burden of proving that he or she is no longer mentally ill. John Hinckley is a case in point. Hospitalized since his acquittal in 1981, Hinckley has argued that his mental illness is now in remission. He has been allowed out of the institution for supervised day trips and visits, and he recently convinced a court to allow him to go to his parents' home for unsupervised, overnight visits. Eventually, Hinckley will almost assuredly seek total release from the institution.

When that happens, the ultimate determination of whether he remains mentally ill will be a critical factor. In 1992, the U.S. Supreme Court placed some limits on the hospital confinement of persons found NGRI. In *Foucha v. Louisiana*, the Court ruled that they may not be held in psychiatric facilities once they are no longer mentally disordered, even if it could be argued that they are dangerous. Foucha had been hospitalized for four years. While a committee of mental health practitioners found his mental illness to be in remission, they could not certify that he was no longer dangerous. Nevertheless, a divided Supreme Court (five to four) ruled that, if no longer mentally ill, Foucha should be discharged. Critics of the *Foucha* decision maintain that the Court did not sufficiently recognize the recurring quality of serious mental disorders. While they may go into remission, persons suffering from them are not necessarily cured (Golding et al., 1999). On the other hand, it is difficult to justify holding an individual who is not disordered on the premise that at some point in the future the disorder is likely to reappear. In many jurisdictions, such individuals are now released conditionally or on community treatment orders. This allows mental health authorities to monitor their progress and assure that they are taking the medication that presumably keeps them stabilized and their mental disorder in remission.

Thus far we have discussed the consequences of a finding of NGRI. In the following section, we cover a variety of standards that courts use to decide whether a defendant was insane at the time of the offense.

Insanity Standards. The insanity defense has been recognized in English courts for over 700 years (Simon, 1983). Since the American legal system is derived from British law, American courts have generally recognized it as well. Standards or tests to determine insanity vary widely among the states, but they usually center around one of three broad models: the M'Naghten Rule, the Brawner Rule, or the Durham Rule (see **Table 6–2**). Moreover, all the insanity

TABLE 6–2   Standards for Criminal Responsibility

STANDARD	YEAR FIRST USED	DESCRIPTION
M'Naghten Rule	1843	It must be clearly proved that at the time of committing the act, the party accused was laboring under such a defect of reason, from disease of the mind, as not to know the nature and quality of the act he was doing; or if he did know it, he did not know he was doing what was wrong.
Durham Rule	1954	An accused is not criminally responsible if the unlawful act was the product of mental disease or mental defect.
Brawner/ALI Rule	1972	A person is not responsible for criminal conduct if at the time of such conduct as a result of mental disease or defect, he lacks substantial capacity to either appreciate the criminality [wrongfulness] of his conduct or to conform his conduct to the requirements of the law.
Insanity Defense Reform Act	1984	A person charged with a criminal offense should be found not guilty by reason of insanity if it is shown that, as a result of mental disease or mental retardation, he was unable to appreciate the wrongfulness of his conduct at the time of his offense.
Guilty but mentally ill	1975	Holds the defendant blameworthy for the offense, but recognizes the presence of a mental disorder

standards are fundamentally based on two criteria: **irrationality** and **compulsion** (Morse, 1986). If it can be established that a person was not in control of his or her mental processes (was thinking irrationally) and/or was not in control of his or her behavior (was driven by compulsion) at the time of the offense, then there are grounds for absolving that person of some or all responsibility for the offense. Jurisdictions, however, differ in the extent to which they accept both these criteria. That is, some jurisdictions accept both criteria, while others accept only the irrationality component.

The M'Naghten Rule: The Right and Wrong Test. The **M'Naghten Rule** has been around in some form since at least the 18th century. The current rule was formulated in 1843, after Daniel M'Naghten, a Scottish woodcutter, was acquitted of killing a man he believed to be the prime minister. M'Naghten thought he was being persecuted by the Tories and their leader, Prime Minister Sir Robert Peel. He fired a shot into a carriage transporting Peel's secretary, Edward Drumond, thinking Peel himself was in the carriage. There was no question that M'Naghten had committed the act, but the court believed he was so mentally deranged that it would be inhumane to convict him. Applying a "wild beast" test in use at the time, the court concluded that it was clear he was not in control of his faculties. He was committed to the Broadmoor Mental Institution, where he remained until his death 22 years later. It was widely believed that M'Naghten "knew" his actions were wrong and that he should have been convicted. Therefore, the law was changed to prevent a similar "miscarriage of justice" in the future. Thus, the rule that bears M'Naghten's name is not the rule under which he was tried.

In 1851, the M'Naghten Rule was adopted in the federal and most state courts in the United States. It is deceptively simple, and therein lies its popularity. It states that a person is not responsible for a criminal act if "at the time of committing the act, the party accused was labouring under such a defect of reason, from disease of the mind, as not to know the nature and quality of the act he was doing; or if he did know it . . . he did not know he was doing what was wrong" (*M'Naghten*, 1843, p. 718). Essentially, the rule states that if a person, because of some mental disease, did not know right from wrong at the time of an unlawful act, or did not know that what he or she was doing was wrong, that person cannot be held responsible for the actions. This is what a jury decided in the case of Deanna Laney, mentioned above.

Thus, the M'Naghten Rule, sometimes referred to as the **right and wrong test**, emphasizes the *cognitive elements* of (1) being aware and knowing what one was doing at the time of the illegal act and (2) knowing or realizing right from wrong in the moral sense. The rule recognizes no degree of incapacity. You are either responsible for the action or you are not. There are no in-betweens.

Some states supplement M'Naghten with an irresistible impulse test, which has similarities to the wild beast test applied in the original M'Naghten case. The irresistible impulse test recognizes or assumes that people may realize the wrongfulness of their conduct, and be aware of what is right or wrong in a particular set of circumstances, but still be powerless to do right in the face of overwhelming pressures from uncontrollable impulses. In other words, there are conditions under which people presumably cannot help themselves. The M'Naghten Rule alone would not cover those circumstances, since it requires that the person did not know right from wrong.

The Brawner Rule and the American Law Institute (ALI) Rule.   The **Brawner Rule**, which is largely based on an insanity rule suggested by the Model Penal Code, is another rule for determining insanity. The Model Penal Code was proposed in 1962 by a group of legal scholars associated with the ALI. The code was drafted to serve as a model for legislatures seeking to modernize their criminal statutes. According to the Brawner Rule, "A person is not responsible for criminal conduct if at the time of such conduct as a result of mental disease or *defect*, he lacks substantial capacity either to appreciate the criminality [wrongfulness] of his conduct or to conform his conduct to the requirements of the law" (*U.S. v. Brawner*, 1972, p. 973, italics added). It must be demonstrated that the disease or mental defect *substantially* and directly (1) influenced the defendant's mental or emotional processes or (2) impaired his or her ability to control behavior. The Brawner Rule, unlike M'Naghten, recognizes *partial* responsibility for criminal conduct as well as the possibility of an irresistible impulse beyond one's control. It also excludes from the definition of mental disease or defect any repeated criminal or otherwise antisocial conduct, an exclusion we referred to earlier in the chapter. This provision (called the **caveat paragraph**) was intended to disallow the insanity defense for criminal psychopaths who persistently violate social mores and often the law. Thus, psychopaths and persons with APDs cannot claim that their abnormal condition is a mental disorder, disease, or defect, even if they have been diagnosed APD.

The Durham Rule: The Product Test.   The **Durham Rule** was created in 1954 in *Durham v. U.S.* by the same court that later rejected it in favor of the Brawner Rule. Monte Durham, a 26-year-old resident of the District of Columbia, had a long history of mental disorder and petty theft. His crime of the moment was burglary, but he was acquitted because his unlawful act was considered to be "the product of a mental disease or mental defect" (*Durham v. U.S.*, 1954, p. 874). While the M'Naghten Rule focuses on knowing right from wrong (the mental element in a crime), the Durham Rule assumes that one cannot be held responsible if an unlawful action is the product of mental disease or defect.

There is nothing in the Durham Rule that relates directly to the person's mental judgment. If the person has a disease or defect, lack of culpability is easily assumed. The rule was later clarified in *Carter v. U.S.* (1957), which held that mental illness must not merely have entered into the production of the act, it must have played a necessary role.

Many states were attracted to the apparent simplicity of the Durham Rule, since it seemed more straightforward and comprehensible to juries. However, it soon became apparent that definitions of "mental illness" are vague and subjective, a situation that fostered the widespread discretionary power of psychiatry and considerable misuse of mental health experts during trial. Moreover, virtually any defendant could be excused, once mental disease or defect had been established, and the Durham Rule quickly lost its popularity.

Until the 1980s, most jurisdictions adopted one of the above rules, with varying degrees of satisfaction. However, the well-publicized Hinckley acquittal sparked a public outcry for the elimination of the insanity defense and prompted legislative bodies and many professional organizations to reexamine it. The American Bar Association and the American Psychiatric Association, for example, proposed new, more restrictive standards (Steadman et al., 1993). Nearly 100 different reforms in 34 jurisdictions occurred soon after Hinckley's acquittal, the most active insanity reform period in American history. In most instances, these reforms reflected a return to the M'Naghten Rule in a modified, more restrictive form (Steadman et al., 1993). Five states—Montana, Idaho, Utah, Nevada, and Kansas—have abolished the insanity defense altogether. Other changes include placing on defendants the burden of proving they were insane (in the past prosecutors had been required to prove defendants were not insane), restricting the role of clinical testimony, and requiring persons found NGRI to prove they were no longer mentally ill before being released from a mental institution. Many of these changes were modeled after the federal law discussed below.

The Insanity Defense Reform Act.   Amid public clamors to abolish the insanity defense completely after the Hinckley acquittal, Congress passed the **Insanity Defense Reform Act of 1984**, which kept the defense in the federal law but modified it in important ways. Rita Simon and David Aaronson (1988, p. 47) assert, "The Hinckley verdict was unquestionably the decisive influence on congressional modifications to the insanity defense." Essentially, Congress made it more difficult for persons using the insanity defense in federal courts to be acquitted. The Insanity Reform Act changed the Brawner/ALI Rule—the rule that has been most consistently adhered to in all federal circuits (except the Fifth Circuit) since its adoption during the early 1970s—to one patterned more along the lines of the M'Naghten Rule. Specifically, a defendant cannot be held responsible if ". . . at the time of the commission of the acts constituting the offense, the defendant, as a result of a severe mental disease or defect, was unable to appreciate the nature and quality or the wrongfulness of his acts. Mental disease or defect does not otherwise constitute a defense" (18 U.S.C., sec 20[a] [1984]).

In addition, the new federal standard changed the Brawner/ALI Rule in three principal ways (Simon & Aaronson, 1988). First, the act abolished the irresistible impulse test (commonly called the **volitional prong**) of the Brawner/ALI Rule. The inability to control one's actions because of mental defect was no longer acceptable as an excusing condition. Second, the act modified the "cognitive" requirement by replacing the phrase "lacks substantial capacity . . . to appreciate" with "unable to appreciate." The intention was to tighten the requirement for defendants to a total lack of ability to appreciate that what they did was wrong (Simon & Aaronson, 1988). Third, under the new law, the mental disease or defect must be severe, to emphasize that certain behavioral disorders (especially personality disorders) do not qualify as a defense. It should be noted that the federal law also bars mental health clinicians from expressing an opinion as to whether the defendant was insane. Clinicians may testify, report on the findings of their evaluations, and provide a diagnosis, but they may not express an ultimate opinion. This is to emphasize that insanity is a legal determination that must be made by the court.

Guilty but Mentally Ill.   Also in response to disenchantment with the insanity defense, some states have introduced a new verdict alternative, **guilty but mentally ill** (GBMI). Michigan was the first to adopt this alternative in 1975, and by 1992, 11 other states had followed Michigan's lead. The GBMI option is intended as an alternative to, not a substitute for, the NGRI verdict. Although states differ in the standards and procedures associated with the GBMI verdict, the major intention of the option was to reduce the number of insanity acquittals, and hold the defendant blameworthy, but still recognize the presence of a mental disorder. Thus, it allows the court to render a "middle-ground" verdict in the case of allegedly mentally disordered defendants. The verdict allows juries, for example, to reconcile their belief that a defendant who commits a crime should be held responsible with their belief that he or she also needs help.

Research on the GBMI laws indicate that they may not have accomplished their intended purposes. In Michigan, for example, insanity acquittals have remained stable, while guilty verdicts have generally declined (G. Smith & Hall, 1982). The same findings have been reported in other states that have adopted the GBMI option (McGinley & Paswark, 1989). Furthermore, defendants found GBMI have received longer sentences and had longer confinements than "sane" defendants found guilty of similar charges (Callahan, McGreevy, Cirincione, & Steadman, 1992; Steadman et al., 1993). In addition, research indicates that those individuals found GBMI are no more likely to receive psychotherapy or rehabilitative services than other mentally disordered defendants in the prison system (Morse, 1985; Slobogin, 1985). Thus, the promise of treatment that is implicit in the statutes remains unfulfilled. Interestingly, there is also evidence that defendants charged with a serious violent crime often elect the GBMI alternative as part of the plea bargaining process. Defense attorneys may be more willing to accept this option than go to trial and risk their client's life (Steadman et al., 1993). Considering the research strongly suggesting that GBMI statutes do not accomplish what was intended, virtually all of the scholarly writing on this issue has questioned the wisdom and efficacy of these laws (Cohen, 2000).

The Mentally Disordered Sex Offender

The third category of mentally disordered individuals appearing before criminal courts is the **mentally disordered sex offender**. Historically, these were persons either charged with or convicted of sexual offenses who were involuntarily committed to civil mental institutions on the basis of their mental disorder and presumed dangerousness to society. Today, the great majority of these offenders are committed under **sexually violent predator** laws, and they do not necessarily require a finding of a diagnosable mental disorder. In some jurisdictions, "mental abnormality" (a vaguer term) will suffice.

Mentally disordered sex offender statutes first appeared on the scene during the early part of the twentieth century and were then called "sexual psychopath" laws. The term psychopath was not really appropriate for a vast majority of these individuals, whose crimes ranged from minor to very serious acts. In most cases, the legislative intention was to provide special dispositional procedures for persons who exhibit a tendency to commit sex offenses, but each state developed its own set of procedures and definitions. Either explicitly or implicitly, the statutes depicted the sexual "psychopath" as a mentally disordered individual who was particularly dangerous to children, women, or both.

Sexual psychopath statutes were challenged in the 1960s and 1970s on a number of constitutional grounds, but particularly because they were vague and overbroad and placed individuals in mental institutions without evidence of their dangerousness. In the late 1980s and 1990s, however, these statutes were resurrected in various forms, most notably sexually violent predator legislation. That is, the term *sexual predator* or *sexually violent predator* is used in place of the outdated sexual psychopath terminology. For example, in 1990, the state of Washington enacted the Sexually Violent Predator Act, which provides for special commitment facilities and allows for the possible lifetime commitment of sexual predators with a mental or personality disorder (F. Cohen, 1998). Other states quickly followed suit. In Iowa the law authorizes involuntary civil commitment for an indefinite period of time for those mentally unstable sex offenders who are a threat to strike again. The law requires that sex offenders be evaluated near the end of their prison terms. If they are determined to be sexual predators, they are confined indefinitely in a high-security treatment facility until no longer a threat to society. Approximately 16 states have passed similar statutes, including Kansas, Washington, Arizona, California, and New York. La Fond (2003) estimates that as many as 2,209 individuals may be held under these laws. In the late 1990s, the U.S. Supreme Court gave its approval to these statutes as long as the state could document (a) a history of sexually violent conduct, (b) a current mental disorder *or abnormality*, (c) a risk of future sexually violent conduct, (d) a connection between the disorder and the conduct, and (e) some inability to control behavior (*Kansas v. Crane*, 2002; *Kansas v. Hendricks*, 1997).

The terms *sexually violent predator* and *sexual predator* are used purposely to avoid the traditional requirements that both mental disorder and dangerousness must be established before an individual can be committed involuntarily to a civil mental institution (F. Cohen, 1998). Additionally, the state wishes to be able to confine the individual for long periods, even after serving a prison term and without proof of a recent overt act (F. Cohen, 1998). Lawmakers reasoned that predators, by their very nature, are dangerous to society and must be kept out of circulation as long as possible. We stress again that the statutes do not necessarily require a finding of mental disorder; in some, "abnormality" is sufficient. Because clinicians recognize that many sexual offenders are not mentally disordered (Janus & Wallbeck, 2000), this allows their confinement even if their behavior does not meet the standard for a diagnosable mental illness. The Supreme Court has emphasized, though, that present dangerousness must be established (it cannot merely be presumed) (*Kansas v. Crane*, 2002).

While it is understandable that the public wishes to be protected from dangerous sex offenders, both the earlier statutes and their latest incarnations have a number of flaws. The early sexual psychopath laws often attempted to intercept sexual psychopaths before they had been convicted of a crime (N. Morris, 1982). They were also based on the false premise that sexual offenders start with minor sexual offenses (e.g., indecent exposure, voyeurism) and move on to serious crimes of violence, like rape. While some do, most do not. The sexual predator laws of today require a conviction, but in some of these statutes the crime can range from relatively minor acts to serious offenses—again seeming to assume that the offender will move from minor to more serious acts. The early laws illustrated "a legislative capacity to conceal excessive punitiveness behind a veil of psychiatric treatment. At base lies the false assumption of a connection between sexual offenses and mental illness" (Morris, 1982, p. 136). Critics of the latest statutes argue that here, too, little has changed. Research has found that many sex offenders do not suffer from mental disorders (Janus & Walbek, 2000), yet the statutes imply that they do. Thus, individuals continue to be committed under the guise that they will receive treatment. In reality, treatment is believed to be sporadic and ineffective (Janus, 2000). Like the GBMI statutes discussed in the previous section, the sexually violent predator statutes appear to be a questionable response to a highly disturbing problem.

Mentally Disordered Inmates and Transfers

The fourth category of mentally disordered relevant to this chapter comprises convicted offenders who exhibit severely disturbed behavior while incarcerated in a jail or prison. In the 1970s and 1980s, it was not unusual for these individuals—particularly those serving time in prison—to be transferred to secure units of civil mental hospitals. As the number of disordered inmates increased, prison systems across the United States began to open treatment facilities within the prison system. Depending on the jurisdiction, then, a seriously mentally disordered inmate might be treated in a separate mental health wing of the prison, transferred to a prison facility specifically designated for the mentally disordered, or transferred to a civil mental hospital. It is also possible that the offender might not receive any treatment, because the extent of the disorder is not recognized or, more soberingly, not acknowledged.

The topic of mentally disordered offenders in jails and prisons is a troubling one, particularly because, as noted earlier in the chapter, the data indicate that their numbers may be increasing. Recall the report from the Bureau of Justice Statistics (Ditton, 1999), wherein 16% of state prisoners, 7% of federal prisoners, and 16% of those held in local jails reported either a mental condition or an overnight stay in a mental hospital. Both researchers and mental health professionals working with jail and prison inmates report significant increases in serious mental health problems (Ashford et al., 2001).

The subgroup of individuals who are transferred to civil mental institutions may be declining with the availability of secure treatment facilities within the prison setting. Because states differ greatly in the treatment and transfer options they provide for mentally disordered prisoners, it is difficult to distinguish a general pattern in either the disorders or the circumstances surrounding the transfers. However, in 1980, the U.S. Supreme Court ruled that the transfer of an inmate to a mental health hospital requires, at a minimum, an administrative hearing to determine whether such transfer is appropriate (*Vitek v. Jones*, 1980). An inmate is entitled to challenge that transfer and to have legal assistance for that purpose. The Supreme Court recognized the special nature of confinement in a mental health facility and the stigma that often accompanies a commitment (Churgin, 1983). Furthermore, transfer to a mental institution not only entails forced treatment of almost any variety, but also may substantially reduce the chances for parole, since parole boards may be reluctant to release into the community a prisoner who was recently in a mental hospital setting. Nevertheless, scholars have observed that transfers to civil mental institutions—or to prison mental hospitals—are not often challenged, despite the due process protections afforded to these inmates by the *Vitek* case (F. Cohen, 1998). Cohen adds that inmates are less likely to resist a transfer than to face delays in getting timely admission to a hospital setting when it is needed.

MENTAL DISORDERS AS UNIQUE DEFENSES

Criminal defendants sometimes use a variety of special mental disorders in an effort to absolve themselves completely of criminal responsibility or to support a claim of diminished capacity or diminished responsibility. Examples of these unique defenses are post–traumatic stress disorder, pathological gambler's syndrome, multiple personality disorder—now referred to as dissociative identity disorder—amnesia, battered woman syndrome, and sexual addiction. In most jurisdictions, the mental disorders will be used as an underlying condition to support a defense of NGRI. However, they also may be used in support of other affirmative defenses. For example, battered woman syndrome—sometimes but not always considered a form of PTSD—may be used to support self-defense.

Post–Traumatic Stress Disorder

According to the DSM-IV, **post–traumatic stress disorder (PTSD)** is

> the development of characteristic symptoms following exposure to extreme traumatic stress or involving direct personal experience of an event that involves actual or threatened death or serious injury, or other threat to one's physical integrity; or witnessing an event that involves death, injury, or threat to the physical integrity of another person; or learning about unexpected or violent death, serious harm, or threat of death or injury experienced by a family member or other close associate. (APA, 1994, p. 424)

The precipitating event would be substantially distressing to almost anyone, and it is "usually experienced with intense fear, terror, and helplessness" (p. 424).

PTSD was formally recognized as a distinct disorder in the 1980 edition of the DSM-III following efforts by veterans' groups to have mental health professionals recognize a "post-Vietnam syndrome" that led to a variety of disabling symptoms (Appelbaum et al., 1993). Since being formally recognized, PTSD has been broadly applied to war veterans, survivors of the Holocaust, survivors of major disasters—such as the events of September 11, 2001—and victims and survivors of rape, child abuse, spousal abuse, and sexual harassment. PTSD falls under the broader category of "dissociative disorders" in the DSM-IV-R. Dissociative disorders are marked by major changes in memory not due to physical causes (Comer, 2004). Other examples of these disorders are certain forms of amnesia, fugues, and DID.

Surveys estimate that between 1% and 2% of all Americans suffer from PTSD (Sutker, Uddo-Crane, & Allain, 1991). One study estimated that PTSD affected 31% of all male and 27% of all female Vietnam veterans (Kulka, et al., 1991).

The symptoms of PTSD include "flashbacks," recurrent dreams or nightmares, or painful, intrusive memories of the traumatic event. A diminished responsiveness, a don't-care attitude, and psychological "numbing" to the external world are common, particularly during the weeks following the event. On the other hand, some research indicates that the symptoms of PTSD may not emerge until considerable time has elapsed, six months to a year or more. In fact, the DSM-IV-TR distinguishes among acute (symptoms last less than three months), chronic (symptoms last longer than three months), and delayed-onset PTSD (when at least six months have passed since the traumatic event). Feelings of alienation or detachment from the social environment are also characteristic, a pattern that leads to difficulty in developing close, meaningful relationships with others. Other symptoms include sleep problems, being easily startled, considerable difficulty concentrating or remembering, and extreme avoidance of anything that reminds them of the event. Even anniversaries of the trauma are often enough to precipitate symptoms. Individuals with a diagnosis of PTSD tend to be moody, depressed, and difficult to be around or work with. They often move from job to job, relationship to relationship.

PTSD has been used to support a defense of NGRI, in both violent and non-violent cases (Monahan & Walker, 1990, 1994). For example, PTSD has been used as an excusing condition for drug trafficking (e.g., *U.S. v. Krutschewski*, 1981). Evidence to date, however, shows that—while courts are willing to admit evidence of PTSD—using it to support an insanity defense is no more successful than using other mental disorders (Appelbaum et al., 1993). Moreover, PTSD defendants, as a rule, do not follow the stereotypic images portrayed by the media as "tortured but essentially upstanding veterans, who at some point, become overwhelmed by their symptoms, 'snap,' and commit a violent crime" (p. 233). Specifically, the research evidence reveals that defendants who use PTSD to support an insanity defense have been in as much trouble and involvement with the criminal justice system as other defendants who use the insanity defense (Appelbaum et al., 1993).

When the PTSD defense has been successful, it usually results in a finding of *diminished responsibility*, rather than the complete absolution of responsibility (NGRI) for the defendant. PTSD has also been cited in plea bargaining and in presentence reports (Monahan & Walker, 1990). That is, prosecutors may be more willing to accept a guilty plea to a reduced charge, and judges more willing to impose a lighter sentence, if evidence of PTSD exists. Appelbaum and colleagues (1993) also found that, in cases involving veterans, PTSD was frequently used as evidence for diminished responsibility in assigning cases to pretrial diversion, in plea bargaining, and in sentencing.

The primary legal argument used by the defense is that defendants were in a PTSD dissociative state when they committed the act. While in that state, persons typically do not remember what they have experienced or even their own identity. In *State v. Felde* (1982), the defendant—a Vietnam veteran who shot a police officer—"claimed that he was in a dissociative state and that he believed that he had been captured by the North Vietnamese at the time he shot the officer" (D. McCord, 1987, p. 65). In *Miller v. State* (1983), the defendant, charged with a prison escape, argued that he thought he was still in Vietnam and his only intention was to get back to the United States.

PTSD has been used to excuse or mitigate criminal responsibility in cases involving battered women who maintain that they have battered woman syndrome, sometimes considered a variant of PTSD (Appelbaum et al., 1993). This is a controversial area for at least two major reasons. First, there is not universal agreement in the psychological literature that a battered woman syndrome exists. Second, advocates for battered women resist the implication that they have a mental disorder or that they are "insane." When PTSD is used, a battered woman may claim that the abuse was so extensive and brutal that, in a dissociative state brought about by the disorder, she killed the abuser. In this case she is more likely to claim "temporary insanity" than "insanity," in the hope that acquittal will not be followed by commitment to a mental institution. However, PTSD in battered woman also may be used to support a claim of self-defense rather than insanity, though courts have not been sympathetic to this approach (Slobogin, 1999). When used in this way, the defendant focuses on other symptoms of PTSD—e.g., heightened fear, anxiety, depression—rather than on the dissociative state. In a different context, evidence that an alleged rape victim shows the symptoms of PTSD has been accepted in some courts as proof that the victim has indeed been raped (Appelbaum et al., 1993). Likewise, PTSD has been used in civil suits involving emotional or physical personal injury, such as sexual harassment suits and civil suits against former abusers.

While courts are increasingly accepting PTSD evidence, some legal scholars and researchers remain skeptical. They believe that objective assessment of PTSD lacks solid validity and the diagnosis depends almost exclusively on self-report. Consequently, critics argue that there is considerable opportunity for faking the disorder, especially if the individual rehearses and practices the symptoms. Appelbaum et al. (1993, p. 230) conclude that the problem of PTSD in the courts as an excusing condition is "particularly acute with something as new, as 'unverifiable,' as potentially useful, and as politically charged as PTSD."

Pathological Gambler's Syndrome

The syndrome of **compulsive gambling** began with psychoanalytic case studies during the early part of the twentieth century (Cunnien, 1985). Compulsive gamblers, the early case studies concluded, are neurotics with an insatiable, unconscious desire to lose what was gained (Cunnien, 1985). The DSM-IV describes pathological gambling as the inability to resist impulses to gamble, despite the dire consequences to family, interpersonal relationships, and daily living. "The essential feature of Pathological Gambling is persistent and recurrent maladaptive gambling behavior that disrupts personal, family, or vocational pursuits" (APA, p. 615). It is a progressive and eventually overwhelming urge to engage in gambling behavior. The disorder may afflict as many as 1% to 3% of the adult population, and is more common among males than females (DSM-IV-TR). In a survey of 1,200 residents of Ontario, Insight Canada Research (1998) found that about 8% of Ontarians could be classified as "problem gamblers," while 0.9% are probable pathological gamblers. Pathological gambling usually begins during adolescence in males and later in life in females (DSM-IV-TR). Pathological gamblers are often overconfident, very energetic, and easily bored but sometimes exhibit stress, anxiety, and depression during their losing streaks.

The characteristic distinguishing pathological gambling from "normal" or social gambling is its "addictive" nature. Addicted gamblers are believed to be unable to walk away from a gamble and are tense and restless if gambling is denied them.

Pathological gambling became fully recognized as a serious mental disorder in the DSM-III in 1980, and since that time the disorder has been used by defendants as an excuse for a variety of illegal activities. The crimes with which defendants have been charged are not gambling offenses but, rather, crimes committed for monetary gain. The defendants contended that money was necessary in order to support their pathological gambling habit (D. McCord, 1987). For example, in *U.S. v. Gillis* (1985), the defendant, who was charged with interstate transportation of stolen vehicles and forged securities, argued that he engaged in these illegal activities to support his gambling habit. The following are additional examples where similar defenses were used: *U.S. v. Davis* (1984), where the defendant was charged with forging and converting government checks payable to deceased relatives; *U.S. v. Gould* (1984), where the defendant was charged with bank robbery; and *U.S. v. Lewellyn* (1985), where the defendant was charged with embezzlement, making a false statement, and mail fraud.

In general, defendants using this defense have been unsuccessful, because they have been unable to demonstrate a connection between "the syndrome and the inability of the defendant to resist the impulse to commit crimes in order to support the gambling urge" (D. McCord, 1987, p. 67). However, it should be noted that the pathological gambling defense has occasionally been successful, as seen in *State v. Lafferty* (1984), a case involving embezzlement, and in *State v. Campanaro* (1980), a case involving forgery.

Cunnien (1985, p. 89) writes, "There are . . . no available data to suggest whether pathological gambling and attendant criminal behavior are uncontrollable or merely uncontrolled." He further concludes, "It remains unproven that impulses to gamble are uncontrollable" (p. 98).

Dissociative Identity Disorder

The essential feature of **dissociative identity disorder** (DID; formerly called **multiple personality disorder** [MPD]) is "the existence within the person of two or more distinct personalities or personality states that recurrently take control of behavior" (APA, p. 484). Furthermore, "each personality state may be experienced as if it has a distinct personal history, self-image, and identity, including a separate name" (p. 484). Periodically, at least two personalities take full control of the individual's behavior. The change or transition from one personality to another is often very sudden (seconds to minutes) and is generally triggered by stress or some relevant environmental stimuli. Often, hypnosis can also bring about this shift into another personality.

According to the DSM-IV, each of the personalities may be aware of some or all the other personalities to varying degrees. There may be as many as a hundred different identities. The disorder occurs about three to nine times more frequently in females than in males. Persons who experience DID are highly suggestible and impressionable and can be readily hypnotized either by themselves or others. Reported cases of what was then called MPD have historically been extremely rare. However, between 1980 and 1989 the number of cases diagnosed in the United States rose dramatically, from 200 to 6,000 (Slovenko, 1989). Part of this increase is due to the APA officially recognizing the disorder in the DSM-III.

There is a good deal of controversy surrounding the existence and prevalence of DID, which in recent years has gained more status among clinicians, while researchers are far more skeptical. The concept of individuals having "multiple personalities" or "alter egos" that control their lives is fascinating to many but remains scientifically questionable. While this phenomenon may exist in a very minute segment of the mentally disordered population, it is also highly susceptible to being overdiagnosed.

On occasion, MPD has been used successfully as an excusing condition for criminal responsibility. In *State v. Rodrigues* (1984), a defendant accused of three counts of sodomy and one count of rape of young girls was acquitted on the basis of MPD. In *State v. Milligan* (1978), Billy Milligan claimed he had 24 separate personalities and was found NGRI in criminal charges of raping three women. In general, however, MPD has not been a successful defense (Slovenko, 1989). One of the more well-known cases in which the MPD defense was tried involved serial killer Kenneth Bianchi, known as the Hillside Strangler. The Hillside Strangler was given wide publicity because of the brutality and sadistic quality of his murders. The victims were young, attractive women who were raped and strangled and whose nude corpses were conspicuously displayed on the hillsides in the Los Angeles area. The Hillside Strangler was responsible for at least a dozen murders during a one-year period (1977–1978).

Much of the following material was acquired from an article written by Martin T. Orne, David F. Dinges, and Emily Carota Orne (1984), and the interested reader is encouraged to study that paper. Throughout his adult life, Bianchi's most consistent career aspiration was to become a police officer, and he even attended a junior college program in police science. Although he repeatedly applied for positions at various police departments, he was not successful at landing a job. However, he did obtain employment as a security guard.

Overall, Bianchi was unable to sustain a successful career pattern, holding at least 12 different jobs during the nine-year period following high school. His background was a series of lies, scams, and illegal activities, ranging from the use of stolen credit cards to the pimping of juvenile prostitutes. During his last year in Los Angeles, Bianchi masqueraded as a psychologist, complete with an office and answering service. He obtained false diplomas and credentials by placing a classified ad in the *Los Angeles Times*, offering a position to a recently graduated psychologist. He requested that the applicants send not only their résumés, but also their official university transcripts. From the hundreds of applications he received, he obtained enough information to forge a transcript and diploma with his name on them.

At age 19, Bianchi married a high school girlfriend, but the marriage lasted less than eight months. At age 26, he began to live with a woman in a common-law relationship; she bore him a son. After the birth of his son, his common-law wife moved to Bellingham, Washington, where Bianchi joined her three months later. In Bellingham, he obtained a job as a supervisor for a private security agency. Bianchi, however, was arrested on January 11, 1979, for the murders of two women in Washington—murders that followed a pattern similar to the Hillside Strangler murders in California.

Despite considerable evidence against him, Bianchi insisted that he was innocent. Eventually, he maintained under hypnosis that his alter personality "Steve" had done the killings. Since Steve did the killings, Ken Bianchi argued that he should not be held responsible and pleaded NGRI under the State of Washington's M'Naghten Rule. The court appointed a team of experts to determine if Bianchi really was suffering MPD. The court (*State v. Bianchi*, 1979) posited that if the experts could agree, the insanity defense might prevail. The team of experts, however, after careful examination of his past and present behavior, found no basis for Bianchi's claim of MPD. Although Bianchi knew the "textbook version" of MPD (probably knowledge gained during the time he impersonated a psychologist), he was less than convincing on the more subtle aspects of the disorder recognized by the experts. The team concluded that Bianchi was a psychopath. Bianchi then quickly changed his plea to guilty in order to avoid the death penalty.

There is considerable debate among practitioners and scholars as to whether the syndrome MPD/DID actually exists, and it is sometimes referred to as the "UFO of psychiatry" (Ondrovik & Hamilton, 1991). In some instances, it may be **iatrogenic**—that is, unintentionally caused by clinicians or practitioners themselves (Comer, 1992). This means that practitioners who firmly believe in and are perceptually sensitive to DID look for and interpret a variety of behaviors as symptoms of the disorder. Clinicians are now told that the symptoms of DID are very subtle and that the average length of time it takes for the disorder to be diagnosed is seven years (Gellinas, 2003). In effect, the practitioner may develop the syndrome in the patient, and the patient, in turn, learns to believe that he or she is afflicted with it. It has also been argued that implicit and explicit suggestions during hypnosis can shape segments of self into the appearance of MPD (Orne et al., 1984). Regardless of whether or not the syndrome is iatrogenic or whether or not it is possible for several personalities to "possess" a physical body, an important point must be made. The syndrome is *subjectively real* to the patient, and the person who allegedly experiences it often plays each of the roles well and convincingly. Martin Orne and his colleagues (Orne et al., 1984, p. 120) observe, "So striking are the behavioral differences between personalities that the assertion is often made that one would need to have the dramatic skills of Sarah Bernhardt or Sir Laurence Olivier, along with a detailed knowledge of psychiatry, to effectively simulate such radically different persons."

Everyone to some degree hosts a number of subpersonalities (Slovenko, 1989). One aspect of our subpersonalities is our moods: One day we may be cool and withdrawn, and the next day, warm and sociable. The situation also makes a big difference. For example, each person is different when at home with parents than when spending time with friends. At home, parents might treat you like the immature 16-year-old they remember, and you find yourself assuming that role quickly and easily. The old conflicts and squabbles with your parents return, just as they did years ago. It is possible that these changes in moods, together with the fact that some clinicians "look hard" for MPD/DID and some patients are happy to oblige, all contribute to the increased prevalence of this disorder.

In summary, the validity of DID as a viable entity is very much open to debate by both the mental health and the legal professions. Supporters of the concept maintain that diagnostic procedures among clinicians are more accurate today than in the past, and clinicians have at their disposal specific diagnostic tests to detect the disorder (Comer, 2004). At present, though, there is very little solid evidence that the syndrome, as a bona fide mental disorder in which one personality completely controls the other(s), actually exists, except possibly in very rare situations. Nevertheless, it is not unusual to be in a roomful of clinicians who seem firmly convinced that DID is a significant problem encountered in their practices and one that mental health practitioners still fail to diagnose. According to this perspective, treatment is a highly complex and multistage process. It involves allowing the alter egos to emerge and enabling the client to confront them. Eventually, the "alters" are left behind, a process that can be very frightening to the client. As one therapist commented, after a long period of treatment, the client had successfully confronted her problems and was ready to move on to a normal life. However, she was concerned about how she would handle financial matters, because "Ruth"—one of her alters—was the one who had always balanced the checkbook.

Amnesia

Amnesia refers to complete or partial memory loss of an event, series of events, or some segment of life's experiences, due to either physical trauma, neurophysiological disturbance, or psychological factors. According to the DSM-IV, "Individuals with an amnestic disorder are impaired in their ability to learn new information or are unable to recall previously learned information or past events" (APA, 1994, p. 156). Amnesia is not simply forgetting a name, a date, or an incident but is reserved for severely impaired ability to remember past material (retrograde amnesia) or to acquire and retain new material (anterograde amnesia).

Some researchers have identified a classification of amnesia called **limited amnesia**, which is "a pathological inability to remember a specific episode, or small number of episodes, from the recent past" (Schacter, 1986b,

p. 48). Limited amnesia may be caused by emotional shock, alcohol or drug intoxication, or a blow to the head. Therefore, limited amnesia is not ongoing, nor does it involve extensive memory loss. Rather, the loss is temporary and restricted to a specific event or incident.

In general, the courts have not been receptive to amnesia either as a valid condition in the insanity defense or as a condition that promotes incompetence to stand trial (Rubinsky & Brandt, 1986). Paull (1993) notes that there have been cases in at least 20 states and five federal circuit courts where the court has held that amnesia per se does not render a defendant incompetent. One reason for this judicial "hard-line" approach to amnesia is the suspicion that the defendant may be faking the memory loss. It is easy for people to simply say they cannot remember committing a crime, and it is difficult for psychologists to determine whether a person can or cannot remember. In recent years, though, psychologists have been able to fine-tune a number of instruments designed to measure malingering—or faking—of various symptoms, including symptoms of amnesia (Rogers, 1997). Additionally, some psychologists believe that amnesia can be evaluated with recognition tests tailored to the information that the client claims not to know (Frederick, 2000).

Amnesia associated with alcoholic intoxication presents a favorite excuse for reprehensible behavior and is the most commonly invoked excusing condition in criminal cases. "When I drink I go blank about some things" is the usual line. It is intriguing to note that 30% to 65% of persons convicted of criminal homicide claim they cannot remember the crime, usually because of alcoholic intoxication at the time of the offense (Schachter, 1986b). A similar pattern exists for other violent crimes (e.g., rape) as well.

However, the courts have not been very sympathetic to defendants who rely on excuses based on alcohol or other drug intoxication. This is because the courts hold the defendants blameworthy since they should have known, at the outset, the risks involved in drinking alcohol or taking drugs. Thus, attempts to use amnesia in this way have met with strong judicial resistance. For example, one court held that "insanity is the incapacity to discriminate between right and wrong while amnesia is simply the inability to remember" (Rubinsky & Brandt, 1986, p. 30). Therefore, amnesia per se fails to qualify as a mental disorder that robs a person of the ability to distinguish between right and wrong.

DANGEROUSNESS AND THE ASSESSMENT OF RISK

Up to this point in the chapter we have covered a range of situations involving mentally disordered individuals and the criminal courts. In many—but not all—of those situations, the courts and other agents of the criminal justice system were concerned about whether the disordered individual was also a danger to society.

The concept of dangerousness pervades much of the criminal law and appears in civil law as well. Defining dangerous behavior is a challenge faced by legislatures, courts, and clinicians. All states and all courts recognize that behavior that is likely to result in *physical harm* is dangerous. They begin to differ when behaviors that lead to property damage or psychological injury are involved. One example of psychological injury is the effect of stalking on the victims, who may be continually shadowed, photographed, contacted by phone or e-mail, and otherwise harassed. Some courts have ruled that this type of behavior can cause irreparable emotional damage. They conclude that a threat of "psychological trauma is . . . as much a menace to the health or safety of others as is possible physical injury" (Developments in the Law, 1974, p. 1237). This form of psychological damage has prompted many state legislatures to pass "stalking laws" stating that persons who continually follow and otherwise harass other individuals can be charged with a criminal offense.

It is fair to say, though, that dangerousness is used primarily in conjunction with violent behavior. Defendants are denied bail because they are judged dangerous, offenders are sentenced to long prison terms to prevent them from committing more crime, and some are sentenced to death because it is feared they will commit more violence. Decisions on whether to parole prisoners convicted of violent crimes are largely based on whether they are dangerous. In civil law, the concept of dangerousness appears in restraining orders, when courts order an individual to refrain from contacting another. As another example, in involuntary civil commitment proceedings, persons may be institutionalized if they are believed to be dangerous to themselves or to others because of a mental disorder.

Implicit in the above decisions is the belief that it is possible to predict an individual's violent behavior. Although some clinicians believe they can do so with a high degree of confidence, most are far more modest about this ability. Since the 1990s, the research and professional literature has increasingly preferred the term *risk assessment* rather than prediction of dangerousness. Risk assessment suggests that clinicians and researchers are more proficient at *assessing the probability* that a given individual—or group of individuals—will engage in harmful behavior than they are at outrightly predicting that someone will be violent. We return to this change in terminology shortly.

Controversy over the ability to predict has been longstanding. Not surprisingly, it has often been fueled by highly publicized incidents. In August 1966, Charles Whitman, a University of Texas student majoring in architectural engineering, murdered his wife and his mother. Shortly thereafter, he carried his personal arsenal in a footlocker to the observation deck of the 307-foot-tall University Tower, where he loaded a number of high-powered, scope-equipped rifles and began randomly shooting at people near the observation deck and on the ground far below. Whitman managed to shoot 44 victims, killing 14, before a police officer and a citizen climbed to the tower and ended the tragedy by shooting Whitman himself.

An investigation revealed that the 25-year-old Whitman had consulted a psychiatrist five months before the incident and, during a two-hour interview, had described "overwhelming violent impulses" and great fear of his inability to control them. He had also revealed a compelling need to "go up on the tower with a deer rifle and start shooting people." Whitman did not return for further consultation after the initial two-hour session. Nevertheless, when the news of his contact with a psychiatrist was disseminated, there was public outcry and many questions about why he was not treated, confined, or referred to the proper authorities. Similar questions were raised when the public learned that James Huberty, who killed 22 fast-food restaurant patrons in the summer of 1984, had also had contact with a mental health clinic. In Huberty's case, social workers had apparently tried without success to return his telephone calls.

In another highly publicized case, an outpatient at a University of California, Berkeley, clinic revealed to his psychiatrist his fantasies about harming, or perhaps even killing, a woman whom he had met at a dance. The psychologist, who learned from one of his patient's friends that he planned to purchase a gun, became increasingly concerned. When the patient discontinued therapy, clinic officials wrote to the police requesting their help in getting the individual committed to a mental institution. Police investigated the case, interviewed the patient, and warned him to stay away from the woman, but did not pursue the commitment, apparently because California's new civil commitment law was difficult to interpret. Two months later, Prosenjit Poddar—the patient—killed Tatiana Tarasoff by stabbing her, though he was carrying his newly purchased gun. He was charged with first-degree murder. Tarasoff's family sued the university clinic, claiming the psychologist had been negligent in not warning the young woman or the family of the danger.

The *Tarasoff* case, undoubtedly familiar to all clinicians, addressed very directly the question of what duty therapists have to warn third parties of possible harmful behavior from their clients. The California Supreme Court first ruled that, when a therapist determines that a patient is a serious danger to another person, the therapist has a duty to warn that individual (*Tarasoff v. Regents of the University of California*, 1974). Two years later (*Tarasoff v. Regents*, 1976), the Court redefined the role as a duty to protect. That is, the therapist need not directly warn the individual, but he or she should take some steps to protect the individual from harm. Following the California court's decisions, courts in many other states issued similar decisions, but others rejected the doctrine. In the 1980s, it was widely applied, but in the 1990s it was rejected altogether or severely limited in many states (Felthous, 2001). Whether or not there exists a statutory duty to warn/protect, many practitioners have interpreted the "spirit" of *Tarasoff* as a standard of practice, believing that the clinician has a professional obligation to take some steps to protect an identifiable potential victim (e.g., Litwack & Schlesinger, 1999).

Courts that have adopted duty to warn/protect rules apparently believe that mental health professionals can predict with considerable accuracy who is or will be dangerous and who will not. The law has been relying on predictions of dangerousness for a long time, dating back at least as far as the sixteenth century (N. Morris & Miller, 1985). Yet researchers and clinicians have long struggled both to define dangerousness and to predict its occurrence. After the *Tarasoff* case, dangerousness generated more controversy than even the insanity defense (Simon & Cockerham, 1977).

When courts consider this question, they often turn to the psychiatric and psychological professions. However, as noted above, many in these professions have resisted the notion that dangerousness can be predicted. Instead, they maintain that, at best, they can offer probabilities based on known factors relating to the individual, often based on data obtained from large groups. (Recall our earlier discussion of the MacArthur Risk Assessment Study of civilly committed psychiatric patients.) Thus, increasingly, the psychological literature has avoided the term prediction of dangerousness and has replaced it with **risk assessment**. Regardless of the terminology, it is clear that some attempt at assessing/predicting the likelihood that an individual will commit violence is warranted.

There is little doubt that a person who has been violent in the past and indicates by word or deed the intent to do serious harm to others is dangerous. Someone who has committed a series of murders, mutilations, or rapes, and who attests to planning to do more of the same, is certainly—by anyone's definition—a dangerous individual. If a person has no history of violence and threatens harm, however, the situation becomes more problematic. Likewise, if a person has been violent in the distant past but has shown no recent signs of violent behavior, the situation is problematic. In these contexts, clinicians have difficulty reaching a consensus on who is dangerous and who is not. This is why current thinking favors surveying a list of "risk factors" in an attempt to determine the likelihood that aggressive behavior will occur. Risk assessment is perhaps the most complicated and controversial issue in the entire field of forensic psychology (Borum, 1996). Many researchers and scholars (e.g., Steadman et al., 1993) consider it one of the most important issues in both criminal and civil matters worldwide. A variety of instruments is available for clinicians engaging in the risk assessment enterprise. Additionally, during a clinical interview, mental health practitioners are often advised to be attuned to background factors. Before reviewing some of these instruments, it is wise to consider conceptual issues relating to prediction.

Until very recently, the psychological research literature consistently concluded that clinicians are unable to specify the type or severity of harm an individual may cause or to predict with great accuracy the probability of harm even occurring. That early literature can best be summarized in the words of Alan Stone (1975, p. 33), who wrote:

> It can be stated flatly on the basis of my own review of the published material on the prediction of dangerous acts that neither objective actuarial tables nor psychiatric intuition, diagnosis, and psychological testing can claim predictive success when dealing with the traditional population of mental hospitals. The predictive success appropriate to a legal decision can be described in three levels of increasing certainty: Preponderance of the evidence, 51%

successful; clear and convincing proof, 75% successful; beyond a reasonable doubt, at least 90% successful.

Stone asserted that mental health professionals have failed to predict dangerous behavior by even the laxest criterion, a *preponderance of the evidence.* Likewise, Cocozza and Steadman (1976)—referring to the involuntary civil commitment of mentally disordered individuals—asserted that "any attempt to commit an individual solely on the basis of dangerousness would be futile if psychiatric testimony were subjected to any of these three standards of proof" (p. 1101). They added that the psychological research has demonstrated "clear and convincing evidence of the inability of psychiatrists or anyone else to predict dangerousness accurately" (p. 1099).

The early research on prediction also demonstrated that clinicians had a strong tendency to overpredict dangerousness, a pattern that held for criminal offenders as well as mentally disordered patients (Monahan, 1981, 1984). At a minimum, the most sophisticated predictive methods yield 60% to 70% false positives (people who were predicted to be dangerous but did not engage in harmful behavior) (Kozol, Boucher, & Garofalo, 1972; B. Rubin, 1972; Wenk, Robison, & Smith, 1972). In a 10-year follow-up investigation of 592 convicted male offenders, mostly sex offenders (Kozol et al., 1972), two of every three persons predicted dangerous were false positives, even after extensive background data and results of independent clinical exams by psychiatrists had been made available to those doing the predicting. Moreover, because of some flaws in the design of the study, the odds for accurate prediction were very much in the researchers' favor (Dix, 1980; Monahan, 1976; Steadman, 1976).

In the 1970s, classic studies that followed individuals after their release from mental institutions also documented the limitations of prediction. Steadman (1976) followed patients who were released from New York hospitals after a landmark U.S. Supreme Court case, *Baxstrom v. Herold* (1966). These "Baxstrom patients" had first been convicted of crimes and had then been transferred to civil mental institutions without hearings shortly before their prison sentences expired. On average they had spent eight years in confinement beyond their prison sentence. The Baxstrom patients were predominantly nonwhite, lower–socioeconomic class, middle-aged males. Although a vast majority had arrest records and many had previous convictions, only 58% had been convicted of violent crimes (Steadman, 1976). On the average, the patients had been institutionalized continuously for 14 years. In its Baxstrom decision, the Supreme Court noted that—like other individuals committed to civil mental institutions—the prisoners had a right to a hearing to determine whether they were mentally disordered and dangerous. As a result, many were released, often against the advice of clinicians who predicted that they were dangerous.

The Baxstrom patients were considered some of New York's most dangerous mental patients, but follow-up reports found that predicted dangerousness had been grossly overstated (false positives) (Monahan, 1976). Steadman and Cocozza (1974) followed up 85 Baxstrom patients and discovered that 20% were rearrested, but only 7% were convicted, usually for minor violations such as vagrancy and public intoxication. An examination of both in-hospital and community behaviors revealed that only 20% of the "extremely dangerous" patients were assaultive toward others during the four-year follow-up period (Steadman, 1976). A prominent variable predicting whether Baxstrom patients demonstrated assaultive behavior was age: The younger the patient, the more likely he or she was to engage in assaultive behavior. Even using the Legal Dangerousness Scale (Cocozza & Steadman, 1976), a measure of four criminal background characteristics, there were two false positives for every three patients predicted to be violent, again underscoring the inaccuracy of clinical prediction.

In a similar research project, Thornberry and Jacoby (1979) followed up a group of mentally disordered offenders in Pennsylvania who were transferred from criminal to civil mental hospitals in that state. These patients had notable histories of mental problems and criminal offenses. Forty-three percent had been hospitalized in the past, and 90% were diagnosed psychotic on current admission. Over 80% had prior arrest records, 64% had previously served jail and prison sentences, and 39% had committed five or more offenses in the past. Until a court ordered their reevaluation (*Dixon v. Attorney General of the Commonwealth of Pennsylvania*, 1971), the patients had been institutionalized indefinitely on the basis of presumed dangerousness.

Thornberry and Jacoby (1979) found that, after their court-ordered transfer to civil and less secure mental hospitals, only 19% were involved in some kind of violence within the hospital setting. Two-thirds of the patients were discharged from the civil hospitals within nine months of the transfer. During a four-year follow-up, about 24% were arrested, and only one-quarter of these arrests were for violent offenses. Overall, the incidence of false positives—in which clinicians had predicted harmful or violent behavior that did not occur—was 67%, or two of every three predictions.

Although we have focused on the above classic studies, it is important to emphasize that other research in the 1970s also supported these findings (e.g., Kozol et al., 1972; B. Rubin, 1972; Wenk et al., 1972). Reviews of the literature led scholars to conclude that, in the area of dangerousness prediction with respect to the mentally disordered, false positives outnumbered true positives by a margin of two to one (Monahan, 1988; Wettstein, 1984).

The ratio of false to true positives deserves some attention. False positive is a descriptor we use for persons who are labeled dangerous (positive) but who do not engage in harmful behavior during a specific period of time after release from custody (false). True positives are persons predicted to be dangerous (positive) who do engage in subsequent harmful behavior (true). (See **Table 6–3**.) For example, assume that a team of mental health professionals concludes that 10 persons are dangerous. If, during a two-year period following release, 6 of them do engage in harmful behavior, we have a 60% rate of true positives and a 40% rate of false positives. On the other hand, the team

TABLE 6–3   Four Possible Outcomes of Prediction

	CRITERION BEHAVIOR	
PREDICTION	DID	DID NOT
Will	True positive	False positive
Will not	False negative	True negative

may predict that 10 people will not engage in violent behavior (negatives). If some of them do, they are called false negatives. True negatives are those who are predicted not to engage in harmful behavior within a certain period of time and who do not. Thus, if the team predicts that 7 out of 10 people will not engage in harmful behavior, and 5 of the 10 do not, the team was wrong in 2 cases. We therefore have a ratio of 20% false negatives to 50% true negatives.

In many ways it is clearly advantageous for mental health professionals to predict more positives than negatives, especially if there is some question about whether a person is dangerous. The *Tarasoff* decision also encourages this trend. Clinicians who fail to warn and protect the community by not detecting persons who eventually commit violent or harmful acts will likely pay a higher social and professional price than clinicians who overpredict dangerousness.

It is quite clear that clinicians tend to overpredict dangerous behavior, under the premise that it is better to be safe than sorry. It is also quite clear that predictions of dangerousness, in general, are inaccurate. Even though researchers have made impressive strides in developing risk assessment instruments, prediction remains a tenuous enterprise. What accounts for this?

First, the behavior being predicted, violence, occurs relatively infrequently in the daily lives of even the most frequent offender. Therefore, the prediction of an infrequent behavior is akin to finding a needle in a haystack of behaviors. Violent behavior happens (or is reported) so infrequently that if you say it will happen, the odds are already against you. Second, while human behavior is generally consistent across time (temporal consistency), it is often inconsistent across situations (transsituational consistency). More specifically, people tend to act the same way during their lifetimes, if the situations eliciting this behavior are basically the same. However, if the situations are different, as is so characteristic of life, people are unlikely to act the same way. As noted earlier, for example, most of us act differently with our parents than we do with our friends, or we act one way with members of the same sex but another way with members of the opposite sex. Thus, mental health professionals would be substantially more accurate if they could be certain that the social environment remained the same. In reality, the social environment is always changing, rendering the predictions based on one situation inapposite for another.

Overall, the best predictor of future behavior is past behavior, but even past behavior will not necessarily be repeated. The best predictor of criminal behavior is a history of criminal behavior, and past violence will suggest a probability of future violence. A history of criminal behavior is the best predictor of criminal recidivism regardless of whether the offender is mentally disordered or normal (Bonta et al., 1998). But again, people change. Furthermore, the more frequently the behavior has occurred in a variety of situations, the more accurate the predictions will be. Someone who frequently manifests violence across many different situations will be far easier to predict than a person who is only occasionally violent in some situations.

Since the 1990s, researchers have made considerable strides in the ability to identify more factors that are associated with violence. In addition to criminal history, recent research strongly indicates that other predictors of criminal recidivism include some combination of age, juvenile delinquency, and substance abuse (Andrews & Bonta, 1994; Bonta et al., 1998; Gendreau, Little, & Goggin, 1996). However, researchers have also warned that risk factors are unique for each individual and that no one factor will necessarily predict violence in any one individual. We now turn to the types of clinical measures that have been offered to help clinicians assess the likelihood that a person will engage in harmful behavior toward others.

Current Risk Assessment Measures

Many of the *risk assessment instruments* have been developed by Canadian psychologists. These instruments generally require a clinician or assessor to evaluate an individual based on information in certain areas of background and behavioral patterns. The first of these instruments was the Dangerous Behavior Rating Scheme, developed by Christopher Webster and Robert Menzies (1993). The scale underwent considerable research development but became a disappointment when it failed to predict dangerousness and violence to a satisfactory level. A second, more promising attempt is the *Violence Risk Assessment Guide* (VRAG), developed by Grant Harris, Marnie Rice, and colleagues (Webster, Harris, Rice, Cormier, & Quinsey, 1994). The VRAG is based on data from 618 men with histories of significant violence who were initially confined at the Oak Ridge Division of the Penetanguishene Mental Health Center in Ontario, Canada. Oak Ridge is a maximum-security facility providing assessment and treatment for persons referred from the courts, correctional services, and other provincial psychiatric hospitals (Webster et al., 1994). Twelve variables believed to predict future violence make up the VRAG. The variables include separation of parents by age 16 or younger, schizophrenia, elementary school maladjustment, a history of alcohol abuse, and symptoms of psychopathy. The 618 violent men in the project were followed for 10 years. Overall, 31% of the subjects committed another violent offense, usually within seven years after release (Rice, 1997). The best predictor of violent recidivism was the score of the psychopathy scale (i.e., PCL-R). "It alone predicted better than any combination of other criminal history variables . . ." (p. 415). On the other hand, the presence of a mental disorder did not predict violence. Based on preliminary research, Rice concludes, "Our work and that of others on the prediction of violence has shown that long-term criminal violence can be predicted with a considerable degree of accuracy among men who have already been apprehended for a violent criminal offense" (p. 418).

Another promising instrument for evaluating risk is the Historical/ Clinical/Risk Management (HCR-20) scale developed by Christopher Webster and his colleagues (Webster, Douglas, Eaves, & Hart, 1997). The HCR bases its predictive power on three major areas: past or historical factors, clinical or current factors, and risk management factors. The HCR contains 10 historical items, 5 clinical items, and 5 risk management items, for a total of 20 items. The historical items include "previous violence," which, as we have learned, is one of the strongest predictors of future violence. Another historical or "H" item is "young age at first violent incident" (p. 267). In other words, the younger the person at the time of the first violent incident, the greater the likelihood that a violent pattern will persist into the future. "Early maladjustment" at home, at school, or in the community is another predictive H item. Other H items in the HCR-20 are relationship instability, employment problems, substance use problems, and major mental illness (particularly psychotic or mood disorders). Clinical or "C" items include lack of insight, negative attitudes (antisocial, hostile, angry), and "active symptoms of major mental illness" (p. 263). Active symptoms of serious mental illness that include delusional systems characterized by sadistic fantasies and homicidal and suicidal ideation are especially related to violence prediction. Risk management or "R" variables are related to the future circumstances of the individuals they are evaluating—that is, whether the person being evaluated is likely to have adequate housing, meals, daily activities, and finances. Research suggests that individuals without these basics are at higher risk for violence than those who have these needs managed and taken care of. Examples of R items are lack of personal support, noncompliance with remediation attempts, feasibility of future plans, and stress. The researchers of the HCR-20 find that the historical (H) items are the strongest for predicting future violent behavior (Webster et al., 1997), and C items are the second strongest (Borum, 1996). The HCR-20 is still in its infancy and needs ongoing research before it receives widespread acceptance as a valid risk assessment instrument.

The MacArthur Network research project discussed earlier in the chapter (Steadman, 1998) represents still another example of efforts to develop a risk assessment measure. The project involves acute psychiatric patients discharged from mental institutions in three locations (Pittsburgh, PA, Worcester, MA, and Kansas City, MO). The goals of the project were threefold: (1) to improve the validity of clinical risk assessment, (2) to improve the effectiveness of clinical risk management, and (3) to provide useful information for reforming mental health policy. The project resulted in the development of the Multiple Iterative Classification Tree, a means of assessing the likelihood that a mentally disordered individual will engage in future aggressive behavior. Among the many factors considered are episodes of violent behavior, violent fantasies, persons in one's positive social network, and substance abuse. Like other researchers, Steadman et al. (1998) emphasize that no one factor can predict that violence will occur.

It should also be emphasized that risk assessment instruments, such as those described above, are not invariably supported in the clinical literature. Many mental health practitioners are suspicious of measures that rely on actuarial data or that were developed on specific populations, such as incarcerated violent offenders or persons held in civil mental hospitals. Some scholars have noted that risk assessment instruments may ignore factors that are specific to the case at hand (Heilbrun et al., 2002) or that clinicians often adjust the scores to incorporate their own clinical impressions (Doren, 2002). Heilbrun et al. acknowledge the value of risk assessment instruments, but they also urge clinicians not to undermine the role of clinical judgment. In essence, one should supplement the other, because neither approach, standing alone, is likely to produce consistent, valid results.

SUMMARY AND CONCLUSIONS

In this chapter, we have focused on the relationship between mentally disordered individuals and crime. In order to begin to understand this relationship, we must go beyond labels, which do not explain why someone behaves in a certain way. Furthermore, labels are assigned by the mental health profession and, along with their definitions, may change with each edition of the DSM, the standard diagnostic manual used by most clinicians. Since the 1980s, however, the DSM has remained relatively stable.

We reviewed some of the major changes in the DSM since it was first introduced in 1952. The DSM of today (DSM-IV-R) is very behaviorally based, providing clinicians detailed presenting symptoms for each of the disorders it lists. In the chapter, we discussed the disorders that are most likely to be associated with criminal conduct (antisocial personality disorder, schizophrenia, psychotic disorders) as well as some of the nontraditional but intriguing disorders that are often highly publicized when used as excusing conditions for crime. Several of these fall under the category of dissociative disorders (e.g., post–traumatic stress disorder, dissociative identity disorder, dissociative amnesia).

With the exception of persons with an antisocial personality disorder, individuals with mental disorders—as a whole—are no more likely than the general population to commit crimes, including violent crimes. However, the subgroup of currently mentally disordered patients who have a history of violence are involved in violent behavior far more often than the nondisordered members in the general population. According to Monahan (1996), this relationship is especially significant if a current mental disorder is accompanied by three symptoms: (1) feeling that others wish to do one harm, (2) feeling that one's mind is dominated by forces beyond one's control, and (3) feeling that others' thoughts are being put into one's head.

Bonta et al. (1998) raise some serious questions as to whether mentally disordered offenders are more likely to recidivate than nondisordered offenders. Preliminary data from recent research suggest that mentally disordered offenders are less likely to commit another crime than non–mentally disordered offenders.

We also reviewed the various categories of mentally disordered individuals who are found in the criminal justice system. These categories include defendants found incompetent to stand trial, defendants found not guilty by reason of insanity, mentally disordered sex offenders, and mentally disordered jail and prison inmates, including those who are transferred to civil mental institutions.

Incompetence to stand trial is a key legal determination of the mentally disordered defendant. In recent literature, the term "adjudicative competence" is gradually replacing competence to stand trial. This is in recognition of the fact that competence pertains to a wide range of court-related situations, including plea bargaining, participating in a variety of pretrial hearings, participating in the trial itself, and sentencing. Although there are always exceptions, persons found IST tend to be marginal members of society, with few family ties, no job, prior hospitalization, and slightly older than most criminal defendants. Recent research indicates that, whereas they are often evaluated in community settings, treatment for restoration to competence continues to take place in institutionalized settings.

Research reveals that fewer than 1% of all criminal cases involve the insanity defense, and when the defense is raised, it usually does not succeed. Although data vary widely according to jurisdiction, it is estimated that about 25% of insanity defenses—which may be raised in felony or misdemeanor crimes—are successful. However, much of the research on the insanity defense was conducted prior to the time when most states modified their statutes to make it more difficult for defendants to raise a successful insanity defense. Additionally, an insanity acquittal is rarely a bargain. The amount of time spent in a mental institution or treatment facility is generally at least as long as the amount of time the offender would have served in prison had he or she been found guilty. Not-guilty-by-reason-of-insanity patients, in most states, must also prove that they are no longer mentally disordered and dangerous before they can be released. Once a person is no longer mentally disordered, however, he or she must be released.

The mentally disordered sex offender category is an extremely controversial one. Many states today prefer the term sexually violent predator and have laws allowing these individuals to be committed to mental institutions following their prison terms. Critics of these statutes believe that mental disorder in these individuals is often wrongfully diagnosed and that the statutes are used to punish offenders beyond their legal sentence. Furthermore, even if these predators are mentally disordered, they apparently do not necessarily receive the treatment that the statutes imply.

Since the 1980s, we have seen the emergence of many special or unique defenses based on psychological states. Although these defenses have received considerable attention from the media, judges and juries have been very reluctant to accept them as excusing or mitigating conditions for criminal actions.

Nevertheless, courts are increasingly allowing defendants to introduce evidence of these mental conditions. Defendants have claimed lack of responsibility, or diminished responsibility, by citing—among other conditions—post–traumatic stress disorder, multiple personality disorder/dissociative identity disorder, compulsive gambling disorder, and amnesia.

Finally, we reviewed the complex literature on dangerousness as it pertains to the mentally disordered. Traditionally, clinicians have overestimated the potential violence of this population, engendering debate about the proper criteria for assessing dangerousness. How many persons are forcefully confined, on the basis of dangerousness, without justification? Accurate predictions of dangerousness are extremely elusive. Today, most clinicians prefer to use the term "risk assessment," indicating that they are offering probabilities that a person will engage in harmful behavior.

Overall, the best predictor available is past behavior. Those who were violent in the past, compared to those without such a history, are more likely to offend in the future. Nevertheless, it is important to emphasize that no one factor—even past violence—is a foolproof predictor of future violence. In the 1980s and 1990s, several risk assessment instruments were developed and tested for use by clinicians involved in the risk assessment enterprise. Among them are the Historical/Clinical/Risk Management scale, the Iterative Classification Tree, and the Violence Risk Assessment Guide. While it is premature to offer ringing endorsements of these measures, they offer promise to clinicians who might otherwise have little guidance in assessing risk beyond their own clinical impressions. Nevertheless, the assessment of risk very probably requires a combination of both risk assessment measures and clinical skills.

CHAPTER 7

HUMAN AGGRESSION AND VIOLENCE

There is ample evidence of the long history of human involvement in aggression and violence. The first 5,600 years of recorded human history, for example, included 14,600 wars, a rate of more than 2.6 per year (Baron, 1983; Montagu, 1976). Some writers argue that aggression has been instrumental in helping people survive. Through centuries of experience, humans learned that aggressive behavior enabled them to obtain material goods, land, and treasures; to protect property and family; and to gain prestige, status, and power. Although some might wonder whether the human species could have survived had it not used aggression, others are quick to point out that both historically and in the present, aggressive behavior is at the root of numerous social and individual problems.

Aggression—a psychological concept that we define shortly—warrants an entire chapter because it is the basic ingredient in violent crime. By studying aggression, psychologists have made substantial contributions to society's efforts to understand both violent and nonviolent crime as well as violent behavior that may not necessarily be defined as crime (e.g., legitimate uses of force). Is human aggression instinctive, biological, learned, or some combination of these characteristics? If it results from an innate, biological mechanism, the methods designed to control, reduce, or eliminate aggressive behavior will differ significantly from the methods used if aggression is learned.

Perspectives of human nature emerge very clearly from the scholarly and research literature on aggression. Some writers and researchers believe that aggressive behavior is basically physiological and genetic in origin, a strong residue of our evolutionary past. This physiological, genetic contention is accompanied by compelling evidence that explanations of human aggressive behavior may be found in the animal kingdom from which it originated. On the other hand, researchers who subscribe to the learning viewpoint believe that, while some species of animals may be genetically programmed to behave aggressively, human beings learn to be aggressive from the social environment. The learning position also offers cogent evidence to support its theory. Other researchers remain on a theoretical fence, accepting and rejecting some aspects of each argument.

If aggression and violence represent a built-in, genetically programmed aspect of human nature, we may be forced, as Baron (1983) suggests, toward a pessimistic conclusion. At best, we can only hope to hold our natural, aggressive urges and drives temporarily in check. Furthermore, we should design the environment and society in such a way as to discourage violence, including administering immediate and aversive consequences (punishment) when it is displayed. Even better—and setting aside ethical or legal considerations for the moment—we might consider psychosurgery, electrode implants, and drug control—all effective methods for the reduction, if not the elimination, of violence.

If, on the other hand, we believe that aggression is learned and is influenced by a wide range of situational, social, and environmental variables, we can be more optimistic. Aggression is not an inevitable aspect of human life. Once we understand what factors play major roles in its acquisition and maintenance, we will be able to change human behavior by manipulating these factors. There are, of course, both positive and negative aspects of human aggression. Many individuals who play in competitive sports, hunt for sport, serve in the military, and work for law enforcement engage in socially permissible forms of aggression that may be necessary or that enhance their quality of life. The focus in this chapter is on the negative aspects, or the forms of aggression that are not socially permissible.

By most accounts, animal aggression reflects the biological programming carried in the genes to ensure the survival of the species. Humans, with their enormously complex and sophisticated cerebral cortex, rely heavily on thought, associations, beliefs, and learning; these become primary determinants of behavior. Theorists differ over the degree to which genetic programming contributes to human behavior. Thus, are people aggressive and violent because their animal instincts continue to promote this particular behavior? And, if the evolutionary aggressive drives still reside within the subcortical structures of the brain (below the cortex in the "old" brain), as some writers tell us they do, are they modifiable? If not, how can we best prevent people from attacking and killing one another? On the other hand, a difference-in-kind perspective suggests that genetic predispositions, or biological precursors of aggression, have a minimal influence on human behavior, if they have any influence at all. After defining aggression, we return to these different points of view.

DEFINING AGGRESSION

The task of defining human aggression is surprisingly difficult, as many social psychologists have discovered. Forcibly jabbing someone in the midsection is certainly defining it by example—Or is it? Now what about jabbing someone more softly, in jest? Would everyone consider football and boxing aggressive behaviors? If someone pointedly ignores a question, is that an example of aggression? What if someone spreads malicious gossip? If a burglar breaks into your home and you reach for your trusty but rusty rifle, aim it at the intruder, and pull the trigger, is yours an act of aggression? Is it any less so if the rifle does not fire? If someone sits passively on a doorstep and blocks your entry, is this aggression?

Some social psychologists define aggression as the intent and attempt to harm another individual, physically or socially or, in some cases, to destroy an object. This definition seems adequate for many situations, but it has several limitations. Refusing to speak does not fit well, since it is not an active attempt to harm someone, nor is the person blocking entry trying to injure anyone. Most psychologists place these two behaviors in a special category of aggressive responses and call them **passive–aggressive behaviors**, since they are generally interpreted as aggressive in intent, although the behavior is passive and indirect.

As fascinating as passive–aggressive behavior may be, it is generally irrelevant when we discuss crime, since the aggression we are concerned with is the type that manifests itself directly in violent or antisocial behavior. We might stretch the point by suggesting that the doorstep sitter is trespassing, in which case he or she might be charged with a criminal offense. Likewise, there are other situations in which passive–aggressive behavior could lead to various types of crime. Refusing to file income tax because one is intensely dissatisfied with the current administration is one example. In general, however, the aggressive behavior we wish to focus on in this chapter is not of the passive–aggressive kind.

In an effort to conceptualize the many varieties of human aggression, Buss (1971) tried to classify them based on the apparent motivation of the aggressor (see **Table 7–1**). You may easily find exceptions and overlapping categories in the Buss scheme, but that emphasizes how difficult it is to compartmentalize human aggressive behavior. It also epitomizes the many definitional dilemmas that hamper social psychologists studying aggression.

Before finally settling on a satisfactory definition of aggression (and we will get there), it may be useful to recognize two types, **hostile** (or **expressive**)

TABLE 7–1 Varieties of Human Aggression

	ACTIVE DIRECT	INDIRECT	PASSIVE DIRECT	INDIRECT
Physical	Punching the victim	Practical joke, booby trap	Obstructing passage, sit-in	Refusing to perform a necessary task
Verbal	Insulting the victim	Malicious gossip	Refusing to speak	Refusing consent, vocal or written

Source: A. H. Buss, "Aggression Pays," in J. L. Singer (ed.), *The Control of Aggression and Violence* (New York: Academic Press, 1971), p. 8.

aggression and **instrumental aggression**, a distinction first made by Feshbach (1964). They are distinguished by their goals, or the rewards they offer the perpetrator. Hostile (or expressive) aggression, which we are most concerned with in this chapter, occurs in response to anger-inducing conditions, such as real or perceived insults, physical attacks, or one's own failures. The aggressor's goal is to make a victim suffer. Most criminal homicides, rapes, and other violent crimes directed at harming the victim are precipitated by hostile aggression. The behavior is characterized by the intense and disorganizing emotion of anger, with anger defined as an arousal state elicited by certain stimuli, particularly those evoking attack or frustration. Angry at the economic system that deprived him of a job, a sniper may open fire on passing motorists and feel satisfaction at having lashed out "successfully" at society.

Instrumental aggression begins with competition or the desire for some object or status possessed by another person—jewelry, money, territory. The perpetrator tries to obtain the desired object regardless of the cost. Instrumental aggression is usually a factor in robbery, burglary, larceny, and various white-collar crimes. The perpetrator's obvious goal in a robbery is to obtain items of value. Usually, there is no intent to harm anyone. However, if someone or something interferes with the perpetrator's objective, he or she may feel forced to harm the victim or risk losing the desired goal. In that sense, a robbery may lead to murder, but the aggression represented is still instrumental. Instrumental aggression is also usually a feature of calculated murder committed by a hired, impersonal killer. Although psychologists make the distinction between hostile and instrumental aggression, the law does not, insofar as responsibility for the crime is concerned. However, certain factors associated with hostile aggression (e.g., if the crime is committed in a particularly heinous fashion) can affect the criminal sentence. On the other hand, a contract killer's instrumental aggression may also bring a longer sentence if information about prior offenses comes to light at sentencing.

Bandura (1973a) notes that most definitions of aggression imply that it is solely concerned with behaviors and intentions residing within the perpetrator (or performer). Going a step further, he suggests that the adequate definition of aggression must consider both the "injurious behavior" of the perpetrator and the "social judgment" of the victim. Thus, a soft poke in the belly may qualify as aggression if it is done derisively and if the recipient interprets it that way. A textbook on criminal behavior, however, must focus on aggression as manifested in conduct, not as it is perceived by a victim. For our purposes, therefore, we define aggression as *behavior perpetrated or attempted with the intention of harming another individual physically or psychologically (as opposed to socially) or to destroy an object*. This definition encompasses all the behaviors described in Buss's typology. Note, however, that aggressive behavior will not always qualify as criminal. A law enforcement officer using *reasonable force* against a criminal suspect is displaying aggressive behavior, but it is not criminal.

Furthermore, we define violence as *destructive physical aggression intentionally directed at harming other persons or things*. Violence may be methodical or random, sustained or fleeting, intensive or uncontrolled. It always harms or destroys the recipient or is intended to do so (Daniels & Gilula, 1970). Therefore, all violent behavior is aggressive behavior, but not all aggressive behavior is violent. Spreading malicious, false information about someone is a case in point.

THEORETICAL PERSPECTIVES ON AGGRESSION

Behavioral and social scientists have debated for over a half-century whether humans are born aggressive and naturally violent or born relatively free of aggressive tendencies. This debate, part of a wider controversy about the respective merits of nature and nurture, touches every school of thought in human behavior. According to the first perspective, humans are programmed aggressive to defend themselves, their family, and their territory from intruders. According to the second, humans become violent by acquiring aggressive models and actions from society. In this section, the topics move from the instinctive and biological perspectives to the more learning-based perspectives.

Psychoanalytical/Psychodynamic Viewpoint

Psychodynamic theorists assume that humans, by their very nature, will always be prone to aggressive impulses and hence are likely to commit violent acts if these impulses are not appropriately managed or held in check. Sigmund Freud, the father of psychoanalysis and a physician by training, was convinced that human beings are susceptible from birth to a buildup of aggressive energy, which must be dissipated or drained off before it reaches dangerous levels. This is known as the **psychodynamic** or **hydraulic model** since it bears a close resemblance to pressure buildup in a container. If excessive pressure accumulates in the container—the human psyche—an explosion is likely to occur, as demonstrated by tirades that may involve violence. According to the traditional Freudian perspective, people who have tirades are blowing off the excess steam of aggressive energy.

Freud suggested that violence in all of its forms is a manifestation of this aggressive energy discharge. Internal energy accumulates to dangerous levels when people have not discharged it appropriately through a process called catharsis, one of the most important concepts in psychoanalytic psychotherapy. Catharsis may be accomplished by actual behavior (playing football, for example) or may occur vicariously (watching football). The Freudian–psychodynamic position predicts that children who participate in or avidly watch school sports will ultimately be less aggressive than children who do not. Freudian psychodynamic followers also maintain that people who engage in violent crime (particularly hostile aggression) have not had sufficient opportunity to "blow off steam" and keep their aggressive energies at manageable levels.

According to the psychoanalytical viewpoint, if violent crime is to be controlled, the human animal must be provided with multiple but appropriate channels for catharsis (e.g., adequate recreational facilities). In this way, children and adults presumably learn to dissipate aggression in socially approved, appropriate ways. Psychotherapy is one such channel, encouraging catharsis under the guidance of a therapist.

Ethological Viewpoints

Ethology is the study of animal behavior in relation to the animal's natural habitat, and it compares that behavior to human behavior. In the mid-1960s, a number of ethologists published books and articles about aggression that interested and appealed to the general public. Three especially popular books were Konrad Lorenz's *On Aggression* (1966), Robert Ardrey's *The Territorial Imperative* (1966), and Desmond Morris' *The Naked Ape* (1967). Lorenz was the chief spokesperson for a theoretical formulation of ethology as it relates to aggression.

A Nobel laureate in biology, Lorenz believed that aggression is an inherited instinct of both humans and animals. One of its main purposes is to enable the animal—and the human being—to defend "staked-out" territory, a territory that ensures sufficient food, water, and space to roam and reproduce. If this space is violated, Lorenz argued, the instinctive or genetically programmed response is to attack, or at least to increase aggressive behavior toward the intruder, thus preventing further territory violation. The tendency to attack space violators is referred to as **territoriality**. Lorenz believed it is an innate propensity developed through the lengthy, complex process of evolution. This innate aggressive behavior among members of the same animal species (intraspecific aggression) prevents overcrowding and ensures the best and most powerful mates for the young.

The more deadly the animal's evolutionarily developed weaponry (e.g., fangs, claws, size, and strength), the more intense the innate inhibitions against engaging in physical combat with members of its own species. This innately programmed inhibition is a form of insurance for species survival,

Lorenz believed, since constant intraspecific physical combat would eventually extinguish the species. Intraspecies aggression is accomplished, therefore, not by actual combat but by complicated displays of force and superiority, such as a show of teeth, size, or color array. These displays are referred to as **ritualized aggression**. Through an intricate communication system not yet understood by scientists, the animals transmit signals, after which the more powerful, dominant animal generally wins out. The losing animal demonstrates defeat by various appeasement behaviors, such as rolling over on its back (characteristic of puppies), lowering its tail or head, and emitting cries of defeat. The weaker animal then leaves the territory of the dominant one.

What does all of this have to do with human aggression? Lorenz and other ethologists believe that it is important to understand animal aggression before we try to understand human aggression, since humans are part of the animal world and probably follow many of its basic principles. In other words, ethologists subscribe to the **difference-in-degree** Darwinian perspective. Efran and Cheyne (1974), for example, observed, after studying invasion of personal space among humans, that "human society may operate through mechanisms which are less uniquely human than is currently fashionable to suggest" (p. 225).

Lorenz raised another issue that, if valid, is more significant to criminal behavior, however. He maintained that human beings have outdistanced the evolutionary process of inhibiting aggression. Instead of developing natural weapons and the species-preserving function of ritualized aggression, humans have developed technological weaponry. Thus, he and many other ethologists believe they can provide at least a partial answer to why human beings wantonly maim and kill members of their own species: They have not developed the ability to engage in the species-preserving behavior of ritualized aggression. Instead, through superior learning ability, they have developed the capacity to annihilate.

The ethological position is intriguing, but it has not been supported by human aggression research (Bandura, 1983; Montagu, 1973; Zillmann, 1983). Zoologists, biologists, and psychologists have tried with little success to apply the Lorenzian tenets to humans. One problem is that the ethological position relies on a strong analogy between animals and humans. Lorenz argued, for example, that the greylag goose is remarkably similar to the human species (Berkowitz, 1973). However, the human brain makes us remarkably unlike the greylag goose and considerably less likely to rely on instinct for determining behavior. Research has yet to delineate any instinctive or invariant genetically programmed behavior determinant in humans. Furthermore, "the capacity to exercise control over one's own thought processes, motivation, and action is a distinctively human characteristic" (Bandura, 1989, p. 1175).

Ethologists also fail to acknowledge and interpret the vast body of existing scientific research that has tested their position and found it wanting. This curious response—or nonresponse—undermines the validity of their whole presentation. Some critics have referred to ethological theorizing as "scientific-sounding misinformation" (Leach, 1973). To date, therefore, there is little evidence to justify portraying humans as *innately* dangerous and brutal or as controlled by instinct. Some contemporary theories do adopt a biological perspective on violence, however, as we will see later in the chapter.

Frustration-Aggression Hypothesis

Around the time of Freud's death in 1939, a group of psychologists at Yale University proposed that aggression is a direct result of frustration (Dollard, Doob, Miller, Mowrer, & Sears, 1939). According to John Dollard and his colleagues, people who are frustrated, thwarted, annoyed, or threatened will behave aggressively, since aggression is a natural, almost-automatic response to frustrating circumstances. Moreover, people who exhibit aggressive behavior are frustrated, thwarted, annoyed, or threatened. "Aggression is always a consequence of frustration" (p. 1).

Because of its simplicity and important implications, the **frustration–aggression hypothesis** drew much research, along with much criticism. Psychologists found it difficult not only to decide what frustration was, but also to determine how it could be measured accurately. Researchers also learned that aggression was a much more complex phenomenon than Dollard and his associates had postulated. Frustration does not always lead to aggression, and aggressive behavior does not always signify "frustration." Experiments indicated that people respond to frustration and anger differently. Some do indeed respond with aggression, but others display a wide variety of responses.

Led by Leonard Berkowitz (1962, 1969, 1973), whose general views on some of the causes of criminality were presented in Chapter 5, researchers began to propose a revised, contemporary version of the frustration–aggression hypothesis. According to Berkowitz, frustration increases the probability that an individual will become angry and soon act aggressively (aggression being defined as a behavior in which the goal is to inflict damage or injury on some object or person). In short, frustration facilitates the performance of aggressive behavior. The behavior may be overt (physical or verbal) or implicit (wishing someone dead). Anger, however, is not the only potentially aggressive emotion. Aversive conditions, such as pain, or pleasant states, such as sexual arousal, may also lead to aggressive behavior (Berkowitz, 1973). We return to this subject shortly.

An important component of the revised frustration–aggression hypothesis is the concept of anticipated goals or expectations. When a behavior directed at a specific goal is thwarted, frustration is likely to result. Thus, the person must have been expecting or anticipating the attainment of a goal or achievement. Mere deprivation of goods will not necessarily lead to frustration. People who are living under deprived conditions may not be frustrated unless they actually expect something better. "Poverty-stricken groups who have never dreamed of having automobiles, washing machines, or new homes are not frustrated because they have been deprived of these things; they are frustrated only after they have begun to hope" (Berkowitz, 1969, p. 15).

Aggression, Berkowitz says, is only one possible response to frustration. The individual may learn others, like withdrawal, doing nothing, or trying to alter the situation by getting out of the situation completely or by compromising. With this approach, Berkowitz not only emphasizes the importance of learning but also stresses the role of individual differences in response to frustrating circumstances.

The revised frustration–aggression hypothesis, therefore, suggests the following steps: (1) The person is blocked from obtaining an expected goal; (2) frustration results, generating anger; and (3) anger *predisposes* or readies the person to behave aggressively. Whether the person actually engages in aggressive actions will depend in part on his or her learning history, interpretation of the event, and individual way of responding to frustration. It will also depend, however, on the presence of aggression-eliciting stimuli in the environment.

Berkowitz notes that the presence of aggressive stimuli in the external environment (or internal environment represented by thoughts) increases the probability of aggressive responses. A weapon is a good example of such a stimulus. Most people in our society associate firearms with aggression. Berkowitz (1983) likens the firearm to a conditioned stimulus in that the weapon conjures aggressive associations, facilitating overt aggression. A gun, even when not used, is more likely to generate aggressive action than is a neutral object. "The mere sight of the weapon might elicit ideas, images, and expressive reactions that had been linked with aggression in the past . . ." (p. 124).

In one experiment designed to test this hypothesis (Berkowitz & LePage, 1967), angry male subjects were more likely to engage in aggressive action in the presence of a gun than a comparable group of angry subjects in the presence of a badminton racket. This suggests that a visible weapon (such as a law enforcement officer might carry) may actually facilitate, rather than inhibit, a violent response in some people.

The Berkowitz–LePage finding generated much controversy as to whether weapons actually do provoke aggressive behavior. A number of studies tried to replicate the finding but failed to find evidence of a *weapons effect* (Penrod, 1983). Some researchers believed that many of the subjects used in some of the studies "saw through" the purpose of the study, a research flaw called demand characteristics. However, a comprehensive review of the research literature found strong evidence that the weapons effect does—in fact—exist (Carlson, Marcus-Newhall, & Miller, 1990). Carlson et al. concluded, "Aggression-related cues present in experimental settings act to increase aggressive responding. This cue effect occurs more strongly when subjects have been negatively aroused before their exposure to aggression-facilitating cues" (p. 632). The weapons effect has also been found in other countries, including Belgium, Croatia, Italy, and Sweden (Berkowitz, 1994).

It should be mentioned that the aggression-eliciting stimuli need not be aggressive or violent in appearance (i.e., a gun, knife, or bomb) but can be seemingly neutral stimuli. That is, the stimuli need only be associated with aversive events or have a decidedly unpleasant meaning to an individual to intensify aggressive reactions. Even some types of music may facilitate or encourage aggressive behavior (Rogers & Ketcher, 1979).

Berkowitz (1989) emphasized two important components to the frustration–aggression equation. Aggressive behavior will be generated (1) to the extent that a person perceives the mistreatment as intentional and (2) to the degree that the frustration experienced is aversive. According to Berkowitz, people become angry and aggressive at being kept from reaching a desired goal if they think someone intentionally blocked them from achieving that goal or deliberately and wrongly tried to hurt them. "They are much more likely to become openly aggressive at someone's blocking their goal attainment if they believe their frustrater had deliberately and unjustifiably attempted to keep them from reaching their goal than if they think the thwarting had not been intentional or had not been directed at them personally" (p. 68). Thus, self-restraint comes into play when people think they have not been deliberately mistreated or that the blocking of the goal was legitimate. On the other hand, people become angry and aggressive when they perceive that they have been treated unfairly or were personally attacked.

Berkowitz also postulates that thwartings or frustrations generate a negative affect, which refers to an emotional state people typically seek to lessen or eliminate. Furthermore, an unexpected interference is more apt to provoke an aggressive reaction than is an anticipated barrier to goal attainment, because the former is usually much more unpleasant. That is, it has more negative affect.

In his reformulation of the frustration–aggression hypothesis, Berkowitz has emphasized the importance of cognitive factors. Currently, it is called the **cognitive–neoassociation model**. It operates in the following manner. During the earlier stages, an aversive event produces a negative affect. This negative affect may be due to physical pain or psychological discomfort. Physical pain as an aversive circumstance is clear, but psychological discomfort needs further elaboration. Being verbally insulted is a good example. While there is no physical pain, personal insults or demeaning comments engender anger, depression, or sadness in just about everyone—all negative affects. Unpleasant feelings or negative affects presumably then give rise, almost automatically, to a variety of feelings, thoughts, and memories that are associated with flight (fear) and fight (anger) tendencies. During this early stage, mediating cognitive processes have little influence beyond the immediate appraisal that the situation is aversive. Some people may act quickly on the basis of these initial emotions without further deliberation or forethought, sometimes engaging in violence. During the later stages, however, cognitive appraisal may go into operation and substantially influence the subsequent emotional reactions and experiences after the initial, automatic responses. These cognitions mediate and evaluate a proper course of action. During the later stages, aroused people make causal attributions about the unpleasant experience, think about the nature of their feelings, and perhaps try to control their feelings and actions.

Berkowitz emphasizes that any unpleasant feeling or arousal can evoke aggressive, even violent responses. A depressed person can murder his or her family, or a thwarted teenager may violently lash out at authority.

Excitation Transfer Theory

Zillmann (1988) has proposed a theory to explain how physiological arousal can generalize from one situation to another. Called **excitation transfer theory**, it is based on the assumption that physiological arousal, however produced, dissipates slowly over time. For example, a person who receives some anger-producing criticism at work is likely to have some residual arousal from that criticism when he or she arrives home later that evening. Encountering some annoying event at home, the person is apt to "fly off the handle" and overreact to the minor home incident. Consequently, the combination of pre-existing arousal, plus anger generated by the irritation at home, may increase the likelihood of aggression. The transfer of arousal from one situation to another is most likely to occur if the person is unaware that he or she is still carrying some arousal from a previous situation to a new, unrelated one.

Aggressive Driving

Aggressive driving illustrates the previous arousal theories of aggression well. Aggressive driving is defined as an incident in which an angry, impatient, or aroused motorist intentionally injures or kills, or tries to injure or kill, another motorist, passenger, or pedestrian, in response to a traffic dispute, altercation, or grievance (Mizell, 1995). It is also considered aggressive driving when an aroused, upset motorist drives his or her vehicle into a building or other structure or property (Mizell, 1995). Aggressive driving, sometimes referred to as *road rage*, apparently is particularly problematic in the United States. The subject even inspired a popular movie, *Changing Lanes*. Road rage is usually reserved for extreme acts of aggression that occur as a direct result of a disagreement between drivers (Joint, 1995). In recent years, aggressive driving and road rage have become increasingly troubling and dangerous phenomena on the nation's highways. In 1996, the AAA Potomac Club found that motorists in the Washington, D.C., area felt more threatened by aggressive drivers than by drunk drivers. It is estimated that an average of over 1,500 men, women, and children is injured or killed each year as a direct result of aggressive driving or road rage.

Studies reveal that the majority of aggressive drivers are young males who have criminal and violent histories and drug or alcohol problems (Mizell, 1995). However, aggressive drivers come from all walks of life, across a variety of socioeconomic levels and occupations. Many have no known history of violence. And celebrities are not immune. "In California, Oscar winner Jack Nicholson believed that a driver of a Mercedes-Benz cut him off in traffic. The 57-year-old actor grabbed a golf club, stepped out of his car at a red light, and repeatedly struck the windshield and roof of the Mercedes" (Mizell, 1995, p. 5).

The weapons most commonly used by aggressive drivers are firearms (37%) and the vehicle itself (35%). Other weapons used are tire irons, jack handles, baseball bats, hurled projectiles, defensive sprays, fists, and feet. Mizell (1995, p. 8) writes, "While the event that sparks the incident may be trivial, in every case there exists some reservoir of anger, hostility, or frustration that is released by the triggering incident." In one case, a man was attacked by fellow motorists because he could not turn off the antitheft alarm on his rented jeep.

Domestic violence is also a very common factor in aggressive driving, when upset spouses and intimate partners vent their anger on the highway. Surprisingly, it is not unusual for angry drivers to use their motor vehicles to attack law enforcement personnel and vehicles. The gender differences in aggressive driving are not as great as might be expected. In one survey, 54% of the women admitted to aggressive driving behavior, compared to 64% of men (Joint, 1995). In that survey, respondents reported that aggressive tailgating (62%) was the most common form of road rage, followed by headlight flashing (59%), obscene gestures (48%), deliberate obstruction of other vehicles (21%), and verbal abuse (16%).

The causes of aggressive driving and road rage are largely minor misunderstandings that are perceived and interpreted by other drivers as aggressive, aversive, or directed personally at them. It also appears that a major factor in the road rage reaction is frustration, followed by emotional arousal that detaches the angry driver from his or her usual cognitive control of appropriate behavior. In most instances, the aggressive driver is already primed for aggressive or violent action due to an incident that happened before reaching the highway (Connell, 1996). A quarrel with a loved one, some difficulty on the job, problems making financial ends meet, or any number of previous events can contribute to the arousal factor. The stimulus that sets off the aggression, as Berkowitz might argue in his cognitive–neoassociation model, is the annoying behavior of another driver. The available weapon is the motor vehicle. Thus, the necessary components of a negative affect and the appropriate stimuli are in place for aggression to occur. Obviously, not all drivers in these circumstances react with rage. In the following section, we focus more on the factors that might distinguish one person's reactions from another's.

Social Learning

Why do some people behave aggressively when intensely frustrated, while others change their tactics, withdraw, or seem not to be affected? One major factor may be past learning experiences. The human being, as we noted in Chapter 5, is very adept at learning and maintaining behavior patterns that have worked in the past, even if they only worked occasionally. This learning process begins in early childhood. Children develop many behaviors merely by watching their parents and significant others in their environment, a process we have called modeling or observational learning. A child's behavior pattern, therefore, is often acquired through the modeling or imitation of other people, real and imagined, in the child's environment (Bandura, 1973a). In fact, available research reveals that the conditions most conducive to the learning of aggression are those in which the child (1) has many opportunities to observe aggression, (2) is reinforced for his or her own aggression, or (3) is often the object of aggression (Huesmann, 1988).

Suppose Harris's father returns home feeling harried after a hot and humid day during which he accomplished nothing (frustration). He finds an official-looking letter from the IRS in the mailbox. He opens it, perhaps muttering mild obscenities under his breath, and finds that the IRS apparently suspects he has shortchanged the U.S. government by several hundred dollars, although he knows he has not (more frustration). He is invited for an audit (even more frustration). In response, he slams his fist on the table, exclaims "Damn it!" or some colorful variation, and kicks the nearest chair (just enough not to damage his toe, since he has learned the painful consequences from past similar episodes). Unknown to his father, Harris has observed this whole scenario. Several hours later, when his block tower crumbles, little Harris pounds his fist, kicks the living room chair, and curses, "Damn it!"

When a child's imitative behavior is reinforced or rewarded by praise and encouragement from significant models, the probability that the behavior will occur in the future is increased. There is evidence that American parents (consciously or inadvertently) encourage or reinforce aggressive behavior in their children, particularly in their sons. For example, Harris's behavior might have been reinforced if Dad or Mom drew attention to it—"Isn't that cute?"—or if they laughed. In a future episode, the kicking behavior might be directed at the family cat. Furthermore, while kicking chairs and towers (or even the family cat, in the minds of some readers) may seem relatively mild, the same behavior becomes very sobering if the parent's anger is taken out on a family member, as too many Harrises in our society have observed. Others are "merely" expected or encouraged to be hard-hitting linebackers and to hold their own against neighborhood bullies, providing they are approximately the same size. They learn that the child who aggresses successfully against others is often rewarded with status, prestige, and the most attractive toys or material goods.

Bandura (1983) identifies three major types of models: family members, members of one's subculture, and symbolic models provided by the mass media. As we noted in Chapter 2, family members, particularly parents, can be very powerful models up until early adolescence. Beginning in early adolescence, peer models are likely to dominate. Not surprisingly, the highest incidence of aggression is found in communities and groups in which aggressive models abound and fighting prowess is regarded as a valued attribute (Bandura, 1983; Short, 1968; Wolfgang & Ferracuti, 1967).

The mass media, including television, movies, magazines, newspapers, and books, provide abundant symbolic models. Television pervades the life of the growing child, even the very young one, and offers hundreds of potentially powerful aggressive and violent models in a variety of formats, ranging from Saturday morning cartoon festivals to triple-X-rated cable and satellite movies. The Internet and computer games have contributed countless additional models. The effects they have on children is a highly debated issue and one we cover later in this chapter.

Since parents are powerful models, we would expect aggressive or antisocial parents to have aggressive or antisocial children. In an old but classic study, Sears, Maccoby, and Levin (1957) interviewed 400 mothers of kindergarten children about their disciplinary techniques, their attitudes about children's aggressiveness, and the children's expressions of aggression toward peers, siblings, and parents. One of the major findings was that physical punishment by parents was related to aggressiveness in the children. This was especially true when physical discipline was supplemented by high permissiveness toward aggression. In support of this finding, some researchers found that preschoolers played more aggressively when they were watched by a permissive adult than when no adult was visible (A. Siegel & Kohn, 1959).

Bandura (1973a) argued persuasively that aggressive behavior can be most productively understood and modified if we give attention to the learning principles like those alluded to earlier. As psychologists learned more about human behavior, they began to agree with him.

Social learning theory hypothesizes that the rudiments of aggressive behavior are initially acquired through observing aggressive models or on the basis of direct experience; aggression is then gradually refined and maintained by reinforcement. Therefore, people may have an aggressive behavioral pattern, but may rarely express it if it has no functional value or is not condoned by significant others in their social environment. The social learning system acknowledges that biological structures can set limits on the types of aggressive responses that can be learned and that genetic endowment influences the rate at which learning progresses (Bandura, 1973a). Biology does not program the individual to specific aggressive behavior, however. These behaviors are learned by observation, either deliberately or inadvertently; they become refined through reinforced practice.

In addition, mere exposure to aggressive models does not guarantee that the observer will try to engage in similar aggressive action at a later date. First, a variety of conditions may prevent observational learning from even taking place. Individuals differ widely in their ability to learn from observation. Some people may fail to notice the essential features of the model's behavior or may have a poor symbolic or visual memory. Alternately, they may not wish to imitate the model. Bandura suggests also that one important component of observational learning may be the motivation to rehearse what has been observed. He notes that a mass murderer, for example, may get an idea from descriptive accounts of another mass killing. The incident remains prominent in his mind long after it has been forgotten by others. He continues to think about the crime and to rehearse the brutal scenario mentally until, under appropriate conditions, it serves as a script for his own murderous actions.

Another restriction on observational learning is what happens to the observed model. If the model is reprimanded or punished either during or immediately after an aggressive episode, this will probably inhibit the observer's behavior. The "bad guy" should not get away with violence, if we are to discourage antisocial behavior via the entertainment media.

If aggressive behavior is to be maintained, it needs periodic reinforcement. According to social learning theory, aggression is maintained by instrumental learning. In the initial stage of learning, observation is important, but in the later stages, reinforcement is essential. The reinforcement may be positive, as when the individual gains material or social rewards, or it may be negative, if it allows the individual to alter or avoid aversive conditions. If aggressive behavior brings rewards in either of these ways, the person is likely to continue it. Research has consistently discovered that aggressive children anticipate more positive outcomes and fewer negative outcomes following their aggressive acts (Hubbard et al., 2001). "When compared with average peers, aggressive children are more likely to believe that aggression will produce tangible rewards, reduce aversive treatment by others, make themselves and peers feel good, increase self-esteem, and help to avoid a negative image" (p. 268).

Youngsters subjected to unmerciful harassment or bullying because of their unusual name or where they live may be able to stop the teasing with their fists. The reinforcement they get from their newly found aggressive behavior is negative, but it is still rewarding. Aggression can also allow individuals to feel in control of a situation if things have not been going their way. A more extreme example is a student who is constantly bullied by peers deciding to put a stop to the aversive circumstances by using a firearm on all those he or she perceives as participants. The psychological reinforcement offered by feeling in control is an extremely powerful component in any human behavior, especially aggressive or violent behavior.

COGNITIVE MODELS OF AGGRESSION

Recent cognitive models for learning aggression have hypothesized that, while observational learning is important in the process, the individual's cognitive capacities and information processing strategies are equally important. Two major cognitive models have emerged in recent years. One that has been proposed by Rowell Huesmann (1997) and his colleagues is a hypothesis called the **cognitive scripts model**. The other model has been developed by Kenneth Dodge and his colleagues (Dodge, 1986; Dodge & Coie, 1987), and is called the **hostile attribution model**. According to Rowell Huesmann (1988), social behavior, in general, and aggressive behavior, in particular, are controlled largely by **cognitive scripts** learned and memorized through daily experiences. "A script suggests what events are to happen in the environment, how the person should behave in response to these events, and what the likely outcome of those behaviors would be" (p. 15). Each script is different and unique to each person, but once established they become resistant to change and may persist into adulthood. For a script to become established, it must be rehearsed from time to time. With practice, the script not only will become encoded and maintained in memory, but will be more easily retrieved and used when the individual faces a problem. Furthermore, the individual's "evaluation of the 'appropriateness' of a script plays an important role in determining which scripts are stored in memory, in determining which scripts are retrieved and utilized, and which scripts continue to be utilized" (p. 19). The evaluation process includes the confidence that one has in predicting outcomes of the script, the extent to which one judges himself or herself capable of executing the script, and the extent to which the script is seen as congruent with one's self-regulating internal standards. Scripts that are inconsistent or violate one's internalized standards are unlikely to be stored or used. An individual with poorly integrated internal standards against aggression, or who is convinced that aggressive behavior is a way of life, is more likely to incorporate aggressive scripts for behavior. Aggressive children, for example, are apt to instigate aggressive reactions from others, confirming their beliefs about the aggressiveness of human nature in a circular, perpetuating fashion.

Kenneth Dodge and his colleagues discovered that highly aggressive children often have a **hostile attributional bias**. That is, children prone to violence are more likely to interpret ambiguous actions as hostile and threatening than are their less aggressive counterparts (Dodge, 1993b). They are twice as likely as average children to see aggression and violence where there is none (Hubbard et al., 2001). Research consistently indicates that violent youth "typically define social problems in hostile ways, adopt hostile goals, and seek few additional facts, generate few alternative solutions, anticipate few consequences for aggression, and give higher priority to their aggressive solutions" (Eron & Slaby, 1994, p. 10). Similarly, Serin and Preston (2001) conclude: "Aggressive juvenile offenders have been found to be deficient in social problem-solving skills and to espouse many beliefs supporting aggression. Specifically, they tend to define problems in hostile ways, adopt hostile goals, seek less confirmatory information, generate fewer alternative solutions, anticipate fewer consequences for aggressive solutions, and choose less effective solutions" (p. 259).

There is research to suggest that some children are especially primed to develop hostile expectations of peers because of earlier exposure to family abuse (Dodge, Bates, & Pettiti, 1990; Hubbard et al., 2001). These children appear to be especially quick at developing hostile attribution biases against a wide range of peers, including new acquaintances. "These children come to have a generalized set of social cognitions that dispose them to draw hostile inferences from the behavior of new peer acquaintances more quickly than their peers do" (Hubbard et al., 2001, p. 277). Some other children, although prone to hostile attribution bias, tend to be more specific in who they identify as hostile, probably due to certain behavioral patterns or interests they find threatening. Overall, research indicates that an interaction involving the social environment and personality factors explains much of the hostile attribution bias in children.

Ronald Blackburn (1998) also reports research evidence suggesting that persistent lawbreaking by adults represents attempts to master a social environment perceived as hostile and threatening. Blackburn hypothesizes that highly criminal offenders approach the world with a well-developed hostile–dominance interpersonal style. That is, rather than being simply a reflection of deficits in conscience (as proposed by Eysenck) or self-control (as proposed by Gotifredson and Hirschi), frequent criminal behavior may represent an ongoing attempt to control and dominate others in the social environment. According to Blackburn, chronic criminality can be understood as "an attempt to maintain status or mastery of a social environment from which they feel alienated" (p. 174). The well-rehearsed cognitive script of persistent, lifelong offenders, therefore, is to dominate—often in a hostile manner—social environments they perceive as hostile.

Aggression is a simple, direct way of solving immediate conflicts. If something is not going your way, approaching the social environment in a threatening, hostile manner is the most direct way (not necessarily the most effective in the long run) of confronting your tormentors. On the other hand, prosocial solutions and alternative nonaggressive scripts are less direct and more complex than aggressive solutions. In essence, they are more difficult to apply. Theoretically, the more cognitively "simple" individual would be more inclined to pursue simplistic and direct solutions to problems. In addition, because prosocial solutions are more complicated and more difficult to apply, they also require effective social skills. However, the development of effective social skills takes time, and those skills will have a spotty reinforcement history until perfected. Aggressive behavior, on the other hand, often receives immediate reinforcement for the aggressor, and therefore is more likely to be retained in one's arsenal of strategies for immediate solutions of conflictual situations. After a 22-year longitudinal study, Eron and Huesmann (1984) concluded that diminished intellectual competence and poor social skills have an early effect in increasing the likelihood that a child will adopt characteristically more aggressive styles of behavior to conflict resolution. For example, research has repeatedly documented the fact that juveniles who are serious sexual offenders have significant deficits in social competence, such as inadequate social skills, poor peer relationships, and social isolation from peers (Righthand & Welch, 2001). Further, the evidence indicates that this aggressive style will persist across situations and time and become a preferred style throughout adulthood. But the relationship is not simply one-way, with limited intellectual competence and inadequate skills causing aggressive behavior. Rather, it appears to be interactive. Aggressive behavior may interfere with positive social interactions with teachers and peers for intellectual and social advancement, perpetuating a chain of mutually influencing events: aggressive behavior influencing the social environment and the social environment, in turn, influencing aggressive behavior.

Dolf Zillmann (1988) proposes an idea similar to the cognitive script theory but, like Berkowitz, emphasizes the importance of physiological arousal and its interaction with cognitions. Zillmann agrees with Hebb (1955, p. 249) that arousal "is an energizer, but not a guide, an engine but not a steering gear." Cognition provides the steering and direction to the energizing effects of anger, fear, or frustration. A long-standing observation in the study of animal and human aggression is that when the organism recognizes or perceives a threat to its welfare and well-being, it can either fight or flee. Following this "recognition of endangerment," physiological arousal quickly sets in, preparing the organism for fight or flight. The "recognition of endangerment," Zillmann reminds us, can be immediate, and the response can be reflexlike. What happens then is also highly dependent on cognition, especially in humans. Very likely, this is when cognitive scripts come in. If the arousal is moderate, the individual with skills and well-integrated standards of prosocial values will probably pursue nonaggressive scripts, although the person may have been angry or threatened at first. However, very high levels of arousal interfere with the complex cognitive processes that mediate our consideration of our internal codes of conduct, as well as our ability to assess the intentions of others and the mitigating circumstances around the incident (Zillmann, 1988). Think of a very stressful or frightening situation that has happened to you and how difficult it was to think clearly. Or think of a time when you became extremely angry and said or did things you wish you hadn't. At high levels of arousal, our cognitions seem to become narrower and more restricted, almost incapacitated at times. Generally, in these high states of arousal, we resort to strongly established habits to guide and dominate our behavior. In essence, we become "impulsive" and largely unthinking, and cognitions that mediate the diminution of hostile or even violent actions are substantially reduced. However, if we have practiced or rehearsed nonviolent or nonaggressive behaviors as solutions, they are likely to be the habits we resort to under high stress, fear, and high arousal.

OVERT AND COVERT ACTS OF AGGRESSION

Rolf Loeber and Magda Stouthamer-Loeber (1998) recommend that researchers on aggression and violence be mindful of two types of aggressive actions: overt and covert. According to Loeber and Stouthamer-Loeber, the two forms of aggression are different in (1) behavior patterns, (2) emotions, (3) cognitions, and (4) development (see **Table 7–2**). Behaviorally, *overt aggression* usually involves direct confrontation with victims and the administration of physical harm or threats of physical harm. *Covert aggression*, on the other

TABLE 7–2   Overt and Covert Aggressive Actions

AGGRESSION	BEHAVIOR PATTERNS	EMOTIONS	COGNITIONS	DEVELOPMENT
Overt	Direct confrontation with victims; generally decreases with age	Anger, high level of arousal and violence	Lacks social cognitions for coming up with nonaggressive solutions	Aggression begins early, especially in boys
Covert	Concealment, dishonesty, sneaky behavior; increases with age	Less emotion; crimes such as fraud, larceny, and theft	Relies on cognitive capabilities, such as planfulness, deceitfulness	Can evolve as well-learned strategy to escape punishment

hand, does not involve direct confrontation but relies on concealment, dishonesty, or sneaky behavior. It is similar to the passive–aggressive behavior discussed earlier in the chapter. In many instances, overt aggression decreases with age, while covert aggression increases with age (Loeber, Lahey, & Thomas, 1991; Stanger, Achenbach, & Verhulst, 1997). However, children who exhibit serious forms of overt aggression (violence) tend to increase their violence as they get older, and often commit both violent and property crimes as adults (Loeber & Stouthamer-Loeber, 1998).

Emotionally, anger is usually an important ingredient in most overt acts of aggression, while more neutral emotions are characteristic of covert actions. Violent actions are usually accompanied by high levels of arousal brought on by anger. Covert actions, on the other hand, tend to be less emotional in nature, such as fraud, theft, embezzlement, burglary, and other white-collar or property offenses.

Covert and overt aggression can also be distinguished on the basis of the cognitions that accompany them. As we explained in this chapter, violent persons (overt aggression) tend to have cognitive deficiencies that make it difficult for them to come up with nonaggressive solutions to interpersonal conflicts and disputes. Overt aggressors also have hostile attributional biases that contribute to violence-prone cognitive processing. On the other hand, people who use covert aggression as a preferred strategy do not demonstrate the degree of cognitive deficiencies in solving their interpersonal problems, nor do they manifest a hostile attributional bias. "Instead, it is postulated that most covert acts are facilitated by specific cognitive capabilities, such as planfulness (i.e., casing situations prior to theft), preoccupations with consumables and property, and lying to escape detection" (Loeber & Stouthamer-Loeber, 1998, p. 250). Occupationally related crimes, for instance, such as theft of company property, misuse of information, and software piracy, are often committed with planning and forethought. Crime committed through the use of computers, called **cybercrime**, is also a good example of covert actions of aggression, and is discussed more fully in Chapter 11.

Developmentally, overt aggression generally begins early, especially in boys, as seen, for example, in the case of life course–persistent offenders. However, Loeber and Stouthamer-Loeber (1998) suggest that development of overt aggressive behavior does not necessarily parallel the development of covert actions. Instead, "some children have never been socialized by their parents to be honest and to respect the property of others. This is common among neglectful parents or parents who hold an indistinct or a weak moral stance in these respects" (p. 251). The formation of honesty and respect for the property of others is instilled by parents' teaching and the prosocial models they offer their children. Some covert actions, especially lying, can also evolve as a well-learned strategy that serves to minimize the chances of detection and punishment by adults.

It should be emphasized that not all overt aggressors who engage in violence start early. As Loeber and Stouthamer-Loeber (1998) note, "It is necessary to account for the emergence of violence in individuals during adulthood who do not have a history of aggression earlier in their lives" (p. 246). These *late-onset types* represent a minority of adult violent offenders, but the hypothesis does suggest that not all highly aggressive and violent individuals manifested aggression in childhood.

Reactive and Proactive Forms of Aggression

Kenneth Dodge and his colleagues (Dodge, Lochman, Harnish, Bates, & Pettit, 1997) have suggested that another way of classifying aggression in children (and adults) is to make a distinction between reactive aggression and proactive aggression. **Reactive aggression** includes anger expressions, temper tantrums, vengeful hostility, and, more generally, "hot-blooded" aggressive acts. **Proactive aggression**, on the other hand, includes bullying, domination, teasing, name-calling, and coercive acts—in other words, more "cold-blooded" aggressive actions. Reactive aggression appears to be a reaction to frustration and is associated with a lack of control due to high states of arousal. In general, reactive aggressive is a hostile act displayed in response to a perceived threat or provocation. Proactive aggression, by contrast, is less emotional, and more driven by expectations of rewards. "Proactive aggression is unprovoked, deliberate, goal-directed behavior used to influence or coerce a peer" (Hubbard et al., 2001, p. 269). The theoretical roots of proactive aggression are found in social learning theory, which, as we learned previously, states that aggression is acquired behavior that is controlled and maintained by reinforcement. It is highly similar to the concept of instrumental aggression. Reliable observations of these two forms of aggression have been found in children (as young as three to six years of age) through teacher ratings, peer ratings, clinical psychiatric records, and direct observations of peer interactions by researchers (Dodge & Coie, 1987; Dodge et al., 1997; Poulin & Boivin, 2000).

Reactively aggressive children, compared to proactively aggressive children, display greater problems in social and psychological adjustment

(Dodge et al., 1997). Psychological adjustment problems include a lack of emotional control when angry accompanied by sleep disorders, depressive symptoms, and personality disorders. On average, these problems emerge at about age 4.5 years. In addition, reactive aggression is related to the tendency to overattribute hostile intent to peers in ambiguous provocation situations (hostile attribution bias) (Hubbard et al., 2001). That is, when a reactive aggressive child interprets a peer's behavior as intentionally harmful or aggressive, he or she is far more prone to respond with angry retaliation or even violence. "Conversely, children who expect that many positive and few negative outcomes will follow aggressive behavior are expected to engage in more goal-directed, deliberate proactive aggression that is not based in anger or retaliation but rather in external contingencies" (p. 269). The external contingencies in the quote refer to rewards.

Gender Differences in Aggression

While boys engage in more overt aggression and direct confrontation as they grow up, it is not clear if boys are generally more aggressive than girls. The current work of cognitive psychologists suggests that there may be socialized differences in the way girls and boys construct their worlds. Social learning theorists have long held that girls are "socialized" differently than boys, or taught not to be overtly aggressive. Anne Campbell (1993, p. 19) argues that "boys are not simply more aggressive than girls; they are aggressive in a different way." Other researchers concur with this observation (Hawkins, Pepler, & Craig, 2001; Lumley, McNeil, Herschell & Bahl, 2002; J. Wood, Cowan, & Baker, 2002). According to Campbell, boys and girls are born with the potential to be equally aggressive, but girls are socialized not to be overtly aggressive, whereas boys are encouraged to be overtly aggressive "to defend" themselves.

Research supports the observation that boys and girls are equally physically aggressive toward their peers when they are toddlers but that this pattern soon changes as children get older and enter their elementary school years (Xie, Farmer, & Cairns, 2003). Loeber and Stouthamer-Loeber (1998, p. 253) conclude from their review of the research that "in general, gender differences in aggression, as expressed by frustration and rage, are not documented in infancy." They note that only in the preschool period (three to five years of age) do observable gender differences begin to emerge, with boys displaying more overt aggression than girls. Overt aggression becomes especially prominent in boys from elementary school age onward. Boys are taught to be tough, not to cry, to take on the bullies, and to physically defend themselves. However, many researchers report that girls are more likely to engage in relationship or interpersonal forms of aggression rather than the physical forms of pushing and hitting (Casey-Cannon, Hayward, & Gowen, 2001; Crick & Zahn-Waxler, 2003; Prinstein, Boergers, & Vernberg, 2001). For example, researchers (Björkqvist, Lagerspetz, & Kaukianinen, 1992; Cairns, Cairns, Neckerman, Ferguson, &

Gariépy, 1989) find that girls and women tend to use more covert, indirect, and verbal forms of aggression, such as character defamation and ostracism. Other researchers report that girls are far more likely to employ *relational aggression*, such as abandoning one friend in favor of another, spreading malicious gossip, or ridiculing another's physical traits (e.g., their attractiveness, weight, or general demeanor) (Crick, 1995; Crick & Grotpeter, 1995; Crick & Zahn-Waxler, 2003; Garside & Klimes-Dougan, 2002; Loeber & Stouthamer-Loeber, 1998).

In conclusion, there is growing recognition that gender differences in aggression are not simply due to biology, but are primarily due to cultural and socialization processes that promote different kinds of aggression. Environmental cues are also important in cognitive scripts and aggressive strategies individuals employ for various situations. Which script or strategy an individual employs is dependent on which environmental cues are present.

ENVIRONMENTAL FACTORS

Population Density

Closely related to the ethological point of view (discussed earlier in the chapter) is one that sees aggression as a result of population density or overcrowded conditions. In areas of high population concentration, personal space is constantly violated. In urban areas, crowded mass transit systems and apartment complexes teeming with people infringe on personal space and territory. Might this overcrowding be a principal factor in crimes of violence and, perhaps, in personal property offenses?

Over 40 years ago, John B. Calhoun (1961, 1962) conducted a series of provocative studies using domestic rats and suggested analogies between the rats and humans. He first allowed groups of rats to propagate freely in a limited physical space with adequate quantities of rat chow and water. Eventually, the rat colonies became overpopulated to such an extent that the rodents demonstrated abnormal behaviors.

Normally, male rats find one or more mates, build a nest, and, together with their mates, produce and raise offspring. Although they roam freely, they rarely show interest in another nest. Under Calhoun's crowded conditions, however, the males either no longer cared about building a nest or could not defend it from bands of marauding male rats. The marauders entered the nests, attacked the females, and tore up the surroundings. Females were so harassed by these marauders that they lost interest in caring for the young. The marauding rats were those that could not build nests of their own because of lack of space. They developed a lifestyle that revolved around attacking other males and females, physically and sexually.

Calhoun also discovered a group of "juvenile delinquents"—male and female rats without nests that were usually too weak to defend or find a mate. These young rats would gather in large clusters and spend their days milling around the floor of the cage, sometimes fighting, sometimes sleeping, sometimes harassing other rats in the vicinity. Rather quickly, the rat society deteriorated and the population declined. Calhoun's studies have been replicated by other researchers using other animals, with generally similar results.

Can we analogize from rats to humans? Obviously, we must do so only very cautiously. The research concerning the effects of crowding on human behavior is far from clear-cut, and at present there is no evidence of a relationship between overcrowding and *crime* among humans. However, some work suggests a link between overcrowding and *aggression*.

Some investigators have exposed people to crowded conditions combined with various room temperatures (Griffith & Veitch, 1971). In general, as population density and temperature increased, so did subjects' negative feelings toward one another. Other investigations (Freedman, Levy, Buchanan, & Price, 1972) found gender differences in response to overcrowding. Males in same-gender, overcrowded groups were more aggressive and hostile than males in same gender, uncrowded groups. The reverse was true for females. In mixed groups, the gender differences did not occur. This evidence could suggest that men are uncomfortable and hostile under crowded same-gender conditions, while women tend to become more affable and friendly. However, the data also lend themselves to other interpretations. Mueller (1983), for instance, finds that the Freedman data indicate that men in the low-density condition were actually less competitive and aggressive, and only slightly more punitive than women. The issue of gender differences in aggressive behavior as a function of crowding or density is far from resolved.

Freedman (1975) conducted a number of correlational studies in various geographical areas throughout the United States and found no relationship between population density and crimes of violence like murder, rape, and aggravated assault. When populations were matched for socioeconomic class and other relevant variables, crimes of violence actually decreased in proportion to the population as density increased. Freedman attributed this finding to the large number of potential witnesses in high-density areas.

Population density studies, therefore, do not clearly support a relationship between overcrowding and aggression (Harries, 1980; Kirmeyer, 1978; Mueller, 1983). While density may play a significant role in engendering aggressive behavior in animals, in the human population the situation is far more complicated. Overall, the available evidence at this point does not support the view that a city's or a neighborhood's density has a significant influence on crime.

Aggression and Ambient Temperature

As temperature increases, violence increases. Or does it? This heat-of-the-night assumption was proposed as a partial explanation for riots and civil disturbances during the late 1960s and early 1970s (Baron, 1977). Later, research spearheaded by Robert Baron (Baron & Bell, 1975; Baron & Lawton, 1972;

Baron & Ransberger, 1978; Bell & Baron, 1977) found support for a relationship between ambient temperature and aggression. The relationship seems complex, however. According to Robert Baron, extremely low and high temperatures tend to inhibit aggression, while intermediate levels tend to be associated with it. Baron suggests that when the temperature becomes very unpleasant (too hot or too cold), the person's major concern is to do something self-protective, such as getting a cold drink or donning thermal clothing. In other words, the individual is attempting, as Berkowitz (1989) suggests, to escape aversive circumstances (negative reinforcement). Slightly lower levels of discomfort tend to enhance the likelihood of aggression in some people, however. Picture yourself on an uncomfortably hot, but not excessively humid, summer day in a large, crowded city. Baron would maintain that your discomfort, compounded by unpleasant odors and other environmental variables, may induce irritability; in potential aggressors, it may produce hostility.

Baron's proposal suggests that collective or individual violence may be prominent at uncomfortable intermediate temperatures, rather than at extremely hot or bitterly cold ones. He hypothesized a similar curvilinear or inverted U-shaped relationship between noise levels and aggression (Baron, 1977). As Penrod (1983) notes, however, these studies do not consider adequately the possible influence of other environmental or situational factors that might be associated with hot weather, such as seasonal unemployment. Subsequent research by Anderson and Anderson (1984) failed to yield the predicted curvilinear relationship. They found that the number of daily violent crimes increased directly as a function of temperature in two different cities. As temperature increased, violent crime increased in a linear fashion. In another study, Anderson (1987) discovered that overall violent crime in the United States was more prevalent in the hotter summer months as well as in the hotter years. The study also revealed that hotter cities have higher violent crime rates than the cooler cities. These relationships also exhibited a linear function rather than a curvilinear one. (See **Figure 7–1**.)

Other investigators have found that a combination of high temperature and air pollution is highly related to family disturbance and violent behavior (Rotton & Frey, 1985). Kenrick and MacFarland (1986) also found a strong linear relationship between horn honking and ambient temperature, at least up to 106 degrees Fahrenheit. The researchers designed a field study in which a car (a 1980 Datsun 200SX) was purposely stalled during a green light at an intersection in the metropolitan Phoenix area. Phoenix, of course, is a city where daily temperatures in excess of 90 degrees are quite common. Results indicated that horn honking was directly linked to the temperature–humidity index. That is, the frequency of horn honking increased as the temperature increased (especially when the humidity was also high). The relationship was particularly strong for those honkers who had their windows down (presumably they did not have an air-conditioner on or did not have one). In addition to frequency of horn honking, the amount of time spent leaning on the horn also increased as a function of the temperature–

FIGURE 7–1 Hypothesized Curvilinear Relationship Between Aggression and Temperature

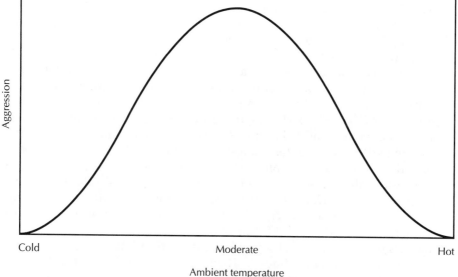

humidity index, often accompanied by verbal and nonverbal signals of hostility. The researchers also observed that the highest levels of horn honking were from young male drivers.

Available data also indicate that hotter regions of the world yield more violence, such as murder, rape, assaults, riots, and spouse abuse. In reviewing the research literature on the relationship between violence and temperature in various contexts, Anderson (1989) concludes that there is little doubt of a strong connection between high temperature and violent crime. Simon Field (1992) writes the following:

> Apart from the criminological universals of age and gender, it would be difficult to find any other factor which is so consistently correlated with violent crime. Under the circumstances the issue receives little attention in the mainstream criminological literature. This is perhaps because the idea that high temperatures induce criminal behaviour is redolent of an outdated environmental determinism, and therefore sits very uneasily with modern sociological theory. Whatever the reasons, the evidence is so compelling that the issue must be addressed. (p. 340)

However, though the relationship seems to be a strong one, it is also likely to be a very complex one. For example, people may be more inclined to drink alcoholic beverages during high temperatures. Therefore, alcohol may be playing a very critical role in the incidence of violence rather than strictly the ambient temperature itself. Field (1992) also suggests that the violence–temperature connection may be due to the increased availability of victims who try to beat the heat by getting outside their homes and doing things besides their usual daily activities—such as going to beaches and amusement parks.

Field (1992) extended the hypothesis of the violence–temperature relationship by examining the *crime–temperature* relationship, including property crime (burglary, theft, robbery, and criminal damage). Although robbery is considered a violent crime—because it involves force or the threat of force—it may justifiably also be considered less violent than murder, rape, or assault. In his study, Field looked at temperature and crime statistics in England and Wales over a 40-year period, with particular emphasis on the very complete monthly data between 1977 and 1987. In addition to temperature, he included rainfall and sunshine in his analysis, since rain is often believed to be the police officer's friend by keeping potential victims and offenders off the street. The results showed a consistent and strong statistical relationship between temperature and crime of most types, but no relationship between crime and rainfall or sunshine. Specifically, high temperatures corresponded to high crime rates, regardless of the type of crime. Field (1992) concludes, ". . . These findings represent compelling evidence that prevailing temperatures affect the level of most types of crimes in England and Wales" (p. 347). Furthermore, Field contends, ". . . The findings cannot generally be explained by the hypothesis that temperature causes aggression, for this would not explain the findings concerning property crime" (p. 348). Therefore, the linear hypothesis propounded by Anderson and others—inasmuch as it is limited to violent crime—is inadequate to explain the findings, suggesting a far more complex relationship than originally supposed. Perhaps temperature affects violence directly and affects other types of crime indirectly by influencing social behavior. That is, temperature affects property crime by influencing routine activities. In hot weather, for example, the family may be more inclined to go to the beach, leaving their home more susceptible to burglary and themselves more vulnerable to robbery and theft.

Other Environmental Factors

The relationships between aggression and other environmental factors, such as noise, air pollution, and even erotica, are relatively new areas of inquiry. With reference to air pollution, for example, some studies indicate that individuals exposed to cigarette smoke are more aggressive than individuals in clean-air conditions (J. W. Jones & Bogat, 1978). Some people are even more aggressive when someone is simply smoking (inappropriately) around them (Zillmann, Baron, & Tamborini, 1981), even if the air is not heavily infiltrated with smoke. Other investigators (e.g., Rotton, 1983) report that malodorous pollution also encourages hostile aggressive behavior. There is also some evidence to suggest that loud, unpredictable, or complex noises may influence aggressive tendencies. For example, Konečni (1975) found that angry subjects exposed to loud or complex noise became more aggressive than angry subjects exposed to soft and simple noise. Apparently, the additional arousal instigated by the noise adds to the arousal effects of anger already felt by the subject. This increase in arousal level presumably facilitates aggressive behavior.

The effects of erotica on aggression and violence, and particularly on sex crimes, is an important topic that has received much research attention in recent years. However, because erotica may be conceptually linked with sexual offenses, we postpone that topic until Chapter 10.

EFFECTS OF THE MASS MEDIA

Ninety-eight percent of American homes have at least one television set (APA Commission on Violence and Youth, 1993). Over 25 years ago, researchers estimated that by the age of 16, the average child had spent more time watching television than sitting in a classroom and had probably witnessed more than 13,000 killings (H. Walters & Malamud, 1975). There is little reason to believe that these numbers have decreased. A more recent estimate suggests that the average American child sees more than 100,000 violent episodes and some 20,000 murders on television before reaching adolescence (D. G. Myers, 1996).

There are four scenes of violence portrayed on network television to every one scene expressing affection. A three-year study (1994–1997), by four universities, on violence on American television revealed that 90% of movies shown on television include violence (National Cable Television Association, 1998). Violence was found most frequently on subscription television (85% on premium cable and 59% on basic cable), while the lowest incidence of violence (18%) was found on Public Broadcasting stations (PBS). Across the three years of the study, nearly 40% of the violent incidents on television were initiated by "good" characters who are likely perceived as attractive role models. In 67% of the programs, violence was portrayed within a humorous context. In general, the study found that most media violence is glamorized and that the long-term negative consequences of violent behavior are rarely depicted. Nearly three-quarters of violent scenes contain no remorse, criticism, punishment, or emotional reactions from the perpetrators. Overall, the survey found that the percentage of programs on television that contain some violence remained unchanged over the three-year study period.

Some surveys have found that news coverage of violence against women and children was not used to educate the public but rather to fascinate and entertain (National Media Archive, 1990). With reference to video game preferences, the most popular game category is fantasy violence and other human violence games (Funk & Buchman, 1996). In that same study, the number of girls who listed violent games was equal to the number of boys who listed violent games. Girls' favorite games were more likely to fall into the fantasy violence category, however, whereas boys preferred the human violent games.

It is not surprising that many people are disturbed by media violence and that social science researchers are intrigued by its possible relationship with the violence in our society. Whether exposure to violent media increases violence has been the focus of several public commissions and reports designed to influence social policy (Wood, Wong, & Chachere, 1991). In general, the bulk of the experimental studies reveals that television violence in particular has a significant effect on the frequency and type of aggressive behavior expressed by some adults and some children, especially children of an impressionable age. The relationship between violent television and aggression appears to be particularly strong for young boys, who closely identify with the violent characters they see on television, and for children who have difficulty in their interpersonal relationships with their peers (Eron & Huesmann, 1986). Let us look at some of this research in more detail.

It is worthwhile citing again the classic study by Bandura (1965) discussed in Chapter 5, in which 66 nursery school children were divided into three groups and shown one of three five-minute films. All three films depicted an adult verbally and physically assaulting a "BoBo," a large inflatable doll with a sand base. One group saw the adult model being rewarded with candy and a soft drink after displaying aggressive behavior. The second group observed the model being spanked and reprimanded verbally. The third group witnessed a situation in which the model received neither punishment nor reward.

After the children saw the film, they were permitted to free-play for 10 minutes in a playroom of toys, including a BoBo doll. The group that had witnessed the adult model being rewarded for the aggressive behavior exhibited more aggression than the other two groups. In addition, boys were more aggressive than girls. The group that saw the adult model being punished exhibited the lowest amount of aggression in the playroom.

Recall that Bandura's research, which included variations on the aforementioned basic design, consistently demonstrated this modeling effect. Furthermore, numerous follow-up studies not only replicated his findings, but also suggested that media violence may have a strong influence on real-life violence in many situations (Baron, 1977). There has also been some suggestion that even news reports of violence may have a **contagion effect** or **copycat effect**, a tendency in some people to model or copy an activity portrayed in the entertainment or news media. Contagion effect is said to occur when action depicted in the media is assessed by certain individuals as a good idea and then mimicked. For example, an ingenious bank robbery, dramatized on television, might be imitated. The contagion effect is not simply restricted to the media portrayals, however. For example, a study by Joiner (1994) illustrates how depression in a college classmate may be contagious. A classmate who is depressed can lower the mood of friends, family, and others who associate with the depressed person and try to help.

A tragic illustration of the copycat effect can be found in a series of school shootings that began in 1997. In October of that year, a 16-year-old, having just stabbed his mother to death, arrived at the high school in Pearl, Mississippi, and began randomly shooting his classmates, killing two and wounding seven. Less than two months later, a 14-year-old male opened fire on a group of fellow high school students participating in a prayer circle in West Paducah, Kentucky. He killed two schoolmates and wounded five others. The West Paducah incident received worldwide media coverage for several weeks, accompanied by extensive stories about the shooter. A few months later, on March 24, 1998, two boys, ages 13 and 11, armed with seven handguns and three rifles, opened fire on their classmates as they gathered on the school playground in Jonesboro, Arkansas, killing four very young girls and their teacher and wounding 10 others. Of the 15 killed or wounded, only 1 was male, indicating that the young shooters were aiming specifically at girls.

Exactly one month after Jonesboro came Edinboro, Pennsylvania, where a 14-year-old male student began shooting during a school dance, killing a teacher. This incident was followed by another shooting less than a month later in Fayetteville, Tennessee, resulting in the death of a student. One week later, a 15-year-old male in Springfield, Oregon, walked into the high school cafeteria and began randomly shooting at fellow students, firing 50 rounds from a .22-caliber semiautomatic rifle in less than a minute. As he stopped to reload, the young shooter was tackled and disarmed by a varsity wrestler. During that one minute, however, he managed to kill two classmates and wounded 22 others. He had shot both his parents prior to leaving for school. Less than two weeks later, on June 15, 1998, a 14-year-old student, armed with a .32-caliber semiautomatic handgun, opened fire in the hallway of a high school as students took final exams, wounding a basketball coach and a volunteer aide. All of these young shooters had an inordinate interest in guns, had troubled backgrounds, knew the details of the previous school shootings, and had a strong fascination with violence presented through the media. And as mentioned in Chapter 2, on April 20, 1999, two teenagers, Eric Harris and Dylan Klebold, in Littleton, Colorado, entered Columbine High School and killed 13 people and injured dozens of others before taking their own lives. The two boys were considered social outcasts and seemed preoccupied with the violence presented in the media, music, and video games.

Exposure to media-portrayed violence does not, of course, automatically promote aggression. Some individuals are affected more than others. Children from low-income families are apparently more influenced by media violence than middle-class children are (Eisenhower, 1969); it is not clear whether this reflects exposure to the violence itself or other factors as well. The young shooters described above came from varied socioeconomic backgrounds. Researchers have found evidence that positive parental models are likely to override violent models on television (Chaffee & McLeod, 1971; J. Goldstein, 1975). Moreover, television violence seems to have substantially less effect on families in which the parents do not rely on aggressive behavior for solving problems (Chaffee & McLeod, 1971).

Researchers have found that aggressive children watch more media violence, identify more with violent characters, and believe more strongly that the violence they observe reflects real life than do nonaggressive children (Huesmann, 1988; Huesmann & Eron, 1986; Lefkowitz, Eron, Walder, & Huesmann, 1977). Does this mean that they learned their aggressive styles from the media? The answer is not very clear. Berkowitz (1970) suggests that people who rely heavily on aggression for meeting their needs are more influenced by media violence than are people who do not usually seek violent solutions. Studies have also shown that extremely aggressive adolescents are most strongly attracted to violence portrayed in media entertainment (Berkowitz, 1970; Eron, 1963; Halloran, Brown, & Chaney, 1969).

Repeated exposure to violence on television may habituate heavy viewers to violence. It may also distort one's perception of the world. Furthermore, television is heavily populated with villainous and unscrupulous people, portrayals that may give frequent viewers a jaded view of the world. There is some evidence that heavy viewers, compared to light viewers, are less trustful of others and overestimate their chances of being criminally victimized (Gerbner & Gross, 1976.

Black and Bevan (1992) report evidence that movies may have a greater impact on aggressive behavior than television. They argue that television programs are interrupted by commercials, that television viewers talk, leave the room, read, and generally have their attention divided with friends and family. However, in a movie theater, the presentation takes place in the dark, in the presence of many strangers, and the film is viewed without interruption and with focused attention. Therefore, the depiction of violence in the movie theater should be more realistic, salient, and memorable than most presentations seen on television. Black and Bevan found that adults (both men and women) who viewed a violent movie (*Missing in Action*) were more aggressive than those who saw a nonviolent film (*Passage to India*), although the aggression probably dissipated rapidly after leaving the theater.

In recent years, hundreds of research articles conclude that *heavy* exposure to televised violence is one of the most significant causes of violence in American society (American Psychological Association, 2003a). For example, Huesmann et al. (2003) conclude from their well-executed research, "Overall, these results suggest that both males and females from all social strata and all levels of initial aggressiveness are placed at increased risk for the development of adult aggressive and violent behavior when they view a high and steady diet of violent TV shows in early childhood" (p. 218). In short, an overwhelming amount of the research indicates that extensive exposure to violent television and movies does increase aggressive tendencies in both children and adults, and the effects seem to be long-lasting.

VICTIM-PRECIPITATED AGGRESSION

So far we have maintained that aggression is principally a learned behavior. Although it may be influenced by a number of variables—temperature, frustration, and situational cues, for example—it occurs because an individual has learned that aggression works. Social learning theory postulates that most aggressive behavior is acquired through modeling and maintained through various forms of reinforcement, especially social reinforcement. However, we have not yet given attention to another parameter, the victim of the aggression. Often, a specific aggressive act is prompted by the behavior of the person who eventually becomes the victim. Specifically, what begins as a heated argument develops into a physical, violent brawl—a process called **escalation**.

Research reviewed by Baron (1977) indicates that most people respond to provocation in kind (e.g., Epstein & Taylor, 1967; Hendrick & Taylor, 1971; M. O'Leary & Dengerink, 1973; S. Taylor, 1967). Furthermore, the reciprocated response approximates in intensity the provocation received. The first person then reacts by increasing the provocation. In this way, verbal attacks often lead to physical retaliation and violence. The implication is that in some crimes, the behavior of the victim plays a role in escalating the offender's actions. This is not to say that the victim should be blamed for the offense. Ultimately, it is each person's individual responsibility to keep him- or herself in check and not react violently to the words and actions of others.

The concept of escalation is consistent with social learning theory. That is, we influence our social environment and the social environment influences us in turn. There is mutual interaction in any interpersonal encounter. Many violent incidents occur between family members or between persons who know one another well. An investigation often reveals escalating anger and arousal between the participants, often ending in serious injury or even death. We return to this topic in Chapter 8. In sum, social learning theory emphasizes that, for some people, violence is a learned response to anger and, sometimes, to provocation from others. Psychologists in clinical practice who adopt a social learning perspective help their client "learn" more appropriate strategies for responding to these stimuli.

THE PHYSIOLOGY OF AGGRESSION

Although most aggressive behavior reflects a learned way of responding to situations, some theorists and students of aggression argue that physiological factors play a significant role. In recent years, the relationship between physiology and aggression has been broached during discussions of premenstrual syndrome, drug treatment for sex offenders, and presumed relationships between certain mental or physical defects (schizophrenia, epilepsy) and crimes of violence. While evidence of a strong relationship between aggression and physiological variables does appear to exist for some species of animals, for humans the evidence is far less compelling.

There is experimental evidence that the nervous and endocrine systems of animals contribute significantly to their aggressive behavior. The endocrine system secretes hormones into the blood or lymph. Differential roles played by male and female hormones have been connected with differential tendencies toward aggressive behavior. Thus, the male hormone testosterone is believed to facilitate aggression in both the male and the female (H. Goldman, 1977; Moyer, 1971). In animals, the female hormone progesterone, when administered to correct hormonal imbalances, may alleviate symptoms of irritability and tension. There is some dated evidence that women taking birth control pills containing progesterone demonstrate less irritability and hostility than do women not on any pill (Hamburg, Moos, & Yalom, 1968).

Some researchers believe that the differential hormonal effects may partly explain why human males overwhelmingly commit more violent crimes than do human females. For example, testosterone levels are significantly higher among male inmates convicted of violent crimes than male inmates convicted of nonviolent crimes (Aronson, Wilson, & Akert, 2005). Research also suggests that violent juvenile delinquents have higher levels of testosterone than nondelinquents (Banks & Dabbs, 1996). In addition, the relationship between the secretion rate of testosterone and the level of overt hostility correlates well in young men but not older men (H. Goldman, 1977). This suggests that testosterone may be released in greater quantities when males are younger than when they are older. The relationship is especially notable in male adolescents with a history of assault or attempted murder. We underscore, however, that learning and social expectations and cognitions play an extremely powerful role in any statistics that indicate gender or age differences in criminal behavior.

Premenstrual Syndrome

At this point, it is relevant to discuss **premenstrual syndrome** (PMS), which refers to the cyclic physiological and psychological changes that occur prior to the onset of menstruation, usually beginning four to seven days before. Although there is considerable debate about whether premenstrual symptoms are validated and present in enough women to merit diagnosis as a syndrome (Sommer, 1983), the fact that some physiological changes do occur is rarely questioned. These changes may include swelling of the extremities and breasts, fatigue, and headaches. On the other hand, some researchers have also reported positive symptoms associated with PMS, such as increased creativity and physical energy.

The symptoms are believed to be due to changes in the hormonal balance between estrogen and progesterone (Moyer, 1976; Tasto & Insel, 1977). During the preovulation phase (menstrual onset to day 14) progesterone dominates over estrogen, a dominance that peaks at approximately day 14 (ovulation) when the estrogen level begins to increase and eventually dominate. Decreases in progesterone have been associated with high risks of suicide, especially violent suicide (Wetzel, McClure, & Reich, 1971), hospital admissions related to depression and schizophrenia (Tasto & Insel, 1977), and criminal offending by women (Dalton, 1964; Moyer, 1971). Because the physiological changes can presumably have a strong influence on behavior, PMS has been used successfully as a criminal defense in British courts. In the United States, a New York case that might have put the syndrome to the test was plea-bargained before it reached the trial stage (Carney & Williams, 1983).

Resistance to a connection between PMS and female criminal behavior is understandable. First, there is too little agreement about whether or not such a *syndrome* actually exists, although many women do experience discomfiting symptoms prior to the onset of menstruation. Second, if society were to accept PMS as an excusing condition for even a portion of the crime committed by women, the social implications would be shattering. What standards would be used to determine which women were susceptible to PMS, and could any woman be trusted during the premenstrual period? Although these questions may seem overly dramatic, they are not irrelevant if one assumes that, during a significant part of their lives, some women are at the mercy of their biology.

The relationship between the premenstrual syndrome and violent crime has yet to be convincingly documented. The first heavily quoted study on the subject was that by Morton and colleagues (Morton, Addison, Addison, Hunt, & Sullivan, 1953). The study was designed to evaluate the effectiveness of various treatments for the relief of premenstrual tension in inmates. Morton, almost as an afterthought, mentioned that 62% of his sample of 249 female prisoners had committed violent crimes (murder, manslaughter, and assault) during their premenstrual week. Another 17% of the sample had committed violent offenses during menstruation. However, the study had many methodological flaws that make it very suspect. The percentages of crimes were indicated for four cycle phases (premenstrual week, midcycle, menstruation, and the end of the period), but the lengths of these phases were not provided (Horney, 1978). Furthermore, no statistical analyses were reported, nor were there any explanations of how the data were gathered (Horney, 1978). Moreover, no one has ever been able to replicate the Morton findings.

In another study, Dalton (1961) interviewed 156 newly convicted women in British prisons on their first weekend after sentencing. She reported that 22% had committed crimes during their premenstrual period, and another 26% during menstruation. Her method for determining these percentages relied exclusively on retrospective memory of the women themselves about their menstrual cycle. Further, Dalton divided the menstrual cycle into seven four-day periods, with menstruation representing days 1 through 4, while the premenstrual period was indicated by days 25 through 28.

There are, however, a number of serious problems with the study. First, crime in the Dalton study did not refer to violence but, rather, to *economic* crimes (*viz.,* shoplifting, burglary, embezzlement, forgery, and prostitution). Second, relying on a one-time estimation of self-reported menstrual cycles is fraught with potential for error, particularly since women do not necessarily accurately remember their menstrual cycles (McFarland, Ross, & DeCourville, 1989). Third, not all women experience regular 28-day cycles. Therefore, dividing the cycles neatly into seven four-day periods is a very questionable procedure.

More recent research also shows that negative emotions (irritability, loneliness, depression, and so on) do not necessarily increase during premenstrual and menstrual phases for most women. For example, McFarland et al. (1989) examined the relationship between women's theories of menstrual distress and their recollections of the physical discomforts and the emotional characteristics that accompany the cycle. Subjects completed daily questionnaires in which they evaluated themselves on emotions and physical symptoms throughout the cycle. Later, the subjects were asked to recall what they had said on the questionnaire during menstruation. The recollections of the women were not only inaccurate, but also consistent with their theories of menstrual distress. "[T]he more a woman believed in the phenomenon of menstrual distress, the more she exaggerated, in recall, the negativity of her symptoms during her last period" (p. 522). Similar observations have been made by Pamela Kato and Diane Ruble (1992), indicating that the intensity of negative emotions experienced during the menstrual state—such as tension, irritability, depression, emotional liability, and anxiety—is open to debate. Research by Dougherty Bjork, Cherek, Moeller, and Huang (1998) found no evidence of an association between the menstrual cycle and aggression in two groups of women who differed in the severity of self-reported premenstrual symptoms.

In summary, there is no evidence to date that the emotions and moods that presumably accompany PMS facilitate or encourage criminal behavior. In fact, it is highly questionable whether pronounced or intense negative moods even occur during the premenstrual or menstrual state for a majority of women, despite what the "current wisdom" assumes. In their careful review of the literature, Harry and Balcer (1987) maintain, "Despite what seems to be substantial interest in the topic, we conclude there is not scientific support for an association between any phases of the menstrual cycle and criminal behavior" (p. 318).

Still, there continues to be debate among scholars of criminal law as to whether hormonal balances or imbalances should excuse violent behavior or at least mitigate responsibility (Carney & Williams, 1983) or should have no relevance whatsoever. Although some researchers would have society accept PMS as a substantive defense in crimes of violence (that is, an excusing condition absolving the individual of moral culpability), others believe that such an approach would undermine gains in women's struggle for economic, social, and political equality. It should be noted, though, that PMS is only one of a number of physiological conditions that are relevant to this issue. For example, individuals have maintained that their aggressive behavior was influenced by such factors as low blood sugar, environmental contaminants, or medications that altered their blood chemistry and prompted them to commit violent acts.

Physiological Control Through Surgery and Drugs

Another controversial issue relating to the physiology of aggression is the treatment of violent offenders. Although treatment in the broad sense can mean psychotherapy or psychoanalysis, in the narrow sense it takes on a medical connotation. Those who advocate such treatment believe that violent individuals should be administered drugs to dull their senses or overcome the effects of presumably overactive aggression hormones. More drastically, they may be submitted to psychosurgery or castration. The former procedure modifies aggressive centers in the brain; the latter excises the testicles, which contain testosterone, or demolishes their functioning.

It is fairly well documented that castration lessens the tendency for animals to be aggressive. In rare instances, castration of prisoners convicted of sex crimes may have significantly reduced their aggressive episodes (Hawke, 1950; Le Maire, 1956). It may surprise you to learn that compulsory castration was legal in the United States until as late as the 1960s. For example, over 370 "voluntary" bilateral orchidectomies (excision of both testes) were performed on mentally disordered sex offenders in San Diego as a "judicial mandate" (Reiss, 1977).

Today, this literal castration for purposes of reducing sexual aggression is no longer an option. Rather, some individuals volunteer or request to be treated with drugs that mimic the chemical composition and action of sexual hormones. For example, medroxyprogesterone (Depo-Provera), which is chemically similar to the female hormone progesterone, is apparently highly effective in lowering testosterone levels (Day & Berney, 2001; Moyer, 1976). Lowered levels of the aggression-inducing male hormone testosterone presumably lessen the male drive to engage in sexual activity. Depo-Provera, the reasoning goes, will inhibit the excessive and impulsive sexual and aggressive behaviors of sex offenders. There is some evidence to support this assumption. Blumer and Migeon (1973), for example, found that ingestion of high levels of Depo-Provera successfully reduced sexual arousal and the need to engage in sexual "deviations."

Medroxyprogesterone and similar antilibidinal drugs (also called antiandrogen drugs) continue to be used by many clinicians as a supplement to psychotherapy for adults with deviant sexual behaviors. Because there is a risk that they will affect bone and testicular maturation, they are not recommended for males under 18 (Day & Berney, 2001). In some cases, antilibinal drugs are used as an initial, short-term measure until other treatment options are investigated. In other cases, they are offered on an "as-needed" basis, such as when the person is under very high stress. However, these drugs may be used as the *principal* therapeutic intervention "in patients who have failed to respond to other treatment approaches and who continue to pose serious problems to their own well being and the safety of others" (Day & Berney, 2001, p. 209).

Recent work in the neuropsychological sciences has provided additional information about aggressive behavior. We must emphasize that about 95% of what is now known about the brain has been learned in the past 10–15 years (Comer, 2004). Advances in technology and instrument sophistication have allowed neuropsychologists to study the potential influence of molecular components, especially substances known as *neurotransmitters*, in facilitating and inhibiting aggression. Neurotransmitters are biochemicals directly involved in the transmission of neural impulses. Without them, communication within the mammalian nervous system would be impossible. Researchers have learned that some of these neurotransmitters—namely, norepinephrine, acetylcholine, and serotonin—may significantly influence the cortical and subcortical mechanisms responsible for aggression and violence. No single neurotransmitter solely excites or inhibits aggression, however.

Recent research suggests that the neurotransmitter **serotonin**, a biochemical that occurs naturally in the midbrain, may play the most significant role in modulating aggression and violence (Coscina, 1997; Lesch & Merschdorf, 2000; Loeber & Stouthamer-Loeber, 1998; Moffitt et al., 1997). Specifically, many individuals who act aggressively toward others or commit violent suicide appear to have abnormally low levels of serotonin (Bear, Connors, & Paradiso, 1996; Davidson, Putnam, & Larson, 2000; Rosenzweig, Leiman, & Breedlove, 1999; Stanley et al., 2000). Since serotonin is difficult to measure directly, the usual procedure is to measure the concentrations of the chemical in the cerebrospinal fluid.

Much of the research has focused on animals rather than humans. In one study, for example, the serotonin concentrations of aggressive rhesus monkeys were lower than normally found in the species (Higley et al., 1992), and in another study, tame silver foxes and laboratory rats appeared to have higher levels of serotonin than their wild, more aggressive counterparts (Pihl & Peterson, 1993; Popova, Voitenko, Kulikov, & Augustinovich, 1991).

In humans, Pihl and Peterson (1993) assert: "Reduced brain serotonin function is associated with heightened vulnerability to depression, increased risk of violent suicide, propensity to exhibit aggressive or impulsive behavior, and susceptibility to alcohol abuse both among persons with psychiatric disorders and among the general public" (p. 114). For example, Mann, Arango, and Underwood (1990), in their review of the literature, found that decreased levels of serotonin were prevalent among suicide victims. Serotonin does seem to play a significant role in some forms of depression, as can be seen by the relative success of antidepressant drugs like Prozac and Zoloft, which keep serotonin concentrations high in various parts of the brain. Some additional preliminary but inconclusive findings suggest that humans who become violent under the influence of alcohol (Virkkunen & Linnoila, 1993) and children who torture animals (Kruesi, 1979; Kruesi et al., 1990) appear to be abnormally low in concentrations of serotonin. Other research suggests that low levels of brain serotonin encourage impulsive forms of aggressive or violent behavior (Kruesi & Jacobsen, 1997).

If certain neurotransmitters are implicated in aggressive behavior, it is not too far-fetched to consider drug regimens for control, similar to the antilibidinal drugs discussed above. Neurotransmitters are strongly affected by drugs. However, since neurotransmitters are the basic chemicals for all behavior, any modification of their levels in the nervous system is likely to affect a large range of behavior and emotions, not just the behavior that researchers are seeking to control. Therefore, although the considerable potential of drugs in controlling and reducing aggression cannot be overlooked, their peripheral effects must be considered.

Some neurophysiologists concentrate their research on trying to identify aggression centers in the brain. Presumably, if the part of the brain that controls or facilitates aggressive or violent behavior could be located, it might be manipulated. The research to date indicates that if an aggression center exists, it is most likely in the general area of the brain stem known as the *limbic system*, which consists of a diverse group of complicated brain structures and circuitry. Specifically, a small, almond-shaped group of nerve cells in the stem called the *amygdala*, another structure called the *hypothalamus*, and a portion of the brain itself called the *temporal lobe* have been the focus of scientific research. To date, however, we know too little about how our brain works, and we do not know where behavioral centers are located.

Until drugs to help control behavior became widely available, researchers examining the relationship between aggression and brain centers often used *stereotaxic* procedures, which they believed had great potential for the control of hostile aggression. By drilling a small hole in the skull, researchers were able to penetrate the brain with small insulated-wire electrodes for electrical stimulation. They also sometimes inserted minute, hollow glass tubes (cannulae) to allow them to chemically stimulate specific sites in the brain and stem. The needle electrode, once properly implanted, could be permanently attached to the skull with screw fittings, allowing a small segment of the electrode to protrude from the skull for the attachment of wires or to receive radio transmission from a distance. This procedure of wireless communication was known as *telemetry*. The external part of the electrode was small enough so that it could be covered with hair and thus not be noticeable. The individual felt no pain from the procedure.

Small electric currents could then be passed through the electrodes to the brain site, stimulating the brain structure (or destroying it, if necessary, with direct current or high-frequency alternating current). In this way, aggressive and violent behavior could be stimulated or inhibited, depending on whether the site had an excitatory (facilitating) or inhibitory effect on aggressive behavior. If the researcher applied low-frequency alternating current to an area with a facilitating function, the individual would probably behave aggressively; conversely, when current was applied to an inhibitory area, the person would be mild-mannered.

Violence also could be controlled by producing permanent alterations of brain tissue (lesions) by surgical, electrical (direct current), or chemical means (collectively called psychosurgery). Lesions in the temporal lobe of the brain were performed on several prisoners in California (Valenstein, 1973). The Japanese neurosurgeon Hirataro Narabayashi claimed success with amygdala operations on a diversity of patients plagued by aggressive, uncontrollable, destructive, and violent behavior. He reported that about 68% of his patients showed a significant decline in aggressive, violent behavior (Valenstein, 1973).

It should be noted that surgery such as that described above is not commonplace today. Psychosurgical procedures are highly refined and are considered primarily experimental. They are used only as a last resort in very severe cases of some mental illnesses (Comer, 2004). However, as a result of the aforementioned research, it is now possible for scientists to implant electrodes into a specific region of the human brain and monitor brain-wave patterns by computer, even when the individual is some distance away from the laboratory. When a brain-wave configuration known to be associated with violent behavior in that particular individual occurs, the computer activates an electrical stimulation to the brain site.

What are the social implications of such scientific practices? To what extent are they justified? In other words, just because we "can," does this mean that we "should"? Some investigators assert that we should control the antisocial elements in our society by any perfected biochemical, electrical, or surgical means necessary. In the early 1970s, then-President of the American Psychological Association, Kenneth B. Clark, urged his colleagues to make full use of these breakthroughs in biological research, which he referred to as **psychotechnology**. Assuming that no individual would choose to be a criminal if "not impelled by some forms of internal, biochemical, or external, social forces—or some combination of both" (Clark, 1971, p. 1056), he made the following comment:

> The implications of an effective psychotechnology for the control of criminal behavior and the amelioration of the moral insensitivities which produce reactive criminality in others are clear. It would seem, therefore, that there would be moral and rational justification for the use of compulsive criminals as pretest subjects in seeking precise forms of intervention and moral control of human behavior. (p. 1056)

Clark also suggested that world leaders be required to submit themselves to perfected forms of psychotechnological and biochemical intervention so that their potentially aggressive, hostile impulses could be controlled. This would be justified, since it would prevent the mass destruction of civilization.

Since Clark's widely quoted address, few psychologists have called for similar drastic interventions, although biochemical intervention and surgical techniques on the human brain (psychosurgery) are increasingly sophisticated. The medical, legal, moral, and ethical ramifications if Clark's proposals were to be carried out on a large scale would be overwhelming, and the questions posed would be unanswerable. Who would decide which technique should be used on whom? Which individuals would be required to submit to psychosurgery, and which would be encouraged to? What are the constitutional rights of the subjects? Although some courts have already begun to answer some of these questions with respect to institutionalized individuals, there remain numerous unsettled issues that are not within the scope of this text.

Furthermore, biological alleviation of aggressive behavior would undoubtedly affect socially desirable behaviors as well. There is evidence to suggest that aspects of a person's emotional, cognitive, and intellectual functioning may be significantly affected by biological manipulation of the brain. Neuronal networks in the central nervous system do not function in physiological isolation. It is estimated that the brain contains between 100 and 200 billion brain cells (neurons) whose interconnecting pathways form the most complex intercommunication network in the known universe. Each nerve cell or neuron may play some role in behavior. Scientists talk about areas or structures in the brain that may account for some type of behavior, but they know that each of these areas contains numerous neurons and supportive cells that contribute to a variety of functions. Thus, surgical, electrical, or chemical intervention to affect aggression may also incidentally affect other behaviors that need not and should not be changed.

Brain Pathology and Aggression

Postmortem examinations on chronically antisocial, violent persons are not routine, but when done they have generally found no noticeable lesion or malformation in the limbic system or other areas of the central nervous system (H. Goldman, 1977). This does not necessarily mean there was no physiological abnormality. The instruments used in the postmortem analysis may not have been sophisticated enough to detect them. Alternately, the individual's violent behavior might have reflected biochemical or neurotransmitter substances rather than malformation or damage to neural structures. In some instances, however, individuals were found to have symptoms of serious brain diseases. Richard Speck, who murdered eight student nurses in Chicago, reportedly displayed such symptoms (Valenstein, 1973). Charles Whitman, who killed passersby from the top of a university tower, was found in an autopsy to have a large tumor in the area of the amygdala (Mark & Ervin, 1970). Even so, it is not clear that these abnormalities directly affected Speck's and Whitman's violent behavior.

Furthermore, despite the fact that we are learning more about the brain than ever before, it is extremely unlikely that a majority of criminals in our society suffer from brain pathology or significant dysfunction. A small proportion of violent crime may be committed by people with brain diseases, but disease does not account for an appreciable portion of the aggression in our society.

Abnormal brain-wave patterns, introduced in Chapter 4, are more common, however. A significant number of prisoners who have committed violent crimes apparently display these patterns (Mark & Ervin, 1970; Valenstein, 1973). You may recall that one category of abnormal brain-wave patterns, slow-wave activity, is especially apparent in the temporal lobe region of the brain. Hare (1970) estimates that 2% of the general population exhibits this phenomenon, compared to 8.2% of the convicted murderer population and

14% of aggressive psychopaths. A second type of abnormal brain-wave activity, positive spike activity, occurs in less than 2% of the general population. However, it has been estimated that anywhere between 20% and 40% of individuals with a history of impulsive, aggressive, and destructive behavior display positive spikes (Hare, 1970). The destructive and violent responses are often precipitated by relatively mild provocations, but they can result in severe damage to property and injury or death to others. Do abnormal brain waves cause violent behavior? Or does violent behavior cause abnormal brain waves? It is impossible to tell. At present, the research on brain-wave patterns has uncovered only correlations, which do not signify cause and effect. The evidence to date indicates only that some forms of brain pathology or dysfunctions are found in a very small percentage of those who are violent—nothing more.

Heredity and the XYY Chromosome

Some early investigators believed that criminal behavior and predispositions to be violent were a result of heredity. The most prominent proponent of this view was Lombroso, who was convinced that a criminal "type" could be identified by specific physical characteristics, such as an unsymmetrical head and jaw, a low forehead, protruding ears, and bushy, connected eyebrows.

Later, mid-twentieth-century inquiries on the relationship between genetics and criminality focused on the so-called XYY chromosomal syndrome. The impetus for this research was a study by Jacobs and his associates (Jacobs, Brunton, Melville, Brittain, & McClemont, 1965), who reported that the presence of an extra Y chromosome in the male is significantly associated with the triad of tall stature, mental retardation, and an unusually high level of aggressive behavior. After the Jacobs study was released, some investigators hypothesized that the XYY chromosomal anomaly was closely related to violent criminal activity in males.

Chromosomes are chains of genetic material known as DNA that contain hereditary instructions for the growth and production of every living cell in the organism. Within each chromosome there are numerous genes; in fact, each cell contains between 30,000 and 40,000 genes (Andreasen, 2001). Chromosomes and their genes control physical traits such as eye and hair color and height, and they may have substantial influence on many psychological predispositions and temperaments. For example, chromosomes may account for a predisposition to depression. Each cell in the human body normally possesses 46 chromosomes, or 23 pairs. One pair in each cell is responsible for sex determination and sex characteristics. One member of the pair is always an X, but the other member may be either an X or a Y, depending on the sex of the individual. They are named after their appearance under a microscope. Each cell of the normal woman has two X chromosomes, while each cell of the normal man has an X and a Y. In rare instances, however, a genetic anomaly occurs in males in that two Y chromosomes pair with a single X—hence the phenomenon XYY. Rather than the usual 46 chromosomes, the individual has 47.

The principal characteristics associated with the presence of an extra Y chromosome include unusual height, episodes of violent aggression, and borderline intelligence—although there are many exceptions. Severe acne or scars from acne are also a characteristic.

A number of infamous murderers apparently had the XYY abnormality. One was Robert Peter Tait, who was convicted of beating to death a 77-year-old woman in Australia (Fox, 1971). The XYY characteristic was discovered after his trial but did not delay his execution. The XYY genotype was first used as a basis for criminal defense in 1968, at the trial of Daniel Hugon in Paris. Hugon was charged with the brutal murder of an elderly prostitute. Although convicted, he received only seven years' imprisonment. It is not certain that the court considered the XYY abnormality a mitigating factor in determining his sentence, however (Fox, 1971). In the United States, criminal defendants have not used the defense successfully. "Big Bad John" (Sean) Farley, a six-foot eight-inch, 240-pound giant who murdered and mutilated a Queens, New York, woman in 1969, was convicted despite his plea of insanity due to chromosomal imbalance. Finally, Richard Speck, the murderer of eight student nurses, possessed some of the physical features associated with the XYY chromosome. After his conviction, researchers examined his chromosomal structure. Although there was considerable confusion at the time the results were released, it has been concluded that Speck's genetic structure does not include the abnormality.

Although XYY has not been used as a criminal defense, there is some empirical support for its relationship with crime. So far, however, there is little evidence that violence and XYY go hand in hand. After an extensive review of the world literature, Jarvik, Klodin, and Matsuyama (1973) concluded that the presence of the XYY configuration in the general population averages between 0.11% and 0.14%; among mental patients it is significantly higher, averaging between 0.13% and 0.20%. However, in criminal populations, Jarvik found that XYY occurred in 1.9% of the cases. Jarvik's research combined information from 26 studies, including 5,066 criminal subjects. The 1.9% figure for the presence of the XYY chromosome, however, constitutes a very small percentage of the total prison population and seems to represent very little of the violence in our society. In another study, XYY prisoners were found to have fewer assault incidents than comparable groups of "normal" XY prisoners (Price & Whatmore, 1967). A great majority of the XYY crimes were against property.

Contemporary researchers have not pursued the extra-Y theory, however, because this particular chromosome does not appear to be a powerful explanatory factor for human violence. However, there is widespread recognition that—as a general principle—the numerous genes contained within a person's chromosomes influence not only one's physical characteristics but perhaps even one's behavior (Comer, 2004). Thus, there may be genetic *susceptibilities* to mood disorders, including severe depression, schizophrenia, and other mental disorders. As we discussed in Chapter 6, some of these disorders have been associated with various crimes. In 2000, an extensive *Human Genome Project* designed to map all of the genes in the human body was completed. Results from that project are expected to contribute significantly to the understanding of human disorders, both medical and psychological (Comer, 2004).

Epilepsy and Violence

Between 1889 and 1970, there were only 15 court cases in the United States in which epilepsy was used as a defense against charges of murder, homicide, manslaughter, or disorderly conduct (Delgado-Escueta, Mattson, & King, 1981). However, during the 1970s medical researchers implied that there was a causal relationship between temporal lobe epilepsy and violence (M. Goldstein, 1974; Pincus, 1980). This implied relationship resulted in a rash of diminished responsibility or insanity defenses for violent acts beginning in 1977. Presumably, the person plagued with this disorder is prone to uncontrollable periods of violence and destruction. However, available research fails to support any relationship between violence and epilepsy in general or violence and psychomotor epilepsy (Valenstein, 1973; Blumer, 1976).

Although angry, irritable behavior between seizures is commonly reported in individuals with chronic temporal lobe seizures, these individuals rarely inflict physical harm (Blumer, 1976). In rare cases, some violence may occur in the confusional state that takes place immediately after an epileptic seizure, if the individual is provoked. During this brief rage attack, the person appears to lose control and may even destroy some furniture or strike a family member. Rarely is there actual physical injury, and rarely are criminal charges brought. Furthermore, it is not clear whether aggression occurs because of the seizure itself, occurs because of associated brain damage that often accompanies psychomotor seizure activity, or is independent of the seizure itself (Herzberg & Fenwick, 1988). Available evidence (e.g., Wong, Lumsden, Fenton & Fenwick, 1994) indicates that if violence does occur during the seizure episode, the violent behavior is probably due to a long-standing response pattern of the individual and is not directly related to the seizure itself.

SUMMARY AND CONCLUSIONS

In this chapter we have reviewed the major psychological perspectives on aggression and violence. Answers to what can be done about aggression and violent crime rest ultimately on one's perspective of human nature. If one believes that aggression is innate and part of our evolutionary heritage, the position held by mainstream psychoanalytic and ethological thought, then the conclusion must be that aggression is part of life and that little can be done to alter this basic ingredient of human nature. Clues for reducing aggression are found in the behavior demonstrated throughout the animal kingdom. If, on the other hand, one believes that human aggression is acquired, then the key becomes principles of human learning and thought, and hope that one can change this acquired behavior for the betterment of humankind. The distinction between the innate and the learning viewpoints has been somewhat over-simplified, but most contemporary theories on aggression fall within one or the other camp. At this point, the learning perspective has garnered considerably more empirical support than the innate perspective. Cognitive factors are especially important in explanations of human aggression.

Complicating the above, though, is the increasing amount of research being done in the biological sciences, most particularly relating to the brain and to human genetics. As noted in this chapter, 95% of everything we know about the human brain has been learned within the last 15 years. Researchers are acquiring extensive information about the contribution of genes to physical characteristics and susceptibility to medical problems. Many believe that they will eventually link genes to a variety of behavioral problems and mental disorders as well. It is crucial to keep in mind, though, that although some genes may *predispose* individuals to certain disorders that may lead to violence or other antisocial behavior, genes do not *determine* behavior.

Furthermore, as more research data are published, even the *learning* perspective becomes increasingly complex, and additional factors must be considered. For one thing, physiological arousal certainly plays a major role in aggressive and violent behavior, as suggested by Berkowitz (1989). High levels of arousal seem to *facilitate* (again, not cause) aggressive behavior in certain situations. Extremely high arousal seems to interfere with our sense of self-awareness and internal control, rendering us more susceptible to environmental cues and to mindless or habitual behaviors. In this sense, under very high arousal, we may not stop to consider the consequences of our violent behavior. This point raises serious questions about the value of capital punishment or life sentences as general deterrents to violent crime. Although there is reason to sentence a person convicted of a serious violent crime to a long term as retribution for the crime or to incapacitate the person, there is little justification for doing so under a deterrence rationale.

The different types of aggressive behavior were also emphasized in this chapter. Overt and covert forms of aggression must be considered in any discussion of crime. Overt aggressors are more likely to be involved in both violent and serious property–economic crimes, whereas covert aggressors are more prone to be involved in property offenses, particularly occupational crime. And although the conventional wisdom has been that boys are more likely to commit highly aggressive crimes, the evidence suggests that girls may be equally involved in aggressive behavior of a different kind. Gender differences in aggressive behavior are believed to be mainly due to socialization factors.

Situational and neurophysiological factors also contribute significantly to aggressive behavior. Aggressive stimuli, crowds, pollution, temperature, smells, and central nervous system pathology all must be entertained as possible contributors. Social learning theorists also note that the media and the models they provide substantially affect our attitudes, values, and overall impressions about violence. Attitudes, beliefs, and thoughts refer to the cognitive processes that are beginning to emerge as contenders for a leading role in the psychological explanation of criminal behavior. Operant and classical conditioning remain important, but they do not adequately address the many intricacies of criminal behavior.

We end the chapter with a concise summary statement by Rowell Huesmann (1997), who, after reviewing the research literature, concludes, "No one causal factor by itself explains more than a small portion of individual differences in aggressiveness" (p. 70). He hastens to add, however, that "early learning and socialization play a key role in the development of habitual aggression" (p. 70).

CHAPTER 8

HOMICIDE, ASSAULT, AND FAMILY VIOLENCE

I f the news and entertainment media are reasonably decent barometers of human interest, homicidal violence must be one of Western civilization's most fascinating subjects and, along with sex, the most marketable. Usually, the more bizarre, senseless, or heinous the murder, the more extensive press coverage it receives, followed shortly thereafter by books, television specials, and movies. Unusual mass murders, serial murders, and so-called motiveless killings are especially popular. Yet on a national level, criminal homicide consistently accounts for only about 1% or 2% of all violent crimes reported in the FBI's Uniform Crime Reports (UCR; Federal Bureau of Investigation, 2003) (see **Figure 8–1**). A total of 16,204 such homicides were reported in 2002. In the same year an estimated 1.4 million violent offenses were reported to law enforcement agencies. The rate for violent crime was 494.6 offenses per 100,000 in the population, a rate that is similar to the data reported for the preceding five years. If we consider its percentage distribution among all index crimes, murder represents only 0.2% of the total. Furthermore, the vast majority of these criminal homicides offer very little mystery or intrigue. In many cases, they involve angry friends, spouses, or acquaintances killing friends, spouses, or acquaintances. During 2002, for example, the relationship between the victims and the perpetrators was known in 57.2% of all homicides. Within those known

FIGURE 8–1   Violent Crime Distribution in the United States, 2002

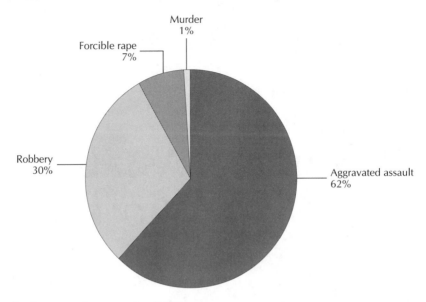

Source: Federal Bureau of Investigation (2003).

relationships, 22.2% of the victims were related to their killer, 53.4% were acquainted with the killer, and 24.4% did not know their killer (Federal Bureau of
Investigation, 2003).

The disproportionate amount of attention paid to criminal homicides may
be explained in a variety of ways. Obviously, this is a highly serious crime, with
death being the ultimate victimization. However, another reason for the attention may be related to our fascination with the occult, the mysterious, and the
macabre. We crave science fiction, tales of terror, even haunted houses. Perhaps
we need a certain amount of excitement and arousal to prevent our lives from
becoming too mundane and boring. Psychologists have long known that novelty
produces arousal and excitement and breaks monotony (Berlyne, 1960). This
human need for stimulation and excitement—which, as we learned in Chapter 3,
is greater in some people (extraverts) than others (introverts)—may partly explain the appeal of roller coasters, skydiving, race car driving, bungee jumping,
and gambling. Extraverts also may enjoy films featuring vampires, werewolves,
psychomurderers, or torture chambers—or these vicarious pleasures might be
enjoyed by ambiverts or introverts not wishing to seek out this type of excitement directly. In any case, tales of murder, fictional or not, add zest to life. For
the family that has been touched by murder, however, this vicarious response on
the part of others must be difficult to understand and to accept.

The marketability of murder might also be explained by curiosity or exploratory behavior, which is very closely related to excitement and arousal.

One purpose of curiosity is to allow organisms to adjust to their environments (Butler, 1954). An individual or an organism explores a new situation to satisfy this curiosity—which is theorized to be a physiological drive state—and, in the process of discovering information, adapts to the new situation. Curiosity about murder might help us prepare for the possibility that a similar event could happen to us. Reading about bizarre, seemingly irrational homicides might help us to identify danger signals. Information about the incident gives clues about who murders, who gets murdered, and in what circumstances. To some extent, we can take preventive measures, even though there is no guarantee that such measures will keep us safe. Furthermore, families and close friends of murder victims would say that nothing can prepare someone for the devastation that is experienced when a loved one is murdered.

The above reactions to depictions of violence—experienced vicariously— may be regarded as adaptive or functional. Extensive exposure to violence also has a dysfunctional side, however. Specifically, it may immunize us from the horror of violence. Many social commentators have advanced cogent arguments that Western civilization has become conditioned or jaded to cruelty and inhumane behavior and that people are desensitized to human suffering. In addition, the constant attention that the news and entertainment media give to violence also makes it seem more widespread and frequent than it really is. This phenomenon is called the **availability heuristic** by social psychologists. Heuristics refer to cognitive shortcuts that people use to make quick inferences about their world. When the media continually show graphic and frightening accounts of violence, people are likely to incorporate these vivid details into cognitive shorthand and have them readily available for future reference. When they think of violence at a later time, they remember the most frequently seen and horrific accounts, increasing their fear of violent crime and augmenting its incidence in their minds.

To speculate about why we are attracted to accounts of murder and violence, or to wonder about the effects of repeated exposure, may not seem to address the main focus of this chapter, which is the violent offender. Speculation becomes relevant, however, when we shift the focus to the individual who is part of a society that seems to have an inordinate need to seek out stimulation or to know details of crimes. When that individual is insensitive to suffering and begins to create his or her own excitement by torturing and murdering, we have a social problem. Psychology, as we will see in this chapter, can offer some suggestions for understanding and solving this problem.

After defining our terms, we examine situational and dispositional factors that occur consistently in homicide and aggravated assault, beginning with statistical data on their incidence and prevalence and their demographic correlates. Thus far in the text, theoretical issues have been introduced with minimum application to specific offenses. Beginning here and throughout the remainder of the book, we interweave the theories and concepts previously outlined with specific categories of criminal behavior. Thus in this chapter we focus on family violence.

DEFINITIONS

Criminologists generally study aggravated assault and homicide together, primarily because they view many aggravated assaults as failed homicide attempts (Doerner, 1988; Doerner & Speir, 1986). Dunn (1976) challenges this practice. He notes that the aggravated assault rate is at least 20 times that of homicide. "Given this disparity in rates, it is difficult to imagine that even one-quarter of all aggravated assaults were attempted homicides or would have been homicides except for the intervention of medical care" (p. 10). Therefore, it may be unwarranted to consider aggravated assault as being in the same league as homicide; the two may differ in important variables, including the motives of the perpetrator. A purist, therefore, would try to maintain an aggravated assault–homicide distinction. And, of course, the distinctions are maintained in crime statistics as well as in criminal law.

For our purposes, it is neither realistic nor desirable to maintain a definitive assault–homicide distinction. Not realistic, since much of the relevant research on offender *characteristics* collapses the categories into one, under the rationale that people who kill usually (but not invariably) have a history of assaultive behavior. It is not desirable, since, from a psychological point of view, the two types of behavior are comparable. Often, the type of weapon used determines the final outcome. The high-powered bullet, as an obvious example, is in most cases far more lethal than the knife (Block, 1977; Gillin & Ochberg, 1970). A stabbing or even a beating may represent behavior similar to that displayed in homicide with a Saturday night special. In law, the distinctions between murder and aggravated assault are crucial, chiefly due to the extent of harm; in psychology, they are less so.

Block (1977) contended that death is a highly plausible outcome of any violent crime, including robbery and rape. Criminal homicide, then, is violent behavior carried too far. In general agreement with Block, we designate criminal homicide and aggravated assault as one form of violent behavior, although the statistics section separates them briefly. In later chapters we discuss other forms of violent behavior, including rape and armed robbery.

Criminal homicide is causing the death of another person without legal justification or excuse. Legally, the term murder is reserved for the "unlawful killing of one human being by another with malice aforethought, either expressed or implied" (H. Black, 1990, p. 1019). "Malice aforethought" refers to premeditation, or the mental state of a person who thinks ahead, plans, and voluntarily causes the death of another, without legal excuse or justification. However, "premeditation" can occur in a very short period of time (even a minute); it does not require weeks of planning. In most states murder is divided into two degrees, a statutory provision that allows courts to impose a more severe penalty for some murders than others. Some states even specify three degrees of murder. The degree system was once a useful and meaningful method of distinguishing between murder that was punishable by death and murder that was not (T. Gardner, 1985). In more recent times, the distinctions between the degrees have become more blurred. Usually, murder in the first degree is a homicide that was committed with particularly vicious, willful, deliberate, and premeditated intent. Murder in the second degree is characterized by the intentional and unlawful killing of another but without the type of malice and premeditation required for first-degree murder. Examples of second-degree murder include "crimes of passion" such as an enraged father who strangles the drunken driver who just killed his son. Although there was no premeditation, the angry father still wanted to kill him. Many states that do not distinguish between degrees of murder would call this an example of nonnegligent manslaughter.

The UCR include both **murder** and **nonnegligent manslaughter** under the rubric criminal homicide for reporting purposes (see **Figure 8–2** for an illustration of their downward trend). Deaths of others that occur as a result of negligence (negligent manslaughter) are not included. The essential difference between murder and nonnegligent manslaughter is that malice aforethought must be present in murder, whereas it must be absent in nonnegligent manslaughter.

Negligent manslaughter is killing another as a result of recklessness or culpable negligence. Although there was no intent to kill, the law says you should have known that your actions could result in the death of another person. For example, a man who recklessly waves a gun around in jest, when the gun discharges and kills someone, is still responsible for that person's death. A driver who turns to look at a passenger, crosses the center lane, and hits an oncoming car, killing its occupant, displayed negligent (not reckless) behavior but is still

FIGURE 8–2   Murder and Nonnegligent Manslaughter in the United States, 1984–2001

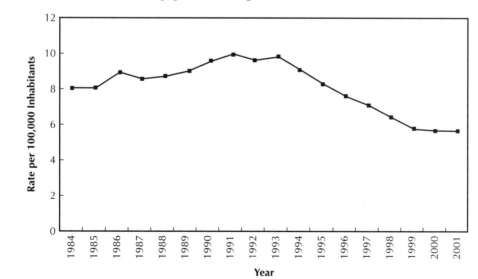

Source: Federal Bureau of Investigation (2003).

responsible for the death. What the above two individuals have in common is that they did not intend to kill anyone. Both situations illustrate negligent manslaughter, as opposed to the nonnegligent manslaughter covered along with murder in the UCR statistics.

The person charged with murder (first or second degree) or with nonnegligent manslaughter intended for the victim to die. In the case of nonnegligent manslaughter, the original intent may not have been to kill the victim. However, in the particular situation, the perpetrator became agitated and emotionally upset to the point of losing control of the self-regulatory system. A man who chokes a woman to death during rough sex is an example. In some states, nonnegligent manslaughter is equivalent to second-degree murder.

In line with UCR classifications, we combine both murder and nonnegligent manslaughter under the general rubric homicide in this chapter. We are not concerned with suicides, accidental deaths, negligent manslaughter, or justifiable homicide (the killing of a person by a law enforcement officer in the line of duty or, in some cases, the killing of a person in the act of committing a violent felony by a private citizen).

Assault is the intentional infliction of bodily injury on another person, or the attempt to inflict such injury. It becomes aggravated assault when the intention is to inflict serious bodily injury. Aggravated assault is often accompanied by the use of a deadly or dangerous weapon. Simple assault is the unlawful, intentional inflicting of less than serious bodily injury without a deadly or dangerous weapon, or the attempt to inflict such bodily injury, again without a deadly or dangerous weapon.

SOCIOLOGICAL CORRELATES OF HOMICIDE

Race/Ethnic Origin

One of the most consistent findings reported in the criminology literature is that African Americans in the United States are involved in criminal homicide—both as offenders and as victims—at a rate that is extremely disproportionate to their numbers in the general population. Although African Americans make up about 13% of the U.S. population, they accounted for more than 50% of all arrests for violent crimes in 2002 (Federal Bureau of Investigation, 2003). About 50% of those arrested for murder and about 40% arrested for aggravated assault are African American (Federal Bureau of Investigation, 2003). In addition, African Americans comprise on the average about 40% of the prisoners in local jails (see **Table 8–1**) and nearly 50% of the prisoners in state and federal facilities, indicating that their conviction rates are also unusually high. Of persons under the sentence of death in 2001, 44% were African American, and 54% were White (Bureau of Justice Statistics, 2003a).

This pattern has been observed for many decades now. Wolfgang (1958, 1961) studied 588 homicides reported in Philadelphia from 1948 to 1952 and

TABLE 8–1 Jail Inmates, 2001

RACE OF INMATE	ESTIMATED GROUP	PER 100,000 RESIDENTS IN GROUP
Total	665,475	231
White	291,800	147
Black	264,900	740
Latino	96,000	256
Other	10,800	72

Source: Bureau of Justice Statistics (2002).

found that about 73% of the offenders and 75% of the victims were African American. Furthermore, in 94% of all reported cases, African Americans killed African Americans or whites killed whites, indicating that most homicide is intraracial. *Intraracial* means that offenders commit crime against members of their own race, whereas *interracial* means that offenders commit crime against members of a different race. More recent data from 2002 continue to show this trend: 92% of the African-American victims were slain by African-American offenders, whereas 85% of the white murder victims were killed by white assailants (Federal Bureau of Investigation, 2003). Nationwide, African-American males have a 1-in-40 chance of becoming homicide victims during their lifetimes (Federal Bureau of Investigation, 2003). White males, on the other hand, have a 1-in-280 chance. African-American females have a 1-in-199 chance of becoming homicide victims while white females have a 1-in-794 chance.

The disproportionate representation of African Americans in the arrest and conviction data for violence probably reflects social inequities, such as lack of employment or educational opportunities, racial oppression in its many forms, racial differences in the reporting of crime to police, discriminatory treatment at the hands of the criminal justice system, and law enforcement practices in inner-city areas where many African Americans reside. There is no evidence to suggest that racial biological or neuropsychological predispositions play a role in the consistently reported differences in violence rates over the years.

Latinos/Hispanics are projected to become the largest ethnic minority group in the United States within the next decade. The Latino/Hispanic population is now equal to the African-American population, and growing (Martinez, 2002). Latinos/Hispanics constitute about 12.5% of the U.S. population and account for about 12% of the arrests for violent crimes. Furthermore, only about 1% of those arrested for homicide are Latinos or Hispanics. However, Latinos/Hispanics make up about 27% of the federal prison population and 17% of the state prison population (Bureau of Justice Statistics, 2003c). In addition, 12% of the inmates under a sentence of death in 2001 were Latino/Hispanic (Bureau of Justice Statistics, 2003a). Overall, though, the research indicates that the Latino/Hispanic violence *victimization* rate falls below the rates found for African-American and white populations, including the *economically disadvantaged* segments of the U.S. population (Martinez, 2002; Reidel, 2003). Persons of Latino/Hispanic origin experience about 11% of all violent crime against persons age 12 or older in the United States, mostly in the form of simple assault (Bureau of Justice Statistics, 2002). Most of the victims receive only minor injury from the assault. Martinez argues that the relatively low violence rates are partly due to the fact that Latinos generally have high rates of participation in the labor force and also have close and highly supportive connections to the local community and extended family.

American Indians and Alaska Natives account for 1.5% of the U.S. population and represented 1.3% of the total arrests reported in 2002 (Federal Bureau of Investigation, 2003). Similarly, they accounted for 1.1% of the arrests for murder and 1.1% of the total arrests for violent crime in 2002. On the other hand, the rate of violent *victimization* of American Indians appears to be well above that of other U.S. racial or ethnic subgroups and is more than twice as high as the national average (Greenfeld & Smith, 1999). In fact, American Indians experience aggravated assault and simple assault at the highest rates of any racial or ethnic group in the United States (Rennison, 2002). Moreover, American Indians are more likely than other races to experience violence at the hands of someone of a different race (interracial violence) (Chaiken, 1999).

Asians account for 4.2% of the U.S. population, and Pacific Islanders another 0.3%. Although available research is limited, the UCR data indicate that Asian Americans/Pacific Islanders are arrested in numbers that fall significantly below their representation in the general population, both in overall arrests (1.1%) and in arrests for violent crime (1.2%) and murder (1.2%) (Federal Bureau of Investigation, 2003). Asian Americans experience the lowest rates of victimization of violence of any racial or ethnic group in the United States (Rennison, 2002).

Although much more research needs to be done on the relationship between racial/ethnic minorities and crime, using rigid categories such as Black, Latino/Hispanic, Asian, Native Americans, and White, represents an oversimplification of the multiethnic and multicultural mixtures across the nation. Cultures and subcultures are highly complex and multidimensional, and meaningful research on the ethnic/minority differences in violence require a knowledgeable sensitivity of this complexity.

Gender Differences

The relationship between homicide and gender is also robust. Wolfgang (1958) reported that 82% of the murderers and 76% of the victims in his Philadelphia sample were male. Specifically, the homicide offender rate per 100,000 was 41.7 for African-American males, 9.3 for African-American females, 3.4 for white males, and only 0.4 for white females. Notice how the race factor emerges strongly in combination with the gender factor. That is, the group displaying by far the highest incidence of homicide is African-American males.

TABLE 8–2 Murder Victims by Race and Gender, 2002

RACE OF VICTIM	TOTAL	GENDER OF VICTIM		
		MALE	*FEMALE*	*UNKNOWN*
White	6,757	4,852	1,905	0
Black	6,730	5,544	1,184	2
Other	377	256	121	0
Unknown	190	127	41	22
Total	14,054	10,779	3,251	24

Source: Federal Bureau of Investigation (2003).

Table 8–2 shows murder victims by race and gender in 2002. The 2002 data also indicated that 92.3% of black murder victims were killed by black offenders and 84.7% of white murder victims were killed by white offenders (Federal Bureau of investigation, 2003).

UCR data consistently reveal that the annual arrest rates for murder run about 90% male, 10% female (Federal Bureau of Investigation, 2003). In 2002, males accounted for about 77% of murder victims (Federal Bureau of Investigation, 2003). In 2002, 83% of all arrests for violent crime offenses were male. (In addition to murder, nonnegligent manslaughter, and aggravated assault, other violent offenses include rape, robbery, and simple assault.) It should be noted, however, that there are substantial situational and victim differences in murders committed by males versus females, a topic that reappears in Chapter 9.

Age

With monotonous regularity, national statistics from all sources continue to underscore the fact that about half of all those arrested for violent crime are between 20 and 29 years of age. In 2002, individuals under age 25 made up 44% of all violent crime arrestees and comprised 51% of all those arrested for murder or nonnegligent manslaughter (Federal Bureau of Investigation, 2003). By far the highest rate of offending occurs among young, African-American males, aged 18 to 22 (Federal Bureau of Investigation, 2003).

The young are also the victims. For example, in 2002, persons aged 12 to 24 sustained violent victimization at rates higher than that for individuals of all other ages combined (Bureau of Justice Statistics, 2003b). Of all murder victims, 50% were under 30 years of age (Federal Bureau of Investigation, 2003).

As we learned in Chapter 2, most offending histories tend to be short, usually dropping off dramatically somewhere between late adolescence and early adulthood (the adolescent-limited, or AL, group). However, a small number of persons (about 6%) continue to engage in violence far beyond early adulthood. Most probably, these violent offenders are life course–persistent offenders.

Socioeconomic Class

Criminologists have long assumed that crime, including violent crime, is found primarily among the lower socioeconomic class. Ongoing research (e.g., Bailey, 1984; Blau & Blau, 1982; Hawkins, 1985; M. Smith & Bennett, 1985; K. Williams, 1984) has supported the observation that violence appears to be associated with the lower class or with economic and social discrimination.

Research and commentary by Tittle (Tittle, 1983; Tittle & Villemez, 1977) challenged both the theory and the empirical research based on class distinctions in criminal activity, however. Tittle argued that criminologists have established their theories and conducted their research on the basis of unfounded assumptions about the lower class. After reviewing 35 self-report studies, Tittle and Villemez (1977) asserted that the supposed link between social class and crime was a myth.

Other criminologists believed that a rejection of the relationship was premature. Braithwaite (1981) reviewed over 100 studies and disagreed with Tittle's conclusions, finding considerable support for the view that individuals in the lower class commit more crime than those in other classes. Elliott et al. (1980), after analyzing data from their self-report youth survey, emphasized the importance of distinguishing between serious crime against persons and property and nonserious offenses. They noted that lower-class youth are proportionately more involved in serious crimes than other youth.

Criminologists today readily acknowledge a relationship between crime and low socioeconomic status. There is little doubt of a relationship between socioeconomic position in society and those adult crimes that tend to come to the attention of police and to appear in official crime statistics, including the violent crimes that are the subject of this chapter. However, we know that violence within families or between intimates and acquaintances, when perpetrated by persons of higher economic status, does not always come to the attention of police. Thus, the official statistics are at least somewhat misleading. Furthermore, as we learned in Chapter 2, the relationship between crime and poverty is complex, involving a myriad of factors. Finally, as we discuss in Chapter 11, persons of high socioeconomic status commit varieties of crime whose enforcement and prosecution are often not considered a high priority in our society.

Victim–Offender Relationship

Research has consistently indicated that offenders and victims of homicide often know one another. Early studies found that in at least two-thirds of all homicides the offender and the victim know one another well (Bullock, 1955; Driver, 1961; Hepburn & Voss, 1970; Svalastoga, 1956; Wolfgang, 1958; M. Wong & Singer, 1973). In the Wolfgang data, the victim and offender were strangers in only about 14% of the cases. In a Chicago investigation, Hepburn and Voss (1970) reported a slightly higher victim–offender unfamiliarity figure, 19%.

Figure 8–3   Murder Victimization by Known Relationship, 2002

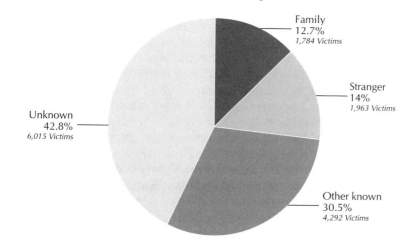

Source: Federal Bureau of Investigation (2003, p. 25).

Recent UCR data (Federal Bureau of Investigation, 2003) show that nearly half the murder victims in 2002 were either related to the offender (12.7%) or acquainted with the offender (30.5%). In 14% of the cases, victims were murdered by strangers. The relationships were unknown for the remaining 42.8% (**Figure 8–3**). Among all female murder victims in 2002, 32% were slain by husbands or boyfriends, while only 3% of male victims were killed by wives or girlfriends. **Table 8–3** takes a very different slant on these data. First, the table lists the percentage of total murders committed over the period 1976–1997. Second, it shows whom male and female murderers tended to kill, in contrast to the previous data, which take a victimization approach. In other words, Table 8–3

Table 8–3   Total Murders by Offender and Victim Over a 20-Year Period, 1976–1997

Victim	Offender (%)	
	Female	*Male*
Spouse	28.3	6.8
Ex-spouse	1.5	0.5
Child/stepchild	10.4	2.2
Other family member	6.7	6.9
Boyfriend/girlfriend	14.0	3.9
Acquaintance	31.9	54.6
Stranger	7.2	25.1

Source: Greenfeld (1999, p. 4).

reports that over the 20-year period, murdered females were killed by spouses more often than were murdered males; the 2002 data also illustrate that when women are killed, they are most often killed by their husbands or boyfriends.

The 2002 data indicate that 26.5% of the murders resulted from arguments and 16.5% were committed in the process of committing felonies such as forcible rape, robbery, arson, and drug trafficking (Federal Bureau of Investigation, 2003). Twenty-three percent involved other types of circumstances—some also involving felonies—such as brawls, sniper attacks, and juvenile and gang killings (see **Table 8–4**).

Men are victimized by violent strangers at an annual rate more than double that for women (Federal Bureau of Investigation, 2003). The chance of becoming the victim of a violent crime perpetrated by a stranger increases with age for women but remains about the same across all ages for men (U.S. Department of Justice, 1989b).

While the homicide offender and his or her victims frequently have similar demographic characteristics, this observation holds primarily for family and acquaintance homicide. When it comes to stranger homicide, there is a

TABLE 8–4   Murder Circumstances by Gender of the Victim During 2002

CIRCUMSTANCE	TOTAL MURDER VICTIMS	MALE	FEMALE	UNKNOWN
Total	14,054	10,779	3,251	24
Felony type total	2,314	1,894	419	1
Rape	43	3	40	0
Robbery	1,092	936	156	0
Burglary	96	68	28	0
Larceny-theft	15	14	1	0
Motor vehicle theft	16	14	2	0
Arson	59	28	31	0
Commercialized vice	8	3	5	0
Other sex offenses	8	1	7	0
Narcotic drug laws	657	595	61	1
Gambling	5	5	0	0
Other—not specified	315	227	88	0
Suspected felony type	67	56	11	0
Other than felony type total	7,097	5,193	1,897	7
Romantic triangle	130	89	41	0
Child killed by babysitter	38	15	23	0
Brawl due to alcohol	153	131	22	0
Brawl due to narcotics	84	72	12	0
Argument over money	203	165	38	0
Other arguments	3,527	2,567	957	3
Gangland killings	73	69	4	0
Juvenile gang killings	911	869	42	0
Institutional killings	12	11	1	0
Sniper attack	11	8	3	0
Other—not specified	1,955	1,197	754	4
Unknown total	4,576	3,636	924	16

Source: Federal Bureau of Investigation (2003, p. 24).

clear tendency for the offender to be younger and of a different race than the victim (Riedel, Zahn, & Mock, 1985).

Weapons

Guns and knives (or other cutting instruments) are the two preferred instruments for inflicting death, but this preference is somewhat influenced by gender (**Table 8–5**), race, geography, and other parameters. For example, in Philadelphia during the early 1950s, stabbing was the most common lethal method (Wolfgang, 1958), whereas in Chicago during the 1960s and early 1970s, shooting was preferred (Block, 1977; Hepburn & Voss, 1970). Later, firearm-related homicides in Chicago increased almost threefold (Block, 1977). However, death inflicted by other weapons increased only slightly.

Nationwide data indicate that firearms were used in over 70% of all homicides committed between 1993 and 2002 (Federal Bureau of Investigation, 2003; Zawitz & Strom, 2000), while knives or cutting instruments were used in less than 13% (Federal Bureau of Investigation, 2003). Approximately 80% of firearm homicides are committed with handguns, 6% with shotguns, 5% with rifles, and 7% with unspecified firearms. Furthermore, in 1998, 400 police officers were injured in firearm assaults, and 58 police officers were killed while responding to a crime (Zawitz & Strom, 2000).

In 1994, 44 million Americans owned 192 million firearms, 65 million of which were handguns (P. Cook & Ludwig, 1997), and an additional 12.5 million firearms were purchased between March 1994 and November 1998 (Bureau of Justice Statistics, 1999). Although there are enough firearms to provide every American adult with one, only 25% of adults actually own guns. Most gun owners, specifically 74%, possess two or more. Interestingly, gun ownership is highest among middle-aged, college-educated people of rural small-town America (P. Cook & Ludwig, 1997). About 14 million adults (approximately one-third of gun owners) carry firearms for protection. Two-thirds of those who carry guns

TABLE 8–5   Weapons' Used by Male and Female Murderers, 1998

WEAPON USED	MURDERER (%)	
	FEMALE	*MALE*
Handgun	42	51
Other firearm	11	16
Knife	31	18
Blunt object	4	6
Other	12	9

Source: Greenfeld (1999, p. 4).

keep them in their vehicles, while the others sometimes carry them on their person. Although it is often pointed out that many individuals own guns for sport, these same individuals typically consider protection a secondary purpose for gun ownership.

About every 14 minutes someone in America dies from a gunshot wound. About half of those deaths are suicides, about 44% are homicides, and 4% are unintentional shootings (Zawitz & Strom, 2000). Moreover, a study in the *New England Journal of Medicine* (Washington Post, October 12, 1993) contradicts the common view that having a gun protects people from violence. The study discovered that in households with guns the death of a household member is three times more likely than in gunless households. Research such as the above suggests that, while guns do not *cause* violent crime, accessibility of guns facilitates it. Furthermore, the harm that results from an individual's anger or from the careless or reckless use of weapons is far greater than the harm that results when less lethal weapons, or no weapons at all, are available. This is the justification for laws such as those that require guns to be registered and to have child-safety locks installed and that forbid convicted felons from owning and carrying weapons. Because of the widespread availability of illegal firearms, these laws are often very difficult to enforce.

Other Factors

Several other factors associated with violent crime are reported consistently in the research.

Temporal Factors.   Homicides are equally distributed across the 12 months of the year, although there is a slight increase during some holidays (December and January) and the summer months. The holidays are the times when many family gatherings and celebrations take place and, also, when interpersonal tensions and alcohol consumption can be at their highest levels. Weekends, especially the hours between 8 PM Saturday and 2 AM Sunday, are clearly the time when homicides most often occur (Block, 1977; Hepburn & Voss, 1970; Wolfgang, 1958).

Victim Precipitation.   In a classic study, Wolfgang (1958) found that about 26% of homicide cases were victim-precipitated: The victim contributed in a significant way to his or her own demise by taking the first step toward violence. Hepburn and Voss (1970) found that about 38% of Chicago homicides seemed to be provoked by the victim. Studies do suggest that offender motives for killing are often based on minor altercations and domestic quarrels in which both parties were actively aggressive. Recall the phenomenon of escalation presented in the previous chapter, where we noted that some people tend to retaliate in kind to insults or blows. Moreover, verbal quarrels very often escalate to physical altercations. Separated from the context in which they took place, the precipitating factors of violent behavior are often pitifully trivial. It should be noted, though, that Wolfgang did not consider verbal taunts or insults a form of victim precipitation; rather, the victim had to actively make the first physically violent move. In that sense, "pure" victim-precipitated homicide, as defined by Wolfgang, may qualify as self-defense on the part of the individual who committed the homicide. We should emphasize, also, that official statistics, such as those represented in the UCR, do not make inferences about the victim's possible role in the offense. Thus, there is no suggestion that a given percentage of homicides was victim-precipitated.

Alcohol. Alcohol continually emerges as a factor associated with homicide. Wolfgang reported that in nearly two-thirds of cases, either the victim, the offender, or both had been drinking immediately prior to the slaying. In 2002, a very small number of homicides (153) were *the result of* a brawl due to the influence of alcohol (Federal Bureau of Investigation, 2003). However, we have no way of knowing from the official statistics how great *a factor* alcohol was in the other homicides. (The noteworthy relationship between alcohol and violence is discussed in detail in Chapter 12.)

Sniper Attacks

On November 25, 2003, while heading to a doctor's appointment, Gail Knisley was killed on Ohio Interstate 270 by a sniper. Throughout that year, at least 23 other reports documented shots fired at vehicles along the same highway, which surrounds Columbus. One shot broke a window at an elementary school. The reports began in May. The shots had been fired at different times of the day, piercing cars, trucks, vans, and horse trailers, shattering windows, and flattening tires (McCarthy, 2003). Charles A. McCoy, Jr., age 28, has been charged with the shootings. McCoy, who is believed to be mentally ill, lived a half-mile north of Interstate 270 where the shootings were concentrated. The mother of the suspect testified in a preliminary hearing that she discovered four guns over a period of several months in the house she shared with her son. At least one of the guns was linked to the sniper attacks.

Perhaps the most frightening sniper attacks in modern times took place over a 23-day period in October 2002. Ten persons, chosen at random, were killed by sniper fire, the first six within the first 27 hours of the incident. The attacks took place in and around the Washington, DC, area. The two alleged snipers, 42-year-old Army veteran John Allen Muhammad and his teenage sidekick, 17-year-old Lee Boyd Malvo, were arrested on October 24, 2002, while sitting in their 1990 Chevrolet Caprice. The beat-up Caprice had been modified to enable the snipers to crawl into the vehicle's trunk from the backseat and shoot a high-powered rifle (a Bushmaster XM-15, a semiautomatic version of the M-16) through a hole sawed just above the license plate. In total, the two men were accused of shooting 19 people, killing 13 and wounding

6, in Alabama, Georgia, Louisiana, Maryland, Virginia, and Washington, DC, in an attempt to extort $10 million from the government.

Muhammad was convicted of two counts of capital murder on November 17, 2003, after a Virginia jury deliberated for six and a half hours. A week later, a seven-woman, five-man panel recommended the death sentence and a judge then sentenced him to death. He was the first person ever charged and sentenced under Virginia's new post–September 11, 2001, terrorism law. The law outlaws attempts to intimidate the civilian population at large or to influence the conduct or activities of the government through intimidation.

Muhammad is an ex-U.S. soldier who served in the Gulf War and who is an award-winning expert marksman. He was trained as a mechanic, truck driver, and metal worker. He is the father of four children, has been married at least twice, and was involved in bitter custody battles for his children. On at least one occasion, he was accused of abducting the children. Malvo and his mother left Jamaica when he was about 14 years old and moved to the island of Antigua and then to Fort Myers, Florida. Muhammad and Malvo were very close, with Muhammad referring to the teenager as his son. Malvo, tried separately, advanced an insanity defense, arguing that he was brainwashed by Muhammad and was thus not responsible for the crimes. He was also convicted in December 2003, but the jury recommended that he be sentenced to life imprisonment without parole rather than given a death sentence. A judge subsequently accepted that recommendation.

Due to the sniper attacks in the Washington, DC area, the FBI began to study other sniper incidents between 1982 and 2001 (Federal Bureau of Investigation, 2003). Much of the material in the remainder of this section pertains to that study. During this 20-year interval, there were an estimated 327 incidents of sniper attacks in which a total of 379 victims were killed. Although the numbers seem large, research demonstrates that sniper attacks are unique circumstances that occur infrequently. More specifically, of the total 364,648 homicides that occurred during the 20-year period, only 0.1% were caused by sniper fire.

Nearly 80% of the victims were males. Although the victims included all age ranges, 14% were under the age of 18. In about 9 of the 10 cases, the victim and the sniper were strangers and/or the relationship was unknown. A breakdown of the data by race indicates that 52.5% of the victims were white, 44.1% were black, and the remaining 3.4% were other races. A handgun was the weapon of choice in two-thirds (63.6%) of the incidents; a rifle or shotgun was used in the remainder. Nearly half of the sniper attacks took place in the western regions of the country.

In the vast majority of cases (96.9%), the sniper was male, usually between 18 and 24 years old. Female offenders cut across all age groups, with no particular age group emerging as the most prevalent. The youngest female sniper identified was 13, and the oldest fell into the 30- to 34-year-old age group. The youngest male sniper identified was in the 10- to 12-year-old age group. In 54.5% of known cases, the offender was white, and 43.7% of the time the offender was black. The remainder of the offenders were either American

Indians/Alaskan Natives or Asians/Pacific Islanders. Other than demographic data, the psychological characteristics of criminal snipers are largely unknown. This is an area in desperate need of well-designed research.

SOCIOLOGICAL CORRELATES OF ASSAULT

Assault has not drawn nearly the amount of research, publications, or popular interest that homicide has. Yet aggravated assault is the most common type of violent crime, accounting for approximately 63% of all violent crimes reported to police in 2002 (Federal Bureau of Investigation, 2003) (see Figures 8–1 and 8–4). On the average, approximately 900,000 to 1 million aggravated assaults and over 600,000 simple assaults are reported annually. In 2002, there were 310.5 reported victims of aggravated assault for every 100,000 people in the United States. This rate was 2.7% lower than in 2001, 14.2% lower than in 1998, and 29.6% lower than in 1993 (Federal Bureau of Investigation, 2003) (see **Figure 8–4**). The frequency of aggravated assaults has been consistently higher during summer months.

African Americans make up about one-third of those arrested for assault, aggravated or simple, a number disproportionate to their representation in the population. As for their disproportionate involvement in homicide, however, we must be careful in the interpretation of these statistics. Similar to the

FIGURE 8–4   Aggravated Assaults in the United States, 1985–2001

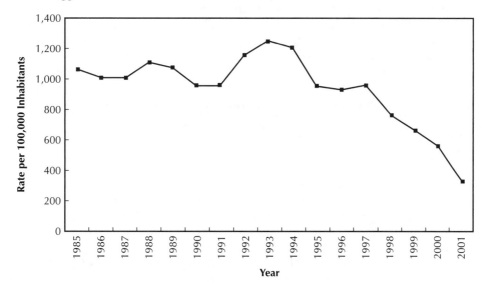

Source: Federal Bureau of Investigation (2003).

statistics for homicides, assaults are overwhelmingly intraracial (Federal Bureau of Investigation, 2003). Nationwide in 2002, law enforcement agencies cleared 56.5% of reported aggravated assaults.

The victim and offender know one another or are relatives in at least 50% of reported assault cases (Federal Bureau of Investigation, 2003; U.S. Department of Justice, 1988, 1989b). As might be expected, the lethal firearm is employed significantly less often in assault than in homicide. In 2002, personal weapons, such as hands, fist, and feet, were used in 27.7% of reported aggravated assaults (Federal Bureau of Investigation 2003). In addition, firearms were used in 19% of aggravated assaults, and knives or cutting instruments were used in 17.8%. Blunt instruments or other dangerous instruments were used in 35.4% of the reported aggravated assaults.

About half of those arrested for assault are young. In 2002, 39% of offenders were younger than 25 and 53% were under age 30 (Federal Bureau of Investigation, 2003). In addition, males outnumber females seven to one in total arrests for assault. Among the 15.4 million college students in 1995, about 1.5 million experienced a violent crime (Greenfeld, 1998). Aggravated assault is the most common form of violent crime reported on college campuses, representing 28% of the total, followed by robbery (12%) and forcible rape (9%) (Seymour, 2000). About 87% of the violent crimes sustained by college students in 2002 occurred off-campus. About one-third of the violent incidents experienced by college students involved alcohol. It should be noted that official college campus statistics, such as those reported by the FBI (2003) above, are gathered as a result of the Student Right-to-Know and Campus Security Act of 1990, which requires that all institutions receiving federal aid report their crime statistics to the public. However, these official campus crime statistics are notoriously limited in value. Such crime is often underreported, and colleges and universities are also allowed to take in-house measures to deal with some incidents (including some date rapes and assaults), so they do not result in arrests (Karmen, 2001).

The remainder of the chapter focuses on family violence and its many variants. And in Chapter 9, we concentrate on specific types of criminal homicide and the psychological explanations for violence in general.

FAMILY VIOLENCE

The passage of the *Violence Against Women Act of 1994* (Public Law 103-322, Title IV) represented a substantial change in the nation's efforts to identify, control, and prevent crimes of domestic violence. "The Act explicitly recognizes that domestic violence is a serious crime that harms not only its immediate victims, but also their families, children, and the larger community" (B. Campbell, 1996, p. 2). The Violence Against Women Act of 2000 (often referred to as VAWA-2) expanded research and services to victims nationwide and focused on the role of courts in combating violence against women through training, education, and technical assistance for judges and other court personnel (Roberts, 2002).

Family violence (also called domestic violence, intimate partner violence, or spouse abuse) refers to any assault, intimidation, battery, sexual assault, sexual battery, or any criminal offense resulting in personal injury or death of one family or household member by another who is or was residing in the same single-dwelling unit (Wallace & Seymour, 2001). The term "battering" is often used in a slightly more specific fashion to describe *physical violence* in intimate relationships, during either a dating relationship, marriage or partnership, or separation and divorce. Moreover, family violence "is an ongoing, debilitating experience of physical, psychological, and/or sexual abuse in the home, associated with increased isolation from the outside world and limited personal freedom and accessibility to resources" (Wallace & Seymour, 2001, chap. 10, p. 4). The perpetrator's misuse of power, control, and authority usually lies at the heart of family violence (American Psychological Association, 2003a).

About one of every five murders and nonnegligent manslaughters in the United States involves a family member killing another family member, with the majority (about 50%) involving spouse killing spouse (Federal Bureau of Investigation, 2003). Similar statistics have also been reported in Canada (Silverman & Mukhergee, 1987). Homicide within the family accounts for 45% of all murders in England and Wales (d'Orban & O'Connor, 1989; Home Office, 1986). A neglected area of research in family violence is homicide followed by suicide, in which a family member kills other family members and then kills him- or herself. One reason for the neglect is that homicide–suicides are relatively rare, accounting for less than 2% of all homicides. Research has consistently shown, however, that a high proportion of homicide–suicides (usually well over 50%) involve spouses, especially separated or ex-spouses.

Research on the incidence of family violence among various races and ethnic/minority groups has been largely neglected. Although indications are that family violence is substantially underreported at all levels of society, this is especially true for families outside the majority culture (American Psychological Association, 2003a). Based on what is known, however, violence within the African-American family is similar to that within white families, except that it occurs at higher rates. "As is the case for all types of homicide, African Americans are victimized by lethal violence at the hands of family members at rates that are many times higher than those for other racial groups in the United States" (Mercy & Salzman, 1989). Exceedingly few studies document the prevalence of domestic violence against Latinas (Santiago, 2002), Asian women (M. Y. Lee, 2002), or other ethnic minorities in general (Roberts, 2002). Very few existing studies on the prevalence of domestic or family violence make reference to race or ethnicity.

In 1995, approximately 19% of all arrests made for aggravated assault and 68% for simple assault involved family members (U.S. Department of Justice, 2000b). Children under 12 comprised 5% of the victims of family aggravated assault and 4% of the victims of family simple assault. Self-report victimization studies also suggest that at least 20% of simple or aggravated assaults involve family members (U.S. Department of Justice, 1989b). Although these official statistics are woefully incomplete, they underscore the considerable magnitude of family violence.

Some variant of family violence has probably existed for as long as individuals have grouped together as families, both nuclear and extended. However, with the notable exception of intrafamilial homicide, domestic or family violence has not traditionally been regarded as serious crime or worthy of criminal prosecution in this country. State governments and the courts have long claimed that family relationships require or deserve special immunity, including the views that parents have a right to discipline children physically, that a husband possesses the divine right to have sexual access to his wife, and that nagging women or disobedient children often provoke and deserve the beatings they receive (Pleck, 1989). This view has been energetically challenged in recent years by various interest groups attempting not only to educate the public about the problem but to activate lawmakers and the criminal justice system toward more stringent legal and social sanctions.

A Brief History of the Modern Era of Family Violence

The modern era of family violence interest and research began in 1962 when a Denver pediatrician (C. Henry Kempe) and four of his medical colleagues published a paper in the *Journal of the American Medical Association* entitled "The Battered Child Syndrome" (Kempe et al., 1962). The paper documented evidence of repeated multiple bone fractures in children suspected of being abused, and the article gradually became instrumental in the "rediscovery" of serious child abuse. The article was certainly not the sole precipitating factor in prompting the reexamination of child abuse, however. During the 1960s, a very large and influential child welfare movement, bent on drawing public and professional attention to the plight of abused and neglected children, was also taking hold.

In the early 1970s, the women's movement was highly influential in the rediscovery of wife beating and, shortly thereafter, drew attention also to marital rape. What began as a women's rights issue soon picked up support as a law-and-order issue (Pleck, 1989). The women's movement spawned legislation to increase or establish penalties for wife beating, to strengthen civil remedies, and to make it easier for women victims to file criminal charges against their assailants (Pleck, 1989). During the 1980s, several other types of family violence, from sibling violence to filial abuse of the elderly, were acknowledged and empirically investigated. Thus, family violence includes spouse or partner abuse, child abuse, sibling violence, abuse of the elderly, and child-to-parent violence. Currently, child abuse research is the most advanced, sophisticated, and extensive in the field of family violence (Finkelhor & Lewis, 1988). The problem of child abuse has also been the most widely publicized. Nationwide polls in 1976 revealed that only 10% of the general population considered child abuse a serious problem. In 1983, however, over 90% of the population considered it a serious problem (Wolfe, 1985).

However, despite the current interest and public concern about family violence, we still know very little about it. Systematic study of family violence is new and often poorly designed. Even definitions, terms, and concepts in the field are excessively broad, ambiguous, and applied inconsistently, jeopardizing the comparability, generalizability, and reliability of research findings (Weis, 1989). For example, it is unclear what behaviors should be included under the rubric family violence. Should verbal threats, shouting, slapping, aggressive gestures, intimidation, and spanking be included as examples of violence? Or only the more serious, physical forms of violence such as punching, stabbing, striking, shooting, and burning? Surveys conducted during the 1960s and 1970s, for example, indicated that between 84% and 97% of all parents used physical punishment at some time to discipline their children (Gelles, 1982). Surely we cannot conclude that 90% of American parents were abusive during that era. Rather, this high incidence of corporal punishment was due to the widespread and firmly held tradition that a spanking now and then did a child some good. Although that view is currently shifting toward less or no corporal punishment, there still remains considerable controversy as to whether parental spankings and slaps constitute abuse.

It is also unclear how the term violence differs from the terms abuse, maltreatment, neglect, and emotional and social deprivation. As noted by Gelles (1982), the battered child syndrome quickly gave way to the terms child abuse, child neglect, and child maltreatment. Child abuse, once restricted by Kempe and his associates to physical violence, has become increasingly broad, encompassing an extensive range of behaviors and misbehaviors by parents and caretakers. Furthermore, it also remains unclear what relatives or intimates should be included in family violence. Should lovers, intimate friends, common-law spouses, distant relatives, ex-spouses, and separated spouses be included? Therefore, a troubling aspect of family violence research is that terms are defined differently and often unclearly, and an assortment of family members is included in the sample, making reliable comparisons between studies difficult and valid conclusions nearly impossible to come by. In addition, each study collects data from a variety of sources and often uses substantially different procedures and methodology to tabulate and analyze the data.

For our purposes, research on family violence is divided into four major questions: (1) How much family violence is there? (2) What are the common characteristics (or correlates) of the offenders and victims? (3) Is family violence fundamentally different from other kinds of violence (such as street violence)? and (4) What are the causes of family violence? We explore the research in these four areas, keeping in mind the critical problems in definition, sampling, and methodology just described. It should be pointed out that intrafamilial sexual abuse, although mentioned in the following sections, is discussed in greater detail in Chapter 9.

Incidence, Prevalence, and Demographics of Child Abuse and Neglect

Estimates of the prevalence and incidence of family violence differ widely. In this section the term *incidence* refers to the total number of cases (frequency) per year. *Prevalence* refers to the proportion or ratio of the population involved, such as the number of children experiencing abuse per 1,000 children in the general population.

In 2001, an estimated 903,000 children nationwide were victims of maltreatment (U.S. Department of Health and Human Services, 2003). This is a prevalence of victimization of approximately 12 per 1,000 children, a rate that has been relatively consistent over the past decade. The data also indicate that child protective services received approximately 2,672,000 reports of *possible* maltreatment in 2001. Maltreatment refers to all forms of abuse and/or neglect. According to the U.S. Department of Health and Human Services (2003), approximately two-thirds (63%) of all victims were neglected, and about one of five children (19%) experienced physical abuse. Approximately 10% were sexually abused, and another 8% were emotionally abused. There is a high probability that emotional abuse is substantially underreported. Over one-quarter of the victims were victims of more than one type of maltreatment. Definitions for each of these terms are given in **Table 8–6**.

The highest victimization rates were for the age 3 and under group, and rates declined as age increased. Child abuse/neglect perpetrators, defined as persons who maltreat a child while in a caretaking relationship to the child, were mostly female (three-fifths). More than four-fifths (87.1%) of the victims

TABLE 8–6   Definitions of Child Abuse and Neglect

TYPE OF ABUSE	DEFINITION
Physical abuse	Occurs when a parent willfully injures, causes injury to, or allows a child to be injured, tortured, or maimed out of cruelty or excessive punishment
Emotional abuse	Chronic pattern of behavior in which the child is belittled, denied love to promote a specific behavior, or subjected to extreme and inappropriate punishment
Emotional neglect	Failure to provide a child with appropriate support, attention, and affection
Sexual abuse	Exploitation of a child or adolescent for another person's sexual and control gratification
Child neglect	Chronic failure of a parent or caretaker to provide a child with basic needs such as food, clothing, shelter, medical care, educational opportunity, protection, and supervision
Missing and exploited children	Kidnapping of a child from a custodial parent, child abduction by strangers, or sexual exploitation for child pornography, child prostitution

Source: Adapted from Whitcomb (2001).

were maltreated by one or both parents. The most common pattern of maltreatment was a child being neglected by a female parent, with no other perpetrators identified (44.7%). In cases involving sexual abuse, more than half (55.5%) of the victims were abused by known male adults.

Boys and girls are about equally neglected and physically or emotionally abused, but girls are four times more likely to be sexually abused. In 2001, an estimated 1,300 children died from abuse and neglect, a rate of approximately 1.81 deaths per 100,000 children in the general population (U.S. Department of Health and Human Services, 2003). This figure for child fatality due to maltreatment is very probably an underestimation, however. The actual figure is probably closer to 2,000 or more. Determining the number of children who die each year from maltreatment is exceedingly difficult. Child fatalities due to maltreatment are probably underreported because some deaths labeled as accidents or sudden infant death syndrome might be attributed to child maltreatment if more comprehensive investigations were conducted.

Interestingly, research has found that pet abuse and child abuse commonly occur together in dysfunctional families (Arkow, 1998). Adults who are cruel and inhumane to children (and their spouses) are often cruel and inhumane to family pet(s) as well. Abusers often threaten to harm or actually kill a pet to frighten a child into secrecy, to punish the child, or to keep the spouse from reporting the abuse to authorities. In one study, more than half of the women at a shelter reported that their pets had been harmed or killed by their partner, and they delayed coming to the shelter for fear of harm to their pets (Ascione, 1997).

Available research indicates that being a victim of childhood abuse and neglect increases the odds of future delinquency and adult criminality by 40%. More specifically, being abused or neglected as a child increases the likelihood of arrest as a juvenile by over 50%, as an adult by 38%, and for a violent crime by 38% (Widom, 1992). More recent research by Widom (2000) confirms these data further. She states, "The odds of arrest for a juvenile offense were 1.9 times higher among abused and neglected individuals than among controls; for crime committed as adult, the odds were 1.6 times higher" (p. 5). In addition, psychological and emotional problems were prevalent among the abused and neglected sample. Specifically, the abused and neglected individuals were significantly more likely than the controls (a comparison group that had not experienced abuse or neglect) to have attempted suicide and to have met the criteria for antisocial personality disorder. We now consider specific forms of abuse that have attracted recent research attention.

Missing, Abducted, Runaway, and Thrown-Away Children

Each year, thousands of children run away, are abducted, or are thrown away. The vast majority of these children run away to escape neglect or abuse in their current home or living arrangement. A thrown-away youth is one whom a parent or caretaker "throws" out of the home. Most of the nationwide data on these children are reported in NISMART Bulletins. NISMART is an acronym for the National Incidence Studies of Missing, Abducted, Runaway, and Thown-away Children, a large nationwide survey of households, juvenile residential facilities, and law enforcement agencies conducted by the Office of Juvenile Justice and Delinquency Prevention. NISMART consists of several studies designed to estimate the size and nature of the missing children problem in the United States. The more recent study is called NISMART-2, which covers the years 1997–1999. Much of the information in this section comes from that report (U.S. Department of Justice, 2002a).

In 1999, an estimated 1,682,900 youth ran away or were thrown away (U.S. Department of Justice, 2002a). In most instances (71%), the runaway/thrown-away youth was endangered during the episode by virtue of "street" factors such as substance dependency, use of hard drugs, sexual or physical abuse, and their presence in places where criminal activity is prevalent.

Child abduction is another form of child abuse. In many instances, a child is abducted from the custodial parent by the other parent. An estimated 203,900 children were victims of family abduction in 1999, and nearly half were younger than 6 years of age (U.S. Department of Justice, 2002a). Abduction of children by nonfamily members is less frequent. A nonfamily abduction is an episode in which a nonfamily perpetrator takes a child by the use of physical force or threat of bodily harm or detains the child for a substantial period of time (at least one hour) in an isolated place without lawful authority or parental permission or an incident in which a child younger than 15 is taken, detained, or voluntarily accompanies a nonfamily person who conceals the child's whereabouts, demands a ransom, or expresses the intention to keep the child permanently. Approximately 58,200 children were abducted by nonfamily perpetrators in 1999. However, abductions usually do not involve elements of the extremely alarming kind of crime that the media lead parents to associate with the word "kidnapping."

Abduction by a stranger is much less common, but when it occurs, the child's chance for survival is lowered significantly (Whitcomb, 2001). In 1999, there were 115 stereotypical kidnappings, defined as abductions perpetrated by a stranger or casual acquaintance and involving a child who was transported 50 miles or more, detained overnight, and held for ransom or with intent to keep the child permanently (U.S. Department of Justice, 2002a). In 40% of the stereotypical abductions, the child was killed, and in another 4%, the child was not recovered (U.S. Department of Justice, 2002a). Nearly half of all child victims of stereotypical kidnappings were sexually assaulted by the perpetrator, and about one-third required medical attention for injuries (U.S. Department of Justice, 2002a). Over two-thirds of the victims of stereotypical kidnapping were female.

One of five nonfamily abductees (21%) and almost half the victims of stereotypical kidnappings (48%) were abducted by multiple perpetrators (U.S. Department of Justice, 2002b). About half of the nonfamily abductors and one-third of the abductors in stereotypical kidnappings were in their twenties.

Most of the abductions took place in streets, parks, wooded areas, and other public areas, but rarely in the home, backyard, or school environment. Most children were taken into vehicles (45%) or into the offender's home (28%). Ransom is rarely demanded by the perpetrator(s) (less than 5% of all nonfamily or stereotypical abductions). Sexual motivations appear to be the primary motive for both types of abductions.

Munchausen Syndrome by Proxy

An unusual but serious type of child abuse is called **Munchausen syndrome by proxy** (MSBP) first described by Roy Meadow, a British pediatrician, in 1977. This is a form of child abuse in which the parent (usually the mother), or parents, *consistently* and *chronically* brings a child in for medical attention with symptoms falsified or directly induced by the parent or parents (Murray, 1997). Munchausen syndrome by itself is the chronic and relentless pursuit of medical treatment for combinations of symptoms of consciously self-inflicted injury and falsely reported symptoms, usually by an adult (Murray, 1997). When undiscovered, the problem may continue for years. MSBP cases are found in homes of all socioeconomic levels (Pearl, 1995), and the victims are most often children between infancy and eight years of age (J. G. Jones et al., 1986). Both male and female children may be victims. In most cases (about 98%), the mother is the offending parent, and the father is unaware of what is happening. There does not seem to be a gender preference regarding the victim, as both male and female children are represented in equal numbers.

Very often, the offending mother is very knowledgeable about medical issues, has a fascination with medical details, has her own medical history of fabricated illnesses, and is a health professional herself. In addition, the mother is unusually attentive to the child and is reluctant to leave the child's side during medical examination or treatment. This in itself is not unusual, as most parents want to stay with their children at this time. A more important sign of MSBP is characterized by a child who has a series of recurring medical conditions that do not respond to treatment or follow an unusual course that is persistent, puzzling, and unexplained. Another MSBP characteristic is a series of physical or laboratory findings that are highly unusual, discrepant with the medical history, or physically or clinically impossible. In extreme cases, the parent may initiate starvation in the child, nearly suffocate the child, inflict vaginal/rectal injuries in order to produce bleeding, add fat to stool samples to produce a lab abnormality, put his or her blood in the child's urine sample before lab testing, or even inject contaminated material intravenously into the child's bloodstream (Murray, 1997; Pearl, 1995). The extreme forms of abuse certainly lead to serious injury or even death. Unfortunately, the prevalence or incidence of MSBP is unknown at this time, probably due partly to the difficulty of identifying actual illnesses as opposed to fabricated ones. However, the problem may be far more common than typically believed (Schreir, 2002). A review of the medical literature revealed 700 cases of MSBP in at least 52 countries (Pasqualone & Fitzgerald, 1999). The literature also suggests that the mortality rate of children exposed to this syndrome may be as high as 10% (McClure, Davis, Meadow, & Silbert, 1996).

In some instances, the family pet may be the victim of MSBP, with the pet owner consistently taking the pet to the veterinarian for a variety of vague or fake symptoms. The pet owner often is trying to get sympathy and attention through the pet's misfortune.

The primary motivation for MSBP appears to be an intense need for attention from, and for manipulation of, powerful professionals such as physicians, therapists, psychologists, social workers, and lawyers (Schreier, 2002). There are other motivations as well, and they may involve a variety of serious risks to the child.

> The mother who falsified symptoms in her child to get help for herself (because she might be overwhelmed) or the child (because she truly believes that the child is not being treated adequately), or the mother who does so because she has a delusional belief that the child is ill, will pose much different risks for that child than the mother whose motivation might be a compulsive need to repeatedly fool the doctor and/or garner attention for herself as an ideal parent. (p. 985)

Shaken Baby Syndrome

Head injury is the most frequent cause of permanent neurological damage or death among abused infants and children (Duhaime, Christian, Rorke, & Zimmerman, 1998; Fulton, 2000; Showers, 1999; Smithey, 1998). Furthermore, "95% of serious intracranial injury and 64% of all head traumas in infants under 1 year of age are attributable to abuse" (Fulton, 2000, p. 43). Eighty-percent of deaths from head injury in infants and children younger than 2 years are believed to be the result of nonaccidental trauma (American Academy of Pediatrics, 2001). A very large proportion of the cases of head trauma is believed to be a direct result of **shaken baby syndrome** (SBS). Nationally, Ellis and Lord (2001) estimate that 10%–12% of all deaths due to abuse and neglect in infants and older children are attributable to SBS. SBS is most often seen in children younger than two, but also may be seen in children up to five years of age (American Academy of Pediatrics, 2001). Pediatric radiologist John Caffey (1974) coined the term "whiplash shaken baby syndrome" to describe clinical findings he frequently encountered when examining abused infants.

SBS occurs when a caretaker or parent becomes so angry or upset that he or she shakes the baby so hard that serious head injury results. Infants are especially prone to head trauma from shaking (called whiplash injury) because they lack the neck muscles and head control to minimize or prevent the head from moving excessively. In addition to death, violent shaking may result in a variety of other types of neurological damage, including blindness, speech and learning disabilities, paralysis, seizures, and hearing loss. In these situations parents or caretakers often claim they shook the child merely to stop him or her from crying and did not mean to cause serious injury. This is especially the case for young parents who are not aware of infant development or needs. For example, inexperienced parents fail to recognize that the average infant spends about 20% of his or her awake time crying, especially those infants that are inconsolable because of colic or newborn babies of drug-addicted mothers (Fulton, 2000).

Research indicates that at least two-thirds of the perpetrators of SBS are males (Child Abuse Prevention Center, 1998; Fulton, 2000). A large number of the male perpetrators tend to be partners of single mothers and are often in their early twenties (Showers, 1999). Moreover, physicians find that the shaking episodes are not isolated incidents. Approximately 33% to 40% of all cases of SBS show evidence of prior head trauma due to violent shaking episodes (American Academy of Pediatrics, 2001). It is also becoming increasingly recognized that babysitters are sometimes perpetrators, usually because of their immaturity and lack of experience in dealing with infants and very young children (Fulton, 2000).

SBS is often difficult to detect, usually because externally visible injuries are not present. Signs range from mild and nonspecific to severe and immediately identifiable. Symptoms may include frequent vomiting, difficulty eating, irritability, hypothermia, sleep difficulties, inability to vocalize or smile, and general failure to thrive (Coody, Brown, Montgomery, Flynn, & Yetman, 1994). In more severe cases, the symptoms are more apparent and life-threatening. They include a decreased level of consciousness, seizures, coma, bulging areas on the head, and apnea (Fulton, 2000).

Computerized tomography (CT) and magnetic resonance imaging (MRI) provide invaluable ways of identifying the extent of brain damage. Retinal hemorrhages occur in about 75% of victims of SBS, and consequently a thorough eye examination is indispensable in the clinical diagnosis. In advising practicing physicians, the American Academy of Pediatrics (2001) asserts that "serious injuries in infants, particularly those that result in death, are rarely accidental unless there is another clear explanation, such as trauma from a motor vehicle crash" (p. 206).

Prevalence, Incidence, and Nature of Intimate Partner Abuse

The National Family Violence Survey of 1995–1996 estimated that the prevalence of battering of women in the United States ranged from 6 to 8.7 million annually (Roberts, 2002). It is further estimated that one in three murders every year are intimate partner homicides (Roberts, 2002). According to estimates from the National Crime Victimization Survey (NCVS), there were 691,710 nonfatal violent victimizations committed by current or former spouses, boyfriends, or girlfriends of the victims during 2001 (Rennison, 2003). Eighty-five percent of victimizations by intimate partners were against women. Overall, **intimate partner violence** comprised 20% of violent crime against women in 2001. In 2002, 32.1% of female murder victims were slain by their husbands, ex-husbands, or boyfriends, compared to the 2.7% of male murder victims who were killed by their wives, ex-wives, or girlfriends (Federal Bureau of Investigation, 2003).

Same-Sex Domestic Violence

In recent years, the nature and extent of same-sex partnerships have received increased attention. Some researchers (Potoczniak, Mourot, Crosbie-Burnett, & Potoczniak, 2003) have discovered some strong similarities in the research literature comparing the violence cycles and stages of abuse between same-sex domestic violence and opposite-sex domestic violence. For example, similar to opposite-sex domestic violence perpetrators, same-sex domestic violence perpetrators are extremely controlling, are threatened by outside influences, are highly selfish, and blame their partners for the abuse. In addition, the same-sex domestic violence victims show many of the same behavioral and thought characteristics as opposite-sex domestic violence victims.

Turrell (2000) examined same-sex domestic violence among lesbians, gay women, and gay men. In the survey, female participants were able to choose between the designations lesbian and gay woman. Turrell found a physical abuse prevalence rate of 44% for gay men, 58% for gay women, and 55% for lesbians in a past or present relationships. With increased attention relating to issues involving civil unions and same-sex marriages across the nation in recent years, it is obvious that a better understanding of and skillful research attention to same-sex domestic violence are important, especially pertaining to the provision of adequate domestic violence and psychological services to the victims and the training of competent criminal justice personnel in handling the incidents.

Prevalence, Incidence, and Nature of Abuse and Neglect of the Elderly

It is estimated that approximately 2.5 million older Americans are victims of abuse each year (National Center on Elder Abuse, 1999). Elder abuse is characterized by the infliction of physical, emotional, or psychological harm on the older adult, usually defined as age 65 or older (C. Marshall, Benton, & Brazier, 2000). "The general concept involved in the numerous definitions of 'elder abuse' is that the victim is injured, neglected, or exploited because of vulnerabilities associated with age, such as impaired physical or mental capacities" (Klaus, 2000, p. 13). Neglect in this instance is "the refusal or failure to fulfill any part of a person's obligation or duties to an elder" (Seymour, 2001, chap. 13, p. 4). More specific elder abuse definitions include "the refusal or failure to provide an elderly person with such life necessities as food, water, clothing, shelter, personal hygiene, medicine, comfort, personal safety, and other essentials included in the responsibility or agreement with an elder" (chap. 13, p. 4). Abandonment may also be included in the definition of neglect and is characterized by such things as the desertion of an elder at a hospital, a nursing facility, or other similar institution, or desertion of an elder at a public location.

Although there are similarities among the various types of family abuse, elder mistreatment is a more complex phenomenon that encompasses both aspects of interpersonal violence and the aging process (Wolf, 1992). That is, elder abuse and neglect are often a result of long-standing troubled family dynamics and interpersonal processes that have been highly charged when the dependency relationship is altered, because of either illness or financial needs.

Most cases of elder abuse are apparently committed in residential rather than institutional settings, and a large number of abusers are family members who are most intimately related and emotionally connected to the victim. The abusers are most often spouses, older children, siblings, relatives, or, less frequently, paid caregivers. About 20% of elder abuse cases are physical, and 45% involve neglect (C. Marshall et al., 2000).

Estimates of the proportion of elderly persons (persons 65 or older) who are abused range from 4% to 10%, but it is difficult to make confident estimates because of a lack of reliable statistics (Klaus, 2000; Pagelow, 1989; Pillemer & Suitor, 1988). The first-ever National Elder Abuse Incidence Study, conducted by the National Center on Elder Abuse (1998), estimated that during 1996, at least one-half million older persons in domestic settings were abused and/or neglected, or experienced self-neglect, and that for every reported incidence of elder abuse, neglect, or self-neglect, approximately five go unreported (Seymour, 2001) (see **Table 8–7**). The same report found that female elders are abused at a higher rate than males, even after accounting for their larger numbers in the aging population. And two-thirds of the perpetrators of elder abuse are adult children or spouses. While there is no one single causal factor to fully explain why family members abuse their seniors, some explanations have focused on caregiver stress and dependency issues (either the caregiver's or the senior's) (Au Coin, 2003a).

TABLE 8–7 Estimated Incidence of Specific Types of Elder Abuse, 1996

TYPE OF ABUSE	ESTIMATED PERCENTAGE
Neglect	48.7
Emotional/psychological	35.4
Financial exploitation	30.2
Physical abuse	25.6
Abandonment	3.6
Sexual abuse	0.3

Source: National Center on Elder Abuse (1998).

Pillemer and Finkelhor (1988) focused on the Boston metropolitan area and found that 3% of the elderly suffered from one of three kinds of abuse: physical abuse, chronic verbal abuse, or neglect. The researchers extrapolated that about 1 million elderly persons are similarly abused throughout the United States. A Canadian survey (Podnieks, Pillemer, & Nicolson, 1990) reported that about 4% of the elderly population living in private homes in that country were subjected to abuse and neglect.

Measures of violence directed at persons age 65 or older indicated that they are most often subjected to simple assaults (Klaus, 2000). In addition, 6% of the total homicide victims in Canada were older Canadians (65 or older), with a family member being responsible for over half of the cases (Au Coin, 2003a). The same statistic (6.4%) was reported for older Americans in the United States (Federal Bureau of Investigation, 2003). The term **eldercide** is usually reserved for the murder of persons age 65 or older. In Canadian incidents involving a family member, the majority of older women were killed by a spouse or ex-spouse (53%), whereas older males were most often killed by an adult son (43%) (Au Coin, 2003a). These data are similar to those for American senior citizens (Klaus, 2000). In Canada, the most common causes of death for older victims of family-related homicides were beating (29%) and shooting (28%), followed by stabbing (23%) (Au Coin, 2003a). Although a similar family breakdown is not currently available in the U.S. data, the most common cause of death for all older victims was shooting (45%), followed by stabbing (20%), beatings with blunt objects (14%), and beatings with fists or feet (13%) (Federal Bureau of Investigation, 2003).

Sibling and Child-to-Parent Abuse

Violence between siblings is believed to be the most common form of intrafamilial violence, but surprisingly little is known about it (Gelles, 1982; Ohlin & Tonry, 1989). While professionals may recognize intrafamilial parent-to-child and spouse-to-spouse violence, they still may find it difficult to recognize sibling violence and abuse. Steinmetz (1981) reported that two-thirds of the adolescent siblings in the family sample she studied used physical violence to resolve conflict. Families having only sons consistently experience more sibling violence than do families with only daughters (Straus, Gelles, & Steinmetz, 1980). It has been estimated that three children in a thousand annually use a gun or knife on a sibling in the United States (Gelles, 1982). Victims of the more extreme forms of sibling violence tend to be younger siblings. For example, Fehrenbach and colleagues (Fehrenbach, Smith, Monastersky, & Deisher, 1986) reported that over 40% of victims of adolescent rape were younger siblings, usually less than 12 years of age.

Child-to-parent abuse has also become an important topic. Three teenagers (ages 15 to 17) in a hundred (3.5%) were reported to kick, bite, punch, hit with an object, beat up, threaten, or use a gun or knife against a parent (Gelles, 1982). The killing of parents (*parricide*) is usually committed by sons (Lubenow, 1983; Pagelow, 1989) but is the rarest form of intrafamily homicide. Teenagers are generally more likely to commit suicide than harm their own families. Dawson and Langan (1994), in their report for the U.S. Bureau of Justice Statistics, estimate that about 2% of murder victims are killed by their children. Mothers are killed (*matricide*) far more often than fathers (*patricide*) by both adolescents and adult sons and daughters. Female parricide is exceptionally rare in all countries in the world (d'Orban & O'Connor, 1989). When daughters are involved in parricide, they often secure the help of a male friend or sibling to commit the violence. In Britain, boys most often kill a parent (or parents) with explosive violence in response to prolonged provocation and parental brutality and abuse (d'Orban & O'Connor, 1989). Kathleen Heide (1993) identifies three types of parricide offenders: (1) the severely abused child, (2) the severely mentally ill child, and (3) the dangerously antisocial child. The complex family dynamics of parricide most often include multiassaultive family patterns, easy access to guns, heavy drinking, and the children's strong feelings of helplessness in coping with stress at home. Sometimes the adolescent murderer, as well as other family members, feels a sense of relief that the parents are dead.

One of the more famous court cases in recent years involved the Menendez brothers. José Menendez and his wife Kitty were killed by their sons in their Beverly Hills mansion on August 20, 1989. The prosecution in the case claimed that the brothers killed their parents to obtain a $14 million inheritance. The defense argued that they had killed in self-defense to end a lifelong pattern of sexual, physical, and psychological abuse that had left them irrationally fearful for their lives. A California jury found the brothers, Lyle and Erik Menendez, guilty of first-degree murder for the shotgun slayings of their parents on March 20, 1996.

Multiassaultive Families

According to recent statistics, at least 7% of all intact families are multiassaultive (Hotaling & Straus, 1989). That is, some families are characterized by continual cycles of intrafamily physical aggression and violence. Siblings hit each other, spouses hit each other, parents hit the children, and the older children hit the parents. Findings support the notion that assault is a generalized pattern in interpersonal relations that crosses settings and is used across targets (Hotaling & Straus, 1989). Men in families in which children and wives are assaulted are five times more likely to have also assaulted a nonfamily person than are men in nonassaultive families. A similar pattern holds for women from multiassaultive families, although the relationship is not as strong. Sibling violence is particularly high in families in which child assault and spouse assault are present, with boys displaying significantly more assaultive behavior (Hotaling & Straus, 1989). Moreover, children from multiassaultive families have an inordinately high rate of assault against nonfamily members (Hotaling & Straus, 1989). These children are also more likely to be involved in property crime, to have adjustment difficulties in school, and to be involved with police (Hotaling & Straus, 1989). Since a vast majority of the studies have been correlational in design, it is not possible to determine causal directions. It is simply extremely difficult to tell what is causing what in this complicated web of interrelated variables. However, it is quite clear that multiassaultive family members are violent and antisocial across a variety of settings, toward both family members and society in general, and may demonstrate this behavioral pattern throughout most of their lifetimes.

Etiology

For some time, the scholarly and popular literature has concluded that both abusive parents and abusive spouses have themselves been the victims of family violence during their childhoods (Megargee, 1982). Some research suggests that highly violent offenders may have been subjected to more severe and frequent physical and psychological abuse during their childhoods than other offenders (Hämäläinen & Haapasalo, 1996). Individuals grow up to be abusive because they were abused themselves, a belief referred to as the cycle-of-violence hypothesis. However, the consequences of physical assault of children are neither as simple nor as absolute as many public pronouncements would have us believe (Garbarino, 1989). Publications supporting the cycle-of-violence hypothesis rarely present empirical data to support their claims (Gelles, 1982; Pagelow, 1989). When data are presented, they are based on small case studies and correlations are marginal or, at best, modest. Much of the literature, however, suffers from the **woozle effect**. The woozle effect, a term first used in a Winnie-the-Pooh story, and later adopted by Houghton (1979), refers to the tendency of one study to cite another study's data or conclusions but without mentioning the methodological limitations and problems inherent in the original study (Gelles, 1982). For example, one study might conduct a self-report survey of a nonrepresentative sample of battering husbands (who were forced by the courts to attend a battering-husband workshop in Appleton, Wisconsin). Many of these battering men, perhaps mindful of the social sanctions and legal consequences facing them, and hoping to reduce culpability, assert that they were victims of severe physical abuse as children. Since no control group was used (nonbattering husbands) and the sample was nonrepresentative (husbands convicted and assigned by the court within a single geographic and cultural area of the country), the researchers make modest or tentative conclusions, stressing the limited external validity of their findings. The woozle effect occurs when other writers or researchers cite this flawed and highly tentative study, without mentioning its acknowledged limitations, as conclusive evidence for the cycle-of-violence hypothesis.

In short, the cycle of violence and the overall consequences of abuse and neglect are not well documented, and the resilience of human beings rules out any simple cause-and-effect relationship between maltreatment and future behavior (Garbarino, 1989). In many cases, rather than abusive parenting occurring as the logical consequence of childhood victimization, the opposite sequence is found. Cognizant and sensitive to the enormous psychological and social costs of family violence, many victims of child abuse may be less likely than their nonabused peers to commit aggressive acts within their families as adults. Garbarino (1989, p. 222) writes, for example, "Many victims of child abuse, probably most, survive it and avoid repeating the pattern in their own child rearing."

A traditional belief is that battered women allow themselves to be battered (Frieze & Browne, 1989). Others have argued that victims of spousal abuse are masochistic, consciously and unconsciously precipitating the violence to which they are subjected (Megargee, 1982). Still others have depicted battered wives as lacking self-esteem, being highly passive and dependent on their husbands, and being willing to place greater value on maintaining the marriage than on their own safety (Megargee, 1982).

Abusive husbands have been depicted as extremely possessive and unreasonably jealous men who treat their wives like property coveted by other men. This depiction has led to other assumptions about the inadequacy, incompetence, and low self-esteem of these abusive husbands who see threats to their masculinity everywhere. Christine Rasche (1993) examined 155 "mate" homicides that occurred in Florida between 1980 and 1986. She was able to identify several motives for these intimate homicides, with possessiveness the most prominent. Her list of motives and related percentages is as follows.

- Possessiveness (48.9%)
- Self-defense (15.5%)
- Abuse by victim (2.6%)
- Feelings arising out of arguments (20.7%)
- Other motives (9.7%)
- Unknown (7.7%)

Alcohol abuse is also often seen as part of the clinical picture. Similarly, men who abuse their children have been seen as incompetent, immature individuals, overwhelmed and frustrated by the responsibilities of parenting. The violence of both the abusive husband and the abusive father was seen as irrational and expressive, precipitated by frustration and extreme anger. Some professionals have suggested that street violence is generally rational and instrumental, whereas family violence is predominantly irrational and expressive (see Hotaling & Straus, 1989; Megargee, 1982).

The empirical evidence for these depictions is meager, equivocal, and confusing. Some studies find some support for these correlates; others provide no support. Despite several attempts at psychological typologies for wife and child abusers (Megargee, 1982), there does not seem to be any evidence of typical psychological profiles for either the abusers or the abused. However, recent research results look promising to provide a typology that might help in the prevention, intervention, and treatment of abusers. In an extensive review of the research literature, Holtzworth-Munroe and Stuart (1994) identified three primary types of male spouse batterers: Type 1 batterers, who abuse family members only; Type 2 batterers, who abuse family members because of emotional problems; and Type 3 batterers, who are generally violent toward both family members and persons outside the family. Type 1 abusers are the most common, tend to be less aggressive than the other two, and also tend to be more remorseful for their actions. They are generally inadequate, passive men who are dependent on others. Type 2 batterers tend to be depressed, inadequate individuals who are emotionally volatile and who display indicators of personality disorders and psychopathology. Type 3 batterers are individuals who are antisocial, criminally prone, and violent across situations. They are more likely to abuse alcohol and are generally more belligerent toward almost everyone. They are also most likely to be involved in serious violence toward a spouse.

The search for demographic variables has been equally mixed and inconclusive (Hotaling & Straus, 1989; Weis, 1989). Wife and child abuse appears to cut across socioeconomic, religious, and ethnic lines. Even current research on gender does not reveal clear trends for women or men as assaulters of spouse, child, or parent.

The abuse of alcohol and drugs seems to play a role as an exacerbater, but not as a cause, of the family violence. Abusive men with severe alcohol or drug problems are apt to abuse their partners both when drunk and when sober. However, abusive husbands who drink heavily are violent more frequently and inflict more serious injuries on their partners than do abusive men who do not have a history of alcohol or drug problems (Frieze & Browne, 1989). A similar pattern holds for men who abuse their children. Many use alcohol as an excusing agent that allows them to escape some culpability for their antisocial or violent actions, as well as to avoid the full impact of legal sanctions. Babcock, Waltz, Jacobson, and Gottman (1993), in some very promising research, examined the interactions of marital power, interpersonal strategies, and communication skills as predictors of marital violence. They reasoned that husbands who are unable to effect their intentions through negotiation or general communication skills are more likely to resort to physical aggression—pushing, slapping, beating—to achieve their intentions. This is especially the case if the wives are more verbally competent, are better educated, or have better jobs than their husbands. For example, previous research suggests that women with jobs that are higher in status than their husband's jobs experience more life-threatening violence than do wives who are occupationally similar to their husbands (Hornung, McCullough, & Sugimoto, 1981). Frustrated with some combination of power discrepancy between him and his wife, the husband's only perceived effective retort may be physical aggression. The study by Babcock et al. (1993, p. 47) showed ". . . that poor husband communication, as well as discrepancies in education and decision-making power favoring the wife, were . . . associated with husband-to-wife aggression." Moreover, husbands who battered their wives were more likely to be in relationships where their demands were met with their wives' withdrawal (e.g., defensiveness, passive inaction, "stonewalling," or the "silent treatment"). The researchers interpreted the withdrawal pattern as one of power (the individual has resources the other partner wants), whereas the demanding role represented a weak position (the individual wants something the other partner has). This research emphasizes the importance of studying the reciprocal interaction of a relationship if we are to understand family violence more fully.

Once violence has occurred in a relationship, it tends to be repeated (Frieze & Browne, 1989). Over time, violence, if not adequately sanctioned, may also become more severe and more frequent. Furthermore, being violently victimized by an intimate over an extended period of time may result in emotional reactions and psychological scars decidedly different from those incurred by victims of violent crime by strangers. We need more research on the patterns of abuse over the life course of a family before we can offer conclusions.

The elderly appear to be maltreated in much the same way that children are maltreated—with one notable exception: financial exploitation (Pagelow, 1989). The likeliest candidates for elder abuse appear to be white women between 75 and 85 years of age, middle to lower class, Protestant, and suffering from some form of physical or mental impairment (Pagelow, 1989). Only 5% of the elderly are placed in institutions or rest homes, although 85% of them have at least one chronic illness (Hudson, 1986). Most live at home. Abusive caretakers tend to lack resources and to feel trapped, and may be abusing drugs or alcohol. Two-thirds of abusive caretakers are 40 years old or older, and most are sons or daughters of the victims. Spouses constitute the second-largest abuser category. Male caretakers are more likely to abuse the elderly physically, while women caretakers are more prone to abuse them psychologically or neglect them. However, both men and women are equally likely to exploit them financially. The most common abuse is a combination of psychological abuse and neglect (Pagelow, 1989).

Is Family Violence Different from General Violence?

As noted earlier, some clinicians and writers have suggested that family violence is fundamentally different from general (or street) violence and thus should be examined separately (Megargee, 1982). Physical violence against children and that against spouses are "special" cases of violence that only family-based theories can explain. Wife abusers are psychologically distressed, and their violence is irrational. As also mentioned earlier, child abusers are depicted as incompetent and immature, unable to cope with the responsibilities of parenting, and holding unrealistic expectations of children. Similarly, child abusers are extremely emotional and irrational in their assaults. Street offenders, on the other hand, presumably use violence in a deliberate, rational way to gain things, such as material goods, status, and other social reinforcements. General violent offenders utilize violence for a purpose, whereas family violent offenders lash out in anger and without discernible purpose.

Empirical evidence for differences between criminal violence in the streets and family violence is weak and equivocal, with most studies being unsystematic or seriously flawed methodologically (Hotaling & Straus, 1989). The evidence we have so far, however, strongly suggests that the etiology of violent behavior may be very similar, whether it is against a family member or a non-family member. Violent people tend to be violent generally, both within and outside the family context. They are aggressive and assaultive toward a large variety of targets and across a wide array of settings.

Battered Woman Syndrome

The term **battered woman syndrome** was coined and developed by Lenore Walker (1979), a psychologist who specializes in domestic abuse. Walker has identified a cluster of behavioral and emotional features that, she believes, are often shared by women who have been physically and psychologically abused over a period of time by the dominant male figure in their lives. Feelings of low self-esteem, depression, and helplessness are among the important components that frequently accompany the syndrome.

Research on domestic violence finds that the great majority of battered women either remain in lifelong abusive relationships, leave the relationship, or are killed by their abusers. Very rarely do battering relationships get better. A small minority of abused women kill their abusers. Although evidence of battered woman syndrome can be admitted into the trials of women who kill their abusers (Schuller & Vidmar, 1992), it is rarely successful in bringing about an acquittal (Browne, 1987; Ewing, 1990).

Currently, there is considerable debate concerning the reliability, validity, and usefulness of the diagnosis "battered woman syndrome" (Bartol & Bartol, 2004b). One of the major problems with the concept is the tendency for mental health and law professionals to regard it as a *single* entity representing some kind of mental or behavioral disorder displayed by all women who experience a severely abusive relationship. In addition, some theorists prefer to view the psychological effects of battering as a form of post–traumatic stress disorder (PTSD), discussed in Chapter 6, rather than as a separate syndrome.

However, battered women demonstrate a wide range of behavioral patterns that often reflect survival skills and adaptation to serious, life-threatening situations rather than a psychological disorder. Many women simply do not exhibit discernible clusters of psychological maladjustment, depression, and helplessness as portrayed by the battered women syndrome or by PTSD, even though they may have experienced high degrees of coercion, domination, and abuse during a lengthy relationship (Stark, 2002). Some victims, regardless of the abuse, may not demonstrate any signs of a syndrome or mental health problems.

Psychological Effects of Domestic Violence on Children

Domestic violence is recognized as a serious problem in our society today, but how such violence affects the children who are exposed to it was not discussed in the research literature until the 1980s. Children who are exposed to violence between adults in their homes have often been referred to as the "silent," "forgotten," and "unintended" victims of domestic violence. These children were initially referred to as simply "witnesses" or "observers," but recent research literature has reported that some not only are directly involved victims themselves but also suffer some troubling consequences.

Children experience domestic violence through a bewildering array of events. Most often, they see or hear the violence, but they experience it in many other ways as well. Direct involvement, such as trying to intervene or calling 911, is one example (Edleson, 1999). Additional examples include a child's being taken hostage to force the mother's return, being used as a physical weapon against the victim, being forced to watch the violence or to participate in the abuse, and being used as a spy or questioned about the mother's activities (Ganley & Schechter, 1996).

Experiencing the aftermath of the violence may be equally traumatic for children (Edleson, 1999). Examples include the child's seeing the mother with physical injuries and possibly in need of medical help, displaying emotions such as anxiety, depression, and stress, and having to move to a shelter for battered women to escape further abuse. The aftermath can also include a father's alternating between physical violence and loving care, as well as police intervention that can result in the removal of the father from the home. In some instances, removal of the children from the home by child welfare agencies is an uncomfortable possibility.

The number of children exposed to domestic violence in the United States each year is largely unknown. Straus (1991, p. 98) estimates that "at least a third of Americans have witnessed violence between their parents, and most have endured repeated instances." This estimation is based on Straus and Gelles's (1990) national survey, which discovered that 30% of parents who admitted that domestic violence existed in their home also reported that their children had witnessed at least one violent incident during the marriage.

Research has also found that 13% to 27% of adults recall witnessing physical violence between their parents (Forrstrom-Cohen & Rosenbaum, 1985). Police arrest data from five U.S. cities revealed that children were directly involved in adult domestic violence incidents about 27% of the time (Fantuzzo, Boruch, Abdullahi, Atkins, & Marcus, 1997). Fantuzzo et al. also found that younger children were disproportionately represented in households where domestic violence occurred. Another study (Silvern et al., 1995) found that exposure to domestic violence may be even higher in some populations. Silvern and colleagues found that 118 (41.1%) of 287 college women and 85 (32.2%) of 263 college men surveyed had witnessed abuse of one parent by the other.

Explanations of how domestic violence affects a child must include an assortment of already existing risk factors. The child's age, the nature and severity of the violence, the family's socioeconomic status, and parental substance abuse all must be entered into the equation.

The child's behavioral and emotional functioning is the area that has received the most attention from researchers. Overall, these studies report the consistent finding that children exposed to domestic violence exhibit many more behavioral and emotional problems compared to other children. For instance, studies using the Child Behavior Checklist (Achenbach & Edelbrock, 1983) and similar measures have found that children who are exposed to domestic violence display more aggressive and antisocial behaviors as well as fearful and inhibited behaviors (Fantuzzo et al., 1991; Hughes, 1988; Hughes, Parkinson, & Vargo, 1989) and show lower social competence and interpersonal skills than other children (Adamson & Thompson, 1998; Fantuzzo et al., 1991; Hughes, 1988). More aggressive and antisocial behaviors are often referred to as "externalized" behaviors, while fearful and inhibited behaviors are referred to as "internalized" behaviors (B. Carlson, 1991; Edleson, 1999; Stagg, Wills, & Howell, 1989).

Domestic violence has also been shown to have dramatic negative effects on children's emotional health and overall adjustment. Both boys and girls in families with spousal violence demonstrate far more depression and aggression (McClosky, Figueredo, & Koss, 1995; Wolfe, Jaffe, Wilson, & Zak, 1985) and lower self-esteem (Hughes & Barad, 1983) compared to other children. In addition, children who are exposed to violence between parents are more likely to show anxiety, depression, trauma symptoms, and temperamental problems (Hughes, 1988; Maker, Kemmelmeier, & Peterson, 1998).

Another consequence of experiencing violence within the home is its overall effects on the child's immediate and long-term cognitive functioning and attitudes about how to deal with violence and conflict resolution in their own lives. Many researchers conclude that children's exposure to adult domestic violence may generate attitudes justifying their own use of violence to solve problems and deal with frustrations. For example, Spaccarelli, Coatsworth, and Bowden's (1995) study found support for such an association by showing that, among a sample of 213 adolescent boys incarcerated for violent crimes, those boys who had experienced family violence were more likely to subscribe to the viewpoint that "acting aggressively enhances one's reputation or self-image" (p. 173). Interestingly, B. E. Carlson (1991) also reported that in a sample of 101 adolescents, boys who witnessed domestic violence were significantly more likely to approve of violence than were girls who had witnessed domestic violence. One possible explanation is that the boys were witnessing violence perpetrated by males and were more likely to condone and perhaps model that behavior.

In conclusion, the empirical evidence reveals that children's exposure to domestic violence is a serious and widespread problem. Such violence affects children indirectly through its effect on the parental relationship and directly through its effects on their behavioral, emotional, cognitive, psychological, and social adjustment.

Infanticide, Neonaticide, and Filicide

In this section, the focus is on that form of child homicide that occurs when a person intentionally kills a child or infant. That is, the homicide is not accidental or the incidental result of abuse or neglect. Although the term **infanticide** literally means the killing of an *infant*, it has become synonymous with the killing of a child by a parent. Some forms of infanticide can be traced back to ancient societies, including ancient Greece, Rome, China, India, and Europe. "In some instances, it took place as part of socially sanctioned religious sacrifice, was meant to dispose of physically defective infants, was a way to dispose of female infants when males were preferred, or was a form of population control" (Smithey, 2002, p. 888).

An estimated 1,200 to 1,500 children are intentionally killed each year by a parent or other person, representing about 12% to 15% of the total homicides in the United States (Emery & Laumann-Billings, 1998). There were 69 children under the age of 18 murdered in Canada in 2001, comprising 12% of the total homicides there that year (Au Coin, 2003b). In the United States and Canada, about two-thirds of murdered children are killed by family members, mostly parents. Child homicide is not randomly distributed but occurs with greater frequency across the globe in areas characterized by poverty, limited opportunity, and urbanization. The majority of child homicides across the globe are committed by parents killing their own children. Interestingly, the United States ranks fifth in homicides of infants under one year of age (with a rate of 5.4 per 100,000 live births) among 18 developed countries (Smithey, 2002).

In Canada between 1974 and 2001, children under age 6 were more likely to have been killed as a result of strangulation or beating than by other methods (Au Coin, 2003b). Older Canadian children, on the other hand, were more likely to die from gunshot wounds: 32% of victims aged 6–8 years and over 50% of victims aged 15–17 years (Au Coin, 2003b).

Several decades ago, Resnick (1970) recommended that the killing of one's children be divided into two separate categories: *neonaticide*, which refers to the killing of a newborn within the first 24 hours after birth, and *filicide*, which refers to the killing of a child older than 24 hours. Newborns, infants, and children ages 1 to 4 are more vulnerable to homicide than are children ages 5 to 9 (A. Reiss & Roth, 1993). The number and rates of homicides of children under age 5 increased during the years 1976 to 1995 but have declined since 1996 (see **Table 8–8** for recent statistics). Of all children under age 5 murdered from

TABLE 8–8   Number of Infanticides by Victim's Age, 2002

	AGE OF VICTIM					
	LESS THAN 1 YEAR	1 YEAR	2 YEARS	3 YEARS	4 YEARS	TOTAL
No. of infanticides	265	125	116	55	39	607

Source: Federal Bureau of Investigation (2003).

1976 to 1999, 31% were killed by fathers, 30% by mothers, 23% by male acquaintances, 6% by other relatives, and 3% by strangers (Bureau of Justice Statistics, 2001a). Of those children killed by someone other than their parents, 82% were killed by males. Most of the children killed were male.

While it appears that men and women are equally likely to be responsible for infanticide, both research and the law tend to view these perpetrators differently. Furthermore, there is more research conducted on women who kill their children than on men who do so. Traditionally, women who kill their children have been viewed by the legal system and the psychiatric profession as suffering from severe emotional problems, rendering them either insane (the legal system) or psychotic (the psychiatric profession). Men who kill their children are more likely to be viewed as evil (Wilczynski, 1997). Nevertheless, women also have been viewed in that way.

Ania Wilczynski (1991, 1997), who conducted research in England and Wales, pointed out that if the woman wasn't considered "crazy," then she was seen as being obviously morally flawed, calloused, or uncaring and cold. These women are thus viewed as either "mad" or "bad." Mothers, after all, are supposed to act in a loving, warm, selfless, and protective fashion—at all costs—toward their children (Wilczynski, 1991). Any deviation from this stereotype promotes the conclusion that a woman either is mentally ill and needs to be treated with sympathy or, alternatively, is fundamentally wicked or callous and, therefore, needs to be punished harshly. Interestingly, in 1938 England passed the Infanticide Act, based primarily on the assumption that a mother who kills her infant is probably mentally disturbed and psychotic. Today, the courts of England continue to convict on the grounds of "infanticide"—that is, the mother killed her child while mentally ill. Rarely is there conviction for murder or manslaughter. In short, the overwhelming perception by the criminal justice system in England (and perhaps throughout North America) is that women who kill their children are "mad" and "abnormal," whereas men who kill their children are "bad" and "normal" (Wilczynski, 1997).

Wilczynski (1991) studied 22 prosecuted cases of maternal infant killings (in which a mother killed her child under the age of 12 months) in England and Wales between 1971 and 1989. In 14 of the cases, the women were seen as emotionally disturbed. They were considered ". . . essentially good women and mothers, for whom something had gone tragically wrong" (p. 74).

Similarly following the psychiatric tradition, Resnick (1969, 1970) concluded that two-thirds of mothers who committed filicide were psychotic, compared to only 17% of women in the neonaticide group. He also found that a vast majority of the filicide group suffered from serious depression, while very few women in the neonaticide group exhibited this feature. Furthermore, suicide attempts accompanied one-third of the filicides but rarely accompanied neonaticide.

More recent research sheds further light on maternal murder of their young. In a cross-national comparison of British and Canadian filicidal women by McKee and Shea (1998), the data suggested that women who were charged with murdering their children usually suffered from a diagnosable mental disorder and were contending with many stressful events in their lives at the time of the murder. In another study, results showed that women suffering from a diagnosed mental disorder were more likely to use a weapon to murder their children than filicidal women not suffering from an apparent mental disorder (C. Lewis, Baranoski, Buchanan, & Benedek, 1998). The Lewis et al. study found that guns were used 13% of the time and knives 12% of the time.

Coramae Richey Mann (1993) investigated the patterns and characteristics of maternal filicide in six major U.S. cities (Chicago, Houston, Atlanta, Los Angeles, New York, and Baltimore) between 1979 and 1983. Although the data set for the study consisted of 296 cleared homicide cases in which the offender was female, Mann restricted her research sample to 25 maternal filicides of preschool children (ages birth to five years). Because of the small sample size, any far-reaching conclusions must be viewed cautiously.

Mann found that 40% of the women who killed their preschool children had arrest records. One offender had 15 misdemeanor arrests, while another had six felony arrests. Twenty-five percent had arrest records for violent crime. Moreover, 12 of the 25 filicide offenders had recorded child abuse histories in which court or social service intervention had taken place. Most of the victims were killed in the bathroom (30%) or the bedroom (26%), usually on Sunday morning. Manual methods were used in 80% of the cases—hands or feet (52%), suffocation or strangulation (16%), or drowning (12%). The killing of older children (age 4 or 5) tended to be more brutal.

Although the most frequent victim was an African-American female infant under the age of two years, Mann cautioned that her sample was too small to advance any firm conclusions about racial patterns. Mann also emphasized that location is a critical variable when examining the racial/ethnic factor in filicide. Large metropolitan cities, for example, are far more likely to have a minority population than more affluent, suburban areas. While a majority of the offenders were initially charged with murder, only 19% were convicted of that charge. Forty percent of the women who killed their preschool children were sent to prison, most often on a conviction of manslaughter, and another 36% received a probation sentence. The remaining six cases either were not processed, were dismissed, or received special treatment from the court and their dispositions were sealed. A determination that the offender had a mental disorder was apparently rare.

In a more recent summary of the data, Dobson and Sales (2000) concluded: "There is certainly little evidence that women who kill their infant within the first 24 hours of birth are seriously mentally ill, and furthermore, many women who kill their infant after the first 24 hours do not exhibit symptomatology that meets the requirements for diminished capacity or insanity" (p. 1109). However, they also concluded that the potential role of psychosis in *some* women should not be underestimated in filicide. In some instances of filicide, such as observed by Resnick, the mothers are psychotic or otherwise seriously mentally disordered, and we should not lose sight of this fact.

In sum, although researchers have expended considerable energy studying infanticide committed by mothers, there is little consensus on the explanation for this behavior. Earlier studies suggested that it must be the result of serious mental disorder, but recent research has questioned this conclusion. In addition, although men and women kill their children in almost equal proportions, researchers have not focused on studying this behavior in men to the extent that they have in women.

THEORETICAL EXPLANATIONS OF FAMILY VIOLENCE

The development of theory requires well-designed and executed research. Without theoretical testing through sound research, speculations and free-floating explanations with no empirical anchoring abound. This describes what is happening in the field of family violence. Gelles and Straus (1979), for example, were able to identify 15 different theories attempting to explain family violence. Weis (1989, p. 123) observed that "the field is, with few exceptions, characterized by descriptive work, with little hypothesis testing, causal modeling, or attempts to construct and test integrated theories of the different types of family violence."

The systematic study of family violence, however, is a new undertaking. Thus, it suffers from a constellation of uncoordinated research and a matrix of poorly integrated theory, as all new sciences do. Furthermore, the family is a difficult social situation to study. It is a complex social system consisting of many roles, and it is a private social group in which interactions and behaviors are invisible to outsiders. Social interactions are more intense, emotional, and consequential than other interactions (Weis, 1989). In addition, family influences do not flow in one direction; they are apt to be multidirectional, a process called reciprocal influence (Bartol & Bartol, 1998). For example, while the parents affect the development of the child, the child also affects the development and psychological growth of the parents, including their marital relationship, relationships with friends, and even level of job satisfaction. Reciprocal influence implies that the social environment influences the individual, and the individual, in turn, has an impact on the social environment. Therefore, theories that are sensitive to the reciprocal interactionism of family dynamics are the best candidates to advance our knowledge about family violence.

CESSATION OF FAMILY VIOLENCE

Although theories of family violence are underdeveloped, the effectiveness of various procedures or strategies to reduce family violence can still be tested. Unfortunately, there have been very few systematic evaluations of the effectiveness of particular strategies in combating family violence (Elliott, 1989).

One of the more influential investigations examining the effectiveness of police responses to spouse abuse was the Minnesota Domestic Violence Experiment (Sherman & Berk, 1984). The police officers participating in this project handled marital conflict in one of three ways: making an arrest, separating the parties, or advising (or mediating) the parties. Follow-up of the effectiveness of these approaches over a six-month period indicated that arrest was the most effective police response for reducing misdemeanor family assaults. However, the study had serious design problems that undermine both its external validity and its internal validity. Subsequent research in other cities failed to replicate the results of the study (Buzawa & Buzawa, 1996). Moreover, there is some evidence that the impact of an arrest wears off over a relatively short period of time (8 to 12 months), and the assaults return to their original level (Elliott, 1989).

The effectiveness of the legal sanctions of prosecution, conviction, and sentencing in deterring subsequent family violence is questionable. There are also many unanswered questions about the effectiveness of community services and care for family violence victims (Saunders & Azar, 1989). Nevertheless, approaches that combine arrest with supportive services for the victims and monitoring of where the abuser lives offer some hope for decreasing the violence.

Much of the contemporary work and commentary has been directed at reducing male abuse of wives or intimate female partners. Fagan (1989) hypothesized that a large segment of the rewards and support men receive for abusing their wives derives from a long-standing cultural stereotype that men must be dominant and show women who is boss. One very "masculine" way of achieving and maintaining this expected dominance is through physical aggression and, if necessary, violence. Some of the reinforcement comes from the satisfaction of maintaining this physical dominance and the positive social status that accompanies domination over wives advocated by one's peer group and subculture. Accordingly, men subscribing to this subculture socialize together, drink together, and participate in male-oriented recreation activities, generally excluding their wives from these activities. This male subculture provides a social milieu that supports and encourages traditional male dominance in male–female relationships, even if it requires violence now and then. Frequent contacts with this exclusive male subculture by the husband, combined with increasing social isolation of the wife, are particularly associated with the more severe forms of wife abuse (Bowker, 1983; Fagan, 1989). Presumably, the more deeply immersed in this subculture a man is, the more likely he is to batter his wife.

To what extent some women also support this male-dominating tradition is largely unknown, but knowledge about the degree to which women explicitly or implicitly favor this belief system may be extremely important for a deeper understanding of the dynamics of the relationship. This is not to imply that a subculture that supports male domination in a marriage necessarily advocates violence in carrying out this dominance, but research does suggest that many wife batterers manage to isolate their families socially while receiving considerable encouragement and support for physical aggression from their social network of friends. It is not unusual in rural areas, for example, for abusive husbands to see to it that their wives and children are physically isolated, while they continually go hunting, fishing, and drinking with their friends.

An effective way of breaking the wife or female partner abuse cycle, therefore, is to change the abuser's attitudinal system and social network of friends who support or at least condone physical male domination of family relationships. Obviously, this strategy would not be easy to apply in many abusive behavioral patterns. Abusers have had a lifelong learning experience in developing belief systems and, probably, have had a history of considerable reinforcement for their aggressive actions toward women from their subculture. "Leaving the subculture is not unlike leaving the world of the addict or the alcoholic" (Fagan, 1989, p. 408).

Initiating motivation to change a behavioral pattern of abuse often requires establishing a series of situations where the psychological costs for the abuse outweigh its psychological benefits. Legal sanctions may be one way, but many batterers realize that these sanctions are normally weak and without teeth. However, serious attempts by the criminal justice system to put some bite into these legal sanctions (such as arrests, criminal charges, and conviction) may begin to prove effective over the long haul, provided that they are accompanied by community support systems for the woman. It is important to note that it is unlikely that any one arrest or single event will promote a wish to change. It is more likely that a series of aversive and costly events, such as strong legal sanctions, combined with social sanctions from the community (public disclosure, visits by social agencies) and emotional sanctions from the victim (reporting the abuse to authorities, leaving the home, separating, threatening divorce) will wear the abuser down to a point at which he makes a decision to change his behavioral patterns.

However, the more severe and protracted the violence is, the more difficult it may be to stop, despite formal external interventions—legal or otherwise (Fagan, 1989). Legal and social sanctions for spousal abuse may work for less chronic and severe situations. However, legal sanctions, regardless of their nature and strength, not only may be ineffective for the more serious cases, but could possibly lead to an escalation of the violence. Therefore, social, legal, and emotional sanctions may be more effective with individuals who do not have an extensive history of repetitive and serious violence. One of the most sobering research findings in recent years is the discovery that a woman's life is in the greatest danger from an abusive partner within the first six months of her leaving the partner.

As we shall see in Chapter 10, it is one thing to get a person to decide to stop acting in a certain way. It is quite another for an individual to continue to avoid that behavior. Research clearly demonstrates that maintenance of positive behavior is far more difficult to achieve than cessation of the negative behavior.

SUMMARY AND CONCLUSIONS

In this chapter, we have begun to narrow our focus to consider specific offenses. Previous chapters were broader, in that they dealt with general theoretical orientations to crime. Here we reviewed the major sociological data on violence and summarized empirical and clinical research on family violence.

Sociological and official data indicate that incidents of homicides are rare compared to the total incidence of violent crime. In the United States, violent crime is often committed by young males living in environments that implicitly or explicitly advocate violence for the resolution of conflict. Guns (especially handguns) are commonly used in the crime. Certain minority groups—African Americans and Hispanics in the United States and Indians in Canada—are overrepresented in violent crime statistics, but there are a number of explanations for this that have nothing to do with racially or ethnically based individual factors. Statistics indicate also that, when the relationship of victim and offender is known, the homicide victim and the offender are usually family members, friends, or acquaintances. The relationship is known in half to two-thirds of the offenses. While assaults are far more common than homicide, the same sociological features appear, particularly for aggravated assault.

Considering the rapidly expanding research on the topic, family violence undoubtedly deserves a chapter of its own. Family violence is a broad subject that encompasses child abuse, spouse or partner abuse, elder abuse, sibling abuse, and child-to-parent abuse. Some researchers also include intimate partner abuse that occurs when the victim and perpetrator occupy separate households. Abuse comes in many forms, including physical, psychological, and sexual. Family violence is found across ethnic, racial, and socioeconomic classes. Children are particularly vulnerable targets for family violence and maltreatment, enduring physical maltreatment, sexual exploitation, medical and emotional neglect, and psychological trauma—all of which are usually lifelong in their consequences. Women are disproportionately subject to spousal violence, stalking, and the dire economic situations that may lead to both victimization and victimizing. In addition to the obvious physical injuries and deaths that result, family violence is often cited in research and clinical studies as contributing to other individual, family, and societal problems. Most of all, family violence and maltreatment highlight the importance of considering a victimological approach for the complete understanding of violent crime and underscore the fact that the family is far from being a safe haven for many. Factors such as family instability and violence have consistently been found to be prevalent among juveniles who engage in sexually abusive and violent behavior (Righthand & Welch, 2001). Many studies conclude that abused children have trouble recognizing appropriate emotions in others, have less empathy for others, and have difficulty taking another person's perspective (Knight & Prentky, 1993). It is very likely that many of the life course–persistent offenders discussed elsewhere in the text spring from families of abuse, violence, and neglect.

CHAPTER 9

CRIMINAL HOMICIDE: A CLOSER LOOK

This chapter takes a more detailed look at criminal homicide, including several psychology-related investigative methods commonly used to identify offenders. We look at various kinds of criminal homicide, including serial murder, sexual sadistic murder, mass murder, product-tampering homicide, murder at the workplace, and terrorism that results in death. Although the homicides covered in this chapter are relatively rare, the social and emotional impact they have on a community—and on a society as a whole—is considerable. The fear and terror they engender can alter the lifestyles of thousands. Moreover, they draw extensive media coverage; some of it is accurate, but much of it lacks a solid understanding of the psychosocial aspects involved in the crime. Therefore, it is important that we give some attention to what we know—and do not know—about these well-publicized offenses. Finally, we end the chapter by discussing some of the current psychological theories and research that try to explain contemporary violence.

INVESTIGATIVE METHODS

According to John Douglas and Corinne Munn (1992a), there are three important features of offender behavior that may be evident at the scene of a crime: (1) the **modus operandi**; (2) the personation or signature; and (3) staging. The modus operandi (MO) refers to the actions and procedures an offender engages in to commit a crime successfully. It is a behavioral pattern that the offender learns as he or she gains experience in committing the offense. Since the offender often changes the MO until he or she learns which method is most effective, however, investigators may make a serious error if they place too much significance on the MO when linking crimes (Douglas & Munn, 1992c).

Anything that goes beyond what is necessary to commit the crime is called the **personation**, or the **signature**. For example, a serial offender may demonstrate a repetitive, almost ritualistic behavior from crime to crime, an unusual pattern that is not necessary to commit the offense. The signature may involve certain items that are left at or removed from the scene or other symbolic patterns, such as writings on the wall. If the victim is murdered, the signature may include unusual body positions or mutilations of the corpse. In very rare instances, the signature may involve a "DNA torch," where the offender pours gasoline over the genital areas of the victim and sets the victim and the structure or motor vehicle on fire in an effort to destroy any evidence of sexual assault. A signature may also involve the repetitive acts of domination, manipulation, and control used by a serial rapist (Douglas & Munn, 1992b). The signature is often thought to be related to the unique cognitive processes of the offender and, in this sense, may be more important to an investigator than the MO.

Staging refers to the intentional alteration of a crime scene prior to the arrival of the police, and it is sometimes done by someone other than the perpetrator. As Douglas and Munn (1992a) note, staging is usually done for one of two reasons: either to redirect the investigation away from the most logical suspect or to protect the victim or the victim's family. Staging is frequently done by someone who has an association or relationship with the victim. For example, staging done by the family with the intent to protect the victim may be seen in autoerotic fatalities. **Autoeroticism**, a term coined by Havelock Ellis, refers to self-arousal and self-gratification of sexual desire without a partner. Holmes and Holmes (2002) identify four types of autoeroticism besides simple masturbation. The most common appears to be *autoerotic hanging*. The second type is *aquaeroticism*, the third is *chemical eroticism*, and the fourth type is *self-suffocation*. Aquaeroticism refers to the use of water to induce near-drowning experiences for sexual enhancement. Chemical eroticism refers to the practice of using chemical substances (such as Freon) to induce states of erotic asphyxiation. Self-suffocation refers to a behavioral pattern where the person will "deliberately attempt to suffocate to the point of almost losing consciousness" (Homes & Holmes, 2002, p. 176). All four types are based on a deficiency of oxygen that presumably enhances sexual stimulation, and they are usually accompanied by masturbation. Ronald Holmes (1991) notes that there is even a national organization for erotic asphyxiates called the Olenspeigel Society.

In some instances, the method of autoeroticism may result in the death of the victim, such as self-strangulation or hanging. Douglas and Munn (1992a) assert that in about one-third of autoerotic fatalities the victim is nude, and in about another one-third the victim is clothed in a costume, such as a male in female clothing. Under these conditions, friends or family members may alter the scene to make the victim more "presentable" to the authorities. They may even stage a criminal homicide.

In some instances, an offender may engage in **undoing**, a behavioral pattern found at the scene in which the offender tries to psychologically "undo" the murder. For example, the offender may wash and dress the victim or place the body on a bed, gently placing the head on a pillow and covering the body with blankets. This pattern typically occurs in offenders who become especially distraught about the death of the victim. Very often, the offender has a close association with the victim. In other cases, an offender may try to dehumanize the victim by engaging in actions that obscure the identity of the victim, such as excessive facial battery. Other offenders may employ more subtle acts of dehumanization, such as covering the victim's face with some material or object or placing the victim face down. Note that the difference between undoing and staging is the reason behind the action. In staging, the offender is trying to alter the crime scene in order to divert suspicion. In the classic case, the offender wipes fingerprints from a weapon and positions it close to the body in such a way that the death looks like a suicide.

Crime scenes are also classified as organized, disorganized, or mixed (see **Tables 9–1** and **9–2**). An **organized crime scene** indicates planning and premeditation on the part of the offender. The crime scene shows signs that the offender maintained control of him- or herself and the victim. Often the victim is moved from the abduction area to another secluded area, and perhaps the body is then moved to still another area. Furthermore, in an organized

TABLE 9–1   Profile Characteristics of Organized and Disorganized Murderers as Classified by the FBI

ORGANIZED	DISORGANIZED
Average to above-average intelligence	Below-average intelligence
Socially competent	Socially inadequate
Skilled work preferred	Unskilled work
High birth-order status	Low birth-order status
Father's work stable	Father's work unstable
Sexually competent	Sexually incompetent
Inconsistent childhood discipline	Harsh discipline as a child
Controlled mood during crime	Anxious mood during crime
Use of alcohol with crime	Minimal use of alcohol
Precipitating situational stress	Minimal situational stress
Living with partner	Living alone
Mobility (car in good condition)	Lives/works near crime scene
Follows crime in news media	Minimal interest in news media
May change job or leave town	Significant behavior change

Source: Federal Bureau of Investigation (1985, p. 19).

TABLE 9–2   Crime Scene Differences Between Organized and Disorganized Murderers as Classified by the FBI

ORGANIZED	DISORGANIZED
Planned offense	Spontaneous offense
Victim a targeted stranger	Victim/location known
Personalizes victim	Depersonalizes victim
Controlled conversation	Minimal conversation
Crime scene reflects control	Crime scene random and sloppy
Demands submissive victim	Sudden violence to victim
Restraints used	Minimal use of restraints
Aggressive acts prior to death	Sexual acts after death
Body hidden	Body left in view
Weapon/evidence absent	Weapon/evidence often present
Transports victim or body	Body left at death scene

Source: Federal Bureau of Investigation (1985, p. 19).

crime the offender usually selects the victims according to some personal criteria. The infamous serial killer Ted Bundy, for example, selected young, attractive women who were similar in appearance. He was successful in the abduction of these young women from highly visible areas, such as beaches, campuses, and ski lodges, indicating considerable planning and premeditation (Douglas, Ressler, Burgess, & Hartman, 1986).

A **disorganized crime scene** demonstrates that the offender very probably committed the crime without premeditation or planning. The crime scene indicators suggest that the individual acted on impulse, in rage, or under extreme excitement. The disorganized offender obtains the victim by chance, often without specific criteria in mind. For example, Herbert Mullin of Santa Cruz, California, killed 14 people of varying types (e.g., an elderly man, a young girl, and a priest) over a 4-month period (Douglas et al., 1986). Generally, the victim's body is found at the scene of the crime. The **mixed crime scene** has ingredients of both organized and disorganized crime aspects. For example, a crime may have begun in a carefully planned fashion but deteriorated into a disorganized crime when things did not go as planned.

PROFILING

The term *profiling* is used to describe the gathering of various kinds of information about a person or persons. For clarity of presentation, we divide the term into five somewhat overlapping categories: (1) psychological profiling, (2) criminal profiling, (3) geographical profiling, (4) equivocal death analysis, and (5) racial profiling. For our purposes, the term **psychological profiling** is reserved for the psychological description of a person or persons *in general*, criminal or noncriminal. It was first used by the Office of Strategic Services during World War II, primarily to profile enemy leaders and their proclivities (Ault & Reese, 1980). It included their preferred strategies and ways of thinking. After the war, profiling was largely shelved until the FBI started using it again during the early 1970s. Essentially, psychological profiling has its basic scientific roots in psychological testing or psychometrics.

It is important to note that psychological profiling is not necessarily designed to describe criminal tendencies but refers to a broad behavioral realm of tendencies, foibles, faults, likes and dislikes, interests, strengths, and so on. Football coaches, business leaders, political leaders, attorneys, and other professionals often prefer to have some idea about, or psychological sketch of, the psychological characteristics of their opponents or adversaries. Consequently, we do not discuss the general category of psychological profiling to great extent in this text but focus on those methods that are directly related to crime.

Criminal profiling is the process of identifying personality traits, behavioral patterns, geographical habits, and demographic features of an offender based on characteristics of the crime. Some researchers (e.g., Knight, Warren, Reboussin, & Soley, 1998) have introduced the term *crime scene analysis*, or the more technical term *criminal investigative analysis*, to describe the practice of developing offender descriptions based on the analysis of the crime scene However, we prefer to use the more straightforward label criminal profiling.

Geographical profiling is a method of identifying the area of probable residence of, or the probable location of the next crime by, an unknown offender based on the location of and the spatial relationships among various crime sites (Guerette, 2002). Geographical profiling, therefore, can help in any criminal investigation of an unknown offender by locating the approximate area in which he or she lives or by narrowing surveillance and stakeouts to places where the next crime by the offender is most likely to occur. This type of profiling basically tries to identify the geographical territory the offender knows well, feels most comfortable in, and prefers to find or take victims in (Rossmo, 1997). Although a *criminal* profile hypothesizes about the demographic, motivational, and psychological features of the crime and offender, geographical profiling focuses on the location of the crime and how it relates to the residence and/or base of operations of the offender. Geographical profiling is useful not only in the search for serial violent offenders but also in the search for property offenders, such as serial burglars.

Equivocal death analysis, also called **reconstructive psychological evaluation**, is the reconstruction of the emotional life, behavioral patterns, and cognitive features of a deceased person. In this sense, it is a postmortem psychological analysis and therefore is frequently referred to simply as a **psychological autopsy** (Brent, 1989; Ebert, 1987; Selkin, 1987). Most often, equivocal death analysis or the psychological autopsy is done to determine whether the death was a suicide, and if it was a suicide, the reasons why the person did it.

The psychological autopsy differs from criminal profiling in two important ways: (1) The profile is constructed on a dead person, and (2) the identity of the person is already known. **Racial profiling** is defined as "police-initiated action that relies on the race, ethnicity, or national origin rather than the behavior of an individual or information that leads the police to a particular individual who has been identified as being, or having been, engaged in criminal activity" (Ramirez, McDevitt, & Farrell, 2000, p. 3).

Because the latter four forms of profiling are relevant to criminal behavior issues, we now cover each in some detail in the remainder of this section.

Criminal Profiling

It is clear that descriptions or profiles of the general characteristics of a person on the basis of a limited amount of information were used long before the Office of Strategic Services or the FBI employed such methods (D. Canter & Alison, 2000). Criminal profiling can be traced back to the case of Jack the Ripper, the serial killer who brutally murdered five prostitutes in separate incidents in London's East End in 1888. Although the case was never solved, the chief forensic pathologist, Dr. George Baxter Phillips, attempted to help police investigators by inferring personality characteristics based on the nature of the wounds inflicted on the victims (Turvey, 2002). That is, he noticed that the wounds were inflicted with considerable skill and knowledge, suggesting that the killer had a sophisticated knowledge of human anatomy. "In particular, he was referring to the postmortem removal of some of Annie Chapman's organs, and what he felt was the cleanliness and preciseness of the incisions involved" (p. 10). Interestingly, the fictional detective Sherlock Holmes, first created by Sir Arthur Conan Doyle in 1887, consistently employed a form of criminal profiling in his intriguing search for the offender. Since then, in virtually every detective or mystery novel the main characters engage in criminal profiling.

The FBI began using criminal profiling when it was introduced by special agent Howard Tegen in 1970 (Turvey, 2002). He taught the first criminal profiling course, called Applied Criminology, at the FBI National Academy and later constructed his first actual profile as an FBI agent in Amarillo, Texas (Turvey, 2002). In 1972, the new FBI Academy was opened and Special Agent Jack Kirsch developed the FBI's Behavioral Science Unit. The unit was a major contributor to criminal profiling during the 1970s and 1980s. Currently, the unit operates under the direction of the National Center for the Analysis of Violent Crime (NCAVC) at the FBI Academy in Quantico, Virginia.

Criminal profiling ". . . is best viewed as a strategy enabling law enforcement to narrow the field of options and generate educated guesses about the perpetrator" (Douglas et al., 1992, p. 21). Other researchers write that a criminal profile ". . . focuses attention on individuals with personality traits that parallel traits of others who have committed similar offenses" (Pinizzotto & Finkel, 1990, p. 215). In short, criminal profiling is an attempt to identify demographic variables, geographical location, and behavioral patterns of an offender based on characteristics of previous offenders who have committed similar offenses.

Pinizzotto and Finkel (1990) conclude from their research that criminal profiling is much more complex than this, involving a "multilevel series of attributions, correlations, and predictions" (p. 230). Much profiling is guesswork based on hunches and anecdotal information accumulated through years of experience, and it is full of error and misinterpretation. Currently, profiling is probably at least 90% an art and speculation and only 10% science. Professional profilers continually provide predictions of some demographic variables (e.g., white male, age 25 to 35), but rarely do they provide accurate information on psychological variables of the offender. Furthermore, very rarely does profiling provide the specific identity of the offender, nor is it intended to. Criminal profiling basically tries to narrow the field of investigation (Douglas, et al., 1986). Broadly, criminal profiling suggests the kind of person who might have committed the crime under investigation, but it is highly unlikely to pinpoint an individual's exact identity.

A profile report normally includes the gender, age, marital status, and education level and some broad identification of the occupation of the offender. There is also some prediction or estimation as to whether the offender will strike again, whether he or she likely has a police record, and what types of victims are at risk. In some instances, the profiler will try to identify possible motivational factors for the crime as well as the offender's personality traits.

Experienced profilers assert that profiling of *serial* offenders is most successful when the offender demonstrates some form of psychopathology at the crime scene, such as sadistic torture, evisceration, postmortem slashings and cuttings, and other mutilations (Pinizzotto, 1984). The reasoning behind this conclusion is that persons who are mentally disordered show great consistency in behavior from situation to situation. Whether mentally disordered persons are more consistent in their behavioral patterns than persons who are not mentally disordered remains an open question, however. It is likely that some are and some are not.

Profiling appears to be particularly useful in serial sexual offenses, such as serial rape and serial sexual homicides (Pinizzotto & Finkel, 1990). This is because we have a more extensive research base on sexual offending than we do on homicide. Profiling is largely ineffective at this time in the identification of offenders involved in fraud, burglary, robbery, political crimes, theft, and drug-induced crime because of the limited research base, although significant gains in these areas have been made in recent years.

Computer-based models of offender profiles developed from extensive statistical data collected on similar offenses hold considerable promise. Over 10 years ago, FBI researchers observed that "there have been no systematic efforts to validate these profile-derived classifications" (Douglas, Burgess, Burgess, & Ressler, 1992, p. 22). To date, there has been very little research on the utility, reliability, and validity of criminal profiling in general (Alison, Smith, & Morgan, 2003; Woodworth & Porter, 2001).

Pinizzotto and Finkel (1990) did try to assess the accuracy of profiling in a study involving four trained FBI experts, six trained police detectives, six experienced detectives without training, six clinical psychologists naive about criminal profiling, and six untrained undergraduate students. The results, in general, were not strongly supportive of profile accuracy. Trained experts were somewhat more accurate in profiling the sexual offender but were not much better than the untrained groups in profiling the homicide offender. The researchers also tried to identify any qualitative differences in the way experts and nonexperts processed the information provided. Overall, the results showed that experts did not process the material any differently than nonexperts. This finding suggests that the cognitive methods and strategies used by expert profilers are not discernibly different from the way nonexperts process the available information about the crime. The artificiality of the experiment and the quality of information given the groups may have been influential factors in this observation, however. What the researchers did find is that some trained profilers were more interested and skillful in certain areas than other profilers. Some profilers, for example, were good at gaining information from the medical reports, whereas others were better at gaining clues from the crime scene photos. This finding indicates that group profiling by a team of trained experts may be more effective than using one single profiler. Canter and Alison (2000) also assert that it is a misconception that there are some special sets of skills and knowledge for profiling available only to those who have worked with criminals or those who have considerable experience in police investigations. Researchers and thoughtful practitioners can also make significant advances and discoveries in criminal profiling.

In recent years, criminal profiling has caught the attention of the general public through popular films (e.g., *Silence of the Lambs*) and widely watched TV series (e.g., *CSI: Crime Scene Investigation, CSI: Miami, Crossing Jordan, Autopsy*). However, despite the media portrayals of highly successful and probing profilers employing sophisticated techniques and thoughtful strategies for identifying the offender, reality is far more sobering. Contemporary researchers on profiling (Alison, et al., 2002; Alison & Canter, 1999) point out that there are two basic flaws in modern-day profiling. One is the assumption that human behavior is consistent across a variety of different situations. The other flaw is the assumption that offense style or evidence gathered at the crime scene is directly related to specific personality characteristics. Psychology has consistently found that behavior varies according to situations or social context, especially if the social contexts are significantly different. Moreover, there are few empirical data that link crime scene characteristics to personality or other psychological features of the offender.

The above points underscore the fact that many professional profilers are prone to rely on outdated personality theory and psychological principles and are basically unfamiliar with the current research literature on profiling and human behavior in general. Some believe that profiling is best done on "gut feelings" and "instinct" based on many years of experience of crime scene investigations. However, the potential usefulness of criminal profiling is too critical to be relegated to the entertainment media and questionable applications by law enforcement. It is important, therefore, that we learn how reliable and valid the various profiling methods currently utilized are and how they can be improved to allow meaningful application in forensic settings.

In summary, much serious research needs to be done on profiling accuracy, usefulness, and processing before any tentative conclusions can be advanced in the area. Raymond Knight and his colleagues (Knight, Carter, and Prentky, 1998) have made a solid step in that direction by conducting a solid empirical study based on crime scene information across a wide variety of incidents.

Geographical Profiling

In 1995, D. Kim Rossmo completed a doctoral dissertation on the method of geographical profiling that has emerged as a promising tool for serial offender identification (Rossmo, 1977). He also developed a computer program called Criminal Geographic Targeting, or CGT, which is designed to analyze the geographical or spatial characteristics of an offender's crimes. CGT generates a three-dimensional map that assigns statistical probabilities to various areas that seem to fall into the offender's territory. The three-dimensional map is then placed over a street or topographical map where the crimes have occurred. The program considers known movement patterns, possible comfort zones, and victim search patterns of the offender. Ultimately, the objective of the program is to pinpoint the location of the offender's residence and/or base of operations.

Rossmo identifies four patterns serial offenders use to hunt for victims: (1) hunter, (2) poacher, (3) troller, and (4) trapper. Rossmo (1997) writes, "Hunters are those criminals who specifically set out from their residence to look for victims, searching through the areas in their awareness space that they believe contain suitable targets" (p. 167). Hunters are geographically stable in that their crimes usually occur near the offender's residence or neighborhood. Poachers are more transient, traveling some distance from their neighborhood in their search for suitable victims. Trollers, on the other hand, do not specifically search for victims but depend on random encounters during the course of other activities. Trappers create situations (traps) to entice victims to come to them.

Although geographical profiling was originally designed to help investigations of murder, rape, and arson, it is now being used for serial bombings, bank robbery, and child abductions (Guerette, 2002). Geographical profiling still has a way to go before it establishes its predictive validity across a variety of serial offenses. Most of the available research has been conducted by Rossmo himself. To his credit, however, Rossmo warns that the method is essentially an investigative tool that does not necessarily solve crimes but should help in identifying appropriate areas for surveillance, patrol saturation, stakeouts, and monitoring.

The Psychological Autopsy

The psychological autopsy was first used to help medical officials determine the cause of deaths that were classified as ambiguous, uncertain, or equivocal (Shneidman, 1994). Today, the psychological autopsy is usually done to determine what may have been in the mind of the deceased person in the hours leading up to and at the time of death—particularly if the death appears to be a suicide (La Fon 2002).

La Fon (2002) notes that there are two basic types of psychological autopsies used in modern practice: (1) suicide psychological autopsy and (2) equivocal death psychological autopsy. The objective of the suicide psychological autopsy is to identify and understand the psychosocial factors that contributed to the suicide. The purpose of the equivocal death psychological autopsy, on the other hand, is to determine the *reasons* (i.e., suicide or otherwise) for the death. In most cases, the equivocal death psychological autopsy is done for insurance claim purposes. Although some insurance policies compensate beneficiaries if death is determined to be the result of a suicide, many policies do not. In that case, it is important for life insurance companies to have a ruling on the *manner* of death before payment claims are honored.

The reliability and validity of the psychological autopsy, however, have yet to be demonstrated and remain open to debate (Poythress et al., 1993). Poythress et al. (1993) write: ". . . Persons who conduct reconstructive psychological evaluations should not assert categorical conclusions about the precise mental state or actions suspected of the actor at the time of his or her demise. The conclusions and inferences drawn in psychological reconstructions are, at best, informed speculations or theoretical formulations and should be labeled as such" (p. 12). Selkin (1994) further notes that clear, definitive procedures for carrying out the psychological autopsy have yet to be developed and that investigators still have a long way to go before standardized methods for conducting the psychological autopsy are established.

Racial Profiling

In the late 1990s, racial profiling became a serious and troubling issue for the country. **Racial profiling** is defined as "police-initiated action that relies on the race, ethnicity, or national origin rather than the behavior of an individual or information that leads the police to a particular individual who has been identified as being, or having been, engaged in criminal activity" (Ramirez et al., 2000). Apparent incidents of racial profiling were experienced so commonly by people of color that they began to label the phenomenon "driving while black" or "driving while brown" (commonly abbreviated DWB), as a play on the legally accepted term DWI (driving while intoxicated). A Gallup Poll released in 1999 revealed that 72% of black men between 18 and 34 years of age who had been stopped by police believed that they were stopped because of their race. By contrast, only 6% of white men believed that their race played a role in being pulled over by the police. More specifically, members of communities of color say they are being stopped for minor traffic violations, such as underinflated tires, failure to signal properly before switching lanes, vehicle equipment failure, and speeding at less than 10 miles above the speed limit. Another common complaint is that police often stop people of color traveling through predominantly white neighborhoods because the officers believe that people of color do not belong in the area and consequently suspect them of engaging in criminal activity.

A large segment of racial profiling is based on beliefs by law enforcement that many minorities are involved in drug trafficking or carrying contraband, such as illegal weapons. However, the available data suggest that this assumption is unjustified. One of the first cases involving the empirical evidence of racial profiling in a court hearing was *Wilkins v. Maryland State Police* (cited in D. Harris, 1999). *Wilkins* was a class-action lawsuit against the Maryland State Police on behalf of Robert L. Wilkins, an African-American attorney who was stopped, detained, and searched by the MSP for no apparent reason (D. Harris, 1999). With the assistance of Dr. John Lambert, a psychology professor at Temple University, the American Civil Liberties Union conducted a survey on traffic violations on Maryland highway I-95. The survey revealed that 74.7% of the 5,354 speeders stopped by Maryland State Police were white, and 17.5% were African American. However, "between January 1995 and September 1996, the Maryland State Police reported searching 823 motorists on I-95, north of Baltimore. Of these, 600, or 72.9% were black. Six hundred and sixty-one, or 80.3%, were black, Hispanic, or other racial minorities. Only 19.7% of those searched in this corridor were white" (p. 23). Based on his analysis of these data, Lambert concluded the following:

> The evidence examined in this study reveals dramatic and highly statistically significant disparities between the percentage of black Interstate 95 motorists legitimately subject to stop by Maryland State Police and the percentage of black motorists detained and searched by MSP troopers on this roadway. While no one can know the motivations of each individual trooper in conducting a traffic stop, the statistics presented herein, representing a broad and detailed sample of highly appropriate data, show without question a racially discriminatory impact on blacks and other minority motorists from state police behavior along I-95. (Harris, 1999, p. 24)

The "war on drugs" during the 1970s and 1980s appears to be the major impetus for developing the "drug courier profile." In 1985 when the war on drugs was intensifying, the Florida Department of Highway Safety and Motor Vehicles issued guidelines for law enforcement on how to identify drug couriers. The guidelines encouraged officers to be suspicious of rental car drivers, drivers who are scrupulously obeying traffic laws, drivers wearing lots of gold, drivers whose status does not "fit" the vehicle, and drivers who represent *"ethnic groups associated with the drug trade."* The unsubstantiated conclusion of various agencies at that time was that African Americans and Latinos were the principal participants in the exploding drug trade business. In 1986, a racially biased drug courier profile was introduced by the Drug Enforcement Administration (DEA) to various law enforcement agencies across the nation. The profile was used extensively in their training methods for officers in "Operation Pipeline" (Harris, 1999). In 1999, a preliminary survey by the San Diego Police Department found that Latino and African-American drivers were far more likely to be stopped and searched than other drivers (Dvorak, 2000). Several studies in New Jersey and New York have reported similar results (Ramirez et al., 2000). In recent years, lawsuits alleging racial profiling by law enforcement agencies have been brought on behalf of minority motorists in Pennsylvania, Florida, Illinois, and Maryland. In 1996, a New Jersey Superior Court judge threw out 19 drug possession cases, concluding that state troopers patrolling the New Jersey Turnpike had improperly singled out and stopped black motorists. Over a dozen states have passed laws against racial profiling, many of them requiring antibias training and the gathering of statistics on every driver who is stopped (Lewin, 2001), and many more states are considering similar laws (Dvorak, 2000). As we discuss shortly, the catastrophic events of September 11, 2001, have led to the racial profiling of still another group of individuals—Middle Easterners.

International data indicate that racial profiling is not restricted to the United States. A 1998 study by the British Government's Home Office investigated the racial and ethnic demographics of the stop-and-search patterns of police agencies in England and Wales. The study found that blacks were 7.5 times more likely to be stopped and searched and 4 times more likely to be arrested than whites (Ramirez et al., 2000). According to 1999 census data, Britain is 93% white and 7% ethnic minority.

In conclusion, empirical research, anecdotal evidence, and survey data confirm that racial profiling is a social problem. It occurs despite the fact that there is no evidence to support a valid profile based strictly on race. Even if there were—and, again, there is not—a profile model that revolves around race or ethnicity as a critical component violates or infringes on civil rights.

MULTIPLE MURDERERS

One of the most frightening and perhaps incomprehensible types of homicide is the random killing of groups of people, either in one episode or individually over a period of time. Although multiple murders are still rare occurrences, when they do happen they cannot escape attention, and they remain etched in the public consciousness. The slaughter of 21 patrons at a McDonald's restaurant in San Ysidro, California, in July 1984, by James Oliver Huberty is a case in point. Another is the mass murder of 22 patrons at Luby's Cafeteria in Killeen, Texas, on October 16, 1991. Many people still recall the planned, separate murders of 33 young men and boys in the cellar of John Wayne Gacy's suburban Chicago home during the late 1970s. During the early 1990s Jeffrey Dahmer lured at least 17 boys and young men into his home in Milwaukee, where he drugged, killed, and dismembered them. The public was shocked to learn the details of how Dahmer ate the victims' flesh and had sex with the corpses. Other notorious multiple murderers include David Berkowitz, known as the infamous Son of Sam; Kenneth Bianchi, the Hillside Strangler; Albert DeSalvo, the Boston Strangler (although recent DNA evidence has led to questions about DeSalvo's guilt; DeSalvo died in prison); Gary Ridgeway, the Green River Killer; Donald Harvey, the nursing-care killer; and Theodore Bundy.

England had Jack the Ripper in earlier times and, more recently, Peter Sutcliffe, the Yorkshire Ripper who killed 13 women in the red-light districts of northern England. Dennis Nilsen became England's first serial killer to prey on the homosexual subculture, committing at least 15 known murders (Jenkins, 1988).

Serial murder is usually reserved for incidents in which an individual (or individuals) kills a number of individuals (usually a minimum of three) over time. The time interval—sometimes referred to as the cooling-off period—may be days or weeks but is more likely months or years. The cooling-off period is the main difference between serial murders and other multiple murders (Douglas et al., 1986). The murders are premeditated and planned, and the offender usually selects specific victims. **Spree murder** normally refers to the killing of three or more individuals without any cooling-off period, usually at two or more locations. A bank robber who kills some individuals within the bank, flees with hostages, and kills a number of people while in flight during a statewide chase is an example of a spree murderer. **Mass murder** involves killing three or more persons at a single location with no cooling-off period between murders.

The FBI identifies two types of mass murder: classic and family (Douglas et al., 1986). An example of a **classic mass murder** is when an individual barricades himself or herself inside a public building, such as a fast-food restaurant, randomly killing the patrons and employees. The shootings of patrons at the McDonald's restaurant and Luby's Cafeteria, mentioned earlier, are examples. Another example is Sylvia Seegrist (nicknamed "Ms. Rambo" because of her military-style clothing), who began shooting people at a Pennsylvania mall in October 1985, killing three and wounding seven (Douglas et al., 1986). A **family mass murder** is when at least three family members are killed (usually by another family member). Very often, the perpetrator kills him- or herself, an incident that is classified as a mass murder/suicide.

SERIAL MURDERERS

Serial murders seem to be on the increase in the United States and England. In the United States during the 1950s and 1960s, there were only two cases of an individual killing 10 or more victims over a period of time. Since 1970, however, there have been at least 40 known individuals who qualify as serial murderers

(Jenkins, 1988). The U.S. Department of Justice concluded that there were about 35 serial murderers active at any given point in the United States during the 1970s and 1980s (Jenkins, 1988). However, it remains debatable whether serial murders are on the increase or whether the dramatic improvement in communication and computer networks among law enforcement agencies and the news media may account—at least in part—for the statistical increments in the crime. Prior to 1970, information exchange between agencies was difficult and primitive by today's standards. Therefore, serial murderers who moved from one geographic location to another (which they commonly do) probably went undetected.

Mass murderers also seem to be on the increase in the United States, although the phenomenon remains rare in England. Available estimates indicate that as many as 3,500 to 5,000 victims are slain by serial or mass murderers in the United States each year (Holmes & DeBurger, 1988). This estimate may be much too high, however, since it accounts roughly for 14% to 20% of all criminal homicides committed each year across the entire country.

Over a decade ago Jenkins (1988) noted that victims of serial murderers tend to be young women, especially active prostitutes. Today, the primary victims of serial killers tend to be children of both sexes (ages 8 to 16). In response to the increase in child victims, then FBI Director Louis Freeh created a specialized unit to focus on investigation of child abduction and murder: the Child Abduction and Serial Killer Unit. In addition, the Missing and Exploited Children's Task Force (MECTF) was created by Congress in the 1994 Omnibus Crime Bill to assist in investigating the most difficult cases of missing and exploited children. Both the Child Abduction and Serial Killer Unit and the MECTF work closely with the National Center for Missing and Exploited Children. In 1987, the Office of Juvenile Justice and Delinquency Prevention conducted six studies in an effort to determine the incidence of abducted children by nonfamily members.

Unlike the typical violent individual, who demonstrates a propensity for violence at an early age, serial murderers generally begin their careers of repetitive homicide at a relatively late age. Jenkins (1988) concludes that most start their careers at the ages of 24 to 40. Interestingly, the median age of arrested serial murderers is 36. Arrests typically occur about four years after they begin killing. While serial murderers have extensive police records, the records reflect a series of petty theft, embezzlement, and forgery, rather than a history of violence (Jenkins, 1988). Surprisingly, they also do not have extensive juvenile records. Jenkins concludes that the English cases do not provide any early indicators or predictors of eventual murderous behavior. When British serial murderers committed their first murder, about half were married, had a stable family life, and had lived in the same house for many years. A majority had stable jobs, and disconcertingly, a good number had been former police officers or security guards.

Serial murderers kill about four people per year, an average that seems to be characteristic of both British and American offenders. However, the evidence does not support any notion that they kill on the basis of some compulsion or irresistible urge. Rather, the murder appears to be more a result of opportunity and the random availability of a suitable victim.

Holmes and DeBurger (1988) have analyzed the characteristics of serial killers in the United States. In general, the patterns and characteristics of the British sample correspond closely to those of the Americans. However, while the British serial murderers generally stay in the same neighborhood, many of their American counterparts prefer to move around the country, committing murders in a number of states and jurisdictions. Holmes and DeBurger also note that serial murderers are predominantly white males killing white females. There are exceptions, of course. Jeffrey Dahmer, a 31-year-old white male, killed at least nine African-American males in 1991 and, apparently, killed many more over a 10-year period. Victims, in both the British and the American samples, tend to be strangers or individuals the killer has met only briefly, a pattern that makes it particularly difficult for law enforcement agencies to identify the assailant. Moreover, the motive for the killing is usually aberrant and extremely difficult for those who seek the murderer's arrest to understand.

Although relatively rare, there have been at least three dozen female serial murderers in U.S. history, including most recently the notorious Aileen Wuornos, a prostitute whose crimes were recounted in the 2003 movie, *Monster*. Hickey (1991) identified 34 documented female serial murderers, with 82% of them acting after 1900. Moreover, there are some discernible differences between female and male serial murderers. For example, only about one-third of the female offenders killed strangers, in contrast to males, who almost exclusively killed strangers (Holmes, Hickey, & Holmes, 1991). Most victims of female serial killers are husbands, former husbands, or suitors. For example, Belle Gunness murdered an estimated 14 to 49 husbands or suitors in La Porte, Indiana (Holmes et al., 1991). Nannie Doss killed 11 husbands and family members in Tulsa, Oklahoma. On the other hand, Aileen Wuornos killed seven men who had picked her up hitchhiking.

Female serial killers murder primarily for material or monetary gain, such as insurance benefits, will allocations, trusts, and estates. Furthermore, the method of killing is usually the administration of poisons (usually cyanide) or overdoses of pills. Approximately half of the known female serial killers had a male accomplice. Some women have murdered because of involvements in cults or with a male serial murderer. A good example of cult-involvement murderers is the female followers of Charles Manson. An example of murder due to involvement with a male serial murderer is Charlene Gallego, the common-law wife of serial killer Gerald Gallego (Holmes et al., 1991). Charlene Gallego helped Gerald select, abduct, and murder at least 10 individuals.

Jenkins (1993) contends that the current popular image of the serial murderer—a white male who kills for sexual motives—may be an inaccurate one. He argues that lack of a **victimological perspective** encourages confusion and distorted information. He suggests that our current knowledge about serial murderers is strongly influenced by two factors: availability of the victims and attitudes of law enforcement agencies toward those victims. Rather than focusing strictly on individual and personality attributes of the offender, he believes we should also examine the *social opportunity* to kill. In other words, what we know about serial murder may be strongly influenced by the nature and type of the potential victims.

To illustrate, Jenkins provides the case of Calvin Jackson, who was arrested in 1974 for murders committed in a New York apartment building. Actually, Jenkins was a serial murderer, but none of his victims led the police to suspect that. Jackson's killings took place in a single-occupancy hotel where the guests were poor, socially isolated and largely forgotten, and mostly elderly. Time after time, the police were called to the hotel to deal with cases of death or injury due to alcohol, drugs, or old age. When foul play was suspected, the police never considered it the work of a serial murderer, because the victims did not fit the stereotypic profile. Since there was no evidence of grotesque sexual abuse of the victim (the victim stereotype), there was little reason for the police to entertain the possibility of a serial murderer. Other serial murderers may set up situations where murders resemble drug-related homicides. Therefore, our current knowledge of serial murderers may be restricted to a certain category of offender.

An examination of the victim selection of known serial murderers will reveal that killers prefer the group of people offering easy access, transience, and a tendency to disappear without seeming to cause much alarm or concern. Victims are often prostitutes, especially streetwalkers, street runaways, young male drifters, and itinerant farm workers. Young women on or near a university or college campus and the elderly and solitary poor appear to be the groups next preferred. The strongest determining factor in victim selection for both groups seems to be easy availability. Rarely do known serial murderers break in and kill middle-class strangers in their homes, for example. It should be pointed out, however, that although serial killers begin their murderous careers by selecting highly vulnerable victims, they may, as their killings continue, gain substantially more confidence in their ability to abduct more "challenging" victims. Fortunately, very few serial killers become this successful before they are arrested.

Jenkins (1993) further suggests that dramatic increases in serial murder are directly related to dramatic increases in potential victims. For example, he notes that serial murders often co-occur with severe downturns in the economy or deinstitutionalization of mental patients, both of which result in putting more vulnerable people on the streets.

Interestingly, 31 of the 52 known cases of serial murders in the United States between 1971 and the early 1990s occurred in the western states, especially California (Jenkins, 1993). Only four occurred in the northeastern states. The reason for this geographical distribution remains largely a mystery, although the answer probably lies in some combination of lifestyles, economic conditions, and availability of potential victims.

Perhaps an effective method for reducing serial murder would be to identify and protect specific high-risk groups and regions and to take whatever social measures are needed to reduce their vulnerability. Focusing on the offender through criminal profiling and other investigative measures is usually of limited usefulness because most serial killers are apprehended by a mixture of fortuitous events and carelessness by the offender. In the meantime, community leaders and authorities should concentrate on reducing the availability of potential victims.

While African Americans are overrepresented in "normal" homicide cases, only one-fifth of known American serial murderers are African American (Hickey, 1997). The number of Latino and other minority-group serial killers is virtually unknown. One reason for this discrepancy may lie in how serial murder is identified and investigated. For example, law enforcement agencies may be less prone to investigate African-American victims as casualties of serial murderers if they are found in a rundown apartment complex located in a poverty-stricken, densely populated, and crime-infested neighborhood. Under these circumstances, law enforcement officials are more likely to conclude that the victim is simply another fatality in the long stream of never-ending violence characteristic of some urban areas.

TYPES OF SERIAL MURDERERS

Holmes and DeBurger (1988) made a gallant attempt to classify serial murderers into a typology based on motive. They identified four major types: (1) visionary, (2) mission oriented, (3) hedonistic, and (4) power/control oriented. The *visionary type* is driven by voices or visions demanding that a particular group of people be destroyed, such as prostitutes, homosexuals, or derelicts. The visionary killer often operates on the basis of a "directive from God." In many instances, this type qualifies as being psychotic or otherwise mentally disordered. *Mission oriented–type* murderers determine on their own that a particular group of people must be destroyed or eliminated. They see no visions, hear no voices, and function on a day-to-day basis without demonstrating psychologically aberrant behavior. The *hedonistic type* strives for pleasure and thrill seeking and feels that people are objects to use for one's own enjoyment. Reportedly, the hedonistic killer gains considerable pleasure from the murder event itself. The *power/control type* strives to get satisfaction by having complete life-or-death control over the victim. Sexual components may or may not be present, but the primary motive is the extreme power over the helpless victim.

At least two more types could be added to the Holmes–DeBurger list: the *recognition seeker* and the *material-gain seeker*. Some serial murderers may kill primarily for the challenge of it and the recognition they receive from the media. Henry Lee Lucas, who claimed to have killed his first victim when he was 15 years old, is a good example of the recognition seeker. Lucas had a devastating history of childhood abuse and neglect, including unspeakable cruelty at the hands of his mother. First he was imprisoned for a series of burglaries. Then at age 24 he killed his mother, served time for that offense, and was paroled 10 years later, in 1970. Over the next 15 years he alternately boasted of and denied killing numerous other individuals, at one point insisting that he and friends had accumulated over 500 murder victims. Although law enforcement officials believed that he exaggerated his deeds, many also believed that he was responsible for 90 to 100 unsolved deaths. Lucas was eventually convicted of murder again in the mid-1980s and sentenced to death. In 1998, his sentence was commuted to life without the possibility of parole.

The material-gain seeker, unlike the recognition seeker, kills serially for money and for material rewards. Examples include many of the female serial murderers discussed previously, who kill husbands and suitors for insurance, will distribution, and other material acquisition.

Despite these various attempts at identifying typologies, Fox and Levin (1998) contend that the primary motive of serial killers is the domination and control of the lives of their victims. "Overwhelmingly, male serial killers prey on strangers whom they select on the basis of some sexual fantasy involving capture and control" (p. 414). They note that serial killers also tend to collect memorabilia and other "trophies" of their victims, such as audio- or videotapes, photographs, clothing, and body parts. These trophies enable them to relive the control, dominance, and sexual fantasies associated with their victims.

Despite the extensive media coverage and numerous interesting books on the subject in recent years, there have been very few well-designed, empirically based studies on serial murderers during the past 10 to 15 years. Much of the available information has been gathered through anecdotal, interview, or case-study methods, which, while informative and interesting, fail to provide a systematic and functionally useful database for predicting and identifying these offenders.

Jenkins (1988) makes some important points about what happens to serial murderers once taken in custody. Almost inevitably they attempt a defense of insanity or diminished responsibility, but very rarely succeed. As we discovered in Chapter 6, the public—in Britain, Canada, and the United States—is consistently very reluctant to attribute insanity to extremely violent offenders, particularly in the case of serial or mass murderers.

In summary, most of the knowledge we have on serial murderers is based on clinical observations, investigative reports, and anecdotal data. Some of the material is sensational and overly dramatic, such as that found in popular paperbacks. On the other hand, much of the clinical and investigative material is in agreement and relatively consistent, and it adds greatly to our understanding of the serial offender. Our knowledge of the serial murderer, however, could be greatly expanded with more quantitative data, such as we would find in extensive, systematic data collection and analysis. However, because serial murder is extremely rare compared to other violent offenses, the numbers necessary for a more complete analysis are simply unavailable at this time.

MASS MURDERERS

Surprisingly little interest has been directed at mass murderers, especially in comparison to the attention given to serial murderers. Perhaps this is because mass murder, while frightening, is not as intriguing or mysterious as serial murder. Furthermore, mass murder happens quickly and unpredictably, without warning—then the killing is usually over. It is often clear who the offender is, and his or her life is usually ended on the spot.

Classic Mass Murder

Mass murderers tend to be frustrated, angry people who feel helpless about their lives. They are usually between 35 and 45 years of age, and they are convinced there is little chance that things will get better for them. Their personal lives have been failures by their standards and they have often suffered some tragic or serious loss, such as a loss of meaningful employment. George Hennard, for example, the 35-year-old who drove his Ford Ranger pickup into the plate glass window of Luby's Cafeteria in Killeen, Texas, and proceeded to shoot and kill 22 patrons, had lost his cherished job as a merchant marine.

In addition, mass murders are usually carefully planned, sometimes over very long periods of time. For example, on November 2, 1991, Gang Lu, a former graduate student at the University of Iowa, sought six specific professors he felt kept him from getting a $1,000 award for his doctoral dissertation. He managed to kill five of the six within 10 minutes before taking his own life. Lu had written five separate letters to people detailing his plans prior to the murder. Likewise, Hennard had apparently planned his onslaught for many months, even studying video documentaries of previous mass murders.

Moreover, the targets selected by mass murderers are either symbolic of their discontent (such as people at their workplace) or are likely to include individuals they hate or blame for their misfortunes. George Hennard, for example, had a lifelong hatred of women, and he knew that Luby's Cafeteria during lunch would be filled with them. Hennard moved from victim to victim, frequently selecting women, and methodically shot each victim in the head at close range as he shouted "Bitch." Fourteen of the 22 people killed that day were women. Marc Lepine walked calmly through the University of Montreal engineering school (Ecole Polytechnique) with a semiautomatic rifle in search of women to kill. In one classroom he shouted "I want to kill women!" and as he proceeded to shoot them he shouted "You're all a bunch of feminists!" He killed 14 women that day and wounded 13 more people (4 of them men) before he took his own life. In his pocket was a three-page suicide note in which he complained that feminists had always ruined his life. James Oliver Huberty, the McDonald's killer, selected a fast-food restaurant in a Hispanic community (San Ysidro) because he apparently disliked Hispanics and children.

Mass murderers often take a very active interest in guns, especially semiautomatics that maximize the number of deaths in a short period of time. In large measure, the availability of high-powered semiautomatic or automatic weaponry accounts for the increasingly large death toll in recent mass murders. Moreover, mass murderers usually plan to die at the scene, either by committing suicide or by being shot down by law enforcement.

Also, mass murderers are often socially isolated and withdrawn people who are without a strong social network of friends or supports. Their isolation is probably due to some combination of an active dislike of people and a lack of adequate interpersonal and social skills. The mass murder is their chance to get even, to dominate others, to take control, to call the shots, and to gain recognition.

Although it is commonly assumed that the traditional mass murderer intends to die at scene, research has indicated that only about one in five apparently have intentions of suicide. For example, Duwe (2000) examined 495 mass murders over a recent 21-year time period and found that only 21% committed suicide, another 2% attempted to commit suicide, and 3% were fatally shot by police. Overall, statistical data suggest that family mass murderers are far more likely to commit suicide than are classic mass murderers.

The remainder of this section addresses some specific offenses that have been used for, or possess the strong possibility of becoming, mass murder and that seem to be increasingly popular in recent years.

Product-Tampering Homicide

Product-tampering homicide refers to death caused by a commercial product that has been sabotaged by someone; it also has the potential to result in multiple deaths. Between 1982 and 1986, there were 12 confirmed deaths directly due to product tampering (Lance, 1988). This form of homicide is rare and is usually committed for financial gain. The offender usually expects financial gain either through litigation on behalf of the victim (wrongful death), through extortion, or through business operations (Douglas et al., 1992). The business operation strategy refers to attempts to damage a competing business by tampering with its products.

The method most commonly employed in product-tampering homicide is to place cyanide within the product, either before (if the offense involves extortion or business operations) or after purchase, in cases claiming wrongful death. Cyanide is often the poison of choice because of its potency (an ounce can kill 250 people) and its availability (Douglas et al., 1992).

Fortunately, although there are numerous threats to tamper, very few are actually carried out. Nearly two-thirds of the threats are directed at retail stores, and the products threatened are usually well-known national brands (Lance, 1988). News of product tampering sometimes prompts a contagion effect (also known as a copycat effect), in which many people either copy or falsely report the offense. For example, when a baby food company was accused by an individual of having glass in its baby food, more than 600 complaints of glass particles were immediately received across the country. The vast majority of the complaints were false claims by consumers seeking monetary reward by claiming that glass in the products had caused them some injury. One individual was arrested for deliberately feeding shards of glass to his developmentally disabled son in an attempt to obtain money from the baby food company.

Workplace Violence

Workplace violence, which includes assaults, sexual assaults, robberies, and murders, has increased to the point that the U.S. Department of Justice proclaimed the workplace to be the most dangerous place in America (Anfuso, 1994). The following statistics, compiled in an overview by Gregorie (2000), explain why.

- Each year, about 2 million Americans are victimized while working.
- Approximately 1,000 workplace homicides occur annually.
- Guns are the primary weapon used in 82% of workplace homicide, followed by knives and physical force.
- About one of every six violent crimes experienced by U.S. residents occurs in the workplace.
- Boyfriends and husbands, both current and former, commit more than 13,000 acts of violence against women in the workplace every year.
- The National Institute for Occupational Safety and Health reports that murder is the leading cause of death for women at work.

Gregorie (2000, pp. 2–3) further identifies four types of offenders who commit violence at the workplace, an effort that is very useful for understanding workplace violence. They are as follows.

- *Type I.* This offender has no legitimate relationship to the workplace or the victim and usually enters the workplace to commit a criminal action such as a robbery or theft. Common victims of Type I offenders work at small, late-night retail establishments including convenience stores and restaurants or as taxi drivers. This type of workplace violence also includes terrorist and hate crimes such as the World Trade Center and Alfred P. Murrah Federal Building bombings, the events of September 11, and attacks at clinics that provide abortion services.
- *Type II.* This offender is the recipient of some service provided by the victim or workplace and may be either a current or a former client, patient, or customer.
- *Type III.* This offender has an employment-related involvement with the workplace, usually a current or former employee, supervisor, or manager who has a dispute with another employee at the workplace. This type of workplace violence offender is usually referred to as the "disgruntled employee."

- *Type IV.* This offender has an indirect involvement with the workplace through a relationship with an employee, such as an employee's current or former spouse or partner, someone who was dating an employee, or an employee's relative or friend. This type of violent offender follows the employee into the workplace from the outside.

In California, the majority (60%) of workplace homicides involve a person entering a small, night-retail establishment, such as a liquor store, gas station, or convenience food store, to commit a robbery (Southerland Collins, & Scarborough, 1997). Robbery is the primary motive for most workplace homicide, accounting for 85% of the deaths (Gregorie & Wallace, 2000).

According to the FBI (Southerland et al., 1997), workplace homicide offenders whose motivation is not robbery are often disgruntled employees (Type III) who believe their job is (or was) their life, are loners, have few friends, and lack a support system. The target of the attack may be a person or persons (usually innocent) working within a building or structure or for an organization that symbolizes the authority (Douglas et al., 1992).

Data collected by the National Institute for Occupational Safety and Health (NIOSH, 1993) between 1980 and 1989 indicated that approximately 750 people per year were murdered at work, making it the third leading cause of occupational death in the United States (Solomon & King, 1993). In fact, homicide was the leading cause of workplace death for women during those 10 years, accounting for 41% of all female worker fatalities (Kelleher, 1997). A vast majority of these victims were killed (often randomly) by disgruntled employees who were fired or felt mistreated by the company or agency. More recent data from the Bureau of Labor Statistics (1999) showed that nearly 1,000 workers were murdered and 1.5 million were assaulted at the workplace each year. The organization that has experienced the most workplace homicides in past years has been the U.S. Postal Service. Between 1986 and mid-1993, 38 postal employees were murdered at the workplace by disgruntled present or former employees (Solomon & King, 1993). Even so, postal workers as a group are not at the highest risk of being victims of workplace *violence*. According to the Bureau of Labor Statistics (1999), the five occupations at the highest risk are police officer, correctional officer, taxi driver, private security guard and bartender.

With respect to homicide, it seems that a particularly autocratic work environment can be a problem, such as found in large, impersonal bureaucratic organizations. As discussed previously, when employees feel frustrated and angry, they may be more likely to strike out.

Similarly to mass murderers in general, offenders who commit authority homicide tend to be white males who have little social support, are socially isolated, and blame others (externalize) for their problems and misfortune, as mentioned earlier. They are often seriously depressed. Very often, offenders expect to die at the scene, killed either by the police or by suicide. Authority offenders also tend to be preoccupied with weapons, accumulating a number of them over a period of time with eventual revenge or "occupational martyrdom" in mind. The weapons are often of maximum lethality, such as automatic assault weapons (e.g., AK-47) (Douglas et al., 1992). In most instances, the offender is middle-aged (over 30 and under 60) (Kelleher, 1997). There is also evidence that workplace offenders tend to have a history of violent behavior and alcohol or drug abuse and will vocalize, or otherwise act out, violent intentions sometime prior to the authority homicide (Kelleher, 1997). Current data suggest that authority homicides are on the increase (Kelleher, 1997).

TERRORISM

An entire nation and much of the world were stunned by the destruction of life and property on September 11, 2001, when two airliners were intentionally flown into the World Trade Center in New York City, a third airliner was flown into the Pentagon in the nation's capital, and a fourth crashed into a field in Somerset County, Pennsylvania. The plane that crashed in Pennsylvania was believed to be heading for the White House, but passengers onboard took over the plane, preventing it from remaining on its original course. At the World Trade Center, 2,823 were killed (including 5 children under age 5), at the Pentagon 184 lives were lost, and all 40 passengers died in the Pennsylvania crash. Nineteen terrorists (all under the age of 35) were directly involved in the airline hijacking (10 at the World Trade Center, 5 at the Pentagon, and 4 in Pennsylvania) (Federal Bureau of Investigation, 2002). The al-Qaeda terrorist group was believed to be responsible.

The United States, in response to the tragedy, decided to launch strong military forces into Afghanistan in an effort to weed out al-Qaeda cells in that country. Soon thereafter the United States launched another military attack in Iraq, again in apparent pursuit of al-Qaeda-sponsored organizations and despite objections from many that such as invasion was unjustified. Many also believe that these military responses are rarely successful in preventing future attacks because they do not address the root conditions that spawn terrorism (Marsella, 2004). Instead, "there must be a response to prevent its emergence and its growth and development as an appealing option" (p. 34). Furthermore, "terrorism may be contained but never defeated as long as there are real or perceived threats or injustices that foster widespread hatred and revenge. There may be small and large military successes, but eventually there must be coming to grips with the strengths and weaknesses of the human psyche and the cultural milieu in which it is fostered" (p. 4).

Definitions

According to the FBI, "A terrorist incident is a violent act or an act dangerous to human life, in violation of the criminal laws of the United States, or of any state, to intimidate or coerce a government, the civilian population, or any segment thereof" (Federal Bureau of Investigation, 1999b, p. ii). Sternberg (2003) defines terrorism simply "as the systematic use of terror, especially as a means of coercion" (p. 299). Hallett (2004) defines the term as a theatrical crime against person or property in which only symbolic or psychological satisfaction to the perpetrators is gained. A quick scan of the literature reveals that there are numerous definitions of terrorism. Moreover, trying to reach a comprehensive definition is complicated by the maxim, "One person's terrorist is another person's freedom fighter" (Marsella, 2004, p. 15).

Despite the vast and sometimes overwhelming array of definitions, Marsella (2004) finds some common ground in all of them. "*Terrorism* is broadly viewed as (a) the use of force or violence (b) by individuals or groups (c) that is directed toward civilian populations (d) and intended to instill fear (e) as a means of coercing individuals or groups to change their political and social positions" (p. 16). However, he further notes that any comprehensive definition of terrorism also requires thoughtful consideration of the psychosocial context, motives, and consequences of the act. Consequently, we organize this section along these three interconnected themes.

Psychosocial Context

The psychosocial context refers to those social and psychological circumstances that encourage certain behaviors to develop and expand. The psychosocial context is a cognitively constructed world that is sustained through the socialization process that is inherent in each culture. Culture in this sense may be as broad as an entire country or as narrow as a small group of individuals. Thus, there is psychosocial context relevant both to the entire society and to the subcultural components of that society.

Ervin Staub (2004) postulates that certain cultural characteristics are conducive to the emergence of terrorist groups One characteristic is what he calls *cultural devaluation*. Cultural devaluation occurs when a group or culture is selected by another group or culture as a scapegoat or an ideological enemy. "It might consist of beliefs that the other is lazy, or of limited intelligence, or manipulative, or morally bad, or a dangerous enemy that intends to destroy society or one's own group" (p. 158). For example, many see the United States as being indifferent to the world's suffering and insensitive to global cultural diversity and to local identity (Marsella, 2004). Many are convinced that this indifference contributes to the political suppression of the poor and the disadvantaged on a global basis (Marsella, 2004). In addition, some people believe the American culture is a real and tangible threat to traditional cultures' identities, religious affiliations, and ways of life (Marsella, 2004).

It is also worth noting that in the United States, persons associated with racial, ethnic, or religious groups often believe the "dominant" values of American society are inconsistent with the values of their own subgroups. The vast majority of these individuals accept this discrepancy or work within the system to change the dominant views. However, some individuals may take a terrorist approach. Thus, although Staub discusses terrorist groups, the principle of cultural devaluation can also apply to individuals or groups who engage in terrorist-like activities but who are not usually considered terrorist groups. Persons who, in the 1980s and 1990s, firebombed women's health clinics where abortions were provided are a case in point.

The second characteristic noted by Staub involves perceptions of *inequality, relative deprivation*, and *injustice*. Disadvantaged, powerless, and shunned peoples are sometimes more likely to join violent or terrorist groups, not only to get some of their basic needs met, but also to gain a sense of identity and community that the terrorist group offers. Staub (2001) calls such situations *difficult life conditions* characterized by hunger, sickness, absence of a sense of community, and lack of shelter for oneself and one's family. "People with few material resources, having little to lose, are prime candidates for joining extremist organizations that promise better living conditions as soon as the haves are removed from power" (Wagner & Long, 2004, p. 211). There is promise not only of better physical living conditions but also of a sense of belonging. D. M. Taylor and Louis (2004) make a similar point when they argue that, in addition to disadvantaged economic and political factors, the need for psychological identity draws some individuals into terrorist groups. They assert, "What makes terrorist groups particularly attractive is their simplistic worldview that offers recruits a clear collective identity" (p. 184). To this end, terrorist groups also fill a necessary psychological void. Some individuals, however, may also join because they "have moral principles that lead them to identify with those who are affected by difficult conditions or are unjustly treated" (Staub, 2004, p. 159).

The third characteristic is that many—perhaps most—terrorist groups have a strong hierarchy, sometimes with leaders who are described as all-powerful, convincing, and charismatic. Staub calls this psychosocial characteristic a *strong respect for authority*. Some persons who join simply wish to relinquish their unfulfilled selves and submit themselves to power leaders and chain-of-command organizations. They feel most comfortable in hierarchical social structures organized for some challenging or exciting mission. Overall, these real or perceived conditions are apt to be productive areas for terrorist recruitment when promises of a better life beckon.

Motives

Clearly, there is no single motive for engaging in terrorism. The motives are multiple and complex, ranging from revenge and anger to paradise, status, respect, and life everlasting (Marsella, 2004). "The roots of terrorism are complex and reside in historical, political, economic, social and psychological factors. Of all of these, psychosocial factors have been among the least studied and the least understood, but arguably the most important" (Moghaddam &

Marsella, 2004a, p. xi). A solid understanding of international terrorism is best achieved by careful consideration of the multicultural perspectives and psychological dynamics in which it is embedded.

Bandura (2004) skillfully takes the explanation for motives of terrorism into the cognitive realm. He posits that terrorists justify their horrific acts through *cognitive restructuring*. Cognitive restructuring involves moral justifications, euphemistic language, and advantageous comparisons. Moral justification enables people to engage in reprehensible conduct by telling themselves that their actions are socially worthy and have an ultimate moral and good purpose. Bandura writes:

> The conversion of socialized people into dedicated fighters is achieved not by altering their personality structures, aggressive drives, or moral standards. Rather, it is accomplished by cognitively redefining the morality of killing, so that it can be done free from self-censuring restraints. Through moral sanction of violent means, people see themselves as fighting ruthless oppressors who have an unquenchable appetite for conquest or as protecting their cherished values and way of life, preserving world peace, saving humanity from subjugation to an evil ideology, and honoring their country's international commitments. (p. 124)

The second cognitive restructuring process of euphemistic language is based on the well-known research finding that language shapes thought patterns on which people base many of their actions. People behave more cruelly when their conduct is given a sanitized or neutral label. Consequently, they use terms such as to "waste" people rather then kill them and "collateral damage" to designate civilians who are killed in bombings. Among the colorful metaphors and euphemisms offered by Bandura to emphasize his point are bombing missions referred to as "serving the target" and bombs themselves called "vertically deployed anti-personnel devices."

The third cognitive restructuring process is advantageous comparison, where terrorists are convinced that their way of life and fundamental cultural values are superior to those of the culture they attack. Advantageous comparison is further advanced when the terrorists are told, and come to believe, that the enemy engages in widespread cruelties and inhumane treatment of the people the terrorists represent. The United States, for example, is seen by people in Arab countries as blameworthy for their problems because of a variety of U.S. policies and practices (Staub, 2004). Advantageous comparison methods draw heavily on history to justify violence. For example, terrorist leaders will indoctrinate their people about the many oppressive policies and tyrannical tactics the targeted organization or country has employed on them in the past. Many people believe, for example, that the United States has historically and consistently supported repressive governments in the Arab world and elsewhere.

Bandura also states that other disengagement practices are also at play in developing motivations, such as dehumanization, displacement of responsibility, and diffusion of responsibility. Dehumanization is based on the premise that mistreating or randomly killing *humanized* or known persons significantly increases the risks of self-condemnation. It is easier to mistreat (and kill) strangers who are divested of human qualities. "Once dehumanized, they are no longer viewed as persons with feelings, hopes, and concerns but as subhuman forms" (Bandura, 2004, p. 136). Now they can justifiably be called "savages," "gooks," "degenerates," "monsters," "the unwashed masses," "evil cowards," and so on.

In displacement of responsibility, terrorists may view their actions as stemming from the dictates of authorities and leaders rather than from their own personal responsibility, similar to the perpetrators of crimes of obedience discussed in Chapter 5. Consequently, they avoid self-condemning reactions because they are not personally responsible for their conduct; they are only following orders, perhaps even from their god. Some serial killers (e.g., "Son of Sam") have used similar justifications for their actions. Diffusion of responsibility is similar to the concept of deindividuation, also discussed in Chapter 5. Terrorism often requires the services of many people in the organization, all pulling together to achieve some purpose. Bandura points out that each person in the organization often performs a relatively small, fragmentary job that, taken individually, seems harmless. The collective sense of identity that results allows members of the group to participate in being part of horrific or heinous actions that individually they might resist doing themselves.

Ditzler (2004) describes a terrorist typology promulgated by the U.S. Army Command and General Staff College (*U.S. Army Field Manual* [Terrorism Research Center, 1997]). The typology also incorporates some of the research conducted at RAND (B. Hoffman, 1993). The typology identifies three motivational categories: (1) the rationally motivated terrorist; (2) the psychologically motivated terrorist; and (3) the culturally motivated terrorist.

Rationally motivated terrorists are those who consider the goals of the organization and the possible consequences of their actions. They develop well-defined and theoretically achievable goals that may involve political, social, economic, or other specific objectives. In many cases, rationally motivated terrorists try to avoid loss of life but focus instead on destroying infrastructures, buildings, and other symbolic structures to get their message across.

Psychologically motivated terrorists are driven by "a profound sense of failure or inadequacy for which the perpetrator may seek redress through revenge" (Ditzler, 2004, p. 202). The attraction to terrorism is usually based on the psychological benefits of group affiliation and collective identity. They are especially drawn to terrorist groups who have a charismatic leader. One variation of the psychologically motivated terrorist is the lone wolf operation, "for whom the validation of the self is not derived through group affiliation, but through the sense of power, mastery, and autonomy that attends to the ability to make unilateral decisions" (p. 203). A classic example of this type of terrorist is Theodore Kaczynski, known as the Unabomber. Often, lone wolf terrorists have strong feelings of social alienation, anger, and extreme antigovernment ideology. In most instances, they view themselves as victims of the "system."

Another variation is the terrorist who operates in a small group, with or without a well-defined organization. However, like the lone wolf, members of the small group feel alienated and consider themselves victims of the system. Timothy McVeigh, Terry Nichols, and perhaps others involved in the Oklahoma City bombing illustrate this type.

Culturally motivated terrorists are driven by fear of irreparable damage to their way of living, national heritage, or culture by an organization, foreign country, or powerful factions. Most often, religion is the aspect that generates the fervor or passion in the group. That is, national or cultural groups who are largely governed or socially defined by a particular system of faith are often constantly vigilant for forces that may eradicate their religious way of life or cultural identity. Ditzler (2004) gives the example of Afghanistan under the Taliban, where "Islam provided not only a system of religious faith as understood in the West, but the entire system of civil and criminal law, political organization, and social behavior" (p. 203). Under such conditions a perceived threat to the faith would be cause for alarm and a threat to the group's existence. However, most members of the religious group do not respond to the threat with acts of terrorism. One of the most troubling outcomes of the events of September 11 is the widespread and unjustified distrust of people of Islamic faiths.

Consequences

The nature of terrorism is basically psychological; its aim is to create crippling fears and psychological debilitation in a civilian population (Levant, 2002). Ditzler (2004, p. 189) writes, "Terrorist acts are defined to a large degree by their impact, and especially their psychological effects." Without a doubt, "the September 11 attack has achieved its purpose: to create a global psychological state of fear, uncertainty, and terror" (Marsella, 2004, p. 39). And given the psychological nature of terrorism, it is clear that psychology has an important role to play in understanding it, counteracting it, and treating its traumatizing effects (Levant, Barbanel, & DeLeon, 2004). Not until September 11, however, did psychologists demonstrate a sudden and dramatic increase in interest in investigating, studying, and writing about terrorism (Marsella, 2004). Since then, the number of books and articles and the amount of commentary on the psychological foundations of modern-day terrorism by psychologists, psychiatrists, and other mental health professionals have increased enormously.

After the attacks of September 11, 44% of the adults in a national survey said they experienced a significant amount of stress and 90% said they felt some degree of stress following the attack (Schuster et al., 2001). However, it has also been shown that ethnic background, gender, and age influence psychological reactions to terrorism (K. Walker & Chestnut, 2003). Many participants in the Walker–Chestnut survey thought that the United States has been overly involved in the affairs of other countries and now those countries are retaliating. In addition, participants felt that the United States has developed a false sense of security in believing that terrorist groups will not retaliate for the U.S. policies imposed on other countries and cultural groups.

Although psychologists and other mental health professionals provide psychological services to persons adversely affected by terrorism, it is equally important to try to prevent it. One important point made at the beginning of this section bears repeating. "The overwhelming majority of evidence indicates that responding to violence with violence only provokes further violence" (Wagner & Long, 2004, p. 215). Aggressive military action is rarely the solution, unless it is in response to an imminent, documented threat to a country and its inhabitants. International terrorism is unlikely to be reduced until the root causes of the violence are addressed and corrected. "These causes often include real or imagined injustice in meeting basic human needs for coping with difficult life conditions, insecurity, lack of self-determination, and disrespect for one's social identity" (p. 219).

In the above section, we have focused almost exclusively on international terrorism, with a few allusions to domestic terrorism on the part of individuals or small groups. Nevertheless, the psychological principles outlined can apply to domestic terrorism as well. Both historically and in modern times we can point to chilling examples of such terrorism, including activities of the Ku Klux Klan, neo-Nazi groups, radical environmentalists, and radical "right-to-life" members and groups. Virtually all of the concepts we have discussed—for example, cognitive reconstruction, strong hierarchical organization, perceptions of relative deprivation, diffusion of responsibility, and dehumanization—may be applied to domestic as well as to international terrorism.

PSYCHOLOGICAL FACTORS IN GENERAL VIOLENT CRIME

Impulsive Violence

Violent crime is often seen as resulting from impulsive, spur-of-the-moment, and unpredictable acts of enraged individuals. The person who savagely assaults and sometimes kills is operating on impulse, slashing out at a victim without much forethought or planned strategy. This point of view, of course, partly supports the argument for gun control. If the gun had not been available, the perpetrator would not have wounded or killed the victim—at least not as easily. We have also seen that with the significant increase in the technology and availability of rapid-fire and automatic weapons, the number of innocent people killed by mass murderers has increased dramatically in the past 10 years. The technology and availability of weapons, however, are only part of the story.

Some theorists believe that certain personalities or dispositions are more likely than others to react violently in certain circumstances. In *Violent Men*, Hans Toch (1969) theorizes that most violent episodes can be traced to well-learned, systematic strategies of violence that some people have found to be effective in dealing with conflictual, interpersonal relationships. Thus, violence is not simply the act of a person acting on impulse; it is the act of one who has habitual response patterns of reacting violently in particular situations. It is Toch's impression that, if we examine the history of violent persons, we discover surprising consistency in their approaches to interpersonal relationships. They learned, probably in childhood, that violence worked for them. They used violent responses effectively to obtain positive and negative reinforcement. They got what they wanted or avoided unpleasant situations by being violent.

Toch posits that humiliating affronts and threats to reputation and status are major contributing factors to violence. A blow to the self-esteem of the person who has few skills for resolving disputes and conflicts (such as verbal skills) may precipitate violence. This is especially true if the person's subculture advocates that disputes be settled through physical aggression.

In a similar vein, Berkowitz (1970) hypothesized that people sometimes react violently, not because they anticipate pleasure or displeasure from their actions, but because "situational stimuli have evoked the response (they) are predisposed or set to make in that setting" (p. 140). That is, individuals have been conditioned—specifically, classically conditioned—to react violently by prior experiences in similar situations. In some instances, according to Berkowitz, powerful environmental stimuli essentially produce impulsive behavior. Under these conditions, one's "thinking" becomes highly simplified and one responds "mindlessly" to stimuli in a well-learned manner. Thus, some people "fall into" a rage, striking out in an impulsive and automatic response to unpleasant feelings brought on by aversive or noxious stimuli. Aversive or noxious stimuli can be anything from a face one "doesn't like" to physical abuse by another. Nevertheless, individuals are not are likely to strike out unless they have been in a rage in past situations.

A similar view was expressed by Zillmann (1979, 1983), who believed that cognitive or thinking processes are greatly impaired at extreme levels of emotional arousal. Under high excitement, such as anger, behavior normally controlled by thought becomes controlled by mindless habits. Therefore, at very high levels of emotional upset, hostile or aggressive behaviors are likely to become "impulsive," a term Zillmann associates with habit strength. The behaviors have been learned so well that they appear quickly and without thought on the part of the individual. In other words, they seem to be "mindless" actions. Impulsive behavior, then, is not unusual, out-of-character behavior; it reflects habitual responses that might be rejected by the individual under low-arousal or normal conditions.

Toch, Berkowitz, and Zillmann all suggest that when experiencing powerful emotional reactions, many people become incapable of considering the consequences of their violent acts. High arousal inhibits cognitive processing to the point that they may not think before acting. The environment and the relevant external stimuli take control over the internal mediation processes, which have been weakened by extremely high levels of arousal. Of course, while these "arousal" perspectives explain the most frequent and common violent incidents found in a majority of societies, many serial and mass murderers, as we have seen in this chapter, are more thoughtful and calculating in their killings. These multicide offenders tend to fantasize, dream, and cognitively rehearse their violence before actually carrying it out.

Overcontrolled and Undercontrolled Offenders

One of the most heuristic explanations of violence was advanced by Edwin Megargee (1966), who identified two distinct personalities in the highly assaultive population: the undercontrolled and the chronically overcontrolled aggressive types. The **undercontrolled personality** has few inhibitions against aggressive behavior and frequently engages in violence when frustrated or provoked. Aggression is a behavioral pattern that becomes the habitual response when the person is upset or angry.

By contrast, the chronically **overcontrolled personality** has well-established inhibitions against aggressive behavior and rigidly adheres to them, even in the face of provocation. This person has learned (or been conditioned) about the consequences (real, imagined, or implied) of engaging in violence. The overcontrolled individual is the socialized, or perhaps oversocialized, person who readily associates violations of social mores and regulations dictated by others with potentially punishing consequences. Even more than others, this individual will say, "If I violate the rules, I will be punished." Recalling Eysenck's dichotomy, we might posit that the introvert is much like the overcontrolled personality, while the extravert exhibits many features of the undercontrolled.

According to Megargee, however, there may come a time when frustration and provocation overwhelm overcontrolled persons. If this happens, they may strike out violently, perhaps even exceeding the violence exhibited by undercontrolled people. The undercontrolled–overcontrolled typology, therefore, suggests that the more brutal and unexpected slayings are often performed by usually inhibited, restricted individuals. It also seems that numerous family mass murders are committed by overcontrolled family members. Thus, neighbors, friends, and relatives are shocked by a homicide committed by a "nice, quiet, well-mannered boy." The following excerpt from a news story is over 25 years old, but it is still representative of a seemingly unexplainable crime committed by someone who may have been overcontrolled.

> A 16-year-old choir boy described as a "hell of a nice kid" was arraigned here Thursday as funeral services were held for three girls he is accused of stabbing to death.
>
> The girls' bodies were found Monday, face down in a stream in deep woods about a quarter of a mile from their homes.
>
> The state medical examiner said two of the girls were stabbed 40 times each and the third eight times. The death weapon was believed to be a hunting knife. (Tom Stuckey, Associated Press release, October 14, 1977)

In an empirical test of Megargee's hypothesis, R. Blackburn (1968) divided a group of violent offenders into extreme assaultives and moderate assaultives. *Extreme assaultives* were defined as those convicted of murder, manslaughter, or attempted murder. *Moderate assaultives* included persons who had wounded with intent to cause serious bodily harm or who had maliciously wounded or assaulted. On the basis of personality measures, extreme assaultives were significantly more introverted, conforming, and overcontrolled and less hostile than moderate assaultives. Moreover, their extreme aggressive behaviors had occurred only after prolonged or repeated provocation (real or imagined).

In another study (Tupin, Mahar, & Smith, 1973), convicted murderers with a history of violent offenses were found to have a much higher incidence of hyperactivity, fighting, temper tantrums, and other extraverted features during childhood than a comparable group of murderers without previous criminal records of violence. These "sudden murderers"—those without a previous record—were also found in other clinical studies to be introverted and plagued by feelings of inadequacy, loneliness, and frustration (e.g., N. Blackburn, Weiss, & Lamberti, 1960; J. Weiss, Lamberti, & N. Blackburn, 1960). These are all features of the overcontrolled personality type.

Lee, Zimbardo, and Bertholf (1977) reported a limited but pertinent study using a small group of 19 murderers. Ten were classified as sudden murderers because their background reflected no other criminal offenses, while nine were regarded as habitual offenders with prior arrests for violent acts. The Stanford Shyness Survey and Minnesota Multiphasic Personality Inventory (MMPI) were administered to both groups. Eight of the ten sudden murderers indicated they were "shy" on the Stanford Scale, compared to only one of the nine habitual offenders. According to MMPI results, the sudden murderer group tended to be significantly more overcontrolled and passive than the habitual offender group, who tended to be more undercontrolled and assertive. These results combined with other observations suggested to the researchers that people who are overcontrolled are capable of more extreme violence when "inner restraints" break down than are individuals who hold their behavior under looser control.

At present, there is some evidence to suggest that violent offenders may differ along a continuum of undercontrolled–overcontrolled, with most at the polar ends of the continuum. We could further hypothesize that undercontrolled violent offenders will be habitual criminals. Overcontrolled offenders, who usually do not have criminal records, are more likely to engage in one quick, highly violent or murderous episode.

There is also some evidence, however, indicating that undercontrols and overcontrols are found in nonviolent populations about as often as found in violent populations (Henderson, 1983). This finding implies that the Megargee schema may not offer as much help in explaining the various types of violence as originally expected. Furthermore, the over- and undercontrolled dimension does not fully account for the role of situational parameters. For example, persons who are passive and unassertive are more likely to experience intense frustrations and to find themselves in many situations where they feel threat-ened, insecure, and powerless. The Lee et al. group (1977) tried to relate this lack of social and verbal skills to sudden murderers, who are typically shy individuals without the necessary interpersonal skills to assert themselves in social situations. Obviously, however, most shy people do not become sudden murderers.

When people lack the skills and strategies to modify at least some of their social situations, feelings of helplessness usually result. These feelings are in turn likely to provoke one of two response patterns: approach (attack) or avoidance (withdrawal). The withdrawal response, as theorized by Martin Seligman (1975), is often called *reactive depression* or **learned helplessness**. People feel there is nothing that can be done about their predicament, so why bother? This response pattern is vividly illustrated by powerless people living under dire poverty conditions, who perceive that they have little opportunity for change—a life without hope.

An alternative response is to attack, to lash out in desperation, especially if individuals believe this response pattern will be effective in improving their cir-cumstances. Sudden murderers, who have been passive and pushed around all their lives, may be resorting to one final attempt to change what is happening to them. Their homicidal violence may be a desperate response to gain immediate control over their lives, without consideration for the future consequences of their act. As we see below, some contemporary psychological research suggests that alternative strategies are available.

COGNITIVE SELF-REGULATION AND VIOLENCE

The subject of impulsive behavior brings us to what some social learning and cognitive theorists call **self-regulatory mechanisms**. Psychological research is finding that this may be an extremely important factor in violent behavior. In fact, considerable research indicates that treatment approaches that improve the self-regulatory systems of violent people hold the greatest promise for reducing violence (Serin & Preston, 2001). According to social learning theory (e.g., Ban-dura, 1983) and social cognition theory (Bandura, 1986, 1989), we are able to ex-ercise considerable cognitive control over our behavior. Cognitive capacity enables us to transcend the present and think about the future as well as the past, even in the absence of immediate environmental cues. This conceptual thinking ability lets us guide our own behavior by thinking about its possible outcomes. However, circumstances sometimes weaken cognitive control and fa-cilitate impulsive actions. Under certain conditions, therefore, our actions are di-rected more by external stimuli than by cognitive self-regulatory mechanisms.

The self-regulatory process presumes the development and refinement of cognitive structures and concepts, which is learning. As stated earlier, the world as we know it is based on our cognitive structures, which are nonspecific but organized representations of prior experiences. Some people possess more structures than others, and some deviate from what the social mainstream regards as "accurate" structures of the world and human nature. People with many sophisticated structures can evaluate behavior in more complex ways than can people with few, crude structures. For example, someone with a large storehouse of sophisticated concepts would be less inclined to label a murderer simply "sick" or "an animal" and, instead, would see him or her as an individual having a complex of different beliefs and motives.

In normal circumstances, we perceive, interpret, compare, and act on the basis of these structures, which we refer to as personal standards. If we do not like what we are doing, we can change our behavior, justify it, or try to stop thinking about it. We can also reward and punish ourselves for our conduct. Self-punishment is expressed as guilt or remorse following actions we consider foreign to our standards. In most instances, however, we prefer self-reinforcement to punishment. Therefore, we behave in ways that correspond to our cognitive structures. We anticipate the feelings of guilt we will experience for alien actions, and thus we restrain ourselves. "Anticipatory self-condemning reactions for violating personal standards ordinarily serve as self-deterrents against reprehensible acts" (Bandura, 1983, p. 30). Therefore, each of us develops personal standards or codes of conduct that are maintained by self-reinforcement or self-punishment, as well as by external reinforcement and punishment.

Our standards may be built around simplistic beliefs: "There is a sucker in every crowd" or "People are basically mean and brutal" or "The surest route to success is to take care of number one." People who have adopted the "me first" or "it's all about me" approach, and who are convinced that rigorous competition and aggression are the best strategies for achieving success, may find that aggression—even violent behavior—is a source of self-reinforcement and pride (Toch, 1977). In the extreme, "number one" individuals lack self-reprimands for aggression and harmful conduct. Their personal standards about human nature are a built-in justification for their cruel acts.

Standards are not confined to individuals but may be characteristic of entire cultures and societies. Some cultures, subcultures, or groups try to develop ethical and moral standards of conduct in their members. We might ask at this point to what extent American society cultivates nonviolent behavior.

Relating all of this specifically to aggression and violence, we can see that personal and group standards dictate much of our behavior. If one's philosophy is that "life is cheap," and if insensitive conduct is the norm, violence can become a way of life. Some people, therefore, are cruel and violent not necessarily to receive reward from the external environment, but because violence reflects their internal standard and implicit theory of human nature. Others, perhaps the majority, have adopted standards and have built cognitive structures that do not condone hurtful or reprehensible conduct.

To some extent, we have oversimplified self-regulatory mechanism theory in an effort to introduce some of its concepts. Self-regulation does not invariably operate across all situations. Otherwise, how do we explain destructive and reprehensible conduct perpetrated by apparently decent, moral people over the centuries in the name of religious principles and righteous ideologies? What, if anything, justifies deliberate, planned, large-scale violence such as bombing or war? What about terrorism in the name of some higher principle? How do we explain mob violence, in which seemingly good people appear to be swept along by their emotions or by the crowd? Why don't self-regulatory mechanisms operate then, when they are most needed?

Social learning theory explains some of this by hypothesizing that in certain circumstances self-regulatory processes become *disengaged* from conduct. "In the social learning analysis, moral people perform culpable acts through processes that disengage evaluative self-reactions for such conduct . . ." (Bandura, 1983, p. 31). This disengagement may be what takes place in impulsive violence. As described by Berkowitz (1983) and Zillmann (1983), high levels of emotional arousal take our attention away from our internal mechanisms of control. When we become extremely angry, for example, we often say and do things we later regret. We feel upset, remorseful, and guilty, and we wish we could take back our words and actions. If we had carefully considered and evaluated the consequences of our behavior, we would probably have acted differently. But in the heat of emotion, our self-regulatory system, with all its standards and values, was held in abeyance. As we get older, however, we generally learn from experience to pay closer attention to our internal control mechanisms, and we engage in fewer impulsive outbursts. This "mellowing" feature may partly account for the lower rates of impulsive violence as age increases.

Treatment approaches that focus on arousal reduction techniques, interpersonal skills acquisition, and correcting faulty cognitive reasoning are most likely to be effective in reducing violent behavior (Serin & Preston, 2001). Research has consistently demonstrated that violent offenders (both juvenile and adult) have a dominant collection of irrational beliefs, hostile attribution biases, and usually uncontrolled anger. A prominent example of irrational beliefs found in rapists is the belief that women want to be raped.

Regardless of our personal standards against violence or doing harm to others, therefore, we all may occasionally engage in harmful or even violent conduct. When this happens, we use several approaches to convince ourselves of the "rightness" of our actions. We may feel, for example, that under certain conditions some people need to be taught a lesson. An errant child may be hit; an experimental subject may be shocked; a murderer may be executed in the service of justice. The problematic logic of these explanations becomes evident when they are turned around and used to justify actions of which most people disapprove. As we saw in the section on terrorism, terrorists justify their acts of violence under the premise that they are accomplishing a greater good, like freeing a society from tyrannical rule. Ideally, then, we should very narrowly define conditions under which physical aggression and violence might be justified (e.g., to save another human life).

We may also neutralize our internal standards to some extent by concluding, "Others are doing it, many of them much more than I am" or "Most people cheat on their income tax returns; it's part of the game." Certainly, this perspective is relevant to participants engaged in corporate or white-collar crime, a topic we return to in Chapter 11. In addition, as we saw in Chapter 2, on juvenile delinquency, some groups neutralize their criminal conduct by removing from it the onus of "badness." In fact, engaging in the "bad" conduct may increase one's status within the group.

Another way in which we may downplay our internal standards, especially those against violence, is by convincing ourselves that some individuals are less than human, more animal-like than most. As we learned earlier in the chapter, we may **dehumanize** people who commit terribly cruel and heinous murders, in effect seeing them as being closer, to animals than most other people. Some people justify capital punishment on the basis that some criminals are subhuman. Dehumanization helps explain the numerous lynchings of African Americans in U.S. history and the treatment of the Jews in Nazi Germany. In war, we dehumanize the enemy by using derogatory epithets. Like justifying the "rightness" of violence, however, dehumanization also works from both perspectives. Thus, the mass or serial murderer and the individual who continually engages in assaultive behavior, as we have seen, view victims as objects divested of humanity. The offender feels little remorse for any suffering inflicted and does not worry about anticipatory self-punishment. As we have seen, it becomes more difficult to behave cruelly toward others as they become personalized and humanized. In other words, if an assailant becomes acquainted with a potential victim, there is less likelihood of cruelty. This would seem to be especially true of crimes in which killing the victim is not the primary goal.

Finally, we may also disengage our personal standards from our conduct when we are told by a legitimate authority to do something reprehensible. Again as we learned in the terrorism section, when someone who possesses legitimate power commands us to do something, we are, in a sense, relieved of personal responsibility for the conduct, even if the conduct is alien to our personal standards. This concept is called *displacement of responsibility* by Bandura (2004), *strong respect for authority* by Staub (2004), and *obedience to authority* by Milgram (1974).

In sum, the self-regulatory system we develop is not invariant or automatic, but dynamic and subject to certain experiences and circumstances. Moreover, many events are ambiguous and do not fit readily into our existing cognitive templates. Under these conditions, we are more likely to seek clues from outside sources. Nevertheless, the value of the self-regulatory system is its tendency to guide our behavior toward what we believe is the right thing to do in a particular situation. The more we believe in our internal standards, the less prone we will be to rely on outside sources, even under stress or pressure situations. This suggests that the best internal standards are those we have developed ourselves, rather than those imposed or advocated by an external group, which we embrace only for convenience or for appearances.

Interestingly, some research suggests that women are more likely to see aggression as a breakdown of self-regulatory mechanisms than are men (A. Campbell, Muncer, & Coyle, 1992). To women, aggressive behavior ". . . represents a personal failure to adhere to standards of behaviour which they (and others) set for themselves, and consequently they view it negatively" (p. 98). Conversely, men are more likely to see aggression as a means of imposing control and dominance over others and, therefore, regard aggressive behavior as more positive.

Fortunately, most people have developed an internal standard that to wantonly harm another person is wrong. Therefore, the fact that a vast majority of people do not engage in violent behavior is not simply because of a classically conditioned reflex. Rather, it is most likely because they have adopted a belief system that subscribes to the view that it is wrong to harm another human being, at least without just cause. Of course, the human tendency to justify one's behavior—the just-cause argument—is often inseparable from the most heinous violence in human history. We justify large-scale organized violence (wars), claiming we must protect ourselves, our families, and our way of life from the brutal (less than human) enemy.

The next section focuses on mob behavior and what happens to the self-regulatory mechanisms of normally gentle people caught up in a madding crowd. The crowd, it seems, often robs the individual of his or her identity, and consequently, his or her usual reliance on personal standards of conduct. Some of the most violent behavior is exhibited not by single individuals, but by excited groups, especially large ones. Physical assaults that occur in the midst of riots, demonstrations, or celebrations, vigilante-instigated lynchings or beatings, gang rapes, and public stonings all illustrate this mob violence.

DEINDIVIDUATION AND CROWD VIOLENCE

The powerful effect of crowds on individual behavior has interested social scientists since the early 1900s. Crowd influence is usually studied under the rubric *collective behavior*, which includes riots, gang rapes, panics, lynchings, demonstrations, and revolutions. For our purposes, we are concerned with collective behavior only as it affects the instigation and maintenance of violence.

One of the first theorists of collective behavior was Gustave LeBon, whose 1896 book *The Crowd* is regarded as the classic study of groups. Because his views were colored by the French Revolution, LeBon did not take kindly to individual behavior swayed by the crowd. Humans in a crowd are like a herd of animals, he said, easily swayed or frightened. LeBon believed that those who normally are nonviolent and law-abiding are capable of the kind of violence, intolerance, and general cruelty found in the most primitive savages. The person enmeshed in the mob loses sensibility and the ability to reason and forfeits his or her own mind to the crowd. The collective mind is dangerously brutal and destructive to people and property. According to LeBon, even educated people become simple-minded and irrational under its influence. Essentially, LeBon claimed, each person comes under the control of the reflexive "spinal cord" rather than the cerebral cortex.

Most of us have seen dramatizations of a "berserk" mob clamoring for the destruction of some political, social, or physical institution or for swift "justice" for an individual or group. Descriptions of mob actions often liken them to brush fires that grow in intensity and are quickly out of control. However, since true mob actions are naturally occurring and spontaneous events, it is difficult to place them under the scrutiny of scientific, systematic investigation. The processes involved in mob action are still not well understood, therefore. Some social psychologists (e.g., Diener, 1980; Zimbardo, 1970) have attempted laboratory studies of mob or group violence, generally by approximating conditions that might bring out aggression and positing that, if allowed to continue, the aggression would likely result in violence. Obviously, they must stop far short of actual violence, so whether it would have occurred remains speculative. The procedure of trying to mimic an event under laboratory conditions is called a **simulation**.

Zimbardo (1970) believed that deindividuation accounts for much of the tendency of otherwise "tame" individuals to engage in antisocial, violent behavior. Recall from Chapter 4 that deindividuation includes a reduction in feelings of personal distinctiveness, identifiability, and personal responsibility. Furthermore, in a crowd the threshold of normally restrained behavior is lowered. In other words, people feel anonymous, less responsible for their behavior, and less inhibited. According to Zimbardo, these conditions encourage the antisocial behavior associated with selfishness, greed, hostility, lust, cruelty, and destruction.

In one widely cited experiment, Zimbardo manipulated two variables, feelings of anonymity and features of the victim. He randomly assigned female college students to deindividuation and "identifiable" groups. Subjects in the deindividuation group wore shapeless white lab coats and hoods over their heads and worked in dimly lit conditions. The experimenters avoided using their names. By contrast, participants in the identifiable groups felt anything but anonymous. They wore large name tags, were greeted by name, worked under fully illuminated conditions, and wore their own clothes with no added lab coats or hoods.

Subjects were told the project was set up to study empathy. The real purpose, of course, was to study the relationship between deindividuation and aggression. Each subject listened to a five-minute recorded interview between her future "victim" and the experimenter. Some victims were portrayed as warm, sincere, honest persons; others, as obnoxious, self-centered, conceited, and critical. After each interview, the subjects were allowed to administer shock to the interviewees they had heard on tape. They were allowed to observe the reactions of their victims via of a one-way mirror. Aggressive behavior of the subjects was measured by the length of time a painful electrical shock was administered. "Victims"—who actually received no shock—were trained to writhe, twist, and grimace.

Recall now that Zimbardo was manipulating two variables, anonymity (loss of personal identity) and features of the victim (environmental stimuli). Thus, some subjects were hooded, while others were well-identified. Some victims were pleasant and likable; others were obnoxious. Zimbardo reasoned that members of the deindividuation group would administer shocks of longer duration because of the diffusion of responsibility and loss of personal identity. He also hypothesized that victim features would be irrelevant, because the heightened arousal experienced under deindividuation would interfere with the ability to discriminate between the victims. Put another way, the excitement and resulting arousal engendered by shocking someone without the threat of any repercussions would prevent discernment of the target (the person receiving the shock).

One additional hypothesis was tested. Zimbardo predicted that subjects in the deindividuation group would administer longer shocks as the experiment progressed. He believed the act of administering shock without responsibility would be exciting and reinforcing for its own sake (what he called "affective proprioceptive feedback"). Zimbardo predicted that members of the deindividuation group would increase the duration of shock administered to the victim as the experiment progressed. In brief, they find that the antisocial behavior feels "so good" each time they do it that the behavior builds on itself in intensity (vigor) and frequency.

Results of the experiment supported all three hypotheses. The deindividuation group shocked victims twice as long as the identifiable group. The deindividuation group also administered the same levels of shock, regardless of the victim's personality features. And finally, this group shocked for longer periods as the experiment progressed.

Zimbardo concluded that deindividuated aggression is not controlled by the social environment; it is unresponsive to both the situation and the state or characteristics of the victim. That is, the high arousal generated by the excitement of a crowd reduces both (1) a person's private self-awareness and (2) his or her ability to discriminate among external stimuli, such as victim characteristics. The participant is no longer guided by self-regulatory mechanisms and is "blind" to such stimuli as the victim's distress or discomfort. The aggressor loses individuality to the collective mind of the crowd; he or she neither feels compassion nor considers the circumstances. The victim may plead, beg, cry, or scream, but these stimuli will have little effect on the crowd behavior. Even a prestigious and powerful authority figure may be unable to stop the violence once self-identity is obliterated by the furor of the crowd.

Zimbardo's research design, like that of Milgram, has been criticized extensively for its questionable use of subject deception and shock (albeit simulated) and its focus on the negative aspects of human behavior. In a sense, these types of experiments constitute a form of psychological entrapment: Would people really act this way if not prompted by an experimenter? In the wake of such experiments, the National Institute of Mental Health, the American Psychological Association, and other organizations have adopted ethical guidelines that are applied to the funding and approval of research. Experiments like Zimbardo's, therefore, are unlikely to be replicated. Nevertheless, their possible implications cannot be ignored.

Diener (1980) disagrees with the tenets of Zimbardo's deindividuation theory, postulating that deindividuated behavior is responsive to situational or victim characteristics. He believes that a person's normal self-regulatory behavior is reduced by the unusual and exciting activity of the crowd and that this reduced private self-awareness creates an internal state of deindividuation. Since individuals have trouble retrieving their standards of appropriate conduct, they become more responsive to environmental cues (Prentice-Dunn & Rogers, 1982, 1983). In crowds, people do report a strong loss of individual identity, an overwhelming tendency to concentrate on the moment rather than the future, and substantially altered thinking and emotion (Prentice-Dunn & Rogers, 1983). They become less aware of thoughts, moods, bodily states, and other internal processes. Think of the athlete caught up in the excitement of the game, who continues to play while seriously injured. After the game, the athlete might exclaim about a fractured arm, "It didn't feel that serious!"

According to Diener, because deindividuated individuals do not pay attention to their internal processes, including their self-regulatory capabilities, they depend more on environmental cues for behavioral direction. Thus, when aggressive and violent cues are present, they are far more likely than usual to engage in violence. It is Diener's contention that if the victim of a mob action could, in some way, be "humanized," the crowd might stop its brutality. In other words, perpetrators' attention should be directed toward the victim rather than the violence being displayed by other actors. Diener also believes that participants in a mob action can be made to pay closer attention to their internal regulation norms. His hypothesis deserves to be tested by further research. Of course, whether the cries and pleas of the victim during an attack actually could alter the crowd behavior is a question unlikely to be answered by laboratory research. Furthermore, because the theories of Zimbardo and Diener are based on laboratory studies, we cannot conclude that they generalize to actual situations. They do, however, suggest possible explanations for violent mob behavior.

SUMMARY AND CONCLUSIONS

This chapter has taken a closer look at specific types of criminal homicide. We have also examined the investigative methods and criminal profiling used to identify offenders, particularly serial offenders. Multiple murder was the focus of the early parts of the chapter. Although these offenses are rare, the social and emotional impacts they have on a community (and society in general) are substantial. We reviewed the empirical data and professional observations on serial, spree, and mass murder, as well as terrorism.

The latter part of the chapter focused on psychological explanations of violence in general. That is, when we survey the vast majority of violent crime, we find very little mystery and few intriguing characteristics. Serial and mass murders are clearly not ordinary, everyday violence. The psychological perspective suggests that three central issues surround common violence, including the violence that results in loss of life: (1) self-control, as dictated by self-regulatory mechanisms; (2) emotional arousal; and (3) individual reference points for behavioral guidance, which may be either internal or external. Violence is most often committed while the participants are under very high levels of emotional arousal, particularly anger. High arousal seems to reduce the ability to attend to internal standards of conduct and general self-awareness. Furthermore, high arousal seems to make people feel less responsible for their actions; they often claim, "I don't know what came over me" or "I couldn't help it." In short, high arousal renders people more susceptible to "mindless" behaviors and places them under the influence of external stimuli or events.

Self-regulatory mechanisms develop through socialization and personal beliefs about what is right or appropriate, wrong or inappropriate. Under normal conditions, self-regulatory mechanisms control behavior by providing cognitive templates for what is proper behavior for a specific situation. The effect of arousal on these self-regulatory mechanisms appears to be especially important in explaining street or domestic violence, in which the violence is spontaneous, highly charged, and often used as a way of settling personal conflicts.

Individual construct systems are highly similar to the self-regulation process but refer in this context to the human ability to justify or neutralize conduct, no matter how reprehensible. Self-regulation refers to behavioral control; the construct system enables a person to perform an act now and deal with it later. Human beings, with their intricate cognitive equipment, have an uncanny knack for neutralizing, disregarding, minimizing, rationalizing, and misjudging their deeds. We have an enormous capacity for disengaging our beliefs and our internal standards from our actions. Bandura (1983) lists six common disengagement practices we use for dealing with our own reprehensible, antisocial conduct. It is instructive to examine each of these strategies here.

First, people do not ordinarily engage in antisocial conduct until they have justified to themselves the rightness or morality of their actions. Reprehensible acts can be made honorable through cognitive restructuring. Thus, a distressed father, convinced that he must save his family from the evil of the world, kills his children, his wife, and then himself. In essence, he reconstructed his construct system to fit what he believed was the right thing to do in the circumstances. Another example is that of a moral young man who believes killing is wrong and who voluntarily goes to war to protect his country. At first, these two actions may seem to have nothing in common. However, they both represent cognitive restructuring.

The second disengagement practice—related to the first—is that of people convincing themselves that their violent acts are really trivial and not all that bad compared to what others have done. In war we convince ourselves that the atrocities committed by the enemy are far worse than anything we do. A rapist might convince himself that rape is not really that serious, since no "real" physical harm comes to the victim.

The third strategy involves the power of language. One of the costs of human intellectual ability is the considerable power of words; they allow us to justify our actions with relative ease. We use euphemisms to neutralize reprehensible behavior. For example, intelligence manuals use words like neutralize and terminate instead of assassinate and kill. The euphemisms carry less onus and cause less disruption to moral beliefs. In Chapter 2, on juvenile delinquency, we noted that youth subcultures employ various euphemisms to neutralize their antisocial acts.

The fourth strategy—one most commonly found in group violence—is the diffusion of responsibility. Statements that best typify this practice include, "I was just following orders," "I was just following the crowd," and "The executive board decided that it was in the best interest of the economy (and the company) to continue production, despite some risk to the health of others." These assertions have the effect of displacing responsibility for one's actions to others or to forces outside oneself.

The fifth strategy is to not even think about the consequences of one's actions. Here, people convince themselves that the consequences are not important. Alternately, they manage to detach themselves from the aftermath of violent actions. For example, the bombardier or the person who pushes the button that will release lethal chemicals onto a civilian population is not only following orders (diffusion of responsibility) but also probably not allowing thoughts about the tragedy that will result.

Finally, the sixth practice is to dehumanize the victim. "She was loose and got what she deserved." "He was scum." The enemies are labeled "gooks" or something akin to vicious animals. Dehumanization removes all the human, dignifying qualities from the victim or intended victim. As Bandura (1983, p. 32) points out: "Many conditions of contemporary life are conducive to dehumanization. Bureaucratization, automation, urbanization, and high social mobility lead people to relate to each other in anonymous, impersonal ways." These impersonal, dehumanizing aspects of life facilitate violence and make living with it possible.

CHAPTER 10

SEXUAL OFFENSES

Sexual behavior in many societies is a subject fraught with moral codes, taboos, norm expectations, religious injunctions, myths, and unscientific conclusions. In the United States, the daring venture of Albert Kinsey and his colleagues in publishing the scientific evidence they had gathered at the Institute for Sexual Research dispelled numerous myths and corrected fallacies about sex. Many still linger, however, especially with reference to the sex offender, for whom society has little tolerance. Moreover, society often does not distinguish between types of sex offenses. "Degenerates" who expose themselves to passersby or watch unsuspecting women undressing are sometimes as likely to be feared or to attract disgust and anger as are rapists and child molesters. Often, the community clamors for the strict and speedy prosecution of the offender, who is considered a deranged or evil person (or animal) driven by some inner sinister force, from whom citizens must be protected.

Sexual offenders are frequently viewed as a homogeneous class of individuals. Research shows, however, that they vary widely in the frequency and type of sexual activity they engage in, and they differ in personal attributes like age, background, personality, race, religion, beliefs, attitudes, and interpersonal skills (Knight, Rosenberg, & Schneider, 1985). There is no single profile that encompasses a majority of sex offenders. The features of their crimes also differ markedly among offenders, including time and place, the gender and age of the victim, the degree of planning the offense, and the amount of violence used or intended (Knight et al., 1985).

Surprisingly, adolescent males commit 20% to 30% of all rapes and 30% to 50% of all child molestations (Becker & Johnson, 2001). And 70% of these adolescent sex offenders come from two-parent homes, most attend school and achieve average grades, and very few suffer from major mental disorders (Becker & Johnson, 2001). The median age of juvenile sex offenders is between 14 and 15, while the median age of their victims is 7 (Righthand & Welch, 2001). Researchers also have begun to focus on sexual offending by girls, a subject that until recently was virtually ignored (Becker & Johnson, 2001). There is also considerable evidence that prepubescent children—both boys and girls—may commit sexual offenses at a rate much higher than commonly supposed. Several studies have reported sexual aggression in children as young as three or four years of age (Araji, 1997). In addition, a surprisingly large number of preadolescent girls are reported to be sexually aggressive toward other children, and these girls often engage in behaviors that are just as aggressive as boys' (Araji, 1997). Victims of preadolescent offenders are generally very young (averaging between age 4 and age 7), most often are female (when the offender is a male), and typically are siblings, friends, or acquaintances (Righthand & Welch, 2001).

Male juvenile sex offenders participate in a variety of sexual activities. In one study, Zolondek, Abel, Northey, and Jordan (2001) found that 10%–30% of the juvenile sex offenders made obscene phone calls and engaged in phone sex as well as a variety of paraphilias, such as exhibitionism, fetishism, frottage, and voyeurism.

Juvenile sex offenders not only participate in sexual activities, but also tend to commit other crimes, such as shoplifting, burglary, cruelty to animals, arson, and physical assaults (Knight & Prentky, 1993). Many also exhibit poor or inadequate interpersonal and social skills (Knight & Prentky, 1993). Research (e.g., Bumby & Bumby, 1997; Mathews, Hunter, & Vuz, 1997; White & Smith, 2004) indicates that a high percentage (over 50%) of juvenile sex offenders have themselves been sexually abused as children. In addition, over half of adult sex offenders report that their first sexual offense occurred when they were adolescents (Abel, Mittelman, & Becker, 1985).

The causes of sexual offending are neither simple nor straightforward. As the knowledge from systematic study accumulates, it is clear that this behavior is influenced by multiple, interactive factors. Past learning experiences, cognitive expectations and beliefs, conditioning, environmental stimuli, and reinforcement contingencies (both rewards and punishments) are all involved. In this chapter we review the major research findings on potential causal factors involved in the crimes of rape, child molestation, and exhibitionism. We also discuss the phenomenon of fetishes, which sometimes leads to minor criminal activity. By far the greatest focus is on the two sexual offenses that are most troubling to society and most tragic to victims—rape and child molestation (pedophilia).

Some studies (e.g., Revitch & Schlesinger, 1988) reveal that many sex offenders are not prone to violence or physical cruelty but, rather, are timid, shy, and socially inhibited. While this may be correct for a large segment of pedophiles, it is not for rapists, whose attacks have strong aggressive features. In fact, their sexual aggression can be divided into at least two major categories: instrumental and expressive. **Instrumental sexual aggression** is when the sexual offender uses just enough coercion to gain compliance from his victim. In **expressive sexual aggression**, the offender's primary aim is to harm the victim physically as well as psychologically. In some cases the expressive aggression is "eroticized" in that the offender becomes sexually aroused in the presence of physical or psychological brutality.

Regardless of the sex offender's characteristics, motivations, and method of attack or coercion, the social and psychological costs to victims and their families are immeasurable and often devastating. A survey of 3,132 households in the Los Angeles Epidemiologic Catchment Area (ECA) illustrates this very well. Researchers found that over 13% of the individuals interviewed had been victims of sexual assault at least once in their lifetimes (Burnam et al., 1988; Siegel, Sorenson, Golding, Burnam, & Stein, 1987; Sorenson, Stein, Siegel, Golding, & Burnam, 1987). Two-thirds of the sexually assaulted subjects reported two or more assaults. Moreover, lifetime sexual assault was more frequently reported by women (16.7%) than men (9.4%). Thirteen percent of the victims were first assaulted between age 6 and age 10; 19%, between 11 and 15; 34%, between 16 and 20; and 15%, between 21 and 25. The experience of being sexually assaulted was associated with substantially higher risks for later onset of serious, self-destructive depression, substance abuse, numerous fears and inhibiting anxieties, and a variety of major interpersonal problems. Overall, the ECA project found that both male and female victims of sexual assault are two to four times more likely to develop serious psychological problems than nonvictims.

Legislation on Sex Offenders

Before proceeding, it is important to understand that several pieces of landmark legislation have been enacted during the past decade that strongly influence how the federal and state governments view sex offenders. Recent data suggest that, nationally, there are approximately 234,000 sex offenders under the care, custody, or control of correction agencies on any given day (Chaiken, 1998b). In recent years, several brutally violent attacks on young, vulnerable victims have been perpetrated by several convicted-but-released sex offenders. These incidents had an enormous influence on state and federal legislation designed to prevent similar offenses. Much of the recent legislation on sex offenders has sprung from the comprehensive *Violent Crime Control and Law Enforcement Act of 1994*. This legislation has formed the basis for the U.S. Department of Justice's strategy for dealing with violent offenders, most particularly violent sex offenders, during the past decade, and should influence policy for many years to come. For our purposes here, we briefly describe three laws that are most relevant to the topics in this chapter.

During the past decade, the U.S. Congress passed three laws that collectively require states to strengthen the procedures they use to keep track of sex offenders or risk the loss of federal funding: (1) *the Jacob Wetterling Crimes Against Children and Sexually Violent Offender Registration Act* (enacted in 1994), (2) the federal version of *Megan's Law* (enacted in 1996), and (3) the *Pam Lychner Sexual Offender Tracking and Identification Act* (also enacted in 1996). All three statutes require states to establish registration programs so that local law enforcement and community officials will know the whereabouts of sex offenders released into their jurisdiction and enforce notification programs so the public can be warned about sex offenders living in the community (Chaiken, 1998b).

The Jacob Wetterling Act encourages states to require convicted child molesters and sexually violent offenders to notify law enforcement of their whereabouts for 10 years after they are released from prison, parole, or community supervision. The required notification time may be longer if the offender is considered a "sexually violent predator" or one whose crimes were especially heinous. The act encourages states to adopt registration systems for convicted child molesters and other persons convicted of sexually violent crimes. The act was named in honor of 11-year-old Jacob Wetterling of St. Joseph, Minnesota, who was abducted at gunpoint by a masked man in 1989. The young boy was never found.

The second legislative act, known as Megan's Law, requires states to release registration information to the public *when it is necessary for public safety*, a requirement often referred to as "mandatory community notification." While the Wetterling Act does not require that communities be notified of the release of sex offenders, Megan's Law specifies that local communities be so notified, although the extent of notification varies according to the offender's level of dangerousness. For example, in the case of Level 3 offenders, officials must notify the community at large; in the case of Level 2 offenders, only certain agencies (e.g., schools, day care centers) must be notified; and in the case of Level 1 offenders, a passive notification process is in effect. That is, members of the community are told if they ask. Megan's Law was named after seven-year-old Megan Kanka of Hamilton Square, New Jersey, who was assaulted, raped, and murdered in 1994 by a twice-convicted pedophile living across the street.

The Lychner Act amended the Violent Crime Control and Law Enforcement Act of 1994 to require the FBI to establish the national offender database and to handle sex offender registration and notification in states unable to maintain "minimally sufficient" programs on their own. Basically, the Lychner Act establishes more stringent registration requirements for sex offenders living within the community. Under the act, offenders considered the most dangerous to public safety are required to register wherever they go for life. The Lychner Act was named for a Houston real estate agent named Pam Lychner. A twice-convicted felon, waiting for her, brutally assaulted Lychner when she went to show a vacant house. Her life was saved when her husband arrived on the scene and interrupted the attack. Tragically, Pam Lychner and her two daughters were later killed in the explosion of TWA Flight 800 off the coast of Long Island, New York, in July 1996.

Although Congress determined that states must have registration and notification laws on the books if they wish to continue to receive federal funds, it was left to the states to determine precisely how these laws would be crafted. Most state laws are modeled on the above federal statutes, with some modifications. In 2002, the U.S. Supreme Court upheld provisions of the registration laws in two states, Alaska and Connecticut, making it highly likely that registration and community notification will continue far into the foreseeable future.

RAPE

Definitions

Definitions of rape vary widely from state to state; in many states the term *sexual assault* has replaced *rape* in the criminal statutes. According to the U.S. Department of Justice (1988), rape is "unlawful sexual intercourse with a female, by force or without legal or factual consent" (p. 2). The UCR defines rape somewhat differently, distinguishing forcible from statutory rape or rape by fraud. **Forcible rape** is "the carnal knowledge of a female forcibly and against her will" (Federal Bureau of Investigation, 2003, p. 29). It includes assaults and attempts to commit rape by force or threat of force. **Statutory rape** without force and other sex offenses are excluded. Statutory rape is the carnal knowledge of a girl (a female under statutory age), with or without her consent.

The critical factor for statutory rape is the age of the victim, an arbitrary legal cutoff point below which a girl is believed not to have the maturity to consent to intercourse or understand the consequences. Age limits vary from state to state, but most set the limit at 16 or 18. Thus, if an adult male engages in sexual relations with a minor female, he may be convicted of statutory rape.

Rape by fraud is having sexual relations with a consenting adult female under fraudulent conditions. Among the most frequently cited examples is that of the psychotherapist who has sexual intercourse with a patient under the guise of offering treatment.

The limitation of the above definitions is that they are usually restricted to female victims. For example, reported rapes of males are not included in the Uniform Crime Reports (UCR) tabulations of rape, although they may be included under the tabulations of aggravated assault. Furthermore, both official crime data and social science research have traditionally emphasized the role of males as perpetrators of rape and other sexual assaults. For these reasons we use the pronoun "he" throughout the chapter in referring to sex offenders. Nevertheless, as noted above, increasingly more research attention is being given to female offenders as well as to male victims.

Many in the general population (including the victims themselves) do not define sexual attacks as rape unless the assailant is a stranger. Thus, if the victim is sexually assaulted by a husband or a boyfriend, she may not report the incident. Criminal justice officials, as well as the general public, often feel that marital or date rapes are unimportant because they are believed to happen so rarely, compared to stranger rape, or to be less psychologically traumatic to the victim. Criminal prosecutors, for example, admit they are reluctant to prosecute marital or date rape cases because of concerns that juries will not believe that a woman could be raped by a husband or male friend (Kilpatrick, Best, Saunders, & Veronen, 1988). However, in a survey of the general population conducted by Kilpatrick and colleagues (1988), subjects who had been raped identified their husbands as assailants in 24% of the cases and male friends in 17% of the cases. These data suggest that over 40% of the rapes were committed by husbands or acquaintances, a significant and frequently overlooked statistic in the tabulation of rape.

Date Rape

Date rapes may be far more common than generally realized. **Date rape** refers specifically to a sexual assault that occurs within the context of a dating relationship. Some recent data suggest that up to one-third of young adults, between 16 and 24 years of age, report being involved in at least one abusive dating incident (Lingren, 2001). Schubot (2001) found that 15% of his sample of female high school students reported being forced to have sexual intercourse while on a date. In a survey of 925 college women conducted by Frintner and Rubinson (1993), over one-fourth of the respondents had experienced sexual assault or attempted sexual assault. Nearly 83% of the college women who had been sexually assaulted said the attacker was someone they knew and that most of these incidents had happened during their freshman year.

Date rape (or acquaintance rape) has many risk factors because the male often feels he is "entitled to payback" since he probably initiated the date, paid all or most of the expenses, and drove his vehicle. Under these conditions, the woman often blames herself for the attack and, as noted earlier, is blamed by others for somehow arousing her date. In addition, sexual assault by a date or acquaintance may be more traumatizing than assault by a stranger because of the implicit trust involved.

Another traumatizing aspect of date rape refers to a phenomenon pointed out by Karmen (1996). Karmen notes a common distinction made in society between a "real rape" and a date rape. In real rapes, the presumption is that the woman is clearly raped if she is ambushed as an unsuspecting victim in a blitz attack by a complete stranger. It is more convincing if the attacker is armed and leaps out of the darkness to surprise his prey. The rape is even more real if the victim suffers some physical injury. A date rape, on the other hand, is often not considered a real rape since it occurred on an arranged date with someone she knew and agreed to go out with. We return to the topic of date rape in Chapter 12, where "date rape drugs" are discussed.

The classification and study of rape offenses are hampered by the fact that jurisdictions vary widely in their definitions of rape, often disagreeing with the Department of Justice or UCR guidelines. In the mid-1970s, the National Institute of Law Enforcement and Criminal Justice funded extensive surveys of law enforcement agencies that illustrate these differences (Chappell, 1977a, 1977b). Most agencies reported that vaginal penetration was the criterion for a minimum alleged offense to qualify as rape. Over half of the law enforcement agencies surveyed also required evidence of both penetration and force, while another third required evidence of penetration, force, a weapon, and/or resistance by the victim. As might be expected, the average number of rapes reported by the latter agencies was significantly lower than the average number reported by other law enforcement agencies accepting less demanding criteria.

Prosecutors require more stringent evidence than law enforcement agencies before accepting an incident as a probable rape. Most of the 150 prosecutors polled in the Chappell survey set four threshold criteria for filing a complaint of forcible rape: (1) evidence of penetration, (2) lack of victim consent, (3) threat of force, and (4) female gender of the victim. It is intriguing to note, however, that 92% of the prosecutors sampled did not have formal guidelines for filing a charge of forcible rape. Therefore, their survey responses were more likely to reflect their own judgments about the minimum threshold requirements for initiating action against an alleged offender.

Although some agencies follow the UCR guidelines for classifying rape, many adopt different classification systems. About one-third have more stringent requirements; one-fifth, less stringent. Some jurisdictions distinguish between attempted rape and forcible rape. Many, especially the larger ones, include different degrees of forcible rape (e.g., first and second degree). In addition, the term sexual assault is now increasingly being used, either to replace rape or in addition to it.

In cases involving multiple offenses (e.g., rape plus burglary, homicide, or robbery), the offense considered the more "serious" takes precedence and is more likely to be tabulated in the offense statistics, while the "lesser" crime committed at the same time is not recorded. For instance, since homicide is considered to be a more serious crime than forcible rape, homicide–rapes traditionally are tabulated under homicide and not under rape. This is the procedure used under the UCR "hierarchy rule" discussed in Chapter 1. With the new incident-based reporting system also discussed in that chapter, accurate statistics are more likely to be gathered. At present, because of the wide variations in defining rape and sexual assault as well as procedures for collecting data, we must view statistical comparisons and information pertaining to the "average" rape very cautiously.

Incidence and Prevalence

From all indications, the United States has the highest incidence of rape in the world. However, the estimated 95,136 forcible rapes reported to law enforcement agencies nationwide in 2002 represented the *tenth consecutive annual decrease* for this offense in the United States (Federal Bureau of Investigation, 2003). The rate rape represents 6% of the total violent crime rate. As mentioned in the previous section, the UCR's definition recognizes only women and girls as victims of rape. Available data suggest that about 10% of the rapes in this country do not conform to the UCR definition (Chaiken, 1998a). Specifically, it is estimated that in about 9% of reported rapes, the victim is male. And in another 1%, both the offender and the victim are female. In 2002, an estimated 64.8 of every 100,000 females (women and girls 12 and over) were reported victims of forcible rape (Federal Bureau of Investigation, 2003). Rapes by force accounted for 91% of the total rapes reported in 2002, with the remaining 9% being attempts to commit forcible rape. Forcible rape had a national clearance rate of 44.5% during 2002 (Federal Bureau of Investigation, 2003).

Of course, we must recognize that the actual rape rate is greatly underestimated, partly because of some of the problems listed in the previous section and partly because of the ordeal women must go through just to report the incident. Victimization studies offer a revealing contrast to the official rates. The National Crime Victimization Survey finds that about two-thirds of the rape and sexual assaults committed in the United States go unreported (Ringle, 1997). Russell (1983) selected at random and interviewed 930 women living in the San Francisco area. She learned that 175 of them (19%) reported at least one completed extramarital rape and 284 (13%) reported at least one attempted extramarital rape. Fifty percent of those reporting these incidents said they had been raped or attacked more than once, and only 8% said they had reported any rape incident to law enforcement authorities. An early study by Hindelang and his associates (Hindelang, Dunn, Sutton, & Aumick, 1976), designed to gather victimization rates on randomly selected households, found that only about one of every four forcible or attempted rapes was reported to law enforcement agencies. Another early study of hitchhike rape estimated that over two-thirds went unreported (Nelson & Amir, 1975). Based on a national sample of college students from 32 U.S. colleges and universities, Koss and her colleagues (Koss, Gidycz, & Wisniewski, 1987) discovered that about 28% of the college women had been victims of rape or attempted rape (as defined by the UCR). More startling, however, was the finding that virtually none of the incidents were reported to the police and thus they were not recorded in official crime statistics. Based on their data, Koss and her colleagues estimated that the victimization rate for women was 3,800 per 100,000, a rate drastically different from the official rates of 65 to 75 per 100,000. More recent data suggest that more than 50% of college women in both the United States and Canada have been victims of some form of sexual assault (Morry & Winkler, 2001).

Additional victimization data indicate that there is an approximately one-in-five chance that a woman will be raped at some time during her life (Furby, Weinrott, & Blackshaw, 1989; Pope & Shouldice, 2001; Schwartz, 1991). If we include *attempted* rape, the chance may be one in three (Russell & Howell, 1983). As mentioned previously, a surprising number of women are sexually victimized while on a date. Approximately 22% of college women surveyed indicated they had been subjected to a forced sexual encounter (e.g., genital fondling, oral sex, or intercourse) by a date at some point in their lives (Dull & Giacopassi, 1987; Yegidis, 1986). Rapaport and Burkhart (1984) found that 15% of a sample of college men acknowledged that they had obtained sexual intercourse against their dates' will. Koss et al. (1987) report that about 8% of their sample of nearly 3,000 college men admitted raping or attempting to rape their dates.

For several years, data suggested that rape reporting by victims was on the increase. Chappell (1977a) found that rates of reported rape more than doubled over a 10-year period, and others noted that the numbers continued to increase steadily until 1991 (see **Figure 10–1**). However, between 1992 and 2001, the reporting of forcible rape in the United States has decreased steadily. (In 2002 there was a *slight* increase [4.7%] from the previous year.) For example, the rate per 100,000 women decreased 19.4% from 1993 to 2002, from a rate of 80.4 per 100,000 in 1993 to 64.8 per 100,000 in 2002 (Federal Bureau of Investigation, 2003). Adult arrests for forcible rape in 2002 declined 25.9%, and juvenile arrests decreased 26.5% compared to arrests in 1993. It is too early to tell exactly why the rate has generally decreased for the past 20 years.

The increase in reporting until 1994 may be attributed to many factors. For example, it may reflect (1) a higher level of community awareness about rape and other sexual assault, (2) the influence of the women's movement, (3) increased training and sensitivity of law enforcement officers, and (4) the gradual revision of statutes and procedures that makes the gathering of legal

FIGURE 10–1   Rape Rate per 1,000 Persons Age 12 or Over, 1973–2001

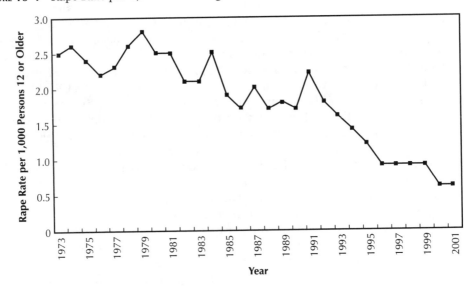

Source: Federal Bureau of Investigation (2003).

evidence less stressful for the victim. In Chappell's national survey of 150 prosecutors' offices (Chappell, 1977b), 61% of the respondents believed that the increased reporting of rape at that time reflected a change in public attitude toward crime. Another third of the prosecutors felt that the increase was a result of the heightened sensitivity of the criminal justice system. It is interesting to note, however, that a vast majority of the prosecutors felt that the increased rape rate also reflected to some extent a "general pattern of increased violence" in America.

The psychological effects on the rape victim, both during and after the assault, are severe and often incalculable. She is frequently victimized twice—by the assailant and by the criminal justice process. Upon reporting the assault, she is expected to recall and describe personally stressful and humiliating events in vivid detail to law enforcement personnel, who are often men. Today, increasingly more police departments take steps to ease the victim's ordeal. These include having victim advocates present, having women officers available, and providing rape sensitivity training for both male and female officers. In addition to the interview with representatives of law enforcement, the victim is required to undergo a medical examination to document penetration and obtain physical evidence, such as DNA from semen. Evidence of physical force—for example, bruises and lacerations—is also relevant and may raise the charge in jurisdictions that recognize degrees of rape.

If the victim is able to withstand these stressful conditions, which are sometimes exacerbated by negative reactions from parents, husband, and friends and even by threats from the assailant, she must then prepare for the courtroom, where her privacy is invaded and her credibility may be attacked. Rape trials are usually covered extensively by the press, although most news organizations do not reveal the victim's name or photograph her. Her reputation, however, is especially vulnerable. Ninety-two percent of the prosecutors surveyed by Chappell asserted that victim credibility was one of the most important elements in convincing juries to convict for forcible rape. Therefore, the defense has often concentrated on the victim's sexual history to destroy her credibility. The strategy of disparaging the victim in this way has come under attack in recent years, and many states have revised their evidentiary rules in an attempt to limit the use of a victim's sexual history. Virtually all states have enacted "rape shield" laws that restrict, to varying degrees, the admissibility of the victim's sexual history into the courtroom (Kilpatrick, Whalley, & Edmunds, 2000). In 1993, Congress extended the federal rape shield law to civil proceedings (such as when a victim sues her aggressor), ruling that a plaintiff's sexual behavior is only admissible if the defendant can show that the evidence it provides to the court outweighs any prejudicial effect on the plaintiff (Fitzgerald, 2003). In addition, victim assistants, whose function it is to offer support, give direct services, and advocate for victims, have been instrumental in easing the victim's burden. It should be emphasized, however, that rape shield laws do not always provide the protection for which they were designed (Ross & Bachar, 2002). Rape shield laws vary from state to state (Kinports, 2002). Consequently, many victims are surprised and dismayed when they are asked questions about their social and sexual histories during adjudication, something they believed would not happen (Ross & Bachar, 2002).

Although criminal justice agencies are beginning to be more sensitive to the painful ordeal a victim must go through, the costs are still high. If the woman reports the sexual assault to the police, she must devote many hours to the process of the investigation and the subsequent court proceedings (Kilpatrick, Whalley, & Edmunds, 2002; Ross & Bachar, 2002). She must bear the costs of missed days of work, child care, medical expenses for the physical and psychological trauma, and transportation. She may feel a need to change lifestyles, move, and install expensive security systems and locks. Sleeplessness, anxiety, and depression must also be factored into the cost equation. We discuss these issues in more detail shortly.

Situational and Victimization Characteristics

Rape is primarily a crime against youth. The National Women's Study (Tjaden & Thoennes, 1998b) reported the following statistical data concerning the age of victims:

- 29% of all forcible rapes occurred when the victim was less than 11 years old,
- 32% occurred when the victim was between 11 and 17 years old,
- 22% occurred between age 18 and age 24,
- 7% occurred between age 25 and age 29, and
- 6% occurred when the victim was older than 29 years old.

The use of alcohol and other disinhibiting substances is common in rapists. The substance abuse is apparent both in the personal history of the rapist and at the time of the offense. Anywhere between 42% and 90% of convicted rapists admit they were under the influence of a disinhibiting substance at the time of the sexual assault, and between 58% and 90% exhibit a history of substance abuse (Marques & Nelson, 1989; Pithers, Beal, Armstrong, & Petty, 1989).

Kilpatrick et al. (2000, p. 12) report cogent evidence that most rapists are intimate partners, not strangers. They list the following victimization information on adult women gathered from the National Women's Survey:

- 24.4% of the rapists were strangers,
- 21.9% were husbands or ex-husbands,
- 19.5% were boyfriends or ex-boyfriends,
- 9.8% were relatives, and
- 14.6% were other nonrelatives, such as friends or neighbors.

Women's fears about being physically harmed in rape are not unfounded. While weapons, especially firearms and knives, are used in only about 25% of the reported assaults (U.S. Department of Justice, 1988), about one-fourth of all rape victims sustain injury serious enough to warrant medical attention or hospitalization. *Severe physical injury*, however, is relatively rare, with about 5% receiving serious, lasting injury (J. Williams & Holmes, 1981). Another 39% receive minor injuries, and 23% receive a variety of cuts and bruises (J. Williams & Holmes, 1981). Further study suggests that women receive more physical and psychological trauma from sexual assault by husbands than by strangers (Kilpatrick et al., 1988). Furthermore, the psychological damage is apparently longer-lasting and more damaging, resulting in serious depression, extensive fears, and problems of sexual adjustment.

Victim surveys also indicate that the most commonly used methods of force during date rapes are verbal persuasion, alcohol, or drugs. While weapons are rarely used, physical overpowering (similar to a wrestling match) is commonly reported (Kanin, 1984). Furthermore, data suggest that date rapes occur most frequently in the male's apartment or room, with the next likely location being the female's apartment or room. Very few occur in a car or outside. About 7% of rape/sexual assaults involved multiple offenders who were strangers to the victim (Greenfeld, 1997).

Rapists often expect more than vaginal intercourse. In approximately 25% of the rapes Chappell studied (1977a), the assailant also demanded oral sexual acts; in about 10%, he demanded both oral and anal sexual acts; in about 6%, anal sexual acts only; and in 4%, other sexual actions. An earlier study (Amir, 1971) reported similar patterns.

Offender Characteristics

What kind of a person rapes? How did he get that way? Why does he do it? Can the "rapist personality" be easily identified? Are rapists mentally disordered? In reading this section, keep in mind that many studies addressing these questions are based on information obtained from convicted offenders located in prisons, forensic evaluation clinics, or secure psychiatric facilities—a very biased sample, since less than 3% of reported rapes in the United States result in a conviction (Battelle Law and Justice Study Committee, 1977).

The most consistent demographic finding is that rapists tend to be young. According to UCR data for 2002, 46.1% of those *arrested* were under age 25 (16.7% were actually under age 18 (Federal Bureau of Investigation, 2003). Henn and his colleagues (1976a) reported that 75% of those accused of rape and referred to a mental health evaluation team in St. Louis between 1952 and 1973 were under age 30. The Queen's Bench Foundation (1978) found that 70% of its sample of 73 convicted rapists were under age 25. The National Crime Victim Survey estimates that nearly one-quarter of the rapes or attempted rapes in any given year are committed by offenders between 12 and 20 years of age.

Another consistent finding is that many men accused of and convicted of rape have been in perpetual conflict with society, long before the current rape offense. About one-fourth of those arrested for forcible rape have raped previously, and about one-third have an arrest history for violent offenses other than rape (Chappell, 1977a). In a sample of 114 convicted rapists studied by Scully and Marolla (1984), 12% had a previous conviction for rape or attempted rape, 39% had previous convictions for burglary and robbery, 29% for abduction, 25% for sodomy, and 11% for first- or second-degree murder. Overall, 82% had a prior criminal record, but only 23% had been convicted of sexual offenses. Gebhard and colleagues (Gebhard, Gagnon, Pomeroy, & Christenson, 1965) reported that 87% of their sample of sexual offenders (mostly rapists) had been convicted of some other crime besides their sexual offense prior to age 26.

The research literature indicates that a significant proportion of sex offenders have been the victims of both sexual abuse and physical/verbal abuse as children, a characteristic found in both adult and juvenile offenders (Craissati & Beech, 2004; Knight & Sims-Knight, 2002). However, the research also suggests that child molesters have experienced more abuse than rapists (Craissati & Beech, 2004).

Occupationally, people arrested for rape tend to come from the so-called blue-collar working class (about 50%) and from the ranks of the unemployed (approximately 30%). In the Scully and Marolla (1984) study, only 20% of all convicted rapists had a high school education or better, and 85% came from working-class backgrounds. Very few individuals from the professional or white-collar occupational fields are arrested for rape—a fact that should not be taken to mean that they do not commit rape or other sexual assault. A study conducted in England (R. Wright, 1980) reported that 75% of those arrested for rape were in the unskilled working class, and only 2% were classified as professional or managerial. Interestingly, for the professional people arrested in the United States, the numbers drop precipitously when the rape charges get to the prosecutor's office—that is, a low proportion is prosecuted—while the numbers of arrested and prosecuted remain about the same for the other occupational groups. At face value, these data suggest that the more affluent or privileged offender is more likely to be filtered out early in the judicial process than is the less privileged, less powerful offender.

According to prosecutors, about one-fourth of those accused of rape admitted that the incident was planned and premeditated (Chappell, 1977b). The problem with this statistic, of course, is that most suspects are unwilling to admit premeditation, since it makes the case against them that much stronger. Therefore, it is highly probable that the number of premeditated rapes is substantially higher than those reported by prosecutors. On the basis of an analysis of reported rapes in Philadelphia, Amir (1971) claimed that 71% were planned. In the Queen's Bench Foundation study (1978), over two-thirds of the convicted rapists interviewed admitted that they had clearly set out to commit a rape.

Traditionally, the rapist has been considered by many clinicians to be the victim of "uncontrollable urges" (Edwards, 1983) or the recipient of a "disordered personality" (Scully & Marolla, 1984). Psychiatric criminology has, for a long time, dominated the popular literature on the sexual offender and continues to have substantial impact on the thinking of Western civilization. As Scully and Marolla (1985) observe, the psychiatric literature, as well as the general public, has traditionally attributed rape behavior to four fundamental causes: (1) uncontrollable impulses or urges, (2) mental illness or disease, (3) momentary loss of control precipitated by unusual circumstances, and (4) victim instigation. Further, Scully and Marolla assert that each of these statements attributes the cause of the rape behavior to parameters outside of the rapist himself—often to the victim. In other words, the traditional psychiatric literature has consistently attributed the causal factors of sexual deviations to circumstances beyond the offender's direct or immediate control. Empirical research has not supported these assumptions, however. After discussing each cause briefly, we outline what researchers have been finding.

Uncontrollable or *irresistible impulse* attribution refers to a psychological state wherein the normal restraints of self-control are substantially reduced or virtually eliminated by an overwhelming sex drive. The major argument from this perspective maintains that high levels of sexual deprivation may cause a bubbling-over of an innate, natural sex drive of such intensity that the individual loses control of his behavior and consequently can no longer help himself. Driven by this powerful, biological force, his only release is immediate sexual gratification. Symons (1979), for example, writes that men's sexual impulses are part of human nature and that men innately seek "no-cost, impersonal copulations."

Mental illness or *disease attribution* contends that rape—and most other sexual deviations—is symptomatic of some deep-seated sickness or mental aberration. All sexual offenders are basically "sick" and in need of help. Inherent in this perspective is the conviction that sexually deviant behaviors are similar in causation and represent a single type of psychopathology, usually some form of character disorder (Lanyon, 1986). According to Lanyon (1986), this belief "tends to be the view held by the judicial system, by social service agencies, and by the general public" (p. 176). And as Scully and Marolla (1985) point out, "Belief that rapists are or must be sick is amazingly persistent" (p. 298). In recent years, although beliefs that sexual offenders are mentally aberrant persist, public opinion has shifted away from offering help and toward more punitive approaches.

The third popular belief, *drug attribution*, argues that one can momentarily lose control of one's urges in certain circumstances, such as through the use of drugs or alcohol. Alcohol, for example, is believed to remove social and moral constraints, leaving some men at the mercy of their sexual appetites. This desire simply becomes overwhelming, causing some men to attack the most convenient victim. In one study, two-thirds of the men who raped their dates attributed their assaults to excessive drinking (Kanin, 1984). They claimed the date rape was caused by their own inebriation together with a loss of judgment due to high levels of sexual excitement. One-fifth were convinced that there was no way the attack would have occurred had they been sober.

The fourth perspective, *victim attribution*, contends that the victim has, in some way, led the perpetrator into temptation. Rape, according to this view, is a sexual act that is promoted unconsciously by the women. "Nice girls don't get raped," or at least they don't "let it get out of hand." Hitchhike rape, for example, is, according to this view, probably victim-precipitated rape. Because of their unconscious desires, women unwittingly cooperate with the rapist by making themselves available to him in various ways. In the Kanin (1984) date rape study, two-thirds of the men said that "although it was probably rape in the legal sense, the fault for the incident resided with the female because of her sexual conduct. According to these males, the sexual demeanor of their victims literally absolved them of guilt so that we are now confronted with something akin to justifiable rape, an analogue to justifiable homicide" (p. 96). Several major surveys conducted on a wide section of the American population strongly suggest that many people continue to believe a victim is at least partially responsible for her rape and that only certain women get raped (Lottes, 1988).

As noted earlier, empirical study has not supported the validity of these four fundamental assumptions; it does, however, support their persistence. In other words, people continue to believe that rape is caused by drugs, precipitated by the victim, or the product of mental illness or the offender's uncontrollable urges or addiction. These misconceptions are held by offenders as well as others. Scully and Marolla (1984) interviewed 114 convicted rapists to obtain information about their perceptions, motivations, and afterthoughts and found that most could be divided into two major groups, "admitters" and "deniers." Admitters essentially corroborated the story told by police and victims. Deniers' versions differed significantly from those of police and victims. The researchers identified 47 admitters and 32 deniers. Apparently, the remainder could not be classified into either category.

Deniers justified their rape behavior primarily by making the victim blameworthy. Five themes ran through these justifications: (1) Women are seductresses; (2) women mean yes when they say no; (3) most women eventually relax and really enjoy it; (4) nice girls don't get raped; and (5) the act was a minor wrongdoing, since the victims were not physically hurt. Thirty-one percent of the deniers said the victim was the aggressor: a seductress who lured them, unsuspecting, into sexual action. About 22% said the victim had not resisted enough or that her no had really meant yes. As one offender put it, despite some struggle, "Deep down inside I think she felt it was a fantasy come true." Most of the deniers justified their behavior by claiming not only that the victim was willing, but also that she enjoyed herself, in some cases to an immense degree. Most of the deniers (69%) were also convinced that "nice girls don't get raped." Their victims, they said, had dressed seductively, were hitchhiking, or were generally known to be "loose."

The belief that bad things happen to bad people and good things happen to good people is called by psychologists the *just world hypothesis* (Lerner, 1980), mentioned in Chapter 1. It is the simplistic belief that one gets what one deserves and deserves what one gets. Just-worlders—people who are most apt to adopt this hypothesis—believe that victims of misfortune or crime deserve their fate. Deniers noted that their victims should not have been in a bar alone, should not have been hitchhiking, or should have worn a bra. The deniers, in this sense, were just-worlders.

A majority of the deniers said that their actions were not reprehensible since they believed they had not physically harmed the victim. Many felt that, although their behavior was not completely proper, it should not have been considered a serious criminal offense, despite the fact that they had threatened their victims with lethal weapons.

Admitters, in contrast to deniers, regarded their behavior as morally wrong and as a serious, harmful attack on their victims. However, most of them tried to diminish their own culpability by asserting that they could not help themselves or were compelled by forces outside their control. Three themes ran through the admitters' justifications: (1) the use of alcohol and drugs, (2) emotional problems, and (3) a "nice guy" self-image. Over three-fourths said they had been under the influence of alcohol or drugs at the time of the attack and that the substance had influenced their judgment and behavior. They were convinced that the ingested substance had, in effect, reduced their awareness as well as their self-control. Normally, they said, they would not have engaged in such a disgusting act.

Forty percent of the admitters said they believed emotional problems were at the root of their rape behavior, and 33% specifically cited an unhappy, unstable childhood or a marital–domestic situation. Furthermore, 80% of the admitters described an upsetting problem or anger-inducing event that occurred prior to the attack. Consistently, Scully and Marolla (1984) found that these men described themselves as being in a rage because of an incident involving a woman with whom they believed they were in love. By contrast, only about 20% of the deniers described such problems.

Most of the admitters described themselves as "nice guys," who in normal circumstances would never dream of doing such a violent thing to a woman. In other words, their actions during that violent episode did not represent their true selves. Many expressed regret and sorrow for their victim and apologized to the researchers. We return to these justifications and excuses later in the chapter.

Classification of Rape Patterns

Since such a wide variety of sexual offenders is involved in rape, some interesting attempts have been made to categorize rapists according to their behavioral patterns. Researchers at the Massachusetts (Bridgewater) Treatment Center (MTC) (Cohen, Garafalo, Boucher, & Seghorn, 1971; Cohen, Seghorn,

& Calmas, 1969; Knight & Prentky, 1987; Prentky & Knight, 1986) recognized that rape involves both sexual and aggressive features and tried to formulate a behavioral classification system that takes these elements into consideration.

Before we proceed, however, it is important to realize that classification systems are permeated with numerous problems and drawbacks. One obvious problem is that individuals do not fit neatly into a category. Furthermore, there may not be many who do. As astutely noted by Gibbons (1988), classification systems or typologies generally consist "of criminological foundations that assume that real life persons can be found in significant numbers who resemble the descriptions of offenders in the various typologies that have been put forth . . . researchers have often failed to uncover many point-for-point real-life cases of these hypothesized types of offenders" (p. 9). However, typologies or classification systems are valuable in organizing an otherwise confusing array of behaviors. They are also useful at correctional facilities for risk management, such as deciding where to place an inmate, or in treatment programming, such as deciding what particular treatment modality might be most beneficial for an inmate. It should be stressed, however, that rape is not a unified behavior pattern but rather is a complicated, often poorly understood, individualized behavior that appears to be precipitated by a variety of internal and external stimuli.

The MTC originally identified four major categories of rapists: (1) displaced aggression, (2) compensatory, (3) sexual aggressive, and (4) impulsive rapists. **Displaced aggression rapists** (also called, in other classification systems, *displaced anger* or **anger retaliation rapists**) are primarily violent and aggressive in their attack, displaying minimal or no sexual feeling. These men use the act of rape to harm, humiliate, and degrade the woman. The victim is brutally assaulted and subjected to sadistic acts like biting, cutting, and tearing. In most instances, the victim is a complete stranger who happens to be the best available object or stimulus for the violence, although she may possess characteristics that attract the assailant's attention. The assault is not sexually arousing for the displaced aggression rapist, and he often demands oral manipulation or masturbation from the victim to become tumescent. Available evidence suggests that resisting this type of rapist only makes him more violent.

According to Knight and Prentky (1987), an offender must demonstrate the following characteristics during the attack in order to be assigned to the displaced aggression category.

1. The presence of a high degree of nonsexualized aggression or rage expressed through verbal and/or physical assault that clearly exceeds what is necessary to force the victim's compliance
2. Clear evidence, in verbalization or behavior, of the intent to demean, degrade, or humiliate the victim
3. No evidence that the aggressive behavior is eroticized or that sexual pleasure is derived from the injurious acts
4. The injurious acts not being focused on parts of the body that have sexual significance

Although many of these rapists are married, they are usually ambivalent toward the women in their lives (Cohen et al., 1971), and their relationships with women are often characterized by frequent irritation and periodic violence. They perceive women as being hostile, demanding, and unfaithful. In addition, they often select as their targets for sexual assault women they consider active, assertive, and independent. The occupational history of these assailants is stable and often shows some level of success. Usually, the work is "masculine," such as truck driving, carpentry, construction, or mechanics. The attack typically follows an incident that has upset or angered the rapist, particularly about women and their behavior. The term *displaced aggression* is derived from the fact that the victim rarely has played any direct role in generating the aggression and arousal. This offender often attributes his offense to "uncontrollable impulses."

Compared to that of other rapists, the childhood of the displaced aggression offender is often chaotic and unstable. Many were physically and emotionally neglected. A large number were adopted or placed in foster homes. About 80% were brought up in single-parent homes.

Compensatory rapists rape in response to an intense sexual arousal initiated by stimuli in the environment, often quite specific stimuli. This type of rapist is sometimes referred to in the clinical and research literature as the "power-reassurance," "sexual aim," "ego dystonic," or "true" sex offender. Aggression is not a significant feature here; the basic motivation is a desire to prove sexual prowess and adequacy. In their day-to-day lives, compensatory rapists tend to be extremely passive, withdrawn, and socially inept. They live in a world of fantasy that centers on images of eagerly yielding victims who will submit to pleasurable intercourse and find the rapist's performance so outstanding that they will plead for a return engagement. The compensatory rapist's fantasies or personal versions of the world may so distort his view of the victim that he may seek further contact with her, even if she strongly resisted the sexual assault.

Although his victim is usually a stranger, the compensatory rapist has probably seen her frequently, watched her, or followed her. Specific stimuli associated with her probably excite him. For example, he may be drawn to college women but may feel the attraction would not be mutual if he approached them via a socially accepted route. He cannot face the prospect of rejection. However, if he can prove his sexual prowess, the victim will appreciate his value. If the victim vigorously resists the compensatory rapist, he is likely to flee; if she submits passively, he will rape without much physical force or violence. This sexually aroused passive assailant will often ejaculate spontaneously, even on mere physical contact with the victim. In general, he does not demonstrate other kinds of antisocial behavior.

The compensatory rapist is often described by others as a quiet, shy, submissive, lonely nice man. Although he is a reliable worker, his withdrawn, introverted behavior, lack of self-esteem, and low levels of need for achievement usually preclude academic, occupational, or social success. His rapes—or attempts at rape—are efforts to compensate for his sense of inadequacy, hence the category to which he is assigned. More recent research by Knight and Prentky (1987) questions the incompetence issue. They found that, compared to the other rapist types, the compensatory rapist evidenced the best heterosexual adaptation and achieved the highest employment skill level. If this finding is replicated, the very term *compensatory rapist* would become misleading.

The **sexually aggressive** or **sadistic rapist** is the one in whom sexual and aggressive features seem to coexist at equal or near-equal levels. In order for him to experience sexual arousal, it must be associated with violence and pain, which excite him. He rapes, therefore, because of the combination of violence and sexual features in the act. He is convinced that women enjoy being forcefully raped and being dominated and controlled by men. This, he believes, is part of woman's nature. Anger and aggression are not always present during the early stages of the assault, which may actually begin as a seduction. In this sense, the sexual aggressive rapist considers the victim's resistance and struggle a game, a form of protesting too much; what she really wants is to be sexually assaulted and raped. This belief appears to be deeply ingrained and widely accepted in many Western societies (Edwards, 1983). Consider the following remarks made by a Scottish attorney general: "M.P.s would do well to remember that rape involves an activity which was normal . . . it was part of the business of men and women that they hunted and were hunted and said 'yes' and 'no' and meant the opposite" (Edwards, 1983, p. 114).

Sexual aggressive offenders are often married, but because they display little commitment or loyalty, they also often have a history of multiple marriages, separations, and divorces. They also may be frequently involved in domestic violence. In fact, their backgrounds include antisocial behaviors beginning during adolescence or before and ranging from truancy to rape–murder. They are severe management problems in school. Throughout their childhood, adolescence, and adulthood, they exhibit poor behavior controls and a low frustration tolerance. Their childhoods are characterized by physical abuse and neglect.

In the extreme, these rapists engage in sexual sadism much like the displaced aggression rapists: Their victims may be viciously violated, beaten, and even killed. The difference between the two types is that the sexual aggressive rapist derives intense sexual satisfaction from aggression, pain, and violence. In order to qualify for assignment to this category, the offender needs to demonstrate (1) a level of aggression or violence that clearly exceeds what is necessary to force compliance of the victim and (2) explicit, unambiguous evidence that aggression is sexually exciting to him.

The fourth type, the **impulsive** or **exploitative rapist**, demonstrates neither strong sexual nor strong aggressive features, but engages in spontaneous rape when the opportunity presents itself. The rape is usually carried out in the context of another crime, such as robbery or burglary. The victims simply happen to be available, and they are sexually assaulted with minimal extrarape violence or sexual feeling. Generally, this offender has a long history of criminal offenses other than rape. In order to be assigned to this group, the offender must show (1) callous indifference to the welfare and comfort of the victim and (2) the presence of no more force than is necessary to gain the victim's compliance.

The MTC:R3

The MTC classification scheme offers a rough framework for conceptualizing and simplifying the behaviors and motives involved in rape. However, it needs refinement and reconstruction, a process the group has been pursuing for a number of years (e.g., Knight & Prentky, 1990; Knight et al., 1998). After a series of analyses and further development, the new MTC classification scheme (called the MTC:R3 [MTC: Rapist, Version 3]) classifies rape offenders into *four* major types and *nine* subtypes. Although the basic four offender types are still in the equation, the researchers have also discovered subtle differences within the original four types. The researchers decided that four primary motivations for rape could improve the original MTC scheme significantly: *opportunity*, *pervasive anger*, *sexual gratification*, and *vindictiveness* (Knight et al., 1998). Knight and his colleagues (1998) concluded that these four motivations appeared to describe enduring behavioral patterns that distinguished most rapists. The opportunistic types (Types 1 and 2) are similar to the fourth type of rapist described earlier. Their sexual assaults appear to be impulsive, predatory acts as a response to being in a situation where the opportunity for the sexual attack arises, and they are not primarily driven by sexual fantasy or explicit anger at women. However, analysis of offender data showed that opportunistic-type rapists can be subdivided on the basis of their social competence (see **Figure 10–2**). Type 1 offenders are higher in social competence and first exhibit their impulsive sexual tendencies in adulthood. Type 2 offenders, on the other hand, are lower in social competence and first demonstrate their impulsive sexual actions during adolescence.

The pervasive anger type (Type 3) is similar to the displaced aggression rapist but with the difference that his generalized anger pervades all areas of his life. His pervasive anger is directed not simply at women but at everyone. Consequently, these rapists often have a long history of antisocial, violent behavior of all kinds and they tend to inflict high levels of physical injury on their victims, especially their rape victims. In many ways they manifest behaviors similar to those of the life course–persistent offender. Sexual motivations and preoccupation characterize four types of rapists in the newly developed MTC classification scheme (Types 4–7; see Figure 10–2). The sadistic rapists (Types 4 and 5) are subdivided into overt and muted types "on the basis of whether their sexual-aggressive fantasies are directly expressed in violent attacks or are only fantasized" (Knight et al., 1998, p. 58). The nonsadistic sexual rapists (Types 6 and 7) are subdivided on the basis of their social competence.

The new MTC:R3 also includes vindictive offender types (Types 8 and 9), characterized by anger directed exclusively at women. These types are highly

FIGURE 10–2   Breakdown of Four Categorizations of Rapist Type into Nine Rapist Subtypes from the MTC:R3

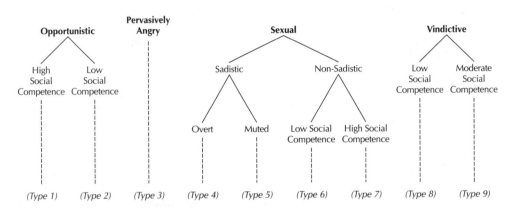

Source: R. A. Knight et al., *Criminal Justice and Behavior*, Vol. 25, p. 57, fig. 2. Copyright © 1998 by Sage Publications, Inc. Reprinted by permission of Sage Publications, Inc.

similar to the displaced aggressive type described in the original MTC. "The sexual assaults of these men are distinguished by behaviors that are explicitly intended to harm the woman physically, as well as to degrade and humiliate her" (Knight et al., 1998, p. 58). Similarly to the opportunistic and nonsadistic rapists, the vindictive types can be subdivided into high–social competence and low–social competence people.

Knight et al. (1998) postulate that these nine rape offender classifications can help substantially in providing additional clues in crime scene investigations. With refinement and continuing research, the MTC:R3 should ultimately enable investigators to identify "type" based on parameters gathered at the crime scene. The MTC:R3 also underscores the multiple strategies and cognitive beliefs possessed by rapists and discourages dogmatic proclamations about why rape occurs. The MTC:R3 increases the understanding of the etiology of sexual offending and helps mental health professions predict recidivism.

A frequently asked question is, To what extent should a woman fight back or resist the attack? The MTC rape categories suggest alternative strategies to women who may wonder to what extent they should resist a rapist. In an interesting study, Sarah Ullman and Raymond Knight (1993) examined the police reports and court testimonies of 274 women who either were raped or avoided rape by violent stranger rapists. They found that forceful resistance (fighting, screaming, fleeing, or pushing the offender) was more effective for avoiding rape than nonresistance. This strategy was especially effective in dangerous situations in which the offender had a weapon. However, although the victim avoided being raped or sexually assaulted, she often received more physical injury when the offender had a weapon, even if the weapon was not used. Nonresistance strategies were largely ineffective in avoiding rape or physical injury. In fact, victims who used nonresistant strategies—such as pleading, crying, and reasoning with the offender—were more likely to be sexually and physically assaulted than women who strongly resisted. Pleading, crying, or reasoning seem to encourage the offender even more. One thing to keep in mind is that the Ullman–Knight study focused on violent, stranger offenders who were committed to the MTC as sexually dangerous. Whether the same results would occur when examining another type of offender, such as date or acquaintance rape, is unclear. Moreover, the MTC rape categories make it fairly clear that compensatory rapists and impulsive rapists—and possibly many sexual aggressive rapists—will be deterred by a victim who struggles. However, displaced aggression rapists are apt to respond with more violence as the victim resists.

In their comprehensive review of the research, D. P. Rosenbaum, Lurigio and Davis (1998) identify four basic strategies of resistance to rape: (1) forceful physical resistance, (2) forceful verbal resistance, (3) nonforceful physical resistance, and (4) nonforceful verbal resistance. Forceful physical resistance involves hitting, kicking, biting, using the fingernails, and using a weapon. Research suggests that using this method of resistance generally helps reduce the probability of severe sexual abuse or rape completion but it also increases the risk that the victim will be attacked and physically injured. Forceful verbal resistance includes screaming, calling for help, and threatening the attacker. While this strategy reduces the probability of rape completion, the degree of physical injury inflicted on the victim is unclear from the research evidence. The third strategy, nonforceful physical resistance, includes trying to flee the scene, pushing the attacker away, and shielding oneself. This type of resistance reduces the probability of rape completion but has little or no effect on the amount of injury received by the victim. Nonforceful verbal resistance, such as pleading, crying, or trying to reason with the attacker, generally leads to an increased probability of rape completion and has no effect in reducing physical injury. Overall, it appears that some type of forceful resistance is most effective in reducing a violent sexual attack and completion of a rape.

The Groth Typology

Groth (1979) has developed a typology with many similarities to the MTC scheme. The Groth proposal is based on the presumed motivations and aims that underlie almost all rapes. Rape is seen as a "pseudo-sexual act" in which sex serves merely as a vehicle for the primary motivations of power and aggression. Groth—rather dogmatically—asserts, "Rape is never the result simply of sexual arousal that has no other opportunity for gratification. . . . Rape is always a symptom of some psychological dysfunction, either temporary and transient or chronic and repetitive" (p. 5). Later, he states, "Rape is always and foremost an aggressive act" (p. 12). Consequently, Groth divides rape behavior into three major categories: anger rape, power rape, and sadistic rape.

In **anger rape**, the offender uses more force than necessary for compliance and engages in a variety of sexual acts that are particularly degrading or humiliating to the female (such as sodomy, fellatio, and even urination on her). He also expresses his contempt for the victim through abusive and profane language. Thus, for the anger rapist, rape is an act of conscious anger and rage toward women, and he expresses his fury physically and verbally. Sex is actually dirty, offensive, and disgusting to him and this is why he uses it to defile and degrade the victim. Very often his attacks are prompted by some previous conflict or humiliation by some significant woman (often a wife, a boss, or a mother). The assault is characterized by considerable physical brutality.

In **power rape**, the assailant seeks to establish power and control over his victim. Thus, the amount of force and threat used depends on the degree of submission shown by the victim. "I told her to undress and when she refused I struck her across the face to show her I meant business" (Groth, 1979, p. 26). His goal is sexual conquest, and he will try to overcome any resistance. Sexual intercourse is his way of asserting identity, authority, potency, mastery, and domination rather than strictly sexual gratification. Often the victim is kidnapped or held captive in some fashion, and she may be subjected to repeated assaults over an extended period of time. The sexual assault is sometimes disappointing to the power rapist because it fails to live up to his frequent fantasies of rape. "Everything was pleasurable in the fantasy, and there was acceptance, whereas in the reality of the situation, it wasn't pleasurable, and the girl was scared, not turned on to me" (p. 27).

The third pattern of rape, **sadistic rape**, includes both sexual and aggressive components. In other words, aggression is eroticized. The sadistic rapist experiences sexual arousal and excitement in the victim's maltreatment, torment, distress, helplessness, and suffering. The assault usually involves bondage and torture, and he directs considerable abuse and injury on various areas of the victim's body. Prostitutes, women he considers promiscuous, or women representing symbols of something he wants to punish or destroy often incur the wrath of the sadistic rapist. The victim may be stalked, abducted, abused, and sometimes murdered.

Groth (1979) reported that over half of the offenders evaluated or treated by his agency (Connecticut Sex Offender Program) were power rapists, 40% were anger rapists, and only 5% were sadistic rapists. The similarities between Groth's scheme and the MTC typology are multiple. The anger rapist is similar to the displaced aggression rapist, the sadistic rapist is similar to the sexual aggressive rapist, and the power rapist shows many commonalities with the compensatory rapist.

Etiology

Generally speaking, sexual socialization plays a crucial role in the rapist's perceptions of what the rape accomplishes and what is "masculine." Sexist attitudes and rape-supporting beliefs have been linked to sexual assault for some time (Forbes, Adams-Curtis, & White, 2004). It is important to realize that sexual socialization (or sexual training) is rarely acquired entirely from home or school; much of it comes from peers, friends, the entertainment media, and experimentation. Most of us, even as children, were fed misconceptions, taboos, and strategies for dealing with the opposite sex. Males often learn that it is "manly" to take the sexual initiative and to persist, even against resistance. Details of a sexual conquest, related to buddies, represent the badge of masculinity and self-worth. On the other hand, if attempts to conquer turn into a comedy of errors, they are seen as personal failure and sexual inadequacy. In addition, some people (both men and women) believe that a woman cannot be raped unless she wants to be. Others learn that women want to be dominated and controlled and that successful lovers demonstrate the "I'm the boss" syndrome. It is interesting to note in this context that some victims actually receive marriage proposals from their assailants (Russell, 1975). Other rapists ask their victims to evaluate their performance during or after the act.

Some researchers have proposed an immaturity hypothesis to account for a large portion of rapes. M. J. Goldstein (1977) found that a sample of convicted sex offenders (who were mostly rapists) continued in adulthood to derive most of their sexual pleasure from fantasizing about sexual stimuli they had derived from the media or from their own imagination. Average males (controls), by contrast, drew much of their sexual pleasure from real-life sexual encounters. Goldstein also discovered that many rapists have pervasive and obsessive preoccupations with sexual matters, to the point where the sexual preoccupation permeates their lives and normally nonerotic material becomes vividly incorporated into sexual fantasies.

Goldstein found that rapists, compared to the average male, relied substantially more on masturbation during adulthood and that this was frequently accompanied by use of erotic material derived from the entertainment media. Furthermore, *all types* of sexual offenders had on the average *fewer* contacts with erotica during their formative years than did most other males. In addition, sexual curiosity was often repressed because of a punitive parental approach to matters sexual. Together, these factors provide a conducive setting for sexual misconceptions and ignorance.

Koss and Dinero (1988) conducted a well-designed survey of approximately 3,000 male students at 32 U.S. colleges and universities. Students were asked questions about the extent of verbal coercion and physical force they had used to become sexually intimate with women without their consent. They were also questioned about attitudes and habits. The results indicated that highly sexually aggressive men expressed greater hostility toward women, frequently used alcohol, frequently viewed violent and degrading pornography (in contrast to Goldstein's finding), and were closely involved with peer groups that reinforced highly sexualized and dominating views of women. In addition, the more sexually aggressive the student, the more likely he was to believe that force and coercion are legitimate ways to gain compliance in sexual relationships. The researchers concluded, "In short, the results provided support for a developmental sequence for sexual aggression in which early experiences and psychological characteristics establish conditions for sexual violence" (p. 144).

In summary, most rapists seem to subscribe to attitudes and ideology that encourage men to be dominant, controlling, and powerful, whereas women are expected to be submissive, permissive, and compliant. Such an orientation seems to have a particularly strong disinhibitory effect on sexually aggressive men, encouraging them to interpret the ambiguous behavior of females as come-ons, to believe that women are not really offended by coercive sexual behaviors, and to perceive rape victims as desiring and deriving gratification from being sexually assaulted (Lipton, McDonel, & McFall, 1987).

Additional evidence of rapists' deviant attitudes and beliefs comes from physiological research. Abel and his associates (Abel, Barlow, Blanchard, & Guild, 1977; Abel, Becker, Blanchard, & Djenderedjian, 1978) have found that rapists show high and nearly equal sexual arousal to audiotaped portrayals of both rape and consenting sexual acts. The degree of sexual arousal was indicated by the subject's penile tumescence, which is measured with a device called a plethysmograph. Male nonrapists, on the other hand, show significantly less penile tumescence in response to rape depictions. In fact, convicted rapists became highly aroused by rape depictions in which the victim experiences abhorrence and pain rather than sexual pleasure. Encouraged by these findings, Abel developed a physiological measure called the *rape index*. The index is arrived at by dividing the average percentage of full penile erection to rape stimuli by the average percentage of full penile erection to consenting sexual stimuli. Avery-Clark and Laws (1984) developed a similar indicator for pedophiles called the *Dangerous Child Abuser Index*. Today, many investigators use this measure in the diagnosis and treatment of rapists as well as child molesters. Generally, research suggests that rapists tend to have a higher rape index than nonrapists. The overall accuracy of the penile plethysmograph and its sensitivity to extraneous factors and faking remain very much in question, however.

Abel and his group also discovered that some rapists became highly sexually aroused even to scenes of *nonsexual aggression*, such as a man beating a woman with his fists. Thus, it appears that some men strongly associate aggression and violence toward women with sexual arousal, a pattern very similar to that of the sexual aggressive rapist described earlier. In fact, in rapists the intensity of this deviant arousal has been found to be positively related to the number of rapes committed and the degree of injury inflicted on victims (Abel et al., 1978). Some rapists apparently find scenes that show women being beaten exciting and pleasurable. In addition, male spouse abusers may, in part, be motivated by such arousal. On the other hand, a majority of men (70%) in the general population find the presence of aggression inhibiting to sexual arousal (Malamuth, Check, & Briere, 1986). Interestingly, men in the general population who are sexually aroused by force also are more accepting of an ideology that justifies male aggression against and dominance over women. These men also admit that they would probably rape if the opportunity were presented.

The role played by fantasy and imagination in the development of sexually aggressive behavior is becoming an increasingly important topic (Laws & Marshall, 1990). Self-reports by sexual offenders find that frequent imagery and fantasy of sexually aggressive scenes are extremely important in motivating and guiding overt sexual aggression. Aggressive fantasies are particularly exciting to men convicted of rape (Abel et al., 1977). Interestingly, in a self-report survey of 114 college men conducted by Greendlinger and Byrne (1987), over one-third indicated they fantasize about aggressively raping a woman, and 54% fantasize about "forcing a woman to have sex."

Related to the role played by fantasy in the development of sexual deviance is the role played by masturbation. The intrinsically physiological pleasure and arousal generated by masturbation can serve as a strong bonding agent, particularly if paired repeatedly with some fantasized object or person. Also, it is important to realize that there are two powerfully reinforcing processes in masturbatory activity: sexual arousal and the reduction of that arousal at orgasm. Fantasized or actual behaviors that are sexually arousing and that result in sexual satisfaction (i.e., orgasm) are likely to increase in strength and frequency. This process is known as "masturbatory conditioning" (W. Marshall & Barbaree, 1988). On the basis of clinical studies (e.g., George & Marlatt, 1989; Groth, 1979; W. Marshall, 1988), it appears that masturbatory conditioning may play an integral part in the development of both normal and deviant sexual behavior.

In sum, the evidence to date indicates overwhelmingly that rapists learn to be rapists and that much of the teaching is done by equally naive peers, parents, significant social models, and the entertainment media. Rape springs from a culture characterized by violence that communicates a dominant ideology that degrades women and justifies coercive sexuality. Fortunately, most males eventually acquire a close approximation of sexual sophistication and some understanding of the needs of others. Many rapists, however, seem to remain sexually and, in some ways socially, immature.

Rape myths have received renewed research attention during the past five years. Rape myths are "attitudes and beliefs that are generally false but widely and persistently held, and that serve to deny and justify male sexual aggression against women" (Lonsway & Firtzgerald, 1994, p. 134). Many—but not all—rapists tend to hold them. Research indicates that men who subscribe to rape myths are hostile towards women in general (Forbes, Adams-Curtis, & White, 2004). Furthermore, attitudes that promote the denigration of women may be widespread. There is distressing evidence that rapists may reflect the explicit and implicit beliefs held by many others. For example, in one study, 35% of male college students on several different campuses felt there was some likelihood that they would rape if they could be sure of getting away with it (Malamuth, 1981). In another study, 60% of a group of 352 male undergraduates indicated there was some likelihood they would rape or force a female to perform a sexual act against her will if given the opportunity (Briere, Malamuth, & Ceniti, 1981).

Malamuth (1989) cautions, however, that one does not conclude that subjects who indicate they would sexually force a woman are necessarily "potential rapists." The scale used in his research, *Attraction to Sexual Aggression,* is designed to measure men's belief that actually engaging in sexual aggression would be an arousing, attractive experience. Whether they would act on that belief is dictated by a myriad of factors across a wide spectrum of influences, including the degree of motivation to commit the act, the internal and external inhibitions present, and the opportunity to commit the act.

Rape and Pornography

The relationship between rape and pornography is shrouded with confusion and surrounded by debate. Two presidential commissions established to study the effect of pornography on crime and human behavior reached opposite conclusions. The first and most comprehensive, established in 1967, was directed not to issue recommendations unless the effects were clear-cut. Because of the complexity it uncovered, the commission could not conclude whether explicit sexual material contributed significantly to sex crimes, prompting then-President Richard M. Nixon to remark that the commission was "morally bankrupt." Many have used this conclusion to support their contention that pornography is not harmful. The second National Commission on Obscenity and Pornography, which issued a report in 1984, recommended widespread restrictions of pornographic material. This commission has been extensively criticized for its lack of scientific objectivity.

Research evidence has suggested that under certain conditions pornography facilitates aggressive, sexual behavior toward women. Studies by Donnerstein (1983) and Malamuth (Malamuth & Check, 1981; Malamuth, Haber, & Feshbach, 1980; Malamuth, Heim, & Feshbach, 1980) indicate, for example, that a general statement that pornography does not negatively influence people needs several qualifiers. In a series of ongoing experiments, Donnerstein found evidence that three factors influence the relationship between erotica and human aggression: (1) the level of arousal elicited by erotic films, (2) the level of aggressive content, and (3) the reactions of the victims portrayed in these films and photographs. Donnerstein and others (e.g., Meyer, 1972; Zillman, 1971) angered male subjects in a variety of ways, then found that erotica shown to these aroused subjects significantly increased their aggressive behavior toward others. Because of their arousing properties, the erotic stimuli apparently may promote aggression under certain conditions. This finding accords with Berkowitz's theory (discussed in Chapter 7) on the relationship between arousal and aggression. Anything—sexual or not—that increases the arousal level of an already aroused subject will increase aggressive behavior in situations where aggression is the dominant behavior. The increased arousal may also draw the subject away from his own internal control or self-regulatory mechanisms, thereby allowing him to be less concerned about the consequences of his behavior. Furthermore, pornography investigations reveal that if the subject was angered by a woman, he would be even more aggressive toward other women after being exposed to the erotic film. These findings corroborate the frequent clinical observation that prior to a rape many rapists had been angered, upset, humiliated, or insulted, often by a woman (e.g., Groth, 1979).

Extremely violent stimuli, both erotic and nonerotic, can also facilitate aggression toward women, even in nonangered males, under certain conditions. The level of violence in the film appears to be significant. Portrayals of women being assaulted, even nonsexually, can increase subsequent aggressive behavior by men toward women, even when the males are not angry. Therefore, highly aggressive and violent acts depicted in the media may facilitate the rape act for some males. Since many rapists regard their act as a direct aggressive attack on women, seeing films where women are physically abused may encourage and support their own violent inclinations.

The reactions of the victims portrayed in films also seem crucial. Films or photographs that depict the female victim enjoying rape (common in pornography) encourage acceptance of the rape myth and promote violence against women (Malamuth & Check, 1981). If, on the other hand, the victim finds the rape both painful and abhorrent (negative aggressive erotica), male observers are disinclined to act aggressively. However, several qualifiers must be attached to this finding. If the male observer is already angered (aroused), seeing the victim suffer may make him more aggressive, since any arousal increase in an already aroused subject will increase subsequent aggressive behavior. The specific content of the film becomes irrelevant, as long as it meets the minimum criterion of being somehow arousing. On the other hand, males who are not upset or aroused before seeing a female victim suffer are less likely to aggress against women.

For some individuals, however, due to their conditioning history, pain cues are reinforcing if they are repeatedly associated with sexual gratification. Precisely how they react to various erotic portrayals is unclear, but it seems reasonable to suggest that they would find depictions of pain both highly arousing and supportive of their belief that pain and sexual gratification go together. They might also conclude that the pain–pleasure relationship is inherently characteristic of everyone's sexual gratification and that women really enjoy being "roughed up."

The relationship between violent pornography and sexual aggression remains complex and troubling. Although sexually arousing nonviolent pornography should be available in a free society and arguably has social value, violent pornography has no redeeming value. Its harmful effects, however, are difficult to document except as they relate to a subgroup of individuals. If all violent pornography were eradicated today, sex crimes would likely decrease. The same argument could be made to support confiscation of handguns and rifles or random, unannounced drug testing of the citizenry. The extent to which a society should be asked to barter freedom in exchange for security remains a topic about which reasonable people consistently disagree.

PEDOPHILIA

Pedophilia, commonly known as "child molestation" or child sexual abuse, is defined in a variety of ways. The DSM-IV (American Psychiatric Association, 1994) defines the term as a condition in which, "over a period of at least 6 months, recurrent, intense sexually arousing fantasies, sexual urges, or behaviors involving sexual activity with a prepubescent child or children (generally age 13 years or younger) occur" (p. 528). The DSM-IV further specifies that some pedophiles are sexually attracted only to children (the exclusive type), whereas others are sexually attracted to both children and adults (nonexclusive type). According to Finkelhor and Araji (1986), pedophilia is a male adult's conscious sexual interest in prepubertal children. One of two behaviors signifies that interest. Either the adult has had some sexual contact with a child (touched the child or had the child touch him with the purpose of arousing him sexually) or the adult has masturbated to sexual fantasies involving children. The last definition recognizes that a male adult may have very strong sexual interest in children and be blocked from acting on it more directly only by circumstances. Occasionally, researchers extend the definition to include ages 13 through 15, but most literature reserves the term **hebephilia** for sexual contact of adult males with young adolescents. Traditionally, most definitions of pedophilia were restricted to sexual contact between an adult and a child who are not closely related. Sexual acts between members of a family when at least one participant is a minor were typically labeled "incest." More recent research and commentary, however, have placed all sexual contacts between an adult and a child in the pedophilia category. For purposes of clarity, we use pedophilia and child molestation interchangeably as umbrella terms for all categories of child sexual abuse.

Incidence and Prevalence

As with sexual offenses in general, a caveat pertaining to the statistics is necessary. Data on pedophilia are difficult to obtain, since there are no central or national objective recording systems for tabulating sexual offenses against children. Also, as just noted, offenders may be arrested and prosecuted under a variety of statutes and for a variety of offenses, including child rape, aggravated assault, sodomy, incest, indecent exposure, and lewd and lascivious behavior. Although the UCR lists sex offenses, it does not differentiate pedophilia from the mixture of other possible sexual offenses. However, a variety of retrospective surveys of the general population indicates that from a quarter to a third of all females and a tenth or more of all males were molested during childhood (Finkelhor & Lewis, 1988; Peters, Wyatt, & Finkelhor, 1986). Moreover, only 35% of the children who are sexually victimized report it to anyone (Finkelhor, 1979). Russell (1984) found that in her sample only 2% of all incestuous abuse cases and 6% of all cases of extrafamilial abuse of females under 18 had ever been reported to the police. From a national survey of about 1,200 American males (Finkelhor & Lewis, 1988), it is estimated that between 5% and 10% of the male population has engaged or will engage in child sexual abuse at some time in their lives. It is important to note, however, that this figure may include a one-time incident that—although still to be condemned—may not represent the offender's usual behavior and would not qualify him as a pedophile for purposes of this chapter. However, these data indicate that children are sexually victimized at levels that far exceed those reported for adults (see Finkelhor & Dziuba-Leatherman, 1994).

In the Russell (1984) survey, 930 randomly selected female residents of San Francisco were interviewed throughout the summer of 1978. The purpose of the project was to obtain an estimate of the incidence and prevalence of rape and other forms of sexual assault, including the amount of sexual abuse respondents experienced as children. Twelve percent of the women said they had been sexually abused by a relative before the age of 14. Twenty-nine percent reported at least one experience of sexual abuse by a nonrelative before reaching the age of 14. Overall, 28% of the 930 women reported at least one incident of sexual abuse before reaching the age of 14.

Situational and Victimization Characteristics

The offender, or pedophile, is almost always male, but the victim may be of either gender. As noted earlier, however, research is beginning to focus more on the sexual offending of women (Becker & Johnson, 2001; L. Ellis, 1998). Although the predominant view remains that men far outnumber women as perpetrators, there is growing recognition that women are not immune to committing this type of crime. We discuss this topic again below. Heterosexual pedophilia—male adult with female child—appears to be the more common type, with available data indicating that three-quarters of pedophiles choose female victims exclusively (Langevin, 1983; Lanyon, 1986). Homosexual pedophilia—male adult preference for male child—appears to be substantially less frequent (about 20% to 23% of reported cases). A small minority of pedophiles choose their victims from both sexes. The behavior of the pedophile or child molester is usually limited to caressing the child's body, fondling the child's genitals, and/or inducing the child to manipulate his or her genitals. Heterosexual penetration is apparently involved in only a small proportion of the total number of offenses.

The offender and the victim know one another in most instances, often very well (McCaghy, 1967; L. Schultz, 1975; Virkkunen, 1975). Many victims were actively seeking natural affection from their offenders, as a child seeks to be hugged or cuddled. Some victims feel kindly and lovingly toward the offender, who sometimes interprets this behavior as "seductive." Clinical observations suggest that pedophiles, as a group, tend to have positive feelings toward their victims, generally perceive them as being willing participants, and frequently victimize children living in their immediate households (Miner, Day, & Nafpaktitis, 1989). It is not uncommon for the sexual behavior between the offender and the victim to have gone on for a sustained period of time.

The form of the sexual contact seems to depend on three factors: the degree to which the offender had previous nonsexual interactions with children, the nature of the relationship between the child and the offender, and the age of each. Offenders who have had limited interaction with children are more likely to perform or expect genital–genital and oral–genital contact, rather than to indulge only in caressing or fondling. Furthermore, the more familiar the offender and the victim are with one another, the greater the tendency for genital–genital or oral–genital contact.

There is some disagreement about the extent to which child molesters harm the child physically or use physical force. According to most research, pedophiles do not usually use overt physical coercion. McCaghy (1967) found no evidence of any kind of coercion, verbal or physical, in three-fourths of the child molestation cases he examined. Research by Groth and his colleagues (Groth, Hobson, & Gary, 1982) supports these findings. Lanyon (1986), summarizing the research, concluded that violence is involved in about 10% to 15% of child sexual abuse cases. However, G. C. N. Hall, Proctor, and Nelson (1988) report that 28% of a sample of convicted pedophiles (122 nonpsychotic patients in a state mental hospital) were officially identified as having used physical force or the threat of force beyond what was necessary to gain the victim's compliance. Marshall and Christie (1981) found that in a sample of 41 pedophiles incarcerated in Canadian federal penitentiaries, 29 had used physical force. In an earlier study of 150 pedophiles, Christie, Marshall, and Lanthier (1979) reported that 58% used excessive force in their attack, and 42% of the child victims sustained notable injuries. The researchers suggested that the offenders in their sample were highly sexually aroused by physical violence, significantly more so than other nonaggressive sex offenders. The reported differences in the use of violence and force by pedophiles appears to be explained by the sample used. Studies reporting a high incidence of violence or aggression focus on incarcerated, relatively hard-core offenders, while those reporting little or no violence sampled less criminal or nonincarcerated pedophiles, generally those on probation.

Groth, Hobson, and Gary (1982) recommend that the few offenders using violence or force and causing physical harm to the child should be labeled "child rapists." On the other hand, those offenders using only psychological pressures should be considered child molesters or pedophiles. Although Groth's suggestion has merit, researchers in this area have used pedophile and child molester as umbrella terms to cover all child sexual abusers.

Research offers strong support for the assumption that sexual abuse in childhood (both violent and nonviolent) produces long-term psychological problems in many children (Briere, 1988). Reports of depression, guilt, feelings of inferiority, substance abuse, suicidality, anxiety, chronic tension, sleep problems, and fears and phobias are common. Depression is the symptom most commonly reported among adults who were molested as children. The extent of psychological damage to the child produced by sexual abuse is dependent on several factors. Groth (1978) contends that the greatest trauma occurs in children who have been victims for long periods of time, in children who are victimized by a closely related person (such as a stepfather), when the victimization involves penetration, and when it is accompanied by aggression. In their careful review of the research literature on pedophilia, Browne and Finkelhor (1986) concluded that (1) younger children appear to be somewhat more vulnerable to trauma than older children, (2) the closer the relationship between offender and victim the greater the trauma, and (3) the greater the force used the greater the trauma. They also concluded, however, that there is no conclusive support for the contention that the longer and more frequent the abuse the greater the trauma. Nor is there any clear evidence that traumas are related to the type of sexual abuse (intercourse, fondling, fellatio, cunnilingus, etc.). This suggests that "mild" abuse may be as traumatizing as intercourse, especially if the victim is young and closely related to the offender. The Browne and Finkelhor review also suggests that, for some unexplained reason, victims of child sexual abuse are more likely than nonvictims to be sexually assaulted again as adults.

Offender Characteristics

Pedophilia is primarily committed by males, but it is not exclusively a male offense. The National Center on Child Abuse and Neglect (1981) reported that 46% of the abusive sexual experiences encountered by children included a female perpetrator. This figure is misleading, however, in that it includes any female caretaker who "permitted acts of sexual abuse to occur" (Russell & Finkelhor, 1984). In other words, leaving the child with a boyfriend who molests the child while babysitting would be considered sexual abuse by the mother. The mother who fails to report her suspicions that her husband is sexually abusing her daughter would also be included in the statistic. If only those women who actually *committed* child sexual abuse are included, the percentage of female offenders drops to 13 in the case of female victims and 24 in the case of males (Russell & Finkelhor, 1984). On the basis of their research, Russell and Finkelhor (1984) suggest that females are involved in about 5% of cases of sexual abuse of girls and about 20% of cases of boys.

More recent research suggests that these figures may be higher, however. Nevertheless, because sexual abuse of children by females is so little explored, we concentrate in the remainder of this chapter on what is known about male pedophiles. It should be noted, as well, that almost all theories and typologies have been developed on male offenders.

Prentky, Knight, and Lee (1997) conclude from their extensive research on the subject that the classification and diagnosis of child molesters are complicated by a high degree of variability among individuals in reference to personal characteristics, life experiences, criminal histories, and reasons or motivations for offending. Essentially, there is no single "profile" that accurately describes all child molesters. With this caveat in mind, we proceed with some commonly observed characteristics of many of the pedophiles.

Although there is considerable age variability, the average age of convicted male child molesters ranges between 36 and 40. While about 75% of convicted rapists are under 30, about 75% of convicted child molesters are over that age (Henn, Herjanic, & Vanderpearl, 1976b). Groth (1978), however, noted that all the child molesters he and colleagues worked with committed their first child molestation offense before age 40. Over 80% were first offenders by age 30, and about 5% committed their first sexual assault before they reached adolescence. However, despite the statistical finding that child molesters tend to be older than most other sexual offenders, there seems to be a pattern of victim preference as a function of age. Older pedophiles (over 50) seek out immature children (10 or younger); younger pedophiles (under age 40) prefer girls between 12 and 15 years old (Revitch & Weiss, 1962). The latter are technically classified as hebephiles.

Perhaps because of the extremely negative attitude society displays toward child molesters, pedophiles almost always resist taking full responsibility for their offenses (McCaghy, 1967). Many claim that they went blank, were too drunk to know what they were doing, could not help themselves, or did not know what came over them. They show a strong tendency to attribute the cause of their behavior to external forces or motivating factors largely beyond their personal control.

However, those charged with child molestation rarely manifest any serious or pronounced behavioral or emotional problems other than the pedophilia (Henn et al., 1976b). When clinical diagnoses are made, they are most often organic brain syndrome (damage) and mental retardation, but these represent only a small percentage of the total pedophile population. Since pedophilia and exhibitionism are the most common sexual offenses committed by senile and arteriosclerotic men (J. Coleman, 1976), the organic brain syndrome classification is not really surprising.

Many aggressive pedophiles demonstrate a large number of similarities with rapists and the prison population in general (Knight, Rosenberg, & Schneider, 1985). The most notable commonalities are the following: (1) They have problems with alcohol, (2) they have a high rate of high school failure and dropout, (3) they tend to have unstable work histories in unskilled occupations, and (4) they tend to come from the low socioeconomic class.

Alcohol abuse is frequently a problem in sex offenders. While about one-third to one-half of convicted rapists have serious problems with alcohol, about one-quarter to one-third of convicted pedophiles have such problems (Knight, Rosenberg, & Schneider, 1985). Research also indicates that a large segment of pedophiles does not progress much beyond the eighth grade in school (Christie, Marshall, & Lanthier, 1979), and many show signs of mental deficiencies on traditional IQ tests (Knight et al., 1985; Swanson, 1968).

About two-thirds of those arrested and convicted for child molestation offenses come from the unskilled or semiskilled occupational groups (McCaghy, 1967; Gebhard et al., 1965). However, other occupational groups may handle the incident quite differently to prevent additional trauma for the victims and social embarrassment for their families during the legal investigation and process. In the 1980s, the media were filled with accounts of the alarming increase in child sex abuse rates. These same accounts note that it knows no economic or social barriers: Child offenders exist at all levels of society and among all occupational groups.

Classification of Child Offender Patterns

The Massachusetts Treatment Center (MTC) (Cohen et al., 1969; Knight, 1988; Rosenberg, & Schneider, 1985) has been developing a widely cited typology of pedophile behavioral patterns, similar to the rape typology presented earlier. Four major pedophiliac patterns have been identified: (1) the fixated type, (2) the regressed type, (3) the exploitative type, and (4) the aggressive or sadistic type.

The **fixated** (or **immature**) **pedophile** demonstrates a long-standing, exclusive preference for children as both sexual and social companions. He has never been able to develop a mature relationship with his adult peers, male or female, and he is considered socially immature, passive, timid, and dependent by most people who know him. He feels most comfortable relating to children, whom he seeks out as companions. Sexual contact usually occurs only after the adult and child have become well acquainted. Fixated pedophiles rarely marry, and their social background lacks much evidence of dating peers or even any sustained, long-term friendship with an adult (outside of relatives). This pedophile wishes to touch, fondle, caress, and taste the child. He rarely expects genital intercourse, and very rarely does he use physical force or aggression.

The fixated pedophile generally has average intelligence. His work history is steady, although it is often work that is below his ability. His social skills are adequate for day-to-day functioning. Probably most troubling about the fixated or immature pedophile is that he is not concerned or disturbed about his exclusive preference for children as companions, nor can he see why others are concerned. Therefore, he is difficult to treat and is most likely to recidivate.

The **regressed pedophile** had a fairly normal adolescence and good peer relationships and heterosexual experiences but later developed feelings of masculine inadequacy and self-doubt. Problems in the individual's occupational, social, and sexual lives followed. The regressed child offender's background commonly includes alcohol abuse, divorce, and a poor employment record. Each pedophilial act is usually precipitated by a significant jolt to the offender's sexual adequacy, by either female or male peers. For example, the pedophile may perceive other males as being more successful with women than he. Unlike the immature child offender, the regressed child offender usually prefers victims who are strangers and who live outside his neighborhood. The victims are nearly always female. Unlike the fixated pedophile, he seeks genital sex with his victim. Because he feels remorseful and expresses disbelief after that act, clinicians usually find him a good prospect for rehabilitation. As long as stressful events are kept to a minimum and he learns to cope adequately with those he does have, he is unlikely to reoffend.

The **exploitative pedophile** seeks children primarily to satisfy his sexual needs. He exploits the child's weaknesses any way he can and tries various kinds of strategies and tricks to get him or her to comply. He is usually unknown to the child and commonly tries to get the child isolated from others and his familiar surroundings. If necessary, he will use aggression and physical force to get the child to comply with his wishes. The exploitative offender does not care about the emotional or physical well-being of the child, but sees the victim only as a sexual object.

The exploitative offender exhibits a long history of criminal or antisocial conduct. His relationships with peers are unpredictable and stormy. He is unpleasant to be around and is often avoided by others who know him. He tends to be highly impulsive, irritable, and moody. His markedly defective interpersonal skills may be the principal reason that he chooses children as victims (Knight et al., 1985). Clinicians find him difficult to treat, as his deficiencies extend to all phases of his daily life.

The **aggressive** (or **sadistic**) **pedophile** is drawn to children for both sexual and aggressive reasons. Pedophiles in this group are apt to have a long history of antisocial behavior and poor adaptation to their environments. Most prefer victims of the same sex (homosexual pedophilia). Since the primary aim is to obtain stimulation without consideration for the victim, this group often assaults the child viciously and sadistically. The more harm and pain inflicted, the more this offender becomes sexually excited. Aggressive or sadistic pedophiles are most often responsible for child abductions and murders. Clinicians find this type not only dangerous to children, but among the most difficult to treat. Fortunately, this type is rare. Although rare, this is the type frequently portrayed in the media and is most associated with the image of the child molester.

An example of an aggressive child molester is Albert Fish (1870–1936), whose background is discussed by Nash (1975). Fish, called the "Moon Maniac," admitted sexually molesting more than 400 children over a span of 20 years. In addition, he confessed to six child murders and made vague reference to numerous others. He was eventually convicted of murdering a 12-year-old girl and was electrocuted in 1936. A more contemporary example might well be John Wayne Gacy Jr., who sadistically murdered 33 teenage boys and young men and buried their bodies in the cellar of his suburban Chicago home.

Fish thought the conditions of his childhood led to a "perverted" life of crime. He was abandoned at an early age and placed in an orphanage, where he first witnessed and experienced brutal acts of sadism. Fish was quoted as saying, "Misery leads to crime. I saw so many boys whipped it ruined my mind." He apparently began his career of child molesting in earnest when his wife deserted him for another man. This suggests that, like regressed offenders, aggressive offenders may begin their crimes in response to precipitating events involving rejection and feelings of sexual inadequacy.

The MTC:CM3

Similar to the MTC classification scheme for rapists, the MTC classification system for child molesters has also undergone some refinement in recent years. In an effort to depict more accurately the complexity involved in classifying pedophiles, the MTC:CM3 (MTC: Child Molester, Version 3) has made some tentative changes to the original scheme described earlier. Three significant changes are recommended: (1) Divide the regressed and fixated types into three separate factors—degree of fixation on children, level of social competence achieved, and amount of contact an offender has with children; (2) incorporate a new narcissistic offender type into the scheme; and (3) partition the violence of the sexual assault into physical injury and sadistic components (Knight, 1989).

The researchers discovered that, although the regressed or fixated pedophile classification is a valid one, it was also more complicated than originally supposed. Researchers found that the regression or fixated (immature) classification could be further subdivided into the molester's style of offending, his interpersonal relationships with children, the intensity of the offender's interest, and the level of social competence achieved by the offender. For example, offenders could be classified according to their level of fixation and social competence. Level of fixation refers to the strength of an offender's sexual interest in children (Knight et al., 1989). For example, to what extent are children the major focus of the offender's thought and attention? If children are the central focus of the offender's sexual and interpersonal fantasies and thoughts for more than 6 months, then the offender qualifies as having high fixation. Social competence refers to the degree to which the offender can participate effectively in daily living. An offender is classified as having high social competence if he has demonstrated at least two of the following behaviors: (1) has had a single job lasting three or more years, (2) has had a sexual relationship with an adult for at least a year, (3) has assumed responsibility in parenting a child for three or more years, (4) has been an active member in an adult-oriented organization (e.g., church group, business group) for one or more years, or (5) has had a social friendship with an adult for at least one year. The dimensions of fixation and social competence result in four types of child molesters: high fixation, low social competence (type 0); high fixation, high social competence (type 1); low fixation, low social competence (type 2); and low fixation, high social competence (type 3). The regressed type was dropped in the MTC:CM3 in favor of the term "low fixation."

Research further revealed that pedophiles can also be distinguished on the basis of how much daily contact with children they seek (see **Figure 10–3**). A high-contact offender demonstrates regular contact with children in both sexual offense and nonsexual contexts (Knight et al., 1989). High-contact offenders often become involved in an occupation or recreation that brings them into considerable contact with children, such as bus driver, school teacher, Boy Scout leader, or Little League coach. Research data revealed that there are two kinds of offenders who seek more extensive involvement with children beyond their sexual offenses. The first high-contact type, the *interpersonal offender* (Type 1), seeks the extensive company of children for both social and sexual needs. He sees the child as an appropriate companion in a relationship and feels his friendship is mutually satisfying. The second type, the *narcissistic offender* (Type 2), solicits the company of children only to increase his opportunities for sexual experiences. Similarly to exploitative offenders, they typically molest children they do not know and their sexual acts with children are typically genitally oriented (Knight, 1989). Furthermore, they have little or no concern about the needs, comfort, or welfare of the child (Knight et al., 1989).

Figure 10–3   Flow Diagram of the Decision Process for Classifying Child Molesters on Axis I and Axis II of the MTC:CM3

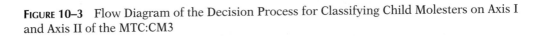
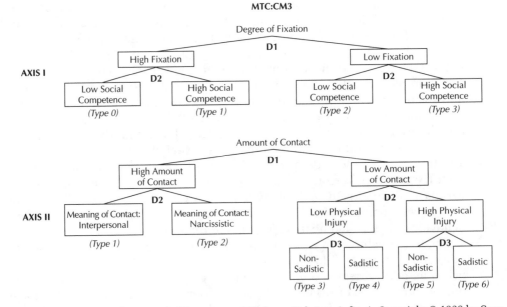

Source: R. A. Knight et al., *Journal of Interpersonal Violence*, Vol. 4, p. 8, fig. 1. Copyright © 1989 by Sage Publications, Inc. Reprinted by permission of Sage Publications, Inc.

Another group of pedophiles is low-contact seekers. Low-contact offenders' only contacts with children are in the context of sexual assault. Low-contact offenders are evaluated according to the amount of physical injury they administer to their victims. Two types of low-contact seekers tend to administer very little physical injury to their victims: the exploitative type and the muted sadistic type. Low injury refers to the absence of physical injury to the victim and the presence of such acts as pushing, shoving, slapping, holding, and verbal threats. None of the acts of low injury results in a lasting injury (e.g., cuts, bruises, contusions). The *exploitative, nonsadistic offender* (Type 3) uses no more aggression or violence than is necessary to secure victim compliance. Furthermore, the assault does not reveal evidence that sadistic actions engender sexual arousal in the offender. The *muted* or *symbolic sadistic offender* (Type 4) engages in a variety of distressing, painful, and threatening acts, none of which causes physical injury to the child.

Finally, the MTC:CM3 classifies two offenders who have often administered a high amount of physical injury to their victims: the aggressive offender and the sadistic offender. High injury is characterized by hitting, punching, choking, sodomy, or forcing the child to ingest urine or feces (Knight et al., 1989). The *aggressive, nonsadistic offender* (Type 5) is similar to the aggressive pedophile described earlier except that sadism is not a primary aim of the assault. This offender is extremely angry about all things in his life and is generally violent toward people in his life, including children. The *sadistic offender* (Type 6) obtains sexual pleasure from the pain, fear, and physical harm he inflicts on the child.

The newly developed MTC:CM3 helps identify offender type based on crime scene information and perhaps presents a more refined classification system of child molester types. However, research beyond the MTC population is needed before investigators will feel comfortable about adopting this promising scheme.

The Groth Classification Model

In a classification system similar to that of the MTC, Groth (1978; Groth & Burgess, 1977) classifies child offenders on the basis of the longevity of the behavioral patterns and the offender's psychological aims. If the sexual preference for children has existed persistently since adolescence, he is classified as an *immature* or *fixated child offender*. As in the MTC classification system, the fixated child offender has been sexually attracted primarily or exclusively to significantly younger people throughout his life, regardless of what other sexual experiences he has had. Groth believes that this fixation is due to an arrest of psychological maturation, resulting from unresolved formative issues that persist and underlie subsequent development. On the other hand, if the offender has managed to develop some normalcy to his relationships with adults but resorts to child offending when he is stressed or suffers a devastating blow to his self-esteem, he is called a *regressed* child offender.

Based on his clinical research, Groth has also subdivided child offenders according to their intentions or psychological aims. He identifies two basic categories: (1) sex pressure offenders and (2) sex force offenders. In sex pressure offenses, the offender's typical modus operandi is to entice children into sexuality through persuasion or cajolement or to entrap them by placing them in a situation in which they feel indebted or obligated. Children may feel they owe something to a person who taught them to swim or bought them a bike. The sex force offense, on the other hand, is characterized by threat of harm and/or use of physical force in the commission of the offense. The offender either intimidates the child by exploiting the child's relative helplessness, naiveté, and awe of adults or attacks and physically overpowers his victim.

Groth finds he can further subdivide the sex force group into the *exploitative type*, in which the threat of force is used to overcome victim resistance, or the *sadistic type*, who derives great pleasure in hurting the child. The exploitative type typically employs verbal threats, restraint, manipulation, intimidation, and physical strength to overcome any resistance on the part of the child. His intent is not necessarily to hurt the child but to obtain compliance. The sadistic type, which fortunately is rare, eroticizes physical aggression and pain. He uses more force than is necessary to overpower the victim and may commit a so-called lust murder. Therefore, physical and psychological abuse and/or degradation of the child is necessary for him to experience sexual excitement and gratification. Often, the child is beaten, choked, tortured, and violently sexually abused.

Certainly the Groth typology has strong commonalities with the MTC typology. The immature and the regressed child offenders display features of the sex pressure offender, and the aggressive child offender shows strong similarities to the sex force offender. It may be more appropriate for the present time to classify the child offender according to the degree of coercion or force he uses rather than according to personality features. The first method focuses on offender behavior, a criterion that is more objective and clear-cut. The second focuses on "understanding" the behavior by assuming a variety of personality constructs. We have too little information on child offenders at this point to do that with total confidence.

Recidivism

If pedophilia is learned, we would expect a fairly high incidence of recidivism. Like the national recidivism rates for most offenses, however, pedophile recidivism rates are difficult to confirm. Moreover, the second time around, the pedophile is undoubtedly more careful to avoid detection. In the California study by Frisbie (1965), recidivism rates over a five-year period were reported to be 18.2% for heterosexual pedophiles and 34.5% for homosexual pedophiles. However, as L. G. Schultz (1975) noted, most pedophile offenses go unreported. Abel and colleagues (Abel, Becker, Murphy, & Flanagan, 1981) reported that incarcerated homosexual pedophiles had, on the average, 31 victims, while heterosexual pedophiles had an average of 62 victims. A Dutch study (Bernard, 1975) reported that at least half of its respondents claimed sexual contacts with 10 or more children. Fourteen percent of the sample—which included both arrested and unarrested pedophiles—admitted to sexual contacts with more than 50 children, and 6% to contacts with between 100 and 300 children. Fifty-six percent of this sample indicated that they had one or more "regular" sexual contacts with children. Fully 90% asserted that they did not want to stop their pedophilial activities.

Abel and colleagues (Abel, Mittelman, Becker, Rathner, & Rouleau, 1988) report that of the 192 nonincarcerated child offenders who voluntarily participated in a treatment program, the men most likely to drop out of treatment were those with a history of considerable and varied pedophilic behavior. That is, 70% of the frequent child offenders who demonstrated no age preference (child or adolescent) or gender preference (male or female) dropped out of treatment, usually early in the process. The treatment program consisted of 30 90-minute group sessions given weekly and directed at decreasing deviant arousal, developing cognitive restructuring of distorted sexual attitudes and beliefs, and increasing subjects' social competence with adults. In addition, those subjects who managed to complete the program and who had varied child offending behaviors and multiple victims were the ones who were most likely to recidivate within one year after treatment.

Further indications of recidivism rates of child offenders can be garnered from the 13-year outpatient treatment program described by Marshall and Barbaree (1988). This Canadian project offered psychological treatment of deviant sexual behavior on a voluntary basis to a variety of sexual offenders. Forty percent of the child offenders refused treatment. The project had access to official records (charges and convictions) throughout North America as well as to information from "unofficial" files of local police departments and Children's Aid Societies in the towns where the offenders lived. Thirty-two percent of the untreated child offenders reoffended, compared to 14% of the treated offenders. The average follow-up period for both groups was approximately three and one-half years. Of the 26 men who recidivated, only 11 were identified "officially" (charges and convictions), whereas the remainder were identified through the "unofficial" information. Even so, the unofficial measures of recidivism were still official in that they were collected by public agencies, which leaves us still wondering how high the "unofficial" recidivism rates for child offenders really are.

Etiology

Most explanations of pedophilia focus on a single factor as the principal cause of sexual and social preferences for children by adults. One clinical hypothesis, for example, suggests that pedophiles select children as sex objects because they are haunted by feelings of masculine and sexual inadequacy in adult re-lationships (e.g., Groth et al., 1982). They are terrified of being ridiculed about their sexual and social behavior in the adult world. In the world of the child, they can be safely curious, awkward, and inexperienced. This observa-tion might help explain why pedophiles rarely engage in heterosexual inter-course. Although this inadequacy hypothesis appears to have some validity, it fails to explain the full range and diversity of pedophilic behavior.

Finkelhor and Araji (1986) find four basic explanations for pedophilia in the research and clinical literature: emotional congruence, sexual arousal, blockage, and disinhibition theories. The most common is what they call *emotional congruence theories*. These theories try to explain why a person would find relating sexually to a child to be emotionally gratifying and con-gruent with their needs. Finkelhor and Araji refer to these explanations as emotional congruence theories, since they convey the idea of a fit between the adult's emotional needs and the child's characteristics. Most congruence theo-ries are psychoanalytic in origin and focus on "arrested psychological devel-opment." According to this perspective, pedophiles see themselves as children with childish emotional needs and dependency, and consequently they feel most comfortable with children. A similar version focuses on the low self-esteem and loss of efficacy pedophiles experience in their daily lives. Relating to a child is congruent, because the inadequate adult finally feels powerful, omnipotent, and in control of a relationship. In short, relating to a child pro-vides a sense of mastery and control in their lives.

The second group of theories tries to explain why pedophiles become sexually aroused by certain characteristics of children. Sexual arousal is typ-ically measured by penile tumescence to the presence of children or to sex-ual fantasies of children. Called *sexual arousal theories*, this perspective contends that pedophiles become sexually aroused to stimuli (features of children) that, for a variety of reasons, do not generate sexual arousal in normal males. One set of theories within this group posits that it is a com-mon childhood experience to engage in sexual play with playmates. For the pedophile, the childhood sexual play may have been particularly vivid, re-warding, and stimulating, and even possibly the most sexually exciting expe-rience he has ever had. Adult sexual play, in comparison, was less arousing, satisfying, or rewarding, perhaps even nonexistent. The pedophile's shyness, for example, may have precluded adult sexual contacts. Under these condi-tions, he probably took the most available sexual avenue, masturbation. As noted earlier, the powerful reinforcing role of masturbatory behavior (mas-turbatory conditioning) has been demonstrated in clinical studies of most sexual offenses (Marshall, 1988). During masturbation, the pedophile's fan-tasies may focus on the satisfying sexual experiences he had during child-hood. Repetitive masturbatory activity, therefore, reinforces the immature level of sexual behavior associated with childhood. Whereas masturbation of itself may be a normal outlet for sexual tension, for the pedophile it becomes an act that reinforces his attraction to children. Continual association between the pleasurable masturbatory activities and fantasies about childhood sexual experiences results in a strong bond between sexual arousal and children. Eventually, children become sexual stimuli capable of arousing high levels of sexual excitation.

Another version of the sexual arousal perspective links traumatic sexual victimization to pedophilic behavior. Many researchers have found unusually high amounts of childhood sexual victimization in the background of pedophiles (Bard et al., 1987). It is unclear, however, how sexual trauma, which is aversive, becomes conditioned or associated with the sexual pleasures of pedophilia.

Blockage theories assume that pedophilia is the result of blockage of normal sexual and emotional gratification from adult relationships. Frustrated in his quest for normal channels of sexual gratification, the offender seeks the company of children. Blockage theories emphasize the unassertive, timid, inadequate, and awkward personalities of the pedophile, arguing that these social deficiencies make it nearly impossible for him to develop normal social and sexual relationships with adult women. When the marital relationship breaks down, for example, the pedophile may turn to his daughter as a substitute.

The fourth set of explanations focuses on the loss of self-control and personal constraints on behavior. *Disinhibition theories* outline a variety of circumstances that presumably propel the offender to his deeds. Poor impulse control, excessive use of alcohol and drugs, and an assortment of stressors could all lead him over the brink to his favorite deviant sexual practices. As mentioned earlier, many pedophiles refuse to take blame, but attribute the cause of their pedophilic behavior to forces outside themselves. "I couldn't help myself" or "I don't know what came over me" are frequent pleas.

Which theoretical perspective has the inside track for the explanation of pedophilia? By itself, none can account for the multiple causes and the full range of learning experiences, beliefs, motivations, and attitudes of pedophiles. Overall, though, it is clear that child molesters think about their victims in a self-serving and cognitively distorted manner (Ward & Keenan, 1999). Child molesters, in general, have beliefs and attitudes that legitimize sexual involvement with children and help them continue their sexual contact. More specifically, child molesters "see children in sexual terms as wanting sex, as not being harmed by sexual contact with an adult, and view themselves as not really being responsible" (Ward & Keenan, 1999, p. 821).

Despite the high media profile of clergy child molesters in recent years, very little is known about them (Saradjian & Nobus, 2003). This lack of knowledge is partly due to researchers' lack of access to the clergy. Saradjian and Nobus (2003) studied 14 clergymen who had sexually abused children. Based on their small sample, the authors were able to conclude that religious professionals seem to hold many of the same cognitive distortions and justifications as nonreligious pedophiles. Religious professionals, like other molesters, minimized and denied the harm caused by sexual activity between an adult and a child. Perhaps the one unsurprising major difference is that the religious professsionals tended to rely more on religion-related cognitive distortions to facilitate their sexual offending. They believed, for example, that God permitted or understood the abuse and would forgive them for their sins. "God knows I' m weak and will forgive me" (Saradjian & Nobus, 2003, p. 919).

EXHIBITIONISM

Exhibitionism is the deliberate exposure of the genitals to another person to achieve sexual gratification. Several authors have reported that in some parts of the world exhibitionism—often called indecent exposure—is the most frequent sexual offense known to the police (e.g., J. Coleman, 1976; Wincze, 1977). In Canada and the United States, exhibitionism—usually called lewd and lascivious behavior in the legal system—accounts for about one-third of all sex crimes (Evans, 1970; Rooth, 1974), and in the United Kingdom it accounts for one-fourth (Feldman, 1977). While exhibitionism, along with other relatively mild offenses such as voyeurism and frottage, make up a substantial number of officially recorded sex offenses, persons convicted of these offenses are rarely incarcerated (Rice, Harris, & Quinsey, 2001). Bancroft (1976) estimates that exhibitionism is the second most common sexual deviation treated at mental health facilities in England.

Rooth (1973, 1974) argued that the practice of exposing oneself is primarily a Western phenomenon. In India, extensive surveys failed to uncover a single case (Rooth, 1974). In Japan, the incidence for one year was 59 convicted cases, compared to 2,767 in England and Wales during the same year. Rooth (1973) also suggested that exhibitionism is rare in Latin America and Third World countries.

To what extent exhibitionism is exclusively a Western phenomenon remains open to debate. Much depends on the culture and police discretion in each country. In Latin American countries, for example, it is a common sight to see men and women openly urinating in public (Rhoads & Borjes, 1981). If a society reacts so casually to nudity or exposure of sexual organs, exhibitionism will lose its shock value. In an effort to determine comparable rates of exhibitionism, Rhoads and Borjes asked working women in both the United States and Guatemala how often men had exposed themselves to them in public. The survey indicated no difference in the number of incidences, but the official records of the two countries were drastically different. This may reflect reluctance on the part of the Guatemalan women to report exhibitionism, since officers are likely to ridicule the victims.

Exhibitionists are almost always males who delight in surprising and shocking their audiences. They differ from "strippers"—both male and female—in that the latter expose themselves for economic gain rather than sexual gratification. In addition, of course, persons watching strippers do so deliberately and voluntarily. Exhibitionists sometimes masturbate during the exposure, but most prefer to do so in private, immediately following their exposure.

Situational Characteristics

If the offender is not particularly brazen, he may habitually hide behind the curtain of a window in his home when school lets out and, as young girls walk by, tap on the window, quickly expose himself, and make a fast retreat behind the curtain. This is risky, however, since his identity is easily traceable. Another favorite procedure is to use a car, drive slowly by a female or group of females, open the car door, show himself, and quickly drive away. The bolder exhibitionist is often the "street flasher" who opens his coat to a selected victim, makes certain the impression registers, and then runs or walks away.

Favorite locations for exposure vary, but most exhibitionists prefer public places like parks, theaters, stores, or relatively uncrowded streets. An early Toronto study (Mohr, Turner, & Jerry, 1964) reported that 74% of a sample studied preferred open places, and most displayed themselves from a parked car. The remainder of the sample generally preferred their own homes, often exhibiting themselves through windows or doorways.

The overwhelming majority of exhibitionists prefer strangers for victims and rarely expose themselves more than once to the same victim. Although the preferred victim is usually female, an exhibitionist will occasionally expose himself to adult males and male children. Exhibitionists who prefer adult women will usually expose to them individually, while those who prefer female children will generally expose to small groups of two or three (Evans, 1970; Mohr, Turner, & Jerry, 1964). Most adult female victims are in their late teens or early twenties, usually unmarried. This supports the theory that most exhibitionists deliberately select their victims on the basis of specific stimuli. For example, one exhibitionist may have a definite preference for exhibiting to young girls between 9 and 11 years old who look "naive." Another may search for a pretty face, dark hair, shapely legs, or various other physical features. Exhibitionists also tend to be consistent in the setting and time of day they choose for exposure. In fact, many are so predictable that, once the incident is reported, they are easily detected and arrested.

Offender Characteristics

Most exhibitionists begin their behavior at puberty, with a peak period occurring between age 15 and age 30 (Evans, 1970). Contrary to popular belief, onset after age 30 is extremely rare, except in men with mental impairment due to organic brain damage or senility. Compared to the general population, exhibitionists usually have at least average intelligence, educational levels, and vocational interests (Blair & Lanyon, 1981). The majority also appear to have a reliable work record (Mohr, Turner, & Jerry, 1964).

Psychosis or other mental disorders are found no more frequently in exhibitionists than in the general population (Blair & Lanyon, 1981). However, exhibitionists show an above-average incidence of previous sexual offenses other than exhibitionism, including voyeurism and even attempted rape. In the main, however, exhibitionists neither assault their audience physically nor desire sexual intercourse with them. It is highly probable that if victims expressed interest in sexual activity, most exhibitionists would be frightened and confused and would flee. In most cases, the primary motive behind the exhibitionism is the sexual excitation (reinforcement) the offender receives from shocking, surprising, or mildly frightening his victims. These reactions generate considerable sexual arousal. Later, he will probably masturbate to that image. On the other hand, if his exposure fails to engender the anticipated fright or surprise, and produces instead a disinterested, noncommittal facial expression, the offender is disappointed and suffers some loss of self-esteem.

Although many exhibitionists are married, most are considered socially and sexually inadequate both by themselves and by those around them. Many are introverted, shy, socially reserved individuals who feel uncomfortable in most social situations. Generally, they are described as unassertive, self-effacing, timid, and passive. A majority of exhibitionists feel the urge to expose following a blow to their fragile self-esteem, which prompts heightened feelings of inadequacy and stress.

Therefore, like other sexual offenses, exhibitionism is a learned behavioral pattern reinforced by sexual arousal and the subsequent tension reduction achieved through masturbation. Many exhibitionists indicate that their behavior was initially acquired through some preadolescent sex play or by chance. For example, the history of most exhibitionists includes a vivid memory of a young girl expressing amazement or fear at their penis, viewed either accidentally or during sexual play. Characteristically, this attention was sexually exciting to the male, and he masturbated to the imagery of the incident. This not uncommon incident by itself is usually not sufficient to establish exhibitionism. However, a repeated pairing of the memory of the event with the sexual arousal derived from masturbation may lead to a proclivity for exhibitionism in individuals who lack sufficient self-control or self-regulatory mechanisms. That is, pleasurable, repetitive masturbatory activities in the presence of this mental imagery strongly encourage eventual exposure of the penis to victims who are perceived as similar to the initial observer. If the first, real-life exposure is sexually arousing, a strongly reinforcing chain of events is established. Each time the exhibitionist exposes and receives this sequence of rewards, the behavior pattern becomes that much more firmly entrenched.

During subsequent periods of stress and inadequacy, exposure becomes an increasingly effective way of dealing with uncomfortable emotions, especially when preferred victims are available. Therefore, because exhibitionism is a learned response, it continues to be repetitive and resistant to extinction. Furthermore, exhibitionists may expose themselves many thousands of times without complaints from victims. Irate adults do not report an incident of exhibitionism unless the victim was their offspring. Even then they may not report it in order to protect the child from having to describe the incident to police.

It is important to note that exhibitionists, in contrast to many pedophiles, often express a desire to change their behavior. Although they may expose themselves numerous times, once detected they are more likely to seek therapeutic help. Moreover, it is not uncommon for an exhibitionist to seek professional help prior to being arrested for his behavior. Reviewing the literature on treatment for sex offenders, Rice, Harris, and Quinsey (2001) note that motivated exhibitionists have been helped by pharmacological or other treatments designed to reduce sexual arousal together with attention to other factors that might facilitate their offending, such as depression and lack of employment. Day and Berney (2001) note that antiandrogen drugs have been shown to be effective in cases of exhibitionism, pedophilia, and fetishism in mentally retarded individuals.

VOYEURISM AND FETISHISM

Voyeurism, also known as scoptophilia or inspectionalism, is the tendency to gain sexual excitement and gratification from observing unsuspecting others naked, undressing, or engaging in sexual activity. The term **fetishism** refers specifically to a sexual attraction to inanimate objects rather than to people. It is distinct from **partialism**, which is an exaggerated sexual interest in some part of the human anatomy not usually associated with sexual arousal, such as the knee. The individual with a fetish may become sexually aroused at the sight of boots, handbags, stockings, panties, fur, or even tailpipes on motor vehicles. The fetish object may be kissed, fondled, tasted, smelled, or just looked at.

Both voyeurism and fetishism are little more than minor sexual offenses, since they usually do not seriously harm the community. They are, of course, egregious violations of other people's privacy, because "victims" are observed without their knowledge or their possessions are appropriated for "deviant" purposes. The voyeur or the fetishist runs afoul of the law when he harasses, trespasses, burglarizes, damages property, or steals objects.

Recall that the voyeur is sometimes an exhibitionist, and vice versa. However, the voyeur is less likely than the exhibitionist to become involved in serious forms of antisocial behavior, such as rape or other forms of violence. He does not harm his victims physically, and like the exhibitionist, he is often described as a passive, shy, introverted, submissive, and harmless person. Clinical studies reveal that he suffers from strong heterosexual anxieties and immaturity.

One observation made in the Queen's Bench Foundation study (1978) demands attention. About 10% of the convicted rapists interviewed stated that they had watched their victim through a window before attacking her. The authors suggested that, in light of this finding, some "peeping Toms" should be watched for possible rape tendencies. However, some distinguishing aspects of voyeurism should be noted. All but one offender had intentions of raping before observing. The one rapist who said that he did not intend to rape when he watched his victim admitted that he did intend to "have sex" with her. In addition, all but one of these offenders had weapons in their possession at the time of their arrest (knives, guns, meat fork), even though they ordinarily did not carry them. Also, forceful entry into the victim's apartment was the common approach, and the victim was often raped with extreme violence.

These rapists, therefore, probably had little in common with the typical voyeur. Their intention from the outset was to attack the victim violently. They apparently watched the victim to determine her habits, whether anyone else was at home, and the best way to get into her residence. In other words, they were stalking their victims. The typical voyeur gets his satisfaction from watching, imagining, and eventually masturbating, with no intention of having sexual contact, forced or otherwise, with the victim.

Voyeurism, like other forms of sexual deviation, is a learned behavior. Although each individual has a unique approach to viewing, many voyeurs report the preadolescent experience of becoming sexually aroused while watching an unsuspecting woman undress. A common theme running through clinical studies is that the mental imagery of that scene is later coupled with sexual arousal, again perhaps satisfied through masturbation. Eventually, this conditioning produces a desire to observe different, realistic sexual scenes. Keep in mind that an important component of the sexual excitement experienced by the voyeur is the victim's unawareness of his presence. Erotic films or pornography, by themselves, are not likely to serve his purpose.

Fetishism is principally a male phenomenon pursued in the privacy of one's home, without interference in the lives of others. A fetish refers to the use of nonliving objects as a repeatedly and strongly preferred method of achieving sexual excitement. The fetish object is most often some item of women's apparel, such as undergarments, shoes, boots, or stockings. The person with a fetish typically masturbates while rubbing, holding, or smelling the fetish object or may ask a sexual partner to wear the object during their sexual encounters (American Psychiatric Association, 1994, p. 526). Through classical conditioning, virtually any object can assume sexual significance. Gosselin and Wilson (1984) described a study of a man who was strongly attracted to safety pins. From the age of eight, he had experienced extreme sexual pleasure from gazing at these shiny objects in the privacy of his bathroom. "When he was 23 his wife observed the complete sequence, which began with him staring at the safety pin for about a minute. This was followed by a glassy-eyed appearance, vocal humming noises, sucking movements of the lips and total immobility for another minute or two" (Gosselin & Wilson, 1984, p. 104).

As mentioned previously, most fetish objects are those worn by the female, such as undergarments, shoes, boots, or hosiery. Chalkley and Powell (1983) found that underwear, stockings, and other types of lingerie were most popular for British fetish collectors. Next most common were rubber and certain rubber articles such as mackintoshes, tubes, dolls, and paraphernalia for giving enemas.

In an excellent, if controversial, demonstration of fetish conditioning, Rachman (1966) showed male subjects a slide of a pair of women's black boots, followed immediately by slides of attractive, naked women (sexual arousal). After a number of such trials, the subjects became sexually excited, as measured by penile circumference, in response to the boots slide itself. There were also indications that the subjects became aroused not only by slides of those particular boots, but also by slides of other boots and shoes as well.

Fetishism merits attention here primarily because the person with a strong attachment to an object might commit larceny or burglary to get it. One of the major avenues for obtaining fetishes is to steal, and since clothes dryers are more in vogue in modern society than clotheslines, the fetishist's traditional method of stealing from the backyard clothesline has been replaced by more daring techniques. Chalkley and Powell (1983), in their British sample of 48 cases of fetishism, found that 38% experienced considerable excitement and sexual arousal when stealing the fetish. In this sense, it is conceivable that an indeterminant number of unexplained burglaries—when minor things are taken but more valuable items remain untouched—are a result of an impatient quest for fetishes! Some fetish burglars find sexual excitement just being in someone's house without his or her knowledge and presence. It is also not unusual for the fetish burglar to take valuable objects along with his fetish, however, either to throw off suspicion or to offer a face-saving "reasonable" explanation for the burglary if he is apprehended. In one serious fetish case described by Hazelwood and Burgess (1987), the offender admitted committing over 5,000 burglaries primarily to obtain panties to satisfy his fetish. He also estimated that he stole valuables in about one-half of his burglaries.

TREATMENT OF SEXUAL OFFENDERS

Sexual offenders are often highly resistant to changing their deviant behavior patterns. Although a wide variety of treatment programs have been tried, very few have been successful in eradicating sexual offending. A 1994 survey of therapeutic services for sex offenders revealed that there were 710 adult and 684 juvenile treatment programs (Longo, Bird, Stevenson, & Fiske, 1995), compared to 297 adult and 346 juvenile treatment programs in 1985 (Knopp, Rosenberg, & Stevenson, 1986). Despite the increase in treatment programs, the success ratio remains disappointingly low. After careful review of the research and clinical literature, Furby, Weinrott, and Blackshaw (1989, p. 27) concluded, "There is as yet no evidence that clinical treatment reduces rates of sex reoffenses in general and no appropriate data for assessing whether it may be differentially effective for different types of offenders." The Furby review included all variants of therapeutic approaches. Likewise, Rice et al. (2001, p. 302) write, "The effectiveness of sex-offender treatment has yet to be demonstrated. . . . Thus the treatment outcome literature is profoundly unhelpful in giving clues about what might be effective with particular kinds of sex offenders." Nevertheless, Rice et al. note that all is not hopeless. They urge clinicians to adopt individualized treatment approaches that take into account an offender's motivation. Specific interventions designed to reduce recidivism should then be undertaken. An essential component of the treatment, they point out, is ongoing supervision.

Prentky et al. (1997) conclude that sex offender therapy can be categorized into four broad approaches. One approach is **evocative therapy**, a treatment that focuses on (1) helping offenders to understand the causes and motivations of their sexual behavior and (2) increasing offenders' empathy for the victims of the sexual assault. Evocative therapy may include individual, group, couples/marital, and family counseling. The second approach is **psychoeducational counseling**, which uses a group or class setting to remedy deficits in social and interpersonal skills. Psychoeducational strategies include anger management, the principles of relapse prevention, and other topics such as human sexuality, dating, and myths about sexuality and relationships. The third approach is **drug treatment**. This approach concentrates on "reducing sexual arousability and the frequency of deviant sexual fantasies through the use of antiandrogen and antidepressant medication" (Prentky et al., 1997, p. 13). The fourth approach is **cognitive behavior therapy**, which focuses on changing beliefs, fantasies, attitudes, and rationalizations that justify and perpetuate sexually violent behavior. Prentky et al. (1997) suggest that the most effective approach probably resides in using some combination of the four, although which specific combination remains unclear. They agree, however, that cognitive-behavioral approaches (complemented on occasion with some medication) continue to offer the most effective technique in the temporary cessation of deviant sexual behavior in motivated individuals. Cognitive-behavior therapy argues that maladaptive sexual behaviors are learned according to the same rules as normal sexual behavior, by means of classical and/or instrumental conditioning, modeling, reinforcement, generalization, and punishment. They are, therefore, modifiable. Cognitive-behavioral therapy, compared to traditional verbal, insight-oriented therapy, has demonstrated short-term effectiveness in eliminating exhibitionism and fetishism (Kilmann, Sabalis, Gearing, Bukstel, & Scovern, 1982), some forms of pedophilia (G. Hall, 1995; Marshall & Barbaree, 1988), and sexual aggression and arousal (Quinsey & Marshall, 1983).

The major problem, however, is not getting the motivated offender to stop his deviant sexual pattern, but preventing his relapse across time and situations. It is analogous to dieting. Most diet regimens do work in getting the motivated individual to lose weight. However, they offer little help in preventing people from eventually relapsing into old eating habits. This is why ongoing therapeutic supervision of sex offenders is critical.

A treatment approach showing some promise in the treatment of sex offenders is called **relapse prevention** (RP). "RP is a self-control program designed to teach individuals who are trying to change their behavior how to anticipate and cope with the problem of relapse" (George & Marlatt, 1989, p. 2). The program emphasizes self-management; clients are considered responsible not for the cause but for the solution of the problem. And as the name implies, the program concentrates on preventing a *relapse* of deviant sexual behavior. Therefore, RP distinguishes treatment from maintenance. As stated earlier, behavior therapy is effective in cessation of the behavior, but RP is specifically designed to be effective in helping the individual *maintain* the "cure." Distinctions are made between the terms *relapse* and *lapse*. "Relapse is a violation of a self-imposed rule or set of rules governing the rate or pattern of a selected target behavior" (George & Marlatt, 1989, p. 6). A *lapse*, on the other hand, refers to "a single instance of violating the rule" (p. 6). "With sex offenders, the term relapse will refer to any occurrence of a sexual offense, thus connoting full-scale reestablishment of the problematic behavior. The term lapse will refer to any occurrence of willful and elaborate fantasizing about sexual offending or any return to sources of stimulation associated with the sexual offense pattern, but short of performance of the offense behavior" (p. 6).

RP, as a system of maintenance-oriented principles and interventions, has two central objectives: It teaches individuals (1) to cope effectively with "high-risk situations" (HRSs) and (2) to identify and respond to early warning signals of urges and "apparently irrelevant decisions." An HRS is any situation that poses a threat to the individual's sense of control over his behavior and consequently increases the probability of lapse or relapse. Examples of HRSs that may predispose an individual toward relapse include negative emotional states, such as anger and depression, interpersonal conflict, and various social pressures (George & Marlatt, 1989). Research by Pithers and associates (Pithers et al., 1989; Pithers, Kashima, Cumming, Beal, & Buell, 1988) has found that rapists often experience anger and use alcohol or other drugs before engaging in sexual aggression. Pedophiles, on the other hand, often experience anxiety or depression before seeking a child. A feeling of low self-esteem is experienced by both groups. These precursors reflect the beginning stages of an HRS. In other words, they psychologically predispose the individual toward a relapse.

Relapse seems to follow a sequence of events, all representing HRSs (Pithers, Marques, Gibat, & Marlatt, 1983; George & Marlatt, 1989). First, an urge, a fleeting thought, or a dream about committing an offense occurs. This is followed by elaborations of fantasies about committing the offense. Then the aroused individual engages in masturbation coupled with fantasies and/or pornography related to the imagined sexual activity. Next he plans how he is going to commit the act. Finally, the individual engages in the act. RP provides a framework within which a variety of behavioral, cognitive, educational, and skill-training techniques is used to train sex offenders to recognize and interrupt this chain of events (Marshall & Barbaree, 1988).

If the individual does not know how to cope with these HRSs, there is a high probability that he may lapse or relapse. On the other hand, if he learns how to cope, and he successfully manages to get through the HRS without violating his newly adopted rules, his perceived control increases and the probability of relapse declines. The individual experiences a sense of mastery and self-efficacy and is better prepared for the next bout with an HRS.

The second component in RP intervention is apparently irrelevant decisions. What at first glance seems to be an innocuous decision, unrelated to an HRS, may well be the first step toward relapse. For example, a pedophile's decision to take walks by parks and schoolyards at times when they are predictably crowded with children might be an early warning sign. It is important, therefore, that the individual learn to recognize and interrupt these apparently irrelevant decisions.

Critical to RP treatment intervention is the motivation of the offender. Without motivation, the program will not work. Remember, another key feature is that RP is for *maintaining* a cessation of the deviant behavior, not cessation itself. Therefore, a behavior therapy program or other conventional treatment intervention that stops the behavior must precede RP. The treatment phase normally takes a relatively short period of time. Another important point outlined by George and Marlatt (1989) is that incarceration without treatment will not prevent reoffending. They offer three reasons for this. First, externally imposed, forced control does little to encourage an offender to seek help in changing his ways. Second, the offender can still maintain attachment to his offense pattern through fantasy. Third, it is conceivable that an offender could continue to actually engage in some semblance of his offense patterns even during confinement.

A volunteer outpatient treatment program for child molesters described by Marshall and Barbaree (1988) illustrates very well some of the procedures used to stop the behavior. The program uses a variety of behavior techniques. First, clinicians use aversive conditioning by linking electric shock to an offender's deviant visual and verbal images. Second, they reduce the attraction of deviant fantasies during masturbation through satiation therapy. Satiation therapy attempts to reduce the sex drive by having the patient masturbate at a frequency that will substantially reduce urges and cravings. Third, they eliminate the occurrence of deviant thoughts elicited by children or by daydreams during their day-to-day living pattern through smelling salts. That is, each patient carries smelling salts, and each time a deviant thought occurs, the patient is instructed to place the salts close to his nose and to inhale deeply. Through aversive conditioning, deviant thoughts are soon strongly associated with the experience of unpleasant smelling salts. Currently, there is no evidence that this aversive therapy has a negative impact on "normal" sexual thoughts and behavior.

The program also enhances the social competence of the child molester by training him in the skills of conversation with adult partners as well as reducing his anxiety in the presence of adult partners. The treatment also addresses training in assertiveness and counsels the patient in financial management, use of leisure time, and alcohol or drug use. So far, Marshall and Barbaree have been able to do a three and a half–year follow-up on 117 patients, some of whom received the treatment described and some who did not. While 32% of the nontreatment group has reoffended, only 14% of the treated group has reoffended. In another RP project, Pithers et al. (1988) found a 10%

relapse rate for rapists and a 3% relapse rate for pedophiles during a short follow-up (less than one year).

RP is a relatively recent development and its long-term success has yet to be established. However, it does have substantial promise for the elimination of deviant behavior in offenders motivated to change. And as noted by Prentky et al. (1997), "Continuity of treatment is considered a critical factor in managing sex offenders. Maintenance is forever, and Relapse Prevention never ends. Community-based clinical management must be supportive, vigilant, and informed by current wisdom about maximally effective maintenance" (p. 14).

SUMMARY AND CONCLUSIONS

This chapter has covered a wide range of sex offenses, focusing particularly on the serious crime of rape. We noted early in the chapter that many researchers, as well as statutes, prefer the term sexual assault. The latter term can encompass both penetration and a variety of behaviors that fall short of that ultimate violation. Rape—as well as other violent sexual offenses—is committed for a variety of reasons by a variety of offenders. A major motivation appears to be to harm, derogate, or embarrass the victim. In some situations, the rapist may interpret his behavior as harmless, believing that his victims enjoy being "roughed up." Nevertheless, the effect is invariably the opposite. The psychological and social damages to the victim are incalculable. Sexual assault by husbands, dates, and intimate friends is more frequent than commonly supposed.

Most rapists are young and often show a history of rape and other violent actions. Traditionally, both rape and other sexual assaults also have been considered almost exclusively a male enterprise. In the 1990s, however, researchers began to question this assumption. Although it is still a fact that men and boys commit the great majority of sexual offenses, we can no longer ignore the reality that women and girls also commit them. Because most theory building and typologies have been developed using males, we have used the male pronoun to refer to offenders throughout the chapter.

Several attempts at typologies or classification systems of sex offenders have been tried, the most notable being those developed by the Massachusetts Treatment Center and Groth. Of the two, the MTC classification system is the most widely used and has been the one most submitted to empirical research.

Rape—and other sexual behavior—appears to be due, in part, to the type of socialization experiences the offender has had. He has constructed, from information received from a variety of sources and models, a belief and value system that encourages and justifies the aggressive behavior. Further, most rapists have attitudes and an ideology that encourage men to be dominant, controlling, and powerful, while expecting women to be submissive, permissive, and compliant. This attitudinal pattern may be much more prevalent in society, in both men and women, than commonly realized.

We also learned that under very high levels of arousal, any consideration of the rightness of a sexual assaulter's behavior or its consequences may be obliterated. As we saw with reference to homicide and assault, high levels of arousal reduce attention to private self-awareness and personal standards of appropriate conduct. Under high levels of excitement, some normally law-abiding persons may become rapists or, at least, use the high excitement as a justification for their rape behavior. Of course, some people possess a value system that justifies rape or the resolution of interpersonal conflict through violence, regardless of their arousal level.

Pedophilia, also potentially a very serious offense from the victim standpoint, appears to involve less aggression and violence, except, of course, for the pedophilia that includes rape and assault. Pedophilia appears to be motivated by both sexual desire and an expectation of sexual adequacy that would not occur in sexual congress with another adult. Like rape, it is engaged in for a variety of reasons by a variety of offenders. There is no such thing as a common "molester profile." Each has his own construct system and beliefs about his behavior and motivations. Some offenders, for whatever reason, are vicious and violent; others are passive, relatively meek people who enjoy the companionship of children. Most pedophiles are the latter. They appear to see themselves as sexually and interpersonally inept adults who feel more comfortable interacting with children. Classical conditioning also appears to play a prominent role in the development of pedophilia, perhaps much more so than in rape.

We also gave some attention to the minor sexual offenses of exhibitionism, voyeurism, and fetishes. Classical conditioning, particularly masturbatory conditioning, also appears to play a crucial role in the development of these sexual deviations. Sexual arousal repeatedly linked with objects and persons seems especially important.

Treatment of sexual offenses can be successful if the offender's motivation to change is evident. Successful treatment strategies must focus not only on cessation of the antisocial sexual conduct, but also on maintenance of prosocial behaviors. Thus, continuing monitoring or supervision should be a part of the treatment regimen. Nevertheless, reviews of the literature on sex offender treatment are not encouraging, particularly for the more serious and violent sexual offenses. The "milder" offenses such as exhibitionism are more likely to yield positive treatment results if the offender is motivated and if a treatment strategy focused on individualized needs is adopted.

CHAPTER 11

ECONOMIC CRIME, PUBLIC ORDER CRIME, AND OTHER CRIME

Economic crimes generally involve the illegal acquisition of money and material goods or the illegal destruction of property for financial gain. Crimes against the public order are actions against public or moral decency or other conduct that is interpreted as a threat to the orderly operations of a given society. Examples include prostitution, pornography, gambling, vagrancy, disorderly conduct, public drunkenness, and drug use. Often, these violations are called "victimless crimes" because of the difficulty of pinpointing an identifiable victim of the offense. Later in this chapter we concentrate on the public order crime of prostitution. In the next chapter we turn our attention to drug use and its relationship to criminal behavior. Most of this chapter focuses on the various kinds of economic offenses.

Economic crimes are similar to the violent offenses discussed in earlier chapters in one important psychological aspect. Most of them involve a dehumanization of the victim, although in a different sense from the dehumanization that often occurs in violence. Dehumanization occurs when a person or group of persons sees and treats certain individuals as objects, rather than human beings. When a person is not responding to the human qualities of other people, it becomes much more possible to act inhumanely toward them. Therefore, offenders find it easier to see their victims as objects rather than as people. In most economic crimes (such as larceny and burglary), the offenders avoid confronting their victims directly. Therefore, they do not directly observe or experience the economic, social, and psychological discomfort of their victims. In the victim's absence, internal values and social constraints are less effective, allowing the offender to repress, deny, or justify the crime more easily. As Gresham Sykes (1956) puts it, the individual's internal sentiments are more easily neutralized by the physical absence of the victim. The offender does not have to think of the effects his or her actions have on the victim, because the offender does not know the victim as a human being, only as a target. The exception, of course, is robbery, but even in this case, victim contact is usually fleeting.

We focus specifically on the economic crimes of robbery, burglary, shoplifting, larceny-theft, and auto theft. It should be noted that, although robbery is an economic crime, it is not classified as a property crime in the UCR. That is, it is considered a violent crime against persons rather than a crime against property. **Figure 11–1** provides a percentage breakdown of the UCR index crimes for 2002. As you can see, larceny-theft, burglary, and motor vehicle theft account for a very large portion of the total index crimes (88%), with larceny-theft accounting for the majority. In 2002, law enforcement reported an estimated 10.5 million property crimes (Federal Bureau of Investigation, 2003). The 2002 property crime rate was estimated to be 3,624 property crimes per 100,000 inhabitants and has declined 10.6% from the 1998 rate and 23.5% from the 1993 rate. The additional statistical facts are as follows.

- In 2002, larceny-theft made up 67.5% of the total property crimes.
- Burglary comprised 20.6% of the total property crimes.

FIGURE 11–1   Percentage Distribution of UCR Index Crimes, 2002

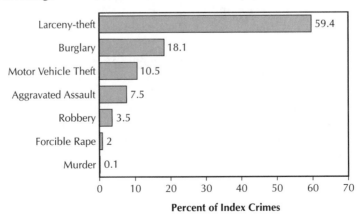

Source: Adapted from Federal Bureau of Investigation (2003).

- Motor vehicle theft accounted for 11.9% of the total property crimes.
- The average loss of property in 2002 was $699.
- The overall clearance rate for property crime in 2002 was 16.5%.
- Robbery comprised 29.5% of the total violent crime rate.
- The overall clearance rate for robbery was 25.7%.

In addition to the crimes specified above, the chapter covers "white-collar" offenses and discusses the difficulty in defining that concept. Specific crimes like fraud and embezzlement are discussed, as is the relatively new cyber-crime. Finally, we touch on hostage taking (kidnapping), bombings, and arson, which could also be classified as crimes against persons or violent offenses. Because they are often motivated by the desire to acquire property, they are included here as economic crimes. However, perpetrators also may be interested in acquiring social status or psychological rewards. Note that crimes discussed here are to be distinguished from the terrorism covered in Chapter 9. Though the actions may be the same (e.g., setting a bomb), the motives are different. Because the UCR does not report crime rate statistics for nonindex crimes, we are unable to include such information here.

Obviously, most people engage in economic and property crime for the money or for other tangible rewards that meet biological, psychological, or social needs. Sykes (1956) notes, however, that this does not tell us why some people commit economic crime under certain social conditions, while others do not. Explanations based strictly on economic necessity and the satisfaction of basic human needs do not go far enough. Sykes proposes the concept of **relative deprivation** as one additional factor. To assess the economic want associated with economic crime, we should consider not what the individuals have or are making in personal income but, rather, how great the discrepancy is between what they have and what they would like to have. Specifically, relative deprivation is the psychological distance between what people perceive they have now and what they feel they can realistically attain—their goal. Goals are strongly influenced by the social groups to which people belong or reference groups with which they identify.

From a psychological perspective, economic crimes cannot be explained simply by biological needs, by material wants, or even in terms of relative deprivation. Powerful cognitive motivators must also be considered. These cognitive factors are in the form of outcome expectations and the capacity to predict and appreciate future consequences of one's behavior. Furthermore, the cognitive forces may be relatively independent of external reinforcements like tangible rewards or even social and status rewards. Self-reinforcements, including self-rewards and self-punishments, may represent a major motivating factor in many economic crimes. That is, the offender may receive pleasure and self-satisfaction from the completion of a crime and from doing it well.

Cognitive factors are also extremely important in another sense: They allow offenders to justify their behavior. A strong theme of this chapter is the tendency of economic offenders to minimize, distort, or deny misconduct or reprehensible behavior. The aforementioned psychological separation from the victim helps them to do this. We expand on these psychological issues of motivation and justification throughout the following pages.

BURGLARY

Burglary is the unlawful entry of a structure, with or without force, with intent to commit a felony or theft. The FBI classifies burglary into three categories: (1) forcible entry, (2) unlawful entry where no force is used, and (3) attempted forcible entry. Approximately 2.15 million burglaries occurred in the United States during 2002 (Federal Bureau of Investigation, 2003). Nationwide, the residential burglary rate is 746.2 per 100,000 inhabitants. The National Crime Victimization Survey (NCVS) reports that about 4 million residential burglaries occurred in 1999. The discrepancy between the burglary data reported in the UCR and the data in the NCVS is due to the fact that not all residential burglaries are reported to the police, even though they are mentioned on victimization surveys.

About 30.8% of burglaries did not involve forced entry in 2002 (Federal Bureau of Investigation, 2003). That is, the offenders entered through an unlatched window or unlocked door or used a key "hidden" in an obvious place, such as under a doormat. Another 6.5% of the 2002 burglaries were *attempts* at forcible entry.

Consistently, year after year, about two-thirds of all reported burglaries involve residential property, while the remaining one-third involves commercial establishments. Burglaries of residences occur more frequently (61.7% in 2002) during the daytime, whereas burglaries of businesses and nonresidential property mostly occur at night (57% in 2002). In 2002, the overall loss due to burglary was estimated to be $3.3 billion, with the average dollar loss per burglary about $1,549 (Federal Bureau of Investigation, 2003). The clearance rate for burglary in 2002 was 13%, not a surprising statistic considering the nature of the crime and the unlikelihood that it will be witnessed.

Burglaries are more likely to occur during the warmer months, especially July and August, apparently because people are more likely to be outdoors or away on vacation and are more likely to leave doors and windows open, making their residences vulnerable. A study by Langer and Miranksy (1983) reveals that a large segment of the population does not take responsibility for burglary prevention. Approximately half of the New York City residents questioned admitted that they did not lock all their doors when away from home, even if they had been burglarized before. Interestingly, while 66% believed that burglary could be prevented, 61% of these subjects did not use all their locks. They believed that it was the responsibility of others (e.g., the police, the landlord, the building superintendent) to guard the premises, rather than their own personal responsibility. Furthermore, those who thought their neighborhoods were unsafe and burglary-prone were less likely to use locks than those who considered their neighborhoods safe and less burglary-prone. Possibly, people in burglary-prone areas are convinced that if someone decides to burglarize their homes, there is not much they can do about it, locks or no locks.

Like other criminal offenses, burglary seems to be primarily a crime committed by the young; nearly two-thirds of those arrested in 2002 were under 25, with the average age being about 22 (Federal Bureau of Investigation, 2003). To some extent, this arrest ratio may reflect the lack of sophistication of younger burglars, who, because of their inexperience, are more likely to be detected. However, researchers have noted that, with increasing age, some burglars find they are not as nimble and athletic as they once were. Crawling through small open windows and climbing fences take their toll, and these strenuous activities become more burdensome with age. Thus, many older burglars turn to shoplifting (Cromwell, Olson, & Avary, 1991). Shoplifting is considerably easier, less risky, and more cost efficient. Shoplifted items are more easily converted to cash and are more profitable than items gained through burglary, because they are new, untraceable, and have their price tags attached. Furthermore, the criminal penalties are significantly less for shoplifting than they are for burglary.

Burglary is largely a male enterprise, with only 13% of those arrested in 2002 being women. Although 70.4% of those arrested in 2002 were white, minorities (30% are African American) are overrepresented in proportion to their numbers in the general population (Eskridge, 1983; Federal Bureau of Investigation, 2003).

As noted earlier, about two of every three burglaries are residential. And burglary of residences usually occurs during the daytime and on weekdays, whereas commercial establishments are usually burglarized late at night and on weekends (Cromwell et al., 1991; Pope, 1977b). This is not surprising, since burglary is a passive crime; the offender selects times and places that will minimize the possibility of an encounter with victims. Almost all experienced burglars (well over 90%) assert they will not even enter a residence when the occupants are believed to be at home (Cromwell et al., 1991). The home is occupied during the day most commonly by women or retired individuals. However, burglars know that occupants develop predictable patterns regarding the use of discretionary time for the purposes of shopping, errands, or visiting friends or relatives. Women who work outside the home also show similar patterns on weekends. Generally, the prime time for these errands and visits tends to be between 10:00 and 11:00 AM and from 1:00 to 3:00 PM (Cromwell et al., 1991). Parents, on the other hand, often develop predictable patterns of taking children to school and picking them up after school.

Of all crimes, burglary also offers the greatest probability of success with the least amount of risk. Not only is it a crime without victim contact and probability of identification, but it does not require weapons. Furthermore, the penalties usually are less severe than those for robbery. Juvenile offenders are more likely than their older counterparts to burglarize during the daytime hours (Pope, 1977c). In fact, a prime time for many juvenile burglaries is at the end of the school day, often between 3 and 6 PM.

Burglary Cues and Selected Targets

The identification of situational cues is especially important in successful burglary. Nee and Taylor (1988) found that there are at least four broad categories of relevant cues used by experienced residential burglars. They are as follows.

1. *Occupancy cues,* such as letters or newspapers visible in the mailbox, motor vehicles present, and windows, blinds, and curtains shut or open.
2. *Wealth cues,* such as the appearance of the house, the neighborhood, the quality of the landscaping, the make(s) of car(s) driven, and the visible furnishings.
3. *Layout cues,* such as how easy it would be to gain access to the house or building, as well as to escape.
4. *Security cues,* such as alarm systems, window locks, and deadbolt locks.

M. Taylor and Nee (1988) designed a study that tested the possible differences in identifying these cues between burglars and homeowners. The burglars consisted of a group of 15 experienced burglars serving time in Cork Prison in Ireland, and the homeowners consisted of 15 Irish homeowners. Each subject was requested to explore a simulated environment made up of slides and maps of five different houses. The researchers found that burglars were better able to discern security provisions and were more concerned about escaping successfully from the scene than were homeowners. Most surprising, however, was the high amount of agreement between burglars and homeowners on which houses were most vulnerable to burglary. More research needs to be done in this area and the range of relevant cues better identified.

Bennett and Wright (1984) conducted an extensive three-year project on convicted burglars confined in various prisons throughout southern England. The researchers' primary interest was to learn the decision-making processes and perceptions of the residential burglars at the time of the crime. The principal method of data collection in the study was through semistructured interviews with the burglars themselves. Although a majority of the burglars had committed a variety of other economic crimes, almost all of them considered burglary their main criminal activity. Therefore, most of them probably qualify as professionals rather than amateurs.

Bennett and Wright discovered that almost all the burglaries were planned. Very few of the burglaries were the result of spur-of-the-moment decisions, nor were there any constant or irrepressible urges to burglarize. The two main aspects that went into the planning were the situational cues of surveillability and occupancy. Surveillability cues were related to the amount of cover or openness around the house, whether it was overlooked by neighboring houses, the availability of access to the rear, and the presence or proximity of neighbors. Occupancy cues were similar to the ones reported by Nee and Taylor, such as a car in the driveway, lights on in the house, the presence of mail, and whether the walks were shoveled or the lawn was cut. Experienced burglars said that "occupancy proxies" were the major deterrents in attempts to burglarize. Specifically, burglar alarms and dogs were extremely important in the prevention of burglary. This was also a consistent finding of Cromwell and colleagues (1991). In fact, they found that the dog does not have to be a large one. Any dog will do, since a large one poses a physical threat and a small dog will be noisy. Cromwell and his associates also found that deadbolts caused burglars considerable difficulty in entry, even though some of the experienced burglars claimed such locks would not be any problem. However, Cromwell et al. not only obtained self-report data from experienced burglars, but also had them demonstrate their claims. Security locks and deadbolts caused all kinds of trouble, even for highly experienced burglars—despite their claims prior to the demonstration. Much of the research on burglary, on the other hand, finds that increased police patrols, and other such strategies, have very little influence on decisions to burglarize or on the burglary success rate. However, watchful neighbors tend to be strong deterrents for burglars. This observation is supported by both experienced burglars and crime statistics.

Research data suggest that, although burglary is a "planned" behavior, burglars identify a large number of potential targets and then select the most vulnerable. Cromwell and his colleagues caution, however, that although much of the research on burglary suggests that a high percentage of burglars make carefully planned, highly rational decisions based on a detailed evaluation of environmental cues, the crime seems to be more of finding the right opportunity from an array of potential targets. Burglary is not generally an impulsive crime, but it is not usually planned to precise detail either.

The Cromwell and colleagues (1991) study found that many burglars engage in what they referred to as **rational reconstruction**. That is, "Our findings indicate that burglars interviewed in prison or those recalling crimes from the past, either consciously or unconsciously, may engage in rational reconstruction—a reinterpretation of past behavior through which the actor recasts activities in a manner consistent with 'what should have been,' rather than 'what was'" (p. 42). Thus, self-report data from burglars may indicate that there was considerable planning involved in the burglary, whereas the crime was actually one of opportunity. The Cromwell project not only gathered data from self-reports, but also had the experienced burglars simulate their burglaries. Moreover, the research team went on "ride-alongs" during which the burglars described their previous burglaries or described how they would burglarize a residence they perceived as vulnerable. Thus, the researchers were able to identify some of the disparities between what the professional burglars told them and what they actually did before, during, and after the real burglary. These findings suggest that research based exclusively on self-report data may be incomplete or suspect.

Cromwell and his colleagues (1991) also found in their systematic study of experienced burglars that one of the most popular entry methods was through sliding glass patio doors. Burglars said that these doors are easily popped out of their sliding tracks by hand or with the aid of a crowbar or screwdriver. Entry is therefore quick and noiseless. Another common method is to remove, cut, or gently break a window pane and crawl through the open window. A skillful burglar will carefully remove the pane, crawl through, and then replace the pane in a professional manner. Other commonly preferred methods for residential burglary include forcing the rear door open with a pry tool or kicking it down or opening the garage door and forcing open the door between the garage and the house.

Who Burglarizes?

National research data on arrested burglars in the United States indicate that a large proportion commit the offense near their own residence. This seems especially true for juvenile offenders (Pope, 1977a). The Santa Clara Criminal Justice Pilot Program (1972) found that over one-half of the apprehended offenders traveled no more than a mile from their own home to commit the offenses. Barker (2000), in a study of serial burglars who operated in a small town in southern England, found that these offenders tended to live surprisingly close to the areas they burglarized. She discovered, however, that the mean home-to-offense distance increased during the later stages of burglary. For example, in her series the average home-to-first-offense distance was 2.16 kilometers, the average distance from home to the middle offense was 3.57 kilometers, and the average distance from home to the last offense was 5.52 kilometers. It is difficult to generalize from these data, however, because apprehended burglars are presumably less skillful and thus more detectable than burglars who succeed. It is possible that successful burglars operate farther away from home. Eskridge (1983) found that those who burglarized commercial establishments were more willing to travel much greater distances.

Over half of the apprehended burglars worked with an accomplice (Chimbos, 1973; Pope, 1977a). Eskridge (1983), who conducted a survey of crime in Lincoln, Nebraska, reported that nearly two-thirds of the identified burglars worked in groups of two or more. On a national level, groups of two or more are responsible for just under half (42%) of all burglary incidents. National data also suggest that very few burglars work with more than three accomplices. Younger offenders and females are more likely to use accomplices than older males (Pope, 1977a). However, this pattern also depends to some extent on the sophistication of the offender. Experienced, competent offenders who realize the formidable challenge presented by protection instruments (alarms or safes) may also be more likely to take on assistants (Shover, 1972).

As for other criminal offenses, the best predictor of burglary is an offender's record. In a California analysis, 80% of the offenders studied had a prior arrest record (Pope, 1977c). Of these, 58% had a prior burglary arrest and 47% had prior drug arrests, usually selling. Males were far more likely to have a previous criminal record than females.

In their study of male *and* female burglars, Decker, Wright, Redfern, and Smith (1993) found that the offending patterns of female burglars were very similar to those of males. One major exception was that male burglars often stole cars, whereas the female burglars did not. Decker and his colleagues found that they could divide the female burglars into two major groups: accomplices and partners. Accomplices committed the burglary because of their subservience to others—usually men—during their burglaries. Partners, on the other hand, participated as equals in the commission of burglary. Although some of the females co-offended with males, they did not take orders from them.

Use of Alcohol and Other Substances

Although a well-known Santa Clara 1972 project concluded that burglars are rarely under the influence of alcohol and other drugs at the time of their crime, the more recent data reported by the Cromwell and associates (1991) study indicate that this is not so. Ninety-three percent of the professional burglars studied by the Cromwell group said they "fixed" or "got high" before entering a residence. These experienced, professional burglars admitted they needed to lower their anxiety levels and reduce their fear prior to the burglary. The vast majority of these burglars reported that moderate amounts of alcohol or drugs simply made them better burglars, because these substances increased their alertness and vigilance and bolstered their nerve to stay in the residences long enough to search for and locate a variety of items to steal. Female burglars did the same thing (Decker et al., 1993). Specifically, the calming effects of drugs and alcohol enabled them to focus more on environmental cues related to risk, as well as valuable items hidden in the house that they normally would not find. Psychologically, this observation makes sense because high levels of arousal do narrow one's attention span and reduce one's focus on environmental cues in certain pressure situations (Easterbrook, 1959). Also, the Cromwell study found that heroin-using burglars tend to be more rational, more professional, and less likely to be arrested than burglars using cocaine or speed (or, more generally, stimulants). Moreover, the heroin user was able to exercise considerable control over the amount of the drug used for maximum proficiency in burglarizing.

What Happens to the Merchandise?

Amateur burglars usually take money or personal items that they need, whereas the professional takes items with excellent resale value, like electronic equipment, cameras, jewelry, and furs (Vetter & Silverman, 1978). The professional usually has access to a "fence," whereas the amateur rarely has that kind of contact. A fence, an integral component in the professional burglary cycle, is a person who knowingly buys stolen merchandise for the purpose of resale. Professional burglars also have individually distinctive methods and not infrequently leave their mark (their signature) to goad the investigators they have foiled. Many professional burglars prefer retail stores over residential homes.

The Cromwell and associates (1991) research raises serious questions concerning the extent to which professional fences are used today. In their investigation of experienced burglars operating in an urban Texas metropolitan area of 250,000, they found considerable diversity in the channels through which stolen property was distributed. Some burglars sold their stolen property to pawnshops, others to friends and acquaintances, and still others traded their property for drugs. Some resold the merchandise to legitimate businesses or strangers. The researchers, therefore, suggest that today the "professional fence may have been displaced by a more diverse and readily accessed market for stolen property" (p. 73).

Motives

As you might expect, the motives for burglary are varied, but the primary factor for professionals is undoubtedly monetary gain. When performed competently, burglary is a lucrative business with low risks and with monetary rewards far surpassing those the burglar might earn in the "noncriminal" world. David (1974) learned that a husband and wife team he interviewed made, on the average, $400 to $500 a day; a solitary offender in his sample made about $500 per week. These figures will obviously be much higher in today's market. Many professionals also conceive of their behavior as a challenging skill to be continually developed and refined. Some even said they get a "rush" of excitement during the planning and commission of the crime, especially if they are good at it (Cromwell et al., 1991). In this sense, burglary is highly adaptive and represents an instrumental behavior supported by strong reinforcement. For many burglars, however, a simple conclusion that they participate in their crimes as their sole profession or lucrative business may be unwarranted. A vast majority of burglary is committed to supplement the offenders' incomes and to improve their quality of life (Rengert & Wasilchick, 1985). The income gained from burglary enables the offender to buy drugs, alcohol, and expensive goods and, more broadly, to be able to "party." Subsistence needs are often met through other sources of income, such as a regular job.

Some burglars may burglarize the same place again, or even repeatedly, in a pattern called *repeat burglary*. Burglars that participate in repeat burglary do it because of the efficiency in time, planning, and risk it provides (Farrell, Phillips & Pease, 1995). Residential locations are especially vulnerable if residents do not change the layout or make entry more difficult after a burglary.

In other words, the burglar knows the layout of the target well, was successful the first time, and may even have seen valuables the first time around that prompted a return visit.

Shover (1972) discusses some of the outstanding features of the competent professional burglar, whom he calls the "good burglar." This burglar demonstrates technical skill, maintains a good reputation for personal integrity among colleagues in the criminal subculture, gets most of his income from burglary, and has been at least relatively successful at the crime. A good reputation means that the burglar is close-mouthed, stands up to police, and is sympathetic to the criminal way of life.

The professional burglar, then, is primarily motivated by money but also by self-satisfaction and accomplishment. When self-satisfaction and self-reinforcement are conditioned on certain accomplishments, people are motivated to expend the effort needed to attain the desired goal, perhaps even independently of monetary gain. Walsh (1980), for example, has emphasized the expressive and psychological components of burglary. He posits that, for some burglars, the challenge of the crime is far more rewarding than the material reward. Based on interviews with victims and offenders, Walsh identifies three kinds of expressive burglars: (1) *the feral threat*, (2) *the riddlesmith*, and (3) *the dominator*. Feral burglars engage in destructive, malicious vandalism during the break-in by spilling things, breaking glass, smashing objects, and urinating and defecating in various areas throughout the house. Riddlesmiths, on the other hand, try to demonstrate their technical skill to the victims and investigators by setting up puzzles, mysteries, and booby traps throughout the house. Riddlesmiths are inventive in the way they cause damage and may leave messages on walls, floors, and mirrors. Dominators enjoy threatening or frightening victims and, therefore, break into homes that are occupied. All three of these expressive burglars are interested in communicating to burglarized victims through a particular style or MO. Thus, burglars who take great pride in developing ingenious techniques and stumping police are even more likely to continue their illegal conduct. While external reinforcements (tangible rewards) are important, internal reinforcement may be a very powerful motivating and regulating factor.

Psychological Impact of Burglary

Merry and Hansent (2000) point out that, for all of us, the home is a sanctuary: "It is a special place that is central to our daily lives, a place that is at the beginning and end of most of our journeys; it is chosen and personalized" (p. 36). The manner in which homes are decorated and arranged and the objects within them represent important aspects of our lives and personalities. When our homes are burglarized, therefore, it is an invasion of our intimate space and an attack on our identity, physically and symbolically. Some victims describe burglary as a rape of their home, especially when the burglar has disturbed personal photographs, letters, and diaries, leaving the feeling of having been violated or at least "touched" by the intruder (Merry & Hansent, 2000). The distress levels experienced by victims are often more pronounced when the invasion extends to private areas, such as bedrooms, closets, chests-of-drawers, bathrooms, and desks. The invasion also endangers the victims' sense of control and threatens their ability to protect their own personal territory. Some victims, after being burglarized, install security systems such as video cameras, increase and improve the locks, buy dogs, or even move to new homes. Overall, the psychological trauma caused by a burglary can be substantial for many victims, and its effects may continue for many years.

Very often the burglar's actions are intended to produce some response from the victim. In other words, some burglars specifically tailor their styles (or signatures) to convey messages to victims and investigators, hoping to induce some strong emotional reactions from the victims. The emotional reactions of burglarized victims often run the gamut from anger and depression to fear and anxiety (B. Brown & Harris, 1989). In addition, the individual style used by the offender probably reflects something about his character and personality. According to Merry and Hansent, this aspect is referred to as the interpersonal dimension of the crime. It is suggested, therefore, that the victim's feelings of fear and vulnerability are psychological losses that are translated into gains for the offender. In this sense, the burglar gains materially and psychologically from the crime. The interpersonal aspects of the burglary (i.e., the style used by the burglar) are areas that provide considerable potential for burglary profiling in future research.

LARCENY AND MOTOR VEHICLE THEFT

McCaghy (1980) refers to the larceny-theft category as a "garbage can" because it is heterogeneous and hard to classify. Larceny-theft is defined as the "unlawful taking, carrying, leading, or riding away of property from the possession or constructive possession of another" (Federal Bureau of Investigation, 1997, p. 43). It differs from burglary in that it does not involve unlawful entry. Larceny includes pickpocketing, purse snatching, shoplifting, stealing from vending machines or from motor vehicles, and theft of property left outdoors (bicycles, pedigreed dogs, lawnmowers). The larceny-theft offenses in the United States during 2002 accounted for 59.4% of the Crime Index total and 67.5% of the property crime total (Federal Bureau of Investigation, 2003). **Figure 11–2** provides a percentage distribution of the more common types of theft known to police. The clearance rate for larceny-theft was 18% in 2002, nationwide.

The 2002 larceny-theft rate in the United States was 2,445.8 per 100,000 people (Federal Bureau of Investigation, 2003). Five- and ten-year trends showed that the rate declined 10.4% from the 1998 rate and 19.4% from the 1993 rate (Federal Bureau of Investigation, 2003). Thefts of motor vehicle parts, accessories, and things left in cars made up the largest portion of reported

FɪɢUʀE 11–2   Larceny-Theft Offenses in the United States, 2002

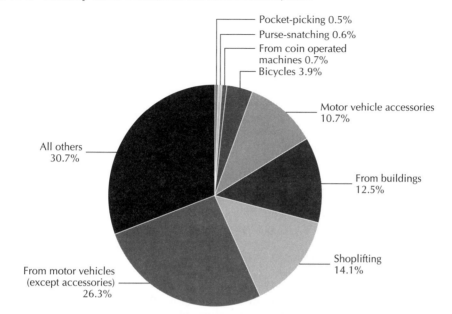

Pocket-picking 0.5%
Purse-snatching 0.6%
From coin operated
machines 0.7%
Bicycles 3.9%

Motor vehicle accessories
10.7%

All others
30.7%

From buildings
12.5%

Shoplifting
14.1%

From motor vehicles
(except accessories)
26.3%

Source: Federal Bureau of Investigation (2003, p. 52).

larcenies (26.5%) in 2002, followed by shoplifting (14%). The average value of property stolen in 2002 was $699.

Motor vehicle theft is defined as the theft or attempted theft of a motor vehicle, including the stealing of automobiles, trucks, buses, motorcycles, motor scooters, and snowmobiles (Federal Bureau of Investigation, 1997). The taking of a motor vehicle for temporary use by persons having lawful access is excluded from the definition (Federal Bureau of Investigation, 2003). An estimated total of 1.25 million thefts of motor vehicles occurred in the United States during 2002 (Federal Bureau of Investigation, 2003). The 2002 national motor vehicle theft rate was about 432.1 per 100,000 people and represents a 28.7% decrease since 1993. The clearance rate for motor vehicle theft in 2002 was 13.8%. **Table 11–1** shows the leading type of motor vehicles stolen in 2001, according to the National Highway Traffic Safety Administration.

Larceny and motor vehicle theft are common and widespread offenses, but research reporting specifically on these areas is rarely available. To some extent, the motivating factors that apply to burglary apply here as well. On the other hand, larceny is more likely to be committed by the nonprofessional and the desperate. Of the estimated 148,943 arrests for motor vehicle theft in 2002, males accounted for 83.5% of those arrested. Persons in the under-18 age group were involved in 30.4% of the motor vehicle thefts cleared nationally in 2002.

TABLE 11–1 Top 10 Stolen Vehicles in 2001, Based on Theft Rates per 1,000 Vehicles Produced

VEHICLE	THEFT RATE/1,000 VEHICLES
Chrysler Town & Country MPV	22.98
Dodge Intrepid	12.72
Chevrolet Metro	12.44
Acura Integra	10.50
Plymouth Neon	10.34
Dodge Neon	10.32
Dodge Stratus	10.23
Mitsubishi Mirage	9.24
Mitsubishi Galant	7.08
Chevrolet Camaro	6.83

Source: National Highway Traffic Safety Administration (2003).

FRAUD AND IDENTITY THEFT

Crimes of fraud involve deception used for the purpose of obtaining illegal financial gain. They often involve the misrepresentation of facts and the deliberate intent to deceive with the promise of goods, services, or other benefits that either do not exist or were never intended to be provided (Deem & Murray, 2000). Fraud includes identity theft, elder financial abuse, counterfeiting, mail fraud, bank fraud, and various corporate or organizational wrongdoings. Over the last two decades, fraud has increased in awareness with such high-profile cases as the Savings and Loan debacle of the 1980s and the massive cases involving Enron, Tyco, and other corporations. However, because fraud is not an index crime, the government does not keep track of fraud rates.

Identity theft occurs when one individual or a group of individuals misappropriates another person's personal identification information, such as name, social security number, date of birth, and mother's maiden name and uses the information to take over existing credit card or bank accounts, apply for a mortgage or car loan, make large purchases, or apply for insurance (Deem & Murray, 2000). In many instances, unsuspecting victims have no idea that anything is amiss until they receive phone calls from creditors or have difficulty applying for a job, loan, or mortgage. According to available data, the amount of identity theft has increased dramatically over the past 10 years, rising to over $745 million in 1997 (Deem & Murray, 2000).

Part of this increase is due to the development of new technologies in the Internet and telecommunications. The emotional impact of identity theft—and fraud in general—on victims is substantial and should not be underestimated. In addition to strong feelings of being victimized, feelings of self-blame and feelings that one can no longer trust one's own ability to handle financial matters, or to judge people, emerge. And then there is the long, drawn-out process of repairing both credit rating and emotional well-being.

SHOPLIFTING

Shoplifting is a frequent and costly type of crime. Although shoplifting comprised about 14% of all arrests for larceny-theft in 2002 (Figure 11–2), it is obviously underreported by a large margin. Based on self-report data, as many as 60% of American consumers have shoplifted in their lives, and 30% to 40% of adolescents admit that they shoplift repeatedly (Krasnovsky & Lane, 1998). Shoplifting activities usually decrease as offenders get older and more mature (Osgood, O'Malley, Bachman, & Johnston, 1989). The National Retail Federation and surveys by the Security Research Project at the University of Florida in Gainesville estimate the total monetary loss due to shoplifting in the United States to be roughly $10.15 billion (C. Coleman, 2000). This figure represents a 14% increase from 1997 to 2000. Interestingly, total losses from employee theft jumped 34%, to $12.85 billion, during that same time period.

The data on all other economic crimes are difficult to obtain, but data acquisition for shoplifting offenses is especially difficult, since store personnel exercise wide discretion in reporting offenses. The best estimates suggest that only 1 in every 40 shoplifters is apprehended (Krasnovsky & Lane, 1998). Hindelang (1974) found that whether charges were filed depended on the retail value of the stolen object, what was stolen, and the manner in which it was taken, rather than demographic and personality characteristics of the shoplifter. Specifically, the offender's race did not seem to matter, or whether the offender was male or female, poor or middle-class. What determined referral for arrest was whether the item was expensive, had resale value, or was stolen in a professional, skillful manner. Later research by M. G. Davis, Lundman, and Martinez (1991) found that shoplifters are more likely to be arrested not only when they take expensive items, but also when they resist being apprehended, have no local address, and/or live in poor neighborhoods. In England, on the other hand, store managers consider the age of the shoplifter as well as the value of the stolen item (Farrington & Burrows, 1993). The British study found that, generally, store managers did not report to the police the very young (under age 17) or very old (over 60), the mentally impaired, or those shoplifters in an advanced stage of pregnancy, unless they were caught repeatedly. In a series of observational studies (also in England) by Abigail Buckle and David Farrington (1984), random samples of customers were followed by trained observers as they shopped. Approximately 1 in 50 was observed to steal. The amount of shoplifting, however, differed dramatically from store to store. Shoplifting characteristics in supermarkets are likely to differ significantly from those exhibited in retail department stores or hardware stores. Buckle and Farrington (1994) conducted a replication of the 1984 study. Again, trained observers randomly followed approximately 500 customers in a small department store located in another city. The proportion of customers who shoplifted was between 1% and 2% and the majority was male. Most of the shoplifters also purchased goods as they checked out of the store, probably to allay suspicion. In general, the items stolen were small, low-cost items. In contrast to the original study, where there was a preponderance of older shoplifters (age 55 or over), Buckle and Farrington found that most of the shoplifters were young (age 25 or less). These studies underscore the warning that estimations concerning the incidence of shoplifting must be placed within a situational, cultural, and historical context. Furthermore, apprehension statistics may tell us more about the store security personnel practices and biases than about the shoplifting population (Klemke, 1992). In fact, it is not uncommon for security personnel to claim that they have developed a "sixth sense" for picking out likely suspects. This "sixth sense" is, in some cases, a bias or stereotype against certain segments of the population more than any all-encompassing, accurate skill.

Who Shoplifts?

It has been assumed that shoplifting is committed primarily by adolescent girls and women. Among the explanations offered for women's greater involvement in shoplifting, the most common is that women have greater opportunity to steal small items from merchants than do men. Nearly 25 years ago Gibbens (1981) noted that women were more likely to be in stores where detectives were stationed. As men joined the ranks of frequent shoppers, however, their shoplifting rates began to increase, and the gap between men and women narrowed (Moore, 1984). Baumer and Rosenbaum (1984), in an extensive review of the available research, concluded that gender ratio appears to be about 50–50. Farrington and Burrows (1993) report a similar gender ratio in England.

There has also been a widespread belief that the vast majority of shoplifters are juveniles under age 18. Most studies indicate that, although juveniles make up a large proportion of shoplifters, they are by no means the majority (Baumer & Rosenbaum, 1984). Moreover, about 70% of apprehended juvenile offenders were working in groups, compared to about 20% of apprehended adult shoplifters (Baumer & Rosenbaum, 1984). It should also be noted that shoplifting by juveniles is more likely to be evenly proportioned among males and females (Baumer & Rosenbaum, 1984; Russell, 1973). This is also apparently true for shoplifting by the elderly, a phenomenon on the increase and engaged in by both men and women in nearly equal numbers (Fyfe, 1984).

Shoplifting activity appears to change dramatically along the lifespan. Self-report data indicate that many individuals reported shoplifting when they were under age 10, but the frequency—for most individuals—declined as they got older (Klemke, 1992). The decline is particularly noticeable between age 17 and age 23. Klemke notes that this pattern supports the **invariance hypothesis**, proposed by Gottfredson and Hirschi (1990), that crime declines with age everywhere and at all times. For some reason, however, the tendency to shoplift reemerges during middle age, especially for women. A majority of apprehended shoplifters are in the middle-income bracket and generally carry enough money or credit cards to pay for the items stolen (Baumer & Rosenbaum, 1984).

Baumer and Rosenbaum outline some of the psychological characteristics and behavioral patterns of shoplifters. They note that such things as extreme nervousness, aimless walking up and down the aisles, looking around frequently, glancing up from the merchandise frequently, and leaving the store and returning a number of times are some of the indicators that suggest shoplifting.

In spite of its traditional prominence in economic crime, shoplifting has received little psychological research attention. The most heavily quoted source on the subject, Mary Owen Cameron's *The Booster and the Snitch: Department Store Shoplifting* (1964), reported data accumulated in the 1940s and early 1950s. Cameron divided her shoplifters into two groups: Commercial shoplifters were "boosters," and amateur pilferers were "snitches." All of her data were subsequently explained with reference to this dichotomy. The boosters were professionals, accepted members of the criminal subculture. They stole for substantial financial gain by choosing items from preselected locations. Boosters used a wide range of techniques such as "booster boxes," packages designed for concealing items inserted through hidden slots or hinged openings, and "stalls," containers with hidden compartments (large handbags, coats with hidden pockets). Snitches, on the other hand, were "respectable" persons who rarely had criminal records. They did not consider themselves thieves, and the idea that they might actually be arrested and prosecuted rarely crossed their minds. Very often, once apprehended, they claimed they stole the item on impulse and did not know what came over them.

Some social science research has focused on elderly shoplifters. Feinberg (1984) found that shoplifting was neither a female-dominated offense nor undertaken for subsistence purposes. Elderly shoplifters, he notes, are neither indigent, lonely, nor victims of poor memory. He attributes their criminal offenses to changes in status that separate the elderly from mainstream society. Often, they must reevaluate their past values and try out different selves and meanings. To what extent Feinberg's research may be generalized to other age groups remains an open question.

Motives

The motives behind commercial shoplifting may be clearer than those behind the amateur type. Whereas boosters take merchandise of value, snitches tend to take inexpensive items they can use. Some research has noted that male snitches prefer items of more value, such as electronic equipment and jewelry. Women snitches seem to take clothing, cosmetics, and food. The boosters shoplift for the money; the snitches, for more obscure reasons.

Theories concerning the intentions of snitches range from economic ones, like attempts to stretch the family budget (Cameron, 1964), to emotional ones, like attempts to satisfy needs centering around matrimonial stress, loneliness, and depression (Russell, 1973). In recent years, some "experts" have even concluded that most shoplifting is an addiction, much like gambling and alcoholism. The notion of shoplifting as a means of alleviating unmet needs or addiction is weak and poorly documented, however. The behavior gains attention, but it also becomes aversive. On the other hand, the contention that shoplifting has primarily an economic motivation seems oversimplified. Shoplifting is pursued by different people for different reasons.

Methods of Shoplifting

Males tend to favor concealing stolen merchandise in pockets or clothing, while females generally prefer purses or shopping bags. The method of concealment, however, depends considerably on the merchandise, the gender of the offender, and the type of store. In clothing stores, shoplifters would more likely attempt to walk out wearing the clothing after leaving the fitting room, for example. Men prefer to hide items beneath their clothing in supermarkets, while pockets are preferred in drug and discount stores. Women tend to prefer purses for concealment in supermarkets or grocery stores and packages and bags in drug and discount stores. Two things that draw the attention of store security personnel are false broken arm casts and large shopping bags obtained from a prior visit. In addition, women with babies in strollers or in backpacks often report that they are carefully watched by store personnel.

The item most commonly stolen in supermarkets or grocery stores is meat, while in drug stores clothing tends to be more common, followed by health and beauty aids. A common trick for some shoplifters in a supermarket is to do a lot of "grazing" while shopping. That is, the shopper eats, drinks (commonly soda), or "tastes" while shopping, especially in the fruit section, and fails to pay for the items when checking out. Klemke (1992) notes that some shoplifters prefer to conceal the items, while others do not. Some walk nonchalantly out the door with the item(s) as though nothing is amiss.

Types of Shoplifters

Moore (1984), studying 300 convicted shoplifters referred for presentence investigation, identified five patterns of offending. Although no shoplifters were considered professional to the degree of Cameron's booster category (the professionals may have escaped detection), 11.7% were semiprofessional, reporting shoplifting behavior at least once a week. Their "take" amounted to approximately $1,250 a year (a significant amount in the early 1980s).

The most frequent type of shoplifter in Moore's study was the "amateur" (56.4%), who stole small personal items when the opportunity arose. The methods used by amateurs were less sophisticated than those of the semiprofessionals, and unlike the semiprofessionals, the amateurs admitted that their behavior was morally wrong or illegal. Both types of shoplifting were premeditated, habitual, and directed toward financial gain. Persons in the amateur category were more likely to exhibit mild personality disorders or to be plagued by psychosocial stressors associated with interpersonal problems, such as family disruption.

Approximately 17% of Moore's offender population were impaired by mental or emotional problems. However, very few individuals (1.7%) had severe mental or emotional problems that directly "compelled" them to shoplift. The persons in the latter category were called "episodic" offenders.

Fifteen percent of the sample were "impulse" shoplifters, and another 15% were "occasional" offenders. Impulse shoplifters typically had seen an item that they desired but were unable to afford. They had picked it up and pocketed it or carried it around the store, often in a daze, trying to decide whether to steal it. Eventually they tried to walk out but were detected. Later, they could not recall at what point they had made the decision to shoplift. Occasional offenders were less impulsive but more likely to steal for excitement or a dare. Both impulse and occasional offenders were extremely embarrassed when detected, pleaded with officials to give them another chance, and were considered unlikely to shoplift again.

Although Moore found no significant gender differences in overall shoplifting, 68% of the teenage offenders were male, whereas 56.5% of the adult offenders were female. Moore also found interesting differences between male and female adult offenders with respect to psychological stress. More women reported being under great stress in their lives than did men (28.9% of the women compared to 13.5% of the men). However, this difference may also be due to the greater reluctance of men to report stress or other emotional problems in general. Mental disorders, found in only a small percentage of the total shoplifter population, appeared twice as often in women as in men. There were no gender differences in the incidence of milder mental disorders, however. Substance abuse, on the other hand, was more common among men than women (52% to 26%).

One thing does appear clear, however. Clinicians and researchers have been unable to substantiate evidence of **kleptomania**, the *irresistible* impulse to steal unneeded objects. Some have even questioned its very existence as a behavior pattern. According to the DSM-IV (American Psychiatric Association, 1994), the kleptomaniac "experiences a rising subjective sense of tension before the theft and feels pleasure, gratification, or relief when committing the theft" (p. 612). A strong argument against kleptomania is that shoplifters display exceedingly low recidivism rates. Once apprehended, the amateur rarely shoplifts again (Cameron, 1964; Russell, 1973). If kleptomania were an important ingredient, we would expect the individual to steal repeatedly as the tension increases.

Lloyd Klemke (1992) suggests that kleptomania is a psychiatric label intended to ease the guilt of affluent women caught stealing at the turn of the twentieth century. Merchants, Klemke points out, did not want to antagonize their affluent clientele. Furthermore, affluent families wanted to keep their moral reputations untarnished and keep their women at home. Nor did the courts want to convict "respectable ladies" as common criminals. Thus, kleptomania (the Greek word for "stealing madness," a term presumably coined by Esquirol in 1838) legitimized the actions of the merchants and the courts to dismiss or acquit the "afflicted" woman and excuse her from being held personally responsible for her actions.

If kleptomania does exist, it seems to be a rare phenomenon. For example, in a recent study conducted by Sarasalo, Bergman, and Toth (1997), 50 shoplifters (29 males, 21 females) were interviewed immediately after being caught red-handed in central Stockholm, Sweden. None of the persons interviewed fulfilled the DSM-IV criteria for kleptomania. Sarasalo et al., however, did find that many of the shoplifters reported a "thrill" and challenge in connection with the crime.

Much of the literature on the causes of kleptomania focuses on its relationship to anxiety, depression, or sexual disturbances (M. Goldman, 1991; Sarasalo, Bergman, & Toth, 1996). Citing sexual disturbances as a cause for kleptomania is primarily based in the psychoanalytic tradition. But as Marcus Goldman (1991) notes, "There are no modern data available to refute or confirm these earlier psychoanalytic findings" (p. 990).

Overall, much of the recent research has found depression to be a common symptom of people who engage in "nonsensical shoplifting" (Lamontagne, Boyer, Hetu, & Lacerte-Lamontagne, 2000), a term sometimes used interchangeably with kleptomania. Yates (1986) claims that 80% of those who engaged in nonsensical shoplifting were depressed. McElroy and colleagues (McElroy, Pope, Hudson, Keck, & White, 1991) found that all 20 patients they studied who engaged in nonsensical shoplifting met the DSM-III-R criteria for a lifetime diagnosis of a major mood (depression) disorder. In addition, many of these patients said they engaged in nonsensical shoplifting far more often when they were depressed. It seems that some depressed people may engage in nonsensical shoplifting as a stimulating, exciting activity that moves them away from feelings of helplessness. In fact, M. Goldman (1991) finds that depressive states are often reported throughout the literature as precursors to many kinds of theft that are not related to profit.

For some unexplained reason, women seem to engage in nonsensical shoplifting more often than men. According to Marcus Goldman (1991), "It would appear that the average person suffering from kleptomania is a 35-year-old married woman who has been apprehended for the theft of objects she could easily afford and does not need" (p. 994). However, statistics on "kleptomania" are incomplete and largely unknown. Therefore, any statement concerning gender differences in either kleptomania or nonsensical shoplifting should be made very cautiously.

Shoplifting can be controlled to some extent by the use of electronic article surveillance or ink tags (Eck, 2000). Electronic article surveillance involves attaching electronic tags on merchandise that only store clerks can remove at the time of payment. Failure to remove the tag sets off an alarm at the door as the customer leaves the store. Ink tags deface the merchandise if it is removed from the store without being paid for, thereby destroying the value of the stolen goods (Eck, 2000). In his review of the research literature, Eck reports that electronic article surveillance measures can reduce shoplifting from 32% to 80%, and are found to be more effective than either security guards or store redesign. (See Bamfield [1994], DiLonardo [1996], and Farrington et al. [1993] for more detail on relevant studies.) Ink tags as an effective prevention of shoplifting have been less studied than electronic article surveillance but appear to be equally promising.

PROSTITUTION

One nonviolent economic crime that has long received attention in the psychological literature is prostitution, often regarded as a victimless crime. Prostitution—essentially sex for sale—is illegal in all states except Nevada. Nevada does, however, prohibit prostitution in counties in the state that exceed 200,000 in population (J. Miller, 1991). People may be arrested for both soliciting and providing sex, but by far the majority of arrests are for the latter. In the popular literature, this crime is blamed for decreases in neighborhood property values, increases in drug abuse and violent crime, and deterioration of the American family. Some commentators note that prostitutes (especially female prostitutes) are more often victims than offenders, and more than one author suggests that the criminal justice system shares the role of victimizer with pimps and persons who patronize prostitutes (James, 1978). Of particular concern to many observers is juvenile prostitution. On the other hand, some social scientists and social commentators suggest that adult prostitution is a lucrative career, and it has even been suggested that prostitutes be recruited to assist in the treatment of some sexual problems (Adler, 1975).

Cogent arguments have been advanced in favor of the legalization or decriminalization of adult prostitution. Traditionally, it has been treated as primarily a female crime, with women comprising the great majority of the arrests. In the past, female prostitutes accounted for approximately one-third of the female jail and prison population (James, 1978), whereas male prostitutes were rarely incarcerated. Today, the arrest figures are more closely parallel, with women accounting for approximately two-thirds of all arrests for prostitution and commercial vice (Federal Bureau of Investigation, 2003). The arrest figures do not distinguish between soliciting and providing services, however. Conservative estimates suggest that prostitution is the primary source of personal income for at least 1 million women and girls in the United States (J. Miller, 1991); no similar estimates are available for male prostitutes. In addition, there are virtually no reliable statistics on the extent to which people procure the illegal services of prostitutes.

Prostitution is relevant to this text because it is a "deviant behavior" that lends itself well to psychological examination. Our purpose in discussing prostitution is not to consider its moral and policy implications, but to focus on the sociological and psychological myths and misconceptions that surround it and to review the available psychological research. That research focuses almost exclusively on the person providing the service, particularly the female prostitute, rather than on the person who obtains it. Consequently, the discussion herein does the same. It should be emphasized, though, that—if prostitution is to remain a crime—researchers should give equal attention to both parties in the transaction. A parallel might be drawn to illegal drug use, where the reverse phenomenon occurs. That is, researchers in psychology are far more likely to study the substance abuser than the seller or distributor. Both are committing a criminal offense.

We do not, however, address the exploitation of juveniles of both sexes for prostitution purposes, a phenomenon quickly gaining the attention of social science researchers. Miller (1991) argues that prostitution is a form of sexual exploitation and a form of sexual coercion for all women, because they are compelled or forced (usually by men), physically and psychologically, to engage in a sexual act.

Prostitution is defined as the offering, agreement to offer, or provision of sexual relations in return for tangible rewards or special favors. Increasingly more jurisdictions are adding solicitation of services to their criminal statutes and thereby rendering illegal the behavior of the "john" as well as the prostitute. Prostitution may involve either a heterosexual or a homosexual pairing or it may involve group behavior. Although it most commonly refers to the procurement of sexual intercourse with a woman by a man, a variety of sexual activities may be involved.

It is impossible to estimate the number of commercial prostitutes in the United States, since police agencies interpret the criminality of the behavior very subjectively and arbitrarily. Arrests are often dependent on social and political pressures. It is generally recognized that prostitutes are often harassed and detained, with or without formal arrest, and for purposes other than the idealized goal of eliminating the practice. Primary clientele of both female and male prostitutes are believed to be white, middle-class men between 30 and 60 years of age (Haft, 1976; Jolin, 1994).

Theorists and researchers have traditionally offered biased, subjective generalizations, all about the female prostitute. They have alternately called her feeble-minded, emotionally disturbed, a latent or manifest homosexual, oversexed, sexually deprived, a primitive creature, or an individual rigidly fixated at her Oedipal (or Electra) stage of psychosexual development. From all indications, none of these labels adequately describes the prostitute. Women who become prostitutes appear to come from many different walks of life, possess varied educational and family backgrounds, demonstrate a wide range of personality types, and express a great variety of motives for their involvement in prostitution. Although research on male prostitutes is less available, there is no reason to believe that the same could not be said of them.

Several researchers have brought attention to a system of class structure among female prostitutes. At the lower end of the continuum are the "streetwalkers," who work the streets; at the uppermost level are "call girls," who cater to a select clientele and are rarely arrested. In recent years, a new category has been documented, which is apparently lower in status than the streetwalker. This is the "lot lizard," a prostitute who works truck stops and highway rest areas (Luxenburg, 2000). (The offensiveness of this term is testimony to the dehumanization so often associated with prostitution.) The call girl is usually more sophisticated and educated than the streetwalker, and is more often protected from the physical brutality and humiliation women at the lower levels of the prostitution hierarchy encounter (D'Emilio & Freedman, 1988). In between are a variety of categories, including stag party workers, escorts, masseuses, conventioneers, bar girls, brothel girls, circuit travelers (who move around in groups to labor camps or lumber camps), and rap booth girls (who occupy glassed-in booths for customer viewing). J. C. Coleman (1976) found that, as we go up the social class structure, the women are increasingly physically attractive, intelligent, well-educated, and sophisticated. Adler (1975) pointed out that the contemporary prostitute is, in many instances, socially and culturally indistinguishable from women in general.

It was generally believed that many prostitutes, especially at the lower status levels, came from lower- or lower- middle-class homes, but even this is now in question. James (1978) noted that a full 64% of her sample of streetwalkers reported their childhood family's income as middle- or upper-class. There seems little doubt, however, that most prostitutes come from conflictual families, where patterns of alienation from a single parent or from both parents are discernible. Many prostitutes also report negative sexual experiences in the home during preadolescence or adolescence. In an oft-cited study, 41% of 136 prostitutes reported incestuous experiences, usually with their fathers (James, 1976). Forty-seven percent reported they had been raped, and 17% had been raped more than once, most before reaching the age of 16. Studies of juvenile prostitutes lend support to these findings. Silberman (cited in Bracey, 1982) interviewed over 200 juvenile prostitutes and reported that 61% had been sexually molested by a member of their household. Bracey (1982) found that 50% of juvenile prostitutes in her sample reported experiencing forcible sexual advances by older men before reaching puberty.

It should be emphasized that while prostitution is regarded as a nonviolent crime, the prostitutes themselves—especially those who operate from the street—are frequent victims of violence (Monto, 2004). Studies have continually shown that a majority of prostitutes working the streets have been raped and physically assaulted during the course of their activities (Farley & Barkan, 1998, 2000; Monto, 2004). In addition, prostitutes are disproportionately represented among female murder victims (Lowman, 2000; Miller & Jayasundara, 2001; Monto, 2004).

However, prostitutes who work indoors are also subjected to high rates of violence. In one study involving three cities in the United Kingdom, while women who worked outdoors did experience significantly more violence than those who worked indoors (81% compared to 48%), the incidence of violence experienced by the indoor women was still very high (Church, Henderson, Barnard, & Hart, 2001). In another study, Raphael and Shapiro (2004) found that not only did indoor prostitutes experience significant amounts of violence but also the type of violence was more serious and the levels were higher than those experienced by women who worked the streets.

Contrary to popular assumption, a majority of prostitutes do not appear to be lured into the activity by organized crime, by brutal pimps, under false pretenses, or to support drug habits. Recruitment by pimps, madames, or organized crime appears to have been a factor for only about 20% of the prostitute population. Nevertheless, rather than "choosing prostitution," they appear to have been precipitated into it by negative effects in their lives, such as the loss of someone close to them or a series of economic setbacks (Luxenburg, 2000). However, juvenile girls, particularly runaways, are more likely to have been recruited. "American society has defined as desirable young, physically perfect women, and girls on the streets, who have little else of value to trade, are encouraged to use this 'resource'" (Chesney-Lind & Shelden, 1998, p. 116). While we do not discuss juvenile prostitution in detail here, it is important to stress that this is a major social problem. According to Chesney-Lind and Shelden (1998), figures have varied widely in the surveys taken, ranging from 600,000 prostitutes under age 16 to close to 1 million.

The assumption of heavy drug use among adult prostitutes also appears questionable. James (1978) suggests that the prostitutes who are apprehended by police (and who thus end up in the criminal statistics) tend to be the "hypes"—the addicts working as prostitutes to support a drug habit. They "form a special, lower class in the hierarchy of the 'fast life'" (p. 306). Inciardi (1980) surveyed 149 female heroin users and found a high incidence of prostitution (about one-third) among them. However, he did not find evidence for a strong causal link. The women who committed crimes to support their drug habits were much more likely to choose economic offenses, like larceny or fraud, rather than prostitution.

Motives

What motivates people to engage in prostitution? An obvious, although oversimplistic answer, is money. It is important to distinguish between financial necessity and financial comfort, however. James (1976) found that only 8.4% of her sample started prostitution out of economic necessity, but 56.5% did so out of a desire for money and material goods. They saw prostitution as a lucrative business that offered material rewards they otherwise might not have attained. Social rewards like parties, dancing, and expensive dining were also a factor.

The James study and others like it have dispelled several alleged motives for entering into prostitution. Early research included numerous studies that portrayed prostitutes as narcissistic, frigid, hating men, fearful of lesbianism, or having an unresolved sexual attachment to their fathers (Electra complex)

(Gibbens, 1957; Greenwald, 1958). Virtually none of these assumptions was verified by later research. For example, James (1976) found that only 1% of her sample demonstrated hostility toward men.

The Freudian theory that prostitution is a result of early sexual love for the opposite-sex parent, and subsequent sexual partners are insufficient surrogates, also seems weak. According to this theory, the bulk of sexual energy and attraction is directed to the initial love object; later partners are unsatisfactory. Therefore, the sexually promiscuous person endlessly but subconsciously searches for the treasured first love object, the father (or, in the case of male prostitutes, the mother). The Freudian perspective sees prostitution as individual psychopathology rather than a social phenomenon. Since a consistent finding in the research literature is that more than half of all prostitutes did not have an available father figure in the home, it is questionable whether they would develop unconscious, imagined incestuous relationships. Because of the dearth of information on backgrounds of male prostitutes, we cannot draw conclusions. However, it is highly unlikely that male prostitutes are subconsciously searching for their treasured first love object, their mother.

As the above should indicate, a continual focus on "explaining" the behavior of women while ignoring the behavior of men who either solicit sex or offer it may seem unwarranted. Prostitution has traditionally been considered a crime that women commit, a judgment that reflects long-standing assumptions about the respective roles of women and men. The theories discussed above should have been applied to male as well as female prostitutes, but there was little if any recognition that male prostitution existed. On the other hand, it could be argued that—because female prostitutes are more likely than male prostitutes to be abused and victimized—the attention placed on them is warranted. Furthermore, numerous questions could be raised about the individuals who patronize prostitutes, if society is to consider this a criminal act.

To conclude that anyone goes into prostitution and remains there for financial gain is premature, and it oversimplifies human behavior. Why do more individuals not opt for that lifestyle? Furthermore, although material gains may provide an initial incentive, it is widely recognized that most female prostitutes—with the possible exception of independent, high-class call girls—do not directly profit much from their work, given the obligatory payoffs to pimps, police, hotel clerks, and taxi drivers. Male prostitutes are likely at a greater advantage, however, because they are less likely to be dependent on the protection offered by pimps.

Human behavior represents an infinite array of learned responses, and prostitution as a complex behavior should be no exception. It is frequently observed that most prostitutes find out about prostitution through friends and get started through their efforts and encouragement (James, 1978). These personal contacts provide significant models and opportunities for imitative learning. In addition, the sex-for-sale behaviors offer greater reward possibilities (money, excitement, adventure) than a previous life predicament. For some, prostitution offers a more positive and potentially exciting alternative than the home situation. In the case of the female prostitute, the relationship with a pimp, who often serves as husband, boyfriend, father, lover, agent, and protector (James, 1976), may be considerably more rewarding than the relationship with family.

Once these expectations and potentially rewarding behaviors are acquired, continued involvement depends partly on the actual rewards obtained. Do the positives of prostitution outweigh the negatives? Even given "good money" and an ideal situation in which the prostitute is relatively independent, few personalities would seem suited for long-term prostitution. To be habitually used solely as a sexual object would appear to require, among other things, a learned method of detachment and the availability of other sources of self-esteem.

Prostitution appears to be an emotionally stressful and psychologically draining occupation. James found that at least 50% of her sample listed emotional stress, worry about physical harm at the hands of a customer, and low self-esteem as major disadvantages. Another 20% listed the stress of worrying about venereal disease, reactions of family and society, personal vulnerability, and feelings of helplessness as primary disadvantages. Contemporary prostitutes have added HIV to the long list of dangers they already face.

In recent years, much attention has been focused away from prostitution as it has traditionally been regarded and toward a related topic, **human trafficking**. In some literature it is referred to as forced prostitution (S. Cook, 2000). Human trafficking has become a highly lucrative criminal market in the United States (Finckenauer & Schrock, 2000). The "commodities" involved in this illicit worldwide trade are women, children, and men and the criminal activity is usually sex related and is committed for long-term exploitation for high profits. Examples include women who agree to come to this country as waitresses or dancers but then are forced into prostitution until they are able to pay off the debt incurred through a smuggling fee. In some Third World countries, parents "sell" their children to traffickers who take them to other parts of the world, including the United States, and profit from their sexual exploitation. Violence, intimidation, and brutality are particularly common with trafficking victims brought in for the sex industry. "Women who are forced into prostitution are often forcibly trafficked between brothels, cities, and countries in what has become the modern slave trade. They experience rape, sexual assault and harassment, physical injury, drug addiction, depression, chronic pain, and serious health problems, including constant exposure to AIDS" (S. Cook, 2000, p. 212). Human trafficking often involves a variety of additional illicit activities, including fraud, extortion, racketeering, money laundering, bribery of public officials, drug use, document forgery, and gambling (Finckenauer & Schrock, 2000; Richard, 1999).

Arguments for the decriminalization or legalization of prostitution are often appealing, particularly if one believes that the present laws are selectively enforced against women or that prostitution is essentially a victimless crime.

However, such decriminalization or legalization approaches must find an alternative way to address the exploitation of juveniles and the many abuses that occur as a result of human trafficking.

ROBBERY

Robbery "is taking or attempting to take anything of value from the care, custody, or control of a person or persons by force or violence and/or by putting the victim in fear" (Federal Bureau of Investigation, 2003, p. 303). There were 420,637 robberies reported in 2002, reflecting a national robbery rate of 145.9 per 100,000 people (Federal Bureau of Investigation, 2003). These figures represent about an 11.8% drop from 1998 and a 43% drop from 1993. Firearms tend to be the weapon used most often in the commission of robberies, followed by strong-arm tactics through the use of hands, feet, and fists.

Interestingly, more than one-third of the robbery incidents in the United States are "acquaintance robberies," in which the victim knows the offender (Felson, Baumer, & Messner, 2000). In these cases, many of the robbery victims are family members, usually women and school-aged youths (Felson et al., 2000). The evidence suggests that acquaintance robbery is relatively minor in that the take is small, offenders are unlikely to use weapons, and injuries are rare (Felson et al., 2000). Moreover, the victim is less likely to report the crime to police.

The national clearance rate for robbery in 2002 was 25.7% (Federal Bureau of Investigation, 2003). Like many other crimes, it is primarily an offense committed by young adults, with individuals under the age of 25 accounting for 61.4% of arrestees. The majority of the arrestees (approximately 90%) were males. The risk of being robbed is highest for young, male, single, poor blacks who live in urban areas (Felson et al., 2000). This risk factor holds whether it is a stranger robbery or an acquaintance robbery.

Robbery accounts for only about 4% of all arrests for economic crimes (but 35% of the violent crimes). However, because of its potential physical harm to victims, it is among the crimes most feared by the American population (Garofalo, 1977). It involves a high probability of physical harm from a stranger, and it can happen to anyone. (Nearly half of robberies occur on streets and highways; see **Table 11–2**.) One in 3 victims are injured in robberies (also called stickups, holdups, muggings), and 1 in 10 seriously enough to require medical attention (U.S. Department of Justice, 1988). Furthermore, robbery offenders are more likely to use weapons than other violent offenders. Yet, despite its dangerousness, robbery is among the least-studied criminal offenses.

One reason for the lack of research interest in the psychology of robbery is that robbery seems so obvious and straightforward: People rob to obtain money. The process is quick, and the potential returns are lucrative. Compared to burglary, however, the risks are great and the penalties substantial.

TABLE 11–2 Locations of Robberies Across the Nation, 2002

LOCATION	%
Street or highway	42.8
Commercial establishment	14.6
Gas or service station	2.7
Convenience store	6.5
Residence	13.5
Bank	2.5
Miscellaneous	17.7

Source: Federal Bureau of Investigation (2003).

Much of this may be true but, as we have seen, human behavior should not be oversimplified. The motives of offenders may be extremely varied. People behave in a certain way because they have convinced themselves that is what works best for them.

Bank Robbery

"A bank robbery is indicated when the crime is robbery and the location is a financial institution" (Federal Bureau of Investigation, 2003). It accounts for 2.4% of all robbery in the United States (Federal Bureau of Investigation, 2003). And although robbery in general had a clearance rate of only 25% in 2001, the clearance rate for bank robbery approached 60%. Only murder had a higher clearance rate.

According to data collected from the Bank Crime Statistics, collected by the Violent Crimes/Fugitive Unit of the FBI, the average amount of money netted from a bank robbery between 1996 through 2000 was $8,000 (Federal Bureau of Investigation, 2003). The amount of money eventually recovered is quite small, averaging about 20% of the total amount taken during the robbery. Bank robbery incidents are most likely to occur on Fridays. Historically, Friday has been payday for much of the nation, requiring large amounts of cash to be delivered to various branch banks. Fridays continue to be the favorite day, even with the reduction of branch bank offices in recent years and the substantial increase in electronic banking. Most bank robberies occur between 9 and 11 AM.

Also according to the Bank Crime Statistics, the percentage of bank robberies that involve the use of a firearm is 32, and the actual shooting of a firearm occurs in about 2% of that total (Federal Bureau of Investigation, 2003). Most (80%) bank robberies are carried out by a single offender. The vast majority of all bank robbers are males (95%) and most are between 18 and 29 years of age.

The great majority of bank robbers (80%) are amateurs who have *not* been convicted of a bank crime in the past (Federal Bureau of Investigation, 2003).

An amateur tends to rob a bank on the spur of the moment without much planning, and primarily to fulfill some need, such as to pay for drugs. Therefore, bank robberies usually do not involve the meticulously planned caper carried out by a group of highly experienced criminals, as often portrayed by the media. A professional, according to the Bank Crime Statistics database, is a bank robber with a prior criminal record, no matter how unsuccessful he (or she) has been at robbing banks in the past.

Robbery: Economic Crime or Violent Crime?

The major distinctions between robbery and other economic crimes like larceny and burglary are the direct contact between the offender and the victim and the threat or use of force. The offender threatens bodily harm if the victim resists or impedes the offender's progress; usually this threat is backed up by a clearly visible lethal weapon, such as a firearm.

The combination of taking property and threatening physical harm to a victim creates problems for the researcher or criminologist classifying the offense. Should robbery be considered an economic crime or a violent crime? Wolfgang and Ferracuti (1967) argue that robbery—like homicide, rape, and aggravated assault—develops within a subculture of violence and should be classified as a violent crime. Normandeau (1968), on the other hand, contends that robbers are generally not violent and are associated with a subculture of theft rather than one of violence. Normandeau based his judgment on a study of Philadelphia robberies, in which he discovered that 44% involved no physical injury to the victim. While 56% of the victims did sustain some injury, only 5% needed to be hospitalized.

If Wolfgang and Ferracuti are correct in saying that robbery is a crime of violence springing from a violent subculture, the backgrounds of offenders should support this. We would expect to find criminal records and a social history peppered with violent incidents. In a study of Boston robberies during 1964 and again during 1968, Conklin (1972) found no "excessive amount" of prior criminal violence in the backgrounds of robbery offenders compared with the "general criminal populations of the country." In addition, fewer than one-third of the robbery victims had sustained injuries in the incidents. Similar findings are reported by C. Spencer (1966) and Normandeau (1968), neither of whom found that robbers had high conviction rates for violent conduct. However, research does suggest that robbers who did rely on violence in the past are more likely to use it in the future, whether in robbery or in other crimes.

One way to solve the problem of classifying robbery is to consider it both an economic crime and a violent crime. In fact, Vetter and Silverman (1978) suggest that it is more accurately catalogued as a violent economic crime. Most robbers, they point out, try to intimidate and frighten victims through threats of violence. Offenders rationalize that the more fear can be induced (without panic), the less resistance will be encountered. If offenders feel that their control over the situation is weakening, they may flee, impose a greater threat, or become more violent.

Strong-arm robbery (without a weapon) is more likely to result in injury to the victim than is robbery with a firearm or knife. Presumably, victims are less fearful (and thus more daring) when confronted by an unarmed individual. In the absence of a gun or other weapon, the victim's resistance to losing valuable personal property is stronger, and he or she is more apt to hamper the progress of the strong-arm offender. The tendency to resist, therefore, may partly account for the higher rates of victim injury in these no-weapon situations. Furthermore, the offender is likely to feel more confident, powerful, and in control of the incident when he or she has a weapon. Because of this increase in confidence, the offender is less likely to be anxious and disorganized in response patterns and, thus, is better able to think clearly and evaluate the consequences of actions.

Assessing skilled robbery, Peter Letkemann (1973) offers pertinent remarks about successful robbers' confidence and victim "management." First, they draw analogies between the technical skills of the burglar and those of the mechanic and between the professional skills of the robber and those of the clinician. Burglars do not have to be concerned with people, but professional robbers must be able to maintain control and handle their victims at all times. Bank robbers, for example, assert that the keys to a successful heist are confidence and the ability to control people under highly stressful conditions. Confidence, they believe, is reflected in the robber's tone of voice and general behavior. High levels of self-confidence are crucial if robbers are to maintain control of the situation. Successful robbers also note that the posture and physical location of the victims are deliberately designed to enhance the offender's control over them.

According to Letkemann, professional robbers often express dismay over media treatment of robbery. Television and movies generally downplay the seriousness of bank robbery, for example; the offenders therefore must work harder to convince their victims that they mean business. The entertainment media also encourage some victims to be heroes; robbers consider heroes irrational and extremely dangerous.

In a revealing study, Richard Wright and Scott Decker (1997) interviewed 86 individuals who were actively engaged in armed robbery on a regular basis in St. Louis. One of the unique aspects about the study is that none of the robbers interviewed were incarcerated, and they were outside the clutches of the criminal justice system (not on probation, not under arrest, not on parole). Most studies of armed robbery feature interviews with prisoners who either admit to engaging in the offense or have been convicted for robbery.

Wright and Decker focused on determining what factors influenced the robbers in their decisions of when, how, and whom to rob. The researchers were also interested in the offenders' thoughts and actions during the commission of the crime. In addition to conducting interviews, the researchers took 10 of the robbers to the site of a recent holdup for which they had not been apprehended and asked them to reconstruct the crime. The sample was overwhelmingly black, poor, male, and uneducated. Although the sample represented all ages, the majority were between 18 and 29 years of age. Most of the offenders had committed numerous robberies in their lifetimes—so many in fact that the majority found it impossible to specify the exact number. Despite the very high number of armed robberies they said they had committed, 60% of the sample had never been convicted of armed robbery. Almost all the sample (96%) reported committing many other offenses, particularly theft, burglary, assault, and drug sales. A majority (85%) typically did their robbery on the street, while 12% preferred to rob commercial establishments (e.g., pawnshops, jewelry stores, liquor stores).

Wright and Decker (1997) found that a vast majority of the offenders did not plan the armed robbery. "The reality for many offenders is that crime commission had become so routinized that it emerges almost naturally in the course of their daily lives, often occurring without substantial planning or deliberation" (p. 30). The researchers discovered that, with few exceptions, the decision to rob was strongly influenced by a pressing need for cash to support their hedonistic, carefree lifestyle. The robbers in this sample were deeply enmeshed in the street culture, where immediate gratification reigned supreme. Many robbers spent their loot with reckless abandon, without much thought to financial obligations or commitments. The offenders chose armed robbery as a lifestyle because it provides quick cash as the need arises. Armed robbery offered immediate cash compared to the delays inherent in disposing of hot merchandise acquired through burglary, shoplifting, and motor vehicle theft.

Although the need for cash was the overwhelming reason for armed robbery, a secondary gain expressed by some robbers was the control they held over their frightened victims. However, this secondary gain seemed to be restricted primarily to law-abiding citizens. In addition, many of these offenders preferred to rob white victims because they usually complied with their demands and did not offer much resistance, particularly white women. According to many of these offenders, black victims were more likely to resist and fight back.

Interestingly, in a study of juvenile robbery trends, Chesney-Lind and Paramore (2001) found that, although females committed fewer robberies than males, they engaged in robbery for basically the same reasons. Money (usually to obtain drugs) and "status conferring goods" (such as jewelry) are the primary motivations for female robbers (Chesney-Lind & Paramore, 2001; Miller, 1998). Although male offenders are most likely to use weapons when committing a robbery, female robbers usually do not use weapons. Chesney-Lind and Paramore (2000) found that in more than 80% of the robberies committed by females, no weapon was used.

One of the favorite targets of the street robbers in the Wright and Decker sample were individuals who themselves were involved in lawbreaking, especially drug sellers and wealthy drug users. Drug dealers carry considerable amounts of cash as a result of their illegal activities. Of course, the risks are higher when targeting drug users because they are more likely to be armed, more likely to resist, and sometimes connected to a powerful drug organization. Wealthy drug users tend to be white persons who come into a neighborhood looking to buy drugs with considerable cash. They can be easily victimized, and like other lawbreakers, they are unlikely to report the robbery to the police.

The Wright and Decker study provides far more meaningful information about the perceptions and cognitive processes of armed robbers than studies that rely exclusively on information gathered from inmates who realize or are fearful that their statements will be reviewed by criminal justice authorities. One of the major findings of the Wright and Decker (1997) project is that there is little psychological mystery behind the motives of armed robbery: They need cash now to support their impulsive, hedonistic lifestyle, and robbery provides the best route to that cash. Some also enjoy dominating their victims and frightening them, but this motive is only secondary to cash acquisition. One caveat about the Wright–Decker study is necessary. Generalizations to other robbers in other cities should be made cautiously until similar studies are conducted in other geographical areas.

Convenience stores appear to be favorite commercial sites for robbery, with an estimated 16,000 to 20,000 robbed per year in the United States. Most convenience stores have no robberies but a few have many robberies (Eck, 2000). One of the debates concerning prevention of convenience store robbery is whether having two or more clerks in the store, rather than one, reduces the robbery attempts. So far, the evidence is unclear, but the two-clerk experiment does not appear to discourage robberies as much as anticipated (Eck, 2000). Cameras and silent alarms do not seem to reduce convenience store robberies, but some preliminary evidence suggests that the installation of interactive CCTV (allowing communication between store personnel and security personnel watching a monitor in a remote location) may be effective in reducing store robberies by nearly one-third (Eck, 2000).

Although convenience stores have traditionally been the favorite robbery sites, America's fast-food restaurants are fast becoming the most preferred target. Many restaurant robberies occur at fast-food restaurants because they are open late, staffed by teenagers, full of cash, and located conveniently near a highway. In describing the vulnerability of fast-food restaurants to armed robbery, Schlosser (2001) writes, "A couple of sixteen-year-old crew members and a twenty-year-old manager are often the only people locking up a restaurant, long after midnight" (p. 84). About two-thirds of the robberies at fast-food restaurants involve current or former employees, and frequently the on-duty manager suffers much of the anger and violence administered during the robbery. In 1998, more fast-food restaurant workers were murdered on the job in the United States than police officers (Schlosser, 2001).

The leading fast-food chains have tried to reduce robbery by spending millions on new security measures, including video cameras, panic buttons, drop-safes, burglar alarms, and additional lighting (Schlosser, 2001). But even the most secure restaurant remains highly vulnerable to robbery.

WHITE-COLLAR AND OCCUPATIONAL CRIME

The term **white-collar crime** was coined by Edwin H. Sutherland in his presidential address to the American Sociological Society in 1939. In his speech, Sutherland urged his fellow sociologists to pay attention to the law-violating behavior of businesses, particularly large corporations. He had uncovered these violations by reviewing government files on 70 large American corporations and had learned that breaking rules was commonplace. In 1949, Sutherland published his now-classic book, *White-Collar Crime*, in which he detailed his findings without naming the corporations. A later edition of the book (Sutherland, 1983) did include the names.

Following Sutherland's lead, a considerable amount of pioneering research was done on white-collar crime between 1939 and 1963 (Geis, 1988). This was followed by a decade of inactivity. Since 1975, there has been a revival of interest in studying the area, although criminological literature pays far less attention to white-collar crime than to other forms of criminal behavior. The highly publicized individual and corporate scandals of recent years have only served to illustrate that this attention is needed.

According to Sutherland (1949), "white-collar crime may be defined approximately as a crime committed by a person of respectability and high social status in the course of his occupation" (p. 9). Although Sutherland used the word "crime," he did not intend it strictly in the legal sense. He recognized that numerous laws and regulations violated by persons of high social status carried civil rather than criminal sanctions, and he wanted these violations to be condemned. In fact, this was a critical factor to Sutherland, who saw a double-standard phenomenon at work. The law-violating behavior of the poor carried criminal penalties; the law-violating behavior of the rich often did not. This was so despite the fact that "the financial cost of white-collar crime is probably several times as great as the financial cost of all the crimes which are customarily regarded as 'the crime problem'" (p. 12).

Although Sutherland's call to study white-collar crime was heeded, his working definition produced numerous problems for subsequent criminologists. Some, most notably Paul Tappan (1947), argued that white-collar "crime" could not really be crime unless it violated the criminal law. The terms *respectability* and *high social status* were considered vague. Over the past three decades, researchers have tried to improve on Sutherland's definition. Marshall Clinard and Richard Quinney (1980) preferred to dichotomize the concept into (1) occupational crime, committed by an individual for his or her own profit, and (2) corporate crime, committed by the corporation through its agents. This dichotomy is probably the most commonly used by criminologists today. Horning (1970) proposed a tripartition to distinguish the various behaviors that might be at issue. He reserved the term *white-collar crime* for illegal acts committed by salaried employees, from which they personally benefit, in which their place of employment is either the victim of or the locale for the commission of the act. Embezzlement is a good example of this. *Corporate crime* refers to illegal acts committed by employees in the course of their employment that primarily benefit the company or corporation. Illegal dumping of hazardous wastes is an example. *Blue-collar crime* refers to the whole array of illegal acts committed by nonsalaried workers against their places of employment. Theft of machinery is an example.

Gary Green (1997) has made significant contributions to clarifying the definitional dilemmas associated with the term white-collar crime by proposing the concept of *occupational crime*. Unfortunately, Green's approach has not been widely adopted. To Green, occupational crime encompasses all of the behaviors previously subsumed under white-collar crime, blue-collar crime, and their variants. Occupational crime is "any act punishable by law that is committed through opportunity created in the course of an occupation that is legal" (p. 15). Green then subdivides occupational crime into four categories: (1) organizational (which includes corporate crime), (2) professional, (3) state-authority, and (4) individual (see **Table 11–3**).

In *organizational occupational crime*, a legal entity such as a company, corporation, firm, or foundation profits from the law-violating behavior. An example is the chief financial officer of a company falsifying the company's tax records with the tacit approval of its board of directors. Other examples are antitrust violations, overcharging the government for products or services, violations of Occupational Safety and Health Administration (OSHA) standards, and bribery of public officials. *Professional occupational crime* includes illegal behavior by persons such as lawyers, physicians, psychologists, and teachers committed through their occupations. A physician's Medicaid fraud or a lawyer's suborning the perjury of a client are illustrations.

State-authority occupational crime encompasses the wide range of law violation by persons imbued with legal authority; the individual who commits state-authority occupational crime is essentially violating the public trust. Bribe-taking by a public official and police brutality are illustrative. Finally, Green uses the category *individual occupational crime* to cover all violations not included in one of the previously discussed categories. The employee who steals equipment from his employer and the person who deliberately underreports income to the IRS are covered in this category.

As evident from the earlier examples, the concept of occupational crime proposed by Green covers a wide variety of offenses, not all of which are

TABLE 11–3   Summary of Green's (1997) Occupational Crime Typology

Occupational Crime	Description
Organizational	Law-violating behavior promoted by the corporation or agency
Professional	Law-violating behavior committed as a result of being in a profession that offers the opportunity for crime
State-authority	Law-violating behavior by those in government
Individual	Law-violating behavior committed by an individual working for a company or organization but committed for his or her own advancement or financial gain

economic in nature and not all of which are committed by persons of high social status. A therapist who sexually assaults a patient and a correctional officer who uses excessive force against an inmate are both committing violent occupational crimes. Neither the therapist's nor the correctional officer's behavior would qualify as white-collar crime in its classic sense. Some criminologists also have contended that certain corporate crimes should qualify as violent crimes, however. James Coleman (1998), for example, cites unsafe working conditions, illegal disposal of toxic waste, and the manufacture of unsafe products as examples of violent crime.

Green argues convincingly that his four-part division allows us to move away from the conceptual quagmire of "white-collar crime" and study a significant amount of workplace-facilitated illegal behavior in a logical, ordered manner. Although the term white-collar crime continues to be widely used, perhaps in deference to Sutherland's contributions to criminology, Green's approach offers an appealing alternative. As noted above, however, the approach that seems to be preferred in the criminological literature is the white-collar dichotomy proposed by Clinard and Quinney, occupational and corporate crime.

Regardless of which term is used, the extent of occupationally linked illegal behavior is extremely difficult to measure. The standard methods of measuring crime discussed in Chapter 1 rarely apply. The typical UCR report, for example, does not tell us whether a reported crime or an arrest was related to the perpetrator's occupation. Fraud, can be committed by a bank executive, a college student, a Fortune 500 Corporation, or a recipient of welfare benefits. Even when uncovered, the violations we have been discussing are often not recorded. Rather than publicize a theft by an employee, for example, a business might prefer to demand restitution, dismiss the employee, or force a resignation. It does not benefit the company's public image to file a criminal complaint.

When an organization is itself the violator, civil suits are often preferred to criminal charges. Additionally, the government regulatory process is widely acknowledged to be inefficient in preventing, uncovering, and punishing violators. When it comes to the professions, law violation is often shielded from the public, because society authorizes them to police themselves by means of standards, codes of ethics, and licensing.

Nevertheless, some attempts have been made to collect data on white-collar offenses, particularly those committed by individuals (Clinard and Quinney's "occupational crime" category). The National White Collar Crime Center (NW3C), a nonprofit organization based in Richmond, Virginia, collects information, publishes a newsletter, and sponsors training sessions and conferences devoted to this issue. In 2003, together with another group—the Coalition for the Prevention of Economic Crime—the NW3C sponsored its seventh annual Economic Crime Summit (The Informant, 2003). Topics that have recently come to the attention of the NW3C are Internet gambling, Internet fraud, online child pornography, insurance crime, and identity theft. Information is available at www.nw3c.org.

Without settling the difficult definitional morass associated with white-collar crime, we nevertheless proceed to discuss one example of this serious crime problem in more detail, specifically, crime committed by corporations and their agents. Sutherland, you will recall, focused on corporations in his original research. Following that discussion, we consider crimes at the opposite end of the continuum, wherein individual employees victimize their employers. Although not necessarily white-collar crimes, the latter behaviors qualify as individual occupational crimes according to Green's approach.

Corporate Crime

For purposes of the criminal law, a corporation is a person; that is, a corporation can be charged, tried, sentenced, and punished. Nevertheless, individuals within that organization are making decisions that render the corporate behavior a crime. Therefore, in discussing explanations for corporate crime, we focus on the behavior of persons, despite the fact that the organizational culture as well as the economic structure of society may facilitate and reward the illegal behavior.

Corporate crime covers offenses ranging from price-fixing to failure to recall a product known to have a serious defect that could potentially cause physical harm. The offenses are so varied, in fact, that most criminologists subdivide the crimes into more manageable categories. Thus, we hear of crimes against consumers, crimes against the environment, institutional corruption, and fiduciary fraud (Rosoff, Pontell, & Tillman, 1998); fraud and deception, manipulation of the marketplace, violation of civil liberties, and—as noted earlier—violent white-collar crimes (J. W. Coleman, 1998); crimes of fraud, offenses against public administration, and regulatory offenses (Albanese, 1995); and false and misleading advertising, defrauding of the government, antitrust crimes, manufacture and sale of unsafe consumer products, unfair labor practices, unsafe working conditions, crimes against the environment, and political bribery (Green, 1997).

The estimated costs of these corporate offenses—both financial and from a human-suffering standpoint—are staggering. However, up-to-date, reliable, or accurate statistics are nearly impossible to find. Although the available research is very dated, the financial cost of corporate crime has been estimated to be between $20 and $40 billion a year (Kramer, 1984). Most scholars in the area would consider this a very conservative estimate for 1984 and even more so today. Kramer (1984) estimated that over 100,000 deaths a year could be attributed to occupationally related diseases, most caused by the knowing and willful violation of occupational health and safety standards by businesses and industries. Annually, 20 million serious injuries are associated with unsafe and defective consumer products—unsafe foods and drugs and defective autos, tires, or appliances. About 110,000 of these injuries result in permanent disability, and 30,000 result in death (Schrager & Short, 1978). Obviously, not all of these accidents, injuries, and deaths are due to corporate neglect or illegal action, but the data suggest that many are (Hochstedler, 1984). Reiman (1995) has estimated that a conservative total of 90,105 Americans die every year as a result of occupational hazard and disease. Although some would argue that these deaths are not necessarily attributable to corporate malfeasance, others would say that corporations should be held responsible for the harms suffered by their workers.

Public attention to corporate crime has focused primarily on the economic crimes that have been highly publicized. These include a variety of practices that constitute fraud, including but not limited to price-fixing, false advertising, deceptive pricing, and securities fraud. Environmental and health-related crimes such as those discussed above have also attracted considerable public attention, however. In the 1990s both the tobacco and the asbestos industries were barraged with law suits brought on behalf of individuals who had either died or been seriously harmed by exposure to these hazardous products.

Explanations for corporate criminality often focus on the criminogenic or crime-producing nature of the business environment; that is, in order to survive, law-breaking is essential. Conklin (1977), for example, argued that law-breaking in American business was normative and that executives often believe that some dishonesty or deceit has to be tolerated in the best interest of the company. In response to comments such as these, corporations proclaim that they have entered an era of social responsibility and that the extent of corporate malfeasance is exaggerated. Business schools note that business ethics courses are a requirement in virtually all programs. Gilbert Geis (1997), however, a prominent scholar in the area of white-collar crime, chastises business schools for using "lulling terms, especially 'ethics,' to camouflage what essentially are considerations of criminal behavior" (p. xii).

You may recall that in Chapter 9, we referred to strategies people use to neutralize some of their violent conduct and separate it from their personal codes. The strategies, proposed by Bandura (1978), are worth repeating here. Although they operate with reference to a wide range of reprehensible conduct, they are particularly relevant to the discussion of corporate crime. The strategies may be used individually or in combination.

One set of neutralizing strategies operates at the level of behavior. What is culpable is made honorable through moral justifications and euphemistic jargon. In other words, a normally reprehensible act becomes personally and socially acceptable when it is associated with beneficial or moral ends. "We did it in the best interest of the company, the employees and their families, and the country." Similarly, corporate decision makers may regard the laws they are violating as unfair, unjust, or simply not in keeping with good business practices. Cressey (1953) called such justifications "vocabularies of adjustment." Conklin (1977) asserted that vocabularies of adjustment may play an even more crucial role in corporate crime than in juvenile delinquency, where they are frequently encountered.

A second set of neutralizing or dissociative strategies obscures or distorts the relationship between actions and their effects. In this group of strategies, people do not see themselves as personally responsible or accountable for their actions. They may disregard or deny the consequences of their actions—"It simply didn't happen the way the press reported it." Alternately, they may displace responsibility to the victim—"Consumers often don't use the appliance properly"—or diffuse the responsibility among the decision-making group—"After careful deliberation the board decided this would be the right decision."

A third set of strategies addresses the effects of the action on the recipients. Here, the dignifying qualities of the victims are removed. "Most consumers are greedy and stupid." "Third World countries are overcrowded anyway." We saw this strategy in action earlier in this text, when aggressors regarded their victims as less than human. This dehumanizing approach also seems to be a hallmark of prejudice and scapegoating.

In sum, through cognitive restructuring supported by corporate norms, decision makers can justify and rationalize behavior that appears reprehensible to outsiders. The restructuring process prevents the manager or executive from labeling him- or herself "criminal." In fact, in some corporations, the extent to which the norms and justifying mechanisms are embraced may well determine how far up the corporate ladder one climbs.

Individual Occupational Crime

When illegal behavior is pursued for the direct benefit of the individual, and the individual is neither a professional nor someone with state authority, Green refers to it as individual occupational crime. In the Clinard–Quinney white-collar crime dichotomy referred to at the beginning of this section, the behavior would simply be "occupational" crime, distinguished from "corporate" crime. In this largely solitary pursuit, offenders are guided primarily by their own personal justifications and reasoning. Embezzlers, for example, are operating outside organizational norms, although they may justify the behavior in much the same way that corporate criminals do. The dissociation strategies identified by Bandura apply here as well. In other words, embezzlers may convince themselves that the activity really is not a crime: They are merely borrowing the money temporarily and will put it to good use. Later, they will reimburse the company (secretly, of course).

One common type of illegal behavior in which the workplace is the victim is employee theft, which is an enormous drain on American business. One estimate has it costing business and industry $5 to $10 billion a year (J. Clark & Hollinger, 1983). In a survey of employees from 47 retail, manufacturing, and service organizations, one-third admitted stealing company property (J. Clark & Hollinger, 1983). The property included merchandise, supplies, tools, and equipment. In addition, almost two-thirds of the employees surveyed reported other types of misconduct, such as sick leave abuse, drug or alcohol use on the job, long lunch and coffee breaks, slow and sloppy workmanship, and falsification of time sheets. Collectively, these are counterproductive behaviors.

They do not involve actual removal of material goods from the organization, but they do reduce production and services.

Modern versions of employee theft involve the Internet and electronic payments. For example, the NW3C reports that some employees are taking advantage of the Automated Clearinghouse network to make personal purchases via the telephone or Web, using the company's corporate checking account numbers, which the employees obtain, often from their own paychecks. Telephone or Internet merchants often accept the account number without verifying the account ownership. Thus, "some companies remain unaware of the fraudulent entries against their accounts for many months, leading to extended problems in regaining their funds" (The Informant, 2003, p. 14).

Explanations for employee theft and counterproductive behaviors are multiple, but most cluster around the themes of age, dissatisfaction, and one's normative group at the workplace. The highest levels of theft and counterproductive behaviors are reported by younger, unmarried male employees (ages 16 to mid-20s). Apparently, these younger employees do not feel any commitment or loyalty to the organization, probably because they do not expect to spend their lives in that situation. Many are college and high school students working only until they graduate. High levels of theft and counterproductive behaviors are also found among employees expressing dissatisfaction with some aspect of their employment, especially with their immediate supervisor. Another component of job dissatisfaction is the workers' perception of the company's attitude toward them. If the workers perceive the organization as caring little about them, job dissatisfaction and the concomitant theft and counterproductive behaviors tend to follow. In these situations, the individuals typically know that what they are doing is "wrong," and if caught, they will admit their guilt and hope for a light sentence. Interestingly, financial restitution may involve more than they actually stole. A woman who admitted to the Automated Clearinghouse debit fraud discussed above made unauthorized transactions of $6,661.08 but was sentenced to 24 months' probation and restitution of $8,126.56 (The Informant, 2003).

While age and job dissatisfaction are highly correlated with theft and counterproductive behavior, normative support offers a viable explanation. Normative support refers to the standards, perceptions, and values the work group has established for itself, with or without the organization's implicit (or explicit) approval. In short, normative support refers to group norms. For example, the group may consider pilfered material a supplement to one's hourly wages, a fringe benefit. Vocabularies of adjustment are frequently employed: "It goes with the job"; "The company expects you to take a little on the side." Another example is the work group verbally neutralizing the societal and organizational prohibitions against theft: "Everyone does it"; "No one cares if we take a few things"; "This is not really stealing." Sieh (1987) found that garment workers took "only what was owed them" and rarely stole items of substantial value.

Whether the group considers it acceptable to take something and where it decides a line should be drawn ("You can help yourself to ballpoint pens, but staplers are hands-off") depend on many variables. For example, the size of the organization is likely to be a factor. Smigel (1970) found that when workers were "forced" (in a questionnaire) to select an organization they would be most inclined to victimize, they first chose large businesses, then government, and, lastly, small businesses. They considered large corporations and big government impersonal bureaucratic giants able to absorb losses more easily than smaller organizations.

Regardless of the explanation, employee theft seems to require some subjective justification on the part of the workers. They often do not perceive their conduct as illegal or even unethical, because the behavior is either in line with group norms, in line with internal standards, or both. From the group's or the worker's perspective, the theft or the counterproductive behavior either is expected or adjusts the imbalances inherent in working for the company. It is interesting to note that employee theft diminishes when an organization clarifies for the workforce precisely what constitutes misconduct and what is expected (J. Clark & Hollinger, 1983). This approach, combined with working conditions that convince employees their organization cares about them, seems to be the most effective in reducing employee theft and counterproductive behavior. Furthermore, improvement in the work environment functions both ways; the worker is also expected to demonstrate loyalty and commitment to the organization, setting up appropriate models for new workers. But loyalty to a company may go too far, as when it represents a higher obligation than commitment to law and ethics. Individual blind loyalty often leads to corporate crime.

CYBERCRIME

> Four high school students, age 14 to 16, hacked into a Bay Area Internet server and then used stolen credit card numbers to go on a giant shopping spree at an on-line auction house. They ordered $200,000 worth of computers, then had United Parcel Service deliver the equipment to vacant homes in San Carlos, where they would pick up the packages after school. (Power, 2000, p. 7)

Cybercrime (or computer crime) refers to any illegal act that involves a computer system. The main types of cybercrime are unauthorized access to computers (hacking), mischief to data (virus generation), theft of communications, copyright violations of computer software, and transmission of pornographic material, including child pornography. In 2003, persons allegedly associated with the Gambino organized crime family were arrested and charged with a $230 million Internet fraud scheme that involved money laundering and a credit card scam perpetrated against individuals who visited a pornographic Web site (The Informant, 2003).

Another cybercrime that is becoming popular is illegal gambling on the Internet. "Since the mid-1990s, Internet gambling operators have established approximately 1,800 e-gaming Web sites in locations outside the U.S., and global revenues from Internet gaming in 2003 are projected to be $5 billion" (The Informant, 2003, p. 23). Not all online gambling is illegal, however. Criminal violations occur when it is conducted from or to a location that prohibits or regulates gambling activities. Authorities stress that a major concern of Internet gambling is its tie to organized crime and to terrorist groups.

Cyberstalking, discussed briefly in Chapter 1, is a serious form of cybercrime that will grow in scope and complexity as more people take advantage of the Internet and other telecommunications technologies. A cyberstalker is able to send repeated, threatening, or harassing messages by the simple push of a button, whereas more sophisticated cyberstalkers can use programs to send messages at regular or random intervals without being physically present at the computer terminal (U.S. Department of Justice, 1999). The anonymity leaves stalkers in an advantageous position for avoiding detection.

The extent of computer crimes is expanding rapidly and its economic impact is staggering (D. Carter & Katz, 1996). The British Banking Association reports that the world loss due to computer fraud alone is approximately $8 billion each year (D. Carter & Katz, 1996). Software piracy is estimated to cost American software companies around $7.5 billion annually.

In May 1999, the Clinton administration established a new national initiative to address the problem in Internet fraud. The initiative encouraged the FBI to join forces with the NW3C to establish the Internet Fraud Complaint Center for strategic information about and analysis of Internet fraud schemes.

The fastest-growing computer-related crime is theft, with the most common stolen commodity being information such as new product plans, new product descriptions, research, marketing plans, and prospective customer lists (D. Carter & Katz, 1996). Since the theft of intellectual property often has no tangible value, the offender does not as readily perceive it as being wrong.

In response to the dramatic increase in computer crimes, the U.S. Congress passed the *Federal Computer Fraud and Abuse Act of 1984*, which was amended and expanded in the *Computer Abuse Amendments Act of 1994*. Computer crime is a serious problem that will continue to draw considerable attention from law enforcement agencies across the globe. In 1997, eight of the world's industrial nations joined forces to fight computer crime, particularly security intrusions and telecommunications fraud. Research focusing on the psychological characteristics of cybercrime is just beginning.

We now turn our attention to some offenses that are somewhat outside the realm of economic or financial crimes but, nonetheless, have many of the same features and motives.

HOSTAGE-TAKING OFFENSES

The hostage-taker holds victims against their will and uses them to obtain material gain or personal advantage. Typically, this offender threatens to take the lives of the victims if certain demands are not met within a specified time period. Included in the broad hostage-taking category are abductions and kidnappings, skyjackings, and some acts of terrorism. Recall that we gave considerable attention in Chapter 9 to acts of international and domestic terrorism. In this chapter, the topic is discussed only as it relates specifically to hostage-taking.

Miron and Goldstein (1978) divide hostage-taking offenses into two major categories based on the offender's primary motivation: **instrumental** and **expressive hostage-taking**. In instrumental hostage-taking, the offender's goal is recognizable—material gain. An example is kidnapping a child and holding him or her for ransom. The goal in expressive hostage-taking is psychological: Offenders want to become significant and to take control over their own fate. Expressive offenders generally feel that they have little control over events in their lives. They want to become important, and they believe the media coverage accompanying their hostage-taking will help them to achieve this goal. To the observer, the conduct of the expressive offender often seems senseless and even suicidal. A skyjacker who demands that a pilot fly an aircraft full of passengers from one continent to another, for no apparent reason, is an example. Hostage-taking offenses sometimes begin as instrumental acts but develop into expressive ones. An offender who initially kidnaps someone for material gain may find that his or her demands are unrealistic and not likely to be met. In this case, the person may decide to play out the scenario for the attention, significance, and control it affords. Sometimes both instrumental and expressive motives are clearly involved from the beginning. That is, the offender expects both material and psychological gain from the abduction.

Since the 1970s, the FBI has classified hostage-takers into four broad categories: terrorists, prisoners, criminals, and the mentally disordered (Fuselier & Noesner, 1990). Research suggests that over 50% of all hostage-taking incidents are perpetrated by mentally disordered individuals (Borum & Strentz, 1993); thus they represent the largest category. Research also indicates that the average terrorist hostage-taker is not as sophisticated as commonly believed (Fuselier & Noesner, 1990). Training for the terrorist activity is marginal or nonexistent. Terrorist hostage-takers are usually young males from deprived socioeconomic backgrounds with little formal education. Moreover, they are very willing to kill innocent victims, and therefore they are considered more dangerous than the more sophisticated hostage-taker. However, "negotiation strategies and tactics for terrorist incidents are identical to those that would be used during any hostage or barricade incident, regardless of the political or religious backgrounds of the subjects" (Fuselier & Noesner, 1990, p. 10).

Criminal and prisoner hostage-taking situations have similar features. Both are likely to be instrumental in nature. In the process of committing a bank robbery, for example, the robber may take a hostage as a human shield to assist in the getaway. Likewise, during a prison riot or escape attempt, inmates may take corrections officers or staff as hostages to help earn their way to freedom or aid in their negotiations with prison officials. Such incidents are extremely rare, and the hostages are not usually harmed, but there are exceptions. A riot in the brutal New Mexico Penitentiary in 1980 was extremely violent, and 7 of

TABLE 11–4   Guidelines for Negotiation

....

Stabilize and contain the situation.

Take your time when negotiating.

Allow the subject to speak: It is more important to be a good listener than a good talker.

Don't offer the subject anything.

Avoid directing frequent attention to the victims; do not call them hostages.

Be as honest as possible; avoid tricks.

Never dismiss any request as trivial.

Never say "no."

Never set a deadline; try not to accept a deadline.

Do not make alternate suggestions.

Do not introduce outsiders (non–law enforcement) into the negotiation process.

Do not allow any exchange of hostages; especially do not exchange a negotiator for a hostage.

....

Source: Fuselier, G. D., and Noesner, G. W., *FBI Law Enforcement Bulletin*, 1990, p. 10.

the 12 officers who were taken as hostages were seriously physically injured (R. Johnson, 1996). However, in the Attica uprising of 1971, prisoners in New York's Attica facility held a number of officers hostage but did not harm them (Wicker, 1976).

Experienced negotiators suggest strategies for dealing with hostage-takers or barricaded individuals (see **Table 11–4**). A **barricade situation** is one in which an individual fortifies or barricades him- or herself in a building or residence and threatens violence, either to him- or herself or to others. First, this person should be denied the excitement and stimulation he or she hopes to initiate. This requires that a potentially chaotic situation be handled as calmly as possible, with minimal media attention. As noted in Chapter 5, very high levels of arousal tend to promote disorganized response patterns and reduce internal thought processes. Under high excitement and chaos, the offender is more likely to revert to "mindless" behavior, which may include violence. The most dangerous phase in most hostage or barricade situations is the first 15 to 45 minutes (Noesner & Dolan, 1992). Therefore, the first officers on the scene should hold their positions until additional resources, including the negotiation team, arrive at the scene. If possible, the officers who are first on the scene should try to engage the hostage-taker in conversation, emphasizing that they wish no harm to the individual. Experienced negotiators believe that conversation distracts the offender from violence and generally calms the situation, especially if the negotiator maintains a calm and steady demeanor.

Second, offenders must be allowed to feel that they are in some control of the situation. Helplessness and powerlessness may have prompted the offense in the first place. If the captors do not feel they have attained any control, they may take steps to prove the opposite, such as shooting one of the hostages.

Third, in hostage or barricade situations time is usually a strong ally of the negotiator. Once the early stages of a crisis have passed and some stability and calm have been achieved, the passage of time plays a positive role. Time has several effects. After the initial high-arousal state, the body winds down and eventually the offender begins to feel tired, sluggish, and depressed. Under these conditions the event takes on aversive properties for the hostage-taker, and he or she is likely to begin to wish the situation were over. Time also promotes some thought processes and greater reliance on internal standards of conduct in the hostage-taker. An offender who has incorporated some values of society may begin to appreciate the ramifications of his or her behavior. However, the hostage-taker may also begin to construct justifications. Either process, however, may enable the offender to accede more easily to police requests. Experienced negotiators strongly recommend that the negotiator act as spokesperson for the authorities and a conduit of information, emphasizing to the hostage-taker that things will take time. Consequently, the negotiator should not be a decision-maker or in command. If the hostage-taker is under the impression that the negotiator (or anyone in the immediate environment) has the power and decision-making authority, he or she will believe that decisions should be made quickly and directly. Under these conditions, any delay generates frustration in the captor and further increases arousal.

Time also affects the relationship with the hostage. According to social psychological research, the more familiar one is with an object or person, the more one tends to become attracted to it (e.g., Freedman, Sears, & Carlsmith, 1978). In many hostage situations, the more the victim and captor get to know one another, the more they begin to accept one another. Furthermore, if the hostage was a stranger to the captor, the hostage takes on human qualities with the passage of time.

The attraction between victim and captor is called the **Stockholm syndrome**, after a hostage-taking incident in Sweden in 1973 that resulted in the marriage of a female hostage and one of her abductors. Police negotiators have noted that on occasion the hostage will side with the captor in working out demands. Although this may simply reflect a wish to end the terrifying ordeal as quickly as possible, it may also signify some attraction to the abductor. When hostages act this way, experts sometimes maintain that they have been brainwashed. An alternate explanation is that they have become attracted to their captors and temporarily identify with their values and goals. In general, though, the Stockholm syndrome is a rare occurrence. According to the FBI's Hostage/Barricade System (HOBAS), a national database that contains data from over 1,200 reported federal, state, and local hostage situations, 92% of the victims of such incidents showed no aspect of the Stockholm syndrome (Fuselier, 1999).

How can a hostage-taking incident, which by its very nature is stressful, generate attraction? We have already noted that mere familiarity can increase attraction to an object or person. There is evidence, also, that unpleasant emotion may intensify attraction (Middlebrook, 1974). Research by S. Schachter (1971) suggests that when people are physiologically aroused, they may have difficulty labeling the arousal with the appropriate emotion, because several conflicting emotional labels may be available. It does not seem to matter whether the arousal derives from negative or from positive circumstances. For example, sexual deprivation may lead to physiological arousal, which may be labeled love. The same process may operate in a highly charged hostage-taking incident, where familiarity combined with very high arousal leads to mutual attraction. If the victim or kidnapper is deindividualized by a hood or a mask, the incident is much less likely to develop into attraction. Also, ideals and purpose may override any tendency to humanize and be attracted to the victims.

Some researchers have suggested that three things must be present before the Stockholm syndrome can take place (Fuselier, 1999). First, the hostage-taker and victim must be together for a significant length of time. Second, the hostage-taker and victim must be in direct social contact during the incident. For example, physical separation of the hostage (such as complete isolation in a separate room) from the hostage-taker will likely prevent development of the effect. Third, the hostage-taker must treat the hostage kindly. Although the first two conditions make sense, the third, in light of the general effects of arousal just discussed, may not be necessary.

Thomas Strentz (1987) outlines some rules to follow should you personally ever be taken hostage, especially if you plan to travel abroad with some regularity. His suggestions are based on the psychological reactions of those hostages who survive (survivors) compared to those who do not (succumbers). Survivors, Strentz notes, are those "who returned to a meaningful existence with strong self-esteem, and who went on to live healthy and productive lives with little evidence of long-term depression, nightmares, or serious stress-induced illness" (p. 4). Although survivors do not ever forget the hostage experience, the experience does not prevent them from living relatively normal lives. Succumbers, on the other hand, are those who either did not live through the ordeal or, upon release or rescue, have considerable difficulty dealing with the emotional trauma caused by the ordeal. They have great trouble getting on with their lives.

Strentz emphasizes, as we did earlier, that the most dangerous phase in any hostage situation is the moment of the abduction and the early minutes thereafter. Arousal levels are extremely high for the abductors and the hostages. Unpredictable and unforeseen things can happen. Strentz asserts that, without exception, any form of resistance is extremely dangerous and should not be tried. He recommends playing the subordinate role immediately. Furthermore, throughout the entire abduction, maintaining a positive mental attitude that things will be all right in the end is absolutely essential. Feelings of hopelessness, abandonment, and isolation can lead to serious depression. On the other hand, a mature, controlled, and stable appearance—even if you are terrified—also helps settle the hostage-taker(s). Anything that calms the situation increases survival for everyone. Furthermore, hostile feelings toward your captors must be masked as best they can, again to keep the situation calm. Do not get into arguments with captors about politics, religion, social issues, or anything else. Strentz refers to the opposite strategy as the **London syndrome**, a behavioral pattern demonstrated by the Iranian press secretary, Abbas Lavasani, during a six-day hostage situation in the Iranian Embassy in London. Lavasani refused to compromise his dedication to his cause, constantly and stubbornly proclaiming his beliefs and seemingly intent on martyrdom. Despite the pleas of his fellow hostages, he kept arguing and was eventually killed by his captors.

Your chances of survival improve greatly if you try to blend in with your fellow captives. The individual who stands out in the crowd "by crying, by being overly polite and helpful, or by doing more than the abductors require, is immediately setting himself or herself up as an easy mark to be exploited" (Strentz, 1987, p. 6). If you are more comfortable in the leadership role, be prepared to take the brunt of the abuse from the captors, and you may be killed as an example to the rest of the hostages. Individuals who have experienced a hostage-taking episode say that being able to fantasize during the many empty hours is one of the critical factors in dealing with the situation. Some imagine travel to various places or dream about what they plan to do after the episode. Also, trying to keep a normal routine as much as possible will relieve stress. Exercise, personal hygiene, writing letters, and keeping logs are examples. This is especially recommended for people who have a strong need to control the situation. Finally, Strentz recommends that no matter what the circumstances, you should never blame yourself or ruminate about what you should have done to avoid the abduction. Accept your status, and follow the patterns described here. The chances for survival will be greatly enhanced if you do.

In sum, the psychological research on hostage-taking focuses more on the effects of the incident on the hostage than on the characteristics of the individual committing the crime. In addition, strategies are offered both to the hostage, for surviving the incident, and to negotiators, for dealing with the hostage-taker effectively in order to prevent escalation and to end the crisis.

ARSON

According to the UCR, **arson** is defined as "any willful or malicious burning or attempt to burn, with or without intent to defraud, a dwelling, house, public building, motor vehicle or aircraft, personal property of another, etc." (Federal Bureau of Investigation, 2000, p. 54). Arson joined the list of UCR index crimes in 1978, signifying both its seriousness and its frequency. About one-fifth of all property loss in the United States is due to arson, exceeding $2 billion annually. In 2002, the average dollar loss associated with arson was $11,252 (Federal Bureau of Investigation, 2003). Tragically, arson claims the lives of an estimated 600 to 700 Americans each year, and 22% of all firefighter injuries in the United States are due to deliberately set fires (U.S. Fire Administration, 1997, 2000, 2002).

Incidence and Prevalence

Arson statistics in the United States are collected by the National Fire Protection Association (NFPA) and the FBI. The NFPA definition, however, focuses on structure fires only and combines both established arsons and suspicious structure fires in compiling its statistics (Douglas et al., 1992). On the other hand, the FBI statistics, as reported in the UCR, exclude fires of suspicious or unknown origins. Still, the statistics reported by the NFPA are similar to the UCR data. According to the NFPA, about 14% of all structure fires can be attributed to arson. The UCR data show that while close to half of arson fires are directed at structures (mostly residential), another 33% involve mobile property, such as motor vehicles and trailers (Federal Bureau of Investigation, 2003) (**Table 11–5**). The remaining arson fires are directed at other types of property, such as crops, timber, and grasslands. In 2002, the nationwide arson clearance rate was approximately 17% (Federal Bureau of Investigation, 2003), slightly higher than the average clearance rate of 15% (Douglas et al., 1992; Federal Bureau of Investigation, 1997).

Arson is difficult to prove or identify because the evidence is often destroyed in the fire. Arson investigators today, however, are extremely knowledgeable and sophisticated and can usually detect when a fire has been deliberately set. However, even with evidence that the fire was set, the motive and the identity of the arsonist are often unknown. Most of the known arsonists are young and male. Some studies have found that between 75% and 85% of all firesetting was done by males, with increasing percentages of females present in the 13- to 17-year old group (Federal Bureau of Investigation, 2003; Stadolnik, 2000). About 50% are under the age of 18, and two-thirds of

TABLE 11–5 Arson by Type of Property, 2002

PROPERTY CLASSIFICATION	NUMBER OF OFFENSES	PERCENTAGE DISTRIBUTION
Total	66,308	100.0
Total structure	27,373	41.3
Single-occupancy residential	11,789	17.8
Other residential	4,821	7.3
Storage	1,940	2.9
Industrial/manufacturing	333	0.5
Other commercial	2,735	4.1
Community/public	3,140	4.7
Other structure	2,615	3.9
Total mobile	21,920	33.1
Motor vehicles	20,736	31.3
Other mobile	1,184	1.8
Other	17,015	25.7

Source: Federal Bureau of Investigation (2003).

arrestees are under age 25 (Federal Bureau of Investigation, 2003). However, it is generally acknowledged that only a small proportion of fires set by juveniles is reported, probably less than 10% (Adler, Nunn, Northam, Lebnan, & Ross, 1994).

Motives

There appears to be a wide variety of motives for arson. In an effort to systematize the reasons, Boudreau and his associates (Boudreau, Kwan, Faragher, & Denault, 1977) listed six primary motives for arson.

- *Revenge, Spite, or Jealousy.* Arsonists in this category include jilted lovers, feuding neighbors, disenchanted employees, and people who want to get back at someone they believe cheated or abused them. Alcohol and/or drugs are often associated with this motive.
- *Vandalism or Malicious Mischief.* Fires set to challenge authority or to relieve boredom are by far the most common of those set by juveniles.
- *Crime Concealment or Diversionary Tactics.* At least 7% to 9% of convicted arsonists are believed to be trying to obliterate evidence of burglaries, larcenies, and murders (Inciardi, 1970; Robbins & Robbins, 1964). The offender in this category expects that the fire will destroy any evidence that a crime was committed. Usually the fire is set near the object or incident the offender wishes to conceal. In some cases, the firesetter may try to cover his or her suicide for insurance purposes. Some arsonists try to destroy records that may link them to embezzlement or other occupational crime. Arson has also been used to divert attention while the offender burglarizes another building or residence.
- *Profit, Insurance Fraud.* This is the category most likely to attract professional or semiprofessional arsonists, who generally escape detection. Consequently, there are few hard data and few statistics to support this motive. However, since the profits gained from arson of this type are so large and the probability of detection so small, actual incidence is believed to be much higher than reported statistically. The property may be residential property, businesses, or modes of transportation (vehicles, boats, planes). According to Douglas et al. (1992), this type of arson usually has two offenders: the primary offender, who is the dominant personality in the offense, and the secondary offender, who is the "torch for hire." The torch for hire is usually male, 25 to 40 years of age, and unemployed. The torch is likely to have a prior arrest record for a variety of offenses, including burglary, assault, and public intoxication.
- *Intimidation, Extortion, Terrorism, Sabotage.* This category refers to fires set for the purpose of frightening or deterring. Examples are fires set by striking workers or employees to intimidate management or by extortionists to show that they mean business. Another example is the

destruction of clinics providing abortions and other health services, presumably set by antiabortionists wishing to intimidate. Members of the radical environmental activist group ELF claimed responsibility in the 1990s for the burnings of very expensive homes built on land that the group argued should not have been developed. By most accounts, arsons in this category are extremely rare. Douglas et al. (1992) refer to these as extremist-motivated arsonists who are committed to further a social, political, or religious case.

- *Pyromania and Other Psychological Motives.* **Pyromania** is a psychiatric term for an "irresistible urge" or passion to set fires along with an intense fascination with flames. Before setting the fire, the individual is said to experience a buildup of tension; once the fire is underway, he or she experiences intense pleasure or release (American Psychiatric Association, 1994). Although the firesetting urge is believed to be uncontrollable, the individual often provides many clues about his or her intention before setting the fire. Pyromania is believed to be a motive in only a small percentage of all arsons, but we will discuss it shortly in more detail to illustrate how some crimes lend themselves well to psychoanalytical interpretation.

Douglas et al. (1992) suggest an additional category that is close to the pyromaniac classification: **excitement-motivated** (E-M) **arson**. E-M arsonists set fires because they crave stimulation that is satisfied by firesetting and by watching all the excitement that accompanies the fighting of the fire. Offenders often select a location that offers a good vantage point from which to safely observe the firefighting and investigation. Sometimes they mingle with the crowd watching the fire, primarily to hear comments and feel the excitement of the crowd. E-M arsonists are usually juveniles or young adults, unemployed, and living with their parents. Generally, E-M arsonists are socially inadequate and have poor interpersonal skills.

In a comprehensive study of 1,016 juveniles and adults arrested for arson and fire-related crimes, Icove and Estepp (1987) reported that vandalism was the most frequently identified motive, accounting for 49% of the arsons in the sample. The second most frequent motive was excitement (25%), followed by revenge (14%), crime concealment (2%), profit (1%), and other or unspecified motives (8%). Research (e.g., Robbins & Robbins, 1964) has consistently shown that most fires set by juveniles appear to be motivated by the wish to get back at authority or gain status or prompted by a dare or a need for excitement. Therefore, it is not surprising that the Icove–Estepp investigation revealed that the vast majority (96%) of vandalism fires were set by juveniles, who often set the fire within one mile from their homes and were accompanied by one or more individuals. About half of these juvenile offenders remained at the scene. E-M fires (69%) also tended to be set by juveniles, who also tended to live within one mile of the crime scene but who preferred to set the blaze alone.

On the other hand, revenge fires tended to be set by adults (81%), who tended to be single males who used alcohol, drugs, or both prior to or during the offense. Earlier research (Inciardi, 1970; Robbins & Robbins, 1964) also concluded that arson for revenge was almost exclusively an adult crime. According to Icove and Estepp, approximately two-thirds of revenge firesetters have a prior arrest record. Crime concealment fires were also most likely set by adults (72%), who were predominantly single, male, and low-income and who also used alcohol and/or drugs prior to or during the offense. Virtually all the concealment firesetters had prior arrest records. Both the revenge and the crime-concealment firesetters usually left the scene of the crime, often to begin establishing an alibi.

Harmon, Rosner, and Wiederlight (1985) studied the psychological and demographic characteristics of 27 women arsonists who were evaluated at the Forensic Psychiatric Clinics for the Criminal and Supreme Courts of New York between 1980 and 1983. Although the sample is small and restricted to a specific geographical area, the researchers found that these female arsonists were somewhat older (mid-30s), were African American, and had a history of alcohol and drug abuse. Generally, the group was uneducated, unmarried, and relying on public assistance for support. Most often, their motivation was revenge, a consistent finding also reported by Icove and Estepp for female arsonists. In their revenge, the women tended to act impulsively, responding to a perceived wrong committed against them or a perceived threat to their persons. In their haste, they used whatever flammable material was handy to set the fire. Generally, they set fires in places where they lived—apartments or common, public spaces in their buildings.

Pyromania

According to the DSM-IV, pyromania is "the presence of multiple episodes of deliberate and purposeful firesetting" (American Psychiatric Association, 1994, p. 614). Moreover, it is characterized by high levels of tension or emotional arousal before the act, and there is relief or reduction of this tension when setting fires or when observing or participating in their aftermath. Pyromaniacs are believed to be regular spectators at fires in their neighborhoods and communities. They are also believed to set off false alarms and to show unusual interest in firefighting paraphernalia.

The term *pyromania* was coined in the early nineteenth century to refer to a form of "insanity" identified by the impulse to set fires without apparent motive (Schmideberg, 1953). Stadolnik (2000) believes the term originated in France in the 1833 writings of a man named Marc, who argued that firesetters suffered from a specific mental illness he called "monomanie incendiaire." According to Stadolnik, firesetting was referred to in the literature of the nineteenth century as "pyromania of Marc." In the mid-1800s, clinicians suggested that there was a relationship between firesetting and sexual disturbances, and psychoanalytic and psychiatric literature, in particular, continued to promote that link throughout the twentieth century. For instance, L. H. Gold (1962, p. 416) contended that the roots of arson are "deep within the personality and have some relationship to sexual disturbance and urinary malfunction." Abrahamsen (1960) wrote, "Firesetting is a substitute for a sexual thrill, and the devastating and destructive powers of fire reflect the intensity of the pyromaniac's sexual desires, as well as his sadism" (p. 129).

Orthodox psychoanalytic thinking draws a connection between pleasurable urination (urethral eroticism) and firesetting. Fenichel (1945) concluded: "Regularly deep-seated relationship to urethral eroticism is to be found. . . . In the same way that there are coprophilic perversions based on urethral eroticism, perversions may also be developed based on the derivative of urethral eroticism, pleasure in fire" (p. 371). This theory is based in part on the presumption that many firesetters are or have been enuretic (bedwetters) (Halleck, 1967). The theory does not suggest that enuretic people are likely to be firesetters, only that firesetters have more than their share of bedwetting behavior. Whether this relationship actually exists is still very unclear from the available research.

The relationship between sexual arousal and firesetting is plausible, since, through the process of classical conditioning, virtually any object or event can become associated with sexual arousal and gratification. The fact that some arsonists have fetishes or records of previous arrests for sexual offenses (MacDonald, 1977) lends some support to this possibility. Individuals who are sexually aroused by fire may, in general, be highly conditionable introverts. We may also expect them to be sexually, socially, and vocationally inadequate (as noted by Levin, 1976). Firesetting could be a way of feeling significant and resolving conflicts.

While some firesetters may obtain sexual arousal and gratification from fire, there is very little evidence that many do. In an extensive analysis of 68 convicted arsonists imprisoned in Florida, South Carolina, and North Carolina, sexual "abnormality" was no more in evidence than it was in a comparable group of controls (nonarsonist offenders) (Wolford, 1972). Nor is there much evidence for the diagnostic label "pyromaniac." Koson and Dvoskin (1982) were unable to find any arsonists in their sample that met the DSM-III criteria of pyromania. More specifically, even though 38% of the sample were repetitive arsonists, none qualified as exhibiting a recurrent failure to resist impulses to set fires compounded by an intense fascination with firesetting and seeing the fires burn.

In their investigation of 1,016 offenders of arson and fire-related crimes in the Prince George's County area of Maryland, Icove and Estepp (1987) reported only two offenders who may have qualified as pyromaniacs. In Canada, Bradford (1982) found only 1 individual of 34 repetitive arsonists who could even remotely qualify as a pyromaniac, and Hill and colleagues (R. Hill et al., 1982), in another Canadian sample of 38 arsonists, found none. Rice and Harris (1991) identified only 6 of their sample of 243 male firesetters who reported being sexually aroused in the presence of fire. Quinsey, Chaplin, and Upfold (1989) reported no differences between normal subjects and firesetters' sexual arousal to fire-related stimuli. Yesavage and associates (Yesavage, Benezech, Ceccaldi, Bourgeois, & Addad, 1983) found no indications that 50 French arsonists were attracted to fire for sexual reasons. Similar findings have been reported for child firesetters (Kuhnley, Hendren, & Quinlan, 1982; Stewart & Culver, 1982).

Repetitive and Persistent Arsonists

Research on repetitive or serial arsonists is beginning to identify some common features. A repetitive or serial arsonist is one who sets three or more separate fires. The time between the firesetting episodes may be days, weeks, or even years. Douglas and colleagues (1992) suggest that a distinction also be made between **spree arsonists** and **mass arsonists**. A spree arsonist sets fires at three or more separate locations, with no emotional "cooling-off" period between them. The **mass arsonist**, on the other hand, sets three or more fires at the same location within a limited period of time. For example, a mass arsonist may set fires to several floors of the same apartment building, simultaneously or within minutes of each other. The most frightening of these repetitive arsonists is the one who randomly selects structures for revenge, excitement, or political (or religious) ideology. An entire community may sleep in fear until the offender either stops or is detected.

The most consistent research finding on the psychology of adult repetitive arsonists is that they, as a group, experience and perceive little control over their environment or personal lives. Adult arsonists who began setting fires as children tend to be unassertive, have limited interpersonal skills, be underemployed or unemployed, and be prone to depression and feelings of helplessness (G. Murphy & Clare, 1996). They are usually from a socially disadvantaged segment of the population (Jackson, Glass, & Hope, 1987) or come from highly disruptive family environments (Fritzon, 2000). Their plight is usually compounded by an assortment of physical, mental, and psychological handicaps (Koson & Dvoskin, 1982). Compared to other criminal groups, their intellectual level (IQ scores) and educational attainment are low (N. Lewis & Yarnell, 1951; Wolford, 1972). They also lack social or interpersonal skills for dealing with their social environment and, consequently, often lack self-esteem (Hurley & Monahan, 1969; Vreeland & Levin, 1980). Depression is commonly reported in other studies, and sometimes the offenders display serious suicidal inclinations (Jackson et al., 1987). Therefore, the overall picture of the adult serial arsonist is one of inadequacy, frequent failure, social passivity, and social isolation.

Theoretically, repetitive firesetting may be motivated by the arsonist's attempt to take control of his or her life and gain some social recognition. For example, the firesetting seems to be precipitated by events that exacerbate the arsonist's feelings of low self-esteem, sadness, and depression (Bumpass, Fagelman, & Birx, 1983). In addition, following a firesetting, many arsonists stay at the scene of the fire, often sound the alarm, and even help fight the fire. In some cases they take heroic action to save lives. The recognition they receive for these actions probably enhances their self-esteem and instills a sense of control in their lives. Jackson et al. (1987) note that most acts of fire-setting by repetitive arsonists progress from small fires to large fires, and the arsonists also become increasingly involved in fighting the fire. Furthermore, repetitive arsonists set fires alone and in secret, with virtually no one aware of their actions until they are caught. If they are caught, their history of fireset-ting presents an additional opportunity for them to gain attention and recog-nition from others.

What are the etiological factors in repetitive firesetting? Fascination and experimentation with fire appear to be common features of normal child de-velopment. Kafrey (1980) discovered that curiosity about fire appears to be nearly universal in children between 5 and 7 years old. Furthermore, this fas-cination with fire begins early, with one in five children setting fires before the age of three. Firesetting behavior seems to decline after age 7, probably be-cause of frequent admonishments of its dangers by parents and other adults. Nearly all children who set fires beyond the normal fascination stage tend to have poor relationships with their parents and are also victims of physical and emotional abuse (Jackson et al., 1987). Also, those children who continue to set fires tend to be more mischievous, energetic, adventurous, and impulsive than their peers. Persistent firesetters are more likely to demonstrate symp-toms of ADHD during childhood (Forehand, Wierson, Frame, Kemptom, & Armistead, 1991), and many are regarded as "conduct problems" by their teachers. Not surprisingly, most persistent firesetters are males (about 80%). Kafrey (1980) refers to these behaviors pattern as the "rascality pattern." The rascality pattern has also been noted by Kolko, Kazdin, and Meyer (1985), Kuhnley, et al. (1982), and Stewart and Culver (1982).

The frequent observation that youthful firesetters are conduct problems, impulsive, more hyperactive, and even more aggressive than their peers appears to be in sharp contrast to the behavior of repetitive adult firesetters, described previously. As noted in Chapter 2, aggressive, acting-out, and hyper-active children are often unpopular with peers (Hartup, 1983; Maccoby, 1986) and demonstrate poor interpersonal and social skills for dealing with others. Patterson (1982) writes that impulsive, hyperactive children with a low frus-tration tolerance and inadequate social skills tend to be social isolates. Moreover, other research (e.g., Caspi, Elder, & Bem, 1987) indicates that ill-tempered children have considerable personal, marital, social, and financial failure throughout their lifetimes, a pattern very similar to that of repetitive arsonists. In addition, both the frequent childhood firesetter and the repetitive adult arsonist exhibit a continual battle against the social environment as demonstrated by frequent contacts with criminal justice agencies. In their conclusion on child and adult firesetting, Vreeland and Levin (1980) write the following:

> The picture turns out to be one of an individual with several maladaptive behaviour patterns, of which firesetting is one. We have identified social ineffectiveness as a common factor in the general tendency of firesetters to have drinking problems, marital, occupational and sexual problems, and to exhibit a variety of other criminal and antisocial behaviours. (p. 44)

Thus, firesetting may be just one component in the constellation of maladaptive behaviors displayed by these individuals. Firesetting may be among these behaviors because of previous experiences with fire. Ritvo, Shanok, and Lewis (1983) found that a surprisingly large number of firesetters had been burned and maltreated with fire as children. They describe how the father of one frequent firesetter had severely burned his feet during his early childhood, as a punishment for lighting fires. Another boy's father had beaten him on his buttocks with a hot spatula. Still another boy's mother had held his hands over a lighted stove burner until they were burned, to punish him for lighting fires. Ritvo et al. (1983, p. 266) speculate that these punishments may have "conveyed the message that the use of fire was an acceptable mode of retaliation."

In this section we have concentrated on the repetitive or serial arsonists who set fires primarily for psychological and social gain. This focus is not to imply that a majority of arson fires are set by these individuals. Obviously, arson is committed for a variety of reasons by a variety of offenders, although much of it is probably committed for monetary gain, such as insurance.

BOMBINGS

In 1995, bombing incidents in the United States decreased 18.5%, to 2,577, from the 3,163 reported in 1994 (Federal Bureau of Investigation, 1996). Bombs killed 193 people in 1995 and injured 744, a dramatic increase from the 31 fatalities and 308 injuries in 1994. This increase is largely due to the tragic bombing incident that killed 168 people and injured 518 in Oklahoma City. In addition, each year there are a substantial number of hoaxes, involving threats of bombing and bogus bomb devices, usually involving businesses. About one-third of these incidences are preceded by a threatening note, letter, or telephone call.

Motives

In over half of all bombings, the motives were unknown. In bombings where the motives were identified, the most frequent was mischief or vandalism (nearly 50%). In about 25% of all incidents, revenge or intimidation was the primary motive. Personal animosity accounted for 15%, and sabotage or subversion another 7%.

Many of the motives for bombing are believed to resemble those for arson. However, it would appear that some bombers are more intent on destruction and injury than arsonists are, and they do not wish to cover up the cause of the destruction. Moreover, the bombing generally requires more technical knowledge than arson and it is more dangerous. The planning, construction, safe transportation, placement, and activation of an explosive device require more skill than dropping a match onto gasoline-soaked rags under a stairwell.

The apparent motives for bombings change with the times. Between 1968 and 1971, nearly half of the bombings in the United States were a result of "social protest" (Moll, 1974), while in 1975 over a third of the bombings were due to "personal animosity," and another third to "malicious destruction" (U.S. Department of Justice, 1976). In 1975 only 10% of the bombings were related to social protest. From 1980 to 1983, there was a steady decline of bombings in this country; the incidence leveled for a couple of years, followed by a dramatic increase since 1987.

While there is certainly no single bomber-type personality, MacDonald (1977) contends that there is a personality pattern that is drawn to bombing that demonstrates most of the characteristics of the "compulsive firesetter"; he calls it the "compulsive bomber." Compulsive implies that the individual is drawn to the activity again and again, the behavior seemingly out of the individual's control.

MacDonald reports that the compulsive bombers he has known exhibited a fascination with bombs from childhood. In addition, he found them to be keenly interested in discussing explosive devices and various techniques of detonating. Large segments of their life appear to be devoted to the study, development, and experience of bombing. More important, they derive excitement from their actions and are aroused by only one aspect of the explosion: the power, the fire, or the noise. One bomber confessed, "I want to become more than what I am" (MacDonald, 1977, p. 40).

In line with the psychoanalytic tradition, however, MacDonald links sexual gratification with bombing, claiming that one in six compulsive bombers obtains sexual pleasure from the explosions. This is apparently based on his observation that sexual deviation is prominent in many bombers.

Two of the more dramatic and best-known bombers are George Metesky, a 56-year-old, known as the Mad Bomber of New York, and Theodore Kaczynski, a 55-year-old mathematical genius known as the Unabomber. Metesky planted 32 different pipe bombs between 1940 and 1956, all supposedly designed to draw attention to the alleged unfair labor practices of a major utility company. Metesky was working for United Electric (now known as Consolidated Edison, or Con Ed) in 1931 when a gush of hot gas from a boiler knocked him down. At the time, he got up and walked away without apparent injury, but he later claimed illness and inability to work as a result of the accident, and he expected compensation. When the company repeatedly denied his requests, Metesky undertook an intense campaign designed to bring attention to Con Ed's "dastardly deeds." He planted bombs in locations that would assure heavy press coverage (Macy's Department Store, the New York Public Library, Grand Central Station), but he maintained that he did not intend to harm anyone. Fortunately, no one was killed during his bombing missions, but some 22 people were injured. Although his first bombing attempt failed, he subsequently became more sophisticated, technically competent, and successful.

At one point Metesky wrote a letter to the editor of a New York newspaper:

> Have you noticed the bombs in your city, if you are worried, I am sorry, and also if anyone is injured. But it cannot be helped, for justice will be served, I am not well and for this I will make the Con Edison sorry. Yes, they will regret their dastardly deeds. I will bring them before the bar of justice, public opinion will condemn them, for beware, I will place more units under theater seats in the near future.   F.P. (MacDonald, 1977, p. 47)

The phrase "dastardly deeds" eventually spelled Metesky's downfall. Investigators searching the files of Con Ed for evidence of disgruntled employees uncovered it in the file folder of Metesky, who had used it in a letter to the company many years before.

Brussel (1978), the consulting psychiatrist in the Mad Bomber case, wrote a detailed account of the events surrounding the search for the bomber and of the arrest, when over a half-dozen law enforcement agents closed in on Metesky's home. He greeted them cordially and immediately guessed their purpose. He smiled frequently and appeared to be in a state of high self-satisfaction at capture. Throughout the trial, Metesky beamed and seemed to be enjoying the excitement he had created and the attention he was gaining. In 1957, the court found him "insane" (Brussel contends he was suffering from "paranoia"), and he was committed to Matteawan State Hospital. Metesky was released in 1973.

Although he was considered insane, he displayed a lifelong pattern of drawing attention to his plight and the perceived injustice done to him. Metesky's behavior probably was his way of coping with his feelings of helplessness. Possibly another principal reason for his bombings was to add excitement to his life or to become famous as the Mad Bomber. Overall, it appears that Metesky was successful in creating some significance for himself.

The search for the Unabomber—Theodore Kaczynski—was one of the longest, most difficult, and most frustrating cases in the history of the FBI. The search took over 17 years until he was apprehended in 1996. In 1993, a UNABOM Task Force (UTF) was established in the search for Kaczynski, with 50 FBI agents assigned to the unit full-time. The UTF investigated more than 2,400 suspects and accumulated 3,600 volumes of information, 175 computer bases, 82 million records, 12,000 event records, 8,182 items of evidence, 22,000 pages of evidentiary documents, and 9,000 evidence photographs.

The Unabomber caused the deaths of three innocent victims and 23 serious injuries by mailing 16 explosive devices to carefully selected target persons. The first few bombings were directed at individuals at universities and airlines—thus the "un" and the "a" in the FBI's code name. His victims included the chief lobbyist for the California Forestry Association, an engineering professor at University of California—Berkeley, a geneticist at University of California—San Francisco, a computer science professor at Yale, the assistant to psychology professor James McConnell, and the president of United Airlines.

The Unabomber continually changed and improved both his bombs and his tactics, indicating a strong intelligence, and he maintained his cover for a long time. Investigators were continually impressed by his combination of intellect, malice, and showmanship during the 17 years. The primary motive of Kaczynski was his desire to have society return to the era before electric power and aircraft. He also believed that mail bombs, mostly sent to universities and airlines, could lead to a massive uprising against technology.

Kaczynski grew up in the Chicago suburb of Evergreen Park and graduated from Harvard University at the age of 20, majoring in mathematics and physics. He went on to earn a Ph.D. in mathematics from the University of Michigan and appeared to be headed for a brilliant career in academics. Instead, he became a recluse who shunned family and friends and lived in a remote, isolated cabin in Montana.

The Unabomber's downfall resulted when his brother, David Kaczynski, recognized his brother's work—a 35,000-word personal and political manifesto—published in *The New York Times* and *The Washington Post*. The piece was published in the *Times* and *Post* after the Unabomber promised he would stop mailing bombs if his statement was published in full. Although his lawyers wanted to use the insanity defense on his behalf before his trial, Kaczynski strongly rejected the defense. On January 22, 1998, Kaczynski pleaded guilty and agreed to a life sentence in prison without possibility of parole. He is currently serving that sentence.

SUMMARY AND CONCLUSIONS

The main theme of this chapter centers on the ways economic offenders minimize, neutralize, deny, and justify their actions to themselves and others. We have reviewed the economic crimes of burglary, larceny, motor vehicle theft, shoplifting, and robbery, white-collar crime, and the tangential economic crimes of arson, bombing, and hostage-taking. Perceived control of one's environment is a secondary theme. We also covered an example of a crime against the public order, namely, prostitution. We found that this "victimless" crime is replete with myths and misunderstandings and is characterized by limited systematic study, almost all of which is directed at female prostitutes. In recent years, considerable attention has been focused on juvenile prostitution, a major social problem, as well as forced prostitution, or human trafficking.

Burglary is not only an instrumental crime designed to acquire property and money, but also an expressive crime. That is, burglars frequently try to communicate symbolically to the victims, often to scare, control, or intimidate or to demonstrate their interpersonal style. These communications usually have significant psychological effects on the victim. However, the major point is that the expressive component provides the potential for the development of scientifically based burglar profiles in a manner similar to the crime scene profiles of murderers and rapists. Other property crimes also have this potential. There certainly is some underlying psychological pattern that is often peculiar to arson, robbery, shoplifting and even motor vehicle theft. The key point here is that there is a critical need for the development of research or scientifically based profiles of property crimes that is equal to the popular demand for crime scene profiles of violent crimes.

While monetary gain is certainly a powerful motive in economic crimes, the cognitive standards against which the offender's behavior is judged and regulated are crucial. These points of reference are strongly influenced by the social context and by one's immediate reference groups, such as fellow workers or peers. Reference groups and the social context are especially powerful influences in white-collar crimes, specifically corporate crime and individual occupational offenses, like employee theft. By restructuring their cognitions to align them with the social climate, white-collar offenders are able to engage in behavior that they would otherwise perceive as reprehensible. Conventional economic offenders are less likely to restructure their cognitions drastically, although they, too, may do so. White-collar, occupational, corporate, and computer offenders often deny they are doing anything wrong; traditional economic offenders are more likely to admit wrongdoing, although like most criminals, they also justify it.

In discussing white-collar crime, we focused on Bandura's strategies for justifying or denying unlawful behavior. Each type of strategy involves either restructuring cognitions or denying consequences of one's conduct. All strategies promote a neutralization of any guilt feelings or self-punishment. The price we pay for the human brain is its powerful ability to justify even heinous and reprehensible actions. Criminologists today are paying increasingly more attention to the crimes of the rich and powerful and are emphasizing the harms they may perpetrate. It may be that, in the long run, we have more to fear from corporate and organizational behavior than from any collection of conventional crime, most particularly the conventional economic offenses discussed in this chapter.

CHAPTER 12

DRUGS AND CRIME

O ver the past 20 years, the United States has been waging a "drug war" against individuals who transport, sell, and use a wide variety of illegal substances. While other periods in history have also seen a focus on drugs, it was in the 1980s that the government began to adopt conservative policies in response to perceived epidemics in the trafficking and use of cocaine, crack cocaine, heroin, and marijuana, among others (Walker, 2001). Billions of dollars have been expended on both reducing the supply of drugs and punishing convicted individuals with long prison sentences. According to Walker (2001), the federal government spent $17.1 billion on drug law enforcement alone in 1999. Many members of the public believe these approaches are justified. For example, in a poll of 1,000 individuals randomly selected across the continental United States (Strasser, 1989), two-thirds of the respondents felt that the sale and usage of drugs were the key cause of crime. In this chapter we review the evidence in support of or against this public perception. Others believe the drug war has in many ways been a colossal failure, neither making significant headway in interdiction nor adequately addressing the widespread problems associated with substance abuse. According to the National Council on Crime and Delinquency (NCCD), substance abuse should be considered *"primarily* as a health-related problem that should reside in the public health domain" (Rosenbaum, 1989, p. 17; emphasis added). Increasingly in recent years, we have heard more such calls for addressing the illegal use of drugs as a health problem at least as much as a crime problem. The drug courts discussed here are a case in point.

The relationship between drugs and crime may be viewed from two perspectives: (1) the use, sale, manufacture, distribution, and possession of illegal drugs, all of which are themselves crimes; and (2) the pharmacological effects certain drugs have on a user's behavior in promoting criminal actions. Research directed at these two perspectives in recent years has reached the following six conclusions, each of which is discussed in this chapter.

1. More individuals are incarcerated or held in jails and prisons for drug offenses than for any other offense, and this has contributed to burgeoning jail and prison populations.
2. Arrestees frequently test positive for illicit drug use.
3. Arrestees and incarcerated offenders were often under the influence of illicit drugs when they committed their offenses.
4. Some offenders commit property crime to support their drug habit.
5. Drug trafficking often engenders violent crime.
6. The drug–crime relationship is difficult to identify and measure.

Let's begin with the first consistent finding, that more individuals are incarcerated or held in jails and prisons for drug offenses than for any other offense. According to the 2002 National Survey on Drug Use and Health, 19.5 million (8.3%) of Americans aged 12 and older are current illicit drug users (Department of Health and Human Services, 2003). Current drug use means the use of an illicit drug during the month prior to the survey. In 2002, 1.1 million people were arrested for drug abuse violations in the United States (Federal Bureau of Investigation, 2003). Another 464,000 were arrested for liquor law offenses. From October 1, 1999, to September 30, 2000, of the 76,952 defendants in U.S. district courts, 27,274 (35.4%) had committed a drug offense (Office of National Drug Control Policy, 2003d). A vast majority of these drug offenders (93.8%) had committed a trafficking offense. Most (91.2%) of these offenders were convicted and most were incarcerated (91.7%). In state courts, 195,133 people were convicted of drug trafficking in 1998, and another 119,443 were convicted of drug possession (Bureau of Justice Statistics, 2001b).

Approximately, in any given year, two-thirds of the inmates in state and county jails had committed a drug offense or used drugs regularly (D. Wilson, 2000). A quarter of those jail inmates had a current charge or conviction for drug law violations. About 15% had a charge or conviction for drug possession, and 9% for drug trafficking. About two-thirds of federal prisoners were also held for drug offenses in 1998 (A. J. Beck, 2000; Mumola, 1999). Eighty-five percent of those federal prisoners incarcerated for a drug offense were involved in trafficking at the time of their arrest, and only 5% were incarcerated for possession of an illicit drug. (**Jails** are operated by local [or sometimes state] governments to hold persons temporarily detained, awaiting trial, or sentenced to confinement for a misdemeanor, usually for less than one year. **Prisons** are operated by state and federal governments to hold persons sentenced under state and federal laws to terms of more than one year.)

As noted above, with the growing recognition that substance abuse is a serious health problem that requires intervention and treatment, many communities have established drug courts. Formally initiated in Miami, Florida, in 1989, they are designed to be a first step in diverting nonviolent offenders with drug problems into treatment and other community-based programs. Offenders who go through the drug court model often are expected to undergo long-term treatment and counseling, sanctions, incentives, and frequent court appearances. If they successfully complete their program, they avoid not only jail or prison but also, in many jurisdictions, a criminal record. In 2003, there were 1,424 drug courts in existence or being planned in the United States (Office of National Drug Control Policy, 2003d). Recidivism among drug court participants ranges between 5% and 28% and is less than 4% for drug court *graduates* (Office of National Drug Control Policy, 2003d).

The second consistent finding from the research is that arrestees frequently test positive for illicit drug use. In 1999, the Arrestees Drug Abuse Monitoring Program (ADAM) collected data from more than 30,000 adult male arrestees in 34 geographical locations (called sites) and more than 10,000 adult female arrestees in 32 sites. In addition, data were collected from more than 2,500 juvenile male detainees in nine sites and more than 400 female juvenile detainees in six sites. The ADAM uses both urinalysis and self-report data to identify the level of recent drug use by the arrestees and detainees.

The ADAM program continually finds that the level of drug use of arrestees is substantial. In 1999, for instance, every site reported that at least 50% of adult male arrestees tested positive for at least one drug (Arrestees Drug Abuse Monitoring Program, 2000). Overall, the median rate for use of any drug was 64% for adult male arrestees, and 67% for adult female arrestees. These figures were basically the same in 1998, with about two-thirds of the adult arrestees and more than half of the juvenile detainees testing positive for at least one drug (Arrestees Drug Abuse Monitoring Program, 1999). Marijuana was the drug most frequently detected in male arrestees, followed by cocaine. Among adult female arrestees, cocaine was the drug most commonly detected, followed by marijuana and methamphetamine. Multiple drug (polydrug) use was also common, with more than one-quarter of the adult male arrestees testing positive for two or more drugs. Marijuana continues to be a very popular drug among all arrestees, particularly among young males, ages 15 to 20. In fact, marijuana was the most commonly used drug for both juvenile and female detainees, with cocaine and methamphetamine detected substantially less frequently. Among adult males, marijuana was the drug most frequently detected, followed by cocaine. Among females, cocaine was the drug most frequently detected, followed by methamphetamine. Among juvenile arrestees, marijuana was far and away the most frequently detected

TABLE 12–1 Overall Average of Positive Test Results for Various Illicit Drugs in Detained Arrestees in the United States and England, 1999

	OVERALL AVERAGE (%)	
DRUG TYPE	IN UNITED STATES	IN ENGLAND
Marijuana	46.9	40.6
Opiates	8.4	17.9
Cocaine	40.7	8.7
Amphetamines	0.5	5.3
Benzodiazepines	9.0	8.2
Methadone	2.8	6.3
Multiple drugs	27.2	21.7

Source: International Arrestee Drug Abuse Monitoring System (2000).

drug. **Table 12–1** shows the types of illicit drugs that persons in the United States and England tested positive for at the time of their arrest. As you can see, marijuana was the drug most often detected in arrestees in both countries. Cocaine was a close second in the United States, but opiates were a very distant second in England.

The third consistent finding of illicit drug research in recent years is that arrestees and incarcerated offenders are often under the influence of illicit drugs when they commit their offenses. **Table 12–2** shows that about one-quarter of federal (prison) inmates and over one-third of state prison inmates admitted they had been using drugs at the time of their offense.

Furthermore, certain professional criminal groups often prefer one drug over another. Professional pickpockets, shoplifters, and burglars, for example—when they use drugs—have a distinct preference for those that steady their nerves and provide relief from the pressures of their occupation (Inciardi, 1981). Professional pickpockets often consider opiates instrumental in furthering their careers. To some extent, this has a cyclical effect, since the material gain from their crimes is used to obtain the drugs.

With reference to the fourth point—that some offenders commit property crime to support their drug habit—in 1997, 19% of state prisoners and 16% of federal prisoners said they committed their current offenses to obtain money for drugs (Bureau of Justice Statistics, 2000b). Table 12–2 suggests that over one-third of all property offenses may have been committed by state prison inmates to support their habit. These figures are actually quite low compared with public perceptions that stealing to support a drug habit is widespread.

The fifth finding of recent research is that drug trafficking often engenders violent crime. There is considerable evidence that violence accompanies drug distribution in the course of territorial disputes between rival organizations and gangs or in conflicts between the buyer and the seller (J. Roth, 1996; S. Walker, 2001). Places where drug deals occur bring together valuable drugs,

TABLE 12–2 Percentage of State and Federal Prison Inmates Who Reported Being Under the Influence of Drugs at the Time of Their Offense, 1997

	INMATES (%)	
TYPE OF OFFENSE	FEDERAL PRISON	STATE PRISON
Total of all inmates	22.4	32.6
Violent offenses	24.5	29.0
Murder	29.4	26.8
Sexual assault	7.9	21.5
Robbery	27.8	39.9
Assault	13.8	24.2
Other	15.9	29.0
Property offenses	10.8	36.6
Burglary	*	38.4
Larceny/theft	*	38.4
Motor vehicle theft	*	39.0
Fraud	6.5	30.5
Other	16.4	30.6
Drug offenses	25.0	41.9
Possession	25.1	42.6
Trafficking	25.9	41.0
Other	17.1	47.1
Public order offenses	15.6	23.1
Weapons	24.4	22.4
Other	8.1	23.3

Source: Office of National Drug Control Policy (2000b).

big money, weapons, and people accustomed to violence. This volatile mix creates a high potential for violence.

The sixth and final point is that the drug–crime relationship is difficult to identify and measure. The relationship between drugs and crimes is complicated by a fourfold interaction: (1) the pharmacological effects of the drug, which refer to the chemical impact of the drug on the body; (2) the psychological characteristics of the individual using the drug; (3) the psychosocial conditions under which the drug is taken; and (4) the interactions a particular drug has with other drugs consumed simultaneously. Discussion of pharmacological effects includes features of the nervous system, such as the amount of neurotransmitter substances within neurons, and body weight, blood composition, and other neurophysiological features that significantly influence the chemical effects of the drug. Psychological variables include the mood of the person at the time the drug is consumed, previous experience with the drug, and the person's expectancies about the drug's effects. Psychosocial variables include the social atmosphere in which the drug is taken. The people who are present and their expectations, moods, and behavior all may influence an individual's reactions to a drug. The interaction factor must be considered in any discussion of drug effects because most illegal drugs are taken in combination, especially with alcohol. For example, it is not unusual to find teenagers and young adults consuming a variety of club drugs in combination with alcohol; more experienced users sometimes combine cocaine powder or crack with heroin (called a "speedball"). More than two-thirds of the arrestees in 1999 who tested positive for opiates also tested positive for another drug (National Drug Control Policy, 2001).

In order to understand the effects of any drug, the pharmacological, psychological, psychosocial, and interacting variables all must be taken into account. Considering the fact that crime is complex to begin with, deciphering the drug–crime connection becomes very difficult, and the conclusions are necessarily that much more elusive and tentative. The relationship between drugs and crime is further complicated by the cultural, subcultural, and ethnographic aspects of drug consumption. The attitudes and perceptions of different age groups and cultures about specific drugs are often in a state of flux. Cultural preferences shift and change depending on drug availability, law enforcement priorities, and changes in cultural attitudes. In addition, demographic studies have shown that drug popularity and epidemics go through four distinct stages: incubation, expansion, plateau, and decline (Golub & Johnson, 1997). During the *incubation* stage, users experiment with the new and emerging drug, learn how to use it, and develop techniques for its use. During the *expansion* stage, prices drop, it becomes easy to use, its availability increases, and word gets around about the drug, all of which contribute to its popularity. During the *plateau* stage, there is a relatively high and constant use of the drug. But during the *decline* stage, the drug is shunned—usually by a new generation of youth—and a new drug emerges in popularity.

Each year, it is estimated that more than 16,000 Americans die due to an overdose or misuse of illegal drugs, and at least 500,000 drug-related emergencies occur in emergency departments throughout the United States (Federal Bureau of Investigation, 1999a). Many of the fatalities and serious reactions involve youth. For example, the availability of higher-purity, lower-cost drugs has led to an increase in widespread experimental drug use among middle school and high school students.

Perhaps a helpful way of understanding the drug–crime relationship is through the **tripartite conceptual model** proposed by Paul Goldstein (1985). Goldstein identifies three principal types of drug-related crime: (1) *psychopharmacologically* driven crime, (2) systemic crime, and (3) economically compulsive crime. Goldstein's psychopharmacological component of the model presupposes that some individuals, as a result of short-term or long-term ingestion of specific drugs or chemical substances, become excitable and/or irrational and demonstrate violent behavior. In other words, the assumption in this component is that some drugs *cause* certain people (even usually nonviolent ones) to become violent and engage in a variety of criminal behaviors. The prevailing view about psychopharmacological violence, however, is that it is rare and attributable mostly to alcohol rather than illicit drugs (MacCoun, Kilmer, & Reuter, 2003).

The *systemic* component of the model hypothesizes that crime arises out of the system of drug trafficking and distribution. Examples of this component include disputes over territory between rival drug dealers and threats, assaults, and murders committed within and by drug dealing organizations. Essentially, it refers to the violence inherent in the enterprise of drug trafficking and distribution and is similar to the fifth observation of research noted previously.

Economically compulsive crime refers to criminal behavior that supports an expensive drug addiction. Robbery committed by drug users to support a costly drug habit is an example. Compulsive drug seeking and use is presumably an overwhelming drive, even in the face of negative health and social consequences (MacCoun et al., 2003). The economically compulsive component is similar to the fourth observation discussed earlier in this section. As each of the major drug categories is examined in the following sections, the pharmacologically driven aspect as a cause for violence and criminal activity is by far, the most difficult to support.

Before entering into this discussion, it is important to stress that we do not in this text give more than passing attention to public policy with respect to drugs. As noted at the beginning of the chapter, there is considerable disagreement over the extent to which the government should continue on its present course of being harsh on drug offenders. The events of September 11, 2001, have shifted priorities to some extent to a war on terrorism. Nevertheless, drug enforcement and harsh punishments continue, and the individuals who are most often affected are members of racial and economic minority groups. Although this book focuses on the individual behavior of drug users, readers also should be aware of the controversy surrounding public policy on this matter.

Major Categories of Drugs

Four major categories of **psychoactive drugs** are covered in the chapter: (1) the hallucinogens or psychedelics, (2) the stimulants, (3) the opiate narcotics, and (4) the sedative–hypnotics or depressants. A psychoactive drug is a chemical substance that influences a person's mood, perception, mode of thinking, and behavior. To keep the chapter within manageable limits, however, we focus only on specific drugs within each category that represent a serious risk to public safety or that are most closely associated with criminal activity, such as the illegal manufacture, sale, and distribution of a **controlled substance**. A controlled substance is any psychoactive drug or chemical substance whose availability is restricted, as designated by state or federal law.

The *Controlled Substances Act* (CSA), Title II of the Comprehensive Drug Abuse Prevention and Control Act of 1970, places all substances of potential

TABLE 12–3   Formal Scheduling as Outlined by the Controlled Substances Act

SCHEDULE	POTENTIAL FOR ABUSE	ACCEPTED MEDICAL USE IN U.S.	PHYSICAL DEPENDENCE	PSYCHOLOGICAL DEPENDENCE	EXAMPLES
I	High	No[a]	High	High	Heroin, LSD, marijuana
II	High	Yes	High	High	PCP, cocaine, morphine methamphetamine
III	Medium	Yes	Moderate	High	Codeine, steroids, barbiturates
IV	Low	Yes	Low	Low	Darvon, Talwin, Valium, Xanax
V	Low	Yes	Low	Low	Cough medicines with codeine

Source: Drug Enforcement Administration (2000).
[a]Although federal law proscribes the use of these drugs for medical purposes, a number of states have passed or are considering "medical marijuana" laws to ease the pain and suffering of seriously ill patients.

abuse into one of five schedules. This placement is based on the substance's medical use, potential for abuse, and dependence potential (see **Table 12–3**). The purpose of the act is to control the distribution, classification, sale, and use of psychoactive drugs that have the potential for abuse. Although the term "potential for abuse" is not specifically defined in the CSA, scheduling classifications are based on available evidence that the drugs can create a hazard to health or jeopardize the safety of other individuals or that there is a significant diversion of the drug from legitimate drug channels. Proceedings to add, delete, or change the schedule of a drug or other substance may be initiated by the Drug Enforcement Administration (DEA), by the Department of Health and Human Services (HHS), or by petition from any interested party (Drug Enforcement Administration, 2000).

The **hallucinogens** or **psychedelics**, which include LSD (lysergic acid diethylamide), mescaline, psilocybin, phencyclidine (PCP), ketamine, marijuana, and hashish, are our first category. So called because they sometimes generate hallucinations, the hallucinogens are chemicals that lead to a change in consciousness involving an alteration of reality. In some respects they replace the real world with an alternative one, although persons using them can generally attend to their altered state and to reality simultaneously. Marijuana, classified as a hallucinogen, is certainly a mild one for the majority who use it. Because of its widespread use and the public's tendency to mistakenly associate it with crime and bizarre behavior, it is the main drug covered under the hallucinogens category. We also include PCP, a powerful drug that has been linked to crime during the past two decades.

Next, we discuss the **stimulants**, so called because they appear to stimulate central nervous system functions. They include amphetamines, clinical antidepressants, cocaine, MDMA, caffeine, and nicotine. Again, because of their alleged relationship with crime, the amphetamines, MDMA, and cocaine are highlighted.

The third group includes the **opiate narcotics**, which generally have sedative (sleep-inducing) and analgesic (pain-relieving) effects. Heroin—a drug whose use appears to be growing at alarming rates in many communities—is featured in this section. The heroin addict appears frequently in crime statistics, since it is believed that he or she often turns to crime—particularly property crime—to finance this expensive habit.

Finally, alcohol and the "club drugs" represent the **sedative–hypnotic** chemicals that depress central nervous system functions. In most instances, the sedative–hypnotics are all capable of sedating the nervous system and reducing anxiety and tension. Examples include alcohol and the benzodiazepines.

Before proceeding, we must distinguish two terms that are consistently used in the drug literature: **tolerance** and **dependence**. Drug tolerance is the "state of progressively decreased responsiveness to a drug" (Julien, 1975, p. 29). Tolerance is indicated if the individual requires a larger dose of the drug to achieve the same effects he or she has previously experienced. In other words, the person has become psychologically and physiologically used to, or habituated to, the drug.

Dependence may be physical or psychological or both. In simple terms, physical dependence refers to the physiological distress and physical pain a person suffers on going without the drug for any length of time. Psychological dependence is difficult to distinguish from physical dependence, but it is characterized by an overwhelming desire to use the drug for a favorable effect. Dependent people are convinced that they need the drug to maintain an optimal sense of well-being. The degree of psychological dependence varies widely from person to person and drug to drug. In extreme dependence the person's mind is permeated with thoughts of procuring and using the drug, and he or she may resort to crime to obtain it. In common parlance, the person who is extremely psychologically and/or physically dependent is an addict.

Secondary psychological dependence may also develop. While primary dependence is associated with the reward of the drug experience (positive reinforcement), secondary dependence refers to expectancies about aversive withdrawal or the painful effects that will accompany absence of the drug. Thus, to avoid the anticipated pain and discomfort associated with withdrawal, the individual continues to take the drug (negative reinforcement).

The data reported in this chapter concerning illicit drug use and abuse were primarily gathered from the *National Household Survey on Drug Abuse* (NHSDA) (sponsored by the Substance Abuse and Mental Health Services Administration), the *2002 National Survey on Drug Abuse and Health* (the updated version of the NDSDA, also sponsored by the Substance Abuse and Mental Health Services Administration), the Office of National Drug Control Policy (sponsored by the Office of the President), the National Drug Intelligence Center (NDIC), the Bureau of Justice Statistics (BJS), the University of Michigan's *Monitoring the Future Study*, the FBI, the DEA, and the National Institute on

Drug Abuse. Most of these organizations and agencies maintain up-to-date Web sites on the Internet, and their addresses are given in the References.

The Hallucinogens: Cannabis

According to the National Survey on Drug Use and Health (Department of Health and Human Services, 2003), marijuana (*cannabis*) continues to be the most commonly used illicit drug in the United States today. Of all the arrests made in 2002, 40% were for marijuana possession and another 5.4% were for marijuana sale, production, or trafficking (Office of National Drug Control Policy, 2003e). An estimated 40% of Americans aged 12 or older had used marijuana or hashish in their lifetime, and 6.2% were current users of marijuana in 2002. Marijuana is commonly used in combination with other drugs and alcohol.

The 2002 Monitoring the Future Study reported that nearly half (47.8%) of high school seniors and 19.2% of eighth graders indicated they had used marijuana at some point in their lives, and 6% of the seniors and 1.2% of the eighth graders said they used marijuana daily in the 30 days before the survey (University of Michigan, 2002). Ninety percent of the seniors said they could obtain marijuana easily. Statistics provided by the Office of National Drug Control Policy (2003d) indicate similar high use of marijuana by high school seniors compared with use of other drugs (**Table 12–4**; see also (**Figure 12–1**).

Marijuana use is most prevalent among 15- to 25-year-olds, whether male or female, and drops off sharply after age 34 (Arrestees Drug Abuse Monitoring Program, 1999). Marijuana has been the drug of choice for adult arrestees since 1970 (Office of National Drug Control Policy, 2003e). Nearly half (41.5%)

TABLE 12–4   Drug Use Among High School Seniors

Drug	Ever Used (%)	Past Year (%)	Past Month (%)
Amphetamines	16.8	11.1	5.5
Cocaine	7.8	5.0	2.3
Crack	3.8	2.3	1.2
Hallucinogens	12.0	6.6	2.3
Heroin	1.7	1.0	0.5
Inhalants	11.7	4.5	1.5
LSD	8.4	36.5	0.7
Marijuana/hashish	47.8	36.2	21.5
MDMA (ecstasy)	10.5	7.4	2.4
Methamphetamine	6.7	3.6	1.7
PCP	3.1	1.1	0.4
Steroids	4.0	2.5	1.4

Source: Office of National Drug Control Policy (2003d).

FIGURE 12–1   Lifetime Marijuana Use, by Age Group, 1965–2002

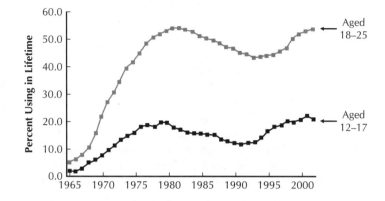

Source: Substance Abuse and Mental Health Services Administration (2003).

of the adult male arrestees and nearly a third (28.4%) of the adult female arrestees in the United States in 2002 tested positive for marijuana use shortly before or at the time of their arrest (National Institute of Justice, 2003).

Historical Background

Marijuana, which apparently originated in Asia, is among the oldest and most frequently used intoxicants. The earliest reference to marijuana was found in a book on pharmacy written by the Chinese emperor Shen Nung in 2737 B.C. (Ray, 1972). It was called the "Liberator of Sin" and was recommended for such ailments as "female weakness," constipation, and absentmindedness. The word marijuana is commonly believed to have derived from "Mary Jane," Mexican slang for cheap tobacco, or from the Portuguese word *mariguano*, meaning intoxicant. Street names for the drug include pot, grass, reefer, weed, Mary Jane, and Acapulco gold.

The drug is prepared from the plant cannabis, an annual that is cultivated or grows freely as a weed in both tropical and temperate climates. There are at least three species of cannabis—sativa, indica, and ruderalis—each differing in psychoactive potency. The psychoactive (intoxicating) properties of the plant reside principally in the chemical delta-9-tetrahydrocannabinol (THC), found mainly in its resin. Thus, the concentration and quality of THC within parts of the plant determine the potency or psychoactive power of the drug.

THC content varies from one preparation to another, partly due to the quality of the plant itself, but also due to its environment. The strain of the plant, the climate, and the soil conditions all affect THC content. For example, the resin is believed to retard the dehydration of the flowering elements and thus is produced in greater quantities in hot, tropical climates than in temperate zones. Consequently, cannabis grown in the tropics (Mexico, Columbia,

Jamaica, and North Africa) presumably has greater psychoactive potential than American-grown hemp. More recent information suggests, however, that THC potency has become more a feature of the species of the cannabis plant than of the geographic area or climatic conditions. Although marijuana produced in Mexico remains the most widely available in the United States, high-potency marijuana also enters the U.S. drug market from Canada (usually grown indoors). Domestically grown marijuana, grown either outdoors or indoors, also represents a substantial proportion of the U.S. drug market.

The THC content in Mexican commercial-grade marijuana ranges from 4% to 6%, whereas in the higher-grade *sinsemilla* the THC content ranges from 15% to 22% (Office of National Drug Control Policy, 2003e). *Sinsemilla* is the Spanish word for "without seed." The on-the-street cost for commercial-grade Mexican marijuana usually ranges from $100 to $200 per ounce, and high potency sinsemilla marijuana may sell up to $1,200 an ounce (Office of National Drug Control Policy, 2003e).

The cannabis extracts used most commonly in the United States are marijuana and hashish. Marijuana is usually prepared by cutting the stem beneath the lowest branches, air-drying, and stripping seeds, bracts, flowers, leaves, and small stems from the plant. There is evidence that the unpollinated female cannabis plant contains more THC than the male. Hashish, the Arabic word for "dry grass," is produced by scraping or in some other way extracting the resin secreted by the flowers. Therefore, hashish, which is usually sold in this country in small cubes, cakes, or even cookielike shapes, has a higher THC content than marijuana. During the 1990s, the THC content of hashish averaged around 6%. Hashish or hash oil is produced by repeated extractions of cannabis plant materials, a process that results in a dark, viscous liquid with a THC content as high as 20% (Abadinsky, 1993) but usually averaging around 15% (Drug Enforcement Administration, 2000). One or two drops of hash oil on a cigarette provide the same psychoactive effects as a joint. When exposed to air over a period of time, marijuana appears to lose its psychoactive potency, since THC is converted to cannabinol and other inactive compounds (Mechoulam, 1970). Cannabis extracts with higher levels of resin deteriorate more rapidly than those with lower levels.

In the United States, marijuana and hashish are usually smoked, most often in hand-rolled cigarettes called "joints" or in hollowed-out commercial cigars called "blunts." It is still popular to lace the joint or blunt with other drugs, such as PCP or crack. A common practice in other countries is to consume cannabis as tea or mixed with other beverages or food.

The psychological effects of cannabis are so subjective and depend on such a wide range of variables that any generalizations must be accompanied by the warning that there are numerous exceptions. Reactions to cannabis, like all psychoactive drugs, depend on the complex interactions of both pharmacological and extrapharmacological factors. As we noted, these include the mood of the user, the user's expectations about the drug, the social context in which it is used, and the user's past experiences with the drug. The strong influence of these extrapharmacological factors together with the widespread variation in THC content in any sample of cannabis makes it exceedingly difficult to obtain comparable research data. Essentially, the effects of cannabis are unique to each individual. Except for increases in heart rate, increases in peripheral blood flow, and reddening of the membranes around the eyes, there are few consistent physiological changes reported for all persons.

Addiction to THC does occur, but only at doses and continued use far above what is now used recreationally. Furthermore, the person who uses marijuana must learn to use the drug to reach a euphoric "stoned" or "high" state. Ray (1983) reports that a three-stage learning process is involved. First, users must inhale the smoke deeply and hold it in their lungs for approximately 20 seconds. Then they must learn to identify and control the effects. Finally, they must learn to label the effects as pleasant.

Cannabis and Crime

Public concern about the connection between cannabis and crime was stimulated as long ago as 1926, by a number of articles printed in a New Orleans newspaper (Ray, 1972). In 1931, a popular article concluded that one of every four persons arrested in New Orleans was addicted to cannabis. With public interest activated, a drive to get the "dangerous" drug outlawed was soon under way. It was spearheaded by then Commissioner of Narcotics, Harry Anslinger, who convinced Congress and many state governments that marijuana often led to serious crime and was a threat to the moral fabric of American society. During this time (the 1930s), marijuana use was often linked with both violent and "perverted" crime.

In 1937, Congress passed the Marijuana Tax Act, a bill intended to add muscle to antimarijuana laws that, by then, existed in 46 states. The Tax Act did not actually outlaw cannabis, but it taxed the grower, distributor, seller, and buyer prohibitively and established so many restrictions that it was nearly impossible to have anything to do with any form of cannabis (Ray, 1972). Interestingly, none of the attitudes or regulations were supported by comprehensive scientific investigations or evidence that marijuana was harmful. The information communicated was anecdotal; the "documentation" consisted of testimony of the "I know a case where" variety. The U.S. Supreme Court eventually declared the Marijuana Tax Act unconstitutional.

In 1939, Bromberg published results of a study conducted in New York between 1932 and 1937. Of a total of 16,854 prisoners, only 67 said they were cannabis users, and only 6 of those had been convicted of a violent crime (cited in Ray, 1972). Bromberg concluded that the relationship between marijuana use and crime was not substantiated, but staunch advocates of the marijuana–crime connection were not swayed.

Numerous research projects directed at the effects of cannabis were launched during the 1950s, 1960s, and early 1970s. Many of these studies had methodological shortcomings and did not control for parity of dosage levels, means of administering the drug, and THC content of the drug itself. Psychological factors associated with the subjects were not considered carefully enough, and experimental settings and instructions were haphazard. At first, some of the research suggested a relationship between cannabis use and criminal behavior. However, with more sophisticated statistical analyses that controlled demographic and criminal background variables, the earlier results were found to be spurious (National Commission on Marihuana and Drug Abuse, 1972). To date, no investigation has established a causal link between the use of cannabis and criminal activity (S. Walker, 2001). Of course, this assertion excludes the illegal acts of selling, possessing, or using the drug.

Both independent research and investigations conducted by government-sponsored commissions strongly indicate that marijuana does not directly contribute to criminal behavior. After an extensive review of available literature, the National Commission on Marihuana and Drug Abuse (1972, p. 470) came to this conclusion: "There is no systematic empirical evidence, at least that is drawn from the American experience, to support the thesis that the use of marijuana either inevitably or generally causes, leads to or precipitates criminal, violent, aggressive, or delinquent behavior of sexual or nonsexual nature." The Commission Report (p. 470), adds, "If anything, the effects observed suggest that marijuana may be more likely to neutralize criminal behavior and to militate against the commission of aggressive acts."

One of the predominant effects of THC is relaxation and a marked decrease in physical activity (Tinklenberg & Stillman, 1970). THC induces muscular weakness and inability to sustain physical effort, so that the user wishes nothing more strenuous than to stay relatively motionless. As Tinklenberg and Stillman (1970, p. 341) note, "'being stoned' summarizes these sensations of demobilizing lethargy." It is difficult to imagine "stoned" users engaging in assaultive or violent activity. If anything, THC should reduce the likelihood of criminal activity, particularly aggressive conduct, as the Commission suggested. There is some evidence to support this conclusion.

Tinklenberg and Woodrow (1974) found that drug users who use mainly marijuana seem less inclined toward violence and aggression than their counterparts who prefer other drugs, such as alcohol or amphetamines. After examining drug usage among lower-class minority youth, Blumer and his associates (Blumer, Sutter, Ahmed, & Smith, 1967) made the same observation. In fact, they found that marijuana users deliberately shunned aggression and violence; in order to maintain one's status in the group, it was important to remain "cool" and nonaggressive, regardless of provocation.

Although the empirical evidence so far indicates that cannabis does not, as a rule, stimulate aggressive behavior or other criminal actions, whenever we deal with human behavior there will be exceptions. Individuals familiar with the effects of cannabis have heard of occasional negative experiences produced by THC. Although the phenomenon is rare, some people do report feelings of panic, hypersensitivity, feelings of being out of contact with their surroundings, and bizarre behavior. Some individuals have experienced rapid, disorganized intrusions of irrelevant thoughts, which prompted them to feel they were losing control of their mind. Under these conditions, it is plausible that one would interpret the actions of others as threatening. It is also possible that these panicked individuals might attack those surrounding them.

However, those who investigate cannabis effects usually agree that people who act violently under the influence of the drug are probably predisposed to act that way, with or without the drug (National Commission on Marihuana and Drug Abuse, 1972). The evidence indicates that violent marijuana users were violent prior to using cannabis. In other words, they learned the behavioral pattern independently of cannabis. In addition, they have come to expect that the drug will "bring out" aggression or violence in them.

In summary, there is no solid evidence to indicate that cannabis contributes to or encourages violent or property crime, in spite of the waning beliefs that this relationship exists. In fact, there is evidence to suggest that cannabis users are less criminally or violently prone under the influence of the drug than users of other drugs, such as alcohol and amphetamines. There are also no supportive data that cannabis is habit-forming to the point where the user must get a "fix" and will burglarize or rob to obtain funds to purchase the drug. Marijuana trafficking and distribution are also not fraught with the extensive systematic violence that accompanies other drugs of abuse. For most people the primary negative effect of marijuana use is diminished psychomotor performance. Thus the public is at risk when someone intoxicated with marijuana drives a motor vehicle.

Marijuana certainly promotes relaxation and interferes with judgment, and probably makes people more daring and more prone to risk taking. It also alters the experience of reality and often improves mood. The drug is clearly used extensively as a recreation enhancer. As noted earlier, nearly 50% of individuals arrested for a variety of offenses had been using marijuana just prior to or at the time of their offense, and it is also very popular among delinquents. Most likely, arrestees and detainees used the drug to improve their sense of well-being, frequently in combination with other drugs. Recall that the drug is classified as a Schedule I drug by the DEA, indicating it is at lowest risk of jeopardizing health and safety. Although it is illegal to produce, possess, sell, or consume marijuana, there is little evidence that the drug propels nonviolent people to become violent or antisocial or to engage in some kind of serious criminal behavior.

Phencyclidine (PCP)

PCP may be classified as a central nervous system depressant, anesthetic, tranquilizer, or hallucinogen. It has many effects, but most pronounced are its barbiturate-like downer effect, perceptual distortions, and hallucinations and its amphetamine-like upper effects, such as excitation and hyperactivity. An overdosed person, for example, may show signs of moving from upper to downer effects while having hallucinations.

PCP was first synthesized in 1957, but due to its psychotic and hallucinogenic effects, it was taken off the market for human consumption in 1965 and limited to use in veterinary medicine as an animal immobilizing agent. Because of its serious and numerous side effects, it is no longer used even in veterinary medicine. Its use increased between 1973 and 1979, then declined briefly between 1979 and 1981. Since 1982, however, it has shown a resurgence in popularity (Crider, 1986), although the popularity remains cyclical. Most users are male, African American, and between 20 and 29 years old (Crider, 1986). The behavior of some individuals under the influence of PCP is highly unpredictable and may lead to life-threatening situations. Under the spell of PCP psychosis, delusions of superhuman strength, persecution, and grandiosity are not uncommon. In general, PCP is associated with a number of serious risks, and many experts believe it is one of the most dangerous illicit drugs on the streets. On occasion, individuals under the influence of PCP may use weapons to defend themselves and to commit other acts of violence.

There is wide variation in the degree of purity and dosage forms of PCP manufactured in clandestine laboratories. It comes in capsules, tablets, liquids, and powder. It may be ingested orally, by inhalation (snorted or smoked), and by intravenous injection. When it is smoked, PCP is often applied to leafy material such as mint, parsley, oregano, or marijuana. Users usually combine PCP with other drugs, particularly marijuana and alcohol. It can cause death, although the majority of fatal doses involved alcohol as well (Brunet, Reiffenstein, Williams, & Wong, 1985–1986). Because of its adverse and negative effects, the reasons for its popularity remain obscure.

The available evidence clearly indicates that PCP users tend to be multiple illicit drug users (polydrug users). To what extent PCP propels a person toward a life of crime is largely unknown, but it does not seem likely that PCP users regularly engage in crime to support their habits. PCP is inexpensive, easily available, and only marginally addictive after chronic use. PCP users are generally polydrug users who have demonstrated a variety of types of antisocial conduct prior to PCP usage. Polydrug usage is more likely to be one symptom within a complicated matrix of other symptoms found in certain individuals habitually "going against" their environment. Currently, PCP is classified as a Schedule I drug of abuse by the DEA.

THE STIMULANTS

Amphetamines

Amphetamines and cocaine are classified as central nervous system stimulants and have highly similar effects. Amphetamines are members of a group of synthetic drugs known collectively as amines. Cocaine (coke, snow, candy) is a chemical extracted from the coca plant (*Erythroxylon coca*), an extremely hardy plant native to Peru. The amines, in particular, produce effects in the sympathetic nervous system, a subdivision of the autonomic nervous system, which arouse users to actions that may include fighting or fleeing from a frightening situation. Amphetamines are traditionally classified into three major categories: (1) amphetamine (Benzedrine), (2) dextroamphetamine (Dexedrine), and (3) methamphetamine (Methedrine or Desoxyn). Of the three, Benzedrine is the least potent. All may be taken orally, inhaled, or injected, and all act directly on the central nervous system, particularly the reticular activating system.

In this section, methamphetamine is the focus of the amphetamine group because it is the drug most preferred by drug users. Methamphetamine has traditionally been the drug of preference when the user injects the amphetamines directly into the bloodstream. Its use has hit a plateau or slowly decreased in the United States since 1998, although in the western and southwestern parts of the country, the drug continues to be popular. One of the reasons for the decline appears to be the decrease in purity and potency of the drug, which produces some unanticipated adverse reactions and negative health consequences (National Institute on Drug Abuse, 2000). According to the Arrestees Drug Abuse Monitoring Program (2000), the proportion of female adult arrestees testing positive in 1999 for methamphetamine was slightly greater than that for male adult arrestees in most areas of the country.

Once the drug is taken, it is rapidly assimilated into the bloodstream, but it is metabolized and eliminated from the body relatively slowly. Both psychological and physiological reactions to these drugs vary dramatically with the dose. In addition, the effects of massive quantities injected intravenously differ substantially from the effects of low doses administered orally. Reactions to the drugs also vary widely among individuals.

The common street names for amphetamines include bennies, dexies, copilots, meth, ice, speed, white cross, uppers, crank, geep, chicken feed, peanut butter, crystal, quill, pep pills, yellow bam, tweek, eye openers, wakeups, hearts, footballs, bombitas, coast-to-coasts, splash, and purple hearts. The street names are derived from the various effects, the purposes to which the drug is put, the shape and color of the drug, and the trade name of the manufacturers.

The amphetamines are synthetic compounds and, unlike cannabis or cocaine, can be easily produced by self-appointed chemists for large-scale illegal distribution. The manufacture of methamphetamine, for example, requires precursor drugs (drugs that are necessary in the manufacture of another) such as ephedrine and pseudoephedrine, which are widely available in Mexico and are believed to be smuggled into the United States in large quantities (Feucht & Kyle, 1996). Over-the-counter cold medicines containing ephedrine or pseudoephedrine and other materials can also be "cooked" to make methamphetamine (Office of National Drug Control Policy, 1999b). Therefore, it is exceedingly difficult to estimate the quantity of amphetamines consumed each year in the Unites States. *The Comprehensive Methamphetamine Act of 1996* was passed, among other things, to control the sale of ephedrine and pseudoephedrine.

Methamphetamine hydrochloride, clear chunky crystals resembling ice (therefore, often referred to as ice, blue, super ice, hot ice, crystal, crank, Mexican crack, or LA glass), is usually smoked, whereas regular methamphetamine is taken orally, injected, or inhaled (snorting the powder). Currently, the popular method of administration is through smoking. Snorting the drug affects the user in about 5 minutes, whereas it takes about 20 minutes after oral ingestion to feel the full effects (Office of National Drug Control Policy, 2003b). Methamphetamine is quite easy to manufacture. The illegal form of the drug is produced in clandestine laboratories (meth labs) that use ingredients purchased in local stores (Office of National Drug Control Policy, 2003b), such as the over-the-counter cold medications mentioned above. The West coast appears to have the majority of meth labs in the United States (Office of National Drug Control Policy, 2003b).

The 2002 data reported by the Monitoring the Future Study indicate that crystal methamphetamine continues to be popular among high school seniors (University of Michigan, 2003). The annual use of methamphetamine by high school seniors in 1999 was 4.7% (University of Michigan, 2002), compared to 1.2% for college students (University of Michigan, 2003) (see also **Table 12–5**). Available research indicates that the majority of methamphetamine users are male, white, and over 26 (Office of National Drug Control Policy, 1999b).

Methamphetamine produces an increase in alertness and a decrease in appetite. The effects can last as long as 12 hours. In high doses, the drug can cause violent behavior, anxiety, insomnia, and symptoms of paranoid behavior, including delusions, hallucinations, and mood swings. Some chronic users develop sores on their bodies from scratching "crank bugs," a delusion that bugs are crawling under their skin.

A more recent drug of abuse in the United States is methcathinone, which is chemically similar to methamphetamine. Known on the streets as "cat," the drug was placed on Schedule I in 1993. Methcathinone is usually snorted, although it can be taken orally by mixing it with some drink or injected intravenously. Its psychoactive effects are identical to those of methamphetamine.

TABLE 12–5   Percentage of Lifetime Methamphetamine Use Among the U.S. Population by Age Group, 2002

AGE GROUP	LIFETIME (%)	PAST YEAR (%)	PAST MONTH (%)
12–17	1.5	0.9	0.3
18–25	5.7	1.7	0.5
26 and older	5.7	0.4	0.2
Total population	5.3	0.7	0.3

Source: Office of National Drug Control Policy (2003b).

Yaba, the Thai name for a tablet form of methamphetamine mixed with caffeine, is being used with some frequency in regions of California and is becoming popular on the rave scene as a club drug (Office of National Drug Control Policy, 2003b). These tablets are popular and produced in Southeast and East Asia.

According to the DEA, the price of methamphetamine in 2001 ranged nationally from $3,500 to $23,000 per pound, $350 to $2,200 per ounce, and $20 to $300 per gram (Office of National Drug Control Policy, 2003b). The average purity of the drug decreased from 71.9% in 1994 to 40.1% in 2001.

Cocaine

Recent data suggest there are approximately 2,707,000 chronic cocaine users and 3,3035,000 occasional cocaine users in the United States (Office of National Drug Control Policy, 2003f). According to the 2002 National Survey on Drug Use and Health, 14.4% of the U.S. population (age 12 or older) had used cocaine at least once in their lifetime (University of Michigan, 2003). More than 8 million Americans (3.6%) had used crack cocaine at lease once in their lifetime. The survey also found that 3.6% of eighth graders and 7.8% of high seniors had used cocaine at least once during their lifetimes. According to the National Drug Intelligence Center's report (National Drug Threat Assessment 2003), cocaine ". . . is the primary drug threat in the United States because of its high demand and availability, its expanding distribution to new markets, the high rate of overdose associated with its use, and its relation to violence" (Office of National Drug Control Policy, 2003f, p. 2).

In 2001, the wholesale price for powder cocaine ranged from $10,000 to $36,000 per kilogram, $400 to $1,800 per ounce, and $20 to $200 per gram (Office of National Drug Control Policy, 2003f). Prices for crack cocaine ranged from $3 to $50 per rock, with prices usually between $10 and $20. Slang names for powder cocaine include candy sugar, pariba, aspirin, mojo, icing, happy dust, oyster stew, and double bubble.

Cocaine has traditionally been much more expensive than the amphetamines, partly because it is a natural organic substance and cannot be produced synthetically. It has to be grown under certain unusual conditions. The coca plant from which it is extracted thrives at elevations of 2,000 to 8,000 feet and with heavy rainfall (100 inches per year). It is an evergreen shrub that grows to about three feet tall and is generally found on the eastern slopes of the Andes. It has long been used by Peruvians living in or near the Andes. Mountain natives were known to chew coca leaves almost continuously and to keep them tucked in their cheek (Ray, 1972). Coca leaves are also used for tea. There are at least 200 strains of coca plants, but the vast majority contain little if any cocaine. However, with North Americans' increasing appetite for cocaine, South American growers and entrepreneurs have developed not only vast new areas for the cultivation of coca but also new, more vigorous strains of the plant (Inciardi, 1986).

In the United States and Canada, cocaine is usually taken nasally (sniffing), inhaled (smoking), or injected intravenously. Cocaine taken orally is poorly absorbed because it is hydrolyzed by gastrointestinal secretions. Cocaine is often used with other illicit drugs, usually alcohol, marijuana, and heroin. Some users alternate snorting lines of cocaine and heroin, known as "crisscrossing," or inject the two drugs together as a "speedball." Light users normally sniff the drug to obtain their "high," but chronic sniffing can result in nasal irritation and inflammation. The common unit in the black market is the "spoon," which approximates one gram of the diluted drug. In most cases, cocaine is diluted 20 to 30 times by weight. It is estimated that there are 6 million (3% of the population) regular cocaine users in the United States.

It is widely believed—but denied by the corportion—that Coca Cola contained cocaine as an active ingredient until 1903, when caffeine was substituted (Kleber, 1988). In fact, around the turn of the century, cocaine was used not only in soft drinks (such as Kos-Kola, Wiseola, and Care-Cola), but even in cigarettes and cigars, various tonics, foods, sprays, and ointments (including hemorrhoid salves) (Smart, 1986). The famous drink "Vin Mariani," so popular among the wealthy at the time, was a combination of vintage French wine and cocaine. However, cocaine began to fall into disfavor when people became concerned about its dangerous and undesirable effects. By 1910, cocaine had become the most hated and feared drug in North America (Kleber, 1988). The Harrison Narcotics Act of 1914 in the United States and the Propriety and Patents Medicines Act of 1908 in Canada sharply curtailed or terminated its usage, and the popularity of cocaine correspondingly declined until the 1960s.

Psychological Effects.   In small doses, both amphetamines and cocaine increase wakefulness, alertness, and vigilance, improve concentration, and produce a feeling of clear thinking. There is generally an elevation of mood, mild euphoria, increased sociability, and a belief that one can do just about anything. The duration of the stimulant's euphoric effects depends on the route of administration. The faster the absorption into the bloodstream, such as by inhaling cocaine vapor into the lungs ("freebasing") rather than snorting the powder form, the more rapid and intense the psychoactive effects. Cocaine vapor is usually produced by igniting the powder form of cocaine. In large doses, the effects may be irritability, hypersensitivity, delirium, panic aggression, hallucinations, and psychosis. Hallucinations sometimes include "coke bugs" that appear to be crawling all over the body. Injected at chronically high doses, these drugs may precipitate "toxic psychosis," a syndrome with many of the psychotic features of paranoid schizophrenia. With the metabolization and elimination of the drug, the psychotic episode usually dissipates. Cocaine, like any psychoactive drug, will engender different experiences for different individuals. Some people under the influence will exhibit violent, erratic, paranoid, or even suicidal behavior; others will display peaceful, friendly, sociable behavior.

Adverse Physical Effects.   Frequent cocaine use may have some strong adverse effects, depending on how it is administered. Regularly snorting cocaine can lead to a loss of the sense of smell, nosebleeds, problems with swallowing, hoarseness, and inflammation of the nasal septum (National Institute on Drug Abuse, 1999). Consuming cocaine orally can cause severe bowel gangrene because of reduced blood flow to the gastrointestinal system. Injecting cocaine can generate some serious allergic reactions, and sometimes results in death. Cocaine is usually processed with a variety of volatile solvents, such as gasoline, benzene, and kerosene, and traces of these toxic substances often remain in the powder form of cocaine.

Cocaine often has a dramatic effect on the cardiovascular system, such as disturbances in heart rhythm and heart attacks. It can adversely affect the respiratory systems, resulting in chest pain or respiratory failure. And it can cause strokes, seizures, blurred vision, nausea, fever, muscle spasms, and coma. Cocaine users who frequently inject the drug are at risk for bacterial infections and other infectious diseases. Sharing needles and using unsterilized drug paraphernalia also put users at considerable risk for HIV, hepatitis, and a variety of other viruses.

There is a potentially very dangerous drug interaction between cocaine and alcohol that should be noted. When the user ingests cocaine and alcohol at once or closely together, the drugs are converted by the body to cocethylene. Cocethylene is substantially more toxic than either drug alone, and available evidence indicates that the mixture of cocaine and alcohol is the most common two-drug combination that results in drug-related death (National Institute on Drug Abuse, 1999).

Partly because of these many serious adverse effects, there has been a downward trend in cocaine use in recent years (National Institute on Drug Abuse, 2000). In 1997, an estimated 1.5 million Americans (0.7% of the entire population) age 12 and older were chronic cocaine users, a significant drop from 1985, when there were 5.7 million chronic users (3% of the population) (National Institute on Drug Abuse, 1999).

Stimulants, Cocaine, and Crime

As pointed out, heavy users of amphetamines typically prefer to inject methamphetamine directly into the bloodstream, cranking up with several hundred milligrams at a time. During these speed "runs" the user may engage in aggressive or violent behavior (F. Hofmann, 1975; National Commission on Marihuana and Drug Abuse, 1973; Tinklenberg & Stillman, 1970). However, it appears that people who behave violently under the effects of amphetamines are very often predisposed to behave violently long before they ingest amphetamines. In other words, there is little evidence to conclude that amphetamines cause people to behave violently but they do increase the likelihood that an already violence-prone person will behave violently. As the data shown in Table 12–1 reveal, very few arrestees test positive for amphetamine use at the time of their arrest.

Research by the Arrestees Drug Abuse Monitoring program consistently reveals, however, that persons arrested frequently test positive for cocaine. Tables 12–1 and 12–4 suggest, for example, that cocaine-based drugs, including crack, are second only to marijuana for abuse in the United States. Both amphetamines and cocaine are considered Schedule II drugs by the DEA. In small doses, these drugs increase alertness and concentration. In large doses, they generally produce negative psychological effects. But to date, virtually no study has shown that stimulants or cocaine facilitate either property crime or violent crime. In an exhaustive review of the literature, the Panel on the Understanding and Control of Violent Behavior concluded that there was no evidence to support the claim that snorting or injecting cocaine stimulates violent behavior (Roth, 1996). Morgan and Zimmer (1997) also conclude that there is very little convincing evidence that cocaine, in either crack or powder form, causes a nonviolent person to suddenly become violent or dangerous to others. Nor is there any evidence to support the assumption that cocaine, especially crack, causes parents to abuse their children. It is more likely the lifestyle of the parent, rather than simply the pharmacologically driven aspect of the drug, that leads to child abuse (Morgan & Zimmer, 1997).

Powder cocaine, however, can be strongly addictive, and the dependence onset can be rapid and severe. It is also expensive, and acquisition of the drug must be accomplished through organized distribution and selling. In other words, powder cocaine is one of the drugs of abuse that encourages systematic violence on a wide scale. In addition, some cocaine abusers may have a difficult time controlling their habit and may rapidly build a tolerance to the drug, requiring larger and larger amounts of the costly drug. Some cocaine users may be forced to engage in shoplifting, theft, drug dealing, and prostitution to support their habit. **Table 12–6** shows percentages of male and female adult arrestees testing positive for cocaine. Because the percentages are so high, the table suggests that cocaine is the drug most commonly used by offenders during the commission of a crime.

TABLE 12–6   Percentage of Male and Female Adult Arrestees Testing Positive for Cocaine in 1999

City	Women (%)	Men (%)
New York	65.1	44.2
Chicago	64.3	41.7
Philadelphia	59.8	39.3
Seattle	48.2	33.4
Detroit	45.9	27.0

Source: National Institute on Drug Abuse (2000, p. 7).

Crack

The most common method of cocaine smoking in the United States is free-basing. Freebase is prepared by dissolving cocaine hydrochloride in water, then adding a strong base such as ammonia or baking soda to the solution (R. Weiss & Mirin, 1987). This cocaine freebase is generally dissolved in ether to extract the cocaine, and then the ether is removed by drying the solution. Other methods may be used that bypass the ether method by heating the mixture. The drying process produces crystalline, smokable pellets or nuggets. The result is a product ranging from 37% to 96% purity (R. Weiss & Mirin, 1987).

During the 1980s, a purified, high-potency form of freebase cocaine—known as crack—exploded in popularity. It was, according to Howard Abadinsky (1993), the drug abuser's answer to fast food. The drug is called crack because it makes a crackling sound when smoked (Abadinsky, 1993; M. Gold, 1984). Crack is several times purer than ordinary street cocaine, and smoking crack generates a very rapid, intense state of euphoria, which peaks in about five minutes. The psychological and physical effects of crack are as powerful as those of intravenously injected cocaine. However, the euphoria is short-lived, ending about 10 to 20 minutes after inhalation, and it is followed by depression, irritability, and often an intense craving for more. It is also extremely dangerous to the user and may result in a rapid and irregular heartbeat, respiratory failure, seizures, or a cerebral hemorrhage. Although most users limit themselves to one or two hits, some users seek multiple hits. Crack smokers, in order to stay high, often find a place where crack can be safely smoked, such as a crack house, because the smoke and smell are difficult to hide.

During the 1980s crack cocaine generated much concern by local officials across the United States because of its popularity, illegal drug trafficking, and health hazards to adolescents and young adults. At one point, some experts regarded crack as the most addictive drug currently available on the street (Weiss & Mirin, 1987). This assumption has been seriously questioned by many research scientists in recent years (Morgan & Zimmer, 1997). Furthermore, it was thought that the craving for the drug might become so severe for some individuals that the user would lie, steal, or commit acts of violence in order to obtain more of the drug (Rosecan, Spitz, & Gross, 1987). Its popularity probably resided in the instantaneous psychological effects it provides, its inexpensiveness, and its wide availability throughout most major U.S. cities. The drug also provided tremendous profits for sellers. For awhile, about one-third of all arrests made by the New York City Narcotics Division involved cocaine, and over half of them involved crack (Cohn, 1986). Because it was so inexpensive and available, it became a very popular drug for the young—including preteenagers.

Since the early 1990s, the use of crack cocaine has begun to decline (Golub & Johnson, 1997). The reasons for the decline are multiple, but the most prominent appear to be its health risks and the changes in attitude among the new generation concerning its use. The youth today consider crack users "dumb" and "crackhead" a dirty word (Golub & Johnson, 1997). In some cities, many youths abuse crackheads or avoid them altogether. Overall, it appears that the primary heavy users of crack cocaine today are those who began using the drug during the 1980s. The more recent generation of youth called "Generation X" tend to avoid using the drug.

The relationship between crack and crime remains obscure. One thing that does emerge from the research literature is that crack users, especially persistent users, are often polydrug users. Surveys indicate that virtually all crack users have been frequent users of other drugs, and most also have an extensive history of drug use, drug sales, and nondrug criminality (Golub & Johnson, 1997). While it is difficult at this point in our knowledge to determine which comes first, drug use or involvement in crime, the evidence does suggest that persistent offenders have engaged in a variety of illegal activities and troublesome conduct throughout their lifetimes, probably before extensive drug abuse. One thing seems clear, though: Crack use by itself does not appear to cause violent behavior in normally nonviolent people (Golub & Johnson, 1997; Morgan & Zimmer, 1997). The association between the crack cocaine black market and systemic violence, on the other hand, is a different matter. The production, distribution, and sale of powder and crack cocaine have been associated with violence for some time, although the amount of violence fluctuates with the illicit market economy.

MDMA

MDMA, or "ecstasy," is a synthetic drug (completely manufactured rather than grown) that is considered a stimulant but has some strong psychedelic effects. MDMA is the abbreviation for methylenedioxymethamphetamine. The drug was first manufactured by a German company in 1912 to be used as a possible appetite suppressant. The drug gained notoriety in the 1990s as the "rave culture" swept over Europe's younger generation. Today, MDMA is known as a "club drug" and is commonly used at all-night dance parties known as "raves." Being under the drug's effects is often referred to as "rolling" because of the up-and-down rolling of emotions it causes. Depending on the dosage, the drug's effects usually last between four and six hours, and normally ecstasy is taken in tablet, capsule, or powder form.

The common psychological effects of MDMA include confusion, depression, anxiety, sleeplessness, drug craving, and paranoia (Office of National Drug Control Policy, 2000a). Its adverse physical effects include muscle tension, involuntary clenching of the teeth, nausea, blurred vision, faintness, tremors, and sweating and chills. Baby pacifiers are often used by MDMA users to prevent damage to or excessive grinding of the teeth. Inhalation of Vick's Vapo Rub is also sometimes used to enhance the drug's psychedelic effects.

The drug's stimulant effects provide an "energy rush" that encourages users to stay physically active for long periods of time, such as dancing all night at rave parties. Although the drug is safer than many other illicit drugs, there are physical risks. At very high doses, MDMA can cause the body temperature to rise as high as 110 degrees, leading to muscle breakdown and kidney or cardiovascular failure (National Institute on Drug Abuse, 2000). Also, all-night raves and extensive dancing in crowded and hot rooms pose the danger of producing not only high body temperatures but dangerous levels of dehydration. Other adverse side effects of MDMA include heart and liver damage, strokes, and long-term brain injury (National Institutes of Health, 1999).

The majority of MDMA found in the United States comes from Europe and is produced in clandestine laboratories located mostly in Western Europe (primarily the Netherlands and Belgium). The drug is usually sold in 300-milligram tablets containing between 75 and 125 milligrams of pure MDMA. To distinguish their product from others', traffickers often put their logos on the tablets, such as butterflies, lightening bolts, stars, and clovers (Office of National Drug Policy, 2000). Common slang names for MDMA include ecstasy, Adam, disco biscuit, hug drug, clarity, and XTC.

The illegal use of MDMA has been increasing at an alarming rate in recent years (**Table 12–7** and **Figure 12–2**). U.S. Customs officials seized more than 5.4 million hits of the drug during 1999, compared with 750,000 hits in 1998 (National Institute on Drug Abuse, 2000), and seized another 9.3 million hits in 2000 (Klam, 2001). A National Institute on Drug Abuse (2000) report on MDMA use in Atlanta, Georgia, 1999 says:

> MDMA use continues to be popular in Atlanta. It has become more available among users age 18 to 25. The price remains stable at $5 to $25. Use remains common at raves and local clubs. Ethnographic research shows that many MDMA users have no idea of the content of the substances they are taking, and that many are using MDMA simultaneously with other substances, including other designer drugs and hallucinogens such as LSD (lysergic acid diethylamide) and mescaline. (p. 15)

FIGURE 12–2   Annual Number of New Users of Ecstasy, LSD, and PCP, 1965–2001

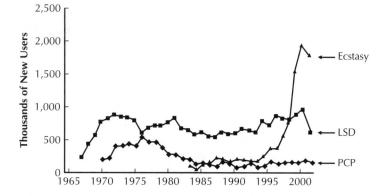

Source: Substance Abuse and Mental Health Services Administration (2003).

TABLE 12–7   Percentage of Lifetime MDMA Use Among the U.S. Population by Age Group, 1998–2000

AGE GROUP	1998 (%)	1999 (%)	2000 (%)
12–17	1.6	1.8	2.6
18–25	5.0	7.6	9.7
26–34	2.6	1.5	1.8
Total population	1.5	2.3	2.9

Source: Office of National Drug Control Policy (2002b).

Outside of the illegal trafficking of the drug, no direct connection has been established between MDMA ingestion and crime. The drug does not appear to be habit forming and is used primarily as an experimental drug that is promoted under group pressure at bars, nightclubs, and rave parties. There is, however, potential for serious physical and neurological damage if MDMA is used frequently and in combination with other drugs. Perhaps the greatest danger to MDMA users is the lack of proper manufacture of the drug. Manufacturing MDMA requires ideal laboratory conditions, and failure to follow procedures precisely can cause contamination or purity problems. Under these conditions, the drug is potentially fatal.

NARCOTIC DRUGS

The word **narcotics** usually provokes intense negative reactions and very often is quickly associated with crime. Like the word dope, it is widely misused to denote all illegal drugs. In this chapter, narcotics refers only to the derivatives of, or products pharmacologically similar to, products of the opium or poppy plant, *Papaver sominferum*.

The opium plant, an annual, grows to about three to five feet in height. Today, most opium is grown in Afghanistan, which produces approximately 75% of the world's opium and opium-based narcotics (Bureau of International Narcotics and Law Enforcement Affairs, 2000). However, the opium poppies that are of most concern to the United States are grown principally in Colombia and Mexico. Although these two countries together cultivate less than 6% of the world's total opium, most of the heroin found in the United States is from Colombian or Mexican suppliers. In fact, Mexico serves as the transit and distribution center for most of the drugs moved into this country.

Narcotic drugs can be divided into three major categories on the basis of the kind of preparation they require: (1) natural narcotics, which include the grown opium; (2) semisynthetic narcotics, which include the chemically prepared heroin; and (3) synthetic narcotics, which are wholly prepared chemically and include methadone, meperidine, and phenazocine. All are narcotics because they produce similar effects: relief of pain, relaxation, peacefulness, and sleep (*narco*, of Greek origin, means "to sleep"). The narcotics are highly addictive for some individuals, who develop a relentless and strong craving for the drug. Many heavy narcotic users, however, lead successful, productive lives, without significant interference in their daily routine. There is no single type of opium user.

Heroin

The most heavily used illegal narcotic in this country is heroin. During the 1970s, it was estimated that there were 400,000 to 600,000 heroin addicts in any given year. During the 1990s, it is estimated that there were 229,000 "casual" users and 500,000 "heavy" users per year (Epstein & Gfroerer, 1997). Data from the 2001 Household Survey on Drug Abuse reports that 1.4% of Americans (3.1 million) had used heroin at least once in their lifetime, and approximately 130,000 Americans said they had used heroin within the month preceding the survey (see **Table 12–8**). It is a safe bet, however, that any self-report survey underestimates the actual drug use by the respondents. The DEA estimates that, in 1999, 208,000 Americans were regular users of heroin, more than tripling the number of regular users in 1993 (68,000) (DEA, 2001). However, more complete estimates conclude that there are 980,000 heroin addicts and 1.2 million casual users in the United States (Bureau of International Narcotics and Law Enforcement Affairs, 2000). Many cocaine users use heroin to cushion the "crash" that often follows the "rush" of using crack. The 1998 Drug Abuse Warning Network (DAWN), which collects data on drug-related hospital emergency departments, reported that 14% of all drug-related emergencies involved heroin.

The availability of heroin continues to be high in almost all areas of the country, although the purity varies considerably from region to region. Most of the heroin seized in 1999 east of the Mississippi River was of Colombian origin, whereas most of the drugs seized west of the Mississippi were of Mexican origin (Bureau of International Narcotics and Law Enforcement Affairs, 2000). High-quality heroin from Afghanistan continues to move in large quantities into Europe, Russia, and other countries of the former Soviet Union.

TABLE 12–8   Percentage of Americans Reporting Lifetime Use of Heroin, by Age Group: 1999–2001

AGE GROUP	1999 (%)	2000 (%)	2001 (%)
12–17	0.4	0.4	0.3
18–25	1.8	1.4	1.6
26–34	1.3	1.1	1.3
Total population	1.4	1.2	1.4

Source: Office of National Drug Control Policy (2003g).

In 2001, heroin was selling for approximately $15–$35 per one-eighth-ounce bag in the United States, or about $100 per gram. In 2001, South American heroin sold from $50,000 to $250,000 per kilogram, depending on purity. Southeast and Southwest Asian wholesale prices ranged from $35,000 to 120,000 per kilogram, and Mexican heroin ranged from $15,000 to $65,000 per kilogram (Office of National Drug Control Policy, 2003g). South American heroin appears to be the most prevalent type sold in the United States. According to the Drug Enforcement Administration (2003b), retail purity levels of heroin ranged from 48.1% for South American heroin, to 34.6% for Southwest Asian heroin, to 20.8% for Mexican heroin.

The heroin "bag"—the common way to sell the drug—may be an actual glassine bag, a balloon, or a number of capsules or pills. When heroin is sold by the "bag," its price does not always depend on its purity. For example, the time of day when it is sold or the location may strongly influence the price due to the risks of detection perceived by the seller. Usually, heroin looks like a white, crystalline material and is characterized by the bitter alkaloid taste. Its appearance is largely dictated by its diluents, which in most cases make up 95 to 98% of its total weight. In some instances, heroin will appear dark-brown due to the impurities left from the manufacturing process or the presence of additives.

Despite the popularity of cocaine, heroin still reigns as the illicit or hard drug of choice in much of the world. Mexican "black tar" heroin has hit the streets in recent years. It is a dark-brown substance that has the appearance of black tar and is sticky like roofing tar or, in some instances, hard like coal. The color and consistency of black tar heroin are due to the crude processing methods used to manufacture it. High-quality Mexican black tar heroin sells for $600 to $800 per gram and ranges in purity from 20% to 80%. In many areas, heroin users combine heroin with cocaine powder (HCl) or with crack and then inject the mixture. As mentioned earlier, this practice is known as speedballing. In some regions, particularly in the West, users often mix heroin and methamphetamine to inject. Heroin is rarely taken orally, because the absorption rate is slow and incomplete. It may be administered intramuscularly, subcutaneously ("skin popping"), or intravenously ("mainlining"), or it may be inhaled ("snorted"). Heroin inhalers usually choose to use heroin and crack simultaneously. In the past, experienced heroin users strongly preferred mainlining because of the sensational thrill, splash, rush, or kick it provided. Injection is probably the most practical and efficient way to administer low-purity heroin. Injection works fast. Intravenous injection provides the most intense and rapid feeling of euphoria, working within seven to eight seconds after injection. Intramuscular injection is slower, taking about five to eight minutes for peak effect. However, in recent years, the dramatic increase in heroin purity has changed the preferred method of administration. The high purity of Colombian heroin available in much of the eastern United States allows the user to snort or sniff the substance like cocaine. In New York, for example, cocaine and heroin are often alternately inhaled, a practice called criss-crossing.

The quality of heroin today also allows it to be smoked. Sniffing or smoking heroin is often preferred over injections now that the fear of contracting HIV or hepatitis from infected needles is so widespread. When heroin is snorted or smoked, peak effects are usually experienced within ten to fifteen minutes.

The effects of heroin depend on the quantity taken, the method of administration, the interval between administrations, the tolerance and dependence of the user, the setting, and the user's expectations. Effects usually wear off in five to eight hours, depending on the user's tolerance. In 1999, heroin-related deaths were rising due to its decreasing price and to the potency of the drug resulting from the significant increases in the purity of Colombian heroin.

Like all narcotics, heroin is a central nervous system depressant. For many users, it promotes mental clouding, dreamlike states, light sleep that may be punctuated by vivid dreams (although the narcotics in general tend to suppress dreaming), and a general feeling of "sublime contentment." The body may become permeated with a feeling of warmth, and the extremities may feel heavy. There is little inclination toward physical activity; the user prefers to sit motionless and in a fog.

Fentanyl, first synthesized in Belgium in the late 1950s (under the trade name Sublimaze), is highly similar to heroin in its biological and psychological effects but may be 100 times more powerful. It is usually administered by intravenous injection, smoked, or snorted.

Heroin and Crime

No other drug family is as closely associated with crime as the narcotics, particularly heroin. The image of the desperate "junkie" looking for a fix is widespread. Furthermore, because of the adverse effects of the drug, it is assumed that the heroin user is bizarre, unpredictable, and therefore dangerous. However, high doses of narcotics produce sleep rather than the psychotic or paranoid panic states sometimes produced by high doses of amphetamines. Therefore, narcotics users rarely become violent or dangerous. Research strongly indicates that addicts do not, as a general rule, participate in violent crimes such as assault, rape, and homicide (Canadian Government's Commission of Inquiry, 1971; National Commission on Marihuana and Drug Abuse, 1973; National Institute on Drug Abuse, 1978; Tinklenberg & Stillman, 1970).

Research evidence does suggest a relationship between heroin addiction and money-producing crime. A study of 573 narcotics users in Miami found that they were responsible for almost 6,000 robberies, 6,700 burglaries, 900 stolen vehicles, 25,000 instances of shoplifting, and 46,000 other incidents of larceny and fraud (Inciardi, 1986). Self-report surveys find that heroin users report financing their habits largely through "acquisitive crime" (Jarvis & Parker, 1989; Mott, 1986). Parker and Newcombe (1987) studied crime patterns and heroin use in the English community of Wirral, located in northwest

England. They found that many heroin users were from the poor sections of the community and were young. The researchers were also able to divide their sample into three groups: (1) the largest group, young offenders who were not known to be using heroin but were highly criminally active; (2) heroin users who engaged in considerable acquisitive crime but were involved in this type of crime prior to their heroin addiction; and (3) heroin users who started engaging in acquisitive crime after developing their habit in order to support the habit. The Parker–Newcombe investigation suggests that some heroin addicts do support their habit through crime.

Ball, Shaffer, and Nurco (1983) found that heroin addicts committed more money-producing crime at times when they were addicted compared to times when they were not. Still, it may be misleading to examine the heroin–crime relationship in isolation without considering the possible interactions between polydrug use and crime or to conclude that heroin addiction causes crime. All we can say with some confidence at this point is that those who use heroin also seem to be deeply involved in money-producing crime. Heroin users, however, may not be driven to crime by the needs of their addiction. Heroin users, particularly polydrug users, may represent a segment of society that runs counter to society's rules and expectations in multiple ways, drug use and larceny among them. It may well be that most heroin-addicted criminals were involved in crime before they became addicted. Research by Faupel (1991) does support this hypothesis. However, studies also suggest that, although many heroin users have criminal records prior to their addiction, their criminal activity increases substantially during periods of heavy drug consumption (Faupel, 1991). Furthermore, polydrug users tend to switch from drug to drug, depending on what is available and inexpensive at the time, and do not seem physiologically desperate for any one particular drug. They simply substitute one drug for the other. Overall, the relationship between heroin use and criminal behavior is a complex one and varies throughout the addict's career.

Other Narcotic Drugs

Other drugs that are often classified as narcotics include thebaine, codeine, morphine, hydromorphone, oxycodone, and hydrocodone. Thebaine is chemically similar to both morphine and codeine but generally produces a high rather than depressant effects. It is considered a Schedule II drug. Hydromorphone (Dilaudid) is a powerful analgesic that is sold in tablet or injectable forms as a painkiller and may substitute for heroin or morphine. Oxycodone is similar to codeine but more powerful. It is often marketed in combination with aspirin (Percodan) or acetaminophen (Percocet) for the relief of pain. Hydrocodone is an orally active analgesic slightly less powerful than morphine.

Although oxycodone products have seen illicit abuse for the 30 years, the oxycodone derivative OxyContin has been used frequently in recent years. Oxy-Contin is a prescription painkiller used to control mild to moderate pain and was first medically marketed in 1995. It was originally available in 10-, 40-, and

80-mg tablets, but in July 2000 a 160-mg tablet became available (National Drug Intelligence Center, 2001). By comparison, Percocet and Tylox contain 5 mg of oxycodone and Percodan-Demi contains just 2.25 mg, and their effects are much shorter-lasting. The drug is chemically classified as an opiate agonist because it provides pain relief by acting on opioid receptors in the spinal cord and brain. It usually comes in the form of a time-release tablet and acts for 12 hour, making it the longest-lasting oxycodone on the market. The pharmacological effects of OxyContin are highly similar to those of heroin, and consequently it tends to attract the same abuser population (National Drug Intelligence Center, 2001). OxyContin is designed to be swallowed whole, but abusers take the drug in a number of ways. They most often chew the tablets or crush them and snort the powder.

According to the National Survey on Drug Use and Health, 1.3% of eighth graders and 4% of high school seniors reported using OxyContin during 2002 (Substance Abuse and Mental Health Services Administration, 2003). Most users tend to be over 30 years old, however. Crimes related to OxyContin are usually nonviolent, and most are burglary, larceny, and other property crimes (Office of National Drug Control Policy, 2002a). The illegal diversion, distribution, and abuse of the drug appear to be concentrated most heavily in the eastern regions of the United States (National Drug Intelligence Center, 2001).

OxyContin abuse has led to a significant increase in the number of pharmacy robberies, thefts, fraudulent prescriptions, and health care fraud incidents (National Drug Intelligence Center, 2001). It is also obtained through what is called "doctor shopping" and improper prescription practices by physicians. Doctor shopping refers to individuals visiting numerous doctors, sometimes in several states, to acquire large amounts of the drug to use or sell to others.

THE DEPRESSANTS

GHB and Rohypnol: The Club Drugs

Rohypnol and gamma-hydroxybutyrate (GHB) are both central nervous system depressants. They are called "club drugs" because they are most often consumed at teenage or young adult nightclubs, raves, or parties.

GHB (also known as "liquid ecstasy," "scoop," "liquid X," "grievous bodily harm," or "Georgia home boy") is a powerful and fast-acting drug most often taken by young users as a pleasure enhancer that produces a rapid state of intoxication. It is usually consumed orally, either as grainy, white- or sandy-colored powder that is often dissolved in alcohol or as a liquid sold in small bottles. GHB is produced primarily in clandestine laboratories and consequently there is no guarantee of quality or purity, making its psychoactive effects unpredictable. The drug can be easily produced by combining gamma-butyrolactone (GBL) with either potassium hydroxide or sodium hydroxide in a container. Recipes or kits for making GHB are sold over the Internet. GHB is also marketed as an antidepressant that suppresses feelings of depression and anxiety, and is promoted and sold on the Internet as such. Prior to 1990, the drug was freely available in health food stores across the United States. In 1990 the Federal Drug Administration (FDA) banned GHB and does not approve the drug for any use at the present time. However, a pharmaceutical formulation of the drug is currently being developed for the treatment of cataplexy, a serious and debilitating disease.

Psychoactive effects of GHB begin within 15 to 30 minutes after consumption and, depending on the purity and dosage, may last as long as six hours. It is often used in conjunction with other drugs, especially alcohol. GHB has many severe and unpredictable side effects, such as nausea, drowsiness, vomiting, delusions, depression, vertigo (dizziness), hallucinations, seizures, respiratory distress, loss of consciousness, slowed heart rate, lowered blood pressure, amnesia, and coma (see **Table 12–9**) (Office of National Drug Control Policy, 1999a). It also interferes with circulation, motor coordination, and balance, and at higher doses (two to four grams), it produces considerable problems in motor and speech control. At these high doses GHB usually produces a very deep sleep, resembling a coma. The drug also produces anterograde amnesia, a condition in which events that occur during the time a person is under the drug's influence are forgotten. In addition, the drug has increasingly been involved in poisonings, overdoses, and fatalities (National Institute on Drug Abuse, 1999).

GHB is tasteless and odorless and mixes easily with alcohol or any nonalcoholic drink. Because it can be mixed with food and drinks without detection, and because of its ability to sedate and intoxicate unsuspecting victims, GHB has been connected to crime in recent years. It is sometimes used in the commission of sexual assault, and it often plays a role in "date rape." It is also used in some instances to pave the way for robbing heavily sedated or unconscious victims.

Because of its increasing use in sexual assaults, the Date-Rape Drug Prohibition Act of 2000 (also known as the Hillary J. Farias and Samantha Reid Date Drug Prohibition Act of 2000) was enacted in January of 2000, specifically to target GHB. Congress found that the abuse of illicit GHB was an imminent hazard to public safety and moved to amend the federal Controlled

TABLE 12–9   Estimated Number of Emergency Department GHB Cases, 1994–2001

	YEAR							
	1994	1995	1996	1997	1998	1999	2000	2001
Total	86	146	638	762	1,282	3,178	4,469	3,340

Source: Office of National Drug Control Policy (2002c).

Substances Act to include the drug as an illegal substance. The act also established a special unit of the Drug Enforcement Administration to assess the abuse of and trafficking in GHB, Rohypnol, ketamine, other controlled substances, and other so-called "designer drugs" whose use has been associated with sexual assault.

The Drug Induced Rape Prevention and Punishment Act of 1996 was enacted into federal law specifically in response to the use of Rohypnol (generic name, flunitrazepam), another club drug that can be used to sexually assault incapacitated individuals. It can mentally and physically incapacitate the victim. The law makes it a crime to give someone a controlled substance without his or her knowledge and with the intent to commit a crime. The law further imposes a penalty of up to 20 years for the distribution and importation of one gram or more of Rohypnol. Simple possession is punishable by up to 3 years in prison and a fine.

Since 1999, Rohypnol tablets have been manufactured to turn blue in a drink to increase visibility and thus be more visually detectable to potential victims (Office of National Drug Control Policy, 2003a). However, the uncolored tablets are still on the market. Furthermore, persons who intend to commit a sexual assault may try to serve blue tropical drinks and punches so that the blue dye can be hidden.

Slang names for Rohypnol include date-rape drug, circles, roofies, Mexican valium, roach-2, forget-me drug, forget pill, or wolfies. Rohypnol is popular among youth because of its low cost, usually less than $5 to $10 per tablet (Office of National Drug Control Policy, 2003a). Rohypnol can be ground into a powder and snorted. Similar to GHB, Rohypnol is tasteless and odorless and can be dissolved in liquids, though not as easily as GHB. It is also sometimes used by bodybuilders for its alleged anabolic effects. It can be taken orally, snorted, or injected. It is often combined with alcohol or used as a remedy for the depression that often follows a stimulant high. The effects of Rohypnol usually begin about 15 minutes after administration and may last for more than 12 hours. In addition, the drug is detectable in urine for up to 72 hours after ingestion (Office of National Drug Control Policy, 2003a).

Lower doses of Rohypnol can cause muscle relaxation. At higher doses, it can cause loss of muscle control, loss of consciousness, and, when combined with alcohol, anterograde amnesia. When combined with alcohol, as is often done, it can be deadly. Chemically, the drug is similar to Valium but 10 times more powerful. Rohypnol is legally manufactured in over 80 countries as a prescribed sedative for the short-term treatment of severe sleep disorders, especially in Europe, but it is neither manufactured nor approved for sale in the United States.

Ketamine, a tranquilizer most often used legitimately by veterinarians on animals, has also recently been found at parties. It produces hallucinatory effects similar to those of PCP and LSD. Ketamine has gained popularity in the past 5 to 10 years and can be produced as a liquid or a powder. The liquid form can be injected, mixed into drinks, or added to smokable materials. The user's senses, judgment, and coordination may be affected for up to 18 to 24 hours after initial use. It carries slang names such as jet, super acid, cat Valium, and honey oil.

The benzodiazepines include chlordiazepoxide (Librium), diazepam (Valium), oxazepam (Serax), and chlorazepate dipotassium (Tranxene), all of which are marketed legally and prescribed as antianxiety tranquilizers or to treat muscle spasms or convulsions. The most common side effects are confusion, drowsiness, and loss of coordination. Table 12–1 points out that 9% of arrestees in the United States and 8.2% of arrestees in England tested positive for benzodiazepines at the time of their arrest.

LSD, commonly referred to as "acid," was first discovered in 1938 at the Sandoz Laboratories in Switzerland. It was marketed initially as a circulatory and respiratory stimulant and later used as a research drug in investigating the causes of schizophrenia. The drug is manufactured from lysergic acid, which is found on the fungus that grows on rye and other grains. It is sold on the street in capsule, tablet, or liquid form. According to the DEA (2003), LSD is the most potent hallucinogen known to science, as well as the most highly studied.

The average effective dose is from 20 to 80 micrograms, which may last for several hours. LSD is often sold in the form of impregnated paper (blotter acid), typically imprinted with colorful graphic designs (DEA, 2003). It has also been manufactured in the form of small tablets (microdots), thin squares of gelatin (window panes), and sugar cubes. The drug is primarily produced on the West Coast, particularly in San Francisco, northern California, and the Pacific Northwest. The production of LSD is complex and time-consuming and requires considerable chemical knowledge.

The effects of LSD are unpredictable and, similarly to those of marijuana, depend on the amount taken, the social environment during ingestion, and the user's personality, expectations, and mood. LSD is not considered an addictive drug, however, since it does not produce compulsive drug-seeking behavior as do cocaine, amphetamine, and heroin (Office of National Drug Control Policy, 2003c).

According to the most recent National Survey on Drug Use and Health (Department of Health and Human Services, 2003), 112,000 Americans aged 12 and older were current LSD users during 2002. Of those surveyed, 10.4% reported using LSD at least once in their lifetime. Most of these users were in the 18 to 25 age group.

Inhalants

The term **inhalant** refers to a thousand or more different household and commercial products that can be abused by sniffing or "huffing" (inhaling though the mouth) for an intoxicating effect. They are found in organic solvents and volatile substances commonly found in adhesives, lighter fluids, cleaning solutions, paint products, and even Wite-Out. The effects of inhalants are usually highly similar to alcohol intoxication, including slurred speech, loss of motor coordination, distortion of perceptions, headache, vomiting, and nausea. Wheezing may be apparent, and in some instances a rash around the glue sniffer's nose and mouth may be evident. While not regulated nationwide, at this writing 37 states have placed restrictions on the sale of these products to minors. Some states have introduced fines, incarceration, or mandatory treatment for the sale, distribution, use, and/or possession of inhalable substances.

Studies have estimated that between 5% and 15% of young people in the United States have tried inhalants (U.S. Department of Justice, 1998), but they are not considered "gateway drugs" that lead to chronic abuse of more powerful illicit drugs. The real danger of inhalants is their potential side effects. Chronic use of inhalants can produce kidney abnormalities and liver damage, and in rare cases heart failure or fatal breathing difficulties may occur.

Alcohol

Despite the public concern over heroin, opium, marijuana, cocaine, and the amphetamines, the number one drug of abuse has been and continues to be alcohol (ethanol, ethyl alcohol, grain alcohol). According to the 2002 National Survey on Drug Use and Health (University of Michigan, 2003), about half of Americans age 12 and older had used alcohol in the past month (51% of the entire population). This represents over 120 million people. About 22.9 million engaged in binge drinking (five or more drinks on at least one occasion in the past month) and about 15.9 million were heavy drinkers (drinking five or more drinks per occasion on 5 or more days in the past 30 days). Approximately 10.7 million of the binge drinkers were between 12 and 20 years of age, and 1.9 million of this age group were heavy drinkers. Men are more likely to be binge drinkers than women (22.8% and 8.7%, respectively), and they are also more likely to be heavy drinkers (9.3% and 1.9%, respectively). An estimated 8 of 10 persons age 12 or older have used alcohol at some point in their lives and half describe themselves as current users (Greenfeld, 1998). About 1 in 18 persons age 18 or older report consuming two or more drinks per day (Greenfeld, 1998) (see **Table 12–10**).

TABLE 12–10   Self-Reported Alcohol Use as a Function of Age

AGE	ALCOHOL USE (%)	
	EVER	CURRENT
12 or older	82	52
12–17	41	21
18–25	84	61
26–34	90	63
35 or older	87	53

Source: Greenfeld (1998, p. 8).

TABLE 12–11   Percentage of Drivers in Fatal Accidents Who Were Intoxicated, 1986 and 1996

AGE	1986 (%)	1996 (%)
All drivers	25.8	18.8
16–20	23.7	14.1
21–24	36.1	27.0
25–34	33.0	26.2
35–44	24.5	21.9
45–64	16.2	13.6
65 or older	6.8	5.4

Source: Greenfeld (1998, p. 13).

Alcohol is responsible for more deaths and violence (it is the third major cause of death) than all other drugs combined. About one in seven Americans age 12 or older drove under the influence of alcohol at least once in the 12 months prior to the National Survey on Drug Use and Health (University of Michigan, 2003). In addition, an estimated 10,000 intoxicated drivers were involved in motor vehicle accidents resulting in 13,400 deaths in 1996 (Greenfeld, 1998). However, motor vehicle death due to alcohol intoxication has steadily decreased in recent years, as have the arrests for DUI nationwide. In 1983, DUI arrests were made for 1 of every 80 licensed drivers, whereas in 1996 the rate had dropped to 1 arrest for every 122 licensed drivers. In addition, rates of intoxication among drivers have declined for every age group between 1986 and 1996. In 1986 an estimated 26% of drivers involved in fatal accidents had a blood alcohol concentration (BAC) of at least 0.10 gram per deciliter, while in 1996 about 19% were estimated to have a BAC at this level (Greenfeld, 1998) (see **Tables 12–11** and **12–12**).

Psychological Effects.   The social, psychological, and physical effects of excessive alcohol use can be just as destructive to the individual, his or her

TABLE 12–12   Blood Alcohol Concentrations (BAC) of Drivers Involved in Fatal Accidents

BAC	PERCENTAGE OF FATAL ACCIDENTS (%)
0	58.6
0.26–0.29	4.7
0.26–0.30	1.9
0.26–0.31	2.4
0.26–0.32	17.2
0.26–0.33	9.1
0.26–0.34	3.5
0.30	2.6

Source: Greenfeld (1998, p. 15).

family, and society in general as heroin abuse. And similar to the heroin addict, the alcoholic can develop a strong psychological and physical dependence on the drug. Society's attitudes toward alcohol are dramatically different from its attitudes toward other drugs of abuse, however. In virtually every part of the United States, alcohol is legal and it is socially acceptable to consume it. In public, drinking behavior is generally unregulated unless it involves heavy intoxication and correspondingly unacceptable conduct, like disturbing the peace or operating a motor vehicle. In private, one can get as drunk as one wishes, a privilege not granted with respect to other drugs.

The effects of alcohol are complex, and we can provide only a cursory treatment here. At low doses (two or four ounces of whiskey, for example) alcohol seems to act as a stimulant on the central nervous system. Initially, it appears to affect the inhibitory chemical process of nervous system transmission, producing feelings of euphoria, good cheer, and social and physical warmth. In moderate and high quantities, however, alcohol begins to depress the excitatory processes of the central nervous system, as well as its inhibitory processes.

Consequently, individuals' neuromuscular coordination and visual acuity are reduced, and they perceive pain and fatigue. The ability to concentrate is also impaired. Very often, self-confidence increases and intoxicated individuals become more daring, sometimes foolishly so. It is believed that alcohol at moderate levels begins to "numb" the higher brain centers that process cognitive information, especially judgment and abstract thought. It should be emphasized at this point that the levels of intoxication are not necessarily dependent on the amount of alcohol ingested; as for other psychoactive drugs, the effects depend on a myriad of interacting variables.

Alcohol and Crime

The belief that alcohol is a major cause of crime appears to be deeply embedded in American society. Surveys, for example, suggest that over 50% of the population is convinced that alcohol is a major factor in crimes of violence (Critchlow, 1986). This pervasive belief appears to be based on the premise that alcohol instigates aggressive conduct in some individuals or somehow diminishes the checks and balances of nonaggressive, nonviolent behavior.

J. C. Coleman (1976) calls alcohol a "catalyst for violence," noting that about one of every three arrests in the United States results from alcohol abuse. The percentage reported years ago by Coleman appears to remain largely the same today. About 36% of the 5.3 million convicted adult offenders under the jurisdiction of probation authorities, jails, prisons, or parole agencies in 1996 had been drinking at the time of the offenses for which they had been convicted (Greenfeld, 1998). Roizen (1997), in summarizing the research on alcohol and violence, found that up to 86% of homicide offenders had been drinking at the time of the offense. Roizen further discovered that 60% of sexual offenders, 37% of assault offenders, 57% of males in marital violence, and 13% of child abusers had also been drinking at the time of the

TABLE 12–13   Percentage of Offenders Drinking at the Time of the Offense, 1996

OFFENSES	ADULTS ON PROBATION	CONVICTED OFFENDERS (%)		
		IN LOCAL JAILS	IN STATE PRISONS	IN FEDERAL PRISONS
All	39.9	39.5	32.3	11.0
Violent	40.7	40.6	37.5	20.4
Property	18.5	32.8	31.8	8.1
Drug	16.3	28.8	18.0	8.2
Public	75.1	56.0	43.0	13.1

Source: Greenfeld (1998, p. 21).

crime. **Table 12–13** identifies the percentage of adult offenders who admitted to drinking at the time of their offense (in 1996). Outside of public order crimes, a higher percentage of offenders reported drinking at the time of violent offenses than during the other offense categories. About 7 of 10 alcohol-involved incidents of violence occurred in a residence, and most of the incidents (about two-thirds) are simple assaults. In addition, two-thirds of victims who suffered violence by an intimate reported that alcohol had been a factor. Ninety percent of alcohol-involved incidents of violence occur off campus (Greenfeld, 1998).

In summary, the evidence is quite clear that approximately one-third of all offenders who commit violent crime were drinking at the time of offense, and many were highly intoxicated. In an up-to-date, extensive literature review, Reiss and Roth (1993, p. 185) conclude, "In studies of prison inmates, those classified as 'heavy' or 'problem' drinkers had accumulated more previous arrests for violent crime, and reported higher average frequencies of assaults than did other inmates." And the National Institute on Alcohol Abuse and Alcoholism (1990, p. 92) asserts, "In both animals and human studies, alcohol more than any other drug, has been linked with a high incidence of violence and aggression." However, the link does not automatically mean that alcohol causes violence. It is most likely that under the influence of alcohol, individuals prone to be aggressive, violent, and antisocial are more likely to be more aggressive, violent, and antisocial. Alcohol may *facilitate* their aggressive tendencies. The available evidence does not allow cogent conclusions that alcohol makes normally nonviolent people act violently.

While the relationship between alcohol and violence has long been suspected, the landmark study by Wolfgang (1958) on 588 Philadelphia homicides brought the alcohol–violence relationship into clear focus and stamped it with some scientific confirmation. The Wolfgang survey reported that in 9% of the homicides, the victims had been drinking alcohol at the time of the offense; 11% of the offenders had been drinking. More important, however, in an additional 44% of the cases, alcohol was present in both the offender and the victim. The Wolfgang findings suggest that some violence-prone people become volatile under the influence of alcohol and that the danger increases greatly when both parties have been drinking. Research does continue to support the *relationship* between alcohol consumption and violence.

A high BAC has been consistently reported in about 50% of homicide victims (e.g., Bensing & Schroeder, 1960; Bowden, Wilson, & Turner, 1958; Cleveland, 1955; Fisher, 1951; Spain, Bradess, & Eggson, 1951; Verkko, 1951; Wilentz, 1953). In one study (Welte & Abel, 1989), 46% of the homicide victims had ingested significant amounts of alcohol, and many, substantial amounts. Specifically, 70% had BAC levels higher than 0.10. This was especially the case for victims involved in fight-related homicides. The high BAC–victim connection, however, should not be read as simply supporting the conclusion that most victims precipitate their own demise. Although this may be the case in a proportion of violent events, the relationship should also be viewed as underscoring the importance of the social context within which violence occurs. Violence frequently occurs in social situations where drinking is heavy, physiological arousal is high (such as anger), interpersonal conflict is evident, and cognitive processes—especially judgment and abstract reasoning—are impaired.

Research in the psychology laboratory also finds strong evidence that drinking alcohol *facilitates* physical aggression. In some laboratory experiments, subjects have been placed in a variety of conditions (independent variables) and allowed to administer "electric shock" (simulated) to another person (the amount and frequency of the shock being the dependent variable). The independent variable could be the drug conditions were to which subjects were randomly assigned (e.g., drug conditions; placebo conditions, in which subjects believed they were receiving a drug but were not; and nondrug conditions, in which believed subjects believe they were not receiving a drug and were not). To create another common independent variable, researchers placed subjects into aroused (usually anger) and nonaroused conditions.

Research using these paradigms has consistently found that drinking alcohol facilitates aggression, measured by shocking behavior (S. Taylor & Leonard, 1983; S. Taylor & Sears, 1988). Furthermore, as the quantity of alcohol consumed increases, so does the tendency to be aggressive, at least up to the point when the subject "passes out." We return to these two findings shortly.

It should be mentioned that the alcohol–violence connection appears to be strongest in the United States, even though the amount of alcohol consumption in this country is by no means the highest in the world. Many countries, including France, Italy, Spain, West Germany, Portugal, and Russia, consume substantially more alcohol per capita than the United States. In addition to obvious cultural differences between the countries, drinking patterns are also different. In some countries, alcohol consumption is spread out across the day, including mealtimes, whereas in the United States drinking is generally reserved for the end of the day, particularly during weekends and holidays. It appears to be this episodic heavy-drinking pattern that is most strongly related to aggression, violence, and antisocial behavior. Interestingly, research indicates that rates of violence associated with alcohol consumption are among the highest in the world in Russia (Pridemore, 2002).

The relationship between episodic heavy drinking of alcohol and aggression or violence is well supported, but how is it explained? Many models and theories have been proposed during the past 20 years, but a majority can be subsumed into two major categories: *disinhibitory models* and *social-cognitive models*. Disinhibitory models contend that alcohol, directly or indirectly, influences neurological or psychological mechanisms that normally control aggressive and antisocial behavior. One disinhibitory perspective hypothesizes that alcohol chemically influences the portion of the brain that controls the expression of aggression. The more intoxicated the person, the less control he or she has of his or her behavior. Another disinhibitory perspective, and by far the most popular in American society, supposes that certain people have a particular sensitivity or susceptibility to alcohol. This perspective views problem drinking as a biological abnormality or disease. This approach, known as the "American disease model" (W. Miller & Hester, 1989), is deeply entrenched in American society and forms the fundamental assumption of Alcoholics Anonymous (AA). Polls show, for example, that 79% of Americans believe that alcoholism is a disease that requires medical treatment (Peele, 1984). The disease conception is not confined to the United States, however. Seventy percent of the general public in Scotland are also convinced that alcoholism is a disease (Crawford & Heather, 1987). The basic AA version is that chronic problem drinking is a disease reflected in an individual's inability to control alcoholic drinking, a disease that exists within the individual even before the first drink is taken. Furthermore, "The condition is irreversible and progressive and requires complete and utter abstinence" (Peele, 1984, p. 1339).

All disinhibitory models assume that alcohol has the power to disinhibit impulses that are normally held in check, and consequently this disinhibition may result in drink-induced criminal behavior (Critchlow, 1986). Furthermore, alcohol also provides a powerful excuse for undesirable behaviors that are often accompanied by such pleas as "I couldn't help myself" or "Alcohol always does this to me." Peele (1984, p. 1348) writes, "Disease conceptions may be alluring to our contemporary society because they are congruent with general ideas about the self and personal responsibility. Alcoholism viewed as an uncontrollable urge is after all part of a larger trend in which premenstrual tension, drug use and drug withdrawal, eating junk foods, and lovesickness are presented as defenses for murder." It should be noted, though, that such defenses to criminal conduct are rarely successful.

While disinhibitory viewpoints focus on internal influences or predispositions, social–cognitive models emphasize the interactions between subjective belief systems or expectancies and the social environment. They reject the disease or loss of control assumptions of disinhibitory models. Social–cognitive models argue that problem drinking and many of the psychoactive influences of alcohol are learned and situationally determined. The contention that one cannot help oneself or that alcohol directly instigates a loss of control is a subjective, cognitive expectancy that feeds on itself, rather than a disease. A person's expectations or cognitions influence how he or she responds to alcohol. Alcohol serves as a cue for acting intoxicated and doing things one normally would not do or acting the way one believes alcohol makes one act.

There is considerable empirical support for social–cognitive models of drinking behavior and actually very little empirical support for disinhibitory models. For example, disinhibitory models advocate total abstinence if alcoholic-prone people are to control themselves, otherwise "one drink leads to one drunk." However, a large body of research shows that the most effective treatment for heavy drinkers is to train them to be responsible light to moderate drinkers rather than have them abstain completely over their lifespans (see Peele, 1984). Research continually shows that total abstinence has a poor track record over the long haul, especially for younger single men, since the abstinence requirement does not dovetail with their lifestyles and the opportunities and pressures to drink that they face (Peele, 1984).

Among the proponents of social–cognitive theory are Marlatt and Rohsenow (1980) and Lang and his colleagues (Lang, Goeckner, Adesso, & Marlatt, 1975), who found that the amount of alcohol consumed may not be as important as what the person expects from the drug. Independent of the pharmacological effects, some people expect to become giddy, or loud, or boisterous after one or more drinks. Some anticipate acting more aggressively under the influence, because alcohol is "supposed" to have that effect. According to Lang, if a person expects alcohol to influence behavior in a preconceived way, it probably will. Moreover, as mentioned earlier, the person avoids blame for some of his or her actions, because society tends to accept the "I was drunk" explanation. In fact, Sobell and Sobell (1973) suggested that one of the rewarding aspects of heavy drinking is that it provides a socially acceptable excuse for engaging in inappropriate behavior.

In Lang and colleagues' (1975) experiment, half of the subjects were told they would be drinking alcohol, which actually was either vodka or tonic water. The other half were told they would be drinking tonic water, not alcohol. However, half the members in this second group were actually given vodka, and the other half received the tonic water they expected. Results indicated that "the only significant determinant of aggression was the expectation factor; subjects who believed they had consumed alcohol were more aggressive than subjects who believed they had consumed a nonalcoholic beverage, regardless of the actual alcohol content of the drinks administered" (p. 508).

According to social–cognitive theory, therefore, the consumer's expectancy becomes the crucial factor. As long as consumers believe they drank alcohol, they expect to feel intoxicated. Furthermore, being "intoxicated," they tend to feel less responsible for their behavior, including violent or criminal behavior. Interestingly, convicted murderers who were intoxicated during the crime often claim they cannot remember the incident at all (Schacter, 1986a). Whether these claims of amnesia are genuine remains very much in doubt.

Critchlow (1986) asserts that the pharmacological action of alcohol cannot account for the many transformations in social behavior that occur when people drink, as those transformations vary widely from culture to culture and in the same culture across time periods. She argues that the effects of alcohol on social behavior are found largely at the cultural level. Expectations about what alcohol can do behaviorally can be learned through a particular culture by anyone, even before taking the first drink. Critchlow writes the following:

> On a cultural level, it seems to be the negative consequences of alcohol that hold the most powerful sway over our thinking. . . . Thus, by believing that alcohol makes people act badly, we give it a great deal of power. Drinking becomes a tool that legitimates irrationality and excuses violence without permanently destroying an individual's moral standing or society's systems of rules and ethics. (pp. 761–762)

While cognitive expectancies play an extremely important role, we should not downplay the pharmacological effects of alcohol. Alcohol does affect the neurochemistry of the central nervous system by depressing many functions. Anyone who has tried to act sober with marginal success, no matter how hard they tried, can attest to this effect. Research confirms that alcohol has a strong pharmacological effect on behavior, somewhat independent of subjective expectancies. For example, Shuntich and Taylor (1972) found that actually intoxicated subjects were more aggressive than both subjects who consumed a placebo beverage (thinking they had consumed alcohol) and subjects who did not consume any beverage. Zeichner and Pihl (1979, 1980) also found that subjects in a nonalcohol condition were as aggressive as placebo subjects who thought they had consumed alcohol.

Social–cognitive theory also predicts that the amount of alcohol consumed should make little difference in overall behavior. If subjects believe they are consuming large amounts, they will, correspondingly, act more intoxicated (and hence more aggressive). If, on the other hand, they do not believe they have consumed much alcohol, even though they actually have, they will be less aggressive and less likely to act intoxicated. In other words, the misled subjects will behave at the level of aggressiveness that corresponds with their expectations, regardless of the amount of alcohol they consume.

In evaluating this implication, a series of studies by Stuart Taylor and his associates (Taylor & Gammon, 1975; Taylor, Gammon, & Capasso, 1976; Taylor, Schmutte, Leonard, & Cranston, 1979; Taylor et al., 1976) is instructive. The Taylor projects found that low doses of alcohol (e.g., 0.5 ounce of vodka or bourbon per 40 pounds of body weight) tend to inhibit aggression, while larger doses (1.5 ounces per 40 pounds) tend to facilitate aggression. Therefore, depending on the amount, alcohol may either inhibit or facilitate expressions of aggression and violence.

The Taylor experiments are in agreement with the known pharmacological effects of alcohol. In small amounts, alcohol appears to stimulate the central nervous system, generating mild euphoria and a sense of well-being. This good cheer becomes readily apparent at a party, when, after the first round of drinks, people tend to take on a happy frame of mind. As alcoholic intake increases, however, the integrating functions of the cortex are depressed, causing some disorganization and impairment of complex cognitive functions. At extreme levels of intoxication, even simple cognitive processes like attention and sustained concentration break down, eventually ending in stupor and sleep. Therefore, violent behavior, if it is to occur, will most likely occur at moderate levels of intoxication.

In the Taylor investigation, when subjects were informed that they would be consuming alcohol, aggression was positively related only to the amount of alcohol actually consumed, not to the amount they thought they had consumed (S. Taylor & Gammon, 1975). In a later study (S. Taylor et al., 1976), subjects were informed that they would be consuming one of three drugs: alcohol, marijuana, or a tranquilizer. Therefore, all subjects within each group had the same drug expectancy. They then received either a high or a low dose of THC or alcohol. The results demonstrated that the high dose of alcohol facilitated aggression, while the high dose of THC suppressed it.

Overall, Taylor's data strongly suggest that the aggression demonstrated by intoxicated subjects is a joint function of the pharmacological state produced by alcohol and cognitive and situational factors. The researchers maintain that alcohol consumption by itself does not produce aggressive behavior (S. Taylor & Leonard, 1983). Physiological effects of alcohol do influence behavior, but they also interact with expectancies and with what is happening in the person's environment at any given time.

Emotions may be important also. Jaffe, Babor, and Fishbein (1988) observe that alcoholics exhibit more aggressive, violent behavior than do nonalcoholics, especially when drinking. Beyond this, however, the researchers also noted that alcoholics frequently report highly negative emotions when drinking, such as anger and depression. They concluded, "Thus it is possible that when these states are experienced by alcoholics with a prior history of aggressive behavior, the likelihood of alcohol-related aggression increases and such behavior can be predicted with some degree of reliability" (p. 217). Similarly, unhappy or depressive thoughts presumably activate other negative memories and feelings and therefore are likely to promote aggressive, violent inclinations (Berkowitz & Heimer, 1989).

Situational factors are crucial. In all of Taylor's studies, aggression was not automatically produced by alcohol, even alcohol in large amounts. Rather, subjects were provoked, were threatened, or at least were in the presence of aggressive cues before they displayed aggressive behavior. Therefore, in order for aggression to occur, there must be provocative, incitive, or instigative cues along with intoxication. Something or someone must anger, threaten, or in some other way arouse the intoxicated subject. But external cues are certainly not the whole story. Internal cues, such as thoughts, beliefs, or even imagined slights or provocations can serve as instigating cues for aggressive or violent behavior.

········➤ ### SUMMARY AND CONCLUSIONS

This chapter has reviewed the relationship between crime and a number of drugs commonly associated with criminal behavior. Four major drug categories were identified: (1) the hallucinogens, (2) the stimulants, (3) the opiate narcotics, and (4) the sedative–hypnotics. Rather than discuss most of the drugs in each category, we considered only those commonly believed to be connected with criminal conduct. Moreover, we did not examine the crimes of drug distribution or possession. We are mainly concerned with whether the substance itself facilitates or instigates illegal action, especially violence, and what damage the drug does to the user. In other words, are persons under the influence of marijuana more violent than they are normally? And how does marijuana affect the health of users? Or, to what extent does alcohol directly contribute to loss of control or reduce self-regulatory mechanisms?

Cannabis, which includes marijuana and hashish, is a relatively mild hallucinogen with few psychological or physiological side effects. No significant relationship between cannabis use and crime has been consistently reported in the research literature. If anything, marijuana seems to reduce the likelihood of violence, since its psychoactive ingredient, THC, induces muscle weakness and promotes feelings of lethargy.

Amphetamines and cocaine (especially crack) represented the stimulant group. Most illegal users do not participate in crime other than the possession or sale of these drugs. Similar to marijuana, amphetamines are plentiful and inexpensive. However, there are some documented cases in which heavy users of amphetamines entered psychological states that presumably predisposed them to violence and paranoia. In addition, several studies have found correlations between violent offenders and a history of amphetamine abuse. As in all correlations, however, it is difficult to determine what contributes to what. Chronic amphetamine use has potential dangerous side effects if used improperly or used in combination with other drugs of abuse. Cocaine, a natural drug that grows only in certain parts of the world, has traditionally been quite expensive. In recent years, the drug has become widely available and its cost less prohibitive. There is no hard evidence, however, that cocaine generally renders one more violent, more out of control, or more likely to engage in property crimes.

We discussed heroin as the representative of the opiate narcotics. Like most other narcotics, heroin appears to be highly addictive, particularly in the sense that it creates a strong psychological dependency. Narcotics in general are so addictive and so expensive that substantial funds are needed to support a user's habit. Thus, some researchers have found a moderate correlation between narcotics and various income-generating crimes. On the other hand, others have noted that most addicts turned to drugs after they had developed criminal patterns.

Of all the drugs reviewed, alcohol—representing the sedative–hypnotic group—shows the strongest relationship with violent offenses, such as rape, homicide, and assault. At intermediate and high levels, alcohol appears to impair or disrupt the brain operations responsible for self-control. Alcohol may also impair information processing, thereby leading a person to misjudge social cues and encouraging overreactions to a perceived threat. However, it is likely that violent behavior associated with alcohol use is a joint function of pharmacological effects, cognitive expectancies, and situational influences. If the individual expects that alcohol will make him or her act aggressively, and if the social environment provides appropriate cues, aggression or violent behavior will be facilitated. The National Institute on Alcohol Abuse and Alcoholism (1997) concluded in its extensive review of the relevant research literature that "alcohol apparently may increase the risk of violent behavior only for certain individuals or subpopulations and only under some situations and social/ cultural influences" (p. 4). Furthermore, the National Institute noted, "intoxication alone does not cause violence" (p. 2). However, the relationship between alcohol consumption and violence is a strong one in Western civilization. The Panel on the Understanding and Control of Violent Behavior concludes "For at least the past several decades, alcohol drinking—by the perpetrator of a crime, the victim, or both—has immediately preceded at least half of all violent events, including murders, in the sample studied by researchers" (J. Roth, 1996, p. 3). While the relationship between alcohol and violence clearly exists, the nature of that relationship is largely unknown. Does alcohol cause violence, or are violent people drawn to alcohol? No drug *directly causes* violence simply through its pharmacological action (Morgan & Zimmer, 1997).

In conclusion, the relationships between crime and all the drugs discussed in this chapter are complex, involving interactions among numerous pharmacological, social, and psychological variables. Research is beginning to ease some data out of the complexity, but additional studies employing well-designed methodology are greatly needed to understand the many possible influences of psychoactive drugs on human behavior, particularly criminal behavior.

At this point in our knowledge, substance abuse appears to be more of a health problem to those who use drugs rather than a "crime problem." This conclusion reflects the continuing controversy over the "right" public policy to adopt with respect to drugs. Although this chapter has not focused on the residual effects of the nation's war on drugs—such as its effect on families, minority groups, prison populations, and individual civil liberties—these effects cannot be ignored. From the psychological perspective, it is unlikely that drugs "cause" people to engage in criminal activity. On the other hand, some drugs clearly allow some people to disengage from their usual constraints against antisocial conduct, including violence. Individuals who are chronic, persistent criminals often are polydrug users, but again it is unlikely that the drugs they ingest directly cause them to engage in criminal activity. It is more likely they were criminally prone prior to and independent of polydrug use.

CHAPTER 13

CORRECTIONAL PSYCHOLOGY

s we have seen throughout this text, people who commit crime do so for a wide range of reasons and display a very broad range of behaviors. Even when we concentrate on the persistent, serious offender—as we have tended to do here—there is wide variability and no "typical" criminal. Persistent offenders engage in various crimes in a variety of ways for a variety of reasons, and they come from divergent social, psychological, neurological, and biological backgrounds. Correctional psychology, the subfield of psychology that is the topic of this chapter, must be highly attuned to these many nuances of criminal behavior. Correctional psychologists consult with the correctional system, provide direct services to persons convicted of crime, and conduct research on psychological issues relevant to prisons, jails, and community corrections.

This chapter deals exclusively with correctional psychology in adult settings. It should be realized, though, that many psychologists consult with and work in juvenile corrections, where they are faced with different challenges. Although we discussed treatment of juveniles briefly in Chapter 2, we by no means were able to present a comprehensive picture of that very important process. Therefore, readers are urged to review other sources for information on juvenile corrections (e.g., Ashford et al., 2001; Bartol & Bartol, 2004a; Grisso & Schwartz, 2000).

Despite our assertion that there is no typical criminal, some generalizations can be made, as long as we recognize that there are always exceptions.

We have learned, for example, that the antisocial behavior of persistent offenders—who comprise a good percentage of the population in jails and prisons—often begins early in life. Some demonstrate a discernible pattern of going against the environment as early as the first grade, ranging from lying, stealing, and truancy to bullying and frequent fighting with peers. Most of the time these early offenders are male. They are often disliked and socially rejected by a majority of their peers, who are not interested in opposing the social environment themselves. In many instances, antisocial children grow up with below-average interpersonal skills for dealing with others in a socially appropriate manner. Their friends tend to be delinquent, antisocial peers.

Antisocial children often do poorly in schoolwork, a pattern that accumulates in disinterest and dropping out—mentally as well as behaviorally. As adults, their work history tends to be spotty, with extended periods of unemployment followed by unskilled labor jobs. For some unknown reasons, persistent offenders often score below the norm on standardized "intelligence" tests, although they often demonstrate other forms of intelligence, including artistic or spatial ability and an impressive street sense of how to survive.

Persistent offenders, particularly those who are aggressive and violent, often come from multiassaultive families where physical and other kinds of abuse are commonplace. In addition, they often have family members, especially parents and/or siblings, who are also frequent offenders and antisocial themselves (Blumstein, Farrington, & Moitra, 1985).

As we discussed in the previous chapter, many persistent offenders tend to be polydrug users, using whatever combinations are on the market at an affordable price. They do not specialize in any one type of offending but tend to demonstrate a wide variety of antisocial behaviors, ranging from theft to aggravated assault. In fact, the frequency, seriousness, and variety of offending are highly correlated (Farrington, 1987). Moreover, the frequency of offending seems to decline with age, especially around age 40, but the reasons for this decline are unknown.

An increasingly recognized exception to all of the above general statements is the persistent white-collar offender, an individual who does not fit neatly into many of the above characteristics. White-collar offenders—whether they be individual occupational offenders or corporate offenders—probably do not have the educational or family backgrounds associated with the typical persistent offender. We may also speculate that their offending may begin later in life rather than in the typical teen or early adult years. Because researchers rarely investigate background or personality variables in these offenders, we have little information at our disposal. Furthermore, white-collar offenders are rarely mentioned in the psychological literature on corrections. The focus is predominantly on violent offenders, substance abusers, sex offenders, and mentally disordered inmates.

Although there are some good indications that persistent offenders have nervous systems that require high amounts of stimulation, there is little reason to believe that these neurological propensities cannot be overcome by learning and cognitive factors, as well as by the influences of the social environment. Human beings are not simply driven by animal instincts, genetic programming, chromosomal anomalies, or primitive biological urges or proclivities from their evolutionary past. They are also thinking, active agents with dreams, goals, and unique perceptions and versions of the world. These versions and goals influence their ongoing behavior, including behavior that violates criminal law. Cognitive processes and constructs can override biology in human action and conduct. Nor is there convincing evidence that any sizable portion of criminal behavior is propelled by some mental disease, biological abnormality, or addiction. As we learned in Chapter 6, serious mental disorder can rob some individuals of the mental state necessary to hold them responsible for their crimes. However, most mentally disordered individuals are not criminal. Furthermore, empirical research does not support the frequent media portrayals that "addictions"—e.g., sexual addiction, alcohol addiction, kleptomania—compel individuals to commit crime.

Human beings are highly adaptable and changeable. Thus, the focus of this chapter is on the work of correctional psychologists in understanding, predicting, and changing criminal behavior patterns.

Careers in Correctional Psychology

Many if not most psychologists working in correctional settings are members of the American Association for Correctional Psychologists, a professional group that sponsors conferences, disseminates research, and promotes standards for the practice of psychology in both institutional and community correctional settings. The standards, last updated in 2000 (Standards Committee, 2000) cover such topics as roles and services, limits of confidentiality, informed consent, screening and evaluation, inmate treatment, staffing requirements, and in-service training.

The three main services provided by correctional psychologists are (1) assessment, diagnosis, and classification; (2) treatment or intervention; and (3) research, planning, and evaluation. Several studies have provided information from correctional psychologists themselves on the work they do in each of these three areas. In one of the earlier projects, Clements (1987) found that a majority of correctional psychologists were located in assessment or reception centers that operated centrally or regionally to screen and classify newly received offenders. Some psychologists also provided treatment services at these centers. Other correctional psychologists treated inmates diagnosed as having mental disorders or adjustment problems within the correctional facility itself. Clements also found that psychologists made up about half of the professionally trained mental health staff in prisons and outnumbered psychiatrists by at least five to one (Clements, 1987).

In a nationwide survey of 120 American correctional psychologists working in institutional settings, Bartol, Griffin, and Clark (1993) discovered that

FIGURE 13–1   Percentage Distribution of What Correctional Psychologists Do

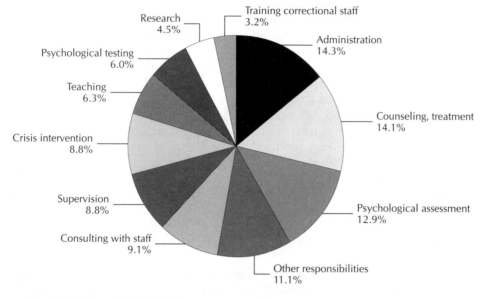

Source: Bartol, Griffin, and Clark (1993).

the *direct* services most commonly provided by psychologists working full-time in the correctional setting were counseling (14.1% of their time) and psychological assessment (12.9%) (**Figure 13–1**). A high percentage of their time was also spent at various administrative duties (14.3%) or consulting with correctional staff (9.1%). Most of the correctional psychologists worked in state institutions or federal facilities (64.2% and 6.2%, respectively). The remainder worked in private, county, or municipal correctional institutions, such as jails and detention centers. The survey revealed that psychologists who work in the federal correctional system were paid a median salary of $60,500, compared to a $50,000 median salary for correctional psychologists working in state systems. A majority of the correctional psychologists (about 80%) thought that employment opportunities for psychologists in corrections would be excellent or very good in the future.

In a more extensive study, Boothby and Clements (2000) surveyed 830 psychologists working in 48 state prisons and the U.S. Federal Bureau of Prisons. Most of the respondents (59%) held doctorate degrees, and most of the remainder held master's degrees as their highest degree (37%). Those respondents working in the Federal Bureau of Prisons all had doctorate degrees, mostly in clinical psychology. Sixty-two percent of the respondents were males, and 38% were females. Doctoral-level psychologists working in the Federal Bureau of Prisons averaged $61,800, whereas doctoral-level psychologists working in the state systems averaged $53,400. According to the Boothby–Clements survey, correctional psychologists spend most of their time on administrative tasks (30%), followed by direct treatment of inmates (26%), and psychological assessment (18%). Very little time was devoted to research (6%).

Boothby and Clements found that the direct treatment provided inmates was mostly one-on-one, with cognitive and behavioral therapies (88% and 69%, respectively) most preferred by the correctional psychologists. When the respondents were asked what emotional problems they most frequently treated, they reported that depression was by far the most common. Anger was a distant second, followed by psychotic symptoms, anxiety, and adjustment problems. In contrast to the more sanguine appraisals of the future of correctional psychology reported in the Bartol et al. (1993) survey, Boothby and Clements (2000) noted that many of their respondents were somewhat pessimistic about the future. They ". . . expressed concern that the number of available jobs will gradually decrease, despite the growing need for psychological services in corrections. Those with doctorate degrees feared their positions would be lost to master's level professions, whereas those with master's degrees expressed concern about losing their jobs to social workers" (p. 726).

Nevertheless, other factors militate against this pessimistic appraisal, particularly in the federal system. The Federal Bureau of Prisons (BOP) offers internships and many career opportunities for psychologists with doctoral degrees. In the BOP, psychologists work independently, not under the supervision of psychiatrists, as in many state facilities. They are involved in a wide variety of tasks, including training staff, conducting forensic evaluations for federal courts, conducting research, and of course providing direct services to prisoners, such as substance abuse treatment, crisis intervention, suicide prevention, and general mental health care. Psychologists working in state and local facilities are less likely to be employed full-time—although many are—and perform similar tasks as those listed above. Finally, it is important not to overlook the opportunities for psychologists consulting with community correctional agencies, such as departments of probation and parole. Community-based treatment has become more common in recent years and offers increased opportunities for psychologists (Heilbrun & Griffin, 1999).

Finally, because diagnosis, classification, and treatment are increasingly guided by evaluation research, the need for psychologists specializing in research is expected to become even greater. We review many of the functions mentioned above in the remainder of this chapter. Before we do, however, it is important that we have some familiarity with the correctional system as a whole.

THE CORRECTIONAL SYSTEM

In the United States, detained, accused, and convicted persons—when incarcerated—are housed in three types of facilities: jails, community-based facilities, and prisons. As described briefly in the previous chapter, **jails** are operated by local (or sometimes state) governments to hold persons temporarily detained, awaiting trial, or sentenced to confinement for a misdemeanor, usually for less than one year. Therefore, jails house a mixture of persons at various stages of criminal justice processing. Nationwide, about 50% to 60% of the jail population at any given time has not been convicted but, rather, is awaiting trial.

Community-based corrections facilities are operated by public or private organizations (under governmental contract). They hold persons for less than 24 hr of each day to allow them limited opportunity to work, attend school, or make other community contacts. Group homes, substance abuse treatment centers, and halfway houses are examples of these facilities. Overall, community-based facilities of this sort house about 4% of all those *confined* in the correctional system. It is not, however, secure confinement. In addition, about two-thirds of all persons under correctional supervision remain in the community, such as on probation or parole (Bureau of Justice Statistics, 2002), without confinement. This is an important distinction to make, because psychologists often work with offenders who are allowed to remain in the community.

Prisons are operated by state and federal governments to hold persons sentenced under state and federal laws after being convicted of felonies, to terms of more than one year. Prisons are often classified according to three levels of security: maximum, medium, and minimum security. In recent years, a new category—the ultramax prison—has appeared on the scene. It is discussed in more detail shortly. In addition to these security classifications among facilities, there are parallel classifications *within* a facility.

Special units within prisons may also hold special categories of offenders, such as those found to be mentally disordered or chronically violent or those with serious physical illnesses. Maximum- or close-security prisons are typically surrounded by a double fence or wall (usually 18 to 25 feet high) guarded by armed correctional officers in observation towers. Medium-security prisons typically are enclosed within double fences topped with razor wire and also typically have armed guards in towers or patrolling perimeters. Virtually all maximum-security and most medium-security prisons have video surveillance, with a control center capable of the remote closing-off of sections of the facility, sometimes including individual cells, in the event of an emergency. Minimum-security prisons usually do not have armed guards and may or may not have fences surrounding the buildings, but video surveillance is still a possibility. In the United States (as of 2000), states operated 1,375 correctional facilities and the BOP operated 96 facilities.

Women comprise 6%–10% of all persons incarcerated, and consequently the great majority of jails and prisons are male facilities. There are few *jails* specifically designed for women: on the whole, women in jail are kept in a separate unit within a predominantly male facility, but there are exceptions. The large New York City jail on Rikers Island, for example, has a separate building for women that is independent of the accommodations for male detainees. The massive Sybil Brand Institute in California is another example.

Most states have no more than one or a few women's *prisons*, which means that women are more likely than men to be imprisoned in areas that are far from their homes. Women's prisons are also rarely classified according to maximum-, medium-, and minimum-security levels. Thus, the one woman's prison in a state is likely to be more rather than less secure, meaning that many women are kept in higher-security levels than they actually need (Owen, 2000).

It is important to note that in six states the concepts of jail and prison are combined. In these jurisdictions, the state controls the entire correctional system, so no distinction is made between locally controlled jails and state-controlled prisons. Thus, the same facility may house detainees, sentenced misdemeanants, and sentenced felons—although the detainees and convicted offenders are usually held in separate units of the facility. Additionally, in these "mixed-system" states, there is typically one or more facilities set aside for special offender populations, such as highly dangerous offenders or the mentally disordered.

At the beginning of the twenty-first century, over 2 million individuals were held in jails and prisons in the United States, representing approximately 1 in 32 adults (Bureau of Justice Statistics, 2002) (**Table 13–1**). Approximately 4 million adults were under correctional supervision in the community, such as on probation or parole. Incarceration rates for women have increased more rapidly than those for men, although women continue to represent less than 10% of the incarcerated population. Black males are significantly overrepresented. An estimated 9% of American black males in their late twenties were incarcerated in 1999, and black males represent nearly 50% of the entire inmate population in all state and federal facilities.

TABLE 13–1 Number of Persons Held in State or Federal Prisons or in Local Jails, 1995–2002

| | TOTAL INMATES IN CUSTODY | PRISONERS IN CUSTODY ON DECEMBER 31 | | INMATES IN JAIL ON JUNE 30 | INCARCERATION RATE |
		FEDERAL	STATE		
1995	1,585,586	89,538	989,004	507,044	601
1996	1,646,020	95,088	1,032,440	518,492	618
1997	1,743,643	101,755	1,074,809	567,079	648
1998	1,816,931	110,793	1,113,676	592,462	669
1999	1,893,115	125,682	1,161,490	605,943	691
2000	1,937,482	133,921	1,176,269	621,149	684
2001	1,961,247	143,337	1,180,155	631,240	685
2002	2,033,331	151,618	1,209,640	665,475	701
Percentage change, 2001–2002	3.7%	5.8%	2.5%	5.4%	
Average annual increase, 1995–2002	3.6%	7.8%	2.9%	4.0%	

[a]Per 100,000 population.

Source: Bureau of Justice Statistics (2003c, p. 2).

In 1999, the BOP had 140,019 inmates under custody in 96 facilities, which includes penitentiaries, federal correctional institutions, federal prison camps, and federal medical centers. The BOP also has some inmates in contract facilities, mostly community corrections centers or detention facilities, which are operated by non-BOP staff. In fact, federal detainees are often kept in local jails because of the dearth of federal detention centers across the country. Interestingly, federal detention centers—particularly those maintained by the military—came to public attention following the terrorist events of September 11, 2001, when the government began to hold persons either suspected of having information about or directly involved in these events. At this writing, the U.S. Supreme Court is considering the extent to which these detainees are entitled to some due process protections, including the right to consult with attorneys and to have the legality of their detentions reviewed by a court.

Over the years, there has been a steady increase in prison and jail populations in the United States, and a similar pattern in Canada (Bonta, Wallace-Capretta, & Rooney, 2000). As noted above, the inmate population for women is increasing at a rate higher than that for men, and has more than doubled since 1990 (Beck, 2000). Since 1990, the number of female prisoners has increased 108%, compared with a male increase of 77% (Bureau of Justice Statistics, 2001b). These increases in prison and jail populations probably reflect a judicial and societal change in attitude about what should be done about offenders, rather than any dramatic increase in crime rates, because crime rates during that same period have either stabilized or gone down.

Nearly 64% of all adult inmates have experienced prior incarceration—in either juvenile facilities, adult institutions, or both. About two-thirds of women confined in state prisons had a history of prior conviction, and three-fourths of men serving time in state prisons had a prior conviction record (Greenfeld, 1999). After release from prison, about 12% are likely to be back in prison within one year. After three years, about 24% of the parolees return to prison. However, more than half of all prison returns are for technical violations of parole, such as failure to notify a parole officer before leaving the state or failure to attend mandated treatment sessions. The remainder is for convictions of a new crime. When former inmates reach age 30, there is a high probability that they will not return to prison. The reasons are multiple, but one viable explanation is that the justice system, in effect, physically "wears down" offenders. In other words, they are tired of repeatedly being arrested, appearing in court, and having to adjust to incarceration. A more optimistic appraisal is that they have aged out of crime and have found alternatives to a criminal lifestyle.

Tables 13–2 and **13–3** list numbers and the types of offenses of which inmates in state and federal prisons have been convicted. Notice that nearly 60% of the inmates serving time in U.S. federal prisons in 1998 were incarcerated for drug offenses.

TABLE 13–2   Estimated Number of Sentenced Prisoners Under State Jurisdiction, by Offense, Gender, Race, and Latino Origin, 1998

OFFENSE	ALL	MALE	FEMALE	WHITE	BLACK	LATINO
Total	1,141,700	1,071,400	70,300	380,400	531,100	194,000
Violent offenses	545,200	525,100	20,100	180,300	257,700	87,600
Murder	134,600	128,500	6,100	42,400	67,100	21,500
Manslaughter	17,600	15,800	1,800	6,200	7,100	3,400
Rape	29,600	29,300	300	13,500	12,100	2,400
Other sex assault	71,200	70,500	700	41,400	17,500	9,300
Robbery	159,600	154,600	5,000	33,000	96,700	25,400
Assault	109,500	104,500	5,000	33,800	48,800	22,000
Other violent	23,100	21,800	1,300	10,000	8,400	3,800
Property offenses	242,900	224,500	18,500	104,200	97,700	34,000
Burglary	118,000	114,400	3,600	49,900	48,100	16,600
Larceny	45,500	39,600	5,900	17,200	20,500	6,100
MV theft	20,100	19,400	800	8,000	7,300	4,400
Fraud	30,200	23,300	6,900	15,700	11,100	2,800
Other property	29,100	27,800	1,300	13,300	10,700	4,100
Drug offenses	236,800	212,900	23,900	46,300	134,800	51,700
Public order	113,900	106,500	7,500	49,200	39,400	20,100
Other	2,800	2,500	200	400	1,500	700

Source: Beck (2000, p. 10).

TABLE 13–3   Number of Sentenced Inmates in U.S. Federal Prisons by Most Serious Offense, 1998

TYPE OF OFFENSE	NUMBER OF INMATES	PERCENTAGE OF TOTAL
Total	108,925	100.0%
Violent offenses	12,656	11.6
Homicide	1,344	1.2
Robbery	8,773	8.0
Other violent	2,539	2.3
Property offenses	8,627	7.9
Burglary	249	0.1
Fraud	6,465	5.9
Other property	1,913	1.8
Drug offenses	63,011	57.9
Public order offenses	22,273	20.5
Immigration	7,430	6.8
Weapons	8,742	8.0
Other public order	6,101	5.6
Other/unspecified	2,358	2.2

Source: Beck (2000 p. 12).

SOCIETAL RATIONALE FOR PUNISHMENT OF OFFENDERS

Four fundamental considerations are usually in operation when offenders are sentenced: (1) protection of others, frequently called **incapacitation**; (2) **rehabilitation**; (3) **retribution**; and (4) **deterrence**. It is important to keep in mind that these goals can be achieved both by imprisonment and by community sanctions. In fact, some people believe that imprisonment should be reserved only for serious, violent offenders or for repeat nonviolent offenders whose criminal activity does not desist.

Incapacitation is the most straightforward justification for punishing individuals, and it is most commonly applied to incarceration. Nevertheless, even persons living in their own homes can be incapacitated to some extent, as by means of house arrest or electronic monitoring. If the criminal is believed to be dangerous to society, on the basis of the crimes he or she has committed, it is obvious that society must be protected from future injury. However, if we rely heavily on incapacitation to remove the offender from the streets, we are in danger of increasing the inmate population dramatically and far beyond the present capacity of correctional facilities. Research has consistently documented that a small percentage—about 6% to 10%—of the criminal population commits an inordinate amount of the crime—perhaps more than 50% of the total (S. Walker, 2001; Wolfgang, 1972). For example, Peterson, Braiker, and Polich (1981) reported that the average prisoner committed about three serious crimes per year of street time, while the most frequent offender (about 8% of the inmate population) committed more than 60 serious crimes per year of street time. Incapacitation directed at this small percentage— a strategy called **selective incapacitation**—might be a more effective means of reducing crime. This was the principle behind the "three-strikes" laws that were passed in many states in the 1980s and remain in the statutes today. Unfortunately, these laws do not necessarily identify the most dangerous chronic offender and are often considered to be very poor policy by criminal justice scholars (Walker, 2001).

Rehabilitation as a justification for confinement often prompts heated debate. Rehabilitation is essentially restoring the person to a useful life, through either education, training, treatment (e.g., psychotherapy, behavior modification), or a combination of these. During the 1970s and 1980s, rehabilitation lost favor with much of society, including courts and criminal justice practitioners. Contributing to this disenchantment was a provocative article by R. M. Martinson (1974), arguing that the concept of rehabilitation, especially in the form of treatment methods then in operation, was ineffective. The concept of rehabilitation has yet to regain a comfortable foothold within the correctional system, but the 1990s saw a resurgence of interest, as we discuss later in the chapter (e.g., Gaes, Flanagan, Motiuk, & Stewart, 1999).

Retribution as a goal of sanctioning refers to the belief that individuals should be held accountable for the harms they do to society and should be punished proportionally to those harms. If we break society's laws, it is only right and just that we be punished. The retributive philosophy is not identical to the concept of revenge, which suggests a more emotional response to a person's criminal behavior. Retribution implies *just* punishment that is not excessive or disproportionate to the crime committed.

Deterrence reflects society's assumption that some form of punishment—defined as aversive consequences for one's behavior—is an effective method of behavior control. In correctional literature, two forms of deterrence, general and specific, are discussed (Andenaes, 1968). **General deterrence** serves as a threat system to society as a whole. Thus, when an individual is sentenced (e.g., to a long prison term), the rest of society is given a message: "If you choose to violate this rule, this is what will happen." The threat and fear of similar punishment should act as a potent deterrent. **Specific** (sometimes called special) **deterrence** applies the threat directly to the person being sentenced. The punishment given should deter him or her from future violations.

Theoretical discussions on the effectiveness of punishment as a deterrent often revolve around the aforementioned dichotomy. The long-debated question surrounding the relationship between deterrence and criminal conduct has never been satisfactorily answered. It is usually assumed that direct application of aversive stimuli is more effective than the observation or knowledge of punishing consequences. In other words, many shoplifters are not deterred from a first offense by signs that warn them of possible prosecution or by reading or hearing about other offenders (general deterrence). However, the embarrassment of actually having one's name published in the local newspaper and the pain of paying a fine or spending time in confinement are much more likely to prevent future violations.

It is reasonable to assume, however, that general deterrence or the threat of punishment does prevent a significant number of people from violating the law. Nevertheless, as we have discussed throughout the book, many crimes occur when individuals are disengaged from their normal constructs or normal inhibitions. Furthermore, crime often brings rewards—monetary gain, status, physiological arousal, a way out of an unbearable situation—that are greater than the threats of possible punishment.

In addition, the general deterrence associated with the legal system may not be as powerful as the threat of punishment established through socialization and moral development. It is reasonable to assume that a very large segment of the population will not engage in serious criminal activity, even if there is no police officer at the elbow. For most people, fear of social, parental, and self-disapproval operates as a sufficient deterrent to persistent offending. In keeping with our theme of the complexity of human behavior, it is probable that some combination of the aforementioned internal and external checks are operating for the majority of people who do not engage in serious crime.

In sum, society punishes criminal offenders under a variety of rationales, not all of which are persuasive from a psychological perspective. Given their choice, most correctional psychologists would probably maintain that rehabilitation is the most justified, because efforts are made to restore the individual to a point whereby he or she can again be a contributing member of society. As we will see shortly, rehabilitation can be a frustrating endeavor, although it is one well worth pursuing. In the following sections we review some of the specific tasks performed by correctional psychologists, including those associated with the rehabilitative goal of corrections.

CLASSIFICATION AND PREDICTION

Classification, whether in jails and prisons or in community settings, is done for two purposes: custody and treatment. Correctional administrators want to know how closely an inmate or a person on parole should be supervised as well as what services and programs should be offered. Classification for custody is not necessarily related to the crime for which a person was convicted, but it may be. For example, individuals with no history of violent behavior in a prison setting, convicted of murdering their spouse, may not require a high-security facility. On the other hand, persons convicted of sexual abuse of children may require placement in protective custody, to protect them from possible victimization at the hands of other prisoners. Likewise, sex offenders in the community may require more frequent and close monitoring than offenders convicted of burglary who have served time in prison and are completing their sentences in the community, on parole.

In sum, then, classification serves a number of important functions within the correctional system. First, it helps corrections officials make decisions about inmate placement in order to provide a safe environment for all inmates and staff. Specifically, classification helps correctional staff to differentiate low-risk offenders from high-risk ones, thereby contributing to institutional security. This is the classification for custody purpose referred to above. Second, it provides information for treatment, intervention, and rehabilitation—the treatment purpose mentioned above. Third, classification helps in making predictions about recidivism and other risks to society. For example, classification helps parole boards in their release decisions, and enables probation and parole officers to assign different levels of supervision according to risk (Bonta & Cormier, 1999).

From a psychological perspective, the process of classification also simplifies and summarizes, enhances prediction, and reminds us that crime and delinquency are behaviorally and psychologically heterogeneous with multiple causation. The psychologist who works with the correctional system is often very closely involved with the classification of offenders. If we do not intend to treat all offenders alike and do not intend to behave haphazardly toward them, some form of classification for treatment is necessary (Sechrest, 1987). Clements (1996), stated the same idea somewhat differently: "Somewhere between the extremes of 'all offenders are alike' and 'each offender is unique' lies a system (or systems) of categorization along pertinent dimensions that will prove to be of value in reaching correctional goals.

Classification systems aggregate individuals into subgroups that share common symptoms, etiology, behavioral attributes, or other relevant characteristics" (p. 123).

Clements (1996) reviewed two decades of research on offender classification. He noted at the outset of his review that a variety of interrelated themes has occurred in the research. It is worthwhile to state these themes, because they provide an excellent illustration of what the classification process involves. The themes appearing in the research include the following:

> risk assessment; the specification of offender typologies leading to differential treatment; process factors that facilitate or impede accurate classification and appropriate assignments; validity and extension studies of various approaches; the use of an offender classification database as a management and planning tool; the development of instruments and systems for both institutional and community correctional settings; assessment of specific offender needs; comparative studies of different approaches to classification assessment; and basic psychometric reports on various factor structures in offender profiles, particularly those based on the MMPI [Minnesota Multiphasic Personality Inventory]. (p. 121)

After highlighting promising trends in these themes, Clements concluded that there was no one "right" classification system, nor was there one assessment instrument that could be integrated across all purposes. In the following section, we focus on a few of the more prominent methods of classification available in the correctional literature.

Classification Systems

One of the earliest classification systems was that proposed by Edward Megargee (Megargee & Bohn, 1979), based on the MMPI. Offenders are identified as 1 of 10 types, each type correlated with a specific behavioral and adjustment profile. Although Megargee's approach is widely recognized for its historical significance, this trait-based classification scheme has its limitations. Clements (1996, p. 132) notes that it has held up "reasonably well," despite questions raised about the reproducibility of its 10 inmate types, its extensions to new correctional settings, and questions about its stability/reliability over time. However, as Clements implies, perhaps even more valuable is Megargee's (1977) list of seven criteria for a good classification system (e.g., sufficient completeness so that most offenders can be classified; provision of clear operational definitions).

Other early classification systems that we do not discuss here have included Quay's (1984) Adult Internal Management System (AIMS), Warren's (1983) Interpersonal Maturity Level (I-level) (Warren, 1983), and the Jesness (1971) Inventory Classification System. In 1994, Patricia Van Voorhis published a text that remains the only contemporary scholarly book devoted exclusively to psychological classification in corrections. In that book, she analyzed the field of correctional classification and also provided a comprehensive research report on five systems (Clements, 1996).

Although a good many schemes or systems of classification have been proposed over the years, corrections research in Canada has led the way in recent development of reliable and valid measures that are based on risk and/or needs appraisal. Examples include the Level of Service Inventory—Revised (LSI-R) (Andrews & Bonta, 1995), the Violence Risk Appraisal Guide (VRAG; G. Harris, Rice, & Quinsey, 1993; Quinsey, Harris, Rice, & Cormier, 1998), the HCR-20 (Webster et al., 1997), the Self-Appraisal Questionnaire (Loza, Dhaliwal, Kroner, & Loza-Fanous, 2000), and, of course, the Psychopathy Checklist—Revised (PCL-R) (Hare, 1991) discussed in Chapter 4. The HCR-20, described briefly in Chapter 6, consists of 10 historical items (H variables), 5 clinical items (C variables), and 5 risk management items (R variables), hence the acronym HCR-20 (Grann, Belfrage, & Tengström, 2000). All of these scales and risk assessment instruments listed earlier have strengths and weaknesses, all show considerable promise, and very active research programs are focused on each.

Most recently, David Simourd (1997; Simourd & Van De Ven, 1999) has advocated a reexamination of the Criminal Sentiments Scale—Modified (CSS-M) as a viable assessment instrument to measure attitudes, values, and beliefs of offenders. This is based on Simourd's contention that criminal attitudes have been identified as a crucial factor in the theoretical understanding and treatment of criminal behavior.

One of the key concepts emerging from the Canadian research is the concept of **dynamic risk factors** (Andrews & Bonta, 1998; Andrews, Bonta, & Hoge, 1990). Dynamic risk factors are the ones that *change* over time and situation. For example, attitudes, values, and beliefs have considerable potential for change, in contrast to the **static risk factors** (or historical factors) of biological parents, gender, birth order, race/ethnic background, and general background variables. Changing attitudes, beliefs, and values is a more challenging but potentially more fruitful goal in corrections than simply identifying which static predictors are associated with criminal behavior. "Dynamic risk factors are characteristics that can change, and when changed, result in a corresponding increase or decrease in recidivism risk" (Hanson & Harris, 2000, p. 7). Dynamic risk factors can be subdivided into *stable* dynamic factors and *acute* dynamic factors (Hanson & Harris, 2000). Stable dynamic factors, although they are changeable, usually change slowly, sometimes taking months or even years to modify. An example is self-esteem. Acute dynamic factors, on the other hand, change rapidly (days, hours, or minutes) and include such things as alcohol or drug intoxication and mood swings. Hanson and Harris (2000), for example, found that acute dynamic factors, such as anger and subjective distress, were better predictors of recidivism for sex offenders (rapists and pedophiles) than were the more stable dynamic factors.

Offenders may have a variety of needs, but not all needs are related to criminal behavior (Bonta et al., 2000). To be effective, treatment or rehabilitation programs must target those needs that will change criminal behavior. Dynamic risk factors that are associated with ongoing criminal behavior are often called **criminogenic needs**, whereas other dynamic factors (e.g., self-esteem, fears) associated with noncriminal behavior are called *noncriminogenic needs*. The concept of criminogenic needs is becoming firmly established in Canadian corrections (Bonta & Cormier, 1999) and is slowly becoming established in U.S. corrections. Therefore, the more effective treatments and rehabilitation strategies in corrections—if a reduction in recidivism is the goal—should be focused on addressing criminogenic needs.

PSYCHOLOGICAL EFFECTS OF IMPRISONMENT

Clinical case studies on the effects of prison life have often concluded that, for many individuals, imprisonment can be brutal, demeaning, and generally devastating. These studies often describe a variety of psychological symptoms believed caused directly by imprisonment, including psychosis, severe depression, inhibiting anxiety, and social withdrawal. However, research (e.g., D. Adams, 1992; Toch & Adams, with Grant, 1989; Toch & Adams, 1989; Zamble & Porporino, 1988) raises serious questions about the extent of serious psychological deterioration that is *caused* by imprisonment. Nevertheless, whether individuals displayed symptoms after imprisonment or came in with these symptoms, it appears that a significant number of incarcerated individuals need mental health attention. It is estimated, for example, that 19% of the U.S. correctional population suffers from a variety of serious mental disorders (Ashford et al., 2001). While this figure relates to both jail and prison populations, most of the research focuses on prisons, probably because prison stays are longer than jail stays. However, jail detainees and inmates are often more in psychological crisis than prison inmates.

Zamble and Porporino (1988) examined the coping strategies and adjustment characteristics of inmates in Canadian penitentiaries. They found that emotional disruption and adjustment were clearly problems for most inmates during the beginning of their sentences, particularly signs of serious to moderate depression. This deleterious reaction came as no surprise, as prison produces a dramatic disruption in customary behavior, compounded by restrictions, deprivations, and constraints. However, these initial reactions soon dissipated for most inmates, and no *lasting* emotional disturbance was discernible as inmates became adjusted to their surroundings and prison routine. Toch and Adams (with Grant, 1989) report a similar pattern in their study on American prisoners. The Toch–Adams data suggest that inmates with serious emotional problems also tend to be disruptive in prison.

Inmate reactions to prison life appear to follow a curvilinear pattern, with stress indicators increasing at the beginning of the term, then dropping, and then rising again as the end of their term approaches (Bukstel & Kilmann, 1980). Many inmates experience what is sometimes referred to as the "short-timer's syndrome," exhibiting signs of distress, sleeplessness, restlessness, and anxiety, probably in anticipation of the new coping strategies required for the outside.

Zamble and Porporino (1988) write, "We conclude that prisons do not produce permanent harm to the psychological well-being of inmates" (p. 149). On the other hand, they did not find positive effects either. "Our data show very little positive behavioral change in prison, just as earlier we could see little evidence for generalized negative effects" (p. 151). Interestingly, Toch and Adams suggest that prison experiences actually temper or even improve inmate misbehavior, most particularly in the young inmate, under age 25. "Young inmates, who are presumably more rambunctious and less mature than older inmates, appear to derive some benefit from this forced environment . . . it is encouraging to find that prison inmates who are initially most resistant to restrictions on their personal liberty demonstrate increasing levels of conformity over time" (pp. 19–20). Why this happens remains largely a mystery, but Toch and Adams (with Grant, 1989) suggest that the maturation process facilitated by *humane* prison environments plays a crucial role. The researchers contend that inmate behavior is likely to improve when inmates learn the association between behavior and its positive or negative consequences within the institution and when they have psychological support, the opportunity to participate in conventional activities, form attachment bonds, and build relationships.

In summary, a vast majority of inmates do not demonstrate *long-lasting* psychological impairment or problems as a result of imprisonment. Nevertheless, a significant number of offenders do need help, if only in crisis situations. In addition, many observers note that the prison environment of today is more violent and impersonal than the prisons of the past (e.g., Haney & Zimbardo, 1998; R. Johnson, 1996), leading to the conclusion that in many places a humane prison may well be an oxymoron. In addition to a violent environment, other factors may exacerbate the stress felt by prisoners, specifically crowding and isolation.

Psychological Effects of Crowding

Prison crowding has become an increasingly important topic as the prison population reaches critical numbers. Prison crowding has probably always been a concern, but the sheer number of offenders being currently processed through the system is without precedent. Nationwide, as noted at the beginning of the chapter, the incarcerated population has reached beyond 2 million, a figure that represents a tripling of the incarceration rate since 1980 (Bureau of Justice Statistics, 2001b). Virtually every state in the United States faces a crowding problem in one or more of its correctional facilities.

Prison and jail overcrowding does seem to be related to a higher incidence of physical illness, socially disruptive behavior, and emotional distress (Bukstel & Kilmann, 1980). Some researchers also have suggested that disruptive behavior in correctional facilities increases directly as the available space decreases (Megargee, 1976; Nacci, Teitelbaum, & Prather, 1977). Indeed, the violence level in U.S. prisons has increased concurrently with the crowding problem (Tonry & Petersilia, 1999).

In a 15-year project on prison crowding, Paulus (1988) concluded that increasing the number of residents in correctional housing units significantly increased the negative psychological (e.g., tension, anxiety, depression) and physical reactions (e.g., headaches, high blood pressure, cardiovascular problems) in inmates. The critical factor appears to be the number of residents sharing a space and not simply the amount of space available. For example, providing some privacy and limiting the visual and physical access of other inmates, such as providing cubicles in open dormitories (for inmates in medium or minimum security), reduce the negative impact of living there.

Paulus also found that socioeconomic level, education level, and prior prison or jail confinements were related to inmate reactions to crowded conditions. Specifically, the higher the socioeconomic and education level, the more difficult the adjustment to, and the lower the tolerance for, crowded conditions. Presumably, many members of the lower socioeconomic class are used to living under crowded conditions and therefore are more tolerant of invasions of privacy and other factors involved in crowded environments. On the other hand, DeRosia (1991) found that inmates from more advantaged socioeconomic backgrounds had, overall, far more personal resources for adjusting to prison life, including crowded conditions, so the research on this is not consistent. Surprisingly, Paulus found that prior confinement interfered with adjustment to crowded conditions. Prisoners who had some history of prior imprisonment exhibited more problems in adjustments than those without prior time. A reason suggested by Paulus is that individuals with extensive prison histories are likely to have spent part of their time in single cells or under less crowded conditions. This may have made them particularly sensitive to crowded conditions, such as living in a dormitory setting or being double-celled. Paulus also found that men and women, and blacks and whites, react similarly to variations in social density.

Paulus hypothesizes that crowding has its primary impact through its influence on social interaction. First, crowding reduces one's sense of control over the social environment, and with the large number of inmates in a prison, things become unpredictable and uncertain. Second, crowded situations interfere with one's goals (such as carrying out desired activities), restrict freedom and privacy, and expose one to a variety of undesired intrusions. And third, crowded situations produce much more activity, noise, interactions, smells, and violations of personal space and generally excessive stimulation.

In summary, the available research does indicate that crowding is related to negative psychological and physical problems in confinement. However, individuals react differently to crowded conditions, some demonstrating much better adjustment than others. There are many other variables that have to be considered also, such as the type of institution, the institution's orientation, the level of violence, the opportunities to move about and to participate in work programs, the type of social milieu, the degree of crowding, and what phase of the sentence an individual is in.

Psychological Effects of Isolation

Prison inmates may be physically isolated or segregated from the general population for a variety of reasons and under a wide range of conditions. For purposes of discussion we can identify the following main categories: (1) **isolation** or **segregation** as a form of punishment; (2) isolation or segregation for an inmate's own protection; and (3) administrative segregation, done for management purposes. For example, administrative segregation might occur while corrections officials are investigating an incident, such as a fight in the prison yard. Most recently, administrative segregation has taken on a new meaning, with the placement of large groups of inmate in high-security—ultramax—facilities. These are discussed shortly.

Segregation as a form of punishment—sometimes called solitary confinement, disciplinary segregation, or punitive isolation—is a temporary condition that is subject to some legal restrictions. For example, depending on the anticipated length of the segregation and loss of "good time" credits, prisoners who are alleged to violate prison rules may be offered a hearing and an opportunity to contest the charges (Palmer & Palmer, 1999). Although this form of segregation may be quite lengthy for some prisoners, it is rarely subjected to empirical psychological research.

Protective custody is a term reserved for isolation that is to protect the inmate, either from himself or herself or from the other inmates. As noted earlier in the chapter, there is no question that many prisons in the United States are violent institutions. It has been estimated that about 25,000 nonsexual assaults and close to 300,000 sexual assaults occur each year in the nation's prisons and jails (Clear & Cole, 2000). Some prisoners voluntarily seek protection from violent others, while others are placed in protective custody—even over their objections—because prison officials believe it is in their best interest. Nevertheless, protective custody does not guarantee that a prisoner is safe. In a highly publicized incident in 2003, a former priest who was convicted of child molestation, and believed to be responsible for other abuses over many years, was strangled to death in his prison cell by another inmate.

Prisoners also may be in protective custody because correctional staff are fearful of possible suicide. This is a problem particularly in jails, which have a higher suicide rate than prisons (Lester & Danto, 1993). Suicide is the leading cause of death in jails across the nation, although in some urban jail facilities,

AIDS-related deaths outnumber suicide (Ashford et al., 2001). On the other hand, suicide is the third leading cause of death in *prisons*, behind natural causes and AIDS. Suicide is usually committed by young, unmarried white males during the early stages of confinement. The most common method is by hanging. A history of mental disorder and previous attempts at suicide are also significantly linked to suicide in both jails and prisons (Ivanoff & Hayes, 2001). Under protective-suicide conditions, the level of social and perceptual–sensory isolation may be even more extreme than in other forms of segregation, because many materials and items must be removed from the cell so that the inmate cannot use the objects to accomplish the suicide. Placement in segregated housing or single cells is especially related to suicide in prisons (Hayes, 1995).

Whether or not they are suicide risks, mentally disordered inmates also may be placed in "observation cells" for short periods of time. These are special cells that may or may not be housed in a mental health unit in the facility. They are typically stripped of all but the barest necessities—such as a metal slab with a mattress for sleeping—and, again, are used on a temporary basis until an individual can be stabilized or transferred to a more appropriate setting.

Systematic knowledge of the psychological effects of isolation comes primarily from the psychological laboratory, using volunteers who allow themselves to be socially isolated, sometimes with sensory restrictions such as a blindfold or earphones, for varying periods of time. The research so far demonstrates that individuals respond differently to such isolation; some show great tolerance and often welcome the quiet solitude from the hustle and bustle of daily living. Others experience stress and anxiety, even after relatively short periods of isolation. In general, however, the research shows that most individuals are able to tolerate and even adjust to isolation, if it is short in duration, such as a few days, or even longer if the individual knows there is a reasonable time limit on the segregation. We must caution against generalizing from isolation studies with volunteers to the isolation imposed by prison officials for administrative, disciplinary, or even protective purposes, however.

In the past, the conditions of disciplinary segregation, in particular, were often deplorable. Offenders were held in cells without adequate ventilation, heat, clothing, light, or sanitary or bathroom facilities for long periods of time. Since no published research has examined the effects of such adverse conditions, it is difficult to determine what the psychological effects might be. Fortunately, the courts—as well as professional correctional standards—eventually called for minimum humane conditions that must be met during isolation, but it would be naïve to believe that abuses in this form of segregation have completely disappeared.

One form of isolation, however, is being extensively criticized in the psychological literature (e.g., Haney & Zimbardo, 1998). This is the administrative segregation popularly known as the **supermax** or **ultramax** prison. These prisons—or sometimes units within a prison—came on the scene in the

1990s and have now been established in many states as well as by the federal government. They are extremely high-security facilities intended for use with the most recalcitrant offenders—or those hardest to manage in a "regular" prison setting. Although procedures vary, in the typical supermax facility prisoners are kept in their cells for as long as 23 hours a day, allowed out for exercise for 1 hour. They do not communicate with each other, and their communication with corrections officers or staff is the minimal necessary to obtain food, medical, legal, or other services. Prisoners are assigned to these facilities for lengthy time periods; some have been confined since the facilities first opened. Such severe isolation has led critics to question the extent to which these individuals can retain their mental health. Indeed, at least one court has already ruled that the conditions in these high-security units are cruel and unusual punishment when used with inmates who are mentally disordered (*Madrid v. Gomez*, 1995).

TREATMENT AND REHABILITATION

In the 1970s, rehabilitation as a goal of corrections experienced a crisis of faith. A typical comment is one made by R. J. Carlson (1976): that rehabilitation by means of psychological treatment "is out of fashion today. It is not dead yet, but the literature is littered with death warrants" (p. 32). He implied that behavioral science professionals (e.g., psychologists, psychiatrists, and social workers) were responsible for overselling their goods to the correctional system.

A broader indictment of rehabilitation had been advanced 2 years earlier. Robert Martinson (1974), who has since gained a reputation as one of the chief critics of rehabilitation during that time period, reviewed 231 studies of prison rehabilitative programs and concluded, "With few and isolated exceptions, the rehabilitative efforts that have been reported so far have had no appreciable effect on recidivism" (p. 25). Martinson had looked at studies on a variety of rehabilitative approaches, not all of which were associated with psychological treatment (e.g., job training programs, education). Although Martinson did not himself conclude that "nothing works," his publication was widely interpreted to have come to that conclusion.

Martinson's article, together with an increasing trend toward punishment in the criminal justice system, had a powerful effect on corrections. There was an immediate shift away from rehabilitation and toward other models of corrections, such as strict punishment with minimal efforts to rehabilitate. Later, the dust settled somewhat and administrators became more reluctant to discard rehabilitative programs in their entirety.

One of the first to criticize the "nothing works" doctrine was Palmer (1975), who noted that Martinson's review tended to reject any type of rehabilitative treatment that was not highly successful. According to Palmer, Martinson was seeking a cure-all approach that would work for everyone, all or almost all of the time. He was not interested in partial success, and he appeared indifferent to the fact that about one-half (48%) of his 231 sample studies showed success with at least some subjects. Interestingly, Martinson himself emphasized this in a later publication in which he attempted to clarify his earlier statements (Lipton, Martinson, & Wilks, 1975).

Supporters of rehabilitation also pointed out that correctional treatments appear to be as effective as the partial success rate achieved thus far by traditional psychotherapy offered to the general population (S. Adams, 1977). Furthermore, Martinson's review spanned research conducted during the years 1945 to 1967, when evaluation and research methodology relating to corrections was in its infancy (Halleck & Witte, 1977). Quay (1977), in a cogent argument against the view that nothing works, noted that evaluations of correctional treatment concentrated too much on the adequacy of the research designs and measurement of outcomes and too little on the integrity of the program being assessed. To evaluate a program, a researcher must consider the rationale and goals of the treatment as well as how that treatment is delivered. Labeling a program "treatment" or "counseling" tells us nothing about what happened in the program. For example, were counseling sessions actually held? How well were they attended? Were inmates coerced into participating in the program, or were they able to volunteer freely without implicit threat?

Quay also advocated scrutinizing the delivery of treatment. Were the "counselors" untrained prison staff or community volunteers? If trained, was the training provided in two-hour lectures by disinterested instructors or was it provided intensively over a period of weeks by interested personnel? Finally, Quay asked, How generalizable is a particular treatment approach to all inmates? To be maximally effective, any treatment–rehabilitative program should be formulated in relation to the needs and capabilities of each person, a concept referred to as **differential treatment**.

The pessimism toward rehabilitation continued throughout the 1980s. In the 1990s, rehabilitation experienced a rebirth, although many of its supporters argued that it never really died. The preferred term among supporters of rehabilitation is that in recent years it has been "reaffirmed" as an important goal of corrections (Cullen & Applegate, 1997). Current correctional literature contains ample support for a wide range of rehabilitation approaches in jails, prisons, and community settings (e.g., Ashford et al., 2001; Cullen & Applegate, 1997; Gaes et al., 1999; MacKenzie, 2000).

As Tonry and Petersilia (1999) have observed, "The pessimism associated with the 'nothing works' findings wrongly attributed to Martinson's famous 1974 article . . . appears to have passed, and there are grounds for cautious optimism about the positive effects, under some conditions, of some cognitive-skills, drug-treatment, vocational training, educational, and other programs in adult prisons" (p. 8).

However, rehabilitation is not enthusiastically or universally embraced by the public or by correctional staff. For example, correctional officers exposed to wide varieties of hard-core offenders on a daily basis and under adverse conditions are apt to view the prison population as incorrigible and to suspect and resist any notion that offenders can be changed. The reasons they committed their crimes are irrelevant; what matters is that little can be done about them now. On the other hand, staff usually will acknowledge that not all prisoners can be characterized in this manner. Furthermore, some scholars have argued cogently that when correctional officers are involved in the rehabilitation effort, their job becomes more meaningful (Toch, 1992).

The fundamental goal of rehabilitation is to develop lawful alternative behavior that will generalize beyond the institution. As indicated by the Tonry/Petersilia comment quoted above, this may be accomplished by nonpsychological approaches, such as education or vocational training, both of which have produced positive results with some offenders in both confined and community settings. In this section, we focus on the psychological approaches or the rehabilitation strategies that comprise a significant portion of the work of correctional psychologists. Recall from the Boothby and Clements (2000) survey that 26% of the time was spent at treatment tasks. In addition, assessment—which comprised 18%—cannot be divorced from treatment. In order to treat effectively, a psychologist must perform ongoing assessment of an individual's status, including his or her needs, risks, and progress.

Some offenders, especially habitually violent ones, are unlikely to benefit from psychological rehabilitation and should remain in prison for society's protection. However, they may still benefit from psychological services, even if they are not rehabilitation-oriented. For example, a habitually violent prisoner who has been seriously assaulted, who is diagnosed with a debilitating medical condition, or who learns of the death of a family member may benefit from crisis intervention provided by psychological staff. In addition, some prisoners do become seriously mentally disordered in the prison setting; for these individuals, psychological treatment that would not necessarily qualify as "rehabilitation" is warranted. (In fact, for serious mental illness, treatment is constitutionally mandated.) As another example, prisoners on death row are often in need of services, particularly as they approach their execution date.

Psychological treatment that *is* rehabilitation-oriented, however, seeks to bring about behavioral and cognitive change that will help the individual adjust both within and outside the prison setting. The overwhelming bulk of the psychological and social research indicates that humans learn behavior, including deviant and unlawful behavior, from significant members of their society. Furthermore, they are constantly perceiving and interpreting their actions and the actions of others in accordance with internal standards and cognitive constructs. To understand their behavior, it seems most fruitful to examine these mediated processes and the justifying mechanisms that accompany them. To change their actions over an extended period of time, it will be necessary to change the cognitive templates or schema they use to perceive, interpret, and expect.

Psychotherapy

The terms psychotherapy, therapy, counseling, and treatment are used interchangeably by clinicians. Broadly, they refer to a set of procedures or techniques used to help individuals or groups alter their maladaptive behavior, develop adaptive behavior, or both. The behavior must be considered maladaptive by the individual, however. In other words, the person must want to change. It has long been a principle that change cannot be forced, but even this principle is being questioned today. For example, a growing body of literature is suggesting that change can be coerced, in the sense that some individuals must first be "forced" into treatment settings and then will gradually come to accept that the treatment is in their best interest (Farabee, 2002).

Treatment programs in jails and prisons are also often handicapped by inadequate facilities, staff, programs, and financial support. Furthermore, particularly in prisons where the length of incarceration is longer, two systems are at work—the formal system dictated by authorities and the informal system run by inmates. In the latter, two processes may be identified: criminalization and prisonization. In **criminalization**, inmates exchange, share, and support one another's construct systems, beliefs, attitudes, and feelings. The system creates a "deviant" culture in which inmates form subgroups and develop friendships, loyalty, and commitment. **Prisonization** is the process whereby inmates learn the specific rules, general culture, and expectation of the prison community. With these two learning processes at work, which are often in conflict with society, it seems that the more time inmates spend in prison, the more likely they will crystallize their thinking and become "better criminals." Despite these challenges, correctional psychologists employ a number of approaches to deliver treatment to inmates.

Psychotherapy can be divided into six very broad and overlapping areas: psychoanalytic, behavioral, humanistic–existential, interpersonal, group, and cognitive therapy. Each approach is designed to change a person's way of thinking about the world to some extent. Most psychotherapies try to change cognitive constructs about ourselves, others, or both. Skinnerian behaviorism is probably least inclined to worry about cognitive constructs, since it focuses heavily on overt behavior, to the exclusion of the mediational processes. Lately, most behaviorists have shifted to a more cognitive–behavioral approach. Within corrections, this is the approach that is associated with the most effective treatment (Gaes et al., 1999). In the following pages we first discuss behavior therapy, then shift to the cognitive–behavioral.

Behavior Therapy

Behavior therapy was developed from learning–conditioning principles derived from well-controlled, precise laboratory environments or small-scale, well-designed demonstration projects. The social and physical environments are crucial considerations in the planning of any behavior therapy program.

Before the treatment program can be effectively implemented, the target behaviors and the environmental events that accompany them must be accurately described and carefully evaluated as to how, when, and where they occur for a particular individual. This information is normally gathered through direct observation of the individual in situations where he or she typically exhibits the target behavior and through interviews with the individual and acquaintances. In the planning stage, these initial data concerning the target behavior (such as frequency) provide baseline or pretreatment information that is useful for later determinations of how effective the treatment plan has been. Once the target behaviors and the conditions under which they occur are determined, the next step usually involves establishing a twofold plan: (1) The associative or reinforcement bond between the target behavior and the environmental event must be weakened, and (2) more desirable behavior must be instituted through reinforcement. When the plan has been implemented, comparing treatment data with baseline data helps to determine whether or not it is working. If the original treatment plan does not work, the conditions are reassessed and a modified plan is introduced.

Behavior therapy (also called behavior modification) seems to have a number of advantages. It has been shown to be highly effective in changing and developing specific behaviors under controlled, experimental conditions. Its apparent simplicity and the ease with which it can be applied by paraprofessionals with minimal training are also appealing. Furthermore, it is economical, because it does not require a legion of high-level, expensive professionals, and it can be immediately beneficial for controlling unmanageable behavior within the institution. Finally, because it quantifies observable behaviors, it lends itself very well to evaluation and research.

However, behavior therapy has a number of problems. While it seems to offer a simple, straightforward method for alleviating pressing behavior problems, it actually requires sophistication on the part of the therapist, stringent environmental control, and a high degree of cooperation and commitment from those even remotely involved in the program. Transferring behavior techniques from the controlled psychological laboratory to the correctional institution, where there are bound to be numerous constraints, is an extremely difficult task. Another flaw is behavior therapy's lack of demonstrated generalizability to the natural environment outside the prison, where powerful, significant models and reference groups often dilute the short-term effectiveness of many behavior therapy approaches. Finally, and perhaps most important, behavior therapy in the correctional setting raises many questions about the rights of inmates, especially if there is any indication that they are being coerced to participate.

Behavior therapy, well applied and with the inmate's willing participation, may be useful for controlling institutional behavior and can promote the acquisition of specific social and academic skills. Furthermore, when combined with social cognitive therapy, it is beginning to demonstrate its effectiveness in inhibiting or even reducing criminal behavior in the natural environment, such as with sex offenders discussed in Chapter 9.

Cognitive Therapy

Criminal behavior is not simply the result of imitating others in the social environment or even the result of external reinforcement. Research in cognitive psychology goes one step further. "If actions were determined solely by external rewards and punishments, people would behave like weathervanes, constantly shifting in different directions to conform to the momentary influence impinging on them. They would act corruptly with unprincipled individuals and honorably with righteous ones, and liberally with libertarians and dogmatically with authoritarians" (Bandura, 1977, p. 128). Instead, most human behavior is motivated and regulated in large part by personally adopted beliefs, values, and expectations.

During the past three decades, cognitive theories have come to dominate the research on learning, memory, personality, motivation, and social psychology (Aronson, Wilson, & Akert, 2005; Mahoney & Lyddon, 1988). The growth of **cognition** has also been very strong in the areas of counseling and psychotherapy. A person's behavior is the result of both external events, such as rewards and reinforcements, and internal events, such as how we think about things and perceive our world. Cognitive treatment, although the strategies differ in form and substance from one another, focuses on cognitive processes that mediate or influence behavior and emotions. Cognitive behavior therapies (CBT) rely on changing individual behavioral patterns by changing the person's thoughts, beliefs, and attitudes. CBT emerged during the past 30 years as a result of dissatisfaction with the theoretical and empirical bases of the strict behavior therapy approach. CBT has become the preferred treatment approach for dealing with certain groups of offenders, including sex offenders, violent offenders, and a variety of persistent property offenders. Bonta and Cormier (1999) rightfully note that "the research on the cognitive-behavioural treatment of offenders has led to wide acceptance of this approach as the preferred method for treating offenders. More traditional counseling techniques (e.g., client-centered, psychodynamic) are slowly losing favour among clinicians working with offenders" (p. 239).

One of the forerunners of the cognitive approaches was **reality therapy**, a form of self-control therapy developed by the psychiatrist William Glasser (1965) and still commonly used in corrections today. The basic principles for the approach were developed at the Ventura (California) School for Girls, whose residents were seriously delinquent adolescent girls. The popularity of reality therapy stems partly from its straightforward approach and easy-to-understand procedures. Because of its apparent simplicity, paraprofessionals and frontline correctional staff can easily be trained to offer personal and group therapy to inmates. Reality therapy is based on the perspective that offenders must face reality—no matter what happened to them in the past—and take full responsibility for their behavior now. In essence, the focus is to teach offenders responsible behavior. A major contribution of reality therapy has been to focus attention on the irresponsible nature of crime and delinquency, rather than viewing them as the result of some psychological sickness or disorder.

Other important forerunners of commonly used cognitive treatment approaches are George Kelly's (1955) *personal construct therapy*, Albert Ellis' (1962) rational-emotive therapy, and Aron T. Beck's (1970) *cognitive therapy*. All of these early approaches have undergone extensive revision since their initial formulation and have splintered into many different therapeutic perspectives.

In the 1980s, **constructivist therapy** emerged as a viable, rapidly growing approach across a wide area of cognitive therapies. "The basic assertion of constructivism is that each individual creates his or her own representational model of the world. This experiential scaffolding . . . in turn becomes a framework from which the individual orders and assigns meaning to new experience" (Mahoney & Lyddon, 1988, p. 200). The basic idea of the constructivist approach is that individuals do not formulate static templates through which ongoing experience is filtered but, rather, develop more dynamic constructs that are always subject to change as a result of new experiences. Thus, "the constructivist does not view cognitive structures as static, storage entities but rather as systems of transformation" (Mahoney & Lyddon, 1988, p. 203).

From a constructivist perspective, developing human beings are active information processors, who explore and adapt to the environment and who continually organize information about the world and themselves into increasingly complex views (Greenberg, 1988). On the other hand, repetitively violent and antisocial individuals may be those who are essentially trapped in an isolated, socially closed-off, and self-constructive cognitive system that relies on simple, straightforward aggressive solutions to survival. Moreover, they continually fall out of mainstream society, which results in their already isolated cognitive systems becoming more narrow, restrictive, and deviant. Instead of becoming more complex and integrative, the world versions of the repetitive offender may stagnate or deteriorate. Many repetitive offenders may become so caught up in their personal versions of the world that they refuse to allow alternative views to pierce their cognitive armor. Yochelson and Samenow (1976), for example, contend that there are 52 basic errors in thinking practiced by hard-core criminals that must be corrected before there is any hope of change. It would seem that cognitive therapies offer the best hope for changing the thinking and belief systems of the repetitive offender.

How successful has CBT been in corrections? Most research concludes that it has been reasonably successful or shows considerable promise in reducing recidivism in violent offenders (Serin & Preston, 2001), juvenile sex offenders (Becker & Johnson, 2001), adult sex offenders (Rice et al., 2001), criminally insane persons (NGRI patients) (Salekin & Rogers, 2001), and serious repetitive offenders (Gacono et al., 2001). However, before sweeping conclusions on the effectiveness of CBT can be made, we still need considerable well-done research using a wide variety of offenders within different contexts. One of the major shortcomings of the current research is the overreliance on self-report measures to determine treatment gain (Serin & Preston, 2001). Although self-report information is important because it may reflect an offender's self-perception, it is also fraught with many serious problems, especially when administered under duress within a correctional environment. In short, self-report answers can be faked or distorted by respondents, who can provide answers they believe authorities want to hear. However, official recidivism measures as indexes of treatment effectiveness also are problematic and may be too insensitive to what really happens after release from a correctional facility. For example, it might be more meaningful to gather information from parole officers concerning the offender's adaptation to life after release or other more subtle adjustment measures rather than relying strictly on official postrelease arrests and conviction records.

Serin and Preston (2001) assert that treatment effectiveness will be increased when it is tailored to the specific needs of the individual offender. Recall the discussion earlier in the chapter about dynamic risk factors and criminogenic needs. Identifying these for any offender is clearly an illustration of tailoring treatment. Becker and Johnson (2001) recommend using multimodal treatment approaches (impulse control techniques, empathy training, anger management) that are firmly based on cognitive–behavioral techniques.

We also need to have a better understanding of the relationships among the vast array of swirling systems that affect delinquent and criminal behavior before we can have highly effective treatment or prevention programs. "Human action is . . . regulated by multilevel systems of control" (Bandura, 1989, p. 1181). One such approach is a social systems theory. A social systems approach facilitates a synthesis of what we know across the various disciplines and perspectives, whether we are discussing social class, neighborhood, community, culture, family, siblings, or the individual (Bartol, 1988). Social systems theory assumes that while it is helpful to study personality variables, family, the neighborhood, and the culture in isolation, it is far more effective to study these variables in relationship to one another. In order to change criminal behavior over long periods of time, we need to study not only the offenders themselves but also their families, peers, schools, neighborhoods, communities, and cultures, all in relationship to one another. The offender affects the other systems and the systems affect the offender in complex, poorly understood ways. Treatment and preventive approaches that are fully able to appreciate this dynamic interplay are far more likely to be successful than those that concentrate on only one aspect of an individual's life. In fact, as we discussed very early in the book, in Chapter 2, one of the most promising approaches to treating juvenile delinquency—multisystemic therapy—uses just such an approach.

SUMMARY AND CONCLUSIONS

As the twentieth century ended, and into the early years of the twenty-first, prison and jail populations across the United States reached record high levels, even while the crime rate was showing signs of stabilizing. The United

States consistently maintains its reputation of being the democratic country with the highest rate of incarceration. Although high numbers of individuals are serving time for violent offenses, nonviolent offenders—e.g., those convicted of drug crimes, burglaries, auto thefts, and other felonies—comprise a substantial percentage of the incarcerated population. In some facilities, nonviolent offenders surpass the 50% mark. Young black males continue to be incarcerated in numbers disproportionate to their representation in the population. We also noted in this chapter that, while women continue to make up less than 10% of all incarcerated individuals, their incarceration rates are increasing more rapidly than those of men.

Although we have focused on imprisoned populations in this chapter, it is important to keep in mind that approximately two-thirds of all persons under correctional supervision in the United States are supervised in community settings, such as on probation or parole. Many psychologists working in corrections offer services to these individuals. For example, probationers and parolees are often required to participate in substance abuse treatment, sex offender treatment, and psychotherapy as a condition of remaining in the community. In addition, psychologists may be asked to conduct presentencing evaluations to determine whether a particular individual would be amenable to treatment. Thus, before deciding whether to send a convicted sex offender to prison or allow him to remain in the community, a judge may request an evaluation of the likelihood that he will reoffend as well as the likelihood that he would benefit from sex offender treatment.

Although psychologists are not the only mental health professionals working in or consulting with corrections, we have emphasized that there are multiple opportunities for psychologists wishing to work in this arena. The tasks we focused on in this chapter included the classification, assessment, and treatment of inmates, but others exist as well. For example, psychologists also may be involved in conducting research, providing hostage negotiation training, offering counseling services to staff, designing programs for families of inmates, and screening and selecting corrections officers.

Classification in corrections is done both to determine the appropriate custody level for a prisoner and to determine what services (e.g., educational, health, psychological) are warranted. Psychologists have been at the forefront of developing classification schemes since Edward Megargee proposed a system based on the Minnesota Multiphasic Personality Inventory (Megargee, 1977). Although the Megargee approach continues to be used in some prison systems, increasingly more attention is given to classification systems proposed by Canadian psychologists, including the Level of Service Inventory—Revised developed by Andrews and Bonta (1995).

Psychological treatment is provided to inmates both to meet their mental health needs and in recognition that rehabilitation is a goal worth pursuing. The growing numbers of individuals with mental health problems in jails and prisons were a topic of concern to correctional officials throughout the 1990s and continue to be into the twenty-first century. In addition, inmates who are generally stable may need crisis intervention services at various points in their incarceration. Most psychological research on treatment deals with the programs intended to aid in rehabilitation. As we noted in the chapter, rehabilitation was dealt a blow in the 1970s and 1980s, when pessimistic reviews questioned the efficacy of many rehabilitation programs. Today, it is recognized that some approaches clearly have merit for some offenders, and rehabilitation has experienced a reaffirmation, although not universally. Of the psychologically oriented approaches, those based on cognitive behavioral principles have received the most positive evaluations. In essence, prisoners are encouraged to "rethink" their assumptions and to find effective ways of managing their lives.

Some aspects of jail and prison life pose major challenges to psychologists working in corrections. From a psychological perspective, overcrowded facilities and isolation for long periods of time are extremely problematic. We have been especially critical of the ultramax facilities that place difficult to manage prisoners in high-security isolation for years at a time. Critics have argued that they are expensive, overused, and conducive to rapid mental deterioration of the prisoners housed within them. However, the facilities as well as the inmates themselves are unique, and we must be cautious in making generalizations. Likewise, all prisons and jails vary widely in the extent to which they are violent, run-down, crowded, and program-oriented as opposed to custody-oriented. Furthermore, inmates vary widely in the degree to which they can adjust to control, threats of violence, isolation from the outside world, isolation from other inmates, boredom, and lack of autonomy.

As we noted at the beginning of the chapter, human beings are highly adaptable and changeable, particularly if they desire to change. The psychologist involved in rehabilitation efforts in jail and prison settings, as well as in the community, provides offenders with necessary skills to achieve this change. Although there are numerous challenges to accomplishing this goal, psychologists and other mental health professionals have made significant strides, particularly when cognitive behavioral treatment can be provided.

GLOSSARY

adjudicative competence The ability to participate in a variety of court proceedings. See also incompetent to stand trial.

adolescent-limited (AL) offender An individual who usually demonstrates delinquent or antisocial behavior only during his or her teen years and then stops offending during the young adult years.

aggression, hostile (expressive) Aggressive behavior characterized by the intent to cause the target discomfort or pain.

aggression, instrumental Aggressive behavior characterized by the intent to gain material or financial rewards from the target.

aggressive (sadistic) pedophile An adult drawn to children for both sexual and aggressive (violent) purposes.

ambiversion Characterized by a score in the average range on the extraversion–introversion scale developed by Hans J. Eysenck.

amnesia Complete or partial memory loss of an incident, series of incidents, or some aspects of life's experiences.

anger rape A rape situation, identified by Groth, in which an offender uses more force than necessary for compliance and engages in a variety of sexual acts that are particularly degrading or humiliating to the victim.

anger retaliation rapist A classification of rapists proposed by the Massachusetts Treatment Center to identify those individuals who are more motivated to humiliate the victim than to gain sexual gratification. See also **displaced anger rapist**.

antisocial behavior Clinical term reserved for serious habitual behavior, especially that involving direct harm to others.

antisocial personality disorder (APD) A disorder characterized by a history of continuous behavior in which the rights of others are violated.

anxiety disorder Mental disorder caused by high levels of physiological arousal that interfere with daily functioning.

arson Any willful or malicious burning or attempt to burn, with or without intent to defraud, a dwelling, house, public building, motor vehicle, aircraft, or personal property of another.

assault The intentional infliction of bodily injury on another person, or the attempt to inflict such injury.

assault, aggravated Inflicting, or attempting to inflict, bodily injury on another person, with the intent to inflict serious injury.

assault, simple The unlawful, intentional infliction of less than serious bodily injury without a deadly or dangerous weapon, or the attempt to inflict such bodily injury, again without a deadly or dangerous weapon.

attention deficit hyperactivity disorder (ADHD) Traditionally considered a chronic neuro-biological condition characterized by developmentally poor attention, impulsivity, and hyperactivity. More contemporary perspectives see the behavioral pattern as a deficiency in interpersonal skills.

autoeroticism A term coined by Havelock Ellis that refers to self-arousal and self-gratification of sexual desire.

availability heuristic The cognitive shortcuts that people use to make quick inferences about their world. It is the information that is most readily available to us mentally, and is usually based extensively on the most recent material we gain from the news or entertainment media.

avoidance learning A process whereby, if a person responds in time to a warning signal, he or she avoids painful or aversive stimuli.

barricade situation A hostage situation in which an individual has fortified him- or herself inside a building or residence, threatening violence to him- or herself or to others.

battered child syndrome A cluster of behavioral and psychological characteristics believed to be common to children who have been abused, physically or emotionally.

battered woman syndrome A cluster of behavioral and psychological characteristics believed to be common to women who have been abused in relationships.

behaviorism A perspective that focuses on observable, measurable behavior and argues that social environment and learning are the key determinants of human behavior.

Brawner Rule A standard for evaluating the insanity defense that recognizes that the defendant suffers from a condition that substantially (1) affects mental or emotional processes or (2) impairs behavior controls. Also called the ALI/Brawner Rule.

burglary The unlawful entry of a structure, with or without force, with intent to commit a felony or theft.

caveat paragraph A section of the ALI/Brawner Rule that excludes abnormality manifested only by repeated criminal or antisocial conduct. It was specifically designed to disallow the insanity defense for psychopaths.

classic mass murder A situation in which an individual enters a public place or barricades him- or herself inside a public building, such as a fast-food restaurant, and randomly kills patrons and other individuals.

classical (Pavlovian) conditioning The process of learning to respond to a formerly neutral stimulus that has been paired with another stimulus that already elicits a response. Also called **Pavlovian conditioning**.

classification In corrections, the process of placing offenders into categories for the purposes of custody and treatment.

clearance rate The proportion of reported crimes that have been "solved" through the arrest and turning-over for prosecution of at least one person. Crimes also may be cleared through exceptional means.

cognitions The internal processes that enable humans to imagine, to gain knowledge, to reason, and to evaluate. The attitudes, beliefs, values, and thoughts that a person holds about the environment, relationships, and him- or herself.

cognitive behavior therapy An approach to therapy that focuses on changing beliefs, fantasies, attitudes, and rationalizations that justify and perpetuate antisocial or other problematic behavior. It is often used in the treatment of sex offenders.

cognitive learning   The formation and development of mental concepts, schemata, theories, attitudes, beliefs, and other mental versions of the world.

cognitive–neoassociation model   A revised theory of the frustration–aggression hypothesis proposed by Leonard Berkowitz.

cognitive scripts   Mental images of how one feels he or she should act in a variety of situations.

cognitive scripts model   Rowell Huesmann's theory that social behavior in general and aggressive behavior in particular are controlled largely by cognitive scripts learned and memorized through daily experiences.

community-based corrections   The broad term for a wide variety of options that allow individuals on probation or parole to be supervised in the community rather than incarcerated. Supervision may occur within their own homes or in special community facilities, such as halfway houses.

compensatory rapist   An offender who rapes in response to an intense sexual arousal initiated by stimuli in the environment, often quite specific stimuli (e.g., dark-haired women). His main motive is to prove his sexual prowess.

compulsion   An action a person feels compelled (driven) by internal thoughts to take, even though it may be irrational.

compulsive gambling   A psychiatric syndrome characterized by anxiety and an insatiable, unconscious desire to lose what was gained in previous gambling.

concordance   A term used in genetics to represent the degree to which related pairs of subjects both show a particular behavior or condition. It is usually expressed in percentages.

conduct disorder   A diagnostic label used to identify children who demonstrate habitual misbehavior.

conformity perspective   The theoretical position that humans are born basically good and generally try to do the right and just thing.

constructivist therapy   Psychotherapy based on the view that the therapist must begin and work with each person's unique version of the world.

contagion effect   A tendency of some people to model or copy a behavior or activity portrayed by the news or entertainment media.

controlled substance   Any psychoactive drug or chemical substance whose availability is restricted, as designated by state or federal law.

copycat effect   See **contagion effect**.

correlation   A mathematical index that reflects the nature of the relationship between two variables.

criminal homicide   A term that encompasses both murder and nonnegligent homicide.

criminal profiling   See **profiling**.

criminal psychopath   A primary psychopath who engages in repetitive antisocial or criminal behavior.

criminalization   The process whereby inmates exchange, share, and support one another's beliefs, attitudes, and feelings, which in the long run promotes criminal activity.

criminogenic needs   Those dynamic risk factors that are empirically found to be related to criminal behavior.

criminology   The multidisciplinary study of crime.

criminology, psychiatric   The branch of criminology that focuses on individual aspects of behavior, particularly internal forces and unconscious drives. Also called **forensic psychiatry**.

criminology, psychological   The branch of criminology that examines the individual behavior and, especially, the mental processes involved in criminal behavior.

criminology, sociological   The branch of criminology that examines the demographic, group, and societal variables related to crime.

cybercrime   Any illegal act that involves a computer system. Also called **computer crime**.

cyberstalking   Threatening behavior or unwanted advances directed at another using the Internet or other forms of online communications.

dark figure   The number of crimes that go unreported in official crime report data.

date rape   A sexual assault that occurs within the context of a dating relationship.

dehumanize   To engage in actions that obscure the identity of the victim, such as excessive facial battery, or to see and treat victims as objects rather than human beings.

deindividuation   A process by which individuals feel they cannot be identified, primarily because they are disguised or are subsumed within a group.

delusional (paranoid) disorder   A mental disorder characterized by a system of false beliefs.

dependence   In substance abuse, a condition that may be physical, psychological, or both, whereby a person develops an intense craving for (and feels he or she cannot live without) a drug.

dependent variable   The variable that is measured to see how it is changed by manipulations of the independent variable.

deterrence   One of the four goals or purposes of sentencing. It refers to the use of punishment to dissuade individuals from committing crime in the future. **General deterrence** refers to the overall symbolic impact punishment has on the population as a whole. **Specific (or special) deterrence** is based on the actual experience of punishment, which presumably will deter the punished individual from engaging in future transgressions.

***Diagnostic and Statistical Manual of Mental Disorders* (DSM)**   The official guidebook or manual, published by the American Psychiatric Association, used to define and diagnose specific mental disorders.

difference in degree   The perspective of human nature that argues that humans are intimately tied to their animal ancestry in important and significant ways and differ only in the extent to which they have developed through the evolutionary process. For example, this perspective might argue that human violence is a result of innate, biological needs to obtain sufficient food supplies, territory, or mates.

differential association–reinforcement theory   A theory of deviance developed by Ronald Akers that combines Skinner's behaviorism and Sutherland's differential association theory. The theory states that people learn deviant behavior through the reinforcements they receive from the social environment.

differential association theory   Formulated by Edwin Sutherland, a theory of crime that states that criminal behavior is primarily due to obtaining values or messages from others, including but not limited to those who engage in crime. The critical factors include those with whom a person associates, how early in life the associations begin, and how frequent and how personally meaningful the associations are.

differential treatment   Any treatment program formulated to meet the individual needs and capabilities of a person in a correctional setting.

discriminative stimuli   Social signals transmitted by subcultural or peer groups to indicate whether certain kinds of behavior will be rewarded or punished within a particular social context.

disorganized crime scene   Demonstrates that the offender committed the crime without premeditation or planning. In other words, the crime scene indicators suggest that the individual acted on impulse, in rage, or under extreme excitement.

displaced aggression rapist   The rapist whose attack is violent and aggressive, displaying minimum or total absence of sexual feeling. Also called **anger retaliation rapist**.

dispositions   In personality theory, a term that signifies internal or personality determinants of human behavior. Dispositional theorists look to inner conflicts, beliefs, drives, personal needs, traits, or attitudes to explain behavior. See also **traits**.

dissociative disorders   Mental disorders characterized by memory loss or loss of identity.

dissociative identity disorder (DID)   A psychiatric syndrome characterized by the existence within an individual of two or more distinct personalities, any of which may be dominant at any given moment. Formerly called **multiple personality disorder (MPD)**.

drug treatment   An approach to therapy that concentrates on reducing the targeted behavior through the use of medication. In sex offender therapy, for example, antiandrogens and antidepressant medications may be used.

DSM   See **Diagnostic and Statistical Manual**.

Durham Rule   A legal standard of insanity that holds that an accused is not criminally responsible if his or her unlawful act was the product of a mental disease or defect. Also known as the **Product Rule**.

dynamic risk factors   Things about a person's developmental history that change over time, such as attitudes, opinions, and knowledge.

dyssocial psychopath   An individual with psychopathic characteristics who is antisocial because of social learning and does not possess the features of the primary psychopath.

ectomorph   A body type characterized by thinness and fragility in structure.

eldercide   The killing of an older person—usually defined as 65 or over—generally by an adult relative or caretaker.

emotional paradox   The research observation that psychopaths seem to be able to talk about emotional cues but lack the ability to use them effectively in the real world.

endomorph   A body type characterized by roundness and fatty tissue.

equivocal death analysis   See **reconstructive psychological evaluation (RPE)**.

escalation   A process whereby each party in a conflict increases the magnitude or intensity of a response in reaction to the increased response received from the other party.

evocative therapy   An approach to sex offender therapy that focuses on (1) helping offenders to understand the causes and motivations of their sexual behavior and (2) increasing their empathy for the victims of the sexual assault.

excitation transfer theory   Theory explaining how physiological arousal can generalize from one situation to another; based on the assumption that physiological arousal, however produced, dissipates slowly over time.

excitement-motivated (E-M) arson   A category suggested by the FBI to classify those people who set fires simply for excitement.

exhibitionism   The deliberate exposure of the genitals to another person to achieve sexual gratification. Also called **indecent exposure**.

expectancy theory   A theory of motivation that takes into account both the expectation of achieving a particular goal and the value placed on it.

exploitative pedophile   An adult who seeks children almost exclusively for sexual gratification.

exploitative rapist   See **impulsive rapist**.

expressive hostage-taking   A hostage-taking situation in which the offender's primary goal is to gain some control over his or her life.

expressive sexual aggression   A rape situation in which the offender's primary aim is to harm the victim physically as well as psychologically.

extinction   The decline and eventual disappearance of a conditioned or learned response when it is no longer reinforced.

extraversion   In Eysenck's theory, a personality dimension that represents needs for stimulation.

factor analysis   A statistical procedure by which underlying patterns, factors, or dimensions are identified among a series of scale items.

false memory syndrome   A mental state wherein an individual believes that an incident has happened, although it actually has not happened.

family mass murder   A situation in which at least three family members are killed (usually by another family member).

fetishism   Sexual attraction to inanimate objects.

fixated pedophile   A male who demonstrates a long-standing, exclusive preference for children as both sexual and social companions. Also called **immature pedophile**.

forcible rape   The carnal knowledge of a female, forcibly and against her will. It includes rape by force, assault to rape, and attempted rape. Although victims may be both female and male, the Uniform Crime Reports definition limits this to female victims.

forensic psychiatry   See **criminology, psychiatric**.

forensic psychology   The production and application of psychological knowledge to the civil and criminal justice systems.

frustration–aggression hypothesis   The theory that frustration leads to aggressive behavior. The theory has been revised several times, with most substantial changes coming from the work of Leonard Berkowitz.

fundamental attribution error   A tendency to underestimate the importance of situational determinants and to overestimate the importance of personality or dispositional factors in identifying the causes of human behavior.

general deterrence   See **deterrence**.

geographical profiling   A type of profiling that focuses on the location of the crime and how it relates to the residence and/or base of operations of the offender. The fundamental assumption of geographical profiling is that serial offenders prefer to commit their crimes near their own residences.

guilty but mentally ill (GBMI)   A verdict alternative in some states that allows defendants to be found guilty while seemingly affording them treatment for mental disorders.

habituation   Getting used to or adapting to a stimulus.

hallucinogens   Those psychoactive drugs that sometimes generate hallucinations and lead to changes in perceptions of reality. Also called **psychedelics**.

Hate Crime Statistics Act   A 1990 federal statute that directs the FBI to collect data on all crimes motivated by racial, ethnic, religious, or sexual orientation hate or bias. Physical or mental disability bias was added in 1997.

hebephilia   The use of young adolescent girls or boys for sexual gratification by adult males.

hostile attribution model   A cognitive model of aggression developed by Kenneth Dodge and colleagues. See also **hostile attributional bias**.

hostile attributional bias   The tendency to perceive hostile intent in others even when it is totally lacking.

human trafficking   The transportation and exploitation of individuals, usually for sex-related purposes and high profits. Children and women from impoverished nations or parts of the United States are particularly vulnerable.

hyperactivity   A behavioral pattern demonstrated by both children and adults wherein there is considerable motor activity in an attempt to gain adequate amounts of cortical stimulation.

iatrogenic   A process whereby mental or physical disorders are unintentionally induced or developed in patients by physicians, clinicians, or psychotherapists.

identity theft   The fraudulent use of another person's personal identification information—such as Social Security number, date of birth, or mother's maiden name—without that person's knowledge or permission.

imitational learning   See **observational learning**.

immature pedophile   See **fixated pedophile**.

impulsive rapist   A rapist who demonstrates neither strong sexual nor strong aggressive features but engages in spontaneous rape when the opportunity presents itself. The rape is usually carried out in the context of another crime, such as robbery or burglary. Also called **exploitative rapist**.

incapacitation   One of the four goals or purposes of punishment. Isolation of the individual from society so that he or she cannot commit more crime.

incompetent to stand trial (IST)   A judicial determination that a defendant lacks sufficient ability to understand the legal charges against him or her and/or to assist a lawyer in the preparation of a defense. See also **adjudicative competence**.

independent variable   The measure whose effect is being studied and, in most scientific investigations, that is being manipulated by the experimenter in a controlled fashion.

index crimes (Part I crimes)   The crimes that are of most concern, as defined by the FBI's Uniform Crime Reports, and are used to indicate the seriousness of the crime problem. The eight index crimes are murder and nonnegligent manslaughter, aggravated assault, robbery, forcible rape, burglary, larceny–theft, arson, and motor vehicle theft.

individual offender   A person who consistently violates the law because of a series of frustrations and disappointments and/or as a matter of personal choice.

infanticide   Although this term literally means the killing of an infant, it has become synonymous with the killing of a child by a parent.

inhalants   Refers to a thousand or more different household and commercial products that can be abused by sniffing or "huffing" (inhaling though the mouth) for an intoxicating effect. They are found in organic solvents and volatile substances commonly found in adhesives, lighter fluids, cleaning solutions, and paint products.

Insanity Defense Reform Act of 1984   A law designed to make it more difficult for defendants using the insanity defense in the federal courts to be acquitted.

instrumental hostage-taking   A hostage situation in which the primary goal of the offender is material or monetary gain.

instrumental learning   A form of learning in which a voluntary response is strengthened or diminished by its consequences. Also called **operant conditioning**.

instrumental sexual aggression   When the sexual offender uses just enough coercion to gain compliance from his victim.

interactionism   The perspective that argues that human behavior is determined or influenced by both internal (biological, psychological, cognitive) and external (social environmental) factors.

intimate partner violence   Crimes committed against persons by their current or former spouses, boyfriends, or girlfriends.

introvert   In Eysenck's theory, a person with low need for stimulation and who conditions easily.

invariance hypothesis   Proposed by Gottfredson and Hirschi, this hypothesis refers to the observation that crime seems to decline with the age of the offender, no matter what historical period or what culture is being considered.

irrationality   A basic ingredient of the insanity standard. Refers to the legal assumption that persons cannot be held criminally responsible for their actions if it is determined that they could not understand the consequences of their behavior.

isolation (or segregation)   In corrections, the separation of the inmate from the general jail or prison population. May be done for disciplinary, protective, or administrative reasons.

jail   A facility operated by a local government to hold persons temporarily detained, awaiting trial, or sentenced to short-term confinement, after having been convicted of a misdemeanor.

just world hypothesis   A belief that one gets what one deserves in this world.

Juvenile Court Act   A statute passed by the Illinois legislature in 1899 that established a separate court for juveniles and marked the official beginning of juvenile justice in the United States.

juvenile delinquent   In the legal sense, a youth who has been adjudicated by a juvenile court and found to have committed a criminal act (distinguished from a status offense).

kleptomania   The irresistible urge to steal unneeded objects. Whether there is such an urge is highly debatable.

learned helplessness   A learned passive and withdrawing response in the face of perceived hopelessness, as theorized by Martin Seligman (1975).

learning perspective   The theoretical position that humans are born basically neutral and behaviorally a blank slate. What they become as individuals depends on their learning experiences rather than innate predispositions.

life course–persistent (LCP) offenders   A term used by Terrie Moffitt to represent offenders who demonstrate a lifelong pattern of antisocial behavior and who are resistant to treatment or rehabilitation.

limited amnesia   A pathological inability to remember a specific episode, or a small number of episodes, from the recent past.

London syndrome   A behavioral pattern observed during a hostage situation at the Iranian Embassy in London. Refers to the explicit and consistent resistance and refusals by hostages to do what is expected by captors. This behavior often results in death or serious injury to the blatant resistors.

major depressive disorder   General label for symptoms that include an extremely depressed state, a general slowing-down of mental and physical activity, and feelings of self-worthlessness.

mass arsonist   A person who sets three or more fires in quick succession at the same location, without a cooling-off period.

mass murder   The murder of three or more persons at a single location with no cooling-off period between murders.

maturation retardation hypothesis   Robert Hare's theory that suggests that the neurological development of psychopaths may be slower than normal.

MDMA   Abbreviation for a drug called "ecstasy," which is a synthetic drug that is considered to be a stimulant with strong psychedelic effects.

mentally disordered sex offender   A classification established by some state legislatures to identify those mentally disordered individuals prone to repetitive sexual attacks on children, women, or both. See also **sexually violent predator**.

mesomorph   A muscular and well-developed body type. Some research has indicated that individuals with this body type are more likely to be involved in violent crime.

minor physical anomalies (MPAs)   Small, nearly undetectable physical abnormalities that some researchers believe may be associated with birth and neurological defects.

mixed crime scene   Indicates that the nature of the crime demonstrates both organized and disorganized behavioral patterns.

M'Naghten Rule   An insanity standard based on the conclusion that if defendants have a defect of reason, or a disease of the mind, so as not to know the nature and quality of their actions, then they cannot be held criminally responsible. Also called **the right and wrong test**.

modus operandi (MO)   The actions and procedures an offender uses to commit a crime successfully.

multiple personality disorder (MPD)   See **dissociative identity disorder**.

multisystemic therapy   A treatment approach for serious juvenile offenders that focuses on the family while being responsive to the many other contexts surrounding the family, such as the peer group, the neighborhood, and the school.

Munchausen syndrome by proxy   An unusual form of child abuse in which the parent (usually the mother), or parents, consistently seeks medical attention for a child with symptoms falsified or directly induced by the parent(s).

murder   The felonious killing of one human being by another with malice aforethought. See also **criminal homicide**.

narcotics   Psychoactive drugs that produce sleep and are derivatives of the poppy plant.

National Incident-Based Recording System (NIBRS)   The FBI's method of collecting data on reported crime and arrests from law enforcement agencies nationwide. Designed to be an improvement on the UCR system.

neurosis   A mild form of mental disorder characterized by anxiety. The term is used infrequently by clinicians today.

neurotic disorders   Anxiety disorders, somatoform disorders, and dissociative disorders.

neuroticism   A dimension of personality according to Hans J. Eysenck that theoretically reflects arousal levels of the autonomic nervous system.

nonconformist perspective   The theoretical perspective that humans will naturally try to get away with anything they can, including illegal conduct, unless social controls are imposed.

nonindex crimes (Part II crimes)   Crimes not considered serious by the FBI and on which only arrest data are gathered in the Uniform Crime Reports. Examples include simple assault, fraud, embezzlement, and vandalism.

nonnegligent manslaughter   The killing of a human being without premeditation but with the intention to kill in the "heat of the moment," such as in high emotional states of anger or passion.

not guilty by reason of insanity (NGRI)   A legal determination that a defendant was so mentally disordered at the time of the crime that he or she cannot be held criminally responsible for his or her actions.

observational learning (modeling)   The process by which individuals learn patterns of behavior by observing another person performing the action.

operant conditioning   See **instrumental learning**.

opiate narcotics   Psychoactive drugs that have sedative (sleep-inducing) and analgesic (pain-relieving) effects.

organized crime scene   Indicates planning and premeditation on the part of the offender. In other words, the crime scene shows signs that the offender maintained control of him- or herself and of the victim, if it is a crime against a person.

overcontrolled personality   A person who has well-established inhibitions against aggressive behavior and rigidly adheres to them, even in the face of provocation.

paranoid disorders   See **delusional disorders**.

partialism   An exaggerated sexual interest in some part of the human anatomy not usually associated with sexual arousal, such as the ankle or elbow.

passive aggressive behaviors   Hostile behaviors that do not directly inflict physical harm, such as refusing to speak to someone against whom one holds a grudge.

Pavlovian conditioning   See **classical conditioning**.

pedophilia   The use of children by adults for sexual gratification and companionship.

personation   See **signature**.

post–traumatic stress disorder (PTSD)   A cluster of behavioral patterns that result from a psychologically distressing event outside the usual range of human experience.

power rape   A rape situation, identified by Groth, in which the assailant seeks to establish power and control over his victim. Thus, the amount of force and threats used depends on the degree of submission shown by the victim.

premenstrual syndrome (PMS)   The cluster of behavioral patterns and psychological changes that are believed to accompany the cyclic physiological changes that occur prior to the onset of menstruation in some women. Although some symptoms are common, the prevalence and existence of a *syndrome* are widely disputed.

primary prevention   An intervention program designed to prevent behavior or disorders before any sign of the behavioral pattern develops.

primary psychopath   Robert Hare's classification of the "true" psychopath. That is, the individual who demonstrates those behavioral features that represent psychopathy—in contrast to secondary psychopaths, who commit antisocial acts because of severe emotional problems or inner conflicts, and dyssocial psychopaths, who are antisocial because of social learning.

prisonization   The process by which inmates adopt and internalize the prisoner subculture within a particular correctional facility.

prisons Correctional facilities operated by state and federal governments to hold persons convicted of felonies and sentenced generally to terms of more than one year.

proactive aggression In children, cold-blooded actions such as bullying, name-calling, and coercive acts.

profiling The process of identifying personality traits, behavioral tendencies, and demographic variables of an offender based on characteristics of the crime. See also **psychological profiling**.

prostitution Offering or agreeing to engage in, or engaging in, a sex act with another in exchange for a fee.

protective custody A form of isolation in which an inmate is separated from others for his or her own safety.

psychedelics The category of psychoactive drugs that produce elevated mood, hallucinations, and altered states of consciousness. Also called **hallucinogens**.

psychoactive drugs Drugs that exert their primary effect on the brain, thus altering mood or behavior.

psychodynamic (hydraulic) model The theoretical perspective that argues that human behavior can be best explained through the use of psychological forces and pressures.

psychoeducational counseling An approach to therapy that uses a group or class setting to remedy deficits in social and interpersonal skills.

psychological autopsy Postmortem analysis often reserved for cases in which suicide occurred or is suspected or alleged. The psychological autopsy is frequently done to determine the reasons and precipitating factors for the death.

psychological profiling The psychological description of a person or persons, whether or not suspected to be or involved in criminal activity.

psychometric approach The perspective that human characteristics, attributes, and traits can be measured and quantified.

psychometric intelligence (PI) A more contemporary designation of intelligence as measured by intelligence or IQ tests.

psychopath An individual who demonstrates a distinct behavioral pattern that differs from that of the general population in its level of sensitivity, empathy, compassion, and guilt. See also **primary psychopath**.

Psychopathy Checklist (PCL) Developed by Robert Hare, currently the best instrument to measure criminal psychopathy. Additional versions include the **Psychopathy Checklist—Screening Version**, the **P-Scan: Research Version**, and the **Psychopathy Checklist: Youth Version**.

psychosis A severe form of mental disorder characterized by hallucinations, delusions, and other indications of loss of contact with reality.

psychotechnology Methods of permanently altering brain tissue through surgical, electrical (direct current), or chemical means.

psychoticism A personality dimension, proposed by Eysenck, characterized by cold cruelty, social insensitivity, unemotionality, high risk-taking, troublesome behavior, and a dislike of others.

punishment An event by which a person receives a noxious, painful, or aversive stimulus, usually as a consequence of behavior.

pyromania   A psychiatric term for an irresistible urge to set fires along with an intense fascination (usually sexual) with fire. The existence of this behavioral phenomenon has been brought into serious question by the available research.

racial profiling   Police-initiated action that relies on the race, ethnicity, or national origin rather than the behavior of an individual or on other information that leads the police to suspect the individual of criminal activity.

rape by fraud   The act of having sexual relations with a supposedly consenting adult female under fraudulent conditions, such as when a physician or psychotherapist has sexual intercourse with a patient under the guise of "effective treatment."

rational reconstruction   A mental process whereby an individual engages in a reinterpretation of past behavior in which he or she recasts activities in a manner consistent with "what should have been" rather than "what was." The term is used in this book specifically for explaining research on burglary.

reactive aggression   In children, hot-blooded aggressive acts, such as temper tantrums and vengeful hostility.

reality therapy   Treatment based on the view that the patient must face reality and take full responsibility for his or her behavior.

reconstructive psychological evaluation   Reconstruction of the personality profile and cognitive features (especially intentions) of deceased individuals.

reductionism   A research approach that argues that in order to understand highly complex events or phenomenon, one must start by examining the simplest parts first.

regressed pedophile   A male who has fairly normal relationships with adults but then reverts to children for sexual and social companionship because of feelings of inadequacy.

rehabilitation   One of the four goals or purposes of sentencing, it is any attempt to bring about change in behavior patterns or attitudes.

reinforcement   Anything that increases the probability of responding.

reinforcement, negative   The reward received for avoiding a painful or aversive condition or stimulus.

reinforcement, positive   The acquisition of something desired as a result of one's behavior.

relapse prevention   A method of treatment designed primarily to prevent a relapse of an undesired behavioral pattern.

relative deprivation   A concept developed by Gresham Sykes for explaining economic crime. It refers to the perceived discrepancy between what an individual has and what he or she would like to have. It is a condition that is especially prominent when people of wealth and people of poverty live in close proximity.

retribution   One of the four purposes of sentencing, it is the principle that individuals should be held accountable for offending against society and should be given appropriate sanctions, proportional to their crime.

right and wrong test   See **M'Naghten Rule**.

risk assessment   The enterprise in which clinicians offer probabilities that a given individual will engage in violent or otherwise antisocial behavior based on known factors relating to the individual.

ritualized aggression   The symbolic display of aggressive intentions or strength without actual physical combat or conflict.

robbery The taking-of or attempt to take anything of value from the care, custody, or control of another by force or the threat of force.

Rohypnol Sometimes referred to as a date-rape drug, it is a powerful depressant commonly abused by young adults and adolescents.

sadistic rapist See **sexually aggressive rapist**.

sadistic rape A rape situation, identified by Groth, in which the offender experiences sexual arousal and excitement as a result of the victim's torment, distress, helplessness, and suffering. The assault usually involves bondage and torture, and the rapist directs considerable abuse and injury on various areas of the victim's body.

schizophrenia Mental disorder characterized by severe breakdowns in thought patterns, emotions, and perceptions.

secondary prevention An intervention program designed for individuals who demonstrate early signs or indicators of behavioral problems or antisocial behavior.

secondary psychopath An individual with psychopathic characteristics but who commits antisocial acts because of severe emotional problems or inner conflicts. Distinct from **primary psychopath**.

sedative–hypnotic Psychoactive drugs that depress central nervous system functioning, generally reducing anxiety and tension.

selective incapacitation The imprisonment for longer terms of offenders who are believed to pose the greatest threat to society.

self-regulatory mechanisms Personal standards that people develop by which they evaluate and compare their own conduct to that of others in their social environment.

self-serving bias The tendency to attribute positive things that happen to us to our abilities and personalities, and to attribute negative events to some cause outside ourselves or beyond our control.

semantic aphasia A characteristic found in psychopaths whereby the words they speak are devoid of emotional sincerity.

serial murder Incidents in which an individual kills a number of victims (usually a minimum of three) over time.

serotonin A chemical enabling nerve cells to communicate with one another. Low levels of this chemical may be related to aggressive behavior.

sexually aggressive rapist A rapist who demonstrates both sexual and aggressive features in his attack. In order for him to experience sexual arousal, it must be associated with violence and pain, which excite him. Also called **sadistic rapist**.

sexually violent predator A legal determination under which states can place restrictive conditions on sex offenders believed to represent a heightened danger to the public. Some statutes allow courts to commit sexually violent predators to civil mental institutions against their will after they have completed their prison sentences.

shaken baby syndrome A form of child abuse in which an adult (usually male) shakes a baby so hard that it causes significant brain damage or death.

signature Any behavior that goes beyond what is necessary to commit the crime. Also called **personation**.

simulation Research conducted in a laboratory setting that is designed to mimic the "real world" as closely as possible.

situationism   A theoretical perspective that argues that environmental stimuli control behavior.

social class   Socioeconomic status, typically based predominantly on one's family's income.

social control theory   A theory proposed by Travis Hirschi that contends that crime and delinquency occur when an individual's ties to the conventional order or normative standards are weak or largely nonexistent.

social learning theory   A theory of human behavior based on learning from watching others in the social environment. This leads to an individual's development of his or her own perceptions, thoughts, expectancies, competencies, and values.

social status   Refers to a person's own socioeconomic status, rather than one's family socioeconomic status.

socialized offender   A person who violates the law consistently because of learning the behavioral patterns from his or her social environment.

sociopath   A person who is repetitively in conflict with the law, apparently with a very limited capacity to learn from past experience. Distinct from Hare's concept of primary psychopath.

somatoform disorders   Mental disorders characterized by vague bodily ailments and dysfunctions caused by psychological factors.

somatotyping   William H. Sheldon's theory relating physique to delinquency; based on delineating three basic body builds: endomorphic, ectomorphic, and mesomorphic.

specific (or **special) deterrence**   See **deterrence**.

spree arsonist   A person who sets fires at three or more locations with no emotional cooling-off period between them.

spree murder   The killing of three or more individuals without any cooling-off period, usually at two or more locations.

staging   The intentional alteration of a crime scene prior to the arrival of the police.

static risk factors   Things about a person's developmental history that normally do not change, such as biological parents, gender, birth order, birth date, and ethnic background. Also called historical factors.

status offenses   A class of illegal behavior that only persons with certain characteristics or status can commit. Used almost exclusively to refer to the behavior of juveniles. Examples include running away from home, violating curfew, buying alcohol, and skipping school.

statutory rape   Rape for which the age of the victim is the crucial distinction, based on the premise that a victim below a certain age (usually 16) cannot validly consent to sexual intercourse with an adult.

stimulants   A broad drug classification that refers to those psychoactive drugs that stimulate the central nervous system and elevate mood.

Stockholm syndrome   A term coined after a hostage situation in Stockholm, Sweden, in 1973, it refers to the phenomenon of hostages becoming attracted to their captors. In the original incident, an escaped convict held four bank employees in the bank vault for 131 hours. One of the bank employees eventually married her captor.

strain theory   A prominent sociological explanation for crime based on Robert Merton's theory that crime and delinquency occur when there is a perceived discrepancy between the materialistic values and goals cherished and held in high esteem by a society and the availability of the legitimate means for reaching these goals.

supermax prisons   See **ultramax prisons**.

territoriality   The tendency to attack violators of one's personal space.

terrorism   The unlawful use of force or violence against persons or property to intimidate or coerce a government, the civilian population, or any segment thereof, in furtherance of political or social objectives.

tertiary prevention   Intervention strategy designed to reduce or eliminate behavioral problems or antisocial behavior that is fully developed in individuals. Treatment or counseling of convicted offenders is an example of tertiary prevention.

theory of moral disengagement   Proposed by Bandura, it supposes that we must disengage our own moral values before committing a criminal act.

tolerance   In substance use, the condition in which only increasing dosages of the drug produce the desired effect.

traits   Relatively stable and enduring tendencies to behave in a particular way across time and place. Traits are believed by some psychologists to be the basic building blocks of personality.

tripartite conceptual model   Identifies three major types of illicit drug crimes. Proposed by Paul Goldstein.

ultramax prisons   Extremely high-security prisons, or units within a prison, in which prisoners are held in isolation, often for 23 hours a day and for extended periods of time.

undercontrolled personality   A person who has few inhibitions against aggressive behavior and frequently engages in violence when frustrated or provoked.

undoing   A behavioral pattern found at the crime scene whereby the offender tries to psychologically "undo" the murder.

Uniform Crime Reports   The FBI's system for collecting data on reported crime and arrests from police agencies nationwide. (See also National Incident Based Reporting System.)

victimological perspective   A proposal that suggests we can gain substantial amounts of knowledge about offender characteristics by also studying the nature and possibly the behavior of the victims selected by offenders.

victimology   The scientific study of the causes, circumstances, individual characteristics, and social contexts of becoming a victim of a crime.

volitional prong   The part of the insanity defense that requires acceptance of the possibility that a defendant could not control his or her behavior to conform to the requirements of the law. The volitional prong is not recognized in federal law or the law of many states.

voyeurism   The tendency to achieve sexual excitement and gratification by observing unsuspecting people naked, undressing, or engaging in sexual activity.

white-collar crime   A broad term, coined in 1939 by Edwin Sutherland, that refers to illegal acts committed by those of high social status in the process of their employment. Contemporary definitions often divide it into corporate crime and individual or occupational crime.

woozle effect   A term, first used in a Winnie-the-Pooh story and later adopted by Houghton (1979), that refers to the tendency of one study to cite a previous study's data or conclusions without mentioning the methodological limitations and problems inherent in the first study.

CASES CITED

Baxstrom v. Herold, 383 U.S. 107 (1966).

Carter v. U.S., 252 F.2d 608 (D.C. Cir. 1957).

Dixon v. Attorney General of the Commonwealth of Pennsylvania, 325 F.Supp. 966 (M.D. Pa. 1971).

Durham v. U.S., 214 F.2d 862 (D.C. Cir. 1954).

Dusky v. U.S., 363 U.S. 402 (1960).

Foucha v. Louisiana, 51 Cr.L. 2084 (1992).

Jackson v. Indiana, 406 U.S. 715 (1972).

Kansas v. Hendricks, 117 S.Ct. 2072 (1997).

Kansas v. Crane, 521 U.S. 346 (2002).

Madrid v. Gomez, 889 F. Supp. 1149 (N.D. Cal. 1995).

M'Naghten, 10 Clark & Fin. 200, 210, 8 Eng.Rep 718, 722 (1843).

Miller v. State, 318 N.W.2d 673 (S.D. 1983).

Sell v. U.S. (2003).

State v. Bianchi, No. 79-10116 (Wash. Super. Ct., Oct. 19, 1979).

State v. Campanaro, Nos. 632-79, 1309-79, 1317-79, 514-80, 707-80 (Superior Court of New Jersey Crim. Div., Union Co., 1980).

State v. Felde, 422 So.2d 370 (La. 1982).

State v. Lafferty, 192 Conn. 571, 472 A.2d 1275 (1984).

State v. Milligan, No. 77-CR-11-2908 (Franklin Co., Ohio, Dec. 4, 1978).

State v. Rodrigues, 679 P.2d 615 (Hawaii 1984).

Tarasoff v. Regents of the University of California, 529 F.2d 553 (Cal. 1974). vac., reheard en banc, & aff'd 131 Cal.Rptr. 1, 551 P.2d 334 (1976).

U.S. v. Brawner, 471 F.2d 969 (D.C. Cir. 1972).

U.S. v. Davis, 772 F.2d 1339 (7th Cir. 1985), cert. denied, 106 S.Ct. 603 (1985).

U.S. v. Gillis, 773 F.2d 549 (4th Cir. 1985).

U.S. v. Gould, 741 F.2d 45 (4th Cir. 1984).

U.S. v. Krutschewski, 509 F.Supp. 1186 (D. Mass. 1981).

U.S. v. Lewellyn, 723 F.2d 615 (8th Cir. 1985).

U.S. v. Weston, 134 F.Supp. 2d 115 (D.D.C. 2001).

Vitek v. Jones, 445 U.S. 480 (1980).

Wilkins v. Maryland State Police, Civil Action No. CEB-93-483 (D.Md., 1993).

REFERENCES

Abadinsky, H. (1993). *Drug abuse* (2nd ed.). Chicago: Nelson–Hall.

Abel, G. G., Barlow, D. H., Blanchard, E. B., & Guild, D. (1977). The components of rapists' sexual arousal. *Archives of General Psychiatry, 34,* 895–903.

Abel, G. G., Becker, J. V., Blanchard, E. B., & Djenderedjian, A. (1978). Differentiating sexual aggressives with penile measures. *Criminal Justice and Behavior, 5,* 315–332.

Abel, G. G., Becker, J. V., Murphy, W. D., & Flanagan, B. (1981). Identifying dangerous child molesters. In R. B. Stuart (Ed.), *Violent behavior: Social learning approaches to prediction, management and treatment.* New York: Brunner/Mazel.

Abel, G. G., Mittelman, M. S., & Becker, J. V. (1985). Sexual offenders: Results of assessment and recommendations for treatment. In H. H. Ben-Aron, S. I. Hucker, & C. D. Webster (Eds.), *Clinical criminology.* Toronto, ON: MM Graphics.

Abel, G. G., Mittelman, M., Becker, J. V., Rathner, J., & Rouleau, J. (1988). Predicting child molesters' response to treatment. In R. A. Prentky & V. L. Quinsey (Eds.), *Human sexual aggression: Current perspectives.* New York: New York Academy of Sciences.

Aber, J. L., Brown, J. L., & Jones, S. M. (2003). Developmental trajectories toward violence in middle childhood course, demographic differnces, and response to school-based intervention. *Developmental Psychology, 39,* 324–348.

Abrahamsen, D. (1952). *Who are the guilty?* Westport, CT: Greenwood Press.

Abrahamsen, D. (1960). *The psychology of crime.* New York: Columbia University Press.

Abt Associates. (1985). *A blueprint for the future of the Uniform Crime Reporting system.* Washington, DC: U.S. Department of Justice.

Achenbach, T. M., & Edelbrock, C. (1983). *Manual for the child behavior checklist and revised child behavior profile.* Burlington: University of Vermont.

Acoca, L., & Austin, J. (1996). *The hidden crisis: The women offenders sentencing study and alternative sentencing recommendations project.* San Francisco, CA: National Council on Crime and Delinquency.

Acoca, L., & Dedel, K. (1998). *No place to hide: Understanding and meeting the needs of girls in the California juvenile justice system.* San Francisco, CA: National Council on Crime and Delinquency.

Adams, D. (1992). Biology does not make men more aggressive than women. In K. Bjorkquist & P. Niemela (Eds.), *Of mice and women: Aspects of female aggression.* San Diego, CA: Academic Press.

Adams, S. S. (1977). Evaluating correctional treatments. *Criminal Justice and Behavior, 4,* 323–340.

Adamson, L. A., & Thompson, R. A. (1998). Coping with interparental verbal conflict by children exposed to spouse abuse from nonviolent homes. *Journal of Family Violence, 13,* 213–232.

Adler, F. (1975). *Sisters in crime.* New York: McGraw–Hill.

Adler, R., Nunn, R., Northam, E., Lebnan, V., & Ross, R. (1994). Secondary prevention of childhood firesetting. *Journal of the American Academy of Child and Adolescent Psychiatry, 33,* 1194–1202.

Akers, R. L. (1977). *Deviant behavior: A social learning approach* (2nd ed.). Belmont, CA: Wadsworth.

Akers, R. L. (1985). *Deviant behavior: A social learning approach* (3rd ed.). Belmont, CA: Wadsworth.

Akers, R. L. (2000). *Criminological theories: Introduction, evaluation and application* (3rd ed.). Los Angeles: Roxbury.

Akers, R. L., & Cochran, J. K. (1985). Adolescent marijuana use: A test of three theories of deviant behavior. *Deviant Behavior, 6,* 323–346.

Akers, R. L., & Lee, G. (1996). A longitudinal test of social learning theory: Adolescent smoking. *Journal of Drug Issues, 26,* 317–343.

Albanese, J. S. (1995). *White-collar crime in America.* Upper Saddle River, NJ: Prentice Hall.

Alison, L., Bennett, C., Ormerod, D., & Mokros, A. (2002). The personality paradox in offender profiling: A theoretical review of the processes involved in deriving background characteristics from crime scene actions. *Psychology, Public Policy, and Law, 8,* 115–135.

Alison, L. J., & Canter, D. V. (1999). Professional, legal and ethical issues in offender profiling. In D. V. Canter & L. J. Alison (Eds.), *Profiling in policy and practice.* Aldershot, UK: Ashgate.

Alison, L., Smith, M. D., & Morgan, K. (2003). Interpreting the accuracy of offender profiles. *Psychology, Crime & Law, 9,* 185–195.

Allsopp, J. F. (1976). Criminality and delinquency. In H. J. Eysenck & G. D. Wilson (Eds.), *A textbook of human psychology.* Baltimore, MD: University Park Press.

Allsopp, J. F., & Feldman, M. P. (1976). Personality and antisocial behaviour in schoolboys: Item analysis of questionnaire measures. *British Journal of Criminology, 16,* 337–351.

American Academy of Pediatrics (APA). (2001). Shaken baby syndrome: Rotational cranial injuries—technical report. *Pediatrics, 108,* 206–210.

American Bar Association. (1979). *Juvenile justice standards project.* Chicago, IL: Author.

American Psychiatric Association (APA). (1968). *Diagnostic and statistical manual of mental disorders* (2nd ed.). Washington, DC: Author.

American Psychiatric Association (APA). (1980). *Diagnostic and statistical manual of mental disorders* (3rd ed.). Washington, DC: Author.

American Psychiatric Association (APA). (1987). *Diagnostic and statistical manual of mental disorders* (rev ed.). Washington, DC: Author.

American Psychiatric Association (APA). (1994). *Diagnostic and statistical manual of mental disorders* (4th ed.). Washington, DC: Author.

American Psychiatric Association (APA). (2000). *Diagnostic and statistical manual of mental disorders—Revised* (DSM-IV-R). Washington, DC: Author.

Amir, M. (1971). *Patterns in forcible rape.* Chicago, IL: University of Chicago Press.

Amsel, A. (1958). The role of frustrative nonreward in noncontinuous reward situations. *Psychological Bulletin, 55,* 102–119.

Andenaes, J. (1968). Does punishment deter crime? *The Criminal Law Quarterly, 11,* 76–93.

Andershed, H., Kerr, M., Stattin, H., & Levander, S. (2002). Psychopathic traits in non-referred youths: Initial test of a new assessment tool. In E. Blaauw & L. Sheridan (Eds.), *Psychopaths: Current international perspectives.* The Hague: Elsevier.

Anderson, C. A. (1987). Temperature and aggression: Effects on quarterly, yearly, and city rates of violent and nonviolent crime. *Journal of Personality and Social Psychology, 52,* 1161–1173.

Anderson, C. A. (1989). Temperature and aggression: Ubiquitous effects of heat on occurrence of human violence. *Psychological Bulletin, 106,* 74–96.

Anderson, C. A., & Anderson, D. C. (1984). Ambient temperature and violent crime: Tests of the linear and curvilinear hypothesis. *Journal of Personality and Social Psychology, 46,* 91–97.

Andreasen, N. C. (2001). *Brave new brain: Conquering mental illness in the era of the genome.* New York: Oxford University Press.

Andreasen, N. C., & Carpenter, W. T. (1993). Diagnosis and classification of schizophrenia. *Schizophrenia Bulletin, 19,* 199–214.

Andrew, J. M. (1978). Laterality on the tapping test among legal offenders. *Journal of Clinical Psychology,7,* 149–150.

Andrews, D. A., & Bonta, J. (1994). *The psychology of criminal conduct.* Cincinnati, OH: Anderson.

Andrews, D. A., & Bonta, J. (1995). *The Level of Service Inventory—Revised.* Toronto, ON: Multi-Health Systems.

Andrews, D. A., & Bonta, J. (1998). *The psychology of criminal conduct* (2nd ed.). Cincinnati, OH: Anderson.

Andrews, D. A., Bonta, J., & Hoge, R. D. (1990). Classification for effective rehabilitation: Rediscovering psychology. *Criminal Justice and Behavior, 17,* 19–52.

Anfuso, D. (1994). Deflecting workplace violence. *Personnel Journal, 73,* 66–77.

APA Commission on Violence and Youth. (1993). *Violence and youth: Psychology's response.* Washington, DC: Public Interest Directorate, American Psychological Association.

Appelbaum, P. S., Jick, R. Z., Grisso, T., Givelbar, D., Silver, E., & Steadman, H. J. (1993). Use of posttraumatic stress. *Psychiatry, 150,* 229–234.

Araji, S. (1997). *Sexually aggressive children: Coming to understand them.* Thousand Oaks, CA: Sage.

Ardrey, R. (1966). *The territorial imperative.* New York: Atheneum.

Arkow, P. (1998). The correlations between cruelty to animals and child abuse and the implications for veterinary medicine. In R. Lockwood & F. R. Ascione (Eds.), *Cruelty to animals and interpersonal violence: Readings in research and application.* West Lafayette, IN: Purdue University Press.

Aronson, E., Wilson, T. D., & Akert, R. M. (2005). *Social psychology* (5th ed.). Upper Saddle River, NJ: Prentice Hall.

Arrestees Drug Abuse Monitoring Program. (1999, April). *1998 annual report on marijuana use among arrestees.* Washington, DC: National Institute of Justice.

Arrestees Drug Abuse Monitoring Program. (2000, June). *1999 annual report on drug use among adult and juvenile arrestees.* Washington, DC: National Institute of Justice.

Arthur, R. G., & Cahoon, E. B. (1964). A clinical and electroencephalographic survey of psychopathic personality. *American Journal of Psychiatry, 120,* 875–882.

Ascione, R. R. (1997). *Animal welfare and domestic violence.* Logan, UT: Utah State University.

Ashford, J. B., Sales, B. D., & Reid, W. H. (2001). Introduction. In J. B. Ashford, B. D. Sales, & W. H. Reid (Eds.), *Treating adult and juvenile offenders with special needs.* Washington, DC: American Psychological Association.

Au Coin, K. (2003a). Family violence against older adults. In Canadian Centre for Justice Statistics (Ed.), *Family violence in Canada: A statistical profile 2003.* Ottawa: Canadian Centre for Justice Statistics.

Au Coin, K. (2003b). Violence and abuse against children and youth by family members. In Canadian Centre for Justice Statistics (Ed.), *Family violence in Canada: A statistical profile 2003.* Ottawa: Canadian Centre for Justice Statistics.

Augustine Fellowship. (1986). *Sex and love addicts anonymous.* Boston: Author.

Ault, R., & Reese, J. T. (1980). A psychological assessment of criminal profiling. *FBI Law Enforcement Bulletin, 49,* 22–25.

Avery-Clark, C. A., & Laws, D. R. (1984). Differential erection response patterns of sexual child abusers to stimuli describing activities with children. *Behavior Therapy, 15,* 71–83.

Babcock, J. C., Waltz, J., Jacobson, N. S., & Gottman, J. M. (1993). Power and violence: The relation between communication patterns, power discrepancies, and domestic violence. *Journal of Consulting and Clinical Psychology, 61,* 40–50.

Bailey, W. C. (1984). Poverty, inequality and city homicide rates. *Criminology, 22,* 531–550.

Ball, J. C., Shaffer, J. W., & Nurco, D. N. (1983). The day-to-day criminality of heroin addicts in Baltimore—A study in the continuity of offense rates. *Drug and Alcohol Dependence, 12,* 119–142.

Bamfield, J. (1994). Electronic article surveillance: Management learning in curbing theft. In M. Gill (Ed.), *Crime at work: Studies in security and crime prevention.* Leiscester, UK: Perpetuity Press.

Bandura, A. (1965). Influence of models' reinforcement contingencies on the acquisition of imitative responses. *Journal of Personality and Social Psychology, 1,* 589–595.

Bandura, A. (1973a). *Aggression: A social learning analysis.* Upper Saddle River, NJ: Prentice Hall.

Bandura, A. (1973b). Social learning theory of aggression. In J. F. Knutson (Ed.), *The control of aggression.* Chicago, IL: Aldine.

Bandura, A. (1977). *Social learning theory.* Upper Saddle River, NJ: Prentice Hall.

Bandura, A. (1978). The self-system in reciprocal determinism. *American Psychologist, 33,* 344–358.

Bandura, A. (1983). Psychological mechanisms of aggression. In R. G. Geen & E. I. Donnerstein (Eds.), *Aggression: Theoretical and empirical reviews* (Vol. 1). New York: Academic Press.

Bandura, A. (1986). *Social foundations in thought and action: A social cognitive theory.* Upper Saddle River, NJ: Prentice Hall.

Bandura, A. (1989). Human agency in social cognitive theory. *American Psychologist, 44,* 1175–1184.

Bandura, A. (1990). Selective activation and disengagement of moral control. *Journal of Social Issues, 46,* 27–46.

Bandura, A. (1991). Social cognitive theory or moral thought and action. In M. W. Kurtines & J. L. Gewirtz (Eds.), *Handbook of moral behavior and development: Vol. I. Theory.* Hillsdale, NJ: Erlbaum.

Bandura, A. (1999). Moral disengagement in the perpetration of inhumanities. *Personality and Social Psychology Review, 3,* 193–209.

Bandura, A. (2004). The role of selective moral disengagement in terrorism and counterterrorism. In F. M. Moghaddam & A. J. Marsella (Eds.), *Understanding terrorism: Psychosocial roots, consequences, and interventions.* Washington, DC: American Psychological Association.

Bandura, A., Barbaranelli, C., Caprara, G. V., & Pastorelli, C. (1996). Mechanisms of moral disengagement in the exercise of moral agency. *Journal of Personality and Social Psychology, 71,* 364–374.

Bandura, A., Caprara, G. V., Barbaranelli, C., Pastorelli, C., & Regalia, C. (2001). Sociocognitive self-regulatory mechanisms governing transgressive behavior. *Journal of Personality and Social Psychology, 80,* 125–135.

Bandura, A., & Huston, A. (1961). Identification as a process of incidental learning. *Journal of Abnormal and Social Psychology, 63,* 311–318.

Bandura, A., Ross, D., & Ross, S. (1963). Vicarious reinforcement and imitative learning. *Journal of Abnormal and Social Psychology, 67,* 601–607.

Bandura, A., & Walters, R. H. (1959). *Adolescent aggression.* New York: Ronald Press.

Banks, T., & Dabbs, J. M., Jr. (1996). Salivary testosterone and cortisol in delinquent and violent urban subculture. *Journal of Social Psychology, 136,* 49–56.

Bard, L. A., Carter, D. L., Cerce, D. D., Knight, R. A., Rosenberg, R., & Schneider, B. (1987). A descriptive study of rapists and child molesters: Developmental, clinical, and criminal characteristics. *Behavioral Sciences & the Law, 5*, 203–220.

Bardone, A. M., Moffitt, T. E., & Caspi, A. (1996). Adult mental health and social outcomes of adolescent girls with depression and conduct disorder. *Development and Psychopathology, 8*, 811–829.

Barker, M. (2000). The criminal range of small-town burglars. In D. Canter & L. Alison (Eds.), *Profiling property crimes*. Dartmouth, UK: Ashgate.

Baron, R. A. (1977). *Human aggression*. New York: Plenum.

Baron, R. A. (1983). The control of human aggression: An optimistic perspective. *Journal of Social and Clinical Psychology, 1*, 97–119.

Baron, R. A., & Bell, P. A. (1975). Aggression and heat: Mediating effects of prior provocation and exposure to an aggressive model. *Journal of Personality and Social Psychology, 31*, 825–832.

Baron, R. A., & Byrne, D. (1977). *Social psychology* (2nd ed.). Boston, MA: Allyn and Bacon.

Baron, R. A., & Lawton, S. F. (1972). Environmental influences on aggression: The facilitation of modeling effects by high ambient temperatures. *Psychonomic Science, 26*, 80–83.

Baron, R. A., & Ransberger, V. M. (1978). Ambient temperature and the occurrence of collective violence: The "long, hot summer" revisited. *Journal of Personality and Social Psychology, 36*, 361–366.

Bartol, C. R. (1988). Understanding delinquency: Causal loops and social systems. *Criminal Justice and Behavior, 15*, 394–401.

Bartol, C. R., & Bartol, A. M. (1994). *Psychology and law: Research and application* (2nd ed.). Pacific Grove, CA: Brooks/Cole.

Bartol, C. R., & Bartol, A. M. (1998). *Delinquency and justice: A psychosocial approach* (2nd ed.). Upper Saddle River, NJ: Prentice Hall.

Bartol, C. R., & Bartol, A. M. (2004a). *Psychology and law: Theory, research, and application* (3rd ed.). Belmont, CA: Wadsworth/Thomson.

Bartol, C. R., & Bartol, A. M. (2004b). *Introduction to forensic psychology*. Thousand Oaks, CA: Sage.

Bartol, C. R., Griffin, R., & Clark, M. (1993, July). *Nationwide survey of American correctional psychologists*. Unpublished manuscript.

Bartol, C. R., & Holanchock, H. A. (1979). A test of Eysenck's theory of criminality on an American prisoner population. *Criminal Justice and Behavior, 6*, 245–249.

Bastian, L. D., & Taylor, B. M. (1991). *School crime: A national crime victimization survey report*. Washington, DC: U.S. Department of Justice.

Battelle Law and Justice Study Committee. (1977). *Forcible rape: An analysis of the legal issue*. Washington, DC: National Institute of Law Enforcement and Criminal Justice.

Baumer, T. L., & Rosenbaum, D. P. (1984). *Combating retail theft: Programs and strategies*. Boston, MA: Butterworth.

Bear, M. F., Connors, B. W., & Paradiso, M. A. (1996). *Neuroscience: Exploring the brain*. Baltimore, MD: Williams & Wilkins.

Beatty, D. (2001). Stalking. In G. Coleman, M. Gaboury, M. Murray, & A. Seymour (Eds.), *1999 National Victim Assistance Academy*. Washington, DC: U.S. Department of Justice.

Beck, A. J. (2000, August). *Prisoners in 1999*. Washington, DC: Bureau of Justice Statistics.

Beck, A. T. (1970). Cognitive therapy: Nature and relation to behavior therapy. *Behavior Therapy, 1*, 184–200.

Becker, J. V., & Johnson, B. R. (2001). Treating juvenile sex offenders. In J. B. Ashford, B. D. Sales, & W. H. Reid (Eds.), *Treating adult and juvenile offenders with special needs*. Washington, DC: American Psychological Association.

Bell, P. A., & Baron, R. A. (1977). Aggression and ambient temperature: The inhibiting and facilitating effects of hot and cold environments. *Bulletin of the Psychonomic Society, 6,* 240–242.

Bennett, T., & Wright, R. (1984). *Burglars on burglary: Prevention and the offender.* Brookfield, VT: Gower.

Bensing, R. C., & Schroeder, O. (1960). *Homicide in an urban community.* Springfield, IL: Charles C Thomas.

Berger, H. (1929). Uber das Electrenkephalogram des Menschen. *Archiv fur Psychiatrie und Nervenkrankheiten, 87,* 527–570.

Berkowitz, L. (1962). *Aggression: A social-psychological analysis.* New York: McGraw–Hill.

Berkowitz, L. (1969). The frustration-aggression hypothesis revisited. In L. Berkowitz (Ed.), *Roots of aggression.* New York: Atherton Press.

Berkowitz, L. (1970). The contagion of violence: An S-R mediational analysis of some effects of observed aggression. In W. J. Arnold & M. M. Page (Eds.), *Nebraska symposium on motivation.* Lincoln: University of Nebraska Press.

Berkowitz, L. (1973). Words and symbols as stimuli to aggressive responses. In J. F. Knutson (Ed.), *The control of aggression.* Chicago, IL: Aldine.

Berkowitz, L. (1983). The experience of anger as a parallel process in the display of impulsive, "angry" aggression. In R. G. Geen & E. I. Donnerstein (Eds.), *Aggression: Theoretical and empirical reviews* (Vol. 1). New York: Academic Press.

Berkowitz, L. (1989). Frustration-aggression hypothesis: Examination and reformulation. *Psychological Bulletin, 106,* 59–73.

Berkowitz, L. (1994). Guns and youth. In L. E. Eron, J. H. Gentry, & P. Schlegel (Eds.), *Reason to hope: A psychosocial perspective on violence and youth.* Washington, DC: American Psychological Association.

Berkowitz, L., & Heimer, K. (1989). On the construction of the anger experience: Aversive events and negative priming in the formation of feelings. In L. Berkowitz (Ed.), *Advances in experimental social psychology* (Vol. 22). New York: Academic Press.

Berkowitz, L., & LePage, A. (1967). Weapons as aggression-eliciting stimuli. *Journal of Personality and Social Psychology, 7,* 202–207.

Berlyne, D. E. (1960). *Conflict, arousal, and curiosity.* New York: McGraw–Hill.

Berman, T., & Paisey, T. (1984). Personality in assaultive and non-assaultive juvenile male offenders. *Psychological Reports, 54,* 527–530.

Bernard, F. (1975). An inquiry among a group of pedophiles. *Journal of Sex Research, 11,* 242–255.

Berndt, T. (1979). Developmental changes in conformity to peers and parents. *Developmental Psychology, 15,* 608–616.

Bernstein, A., Newman, J. P., Wallace, J. F., & Luh, K. E. (2000). Left hemisphere activation and deficient response modulation in psychopaths. *Psychological Science, 11,* 414–418.

Berrueta-Clement, J. R., Schweinhart, L. J., Barnett, W. S., & Weikart, D. P. (1987). The effects of early educational intervention in adolescence and early adulthood. In J. D. Burhcard & S. N. Burchard (Eds.), *Prevention of delinquent behavior.* Newbury Park, CA: Sage.

Binder, A. (1988). Juvenile delinquency. *Annual Review of Psychology, 39,* 253–282.

Björkqvist, K., Lagerspetz, M. J., & Kaukianinen, A. (1992). Do girls manipulate and boys fight? Developmental trends in regard to direct and indirect aggression. *Aggressive Behavior, 18,* 117–127.

Black, H. C. (1990). *Black's law dictionary.* St. Paul, MN: West Publishing.

Black, S. L., & Bevan, S. (1992). At the movies with Buss and Durkee: A natural experiment on film violence. *Aggressive Behavior, 18,* 37–45.

Blackburn, N., Weiss, J., & Lamberti, J. (1960). The sudden murderer. *Archives of General Psychiatry, 2,* 670–678.

Blackburn, R. (1968). Personality in relation to extreme aggression in psychiatric offenders. *British Journal of Psychiatry, 114,* 821–828.

Blackburn, R. (1988). On moral judgments and personality disorders. *British Journal of Psychiatry, 153,* 505–512.

Blackburn, R. (1993). *The psychology of criminal conduct: Theory, research and practice.* Chichester, UK: Wiley.

Blair, C. D., & Lanyon, R. I. (1981). Exhibitionism: An etiology and treatment. *Psychological Bulletin, 89,* 439–463.

Blau, J. R., & Blau, P. M. (1982). Metropolitan structure and violent crime. *American Sociological Review, 47,* 114–128.

Block, R. (1977). *Violent crime.* Lexington: MA: Lexington Books.

Blumenthal, D. R. (1999). *The banality of good and evil: Moral lessons from the Shoah and Jewish tradition.* Washington, DC: Georgetown University Press.

Blumer, D. (1976). Epilepsy and violence. In D. J. Madden & J. R. Lion (Eds.), *Rage • hate • assault • and other forms of violence.* New York: Spectrum.

Blumer, D., & Migeon, C. (1973). *Treatment of impulsive behavior disorders in males with medroxyprogesterone acetate.* Paper presented at the Annual Meeting of the American Psychiatric Association, Washington, DC.

Blumer, H., Sutter, A., Ahmed, S., & Smith, R. (1967). *ADD center final report: The world of youthful drug use.* Berkeley: University of California Press.

Blumstein, A., Farrington, D. P., & Moitra, S. (1985). Delinquency careers: Innocents, desisters and persisters. In M. Tonry & N. Morris (Eds.), *Crime and justice: An annual review of research* (Vol. 6). Chicago, IL: University of Chicago Press.

Boehnert, C. E. (1989). Characteristics of successful and unsuccessful insanity pleas. *Law and Human Behavior, 13,* 31–39.

Bonnie, R. J., & Grisso, T. (2000). Adjudicative competence and youthful offenders. In T. Grisso & R. G. Schwartz (Eds.), *Youth on trial.* Chicago, IL: University of Chicago Press.

Bonta, J., & Cormier, R. B. (1999). Corrections research in Canada: Impressive progress and promising prospects. *Canadian Journal of Criminology, 41,* 235–245.

Bonta, J., Law, M., & Hanson, K. (1998). The prediction of criminal and violent recidivism among mentally disordered offenders: A meta-analysis. *Psychological Bulletin, 123,* 123–142.

Bonta, J., Wallace-Capretta, S., & Rooney, J. (2000). A quasi-experimental evaluation of an intensive rehabilitation supervision program. *Criminal Justice and Behavior, 27,* 312–329.

Boothby, J. L., & Clements, C. B. (2000). A national survey of correctional psychologists. *Criminal Justice and Behavior, 27,* 716–732.

Borduin, C. M., Mann, B. J., Cone, L. T., Henggeler, S. W., Fucci, B. R., Blaske, D. M., & Williams, R. (1995). Multisystemic treatment of serious juvenile offenders: Long-term prevention of criminality and violence. *Journal of Consulting and Clinical Psychology, 63,* 569–578.

Borgstrom, C. A. (1939). Eine Serie von Kriminellen Zwillingen. *Archiv fur Rassenbiologie, 12,* 18–44.

Borum, R. (1996). Improving the clinical practice of violence risk assessment. *American Psychologist, 51,* 945–956.

Borum, R., & Strentz, T. (1993, April). The borderline personality: Negotiation strategies. *FBI Law Enforcement Bulletin,* 6–10.

Boudreau, J., Kwan, Q., Faragher, W., & Denault, G. (1977). *Arson and arson investigation.* Washington, DC: U.S. Government Printing Office.

Bowden, K. M., Wilson, D. W., & Turner, L. K. (1958). A survey of blood alcohol testing in Victoria (1951–56). *Medical Journal of Australia, 45,* 13–15.

Bowker, L. H. (1983). *Beating wife-battering*. Lexington, MA: Lexington Books.

Boykin, A. W. (1986). The triple quandary and the schooling of Afro-American children. In U. Neisser (Ed.), *The school achievement of minority children*. Hillsdale, NJ: Erlbaum.

Boykin, A. W. (1994). Harvesting talent and culture: African-American children and educational reform. In R. Rossi (Ed.), *Schools and students at risk*. New York: Teachers College Press.

Bracey, D. H. (1982). Concurrent and consecutive abuse: The juvenile prostitute. In B. R. Price & N. Sokoloff (Eds.), *The criminal justice system and women*. New York: Clark Boardman.

Bradford, J. M. W. (1982). Arson: A clinical study. *Canadian Journal of Psychiatry, 27*, 188–193.

Brady, J. (1983). Arson, urban economy, and organized crime: The case of Boston. *Social Problems, 31*, 1–27.

Braithwaite, J. (1981). The myth of class and criminality reconsidered. *American Sociological Review, 46*, 36–57.

Brandt, J. R., Kennedy, W. A., Patrick, C. J., & Curtain, J. J. (1997). Assessment of psychopathy in a population of incarcerated adolescent offenders. *Psychological Assessment, 9*, 429–435.

Brennan, P., Mednick, S. A., & Kandel, E. (1993). Congenital determinants of violent and property offending. In D. J. Pepler & K. H. Rubin (Eds.), *The development and treatment of childhood aggression*. Hillsdale, NJ: Erlbaum.

Brent, D. A. (1989). The psychological autopsy: Methodological issues for the study of adolescent suicide. *Suicide and Life Threatening Behavior, 19*, 43–57.

Brier, N. (1989). The relationship between learning disability and delinquency: A review and reappraisal. *Journal of Learning Disabilities, 22*, 546–553.

Briere, J., Malamuth, N., & Ceniti, J. (1981). *Self-assessed rape proclivity: Attitudinal and sexual correlates*. Paper presented at APA Meeting, Los Angeles, CA.

Brittain, R. P. (1970). The sadistic murderer. *Medicine, Science and the Law, 10*, 198–207.

Brodsky, S. L. (1973). *Psychologists in the criminal justice system*. Urbana: University of Illinois Press.

Brodsky, S. L. (1977). Criminal and dangerous behavior. In D. Rimm & J. Somervill (Eds.), *Abnormal psychology*. New York: Academic Press.

Broidy, L. M., Nagin, D. S., Tremblay, R. E., Bates, J. E., Brame, B., Dodge, K. A., Fergusson, D. Horwood, J. L., Loeber, R., Laird, R., Lynam, D. R., Moffitt, T. E., Pettit, G. S., & Vitaro, F. (2003). Developmental trajectories of childhood disruptive behaviors and adolescent delinquency: A six-site, cross-national study. *Developmental Psychology, 39*, 222–245.

Brown, B. B., & Harris, P. B. (1989). Residential burglary victimization: Reactions to the invasion of a primary territory. *Journal of Environmental Psychology, 9*, 119–132.

Brown, J. S., & Farber, I. E. (1951). Emotions conceptualized as intervening variables—with suggestions toward a theory of frustration. *Psychological Bulletin, 48*, 465–495.

Brown, S. E. (1984). Social class, child maltreatment, and delinquent behavior. *Criminology, 22*, 259–278.

Brown, T. L., Borduin, C. M., & Henggeler, S. W. (2001). Treating juvenile offenders in community settings. In J. B. Ashford, B. D. Sales, & W. H. Reid (Eds.), *Treating adult and juvenile offenders with special needs*. Washington, DC: American Psychological Association.

Browne, A. (1987). *When battered women kill*. New York: Free Press.

Browne, A., & Finkelhor, D. (1986). Impact of child sexual abuse: A review of the research. *Psychological Bulletin, 99*, 66–77.

Brunet, B. L., Reiffenstein, R. J., Williams, T., & Wong, L. (1985–1986). Toxicity of phencyclidine and ethanol in combination. *Alcohol and Drug Research, 6*, 341–349.

Brussel, J. A. (1978). *Casebook of a crime psychiatrist*. New York: Bernard Geis Associates.

Bryant, J., & Zillmann, D. (Eds.). (2002). *Media effects: Advances in theory and research* (2nd ed.). Mahwah, NJ: Erlbaum.

Buckle, A., & Farrington, D. P. (1984). An observational study of shoplifting. *British Journal of Criminology, 24,* 63–73.

Buikhuisen, W., & Hemmel, J. J. (1972). Crime and conditioning. *British Journal of Criminology, 17,* 147–157.

Bukstel, L. H., & Kilmann, P. R. (1980). Psychological effects of imprisonment on confined individuals. *Psychological Bulletin, 88,* 469–493.

Bullock, H. A. (1955). Urban homicide in theory and fact. *Journal of Criminal Law, Criminology and Police Science, 45,* 565–575.

Bumpass, E. R., Fagelman, F. D., & Birx, R. J. (1983). Intervention with children who set fires. *American Journal of Psychotherapy, 37,* 328–345.

Bureau of International Narcotics and Law Enforcement Affairs. (2000, March). *International narcotics control strategy report, 1999.* Washington, DC: U.S. Department of State. Available: www.state.gov/www/global/narcotics

Bureau of Justice Assistance. (2000, April). *Emerging judicial strategies for the mentally ill in the criminal caseload: Mental health courts.* Washington, DC: U.S. Department of Justice.

Bureau of Justice Statistics. (1999, July). *Mental health and treatment of inmates and prisoners.* Washington, DC: Author.

Bureau of Justice Statistics. (2000a, June). *An estimated 312,000 handgun sales blocked during the 1994–1998 Brady interim period.* Washington, DC: Author. Available: www.ojp.usdoj.gov/bjs/pub/press/phc98.pr

Bureau of Justice Statistics. (2000b, June). *Drugs and crime facts: Drug use and crime.* Washington, DC: Author. Available: www.ojp.usdoj.gov/bjs/dcf/duc.htm

Bureau of Justice Statistics. (2001a, January). *Homicide trends in the United States: Infanticide.* Washington, DC: Author. Available: www.ojp.usdoi.gov/bjs/homicide/children.htm

Bureau of Justice Statistics. (2001b). *Prisoners in 2000.* Washington, DC: U.S. Department of Justice.

Bureau of Justice Statistics. (2002, April). *Hispanic vicitms of violent crime, 1993–2000.* Washington, DC: Author.

Bureau of Justice Statistics. (2003a). *Capital punishment statistics.* Washington, DC: Author.

Bureau of Justice Statistics. (2003b). *Victim characteristics.* Washington, DC: Author.

Bureau of Justice Statistics. (2003c, July). *Prisoners in 2002.* Washington, DC: Author.

Bureau of Labor Statistics. (1999). *National census of fatal occupational injuries, 1998.* Washington, DC: U.S. Department of Labor.

Burgess, P. K. (1972). Eysenck's theory of criminality: A test of some objectives of disconfirmatory evidence. *British Journal of Social and Clinical Psychology, 11,* 248–256.

Burgess, R. L., & Akers, R. L. (1966). A differential association-reinforcement theory of criminal behavior. *Social Problems, 14,* 128–147.

Burnam, M. A., Stein, J. A., Golding, J. M., Siegel, J. M., Sorenson, S. B., Forsythe, A. B., & Telles, C. A. (1988). Sexual assault and mental disorders in a community population. *Journal of Consulting and Clinical Psychology, 56,* 843–850.

Buss, A. H. (1971). Aggression pays. In J. L. Singer (Ed.), *The control of aggression and violence.* New York: Academic Press.

Butler, R. A. (1954). Curiosity in monkeys. *Scientific American* (reprint 426). San Francisco, CA: W. H. Freeman.

Butts, J., Hoffman, D., & Buck, J. (2000). *Teen courts in the United States: A profile of current programs. Fact Sheet.* Washington, DC: Office of Juvenile Justice and Delinquency Prevention.

Buzawa, E. S., & Buzawa, C. G. (1996). *Domestic violence: The criminal justice response* (2nd ed.). Thousand Oaks, CA: Sage.

Cacioppo, J. T., Berntson, G. G., Sheridan, J. F., & McClintock, M. K. (2000). Multilevel integrative analyses of human behavior: Social neuroscience and the complementing nature of social and biological approaches. *Psychological Bulletin, 6,* 829–843.

Caffey, J. (1974). The whiplash shaken baby syndrome. *Pediatrics, 54,* 396–403.

Cairns, R. B., & Cairns, B. D. (1991). Social cognition and social networks: A developmental perspective. In D. J. Pepler & K. H. Rubin (Eds.), *The development and treatment of childhood aggression.* Hillsdale, NJ: Erlbaum.

Cairns, R. B., Cairns, B. D., Neckerman, H. J., Ferguson, L. L., & Gariépy, J. L. (1989). Growth and aggression: I. Childhood to early adolescence. *Developmental Psychology, 25,* 320–330.

Cairns, R. B., Cairns, B. D., Neckerman, H. J., Gest, S. D., & Gariépy, J. L. (1988). Social networks and aggressive behavior: Peer support or peer rejection. *Developmental Psychology, 24,* 815–826.

Calhoun, J. B. (1961). Phenomena associated with population density. *Proceedings of the National Academy of Sciences, 47,* 428–429.

Calhoun, J. B. (1962). Population density and social pathology. *Scientific American, 206,* 139–148.

Callahan, L. A., McGreevy, M. A., Cirincione, C., & Steadman, H. J. (1992). Measuring the effects of the guilty but mentally ill (GBMI) verdict. *Law and Human Behavior, 16,* 447–462.

Callahan, L. A., Steadman, H. J., McGreevy, M. A., & Robbins, P. C. (1991). The volume and characteristics of insanity defense pleas: An eight-state study. *Bulletin of Psychiatry and the Law, 19,* 331–338.

Cameron, M. O. (1964). *The booster and the snitch.* New York: Free Press.

Campbell, A. (1993). *Men, women, and aggression.* New York: Basic Books.

Campbell, A., Muncer, S., & Coyle, E. (1992). Social representation of aggression as an explanation of gender differences: A preliminary study. *Aggressive Behavior, 18,* 95–108.

Campbell, B. J. (1996). *Validity and use of evidence concerning battering and its effects in criminal trials.* Washington, DC: U.S. Department of Justice, Violence Against Women Office.

Campbell, M. A., Porter, S., & Santor, D. (2004). Psychopathic traits in adolescent offenders: An evaluation of criminal history, clinical, and psychosocial correlates. *Behavioral Sciences & the Law, 22,* 23–47.

Canadian Government's Commission of Inquiry. (1971). *The non-medical use of drugs: Interim report.* London: Penguin Books.

Canter, D. (1999). Equivocal death. In D. Canter & L. J. Alison (Eds.), *Profiling in policy and practice.* Burlington, VT: Ashgate.

Canter, D., & Alison, L. (2000). Profiling property crimes. In D. Canter & L. J. Alison (Eds.), *Profiling property crimes.* Burlington, VT: Ashgate.

Canter, S. (1973). Personality traits in twins. In G. Claridge, S. Canter, & W. I. Hume (Eds.), *Personality differences and biological variations: A study of twins.* Oxford, UK: Pergamon Press.

Carlson, B. E. (1991). Outcomes of physical abuse and observation of marital violence among adolescents in placement. *Journal of Interpersonal Violence, 6,* 526–534.

Carlson, M., Marcus-Newhall, A., & Miller, N. (1990). Effects of situational aggression cues: A quantitative review. *Journal of Personality and Social Psychology, 58,* 622–633.

Carlson, R. J. (1976). *The dilemmas of corrections.* Lexington, MA: Lexington Books.

Carnes, P. (1983). *Out of the shadows: Understanding sexual addiction.* Minneapolis, MN: Compcare Publications.

Carney, R. M., & Williams, B. D. (1983). Premenstrual syndrome: A criminal defense. *Notre Dame Law Review, 59,* 253–269.

Carraher, T. N., Carraher, D., & Schliemann, A. D. (1985). Mathematics in the streets and schools. *British Journal of Developmental Psychology, 3,* 21–29.

Carter, D. L., & Katz, A. J. (1996). *Computer crime: An emerging challenge for law enforcement.* Washington, DC: U.S. Department of Justice. Available: www.fbi.gov/leb/dec961.txt

Carter, R. (1980). Arson and arson investigation in the United States. *Fire Journal, 74,* 40–47.

Casey-Cannon, S., Hayward, C., & Gowen, K. (2001). Middle-school girls' reports of peer victimization: Concerns, consequences, and implications. *Professional School Counseling, 5,* 138–148.

Caspi, A., Elder, G. H., & Bem, D. J. (1987). Moving against the world: Life course patterns of explosive children. *Developmental Psychology, 23,* 308–313.

Cavior, N., & Howard, L. R. (1973). Facial attractiveness and juvenile delinquency among black offenders and white offenders. *Journal of Abnormal Child Psychology, 1,* 202–213.

Chabot, R. A., & Serfontein, G. (1996). Quantitative elctroencephalographic profiles of children with attention deficit disorder. *Biological Psychiatry, 40,* 951–963.

Chaffee, S. H., & McLeod, J. M. (1971). *Adolescents, parents, and television violence.* Paper presented at the meeting of the American Psychological Association, Washington, DC.

Chaiken, J. M. (1998a, April). Learning more from national data collection programs. *National Conference on Sex Offender Registries.* Sacramento, CA: SEARCH group. Available: www. ojp.usdoj.gov/bjs/pub/

Chaiken, J. M. (1998b, April). Foreword. *National Conference on Sex Offender Registries.* Sacramento, CA: SEARCH group. Available: www.ojp.usdoj.gov/bjs/pub/

Chaiken, J. M. (1999, February). Foreword. *American Indians and crime.* Washington, DC: U.S. Department of Justice.

Chalkley, A. J., & Powell, G. E. (1983). The clinical description of forty-eight cases of clinical fetishism. *British Journal of Psychiatry, 142,* 292–295.

Chamberlain, P. (1996). Treatment foster care for adolescents with conduct disorders and delinquency. In P. S. Jensen & D. Hibbs (Eds.), *Psychological treatment with research with children and adolescents.* Rockville, MD: National Institute of Mental Health.

Chappell, D. (1977a). *Forcible rape: A national survey of the response by police (LEAA).* Washington, DC: U.S. Government Printing Office.

Chappell, D. (1977b). *Forcible rape: A national survey of the response by prosecutors (LEAA).* Washington, DC: U.S. Government Printing Office.

Charney, J. (1980). The new diagnostic and statistical manual of mental disorders: Or, what's in a name? *Philosophical Psychology, 1,* 59–71.

Chesney-Lind, M., & Paramore, V. V. (2001). Are girls getting more violent? Exploring juvenile robbery trends. *Journal of Contemporary Criminal Justice, 17,* 142–166.

Chesney-Lind, M., & Shelden, R. (1998). *Girls, delinquency, and juvenile justice* (2nd ed.). Belmont, CA: West/Wadsworth.

Chesno, F. A., & Kilmann, P. R. (1975). Effects of stimulation intensity on sociopathic avoidance learning. *Journal of Abnormal Psychology, 84,* 144–150.

Child Abuse Prevention Center. (1998). *Shaken baby syndrome fatalities in the United States.* Ogden, UT: Author.

Chorover, S. L. (1980). Violence: A localizable problem? In E. S. Valenstein (Ed.), *The psychosurgery debate.* San Francisco, CA: W. H. Freeman.

Christiansen, K. O. (1977). A review of studies of criminality among twins. In S. Mednick & K. O. Christiansen (Eds.), *Biosocial bases of criminal behavior.* New York: Gardiner Press.

Christie, M. M., Marshall, W. L., & Lanthier, R. D. (1979). *A descriptive study of incarcerated rapists and pedophiles.* Ottawa, ON: Report to the Solicitor General of Canada.

Church, S., Henderson, M., Barnard, M., & Hart, G. (2001). Violence by clients towards female prostitutes in different work settings: Questionnaire survey. *British Medical Journal, 322,* 524–525.

Churgin, M. M. (1983). The transfer of inmates of mental health facilities: Developments in the law. In J. Monahan & H. J. Steadman (Eds.), *Mentally disordered offenders.* New York: Plenum.

Chute, C. L. (1949). Fifty years of the juvenile court. In M. Bell (Ed.), *Current approaches to delinquency.* New York: National Probation and Parole Association.

Cirincione, C., & Jacobs, C. (1999). Identifying insanity acquittals: Is it any easier? *Law and Human Behavior, 23,* 487–497.

Claridge, G. (1973). Final remarks. In G. Claridge, S. Canter, & W. I. Hume (Eds.), *Personality differences and biological variations.* Oxford, UK: Pergamon Press.

Clark, J. P., & Hollinger, R. C. (1983). *Theft by employees in work organizations.* Washington, DC: U.S. Government Printing Office.

Clark, K. B. (1971). The pathos of power: A psychological perspective. *American Psychologist, 26,* 1047–1057.

Clear, T. R., & Cole, G. F. (2000). *American corrections* (5th ed.). Belmont, CA: West/Wadsworth.

Cleckley, H. (1976). *The mask of sanity* (5th ed.). St. Louis, MO: Mosby.

Clements, C. B. (1987). Psychologists in adult correctional institutions: Getting off the treadmill. In E. K. Morris & C. J. Braukmann (Eds.), *Behavioral approaches to crime and delinquency.* New York: Plenum.

Clements, C. B. (1996). Offender classification: Two decades of progress. *Criminal Justice and Behavior, 23,* 121–143.

Cleveland, F. P. (1955). Problems in homicide investigation IV: The relationship of alcohol to homicide. *Cincinnati Journal of Medicine, 36,* 28–30.

Clinard, M. B., & Quinney, E. R. (1980). *Criminal behavior systems: A typology.* New York: Holt, Rinehart & Winston.

Cochrane, R. (1974). Crime and personality: Theory and evidence. *Bulletin of the British Psychological Society, 27,* 19–22.

Cochrane, R. E., Grisso, T., & Frederick, R. I. (2001). The relationship between criminal charges, diagnoses, and psycholegal opinions among federal defendants. *Behavioral Sciences and the Law, 19,* 565–582.

Cocozza, J. J., & Steadman, H. J. (1976). The failure of psychiatric prediction of dangerousness: Clear and convincing evidence. *Rutgers Law Review, 29,* 1084–1101.

Cohen, F. (1998). *The mentally disordered inmate and the law.* Kingston, NJ: Civic Research Institute.

Cohen, M. L., Garafalo, R., Boucher, R., & Seghorn, T. (1971). The psychology of rapists. *Seminars in Psychiatry, 3,* 307–327.

Cohen, M., Seghorn, T., & Calmas, W. (1969). Sociometric study of the sex offender. *Journal of Abnormal Psychology, 74,* 249–255.

Cohen, P., Cohen, J., & Brook, J. (1993). An epidemiological study of disorders in late childhood and adolescence—II. Persistent disorders. *Journal of Child Psychology and Psychiatry, 34,* 869–877.

Cohn, V. (1986). Crack use. *NIDA Notes, 1,* 6.

Coie, J. D., Belding, M., & Underwood, M. (1988). Aggression and peer rejection in childhood. In B. Lahey & A. Kazdin (Eds.), *Advances in clinical child psychology* (Vol. 2). New York: Plenum.

Coie, J. D., Dodge, K., & Kupersmith, J. (1990). Peer group behavior and social status. In S. R. Asher & J. D. Coie (Eds.), *Peer rejection in childhood.* Cambridge, UK: Cambridge University Press.

Coie, J. D., Underwood, M., & Lochman, J. E. (1991). Programmatic intervention with aggressive children in the school setting. In D. J. Pepler & K. H. Rubin (Eds.), *The development and treatment of childhood aggression*. Hillsdale, NJ: Erlbaum.

Coleman, C. (2000, September 8). As thievery by insiders overtakes shoplifting, retailers crack down. *Wall Street Journal, 1,* A6.

Coleman, J. C. (1976). *Abnormal psychology and modern life* (5th ed.). Glenview, IL: Scott, Foresman.

Coleman, J. W. (1998). *The criminal elite* (4th ed.). New York: St. Martin's Press.

Coles, E., Freitas, T., & Tweed, R. (1996). Assessment of understanding by people manifesting mental retardation: A preliminary report. *Perceptual and Motor Skills, 83,* 187–192.

Collins, A. F. (1999). The enduring appeal of physiognomy: Physical appearance as a sign of temperament, character, and intelligence. *History of Psychology, 2,* 251–276.

Comer, R. J. (1992). *Abnormal psychology*. New York: W. H. Freeman.

Comer, R. J. (2004). *Abnormal psychology* (5th ed.). New York: Worth.

Community Research Associates. (1998). *Female juvenile offenders: A status of the states report*. Washington, DC: U.S. Department of Justice.

Conklin, J. E. (1972). *Robbery and the criminal justice system*. Philadelphia, PA: Lippincott.

Conklin, J. E. (1977). *"Illegal but not criminal."* Upper Saddle River, NJ: Prentice Hall.

Coody D., Brown, M., Montgomery, D., Flynn, A., & Yetman, R. (1994). Shaken baby syndrome: Identification and prevention for nurse practitioners. *Journal of Pediatric Health Care, 8,* 50–56.

Cook, P. J., & Ludwig, J. (1997). Guns in America: National survey on private ownership and use of firearms. *NIJ Research in Brief*. Washington, DC: National Institute of Justice.

Cook, S. E. (2000). Forced prostitution. In N. H. Rafter (Ed.), *Encyclopedia of women and crime*. Phoenix: Oryx Press.

Cooke, D. J., & Michie, C. (1997). An item response theory analysis of the Hare Psychopathy Checklist—Revised. *Psychological Assessment, 9,* 3–14.

Cooke, D. J., & Michie, C. (2001). Refining the construct psychopathy: Toward a hierarchical model. *Psychological Assessment, 13,* 171–188.

Cooke, D. J., Michie, C., Hart, S. D., & Hare, R. D. (1999). Evaluation of the screening version of the Hare Psychopathy Checklist—Revised (PCL:SV): An item response theory analysis. *Psychological Assessment, 11,* 3–13.

Coordinating Council on Juvenile Justice and Delinquency Prevention. (1996). *Combating violence and delinquency: The national juvenile justice action plan*. Washington, DC: U.S. Government Printing Office.

Corrado, R. R., Vincent, G. M., Hart, S. D., & Cohen, I. M. (2004). Predictive validity of the Psychopathy Checklist: Youth Version for general and violent recidivism. *Behavioral Sciences & the Law, 22,* 5–22.

Correctional Service of Canada. (1990). *Forum on corrections research,* 2(1). Ottawa, ON: Author.

Cortes, J. B., & Gatti, F. M. (1972). *Delinquency and crime: A biopsychosocial approach*. New York: Seminar Press.

Coscina, D. V. (1997). The biopsychology of impulsivity: Focus on brain serotonin. In C. D. Webster & M. A. Jackson (Eds.), *Impulsivity: Theory, assessment, and treatment*. New York: Guilford Press.

Costello, J. C. (2003). "Wayward and noncompliant" people with mental disability: What advocates of involuntary outpatient commitment can learn from the juvenile court experience with status offense jurisdiction. *Psychology, Public Policy, and Law, 9,* 233–257.

Cowley, G. (1993, July 26). The not-young and the restless. *Newsweek,* 48–49.

Craft, M. (1966). The meanings of the term "psychopath." In M. Craft (Ed.), *Psychopathic disorders and their assessment*. Oxford, UK: Pergamon Press.

Craissati, J., & Beech, A. (2004). The characteristics of a geographical sample of convicted rapists. *Journal of Interpersonal Violence, 19*, 371–388.

Crawford, J., & Heather, N. (1987). Public attitudes to the disease concept of alcoholism. *The International Journal of Addiction, 22*, 1129–1138.

Cressey, D. R. (1953). *A study in the social psychology of embezzlement: Other people's money*. Glencoe, IL: Free Press.

Crick, N. R. (1995). Relational aggression: The role of intent attributions, feelings of distress, and provocation type. *Development and Psychopathology, 7*, 313–322.

Crick, N. R., & Grotpeter, J. K. (1995). Relational aggression, gender, and social-psychological adjustment. *Child Development, 66*, 710–722.

Crick, N. R., & Zahn-Waxler, C. (2003). The development of psychopathology in females and males: Current progress and future challenges. *Development and Psychopathology, 15*, 719–742.

Crider, R. (1986). Phencyclidine: Changing abuse patterns. In D. H. Clovet (Ed.), *Phencyclidine: An update*. Rockville, MD: National Institute of Drug Abuse.

Critchlow, B. (1986). The powers of John Barleycorn: Beliefs about the effects of alcohol on social behavior. *American Psychologist, 41*, 751–764.

Critchton, R. (1959). *The great imposter*. New York: Random House.

Crocker, A. G., & Hodgins, S. (1997). The criminality of a noninstitutionalized mentally retarded person: Evidence from a birth cohort followed to age 30. *Criminal Justice and Behavior, 24*, 432–454.

Cromwell, P. F., Olson, J. F., & Avary, D. W. (1991). *Breaking and entering: An ethnographic analysis of burglary*. Newbury Park, CA: Sage.

Crowe, R. R. (1974). An adoptive study of antisocial personality. *Archives of General Psychiatry, 31*, 785–791.

Cruise, K. R., & Rogers, R. (1998). An analysis of competency to stand trial: An integration of case law and clinical knowledge. *Behavioral Sciences & the Law, 16*, 35–50.

Culberton, F. M., Feral, C. H., & Gabby, S. (1989). Pattern analysis of Wechlser Intelligence Scale for Children-Revised profiles of delinquent boys. *Journal of Clinical Psychology, 45*, 651–660.

Cullen, F. T., & Applegate, B. K. (1997). *Offender rehabilitation*. Brookfield, VT: Ashgate.

Cunnien, A. J. (1985). Pathological gambling as an insanity defense. *Behavioral Sciences & the Law, 3*, 85–101.

Dåderman, A. M., & Kristiansson, M. (2003). Degree of psychopathy: Implications for treatment in male juvenile delinquents. *International Journal of Law and Psychiatry, 26*, 310–315.

Dalgaard, O. S., & Kringlen, E. (1976). A Norwegian twin study of criminality. *British Journal of Criminology, 16*, 213–233.

Dalton, K. (1961). Menstruation and crime. *British Medical Journal, 2*, 1752–1753.

Dalton, K. (1964). *The premenstrual syndrome*. Springfield, IL: Charles C Thomas.

David, P. R. (1974). *The world of the burglar*. Albuquerque: University of New Mexico Press.

Davidson, R., Putnam, K., & Larson, C. (2000). Dysfunction in the neural circuitry of emotional regulation: A possible prelude to violence. *Science, 289*, 591–594.

Davis, G. E., & Leitenberg, H. (1987). Adolescent sex offenders. *Psychological Bulletin, 101*, 417–427.

Davis, M. G., Lundman, R. J., & Martinez, R. (1991). Private corporate justice: Store police, shoplifters, and civil recovery. *Social Problems, 38*, 395–411.

Dawson, J. M., & Langan, P. A. (1994). *Murder in families*. Washington, DC: Bureau of Justice Statistics.

Day, K., & Berney, T. (2001). Treatment and care for offenders with mental retardation. In Ashford, J. B., Sales, B. D., & Reid, W. H. (Eds.), *Treating adult and juvenile offenders with special needs*. Washington, DC: American Psychological Association.

Day, R., & Wong, S. (1996). Anomalous perceptual asymmetries for negative emotional stimuli in the psychopath. *Journal of Abnormal Psychology, 105,* 648–652.

Decker, S., Wright, R., Redfern, A., & Smith, D. (1993). A woman's place is in the home: Females and residential burglary. *Justice Quarterly, 10,* 143–163.

Deem, D., & Murray, M. (2000). Financial crime. In G. Coleman, M. Gaboury, M. Murray, & A. Seymour (Eds.), *1999 National Victim Assistance Academy*. Washington, DC: U.S. Department of Justice.

Delgado-Escueta, A., Mattson, R., & King, L. (1981). The nature of aggression during epileptic seizures. *New England Journal of Medicine, 305,* 711–716.

D'Emilio, J., & Freedman, E. B. (1988). *Intimate matters: A history of sexuality in America*. New York: Harper & Row.

Department of Health and Human Services. (2003, September). *Overview of findings from the 2002 national survey on drug use and health*. Rockville, MD: Substance Abuse and Mental Health Services, Office of Applied Studies.

DeRosia, V. R. (1995). *Living inside prison walls: Adjustment behavior*. Westport, CT: Praeger.

Developmental Disabilities Branch. (2000, December). *Attention-deficit/hyperactivity disorder*. Atlanta, GA: Centers for Disease Control and Prevention.

Developments in the Law. (1974). Civil commitment of the mentally ill. *Harvard Law Review, 87,* 1190–1406.

Diener, E. (1980). Deindividuation: The absence of self-awareness and self-regulation in group members. In P. Paulus (Ed.), *The psychology of group influence*. Hillsdale, NJ: Erlbaum.

Dietz, P. E., Hazelwood, R. R., & Warren, J. (1990). The sexually sadistic criminal and his offenses. *Bulletin of the American Academy of Psychiatry and Law, 18,* 163–178.

DiLonardo, R. L. (1996). Defining and measuring the economic benefit of electronic article surveillance. *Security Journal, 7,* 3–9.

Dion, K. (1972). Physical attractiveness and evaluations of children's transgressions. *Journal of Personality and Social Psychology, 24,* 207–213.

Dion, K., Berscheid, E., & Walster, E. (1972). What is beautiful is good. *Journal of Personality and Social Psychology, 24,* 285–290.

Diserens, C. M. (1925). Psychological objectivism. *Psychological Review, 32,* 121–152.

Dishion, T. J., & Andrews, D. W. (1995). Preventing escalation in problem behaviors with high-risk young adolescents: Immediate and 1-year outcomes. *Journal of Consulting and Clinical Psychology, 63,* 538–548.

Dishion, T. J., & Bullock, B. M. (2002). Parenting and adolescent problem behavior: An ecological analysis of the nuturance hypothesis. In J. G. Borkowski, S. L. Ramey, & M. Bristol-Power (Eds.), *Parenting and the child's world: Influences on academic, intellectual, and social-emotional development*. Mahwah, NJ: Erlbaum.

Ditton, P. M. (1999). *Mental health and treatment of inmates and probationers: Special report*. Washington, DC: U.S. Department of Justice, Bureau of Justice Statistics.

Ditzler, T. F. (2004). Malevolent minds: The teleology of terrorism. In F. M. Moghaddam & A. J. Marsella (Eds.), *Understanding terrorism: Psychosocial roots, consequences, and interventions*. Washington, DC: American Psychological Association.

Dix, G. E. (1980). Clinical evaluation of the "dangerous" if "normal" criminal defendants. *Virginia Law Review, 66,* 523–581.

Dobson, V., & Sales, B. (2000). The science of infanticide and mental illness. *Psychology, Public Policy, and Law, 6,* 1098–1112.

Dodge, K. A. (1986). A social information processing model of social competence in children. In M. Perlmutter (Ed.), *The Minnesota symposium on child psychology.* Hillsdale, NJ: Erlbaum.

Dodge, K. A. (1993a). The future of research on the treatment of conduct disorder. *Development and Psychopathology, 5,* 311–319.

Dodge, K. A. (1993b). Social-cognitive mechanisms in the development of conduct disorder and depression. *Annual Review of Psychology, 44,* 559–584.

Dodge, K. A., Bates, J. E., & Pettit, G. S. (1990). Mechanisms in the cycle of violence. *Science, 250,* 1678–1683.

Dodge, K. A., & Coie, J. D. (1987). Social information processing factors in reactive and proactive aggression in children's peer groups. *Journal of Personality and Social Psychology, 53,* 1146–1158.

Dodge, K. A., Lochman, J. E., Harnish, J. D., Bates, J. E., & Pettit, G. S. (1997). Reactive and proactive aggression in school children and psychiatrically impaired chronically assaultive youth. *Journal of Abnormal Psychology, 106,* 37–51.

Dodge, K. A., & Pettit, G. S. (2003). A biopsychological model of the development of chronic conduct problems in adolescence. *Developmental Psychology, 39,* 349–371.

Doerner, W. G. (1988). The impact of medical resources on criminally induced lethality: A further examination. *Criminology, 26,* 171–179.

Doerner, W. G., & Speir, J. C. (1986). Stitch and sew: The impact of medical resources upon criminally induced lethality. *Criminology, 24,* 319–330.

Dollard, J., Doob, L. W., Miller, N. E., Mowrer, O. H., & Sears, R. R. (1939). *Frustration and aggression.* New Haven, CT: Yale University Press.

Donnerstein, E. (1983). Erotica and human aggression. In R. G. Geen & E. I. Donnerstein (Eds.), *Aggression: Theoretical and empirical reviews* (Vol. 2). New York: Academic Press.

d'Orban, P. T., & O'Connor, A. (1989). Women who kill their parents. *British Journal of Psychiatry, 154,* 27–33.

Dougherty, D. M., Bjork, J. M., Cherek, D. R., Moeller, F. G., & Huang, D. B. (1998). Effects of menstrual cycle phase on aggression measured in the laboratory. *Aggressive Behavior, 24,* 9–26.

Douglas, J. E., Burgess, A. W., Burgess, A. G., & Ressler, R. K. (1992). *Crime classification manual.* New York: Lexington Books.

Douglas, J. E., & Munn, C. (1992a). The detection of staging and personation at the crime scene. In J. E. Douglas, A. W. Burgess, A. G. Burgess, & R. K. Ressler (Eds.), *Crime classification manual.* New York: Lexington Books.

Douglas, J. E., & Munn, C. (1992b). Modus operandi and the signature aspects of violent crime. In J. E. Douglas, A. W. Burgess, A. G. Burgess, & R. K. Ressler (Eds.), *Crime classification manual.* New York: Lexington Books.

Douglas, J. E., & Munn, C. (1992c, February). Violent crime scene analysis. *FBI Law Enforcement Bulletin,* 1–10.

Douglas, J. E., Ressler, R. K., Burgess, A. W., & Hartman, C. R. (1986). Criminal profiling from crime scene analysis. *Behavioral Sciences & the Law, 4,* 401–421.

Down, J. L. H. (1866). Observations on ethnic classification of idiots. *London Hospital and Lecture Reports, 3,* 259–262.

Driver, E. D. (1961). Interaction and criminal homicide in India. *Social Forces, 40,* 153–158.

Drug Enforcement Administration. (2000). *Drugs of abuse.* Washington, DC: U.S. Department of Justice. Available: www.usdoj.gov/dea/concern/abuse

Drug Enforcement Adminstration. (2001). *Overview of drug use in the United States.* Washington, DC: U.S. Department of Justice. Available: http//.usdoj.gov/dea/stats/overview.htm

Drug Enforcement Administration. (2003). *Lysergic acid diethylamide (LSD).* Washington, DC: U.S. Department of Justice.

DSM-II. (1968). *Diagnostic and statistical manual of mental disorders* (2nd ed.). Washington, DC: American Psychiatric Association.

DSM-III. (1980). *Diagnostic and statistical manual of mental disorders* (3rd ed.). Washington, DC: American Psychiatric Association.

DSM-III-R. (1987). *Diagnostic and statistical manual of mental disorders* (rev. ed.). Washington, DC: American Psychiatric Association.

DSM-IV. (1994). *Diagnostic and statistical manual of mental disorders* (4th ed.). Washington, DC: American Psychiatric Association.

Duhaime, A., Christian, C. W., Rorke, L. B., & Zimmerman, R. A. (1998). Nonaccidental head injury in infants: The "shaken-baby syndrome." *New England Journal of Medicine, 338,* 1822–1829.

Dull, R. T., & Giacopassi, D. J. (1987). Demographic correlates of sexual and dating attitudes: A study of date rape. *Criminal Justice and Behavior, 14,* 175–193.

Dunn, C. S. (1976). *The patterns and distribution of assault incident characteristics among social areas.* Analytic Report 14. Albany, NY: Criminal Justice Research Center.

Dvorak, J. A. (2000, December 21). *Kansas launches racial profiling study. The Kansas City Star, 1,* 11.

Duwe, G. (2000). Body-count journalism: The presentation of mass murder in the news media. *Homicide Studies, 4,* 364–399.

Easterbrook, J. A. (1959). The effect of emotion on cue utilization and the organization of behavior. *Psychological Review, 66,* 183–201.

Eaton, J., & Polk, K. (1961). *Measuring delinquency.* Pittsburgh, PA: University of Pittsburgh Press.

Ebert, B. W. (1987). Guide to conducting a psychological autopsy. *Professional Psychology: Research and Practice, 18,* 52–56.

Eck, J. (2000). Preventing crime at places. In L. W. Sherman, D. Gottfresson, D. MacKenzie, J. Eck, P. Reuter, & S. Bushway (Eds.), *Preventing crime: What works, what doesn't, what's promising.* A Report to the United State Congress. Available: www.ncjrs.org/works

Edens, J. F., Petrila, J., & Buffington-Vollum, J. K. (2001). Psychopathy and the death penalty: Can the Psychopathy Checklist-Revised identify offenders who represent "a continuing threat to society?" *Journal of Psychiatry and Law, 29,* 433–481.

Edens, J. F., Skeem, J. L., Cruise, K. R., & Cauffman, E. (2001). Assessment of 'juvenile psychopathy' and its association with violence: A critical review. *Behavioral Sciences & the Law, 19,* 53–80.

Edleson, J. L. (1999). Children's witnessing of adult domestic violence. *Journal of Interpersonal Violence, 14,* 839–870.

Edwards, S. (1983). Sexuality, sexual offenses, and conception of victims in the criminal justice process. *Victimology: An International Journal, 8,* 113–128.

Efran, M. G., & Cheyne, J. A. (1974). Affective concomitants of the invasion of shared space: Behavioral, physiological, and verbal indicators. *Journal of Personality and Social Psychology, 29,* 219–226.

Ehrlich, S. K., & Keogh, R. P. (1956). The psychopath in a mental institution. *Archives of Neurology and Psychiatry, 76,* 286–295.

Eidelson, R. J., D'Alessio, G. R., & Eidelson, J. I. (2003). The impact of September 11 on psychologists. *Professional Psychology: Research and Practice, 34,* 144–150.

Elliott, D. S. (1989). Criminal justice procedures in family violence crimes. In L. Ohlin & M. Tonry (Eds.), *Family violence* (Vol. 11). Chicago, IL: University of Chicago Press.

Elliott, D. S., Ageton, S. S., & Huizinga, D. (1980). *The national youth survey.* Boulder, CO: Behavioral Research Institute.

Elliott, D. S., Dunford, T. W., & Huizinga, D. (1987). The identification and prediction of career offenders utilizing self-reported and official data. In J. D. Burchard & S. N. Burchard (Eds.), *Prevention of delinquent behavior.* Newbury Park, CA: Sage.

Ellis, A. (1962). *Reason and emotion in psychotherapy.* New York: Lyle Stuart.

Ellis, C. A., & Lord, J. (2001). Homicide. In G. Coleman, M. Gaboury, M. Murray, & A. Seymour (Eds.), *1999 National Victim Assistance Academy*. Washington, DC: U.S. Department of Justice.

Ellis, L. (1982). Genetics and criminal behavior: Evidence through the end of the 1970s. *Criminology, 20*, 43–66.

Ellis, L. (1998). Why some sexual assaults are not committed by men: A biosocial analysis. In P. Anderson & C. Struckman-Johnson (Eds.), *Sexually aggressive women.* New York: Guilford Press.

Emery, R. E., & Laumann-Billings, L. (1998). An overview of the nature, causes, and consequences of abusive family relationships. *American Psychologist, 53*, 121–135.

Epstein, J. F., & Gfroerer, J. C. (1997, August). *Heroin abuse in the United States.* Rockville, MD: Substance Abuse and Mental Health Services Administration.

Epstein, S., & Taylor, S. P. (1967). Instigation to aggression as a function of degree of defeat and perceived aggressive intent of the opponent. *Journal of Personality, 35*, 265–289.

Ermulf, K. E., & Innala, S. M. (1995). Sexual bondage: A review and unobtrusive investigation. *Archives of Sexual Behavior, 24*, 631–655.

Eron, L. D. (1963). Relationship of TV violence habits and aggressive behavior in children. *Journal of Abnormal and Social Psychology, 67*, 193–196.

Eron, L. D., & Huesmann, L. P. (1984). The relation of prosocial behavior to the development of aggression and psychopathology. *Aggressive Behavior, 10*, 201–211.

Eron, L. D., & Huesmann, L. R. (1986). The role of television in the development of prosocial and antisocial behavior. In D. Olweus, J. Block, & M. Radke-Yarrow (Eds.), *Development of antisocial and prosocial behavior: Research, theories and issues.* Orlando, FL: Academic Press.

Eron, L. D., Huesmann, L. P., & Zelli, A. (1991). The role of parental variables in the learning of aggression. In D. J. Pepler & K. H. Rubin (Eds.), *The development and treatment of childhood aggression.* Hillsdale, NJ: Erlbaum.

Eron, L. D., & Slaby, R. G. (1994). Introduction. In L. D. Eron, J. H. Gentry, & P. Schlegel (Eds.), *Reason to hope: A psychosocial perspective on violence and youth.* Washington, DC: American Psychological Association.

Eskridge, C. W. (1983). Prediction of burglary: A research note. *Journal of Criminal Justice, 11*, 67–75.

Evans, D. (1970). Exhibitionism. In C. G. Costello (Ed.), *Symptoms of psychopathology: A handbook.* New York: Wiley.

Ewing, C. P. (1990). Psychological self-defense: A proposed justification for battered women who kill. *Law and Human Behavior, 14*, 579–594.

Eysenck, H. J. (1964). *Crime and personality.* London: Routledge & Kegan Paul.

Eysenck, H. J. (1967). *The biological basis of personality.* Springfield, IL: Charles C Thomas.

Eysenck, H. J. (1973). *The inequality of man.* San Diego, CA: EDITS.

Eysenck, H. J. (1977). *Crime and personality* (2nd ed.). London: Routledge & Kegan Paul.

Eysenck, H. J. (1981). *A model for personality.* New York: Springer.

Eysenck, H. J. (1983). Personality, conditioning, and antisocial behavior. In W. S. Laufer & J. M. Day (Eds.), *Personality theory, moral development, and criminal behavior.* Lexington, MA: Lexington Books.

Eysenck, H. J. (1996). Personality and crime: Where do we stand? *Psychology, Crime & Law, 2,* 143–152.

Eysenck, H. J., & Gudjonsson, G. H. (1989). *The causes and cures of criminality.* New York: Plenum.

Eysenck, H. J., & Rachman, S. (1965). *The causes and cures of neurosis.* San Diego, CA: Robert R. Knapp.

Eysenck, S. B. G., & Eysenck, H. J. (1970). Crime and personality: An empirical study of the three-factor theory. *British Journal of Criminology, 10,* 225–239.

Fagan, J. (1989). Cessation of family violence. In L. Ohlin & M. Tonry (Eds.), *Family violence* (Vol. 11). Chicago, IL: University of Chicago Press.

Fantuzzo, J. W., Boruch, R., Abdullahi, B., Atkins, M., & Marcus, S. (1997). Domestic violence and children: Prevalence and risk in five major U.S. cities. *Journal of American Academy of Child and Adolescent Psychiatry, 36,* 116–122.

Fantuzzo, J. W., DePaola, L. M., Lambert, L., Martino, T., Anderson, G., & Sutton, S. (1991). Effects of interparental violence on the psychological adjustment and competencies of young children. *Journal of Consulting and Clinical Psychology, 59,* 258–265.

Farabee, D. (Ed.). (2002). Making people change (special issue). *Criminal Justice and Behavior, 29,* 3–109.

Farley, M., & Barkan, H. (1998). Prostitution, violence against women, and post-traumatic stress disorder. *Women and Health, 27,* 37–49.

Farley, M., & Kelly, V. (2000). Prostitution: A critical review of the medical and social sciences literature. *Women and Criminal Justice, 27,* 37–49.

Farrell, G., Phillips, C., & Pease, K. (1995). Like taking candy, why does repeat victimization occur? *British Journal of Criminology, 35,* 384–399.

Farrington, D. P. (1987). Predicting individual crime rates. In D. M. Gottfredson & M. Tonry (Eds.), *Prediction and classification* (Vol. 10). Chicago, IL: University of Chicago Press.

Farrington, D. P. (1991). Childhood aggression and adult violence: Early precursors and later life outcomes. In D. J. Pepler & K. H. Rubin (Eds.), *The development and treatment of childhood aggression.* Hillsdale, NJ: Erlbaum.

Farrington, D. P., Biron, L., & LeBlanc, M. (1982). Personality and delinquency in London and Montreal. In J. Gunn & D. P. Farrington (Eds.), *Abnormal offenders, delinquency, and the criminal justice system.* Chichester, UK: Wiley.

Farrington, D. P., Bowen, S., Buckle, A., Burns-Howell, T., Burrows, J., & Speed, M. (1993). An experiment on the prevention of shoplifting. In R. V. Clarke (Ed.), *Crime prevention studies* (Vol. 1). Monsey, NY: Criminal Justice Press.

Farrington, D. P., & Burrows, J. N. (1993). Did shoplifting really decrease? *British Journal of Criminology, 33,* 57–59.

Faupel, C. E. (1991). *Shooting dope: Career patterns of hard-core heroin users.* Gainesville: University of Florida Press.

Federal Bureau of Investigation. (1985, August). Crime scene and profile characteristics of organized and disorganized murders. *FBI Law Enforcement Bulletin, 54,* 18–25.

Federal Bureau of Investigation. (1992). *Killed in the line of duty: A study of selected felonious killings of law enforcement officers.* Washington, DC: U.S. Department of Justice.

Federal Bureau of Investigation. (1996). *Terrorism in the United States, 1995.* Washington, DC: U.S. Government Printing Office.

Federal Bureau of Investigation. (1997). *Uniform Crime Reports—1996.* Washington, DC: U.S. Government Printing Office.

Federal Bureau of Investigation. (1999a, August). *The FBI's national drug strategy.* Washington, DC: U.S. Department of Justice.

Federal Bureau of Investigation. (1999b). *Terrorism in the United States—1998.* Washington, DC: U.S. Department of Justice, Counterterrorism Threat Assessment and Warning Unit.

Federal Bureau of Investigation. (2000). *Uniform Crime Reports—1999.* Washington, DC: U.S. Department of Justice.

Federal Bureau of Investigation. (2001). *Hate crime statistics,* 1999. Washington, DC: U.S. Department of Justice.

Federal Bureau of Investigation. (2002). *Uniform Crime Reports—2002.* Washington, DC: U.S. Department of Justice.

Federal Bureau of Investigation. (2003). *Uniform Crime Reports—2002.* Washington, DC: U.S. Department of Justice.

Fehrenbach, P. A., Smith, W., Monastersky, C., & Deisher, R. W. (1986). Adolescent sexual offenders: Offender and offense characteristics. *American Journal of Orthopsychiatry, 56,* 225–233.

Feinberg, G. (1984). Profile for the elderly shoplifter. In E. S. Newman, D. J. Newman, & M. L. Gewirtz (Eds.), *Elderly criminals.* Cambridge, MA: Oelgeschlager, Gunn & Hain.

Feld, B. C. (1988). In re Gault revised: A cross-state comparison of the right to counsel in juvenile court. *Crime and Delinquency, 34,* 393–424.

Feldman, M. P. (1977). *Criminal behavior: A psychological analysis.* London: Wiley.

Felson, R. B., Baumer, E. P., & Messner, S. F. (2000). Acquaintance robbery. *Journal of Research in Crime and Delinquency, 37,* 284–305.

Felthous, A. R. (2001). Introduction to this issue: The clinician's duty to warn or protect. *Behavioral Sciences & the Law, 19,* 321–324.

Fenichel, O. (1945). *The psychoanalytic theory of neurosis.* New York: W. W. Norton.

Ferrero, G. (1972). *Criminal man.* Montclair, NJ: Patterson Smith.

Feshbach, S. (1964). The function of aggression and the regulation of aggressive drive. *Psychological Review, 71,* 257–272.

Festinger, L., Pepitone, A., & Newcomb, T. (1952). Some consequences of de-individuation in a group. *Journal of Abnormal and Social Psychology, 47,* 382–389.

Feucht, T. W., & Kyle, G. M. (1996, November). Methamphetamine use among adult arrestees: Findings of the DUF program. *NIJ Research in Brief.* Washington, DC: U.S. Department of Justice.

Field, S. (1992). The effect of temperature on crime. *British Journal of Criminology, 32,* 340–351.

Finckenauer, J. O., & Schrock, J. (2000). *Human trafficking: A growing criminal market in the U.S.* Washington, DC: National Institute of Justice, International Center. Available: www.ojp.usdoj.gov/nij/international/ht.html

Finkelhor, D., & Araji, S. (1986). Explanations of pedophilia: A four factor model. *The Journal of Sex Research, 22,* 145–161.

Finkelhor, D., & Dziuba-Leatherman, J. (1994). Children as victims of violence: A national survey. *Pediatrics, 94,* 413–420.

Finkelhor, D., & Lewis, I. A. (1988). An epidemiologic approach to the study of child molestation. In R. A. Prentky & V. L. Quinsey (Eds.), *Human sexual aggression: Current perspectives.* New York: New York Academy of Sciences.

Firestone, P., Bradford, J. M., Greenberg, D. M., & Larose, M. R. (1998). Homicidal sex offenders: Psychological, phallometric, and diagnostic features. *Journal of the American Academy of Psychology and Law, 26,* 537–552.

Fishbein, D. (2001). *Biobehavioral perspectives in criminology.* Belmont, CA: Wadsworth/Thomson Learning.

Fisher, R. S. (1951). Symposium on the compulsory use of chemical tests for alcoholic intoxication. *Maryland Medical Journal, 3,* 291–292.

Fiske, D. E., & Maddi, S. R. (1961). *Functions of varied experience.* Homewood, IL: Dorsey.

Fitzgerald, L. F. (2003). Sexual harassment and social justice: Reflections and distance yet to go. *American Psychologist, 11,* 915–924.

Fitzhugh, K. B. (1973). Some neuropsychological features of delinquent subjects. *Perceptual and Motor Skills, 36,* 494.

Flor-Henry, P. (1973). Psychiatric syndromes considered as manifestations of lateralized temporal-limbic dysfunction. In L. V. Latiner & K. E. Livingston (Eds.), *Surgical approaches in psychiatry.* Lancaster, UK: Medical and Technical.

Flor-Henry, P., & Yeudall, L. T. (1973). Lateralized cerebral dysfunction in depression and in aggressive criminal psychopathy. *International Research Communications, 7,* 31.

Flynn, E. E. (1983). Crime as a major social issue. *American Behavioral Scientist, 27,* 7–42.

Flynn, J. R. (1999). Searching for justice: The discovery of IQ gains over time. *American Psychologist, 54,* 5–20.

Fois, A. (1961). *The electroencephalogram of the normal child.* Springfield, IL: Charles C Thomas.

Forbes, G. B., Adams-Curtis, L. E., & White, K. B. (2004). First- and second-generation measures of sexism, rape myths and related beliefs, and hostility toward women. *Violence Against Women, 10,* 236–261.

Forehand, R., Wierson, M., Frame, C. L., Kemptom, T., & Armistead, L. (1991). Juvenile firesetting: A unique syndrome or an advanced level of antisocial behavior? *Behavioral Research and Therapy, 29,* 125–128.

Forrstrom-Cohen, B., & Rosenbaum, A. (1985). The effects of parental marital violence on young adults: An exploratory investigation. *Journal of Marriage and Family, 47,* 467–472.

Forth, A. E., Kosson, D. S., & Hare, R. D. (1997). *Hare Psychopathy Checklist: Youth Version.* Toronto: Multi-Heath Systems.

Fox, J. A., & Levin, J. (1998). Multiple homicide: Patterns of serial and mass murder. In M. Tonry (Ed.), *Crime and justice: A review of research* (Vol. 23). Chicago, IL: University of Chicago Press.

Fox, R. G. (1971). The XYY offender: A modern myth? *Journal of Criminal Law, Criminology, and Police Science, 62,* 59–73.

Franke, D. (1975). *The torture doctor.* New York: Avon.

Frederick, R. I. (2000). Mixed group validation: A method to address the limitations of criterion group validation in research on malingering detection. *Behavioral Science & the Law, 18,* 693–718.

Freedman, J. L. (1975). *Crowding and behavior.* San Francisco, CA: W. H. Freeman.

Freedman, J. L., Levy, A., Buchanan, R. W., & Price, J. (1972). Crowding and human aggressiveness. *Journal of Experimental Social Psychology, 8,* 528–548.

Freedman, J. L., Sears, D. O., & Carlsmith, J. J. (1978). *Social psychology* (3rd ed.). Upper Saddle River, NJ: Prentice Hall.

French, J. D. (1957). The reticular formation. *Scientific American, 196,* 54–60.

Frese, B., Moya, M., & Megias, J. I. (2004). Social perception of rape. *Journal of Interpersonal Violence, 19,* 143–161.

Frick, P. J., Bodin, S. D., & Barry, C. T. (2000). Psychopathic traits and conduct problems in community and clinic-referred samples of children: Further development of the psychopathy screening device. *Psychological Assessment, 12,* 382–393.

Frick, P. J., O'Brien, B. S., Wootton, J., & McBurnett, K. (1994). Psychopathy and conduct problems in children. *Journal of Abnormal Psychology, 103,* 700–707.

Frieze, I. H., & Browne, A. (1989). Violence in marriage. In L. Ohlin & M. Tonry (Eds.), *Family violence* (Vol. 11). Chicago, IL: University of Chicago Press.

Frintner, M., & Rubinson, L. (1993). Acquaintance rape: The influence of alcohol, fraternity membership and sports team membership. *Journal of Sex Education and Therapy, 19,* 272–284.

Frisbie, L. V. (1965). Treated sex offenders who reverted to sexually deviant behavior. *Federal Probation, 29,* 52–57.

Fritzon, K. (2000). The contribution of psychological research to arson investigation. In D. Canter & L. Alison (Eds.), *Profiling property crimes.* Dartmouth, UK: Ashgate.

Fulton, D. R. (2000). Shaken baby syndrome. *Critical Care Nursing Quarterly, 23,* 43–50.

Funk, J. B., & Buchman, D. D. (1996). Playing violent video and computer games and the adolescent self-concept. *Journal of Communications,* Spring, 84–89.

Furby, L., Weinrott, M. R., & Blackshaw, L. (1989). Sex offender recidivism: A review. *Psychological Bulletin, 105,* 3–30.

Fuselier, G. D. (1999, July). Placing the Stockholm syndrome in perspective. *FBI Law Enforcement Bulletin,* 9–12.

Fuselier, G. D., & Noesner, G. W. (1990, July). Confronting the terrorist hostage taker. *FBI Law Enforcement Bulletin,* 6–11.

Fyfe, J. F. (1984). Police dilemmas in processing elderly offenders. In E. S. Newman, D. J. Newman, & M. L. Gewirtz (Eds.), *Elderly criminals.* Cambridge, MA: Oelgeschalger, Gunn & Hain.

Gabrielli, W. F., & Mednick, S. A. (1983). Genetic correlates of criminal behavior. *American Behavioral Scientist, 27,* 59–74.

Gacono, C. B., Nieberding, R. J., Owen, A., Rubel, J., & Bodholdt, R. (1997). Treating conduct disorder, antisocial, and psychopathic personalities. In J. B. Ashford, B. D. Sales, & W. H. Reid (Eds.), *Treating adult and juvenile offenders with special needs.* Washington, DC: American Psychological Association.

Gacono, C. B., Nieberding, R. J., Owen, A., Rubel, J., & Bodholdt, R. (2001). Treating conduct disorder, antisocial, and psychopathic personalities. In J. B. Ashford, B. D. Sales, & W. H. Reid (Eds.), *Treating adult and juvenile offenders with special needs.* Washington, DC: American Psychological Association.

Gaes, G. G., Flanagan, T. J., Motiuk, L. L., & Stewart, L. (1999). Adult correctional treatment. In M. Tonry & J. Petersilia, (Eds.), *Prisons: Crime and justice. Review of the research* (Vol. 26). Chicago: University of Chicago Press.

Galanter, M. (1974). Why the "haves" come out ahead: Speculations on the limits of social change. *Law & Society Review, 9,* 95–160.

Gangestad, S. W., & Yeo, R. A. (1994). Parental handedness and relative hand skill: A test of the developmental instability hypothesis. *Neuropsychology, 8,* 572–578.

Ganley, A. L., & Schechter, S. (1996). *Domestic violence: A national curriculum for children's protective services.* San Francisco, CA: Family Violence Prevention Fund.

Garbarino, J. (1989). The incidence and prevalence of child maltreatment. In L. Ohlin & M. Tonry (Eds.), *Family violence* (Vol. 11). Chicago, IL: University of Chicago Press.

Garbarino, J., & Asp, C. E. (1981). *Successful schools and competent students.* Lexington, MA: Lexington Books.

Gardner, T. J. (1985). *Crime law: Principles and cases.* St. Paul, MN: West.

Garofalo, J. (1977). *Public opinion about crime: The attitudes of victims and nonvictims in selected cities.* Washington, DC: U.S. Government Printing Office.

Garside, R. B., & Klimes-Dougan, B. (2002). Socialization of discrete negative emotions: Gender differences and links with psychological distress. *Sex Roles: A Journal of Research, 14,* 115–129.

Gebhard, P. H., Gagnon, J. H., Pomeroy, W. B., & Christenson, C. V. (1965). *Sex offenders.* New York: Harper & Row.

Geis, G. (1988). From Deuteronomy to deniability: A historical perlustration on white-collar crime. *Justice Quarterly, 5,* 7–32.

Geis, G. (1997). Preface. In G. Green, *Occupational crime* (2nd ed.). Chicago, IL: Nelson–Hall.

Gelinas, D. J. (1993, October 3). *Recognizing and treating dissociative processes in trauma survivors*. Professional workshop sponsored by the Vermont Trauma Institute, Burlington.

Gelles, R. J. (1982). Domestic criminal violence. In M. E. Wolfgang & N. A. Weiner (Eds.), *Criminal violence*. Beverly Hills, CA: Sage.

Gelles, R. J., & Straus, M. A. (1979). Determinants of violence in the family: Toward a theoretical integration. In W. R. Burr, F. I. Nye, & I. L. Reiss (Eds.), *Contemporary theories about the family*. New York: Free Press.

Gendreau, P. (1996). The principles of effective interventions with offenders. In A. T. Harland (Ed.), *Choosing correctional options that work*. Thousand Oaks, CA: Sage.

Gendreau, P., & Goggin, C. (1996). *Principles of effective correctional programming*. Toronto, ON: Forum on Correctional Research.

Gendreau, P., Little, T., & Goggin, C. (1996). A meta-analysis of the predictors of adult offender recidivism: What works! *Criminology, 34*, 575–607.

George, W. H., & Marlatt, G. A. (1989). Introduction. In D. R. Laws (Ed.), *Relapse prevention with sex offenders*. New York: Guilford Press.

Gerbner, G., & Gross, L. (1976). Living with television: The violence profile. *Journal of Communications, 26*, 173–199.

Gerbner, G., Gross, L., Morgan, M., & Signorielli, N. (1981). Health and medicine on television. *The New England Journal of Medicine, 305*, 901–904.

Gibbens, T. C. (1957). Female offenders. *British Journal of Delinquency, 8*, 23–25.

Gibbens, T. C. (1981). Female crime in England and Wales. In F. Adler (Ed.), *The incidence of female criminality in the contemporary world*. New York: New York University Press.

Gibbens, T. C., Pond, D. A., & Stafford-Clark, D. (1955). A follow-up study of criminal psychopaths. *British Journal of Delinquency, 5*, 126–136.

Gibbons, D. C. (1977). *Society, crime and criminal careers* (3rd ed.). Upper Saddle River, NJ: Prentice Hall.

Gibbons, D. C. (1988). Some critical observation on criminal types and criminal careers. *Criminal Justice and Behavior, 15*, 8–23.

Gibson, H. B. (1967). Self-reported delinquency among schoolboys, and their attitudes to the police. *British Journal of Social and Clinical Psychology, 6*, 168–173.

Gillin, J. C., & Ochberg, F. M. (1970). Firearms control and violence. In D. N. Daniels, M. F. Gilula, & F. M. Ochberg (Eds.), *Violence and the struggle for existence*. Boston, MA: Little, Brown.

Glasser, W. D. (1965). *Reality therapy*. New York: Harper & Row.

Glueck, S., & Glueck, E. (1950). *Unraveling juvenile delinquency*. New York: Harper & Row.

Glueck, S., & Glueck, E. (1956). *Physique and delinquency*. New York: Harper & Row.

Gold, L. H. (1962). Psychiatric profile of the firesetter. *Journal of Forensic Sciences, 7*, 404–417.

Gold, M. S. (1984). *800-cocaine*. New York: Bantam.

Golding, S. L., Skeem, J. L., Roesch, R., & Zapf, P. A. (1999). The assessment of criminal responsibility: Current controversies. In I. B. Weiner & A. K. Hess (Eds.), *Handbook of forensic psychology* (2nd ed.). New York: Wiley.

Goldman, H. (1977). The limits of clockwork: The neurobiology of violent behavior. In J. P. Conrad & S. Dinitz (Eds.), *In fear of each other*. Lexington, MA: Lexington Books.

Goldman, M. J. (1991). Kleptomania: Making sense of the nonsensical. *American Journal of Psychiatry, 148*, 986–995.

Goldstein, J. H. (1975). *Aggression and crimes of violence*. New York: Oxford University Press.

Goldstein, M. (1974). Brain research and violent behavior. *Archives of Neurology, 30*, 1–34.

Goldstein, M. J. (1977). A behavioral scientist looks at obscenity. In B. D. Sales (Ed.), *The criminal justice system* (Vol. 1). New York: Plenum.

Goldstein, P. J. (1985). The drugs-violence nexus: A tri-partite conceptual framework. *Journal of Drug Issues, 15,* 493–506.

Golub, A. L., & Johnson, B. D. (1997, July). Crack's decline: Some surprises across U.S. cities. *NIJ Research in Brief.* Washington, DC: U.S. Department of Justice.

Gorenstein, E. E. (1982). Frontal lobe functions in psychopaths. *Journal of Abnormal Psychology, 91,* 368–379.

Goring, C. (1913/1972). *The English convict: A statistical study.* Montclair, NJ: Patterson Smith.

Gorman-Smith, D., Tolan, P. H., Huesmann, L. R., & Zelli, A. (1996). The relation of family functioning to violence among inner-city minority youths. *Journal of Family Psychology, 10,* 115–129.

Gosselin, C., & Wilson, G. (1984). Fetishism, sadomasochism and related behaviours. In K. Howells (Ed.), *The psychology of sexual diversity.* London: Basil Blackwell.

Gossop, M. R., & Kristjansson, I. (1977). Crime and personality. *British Journal of Criminology, 17,* 264–273.

Gottfredson, G. D., & Gottfredson, D. C. (1985). *Victimization in schools.* New York: Plenum.

Gottfredson, M. R., & Hirschi, T. (1990). *A general theory of crime.* Stanford, CA: Stanford University Press.

Gottman, J. M. (2001). Crime, hostility, wife battering, and the heart: On the Meehan et al. (2001) failure to replicate the Gottman et al. (1995) typology. *Journal of Family Psychology, 15,* 409–414.

Gove, W. R., & Crutchfield, R. D. (1982). The family and delinquency. *The Sociological Quarterly, 23,* 301–319.

Grann, M., Belfrage, H., & Tengström, A. (2000). Actuarial assessment of risk for violence: Predictive validity of the VRAG and the historical part of the HCR-20. *Criminal Justice and Behavior, 27,* 97–114.

Grant, V. (1977). *The menacing stranger.* New York: Dover.

Green, G. S. (1997). *Occupational crime* (2nd ed.). Chicago, IL: Nelson–Hall.

Greenberg, L. S. (1988). Constructive cognition: Cognitive therapy coming of age. *The Counseling Psychologist, 16,* 235–238.

Greendlinger, V., & Byrne, D. (1987). Coercive sexual fantasies of college men as predictors of self-reported likelihood to rape and overt sexual aggression. *Journal of Sex Research, 23,* 1–11.

Greenfeld, L. A. (1997, February). *Sex offenses and offenders: An analysis of data on rape and sexual assault.* Washington, DC: U.S. Department of Justice, Bureau of Justice Statistics.

Greenfeld, L. A. (1998, April). *Alcohol and crime: An analysis of national data on the prevalence of alcohol involvement in crime.* Washington, DC: U.S. Department of Justice.

Greenfeld, L. A. (1999, December). *Women offenders.* Washington, DC: U.S. Department of Justice.

Greenfeld, L. A., & Smith, S. K. (1999, February). *American Indians and crime.* Washington, DC: U.S. Department of Justice.

Greenwald, H. (1958). *The call girl.* New York: Ballantine Books.

Gregorie, T. (2000). Workplace violence. In G. Coleman, M. Gaboury, M. Murray, & A. Seymour (Eds.), *1999 National Victim Assistance Academy.* Washington, DC: U.S. Department of Justice.

Gregorie, T., & Wallace, H. (2000). Workplace violence: Supplement. In A. Seymour, M. Murray, J. Sigmon, M. Hook, C. Edmunds, M. Gaboury, & G. Coleman (Eds.), *2000 National Victim Assistance Academy.* Washington, DC: U.S. Department of Justice.

Gretton, H. M., McBride, M., Hare, R. D., O'Shaughnessy, R., & Kumka, G. (2001). Psychopathy and recidivism in adolescent sex offenders. *Criminal Justice and Behavior, 28,* 427–449.

Griffith, W., & Veitch, R. (1971). Hot and crowded: Influences of population density and temperature on interpersonal affective behavior. *Journal of Personality and Social Psychology, 17*, 92–98.

Grisso, T. (1986). *Evaluating competencies: Forensic assessments and instruments.* New York: Plenum.

Grisso, T., & Schwartz, R. G. (Eds.). (2000). *Youth on trial: Developmental perspectives on juvenile justice.* Chicago: University of Chicago Press.

Groth, A. N. (1978). Patterns of sexual assault against children and adolescents. In A. W. Burgess, A. N. Groth, L. L. Holmstrom, & S. M. Sgroi (Eds.), *Sexual assault of children and adolescents.* Lexington, MA: Lexington Books.

Groth, A. N. (1979). *Men who rape: The psychology of the offender.* New York: Plenum.

Groth, A. N., & Burgess, A. W. (1977). Motivational intent in the sexual assault of children. *Criminal Justice and Behavior, 4*, 253–271.

Groth, A. N., Hobson, W. F., & Gary, T. S. (1982). The child molester: Clinical observation. *Journal of Social Work and Human Sexuality, 1*, 129–144.

Guerette, R. T. (2002). Geographical profiling. In D. Levinson (Ed.), *Encyclopedia of crime and punishment.* Thousand Oaks, CA: Sage.

Guerra, N. G., Huesmann, L. R., Tolan, P. H., Van Acker, R., & Eron, L. D. (1995). Stressful events and individual beliefs as correlates of economic disadvantage and aggression among urban children. *Journal of Consulting and Clinical Psychology, 63*, 518–528.

Guze, S. B. (1976). *Criminality and psychiatric disorders.* New York: Oxford University Press.

Häfner, H., & Böker, W. (1973). Mentally disordered violent offenders. *Social Psychiatry, 8*, 220–229.

Haft, M. G. (1976). Hustling for rights. In L. Crites (Ed.), *The female offender.* Lexington, MA: Lexington Books.

Hall, C. S., & Lindzey, G. (1970). *Theories of personality* (2nd ed.). New York: Wiley.

Hall, D. M. (1998). The victims of stalking. In J. R. Meloy (Ed.), *The psychology of stalking: Clinical and forensic perspectives.* San Diego, CA: Academic Press.

Hall, G. C. N. (1995). Sexual offender recidivism revisited: A meta-analysis of recent treatment studies. *Journal of Consulting and Clinical Psychology, 63*, 802–809.

Hall, G. C. N., Proctor, W. C., & Nelson, G. M. (1988). Validity of physiological measures of pedophilic sexual arousal in a sexual offender population. *Journal of Consulting and Clinical Psychology, 56*, 118–122.

Halleck, S. L. (1967). *Psychiatry and the dilemmas of crime.* New York: Harper & Row.

Halleck, S. L., & Witte, A. D. (1977). Is rehabilitation dead? *Crime and Delinquency, 23*, 372–382.

Hallett, B. (2004). Dishonest crimes, dishonest language: An argument about terrorism. In F. M. Moghaddam & A. J. Marsella (Eds.), *Understanding terrorism: Psychosocial roots, consequences, and interventions.* Washington, DC: American Psychological Association.

Halloran, J. D., Brown, R. L., & Chaney, D. (1969). *Mass media and crime.* Leicester, UK: Leicester University Press.

Halverson, C. F., & Victor, J. B. (1976). Minor physical anomalies and problem behavior in elementary school children. *Child Development, 47*, 281–285.

Hämäläinen, T., & Haapasalo, J. (1996). Retrospective reports of childhood abuse and neglect among violent and property offenders. *Psychology, Crime & Law, 3*, 1–13.

Hamburg, D. A., Moos, R. H., & Yalom, I. D. (1968). Studies of distress in the menstrual cycle and the postpartum period. In R. O. Michael (Ed.), *Endocrinology and human behaviour.* London: Oxford University Press.

Hammond, W. R., & Yung, B. (1994). African Americans. In L. D. Eron, J. H. Gentry, & P. Schlegel (Eds.), *Reason to hope: A psychosocial perspective on violence and youth*. Washington, DC: American Psychological Association.

Haney, C. W. (1983). The good, the bad, and the lawful: An essay on psychological injustice. In W. S. Laufer & J. M. Day (Eds.), *Personality theory, moral development, and criminal behavior*. Lexington, MA: Lexington Books.

Haney, C., & Zimbardo, P. (1998). The past the future of U.S. prison policy: Twenty-five years after the Stanford prison experiment. *American Psychologist, 53*, 709–727.

Hanson, R. K., & Harris, A. J. R. (2000). Where should we intervene? Dynamic predictors of sexual offense recidivism. *Criminal Justice and Behavior, 27*, 6–35.

Hare, R. D. (1965a). A conflict and learning theory analysis of psychopathic behavior. *Journal of Research in Crime and Delinquency, 2*, 12–19.

Hare, R. D. (1965b). Acquisition and generalization of a conditioned-fear response in psychopathic and nonpsychopathic criminals. *Journal of Psychology, 59*, 367–370.

Hare, R. D. (1968). Psychopathy, autonomic functioning, and the orienting response. *Journal of Abnormal Psychology, 73*, 1–24.

Hare, R. D. (1970). *Psychopathy: Theory and research*. New York: Wiley.

Hare, R. D. (1980). A research scale for the assessment of psychopathy in criminal populations. *Personality and Individual Differences, 1*, 111–119.

Hare, R. D. (1984). Performance of psychopaths on cognitive tasks related to frontal lobe function. *Journal of Abnormal Psychology, 93*, 133–140.

Hare, R. D. (1986). Criminal psychopaths. In J. C. Yuille (Ed.), *Selection and training: The role of psychology*. Boston, MA: Martinus Nijhoff.

Hare, R. D. (1991). *The Hare psychopathy checklist-revised*. Toronto, ON: Multi-Health Systems.

Hare, R. D. (1996). Psychopathy: A clinical construct whose time has come. *Criminal Justice and Behavior, 23*, 25–54.

Hare, R. D. (1998). Emotional processing in psychopaths. In D. J. Cooke, R. D. Hare, & A. Forth (Eds.), *Psychopathy: Theory, research, and implications for society*. Dordrecht, the Netherlands: Kluwer Academic.

Hare, R. D., Clark, D., Grann, M., & Thornton, D. (2000). Psychopathy and the predictive validity of the PCL-R: An international perspective. *Behavioral Sciences & the Law, 18*, 623–645.

Hare, R. D., & Connolly, J. F. (1987). Perceptual asymmetries and information processing in psychopaths. In S. A. Mednick, T. E. Moffitt, & S. A. Stack (Eds.), *The causes of crime: New biological approaches*. Cambridge, UK: Cambridge University Press.

Hare, R. D., & Craigen, D. (1974). Psychopathy and physiological activity in a mixed-motive game. *Psychophysiology, 11*, 197–206.

Hare, R. D., Forth, A. E., & Stachan, K. E. (1992). Psychopathy and crime across the life span. In R. D. Peters, R. J. McMahon, & V. L. Quinsey (Eds.), *Aggression and violence throughout the life span*. Newbury Park, CA: Sage.

Hare, R. D., Hart, S. D., & Harpur, T. J. (1991). Psychopathy and the DSM-IV criteria for antisocial personality disorder. *Journal of Abnormal Psychology, 100*, 391–398.

Hare, R. D., & Jutai, J. W. (1983). Criminal history of the male psychopath: Some preliminary data. In K. T. Van Dusen & S. A. Mednick (Eds.), *Prospective studies of crime and delinquency*. Boston, MA: Kluwer–Nijhoff.

Hare, R. D., & McPherson, L. M. (1984). Violent and aggressive behavior by criminal psychopaths. *International Journal of Law and Psychiatry, 7*, 35–50.

Hare, R. D., McPherson, L. M., & Forth, A. E. (1988). Male psychopaths and their criminal careers. *Journal of Consulting and Clinical Psychology, 56*, 710–714.

Hare, R. D., & Quinn, M. (1971). Psychopathy and autonomic conditioning. *Journal of Abnormal Psychology, 77*, 223–239.

Harmon, R. B., Rosner, R., & Wiederlight, M. (1985). Women and arson: A demographic study. *Journal of Forensic Sciences, 10*, 467–477.

Harpur, T. J., Hakstian, A., & Hare, R. D. (1988). Factor structure of the Psychopathy Checklist. *Journal of Consulting and Clinical Psychology, 56*, 741–747.

Harpur, J. T., & Hare, R. D. (1994). The assessment of psychopathy as a function of age. *Journal of Abnormal Psychology, 103*, 604–609.

Harries, K. D. (1980). *Crime and the environment.* Springfield, IL: Charles C Thomas.

Harris, D. A. (1999, June). *Driving while Black: Racial profiling on our nation's highways.* New York: American Civil Liberties Union. Available: www.aclu.org/profiling/report/index.html

Harris, G. T., Rice, M. E., & Quinsey, V. L. (1993). Violent recidivism of mentally disordered offenders: The development of a statistical prediction instrument. *Criminal Justice and Behavior, 20*, 315–335.

Harry, B., & Balcer, C. M. (1987). Menstruation and crime: A critical review from a clinical criminology perspective. *Behavioral Sciences & the Law, 5*, 307–321.

Hart, H. M., Jr., & Sacks, A. M. (1958). *The legal process: Basic problems in the making and application of law.* Unpublished manuscript.

Hart, S. D., Cox, D. N., & Hare, R. D. (1995). *The Hare Psychopathy Checklist: Screening Version.* Toronto, ON: Multi-Health Systems.

Hart, S. D., & Dempster, R. J. (1997). Impulsivity and psychopathy. In C. D. Webster & M. A. Jackson (Eds.), *Impulsivity: Theory, assessment and treatment.* New York: Guilford.

Hart, S. D., Hare, R. D., & Forth, A. E. (1993). Psychopathy as a risk marker for violence: Development and validation of a screening version of the Revised Psychopathy Checklist. In J. Monahan & H. Steadman (Eds.), *Violence and mental disorder: Development in risk assessment.* Chicago, IL: University of Chicago Press.

Hart, S. D., Watt, K. A., & Vincent, G. M. (2002). Commentary on Seagrave and Grisso: Impressions of the State of the Art. *Law and Human Behavior, 26*, 241–245.

Hartl, E. M., Monnelly, E. P., & Elderkin, R. D. (1982). *Physique and delinquent behavior.* New York: Academic Press.

Hartup, W. W. (1983). Peer relations. In P. H. Mussen (Ed.), *Manual of child psychology.* New York: Wiley.

Hawke, C. C. (1950). Castration and sex crimes. *American Journal of Mental Deficiency, 55*, 220–226.

Hawkins, D. F. (1985). Black homicide: The adequacy of existing research for devising prevention strategies. *Crime and Delinquency, 31*, 83–103.

Hawkins, D. L., Pepler, D. J., & Craig, W. M. (2001). Naturalistic observations of peer interventions in bullying. *Social Development, 10*, 512–527.

Hayashi, G. (1967). A study of juvenile delinquency in twins. In H. Misuda (Ed.), *Clinical genetics in psychiatry.* Tokyo: Ogaku Shain.

Hayes, L. M. (1995). Prison suicide: An overview and guide to prevention. *The Prison Journal, 75*, 431–456.

Hazelwood, R. R., & Burgess, A. W. (1987, September). An introduction to the serial rapist. *FBI Law Enforcement Bulletin*, 16–24.

Hebb, D. O. (1955). Drives and the C. N. S. (Conceptual Nervous System). *Psychological Review, 62*, 243–254.

Heide, K. (1993). Adolescent parricide offenders: Synthesis, illustration and future directions. In A. V. Wilson (Ed.), *Homicide—The victim/offender connection.* Cincinnati, OH: Anderson.

Heilbrun, K., & Griffin, P. (1999). Forensic treatment: A review of programs and research. In R. Roesch, S. D. Hart, & J. R. P. Ogle (Eds.), *Psychology and law: The state of the discipline*. New York: Kluwer Academic/Plenum.

Henderson, M. (1983). An empirical classification of non-violent offenders using the MMPI. *Personality and Individual Differences, 4*, 671–677.

Hemphill, J. F., & Hare, R. D. (2004). Some misconceptsions about the Hare PCL-R and risk assessment: A reply to Gendreau, Goggin, and Smith. *Criminal Justice and Behavior, 31*, 203–243.

Hemphill, J. F., Hare, R. D., & Wong, S. (1998). Psychopathy and recidivism: A review. *Legal and Criminological Psychology, 3*, 139–170.

Hendrick, C., & Taylor, S. P. (1971). The effects of belief similarity and aggression on attraction and counter-aggression. *Journal of Personality and Social Psychology, 17*, 342–349.

Henggeler, S. W. (1994). *Home-based services for serious and violent juvenile offenders*. Philadelphia: Center for the Study of Youth Policy, University of Pennsylvania.

Henggeler, S. W., & Borduin, C. M. (1990). *Family therapy and beyond: A multisystemic approach to treating the behavior problems of children and adolescents*. Pacific Grove, CA: Brooks/Cole.

Henggeler, S. W., Melton, G. B., & Smith, L. A. (1992). Family preservation using multisystemic therapy—An effective alternative to incarcerating serious juvenile offenders. *Journal of Consulting and Clinical Psychology, 60*, 953–961.

Henker, B., & Whalen, C. K. (1989). Hyperactivity and attention deficits. *American Psychologist, 44*, 216–244.

Henn, F. A., Herjanic, M., & Vanderpearl, R. H. (1976a). Forensic psychiatry: Profiles of two types of sex offenders. *American Journal of Psychiatry, 133*, 694–696.

Henn, F. A., Herjanic, M., & Vanderpearl, R. H. (1976b). Forensic psychiatry: Diagnosis of criminal responsibility. *Journal of Nervous and Mental Disease, 162*, 423–429.

Hepburn, J., & Voss, H. L. (1970). Patterns of criminal homicide: A comparison of Chicago and Philadelphia. *Criminology, 8*, 19–45.

Herpertz, S. C., & Sass, H. (2000). Emotional deficiency and psychopathy. *Behavioral Sciences & the Law, 18*, 567–580.

Herzberg, J. L., & Fenwick, P. B. C. (1988). The aetiology of aggression in temporal lobe epilepsy. *British Journal of Psychiatry, 153*, 50–55.

Hetherington, E. M., & Parke, R. D. (1975). *Child psychology: A contemporary viewpoint*. New York: McGraw–Hill.

Hickey, E. (1991). *Serial killers and their victims*. Pacific Grove, CA: Brooks/Cole.

Hickey, E. W. (1997). *Serial murderers and their victims*. Belmont, CA: Wadsworth.

Higley, J., Mehlman, P., Taub, M., Higley, B., Surmi, S., Linnoila, M., & Vickers, J. (1992). Cerebrospinal fluid monoamine and adrenal correlates of aggression free-ranging rhesus monkeys. *Archives of General Psychiatry, 49*, 436–441.

Hill, D., & Watterson, D. (1942). Electroencephalographic studies of the psychopathic personality. *Journal of Neurology and Psychiatry, 5*, 47–64.

Hill, H. M., Soriano, F. I., Chen, S. A., & LaFromboise, T. D. (1994). Sociocultural factors in the etiology and prevention of violence among ethnic minority youth. In L. D. Eron, J. H. Gentry, & P. Schlegel (Eds.), *Reason to hope: A psychosocial perspective on violence and youth*. Washington, DC: American Psychological Association.

Hill, P. (1960). *Portrait of a sadist*. New York: Avon.

Hill, R. W., Langevin, R., Paitich, D., Handy, L., Russon, A., & Wilkinson, L. (1982). Is arson an aggressive act or a property offense? *Canadian Journal of Psychiatry, 27*, 648–654.

Hindelang, M. J. (1974). Decisions of shoplifting victims to invoke the criminal justice process. *Social Process, 21*, 580–593.

Hindelang, M. J., Dunn, C. S., Sutton, L. P., & Aumick, A. (1976). *Sourcebook of criminal justice statistics, 1975*. Washington, DC: U.S. Government Printing Office.

Hindelang, M. J., Hirschi, T., & Weis, J. G. (1981). *Measuring delinquency*. Beverly Hills, CA: Sage.

Hirschi, T., & Hindelang, M. J. (1977). Intelligence and delinquency. *American Sociological Review, 42*, 571–587.

Hockenbury, D. H., & Hockenbury, S. E. (2004). *Discovering psychology* (3rd ed.). New York: Worth.

Hochstedler, E. (Ed.). (1984). *Corporations as criminals*. Beverly Hills, CA: Sage.

Hoffman, B. (1993). *"Holy terror": The implications of terrorism motivated by a religious imperative* (RAND Research Paper P-7834). Santa Monica, CA: RAND.

Hoffman, J. J., Hall, R. W., & Bartsch, T. W. (1987). On the relative importance of "psychopathic" personality and alcoholism measures of frontal lobe dysfunction. *Journal of Abnormal Psychology, 96*, 158–160.

Hofmann, F. G. (1975). *A handbook on drug and alcohol abuse: The biomedical aspects*. New York: Oxford University Press.

Hoge, S. K., Poythress, N., Bonnie, R., Eisenberg, M., Monahan, J., Feucht-Haviar, T., & Oberlander, L. (1996). Mentally ill and non-mentally ill defendants' abilities to understand information relevant to adjudication: A preliminary study. *Bulletin of the American Academy of Psychiatry and the Law, 24*, 187–197.

Hoge, S. K., Poythress, N., Bonnie, R., Monahan, J., Eisenberg, M., & Feucht-Haviar, T. (1997). The MacArthur adjudicative competence study: Diagnosis, psychopathology, and competence-related abilities. *Behavioral Sciences & the Law, 15*, 329–345.

Hoghughi, M. S., & Forrest, A. R. (1970). Eysenck's theory of criminality: An examination with approved school boys. *British Journal of Criminology, 10*, 240–254.

Hollinger, R. (1986). Acts against the workplace: Social bonding and employee deviance. *Deviant Behavior, 7*, 53–75.

Holmes, R. M. (1991). *Sex crimes*. Newbury Park, CA: Sage.

Holmes, R. M., & DeBurger, J. (1988). *Serial murder*. Newbury Park, CA: Sage.

Holmes, R. M., & Holmes, S. T. (2002). *Profiling violent crimes: An investigative tool* (3rd ed.). Thousand Oaks, CA: Sage.

Holmes, S. T., Hickey, E., & Holmes, R. M. (1991). Female serial murderesses: Constructing differentiating typologies. *Journal of Contemporary Criminal Justice, 7*, 245–256.

Holt, S. E., Meloy, J. R., & Stack, S. (1999). Sadism and psychopath in violent and sexual violent offenders. *Journal of the American Academy of Psychiatry and Law, 27*, 23–32.

Holtzworth-Monroe, A., & Stuart, G. L. (1994). Typologies of male batterers: Three subtypes and the differences among them. *Psychological Bulletin, 116*, 476–497.

Home Office. (1986). *Criminal statistics: England and Wales 1985*. London: HMSO.

Horney, J. (1978). Menstrual cycles and criminal responsibility. *Law and Human Behavior, 2*, 25–36.

Horning, D. N. M. (1970). Blue-collar theft: Conceptions of property, attitudes toward pilfering, and work group norms in a modern industrial plant. In E. O. Smigel & H. L. Ross (Eds.), *Crimes against bureaucracy*. New York: Van Nostrand Reinhold.

Hornung, C. A., McCullough, B. C., & Sugimoto, T. (1981). Status relationships in marriage: Risk factors in spouse abuse. *Journal of Marriage and the Family, 43*, 675–692.

Hotaling, G. T., & Straus, M. A. (1989). Intrafamily violence, and crime and violence outside the family. In L. Ohlin & M. Tonry (Eds.), *Family violence* (Vol. 11). Chicago, IL: University of Chicago Press.

Howell, J. C. (1998). A new approach to juvenile crime. *Corrections Compendium, 23,* 1–5, 23–24.

Hubbard, J. A., Dodge, K. A., Cillessen, A. H. N., Coie, J. D., & Schwartz, D. (2001). The dyadic nature of social information processing in boys' reactive and proactive aggression. *Journal of Personality and Social Psychology, 80,* 268–280.

Hudson, M. I. (1986). Elder maltreatment: Current research. In K. A. Pillemer & R. S. Wolf (Eds.), *Elder abuse: Conflict in the family.* Dover, MA: Auburn House.

Huesmann, L. R. (1988). An information processing model for the development of aggression. *Aggressive Behavior, 14,* 13–24.

Huesmann, L. R. (1997). Observational learning of violent behavior: Social and biosocial processes. In A. Raine, P. A. Brennan, D. P. Farrington, & S. A. Mednick (Eds.), *Biosocial bases of violence.* New York: Plenum.

Huesmann, L. R., & Eron, L. D. (1986). *Television and the aggressive child: A cross-national comparison.* Hillsdale, NJ: Erlbaum.

Huesmann, L. R., Moise-Titus, J., Podolski, C., & Eron, L. D. (2003). Longitudinal relations between children's exposure to TV violence and their aggressive and violent behavior in young adulthood: 1977–1992. *Developmental Psychology, 39,* 201–221.

Hughes, H. M. (1988). Psychological and behavioral correlates of family violence in child witnesses and victims. *American Journal of Orthopsychiatry, 58,* 77–90.

Hughes, H. M., & Barad, S. J. (1983). Psychological functioning of children in a battered women's shelter: A preliminary investigation. *American Journal of Orthopsychiatry, 53,* 525–531.

Hughes, H. M., Parkinson, D., & Vargo, M. (1989). Witnessing spouse abuse and experiencing physical abuse: A "double whammy"? *Journal of Family Violence, 4,* 197–209.

Hurley, W., & Monahan, T. M. (1969). Arson: The criminal and the crime. *British Journal of Criminology, 9,* 4–21.

Hutchings, B., & Mednick, S. A. (1975). Registered criminality in the adoptive and biological parents of registered male criminal adoptees. In R. R. Fieve, D. Rosenthal, & H. Brill (Eds.), *Genetic research in psychiatry.* Baltimore, MD: Johns Hopkins University Press.

Icove, D. J., & Estepp, M. H. (1987, April). Motive-based offender profiles of arson and fire-related crime. *FBI Law Enforcement Bulletin,* 17–23.

Inciardi, J. A. (1970). The adult firesetter, a typology. *Criminology, 3,* 145–155.

Inciardi, J. A. (1980). Women, heroin, and property crime. In S. K. Datesman & F. R. Scarpitti (Eds.), *Women, crime and justice.* New York: Oxford University Press.

Inciardi, J. A. (1981). Crime and alternative patterns of substance abuse. In S. E. Gardner (Ed.), *Drug and alcohol abuse.* Rockville, MD: National Institute on Drug Abuse.

Insight Canada Research. (1998). *Prevalence of problem and pathological gambling in Ontario using the South Oaks Gambling Screen.* Ottawa, ON: Canadian Foundation on Compulsive Gambling. Available: www.cfcg.on.ca

International Arrestee Drug Abuse Monitoring Program. (2000). *Comparing drug use rates of detained arrestees in the United States and England.* Washington, DC: U.S. Department of Justice.

Ishikawa, S. S., Raine, A., Lencz, T., Bihrle, S., & Lacasse, L. (2001). Autonomic stress reactivity and executive fucntions in successful and unsuccessful criminal psychopaths from the community. *Journal of Abnormal Psychology, 110,* 423–432.

Ivanoff, A., & Hayes, L. M. (2001). Preventing, managing, and treating suicidal actions in high-risk offenders. In J. B. Ashford, B. D. Sales, & W. H. Reid (Eds.), *Treating adult and juvenile offenders with special needs.* Washington, DC: American Psychological Association.

Jackson, H. F., Glass, C., & Hope, S. (1987). A functional analysis of recidivistic arson. *British Journal of Clinical Psychology, 26,* 175–185.

Jacobs, G. D., & Snyder, D. (1996). Frontal brain asymmetry predicts affective style in men. *Behavioral Neuroscience, 110,* 3–6.

Jacobs, P. A., Brunton, M., Melville, H. M., Brittain, R. P., & McClemont, W. F. (1965). Aggressive behavior, mental subnormality and the XYY male. *Nature, 208,* 1351–1352.

Jaffe, J. H., Babor, T. F., & Fishbein, D. H. (1988). Alcoholics, aggression and antisocial behavior. *Journal of Studies on Alcohol, 49,* 211–218.

James, J. (1976). Motivations for entrance into prostitution. In L. Crites (Ed.), *The female offender.* Lexington, MA: Lexington Books.

James, J. (1978). The prostitute as victim. In J. R. Chapman & M. Gates (Eds.), *The victimization of women.* Beverly Hills, CA: Sage.

Jamison, R. N. (1980). Psychoticism, deviancy, and perception of risk in normal children. *Personality and Individual Differences, 1,* 87–91.

Janus, E. S. (2000). Sexual predator commitment laws: Lessons for law and the behavioral sciences. *Behavioral Sciences & the Law, 18,* 5–21.

Janus, E. S., & Walbek, N. H. (2000). Sex offender commitments in Minnesota: A descriptive study of second generation commitments. *Behavioral Sciences & the Law, 18,* 343–374.

Jarvik, L. F., Klodin, V., & Matsuyama, S. S. (1973). Human aggression and the extra Y chromosome. *American Psychologist, 28,* 674–682.

Jarvis, G., & Parker, H. (1989). Young heroin users and crime. *British Journal of Criminology, 29,* 175–185.

Jeffrey, C. R. (1965). Criminal behavior and learning theory. *The Journal of Criminal Law, Criminology and Police Science, 56,* 294–300.

Jenkins, P. (1988). Serial murder in England 1940–1985. *Journal of Criminal Justice, 16,* 1–15.

Jenkins, P. (1993). Chance or choice: The selection of serial murder victims. In A. V. Wilson (Ed.), *Homicide: The victim/offender connection.* Cincinnati, OH: Anderson.

Jenson, B. (1996, May). *Cyberstalking: Crime, enforcement and personal responsibility in the online world.* Available: www.law.ucla.edu/Classes/Archive. S96/340/cyberlaw.htm

Jesness, C. (1971). Jesness Inventory Classification System. *Criminal Justice and Behavior, 15,* 78–91.

Johns, J. H., & Quay, H. C. (1962). The effect of social reward on verbal conditioning in psychopathic military offenders. *Journal of Consulting Psychology, 26,* 217–220.

Johnson, R. (1996). *Hard time: Understanding and reforming the prison* (2nd ed.). Belmont, CA: Wadsworth.

Johnson, R. E., Marcos, A. C., & Bahr, J. (1987). The role of peers in the complex etiology of adolescent drug use. *Criminology, 25,* 323–340.

Johnstone, L., & Cooke, D. J. (2004). Psychopathic-like traits in childhood: conceptual and measurement concerns. *Behavioral Sciences & the Law, 22,* 103–125.

Joint, M. (1995, March). *Road rage.* Washington, DC: Automobile Association Group Public Policy Road Safety Unit.

Jolin, A. (1994). On the backs of working prostitutes: Feminist theory and prostitution policy. *Crime and Delinquency, 40,* 69–83.

Jones, C., & Aronson, E. (1973). Attribution of fault to a rape victim as a function of respectability of the victim. *Journal of Personality and Social Psychology, 26,* 415–419.

Jones, J. G., Butler, H. L., Hamilton, B., Perdue, J. D., Stern, H. P., & Woody, R. C. (1986). Munchausen syndrome by proxy. *Child Abuse and Neglect, 10,* 33–40.

Jones, J. W., & Bogat, G. A. (1978). Air pollution and human aggression. *Psychological Reports, 43,* 721–722.

Julien, R. M. (1975). *A primer of drug action*. San Francisco, CA: W. H. Freeman.

Julien, R. M. (1992). *A primer of drug action* (6th ed.). New York: W. H. Freeman.

Kafrey, D. (1980). Playing with matches: Children and fire. In D. Canter (Ed.), *Fires and human behaviour*. Chichester, UK: Wiley.

Kahn, E. (1931). *Psychopathic personalities*. New Haven, CT: Yale University Press.

Kanaya, T., Scullin, M. H., & Ceci, S. (2003). The Flynn effect and U.S. policies: The impact of rising IQ scores on American society via mental retardation diagnoses. *American Psychologist, 58*, 778–790.

Kandel, E., Mednick, S. A., Kirkegaard-Sorenson, L., Hutchings, B., Knop, J., Rosenberg, R., & Schulsinger, F. (1988). IQ as a protective factor for subjects at high risk for antisocial behavior. *Journal of Consulting and Clinical Psychology, 56*, 224–226.

Kanin, E. J. (1984). Date rape: Unofficial criminals and victims. *Victimology, 9*, 95–108.

Karmen, A. (1996). *Crime victims: An introduction to victimology* (3rd ed.). Belmont, CA: Wadsworth.

Karmen, A. (2001). *Crime victims* (4th ed.). Belmont, CA: Wadsworth/Thomson Learning.

Kato, P. S., & Ruble, D. N. (1992). Toward an understanding of women's experience of menstrual cycle symptoms. In V. Adesso, D. Reddy, & R. Fleming (Eds.), *Psychological perspectives in women's health*. Washington, DC: Hemisphere.

Kelleher, M. D. (1997). *Profiling the lethal employee: Case studies of violence in the workplace*. Westport, CT: Praeger.

Kelly, D. H. (1980). The educational experience and evolving delinquent careers: A neglected institutional link. In D. Schichor & D. H. Kelly (Eds.), *Critical issues in juvenile delinquency*. Lexington, MA: Lexington Books.

Kelly, G. A. (1955). *The psychology of personal constructs*. New York: Norton.

Kelman, H. C., & Hamilton, V. L. (1989). *Crimes of obedience: Toward a social psychology of authority and responsibility*. New Haven, CT: Yale University Press.

Kempe, C. H., Silverman, F. N., Steele, B. B., Droegemueller, W., & Silver, H. K. (1962). The battered-child syndrome. *Journal of the American Medical Association, 181*, 17–24.

Kenrick, D. T., & MacFarland, S. W. (1986). Ambient temperature and horn honking. *Environment and Behavior, 18*, 179–191.

Kilmann, P. R., Sabalis, R. F., Gearing, M. L., Bukstel, L. H., & Scovern, A. W. (1982). The treatment of sexual paraphilias: A review of the outcome research. *The Journal of Sex Research, 18*, 193–252.

Kilpatrick, D. G., Best, C. L., Saunders, B. E., & Veronen, L. J. (1988). Rape in marriage and in dating relationships: How bad is it for mental health? In R. A. Prentky & V. L. Quinsey (Eds.), *Human sexual aggression: Current perspectives*. New York: New York Academy of Sciences.

Kilpatrick, D. G., Whalley, A., & Edmunds, C. (2000). Sexual assault. In A. Seymour, M. Murray, J. Sigmon, M. Hook, C. Edmunds, M. Gaboury, & G. Coleman (Eds.), *2000 National Victim Assistance Academy*. Washington, DC: U.S. Department of Justice.

Kilpatrick, D. G., Whalley, A., & Edmunds, C. (2002). Sexual assault. In A. Seymour, M. Murray, J. Sigmon, M. Hook, C. Edmunds, M. Gaboury, & G. Coleman (Eds.), *2002 National Victim Assistance Academy*. Washington, DC: U.S. Department of Justice.

Kinports, K. (2002). Sex offenses. In K. L. Hall (Ed.), *The Oxford companion to American law*. New York: Oxford University Press.

Kirmeyer, S. L. (1978). Urban density and pathology—A review of research. *Environment and Behavior, 10*, 247–269.

Klam, M. (2001, January 21). Experiencing ecstasy. *The New York Times Magazine*, 8–43, 64, 68–70, 78–80.

Klassen, D., & O'Connor, W. (1988). Crime, inpatient admissions, and violence among male mental patients. *International Journal of Law and Psychiatry, 11*, 305–312.

Klassen, D., & O'Connor, W. (1990). Assessing the risk of violence in released mental patients: A cross-validation study. *Psychological Assessment: A Journal of Consulting and Clinical Psychology, 1*, 75–81.

Klaus, P. A. (2000, January). *Crimes against persons age 65 or older, 1992–97* (NCJ 176352). Washington, DC: U.S. Department of Justice, Bureau of Justice Statistics.

Kleber, H. D. (1988). Epidemic cocaine abuse: America's present, Britain's future. *British Journal of Addiction, 83*, 1359–1371.

Klemke, L. W. (1992). *The sociology of shoplifting: Boosters and snitches today*. Westport, CT: Praeger.

Klinteberg, B., Magnusson, D., & Schalling, D. (1989). Hyperactive behavior in childhood and adult impulsivity: A longitudinal study of male subjects. *Personality and Individual Differences, 10*, 43–50.

Knight, R. A. (1989). An assessment of the concurrent validity of a child molester typology. *Journal of Interpersonal Violence, 4*, 131–150.

Knight, R. A., Carter, D. L., & Prentky, R. A. (1989). A system for the classification of child molesters: Reliability and application. *Journal of Interpersonal Violence, 4*, 3–23.

Knight, R. A., & Prentky, R. A. (1987). The developmental antecedents and adult adaptations of rapist subtypes. *Criminal Justice and Behavior, 14*, 403–426.

Knight, R. A., & Prentky, R. A. (1990). Classifying sexual offenders: The development and corroboration of taxonomic models. In W. L. Marshall, D. R. Laws, & H. E. Barbaree (Eds.), *The handbook of sexual assault: Issues, theories, and treatment of the offender*. New York: Plenum.

Knight, R. A., Rosenberg, R., & Schneider, B. A. (1985). Classification of sexual offenders: Perspectives, methods, and validation. In A. W. Burgess (Ed.), *Rape and sexual assault*. New York: Garland.

Knight, R. A., Warren, J. I., Reboussin, R., & Soley, B. J. (1998). Predicting rapist type from crime-scene variables. *Criminal Justice and Behavior, 25*, 46–80.

Knopp, F. H., Rosenberg, J., & Stevenson, W. (1986). *Report on nationwide survey of juvenile and adult sex-offender treatment programs and providers*. Syracuse, NY: Safer Society Press.

Knott, J. R., Platt, E. B., Ashby, M. C., & Gottlieb, J. S. (1953). A familial evaluation of the electroencephalogram of patients with primary behavior disorder and psychopathic personality. *EEG and Clinical Neurophysiology, 5*, 363–370.

Kolko, D. J., Kazdin, A. E., & Meyer, E. C. (1985). Aggression and psychopathology in childhood firesetters: Parent and child reports. *Journal of Consulting and Clinical Psychology, 53*, 377–385.

Konečni, V. J. (1975). The mediation of aggressive behavior: Arousal levels vs. anger and cognitive labeling. *Journal of Personality and Social Psychology, 32*, 706–712.

Korman, A. (1974). *The psychology of motivation*. Upper Saddle River, NJ: Prentice Hall.

Kornhauser, R. R. (1978). *Social sources of delinquency*. Chicago, IL: University of Chicago Press.

Koson, D. F., & Dvoskin, J. (1982). Arson: A diagnostic study. *Bulletin of the American Academy of Psychiatry and the Law, 10*, 39–49.

Koss, M. P., & Dinero, T. E. (1988). Predictors of sexual aggression among a national sample of male college students. In R. A. Prentky & V. L. Quinsey (Eds.), *Human sexual aggression: Current perspectives*. New York: New York Academy of Sciences.

Koss, M. P., Gidycz, C. A., & Wisniewski, N. (1987). The scope of rape: Incidence and prevalence of sexual aggression and victimization in a national sample of higher education students. *Journal of Consulting and Clinical Psychology, 55*, 162–170.

Kosson, D. S. (1998). Divided visual attention to psychopathic and nonpsychopathic offenders. *Personality and Individual Differences, 24*, 373–391.

Kosson, D. S., Cyterski, T. D., Steverwald, B. L., Neuman, C. S., & Walker-Matthes, S. (2002). The reliability and validity of the Psychopathy Checklist Youth Version (PCL:YV) in nonincarcerated adolescent males. *Psychological Assessment, 14*, 97–109.

Kosson, D. S., Smith, S. S., & Newman, J. P. (1990). Evaluating the construct validity of psychopathy in black and white male inmates: Three preliminary studies. *Journal of Abnormal Psychology, 99*, 250–259.

Kosson, D. S., Suchy, Y., Mayer, A. R., & Libby, J. (2002). Facial affect recogntion in criminal psychopaths. *Emotion, 2*, 398–411.

Kovacs, M. (1996). Presentation and course of major depressive disorder during childhood and later years of the life span. *Journal of the American Academy of Child and Adolescent Psychiatry, 35*, 705–715.

Kozol, H. L., Boucher, R. L., & Garofalo, P. F. (1972). The diagnosis and treatment of dangerousness. *Crime and Delinquency, 8*, 371–392.

Kranz, H. (1936). *Lebensschicksale kriminellen Zwillinge*. Berlin: Julius Springer.

Krapelin, E. (1913). *Clinical psychiatry: A textbook for physicians*. New York: Macmillan.

Krasnovsky, T., & Lane, R. (1998). Shoplifting: A review of the literature. *Aggression and Violent Behavior, 3*, 219–235.

Kratzer, L., & Hodgins, S. (1999). A typology of offenders: A test of Moffitt's theory among males and females from childhood to age 30. *Criminal Behaviour and Mental Health, 9*, 57–73.

Kretschmer, E. (1925). *Physique and character*. New York: Harcourt Brace Jovanovich.

Krisberg, B. (1992). Youth crime and its prevention: A research agenda. In I. M. Schwartz (Ed.), *Juvenile justice and public policy*. New York: Lexington Books.

Krisberg, B. (1995). The legacy of juvenile corrections. *Corrections Today, 57*, 122–126.

Krisberg, B., & Schwartz, I. (1983). Rethinking juvenile justice. *Crime and Delinquency, 29*, 333–364.

Krohn, M. D., Akers, R. L., Radosevich, M. J., & Lanza-Kaduce, L. (1982). Norm qualities and adolescent drinking and drug behavior: The effects of norm quality and reference group on using and abusing alcohol and marijuana. *Journal of Drug Issues, 4*, 343–360.

Kruesi, M. J. P. (1979). Cruelty to animals and CSF 5HIAA. *Psychiatry Research, 28*, 115–116.

Kruesi, M. J. P., & Jacobsen, T. (1997). Serotonin and human violence: Do environmental mediators exist? In A. Raine, P. A. Brennan, D. P. Farrington, & S. A. Mednick (Eds.), *Biological bases of violence*. New York: Plenum.

Kruesi, M. J. P., Rapoport, J., Hamburger, S., Hibbs, E., Potter, W., Levane, M., & Brown, G. (1990). Cerebrospinal fluid monoamine metabolites, aggression, and impulsivity in disruptive behavior disorders of children and adolescents. *Archives of General Psychiatry, 47*, 419–426.

Kuhnley, E. J., Hendren, R. L., & Quinlan, D. M. (1982). *Journal of the American Academy of Child Psychiatry, 21*, 560–563.

Kulka, R. A., Schlenger, W. E., Fairbank, J. A., Jordan, B. K., Hough, R. L., Marmar, C. R., & Weiss, D. S. (1991). Assessment of post-traumatic stress disorder in the community: Prospects and pitfalls from recent studies of Vietnam veterans. *Psychological Assessment: A Journal of Consulting and Clinical Psychology, 4*, 547–560.

Kurland, H. D., Yeager, C. T., & Arthur, R. J. (1963). Psychophysiologic aspects of severe behavior disorders. *Archives of General Psychiatry, 8*, 599–604.

Kurtzberg, R. L., Mandell, W., Lewin, M., Lipton, D. S., & Shuster, M. (1978). Plastic surgery on offenders. In N. Johnson & L. Savitz (Eds.), *Justice and corrections*. New York: Wiley.

Labato, A. (2000). Criminal weapon use in Brazil: A psychological analysis. In D. Canter & L. Alison (Eds.), *Profiling property crimes*. Dartmouth, UK: Ashgate.

La Fon, D. S. (2002). The psychological autopsy. In B. E. Turvey (Ed.), *Criminal profiling: An introduction to behavioral evidence analysis*. San Diego, CA: Academic Press.

La Fond, J. Q. (2003). Outpatient commitment's next frontier: Sexual predators. *Psychology, Public Policy, and Law, 9*, 159–182.

Lamontagne, Y., Boyer, R., Hetu, C., & Lacerte-Lamontagne, C. (2000). Anxiety, significant losses, depression, and irrational beliefs in first-offence shoplifters. *Canadian Journal of Psychiatry, 45*, 63–66.

Lance, D. (1988, April). Product tampering. *FBI Law Enforcement Bulletin*, 20–23.

Landy, D., & Aronson, E. (1969). The influence of the character of the criminal and his victim on the decisions of simulated jurors. *Journal of Experimental Social Psychology, 5*, 141–152.

Lane, D. A. (1987). Personality and antisocial behaviour: A long-term study. *Personality and Individual Differences, 8*, 799–806.

Lang, A. R., Goeckner, D. J., Adesso, V. G., & Marlatt, G. A. (1975). Effects of alcohol on aggression in male social drinkers. *Journal of Abnormal Psychology, 84*, 508–518.

Lange, J. (1929). *Vebrechen als Schicksal*. Leipzig, Germany: Georg Thieme Verlag.

Langer, E. J., & Miransky, J. (1983). Burglary (non)prevention. In E. J. Langer (Ed.), *The psychology of control*. Beverly Hills, CA: Sage.

Langevin, R. (1983). *Sexual strands*. Hillsdale, NJ: Erlbaum.

Langlois, J. H., Kalakanis, L., Rubenstein, A. J., Larson, A., Hallam, M., & Smoot, M. (2000). Maxims or myths of beauty? A meta-analytic and theoretical review. *Psychological Bulletin, 126*, 390–423.

Lanyon, R. I. (1986). Theory and treatment in child molestation. *Journal of Consulting and Clinical Psychology, 54*, 176–182.

Lawrence, R. (1998). *School crime and juvenile justice*. New York: Oxford University Press.

Laws, D. R., & Marshall, W. L. (1990). A conditioning theory of the etiology and maintenance of deviant sexual preference and behavior. In W. L. Marshall, D. R. Laws, & H. E. Barabaree (Eds.), *Handbook of sexual assault*. New York: Plenum.

Leach, E. (1973). Don't say "boo" to a goose. In A. Montagu (Ed.), *Man and aggression* (2nd ed.). London: Oxford University Press.

Le Bon, G. (1995). *The crowd: A study of the popular mind*. London: Transaction (original work published in 1895).

Lee, M., Zimbardo, P. G., & Bertholf, M. (1977, November). Shy murderers. *Psychology Today*, 68–70, 148.

Lee, M. Y. (2002). Asian battered women: Assessment and treatment. In A. R. Roberts (Ed.), *Handbook of domestic violence intervention strategies: Policies, programs, and legal remedies*. New York: Oxford University Press.

Lefkowitz, M., Eron, L., Walder, L., & Huesmann, L. (1977). *Growing up to be violent: A longitudinal study of the development of aggression*. New York: Pergamon Press.

Legras, A. M. (1932). *Psychese en Criminaliteit bij Twellingen*. Utrecht, the Netherlands: Keminken ZOON N.V.

Le Maire, L. (1956). Danish experiences regarding the castration of sexual offenders. *Journal of Criminal Law and Criminology, 47*, 294–310.

Lemon, N. K. D. (1994, December). *Domestic violence & stalking: A comment on the Model Anti-Stalking Code proposed by the National Institute of Justice*. Duluth, MN: Battered Women's Justice Project.

Lerner, M. J. (1970). The desire for justice and reactions to victims. In J. Macaulay & L. Berkowitz (Eds.), *Altruism and helping behavior*. New York: Academic Press.

Lerner, M. J. (1980). *The belief in a just world: A fundamental delusion*. New York: Plenum.

Lesch, K. P., & Merschdorf, U. (2000). Impulsivity, aggression, and serotonin: A molecular psychobiological perspective. *Behavioral Sciences & the Law, 18*, 581–604.

Lester, D., & Danto, B. L. (1993). *Suicide behind bars: Prediction and prevention*. Philadelphia, PA: The Charles Press.

Letkemann, P. (1973). *Crime as work*. Upper Saddle River, NJ: Prentice Hall.

Levant, R. F. (2002). Psychology responds to terrorism. *Professional Psychology: Research and Practice, 33*, 507–509.

Levant, R. F., Barbanel, L., & DeLeon, P. H. (2004). Psychology's response to terrorism. In F. M. Moghaddam & A. J. Marsella (Eds.), *Understanding terrorism: Psychosocial roots, consequences, and interventions*. Washington, DC: American Psychological Association.

Levin, B. (1976). Psychological characteristics of firesetters. *Fire Journal, 70*, 36–41.

Lewin, T. (2001, January 1). New state laws tackle familiar national issues. *The New York Times*. Available: www.nytimes.com/2001/01/01/politics/01laws.html

Lewis, C. F., Baranoski, M. V., Buchanan, J. A., & Benedek, E. P. (1998). Factors associated with weapon use in maternal filicide. *Journal of Forensic Sciences, 43*, 613–618.

Lewis, N. D. C., & Yarnell, H. (1951). Pathological firesetting (pyromania). *Nervous and Mental Disease Monographs*, No. 82.

Lilienfeld, S. O., Gershon, J., Duke, M., Marion, L., & de Waal, F. B. M. (1999). A preliminary investigation of the construct of psychopathic personality (psychopathy) in chimpanzees (*Pan troglodytes*). *Journal of Comparative Psychology, 113*, 365–375.

Lingren, H. G. (2001). *Dating violence and acquaintance assault*. Lincoln: Nebraska Cooperative Extension, University of Nebraska.

Lipsey, M. W., & Wilson, D. B. (1998). Effective interventions with serious juvenile offenders: A synthesis of research. In R. Loeber & D. P. Farrington (Eds.), *Serious and violent juvenile offenders: Risk factors and successful intervention*. Thousand Oaks, CA: Sage.

Lipton, D. N., McDonel, E. C., & McFall, R. M. (1987). Heterosocial perception in rapists. *Journal of Consulting and Clinical Psychology, 55*, 17–21.

Little, A. (1963). Professor Eysenck's theory of crime: An empirical test on adolescent offenders. *British Journal of Criminology, 4*, 152–163.

Litwack, T. R., & Schlesinger, L. B. (1999). Dangerous risk assessments: Research, legal, and clinical considerations. In A. K. Hess & I. B. Weiner (Eds.), *The handbook of forensic psychology* (2nd ed.). New York: Wiley.

Loeber, R. (1990). Development and risk factors of juvenile antisocial behavior and delinquency. *Clinical Psychology Review, 10*, 1–41.

Loeber, R., & Dishion, T. (1983). Early predictors of male delinquency: A review. *Psychological Bulletin, 94*, 68–99.

Loeber, R., Lahey, B. B., & Thomas, C. (1991). The diagnostic conundrum of oppositional defiant disorder and conduct disorder. *Journal of Abnormal Psychology, 100*, 379–390.

Loeber, R., & Stouthamer-Loeber, M. (1986). Family factors as correlates and predictors of juvenile conduct problems and delinquency. In N. Morris & M. Tonry (Eds.), *Crime and justice: An annual review of research* (Vol. 7). Chicago, IL: University of Chicago Press.

Loeber, R., & Stouthamer-Loeber, M. (1998). Development of juvenile aggression and violence: Some common misconceptions and controversies. *American Psychologist, 53*, 242–259.

Loehlin, J. C. (1992). *Genes and environment in personality development*. Newbury Park, CA: Sage.

Lombardo, V. S., & Lombardo, E. F. (1991). The link between learning disabilities and juvenile delinquency: Fact or fiction? *International Journal of Biosocial and Medical Research, 13*, 112–117.

Lombroso, C. (1876). *L'uomo delinquente*. Milan, Italy: Torin.

Lombroso, G. (1911/1968). *Crime: Its causes and remedies*. Montclair, NJ: Patterson Smith.

Longo, R. F., Bird, S., Stevenson, W. F., & Fiske, J. A. (1995). *1994 nationwide survey of treatment programs and models*. Brandon, VT: Safer Society Program and Press.

Lonsway, K. A., & Fitzgerald, L. F. (1994). Rape myths: In review. *Psychology of Women Quarterly, 18*, 133–164.

Lorenz, A. R., & Newman, J. P. (2002). Deficient response modulation and emotion processing in low-anxious caucasian psychopathic offenders: Results from a lexical decision task. *Emotion, 2*, 91–104.

Lorenz, K. (1966). *On aggression*. New York: Harcourt Brace Jovanovich.

Lottes, I. L. (1988). Sexual socialization and attitudes toward rape. In A. W. Burgess (Ed.), *Rape and sexual assault II*. New York: Garland.

Lowman, J. (2000). Violence and outlaw status of (street) prostitution in Canada. *Violence Against Women, 6*, 987–1011.

Loza, W., Dhaliwal, G., Kroner, D. G., & Loza-Fanous, A. (2000). Reliability, construct, and concurrent validity of the Self-Appraisal Questionnaire. *Criminal Justice and Behavior, 27*, 356–374.

Lubenow, G. C. (1983, June 27). When kids kill their parents. *Newsweek*, 35–36.

Lumley, V. A., McNeil, C. B., Herschell, A. D., & Bahl, A. B. (2002). An examination of gender differences among young children with disruptive behavior disorders. *Child Study Journal, 32*, 89–100.

Lunde, D. T. (1976). *Murder and madness*. San Francisco, CA: San Francisco Book.

Luxenburg, J. (2000). Prostitution. In N. H. Rafter (Ed.), *Encyclopedia of women and crime*. Phoenix, AZ: Oryx Press.

Lykken, D. T. (1955). *A study of anxiety in the sociopathic personality* (Doctoral dissertation, University of Minnesota). University Microfilms No. 55–944.

Lykken, D. T. (1957). A study of anxiety in the sociopathic personality. *Journal of Abnormal and Social Psychology, 55*, 6–10.

Lykken, D. T. (1978). The psychopath and the lie detector. *Psychophysiology, 15*, 137–142.

Lynam, D. (1997). Pursuing the psychopath: Capturing the fledgling psychopath in a nomological net. *Journal of Abnormal Psychology, 106*, 425–438.

Lynam, D., Moffitt, T., & Stouthamer-Loeber, M. (1993). Explaining the relation between IQ and delinquency: Class, race, test motivation, school failure, or self control? *Journal of Abnormal Psychology, 102*, 187–196.

Maccoby, E. E. (1986). Social groupings in childhood. In D. Olweus, J. Block, & M. Radke-Yarrow (Eds.), *Development of antisocial and prosocial behavior: Research, theories, and issues*. New York: Academic Press.

MacCoun, R., Kilmer, B., & Reuter, P. (2003, July). Research on drugs-crime linkages: The next generation. *NIJ Special Report: Toward a drug and crime research agenda for the 21st century*. Washington, DC: National Institute of Justice.

MacDonald, J. M. (1977). *Bombers and firesetters*. Springfield, IL: Charles C Thomas.

MacKenzie, D. L. (2000). Evidence-based corrections: Identifying what works. *Crime & Delinquency, 46*, 457–471.

Mahoney, M. J., & Lyddon, W. J. (1988). Recent developments in cognitive approaches to counseling and psychotherapy. *The Counseling Psychologist, 16*, 190–234.

Maker, A. H., Kemmelmeier, M., & Peterson, C. (1998). Long-term psychological consequences in women witnessing parental physical conflict and experiencing abuse in childhood. *Journal of Interpersonal Violence, 13*, 574–589.

Malamuth, N. M. (1981). Rape proclivity among males. *Journal of Social Issues, 37*, 138–157.

Malamuth, N. M. (1989). The attraction to sexual aggression scale: Part one. *The Journal of Sex Research, 26*, 26–49.

Malamuth, N. M., & Check, J. V. P. (1981). The effects of violent-sexual movies: A field experiment. *Journal of Research in Personality, 15*, 436–446.

Malamuth, N. M., Check, J. V. P., & Briere, J. (1986). Sexual arousal in response to aggression: Ideological, aggressive, and sexual correlates. *Journal of Personality and Social Psychology, 50*, 330–340.

Malamuth, N. M., Haber, S., & Feshbach, S. (1980). Testing hypothesis regarding rape: Exposure to sexual violence, sex differences, and the "normality" of rape. *Journal of Research in Personality, 14*, 121–137.

Malamuth, N. M., Heim, M., & Feshbach, S. (1980). The sexual responsiveness of college students to rape depictions: Inhibitory and disinhibitory effects. *Journal of Personality and Social Psychology, 38*, 399–408.

Mann, C. R. (1993). Maternal filicide of preschoolers. In A. V. Wilson (Ed.), *Homicide: The victim/offender connection*. Cincinnati, OH: Anderson.

Mann. J., Arango, V., & Underwood, M. (1990). Serotonin and suicidal behavior. *Annals of the New York Academy of Sciences, 600*, 476–485.

Mark, V. H., & Ervin, F. R. (1970). *Violence and the brain*. Hagerstown, MD: Harper & Row.

Marlatt, G. A., & Rohsenow, D. J. (1980). Cognitive processes in alcohol use: Expectancy and the balanced placebo design. In N. K. Mello (Ed.), *Advances in substance abuse: Behavioral and biological research*. Greenwich, CT: JAI Press.

Marques, J. K., & Nelson, C. (1989). Elements of high-risk situations for sex offenders. In D. R. Laws (Ed.), *Relapse prevention with sex offenders*. New York: Guilford.

Marsella, A. J. (2004). Reflections on international terrorism: Issues, concepts, and directions. In F. M. Moghaddam & A. J. Marsella (Eds.), *Understanding terrorism: Psychosocial roots, consequences, and interventions*. Washington, DC: American Psychological Association.

Marshall, C. E., Benton, D., & Brazier, J. M. (2000). Elder abuse: Using clinical tools to identify clues of mistreatment. *Geriatrics, 55*, 42–53.

Marshall, L. A., & Cooke, D. J. (1999). The childhood experiences of psychopaths: A retrospective study of familial and societal factors. *Journal of Personality Disorders, 13*, 211–225.

Marshall, W. L., & Barbaree, H. E. (1988). An outpatient treatment program for child molesters. In R. A. Prentky & V. L. Quinsey (Eds.), *Human sexual aggression: Current perspectives*. New York: New York Academy of Sciences.

Marshall, W. L., & Christie, M. M. (1981). Pedophilia and aggression. *Criminal Justice and Behavior, 8*, 145–158.

Martinez, R., Jr. (2002). *Latino homicide: Immigration, violence, and community*. New York: Routledge.

Martinson, R. M. (1974). What works—Questions and answers about prison reform. *Public Interest, 35*, 22–54.

Maslow, A. H. (1954). *Motivation and personality*. New York: Harper.

Matheny, A. P. (1989). Children's behavioral inhibition over age and across situations: Genetic similarity for a trait durign change. *Journal of Personality, 57*, 215–235.

Mazerolle, P., Brame, R., Paternoster, R., Piquero, A., & Dean, C. (2000). Onset age, persistence, and offending versatiltiy: Comparisons across gender. *Criminology, 38*, 1143–1172.

McCabe, K. M., Hough, R., Wood, P. A., & Yeh, M. (2001). Childhood and adolescent onset conduct disorder: A test of the developmental taxonomy. *Journal of Abnormal Child Psychology, 29*, 305–316.

McCaghy, C. H. (1967). Child molesters: A study of their careers as deviants. In M. Clinard & R. Quinney (Eds.), *Criminal behavior systems: A typology*. New York: Holt, Rinehart & Winston.

McCaghy, C. H. (1980). *Crime in American society*. New York: Macmillan.

McCandless, B. R., Persons, W. S., & Roberts, A. (1972). Perceived opportunity, delinquency, race and body build among delinquent youth. *Journal of Consulting and Clinical Psychology, 38*, 281–287.

McCarthy, J. (2003, November 29). Police link 2 shootings on stretch of highway. *The Boston Globe*, pp. 1, 13.

McClearn, G. E., & DeFries, J. C. (1973). *Introduction to behavioral genetics*. San Francisco, CA: W. H. Freeman.

McClosky, L. A., Figueredo, A. J., & Koss, M. P. (1995). The effects of systemic family violence on children's mental health. *Child Development, 66*, 1239–1261.

McClure, R., Davis, P., Meadow, S., & Silbert, J. (1996). Epidemiology of Munchausen syndrome by proxy, non-accidental poisoning, and non-accidental suffocation. *Archives of Disease in Childhood, 75*, 57–61.

McCord, D. (1987). Syndromes, profiles and other mental exotica: A new approach to the admissibility of nontraditional psychological evidence in criminal cases. *Oregon Law Review, 66*, 19–108.

McCord, J. (1979). Some child rearing antecedents of criminal behavior in adult men. *Journal of Personality and Social Psychology, 37*, 1477–1486.

McCord, W., McCord, J., & Zola, I. K. (1959). *Origins of crime: A new evaluation of the Cambridge–Somerville Youth Study*. New York: Columbia University Press.

McElroy, S. L., Pope, H. G., Hudson, J. I., Keck, P. E., & White, K. L. (1991). Kleptomania: A report of 20 cases. *American Journal of Psychiatry, 148*, 652–657.

McFarland, C., Ross, M., & DeCourville, N. (1989). Women's theories of menstruation and biases in recall of menstrual symptoms. *Journal of Personality and Social Psychology, 57*, 522–531.

McGinley, H., & Paswark, R. A. (1989). National survey of the frequency and success of the insanity plea and alternate pleas. *Journal of Psychiatry and Law, 17*, 205–221.

McKee, G. R., & Shea, S. J. (1998). Maternal filicide: A cross-national comparison. *Journal of Clinical Psychology, 54*, 679–687.

McShane, D. A., & Plas, J. M. (1984a). Response to a critique of the McShane & Plas review of American Indian performance on the Wecshler Intelligence Scales. *School Psychology Review, 13*, 83–88.

McShane, D. A., & Plas, J. M. (1984b). The cognitive functioning of American Indian children: Moving from the WISC to the WISC-R. *School Psychology Review, 13*, 61–73.

Mechoulam, R. (1970). Marihuana chemistry. *Science, 168*, 1159–1166.

Mednick, S. A., Gabrielli, W. F., & Hutchings, B. (1984). Genetic influences in criminal convictions: Evidence from an adoption cohort. *Science, 234*, 891–894.

Mednick, S. A., Gabrielli, W. F., & Hutchings, B. (1987). Genetic factors in the etiology of criminal behavior. In S. A. Mednick, T. F. Moffitt, & S. A. Stack (Eds.), *The causes of crime: New biological approaches*. Cambridge, UK: Cambridge University Press.

Mednick, S. A., & Kandel, E. (1988). Genetic and perinatal factors in violence. In S. A. Mednick & T. Moffitt (Eds.), *Biological contributions to crime causation*. Dordrecht: North-Holland, Martinus Nijhoff.

Megargee, E. I. (1976). Population density and disruptive behavior in prison settings. In A. K. Cohen, F. G. Cole, & R. G. Bailey (Eds.), *Prison violence*. Lexington, MA: Lexington Books.

Megargee, E. I. (1982). Psychological determinants and correlates of criminal violence. In M. E. Wolfgang & N. A. Weinder (Eds.), *Criminal violence*. Beverly Hills, CA: Sage.

Megargee, E. I., & Bohn, M. J. (1979). *Classifying criminal offenders*. Newbury Park, CA: Sage.

Meloy, J. R. (1998). The psychology of stalking. In J. R. Meloy (Ed.), *The psychology of stalking: Clinical and forensic perspectives*. San Diego, CA: Academic Press.

Mercy, J., & Salzman, L. (1989). Fatal violence among spouses in the United States, 1986–1987. *American Journal of Public Health, 79*, 595–599.

Merry, S., & Hansent, L. (2000). Intruders, pilferers, raiders, and invaders: The interpersonal dimension of burglary. In D. Canter & L. Alison (Eds.), *Profiling property crimes*. Dartmouth, UK: Ashgate.

Messner, S., & Rosenfeld, R. (1994). *Crime and the American dream*. Belmont, CA: Wadsworth.

Meyer, T. P. (1972). The effects of sexually arousing and violent films on aggressive behavior. *Journal of Sex Research, 8*, 324–333.

Middlebrook, P. M. (1974). *Social psychology and modern life*. New York: Knopf.

Milgram, S. (1963). Behavioral study of obedience. *Journal of Abnormal and Social Psychology, 67*, 371–378.

Milgram, S. (1974). *Obedience to authority*. New York: Harper & Row.

Milgram, S. (1977). *The individual in a social world*. Reading, MA: Addison–Wesley.

Miller, J. (1998). Up it up: Gender and the accomplishment of street robbery. *Criminology, 36*, 37–65.

Miller, J., & Jayasundara, D. (2001). Prostitution, the sex industry, and sex tourism. In C. M. Renzetti, J. L. Edleson, & R. K. Bergen (Eds.), *Sourcebook on violence against women*. Thousand Oaks, CA: Sage.

Miller, J. L. (1991). Prostitution in contemporary American society. In E. Graverholtz & M. A. Koralewski (Eds.), *Sexual coercion: A sourcebook on its nature, causes, and prevention*. Lexington, MA: Lexington Books.

Miller, R. D. (2003). Hospitalization of criminal defendants for evaluation of competence to stand trial or for restoration of competence: Clinical and legal issues. *Behavioral Sciences & the Law, 21*, 369–391.

Miller, W. R., & Hester, R. K. (1989). Treating alcohol problems: Toward an informed eclecticism. In R. K. Hester & W. R. Miller (Eds.), *Handbook of alcoholism treatment approaches: Effective alternatives*. New York: Pergamon Press.

Milstein, V. (1988). EEG topology in patients with aggressive violent behavior. In T. E. Moffitt & S. A. Mednick (Eds.), *Biological contributions to crime causation*. Dordrecht: North-Holland, Martinus Nijhoff.

Miner, M. H., Day, D. M., & Nafpaktitis, M. K. (1989). Assessment of coping skills: Development of situational competency test. In D. R. Laws (Ed.), *Relapse prevention with sex offenders*. New York: Guilford.

Miron, M. S., & Goldstein. A. P. (1978). *Hostage*. Kalamazoo, MI: Behaviordelia.

Mischel, W. (1976). *Introduction to personality* (2nd ed.). New York: Holt, Rinehart & Winston.

Mischel, W. (1990). Personality dispositions revisited and revised: A view after three decades. In L. Pervin (Ed.), *Handbook of personality: Theory and research* (2nd ed.). New York: Guilford Press.

Mizell, L. (1995). *Aggressive driving*. Washington, DC: AAA Foundation for Traffic Safety.

Moffitt, T. E. (1990a). The neuropsychology of juvenile delinquency: A critical review. In M. Tonry & N. Morris (Eds.), *Crime and justice: A review of research*. Chicago, IL: University of Chicago Press.

Moffitt, T. E. (1990b). Juvenile delinquency and attention deficit disorder: Boys' developmental trajectories from age 13 to age 15. *Child Development, 61*, 893–910.

Moffitt, T. E. (1993a). Adolescence-limited and life-course-persistent antisocial behavior: A developmental taxonomy. *Psychological Review, 100*, 674–701.

Moffitt, T. E. (1993b). The neuropsychology of conduct disorder. *Development and Psychopathology, 5*, 135–151.

Moffitt, T. E., & Caspi, A. (2001). Childhood predictors differentiate life-course persistent and adolescence-limited antisocial pathways among males and females. *Development and Psychopathology, 13*, 355–375.

Moffitt, T. E., Caspi, A., Dickson, N., Silva, P., & Stanton, W. (1996). Childhood-onset versus adolescent-onset antisocial conduct problems in males: Natural history from ages 3 to 18. *Development and Psychopathology, 8*, 399–424.

Moffitt, T. E., Caspi, A., Fawcett, P., Brammer, G. L., Raleigh, M., Yuwiler, A., & Silva, P. (1997). Whole blood serotonin and family background relate to male violence. In A. Raine, P. A. Brennan, D. P. Farrington, & S. A. Mednick (Eds.), *Biological bases of violence*. New York: Plenum.

Moffitt, T. E., Caspi, A., Harrington, H., & Milne, B. J. (2002). Males on the life-course-prsistent and adolescence-limited antisocial pathways: Follow-up at age 26 years. *Development and Psychopathology, 14*, 179–207.

Moffitt, T. E., & Silva, P. A. (1988). Self-reported delinquency, neuropsychological deficit, and history of attention deficit disorder. *Journal of Abnormal Child Psychology, 16*, 553–569.

Moghaddam, F. M., & Marsella, A. J. (2004a). Preface. In F. M. Moghaddam & A. J. Marsella (Eds.), *Understanding terrorism: Psychosocial roots, consequences, and interventions*. Washington, DC: American Psychological Association.

Moghaddam, F. M., & Marsella, A. J. (2004b). Introduction. In F. M. Moghaddam & A. J. Marsella (Eds.), *Understanding terrorism: Psychosocial roots, consequences, and interventions*. Washington, DC: American Psychological Association.

Mohr, J. W., Turner, R. E., & Jerry, N. B. (1964). *Pedophilia and exhibitionism*. Toronto, ON: University of Toronto Press.

Moll, K. D. (1974). *Arson, vandalism and violence: Law enforcement problems affecting fire departments (LEAA)*. Washington, DC: U.S. Government Printing Office.

Monahan, J. (1976). The prevention of crime. In J. Monahan (Ed.), *Community mental health and the criminal justice system*. New York: Pergamon Press.

Monahan, J. (1981). *Predicting violent behavior*. Beverly Hills, CA: Sage.

Monahan, J. (1984). The prediction of violent behavior: Toward a second generation of theory and policy. *American Journal of Psychiatry, 141*, 10–15.

Monahan, J. (1988). Risk assessment of violence among the mentally disordered: Generating useful knowledge. *International Journal of Law and Psychiatry, 11*, 249–257.

Monahan, J. (1992). Mental disorder and violent behavior: Perceptions and evidence. *American Psychologist, 47*, 511–521.

Monahan, J. (1996). *Mental illness and violent crime*. NIJ Research Preview. Washington, DC: National Institute of Justice.

Monahan, J., Steadman, H. J., Silver, E., Appelbaum, P. S., Robbins, P. C., Mulvey, E. P., Roth, L. H., Grisso, T., & Banks, S. (2001). *Rethinking risk assessment: The MacArthur Study of Mental Disorder and Violence*. New York: Oxford University Press.

Monahan, J., & Walker, L. (1990). *Social science and law: Cases and materials* (2nd ed.). Westbury, NY: Foundation Press.

Monahan, J., & Walker, L. (1994). *Social science and law: Cases and materials* (3rd ed.). Waterbury, NY: Foundation Press.

Monahan, T. P. (1957). Family status and the delinquent child: A reappraisal and some new findings. *Social Forces, 35*, 250–258.

Monastra, V. J., Lubar, J. F., VanDeusen, P., Green, G., Wing, W., Phillips, A., & Fenger, T. N. (1999). Assessing attention deficit hyperactivity disorder via quantitative electroencephalography: An initial validation study. *Neuropsychology, 13*, 424–433.

Montagu, A. (1973). *Man and aggression* (2nd ed.). London: Oxford University Press.

Montagu, A. (1976). *The nature of human aggression*. New York: Oxford University Press.

Monto, M. A. (2004). Female prostitution, customers, and violence. *Violence Against Women, 10*, 160–188.

Moore, R. H. (1984). Shoplifting in middle America: Patterns and motivational correlates. *International Journal of Offender Therapy and Comparative Criminology, 28*, 53–64.

Morgan, A. B., & Lilienfeld, S. O. (2000). A meta-analytic review of the relation between antisocial behavior and neuropsychological measures of executive function. *Clinical Psychology Review, 20*, 113–146.

Morgan, J. P., & Zimmer, L. (1997). The social pharmacology of smokeable cocaine: Not all it's cracked up to be. In C. Reinarman & H. G. Levine (Eds.), *Crack in America: Demon drugs and social justice*. Berkeley: University of California Press.

Morris, D. (1967). *The naked ape*. New York: McGraw–Hill.

Morris, N. (1982). *Madness and the criminal law*. Chicago, IL: University of Chicago Press.

Morris, N., & Miller, M. (1985). Prediction of dangerousness. In M. Tonry & N. Morris (Eds.), *Crime and justice: An annual review of research* (Vol. 6). Chicago, IL: University of Chicago Press.

Morse, S. J. (1978). Behavior, morals, and science: An analysis of mental health law. *Southern California Law Review, 51*, 527–654.

Morry, M. M., & Winkler, E. (2001). Student acceptance and expectation of sexual assault. *Canadian Journal of Behavioral Science, 33*, 188–192.

Morse, S. J. (1985). Excusing the crazy: The insanity defense reconsidered. *Southern California Law Review, 58*, 777–836.

Morse, S. J. (1986). Why amnesia and the law is not a useful topic. *Behavioral Sciences & the Law, 4*, 99–102.

Morton, J., Addison, H., Addison, R., Hunt, L., & Sullivan, J. (1953). A clinical study of premenstrual tension. *American Journal of Obstetrics and Gynecology, 65*, 1182–1191.

Mott, J. (1986). Opioid use and burglary. *British Journal of Addiction, 81*, 671–677.

Moyer, K. E. (1971). The physiology of aggression and the implication for aggression control. In J. L. Singer (Ed.), *The control of aggression and violence*. New York: Academic Press.

Moyer, K. E. (1976). *The psychobiology of aggression*. New York: Harper & Row.

Mueller, C. W. (1983). Environmental stressors and aggressive behavior. In R. G. Geen & E. I. Donnerstein (Eds.), *Aggression: Theoretical and empirical reviews* (Vol. 2). New York: Academic Press.

Mulder, R. T., Wells, J. E., Joyce, P. R., & Bushnell, J. A. (1994). Antisocial women. *Journal of Personality Disorders, 8*, 279–287.

Mulvey, E. P., Arthur, M. W., & Reppucci, N. D. (1993). The prevention and treatment of juvenile delinquency: A review of the research. *Clinical Psychology Review, 13*, 133–167.

Mumley, D. L., Tillbrook, C. E., & Grisso, T. (2003). Five year research update (1996–2000): Evaluations for competence to stand trial (adjudicative competence). *Behavioral Sciences & the Law, 21*, 329–350.

Mumola, C. J. (1999). *Substance abuse and treatment, state and federal prisoners*. Washington, DC: Bureau of Justice Statistics.

Murphy, G. H., & Clare, C. H. (1996). Analysis of motivation in people with mild learning disabilities (mental handicap) who set fires. *Psychology, Crime, & Law, 2*, 153–164.

Murray, J. B. (1997). Munchausen syndrome/Munchausen syndrome by proxy. *The Journal of Psychology, 131*, 343–350.

Murrie, D. C., & Cornell, D. G. (2000). The Millon Adolescent Clinical Inventory and psychopathy. *Journal of Personality Assessment, 75*, 110–125.

Murrie, D. C., & Cornell, D. G. (2002). Psychopathy screening of incarcerated juveniles: A comparison of measures. *Psychological Assessment, 14*, 390–396.

Murrie, D. C., Cornell, D. G., Kaplan, S., McConville, D., & Levy-Elkon, A. (2004). Psychopathy scores and violence among juvenile offenders: A multi-measure study. *Behavioral Sciences & the Law, 22* 49–68.

Myers, D. G. (1996). *Social psychology* (5th ed.). New York: McGraw–Hill.

Myers, D. L. (2000). *Excluding violent youths from juvenile court: The effectiveness of legislative waiver.* Unpublished dissertation. University of Maryland, Department of Criminology and Criminal Justice. Available: www.preventingcrime.org

Nacci, P. L., Teitelbaum, H. E., & Prather, J. (1977). Population density and inmate misconduct rates in the federal prison system. *Federal Probation, 41,* 26–31.

Nachshon, I. (1983). Hemisphere dysfunction in psychopathy and behavior disorders. In M. Myslobodsky (Ed.), *Hemisyndromes: Psychobiology, neurology, psychiatry.* New York: Academic Press.

Nachshon, I., & Denno, D. (1987). Violent behavior and cerebral hemisphere function. In S. A. Mednick, T. E. Moffitt, & S. A. Stack (Eds.), *The causes of crime: New biological approaches.* Cambridge, UK: Cambridge University Press.

Nagin, D. S., Farrington, D. P., & Moffitt, T. (1995). Life-course trajectories of different types of offenders. *Criminology, 33,* 111–139.

Nagin, D. S., & Land, K. C. (1993). Age, criminal careers, and population heterogeneity: Specification and estimation of a nonparametric mixed Poisson model. *Criminology, 31,* 163–189.

Nash, J. R. (1975). *Bloodletters and badmen: Book 3.* New York: Warner Books.

National Cable Television Association. (1998). *National Television Violence Study* (Vol. 3). Thousand Oaks, CA: Sage.

National Center for Education Statistics. (2003). *Executive summary. Indicators of school crime and safety,* 2003. Available http://NCES.ed.gov/pubs2004/crime03/

National Center for Juvenile Justice. (2003, July). *Juvenile court statistics 1999.* Washington, DC: U.S. Department of Justice, Office of Juvenile Justice and Delinquency Prevention.

National Center on Child Abuse and Neglect. (1981). *Study findings: National study of the incidence and severity of child abuse and neglect.* Washington, DC: U.S. Department of Health and Human Services.

National Center for Victims of Crime. (2000). *Cyberstalking.* Available: www.ncvc/special/cyber_stk.htm

National Center on Elder Abuse. (1999). *Types of elder abuse in domestic settings.* Washington, DC: Author.

National Commission on Marihuana and Drug Abuse. (1972). *Marihuana: A signal of misunderstanding* (Appendix, Vol. 1). Washington, DC: U.S. Government Printing Office.

National Commission on Marihuana and Drug Abuse. (1973). *Drug use in America: Problem in perspective* (2nd report). Washington, DC: U.S. Government Printing Office.

National Drug Control Policy. (2001). *2001 Annual Report.* Washington, DC: U.S. Office of National Drug Control Policy.

National Drug Intelligence Center. (2001, January). *OxyContin diversion and abuse.* Washington, DC: Author.

National Highway Traffic Safety Administration. (2003). *Motor vehicle theft rates.* Washington, DC: Author.

National Information Support and Referral Service (1998). Available: www.ojp.usdoij.gov/nisrs

National Institute of Education. (1977). *Violent schools—Safe school: The safe school study report to the Congress—Executive summary.* Washington, DC: U.S. Department of Health, Education, and Welfare.

National Institute of Justice. (2003). *Preliminary data on drug use and related matters among adult arrestees and juvenile detainees, 2002.* Washington, DC: Author.

National Institute on Alcohol Abuse and Alcoholism. (1990). *Alcohol and health: Neuroscience.* Rockville, MD: U.S. Government Printing Office.

National Institute on Alcohol Abuse and Alcoholism. (1997, October). Alcohol, violence, and aggression. *Alcohol alert.* Rockville, MD: U.S. Government Printing Office.

National Institute on Drug Abuse. (1978). Drug abuse and crime. In L. D. Savitz & N. Johnson (Eds.), *Crime in society.* New York: Wiley.

National Institute on Drug Abuse. (1999, May). *Cocaine: Abuse and addiction.* Rockville, MD: USGPO. Available: www.nida.nih.gov/researchreports/cocaine/cocaine.html

National Institute on Drug Abuse. (2000, June). *Epidemiologic trends in drug abuse.* Rockville, MD: U.S. Government Printing Office. Available: www.nida.gov/CEWG/AdvancedRep/6_20ADV/0600adv.html

National Institutes of Health. (1999, June). *NIDA news release: Long-term brain injury from use of "ecstasy.* Rockville, MD: National Institute of Drug Abuse. Available: www.nida.nih.gov/MedAdv/99/NR-614b.html

National Media Archive. (1990, September). Stories emphasized violence against women and children. *On Balance, 3,* No. 8.

Nebylitsyn, V. D., & Gray, J. A. (1972). *Biological bases of individual behavior.* New York: Academic Press.

Nee, C., & Taylor, M. (1988). Residential burglary in the Republic of Ireland: A situational perspective. *Howard Journal, 27,* 105–116.

Neisser, U., Boodoo, G., Bouchard, T., Boykin, A. W., Brody, N., Ceci, S. J. et al. (1996). Intelligence: Knowns and unknowns. *American Psychologist, 51,* 77–101.

Nelson, S., & Amir, M. (1975). The hitchhike victim of rape: A research report. In I. Drapkin & E. Viano (Eds.), *Victimology: A new focus* (Vol. 5). Lexington, MA: Lexington Books.

Nettler, G. (1984). *Explaining crime* (3rd ed.). New York: McGraw–Hill.

Newman, J. P. (1987). Reaction to punishment in extroverts and psychopaths: Implications for the impulsive behavior of disinhibited individuals. *Journal of Research in Personality, 21,* 464–480.

Newman, J. P., & Kosson, D. S. (1986). Passive avoidance learning in psychopathic and nonpsychopathic offenders. *Journal of Abnormal Psychology, 95,* 252–256.

Newman, J. P., Patterson, C. M., Howland, E. W., & Nichols, S. L. (1990). Passive avoidance in psychopaths: The effects of reward. *Personality and Individual Differences, 11,* 1101–1114.

Newman, J. P., Patterson, C. M., & Kosson, D. S. (1987). Response preservation in psychopaths. *Journal of Abnormal Psychology, 96,* 145–148.

Nicholson, R. A., & Kugler, K. E. (1991). Competent and incompetent criminal defendants: A quantitative review of comparative research. *Psychological Bulletin, 109,* 355–370.

Nicholson, R. A., & Norwood, S. (2000). The quality of forensic psychological assessments, reports, and testimony: Acknowledging the gap between promise and practice. *Law and Human Behavior, 24,* 9–44.

Niedermeyer, A. A. (1963). *Der Nervenarzt, 34,* 168.

Nietzel, M. T. (1979). *Crime and its modification: A social learning perspective.* New York: Pergamon.

Noesner, G. W., & Dolan, J. T. (1992, August). First responder negotiation training. *FBI Law Enforcement Bulletin,* 1–4.

Normandeau, A. (1968). Patterns in robbery. *Criminologica, 1,* 2–13.

Obeidallah, D. A., & Earls, F. J. (1999). *Adolescent girls: The role of depression in the development of delinquency.* Washington, DC: National Institute of Justice.

Office of Juvenile Justice and Delinquency Prevention. (1999). *Promising strategies to reduce gun violence.* Washington, DC: U.S. Department of Justice.

Office of Juvenile Justice and Delinquency Prevention. (2000). *Census of juveniles in residential placement*. Washington, DC: U.S. Department of Justice.

Office of National Drug Control Policy. (1999a, November). *Gamma hydroxybutyrate (GHB)*. Washington, DC: Executive Office of the President. Available: www.whitehousedrugpolicy. gov

Office of National Drug Control Policy. (1999b, May). *Methamphetamine*. Washington, DC: Executive Office of the President. Available: www.whitehousedrugpolicy.gov

Office of National Drug Control Policy. (2000a, June). *MDMA*. Washington, DC: Executive Office of the President. Available: www.whitehousedrugpolicy.gov

Office of National Drug Control Policy. (2000b). *National drug control strategy 2000: The link between drugs and crime*. Washington, DC: Executive Office of the President.

Office of National Drug Control Policy. (2002a, November). *Pulse check: Trends in drug abuse*. Washington, DC: Author.

Office of National Drug Control Policy. (2002b, April). *MDMA (Ecstasy)*. Washington, DC: Author.

Office of National Drug Control Policy. (2002c, November). *Gamma hydroxybutyrate (GHB)*. Washington, DC: Author.

Office of National Drug Control Policy. (2003a, February). *Rohypnol*. Washington, DC: Author.

Office of National Drug Control Policy. (2003b, November). *Methamphetamine*. Washington, DC: Author.

Office of National Drug Control Policy. (2003c, September). *LSD*. Washington, DC: Author.

Office of National Drug Control Policy. (2003d, November). *Drug data summary*. Washington, DC: Author.

Office of National Drug Control Policy. (2003e, October). *Marijuana*. Washington, DC: Author.

Office of National Drug Control Policy. (2003f, November). *Cocaine*. Washington, DC: Author.

Office of National Drug Control Policy. (2003g, June). *Heroin*. Washington, DC: Author.

Offord, D. R., Boyle, M. C., & Racine, Y. A. (1991). The epidemiology of antisocial behavior in childhood and adolescence. In D. J. Pepler & K. H. Rubin (Eds.), *The development and treatment of childhood aggression*. Hillsdale, NJ: Erlbaum.

Ogloff, J. R., & Wong, S. (1990). Electrodermal and cardiovascular evidence of a coping response in psychopaths. *Criminal Justice and Behavior, 17*, 231–245.

Ohlin, L. E. (1983). The future of juvenile justice policy and research. *Crime and Delinquency, 29*, 463–472.

Ohlin, L. E., & Tonry, M. (1989). Family violence in perspective. In L. Ohlin & M. Tonry (Eds.), *Family violence* (Vol. 11). Chicago, IL: University of Chicago Press.

O'Leary, M. R., & Dengerink, H. A. (1973). Aggression as a function of the intensity and pattern of attack. *Journal of Experimental Research in Personality, 7*, 61–70.

Olweus, D. (1978). *Aggression in the schools*. New York: Wiley.

Ondrovik, J., & Hamilton, D. (1991). Credibility of victims diagnosed as multiple personality: A case study. *American Journal of Forensic Psychology, 9*, 13–17.

Orne, M. T., Dinges, D. F., & Orne, E. C. (1984). On the differential diagnosis of multiple personality in the forensic context. *The International Journal of Clinical and Experimental Hypnosis, 32*, 118–169.

Orris, J. B. (1969). Visual monitoring performance in three subgroups of male delinquents. *Journal of Abnormal Psychology, 74*, 227–229.

Osgood, W. D., O'Malley, P. M., Bachman, G. G., & Johnston, L. D. (1989). Time trends and urge trends in arrests and self-reported illegal behavior. *Criminology, 27*, 389–415.

O'Toole, M. E. (2000). *The school shooter: A threat assessment perspective*. Quantico, VA: Critical Incident Response Group, National Center for the Analysis of Violent Crime.

Owen, B. (2000). Prison security. In N. H. Rafter (Ed.), *The encyclopedia of women and crime*. Phoenix, AZ: Oryx Press.

Pagelow, M. D. (1989). The incidence and prevalence of criminal abuse of other family members. In L. Ohlin & M. Tonry (Eds.), *Family violence* (Vol. 11). Chicago, IL: University of Chicago Press.

Palmer, J. W., & Palmer, S. E. (1999). *Constitutional rights of prisoners* (6th ed.). Cincinnati, OH: Anderson.

Palmer, T. (1975). Martinson revisited. *Journal of Research in Crime and Delinquency, 12,* 3–14.

Parker, H., & Newcombe, R. (1987). Heroin use and acquisitive crime in an English community. *British Journal of Sociology, 38,* 331–350.

Pasqualone, G. A., & Fitzgerald, S. M. (1999). Munchausen by proxy syndrome: The forensic challenge of recognition, diagnosis, and reporting. *Critical Care Nursing Quarterly, 22,* 52–64.

Passingham, R. E. (1972). Crime and personality: A review of Eysenck's theory. In V. D. Nebylitsyn & J. A. Gray (Eds.), *Biological bases of individual behavior.* New York: Academic Press.

Patrick, C. J., Bradley, M. M., & Lang, P. J. (1993). Emotion in the criminal psychopath: Start reflex modulation. *Journal of Abnormal Psychology, 102,* 82–92.

Patterson, G. R. (1982). *Coercive family processes.* Eugene, OR: Castalia Press.

Patterson, G. R. (1986). Performance models for antisocial boys. *American Psychologist, 41,* 432–444.

Paulhus, D. L., & Martin, C. L. (1986). Predicting adult temperament from minor physical anomalies. *Journal of Personality and Social Psychology, 50,* 1235–1239.

Paull, D. (1993). *Fitness to stand trial.* Springfield, IL: Charles C Thomas.

Paulus, P. B. (1988). *Prison crowding: A psychological perspective.* New York: Springer-Verlag.

Pearl, P. T. (1995). Identifying and responding to Munchausen syndrome by proxy. *Early Child Development and Care, 106,* 177–185.

Peele, S. (1984). The cultural context of psychological approaches to alcoholism. *American Psychologist, 39,* 1337–1351.

Pennington, L. A. (1966). Psychopathic and criminal behavior. In L. A. Pennington & I. A. Berg (Eds.), *An introduction to clinical psychology.* New York: Ronald Press.

Penrod, S. (1983). *Social psychology.* Upper Saddle River, NJ: Prentice Hall.

Pepler, D. J., & Slaby, R. G. (1994). Theoretical and development perspectives on youth and violence. In L. D. Eron, J. H. Gentry, & P. Schlegel (Eds.), *Reason to hope: A psychosocial perspective on violence and youth.* Washington, DC: American Psychological Association.

Peters, S. D., Wyatt, G. E., & Finkelhor, D. (1986). Prevalence. In D. Finkelhor (Ed.), *Sourcebook on child sexual abuse.* Beverly Hills, CA: Sage.

Peterson, M. A., Braiker, H. B., & Polich, S. M. (1981). *Who commits crimes?* Cambridge, MA: Oelgeschlager, Gunn & Hain.

Pettit, G. S., Laird, R. D., Bates, J. E., & Dodge, K. A. (1997). Patterns of after-school care in middle childhood: Risk factors and developmental outcomes. *Merrill-Palmer Quarterly, 43,* 515–538.

Pihl, R. O., & Peterson, J. B. (1993). Alcohol, serotonin, and aggression. *Alcohol, Health & Research World, 17,* 113–116.

Pillemer, K., & Finkelhor, D. (1988). The prevalence of elder abuse: A random sample survey. *The Gerontologist, 28,* 51–57.

Pillemer, K., & Suitor, J. J. (1988). Elder abuse. In V. B. van Hasselt, R. L. Morrison, A. S. Morrison, A. S. Bellak, & M. Hersen (Eds.), *Handbook of family violence.* New York: Plenum.

Pillmann, F., Rohde, A., Ullrich, S., Draba, S., Sannemueller, U., & Marnerous, A. (1999). Violence, criminal behavior, and the EEG: Significance of left hemispheric focal abnormalities. *Journal of Neuropsychiatry & Clinical Neurosciences, 11,* 454–457.

Pincus, J. H. (1980). Can violence be a manifestation of epilepsy? *Neurology, 30*, 304–306.

Pine, D. S., Shaffer, D., Schonfeld, I. S., & Davies, M. (1997). Minor physical anomalies: Modifiers of environmental risks for psychiatric impairment? *Journal of the American Academy of Child and Adolescent Psychiatry, 36*, 395–404.

Pinizzotto, A. J. (1984). Forensic psychology: Criminal personality profiling. *Journal of Police Science and Administration, 12*, 32–40.

Pinizzotto, A. J., & Finkel, N. J. (1990). Criminal personality profiling: An outcome and process study. *Law and Human Behavior, 14*, 215–234.

Pithers, W. D., Beal, L. S., Armstrong, J., & Petty, J. (1989). Identification of risk factors through clinical interviews and analysis of records. In D. R. Laws (Ed.), *Relapse prevention with sex offenders*. New York: Guilford.

Pithers, W. D., Kashima, K. M., Cumming, G. F., Beal, L. S., & Buell, M. M. (1988). Relapse prevention of sexual aggression. In R. A. Prentky & V. L. Quinsey (Eds.), *Human sexual aggression: Current perspectives*. New York: New York Academy of Sciences.

Pithers, W. D., Marques, J. K., Gibat, C. C., & Marlatt, G. A. (1983). Relapse prevention with sexual aggressives. In J. G. Greer & I. R. Stuart (Eds.), *The sexual aggressor: Current perspectives on treatment*. New York: Van Nostrand Reinhold.

Pleck, E. (1989). Criminal approaches to family violence, 1640–1980. In L. Ohlin & M. Tonry (Eds.), *Family violence* (Vol. 11). Chicago, IL: University of Chicago Press.

Plomin, R. (1986). *Development, genetics, and psychology*. Hillsdale, NJ: Erlbaum.

Podnieks, E., Pillemer, K., & Nicolson, J. P. (1990). *National survey on abuse of the elderly in Canada: Final report*. Toronto, ON: Ryerson Polytechnic Institute.

Pope, C. E. (1977a). *Crime-specific analysis: An empirical examination of burglary offender characteristics (LEAA)*. Washington, DC: U.S. Government Printing Office.

Pope, C. E. (1977b). *Crime-specific analysis: The characteristics of burglary incidents (LEAA)*. Washington, DC: U.S. Government Printing Office.

Pope, C. E. (1977c). *Crime-specific analysis: An empirical examination of burglary offense and offense characteristics (LEAA)*. Washington, DC: U.S. Government Printing Office.

Pope, E., & Shouldice, M. (2001). Drugs and sexual assault. *Trauma, Violence, & Abuse, 2*, 51–55.

Popova, N., Voitenko, N., Kulikov, A., & Augustinovich, D. (1991). Evidence for the involvement of central serotonin in mechanism of domestication of silver foxes. *Psychopharmacology: Biochemistry and Behavior, 40*, 751–756.

Porter, S., Birt, A. R., & Boer, D. P. (2001). Investigation of the criminal and conditional release histories of Canadian federal offenders as a function of psychopathy and age. *Law and Human Behavior, 25*, 647–661.

Porter, S., Fairweather, D., Drugge, J., Herve, H., Birt, A. R., & Boer, D. (2000). Profiles of psychopathy in incarcerated sexual offenders. *Criminal Justice and Behavior, 27*, 216–233.

Porter, S., Woodworth, M., Earle, J., Drugge, J., Boer, D. (2003). Characteristics of sexual homicides committed by psychopathic and nonpsychopathic offenders. *Law and Human Behavior, 27*, 459–470.

Postmes, T., & Spears, R. (1998). Deindividuation and antinormative behavior: A meta-analysis. *Psychological Bulletin, 123*, 238–259.

Potoczniak, M. J., Mourot, J. E., Crosbie-Burnett, M., & Potoczniak, D. J. (2003). Legal and psychological perspectives on same-sex domestic violence: A mutlisystematic approach. *Journal of Family Violence, 17*, 252–259.

Poulin, F., & Boivin, M. (2000). Reactive and proactive aggression: Evidence of a two-factor model. *Psychological Assessment, 12*, 115–122.

Powell, G. E., & Stewart, R. A. (1983). The relationship of personality to antisocial and neurotic behaviours as observed by teachers. *Personality and Individual Differences, 4*, 97–100.

Power, R. (2000, Spring). 2000 CSI/FBI computer crime and security survey. *Computer Security: Issues & Trends, 6*(1).

Poythress, N., Dembo, R., Wareham, J., & Greenbaum, P. E. (in press). Construct validity of the Youth Psychopathic features Inventory (YPI) and the Antisocial Process Screening Device (APSD) with justice-involved adolescents. *Criminal Justice and Behavior*. Forthcoming.

Poythress, N. G., Otto, R. K., Darkes, J., & Starr, L. (1993). APA's expert panel in the Congressional review of the USS Iowa incident. *American Psychologist, 48*, 8–15.

Prentice-Dunn, S., & Rogers, R. (1982). Effects of public and private self-awareness on deindividuation and aggression. *Journal of Personality and Social Psychology, 43*, 503–513.

Prentice-Dunn, S., & Rogers, R. (1983). Deindividuation in aggression. In R. G. Geen & E. I. Donnerstein (Eds.), *Aggression: Theoretical and empirical reviews* (Vol. 2). New York: Academic Press.

Prentky, R. A., & Knight, R. A. (1986). Impulsivity in the life style and criminal behavior of sexual offenders. *Criminal Justice and Behavior, 13*, 141–164.

Prentky, R. A., Knight, R. A., & Lee, A. F. S. (1997). *Child sexual molestation: Research issues*. NIJ Research Report. Rockville, MD: National Criminal Justice Reference Service. Available: www.ncjrs.org/txtfiles/163390.txt

President's Commission on Law Enforcement and Administration of Justice. (1967). *The challenge of crime in a free society*. Washington, DC: U.S. Government Printing Office.

Price, J. B. (1968). Some results on the Maudsley Personality Inventory from a sample of girls in Borstal. *British Journal of Criminology, 8*, 383–401.

Pridemore, W. A. (2002). Vodka and violence: Alcohol consumption and homicide rates in Russia. *American Journal of Public Health, 92*, 1921–1940.

Prinstein, M. J., Boergers, J., & Vernberg, E. M. (2001). Overt and relational aggression in adolescents: Social-psychological adjustment of aggressors and victims. *Journal of Clinical Child Psychology, 30*, 479–491.

Quay, H. C. (1964). Dimensions of personality in delinquent boys as inferred from the factor analysis of case history data. *Child Development, 35*, 479–484.

Quay, H. C. (1965). Psychopathic personality: Pathological stimulation-seeking. *American Journal of Psychiatry, 122*, 180–183.

Quay, H. C. (1972). Patterns of aggression, withdrawal, and immaturity. In H. Quay & J. Werry (Eds.), *Psychopathological disorders of childhood*. New York: Wiley.

Quay, H. C. (1977). The three faces of evaluation: What can be expected to work. *Criminal Justice and Behavior, 4*, 341–354.

Quay, H. C. (1984). *Managing adult inmates: Classification for housing and program assignment*. College Park, MD: American Correctional Association.

Quay, H. C. (1987). Intelligence. In H. C. Quay (Ed.), *Handbook of juvenile delinquency*. New York: Wiley.

Queen's Bench Foundation. (1978). The rapist and his crime. In L. D. Savitz & N. Johnson (Eds.), *Crime in society*. New York: Wiley.

Quinsey, V. L., Chaplin, T. C., & Upfold, D. (1989). Arsonists and sexual arousal to firesetting: Correlation unsupported. *Journal of Behaviour Therapy and Experimental Psychiatry, 20*, 203–209.

Quinsey, V. L., Harris, G. T., Rice, M. E., & Cormier, C. A. (1998). *Violent offenders: Appraising and managing risk*. Washington, DC: American Psychological Association.

Quinsey, V. L., & Marshall, W. L. (1983). Procedures for reducing inappropriate sexual arousal: An evaluation review. In J. G. Greer & I. R. Stuart (Eds.), *The sexual aggressor*. New York: Van Nostrand Reinhold.

Quinsey, V. L., Rice, M. E., & Harris, G. T. (1995). Actuarial prediction of sexual recidivism. *Journal of Interpersonal Violence, 10*, 85–105.

Rabkin, J. G. (1979). Criminal behavior of discharged mental patients: A critical appraisal of the research. *Psychological Bulletin, 86*, 1–27.

Rachman, S. J. (1966). Sexual fetishism: An experimental analogue. *Psychological Record, 16*, 293–296.

Rafter, N. H. (1992). Criminal anthropology in the United States. *Criminology, 30*, 525–546.

Raine, A. (1993). *The psychopathology of crime: Criminal behavior as a clinical disorder.* San Diego, CA: Academic Press.

Ramirez, D., McDevitt, J., & Farrell, A. (2000, November). *A resource guide on racial profiling data collection systems: Promising practices and lessons learned.* Boston, MA: Northeastern University Press. Available: www.usdoj.gov

Rapaport, K., & Burkhart, B. R. (1984). Personality and attitudinal characteristics of sexually coercive college males. *Journal of Abnormal Psychology, 93*, 216–221.

Raphael, J., & Shapiro, D. L. (2004). Violence in indoor and outdoor prostitution venues. *Violence Against Women, 10*, 126–139.

Rasche, C. (1993). Given reason for violence in intimate relationships. In A. Wilson (Ed.), *Homicide.* Cincinnati, OH: Anderson.

Raskin, D. C., & Hare, R. D. (1978). Psychopathy and detection of deception in a prison population. *Psychophysiology, 15*, 126–136.

Ray, O. (1972). *Drugs, society and human behavior.* St. Louis, MO: C. V. Mosby.

Ray, O. (1983). *Drugs, society and human behavior* (3rd ed.). St. Louis, MO: C. V. Mosby.

Reid, J. B. (1993). Prevention of conduct disorder before and after school entry: Relating interventions to developmental findings. *Development and Psychopathology, 5*, 243–262.

Reidel, M. (2003). Homicide in Los Angeles County: A study of Latino victimization. In D. F. Hawkins (Ed.), *Violent crime: Assessing race and ethnic differences.* Cambridge: Cambridge University Press.

Reiman, J. (1995). *The rich get richer and the poor get prison* (4th ed.). Needham Heights, MA: Allyn & Bacon.

Reiss, A. J., & Roth, J. A. (Eds.) (1993). *Understanding and preventing violence.* Washington, DC: National Academy Press.

Reiss, J. (1977). "Voluntary" castration of mentally disordered sex offenders. *Criminal Law Bulletin, 13*, 30–48.

Rengert, G., & Wasilchick, J. (1985). *Suburban burglary: A time and place for everything.* Springfield, IL: Charles C Thomas.

Rennison, C. M. (2002, April). *Hispanic victims of violent crime, 1993–2000* (NCJ 191208). Washington, DC: U.S. Department of Justice, Bureau of Justice Statistics.

Rennison, C. M. (2003, February). *Intimate partner violence, 1993–2001* (NCJ 197838). Washington, DC: U.S. Department of Justice, Bureau of Justice Statistics.

Rennison, C. M., & Rand, M. R. (2003, August). *Criminal victimization, 2002.* Washington, DC: U.S. Department of Justice, Bureau of Justice Statistics.

Rennison, C. M., & Welchans, S. (2000, May). *Intimate partner violence.* Washington, DC: U.S. Department of Justice.

Resnick, P. J. (1969). Child murder by parents. *American Journal of Psychiatry, 126*, 325–334.

Resnick, P. J. (1970). Murder of the newborn: A psychiatric review of neonaticide. *American Journal of Psychiatry, 126*, 1414–1420.

Revitch, E., & Schlesinger, L. B. (1988). Clinical reflections on sexual aggression. In R. A. Prentky & V. L. Quinsey (Eds.), *Human sexual aggression: Current perspectives.* New York: New York Academy of Sciences.

Revitch, E., & Weiss, R. G. (1962). The pedophiliac offender. *Diseases of the Nervous System, 23*, 73–78.

Rhee, S. H., & Waldman, I. D. (2002). Genetic and environmental influences on antisocial behavior: A meta-analysis of twin and adoption studies. *Psychological Bulletin, 128,* 490–529.

Rhoads, J. M., & Borjes, E. D. (1981). The incidence of exhibitionism in Guatemala and U.S. *British Journal of Psychiatry, 139,* 242–244.

Rice, M. E. (1997). Violent offender research and implications for the criminal justice system. *American Psychologist, 52,* 414–423.

Rice, M. E., & Harris, G. T. (1991). Firesetters admitted to a maximum security psychiatric institution. *Journal of Interpersonal Violence, 6,* 461–475.

Rice, M. E., Harris, G. T., & Cormier, C. A. (1992). An evaluation of a maximum security therapeutic community for psychopaths and other mentally disordered offenders. *Law and Human Behavior, 16,* 399–412.

Rice, M. E., Harris, G. T., & Quinsey, V. L. (2001). Research on the treatment of adult sex offenders. In J. B. Ashford, B. D. Sales, & W. H. Reid (Eds.), *Treating adult and juvenile offenders with special needs.* Washington, DC: American Psychological Association.

Richard, A. (1999, November). *International trafficking in women to the United States: A contemporary manifestation of slavery and organized crime.* Washington, DC: Center for the Study of Intelligence.

Richards, H., Casey, J., & Lucente, S. (2003). Psychopathy and treatment response to incarcerated female substance abusers. *Criminal Justice and Behavior, 30,* 251–276.

Riedel, M., Zahn, M., & Mock, L. F. (1985). *The nature and patterns of American homicide.* Washington, DC: U.S. Government Printing Office.

Righthand, S., & Welch, C. (2001, March). *Juveniles who have sexually offended: A review of the professional literature.* Washington, DC: Office of Juvenile Justice and Delinquency Prevention.

Riley, S. (1998). Competency to stand trial adjudication: A comparison of female and male defendants. *Journal of the American Academy of Psychiatry and the Law, 26,* 223–240.

Ringel, C. (1997, November). *Criminal victimization in 1996: Changes 1995–1996 with trends 1993–1996.* Washington, DC: U.S. Department of Justice.

Ritvo, E., Shanok, S. S., & Lewis, D. O. (1983). Firesetting and nonfiresetting delinquents. *Child Psychiatry and Human Development, 13,* 259–267.

Robbins, E., & Robbins, L. (1964). Arson with special reference to pyromania. *New York State Journal of Medicine, 2,* 795–798.

Roberts, A. R. (2002). Preface. In A. R. Roberts (Ed.), *Handbook of domestic violence intervention strategies: Policies, programs, and legal remedies.* New York: Oxford University Press.

Robins, L. N. (1966). *Deviant children grow up.* Baltimore, MD: Williams & Wilkins.

Robins, L. N., & Regier, D. A. (1991). *Psychiatric disorders in America: The epidemiologic catchment area study.* New York: Free Press.

Roche, P. Q. (1958). *The criminal mind: A study of communication between criminal law and psychiatry.* New York: Grove Press.

Rodman, H., & Grams, P. (1967). *Juvenile delinquency and the family: A review and discussion.* Task Force Report: Juvenile delinquency and youth crime. Washington, DC: U.S. Government Printing Office.

Roesch, R., Zapf, P. A., Golding, S. L., & Skeem, J. L. (1999). Defining and assessing competency to stand trial. In A. K. Hess & I. B. Weiner (Eds.), *The handbook of forensic psychology* (2nd ed.). New York: Wiley.

Rogers, R. (1997). *Clinical assessment of malingering and deception* (2nd ed.). New York: Guilford.

Rogers, R. W., & Ketcher, C. M. (1979). Effects of anonymity and arousal on aggression. *Journal of Psychology, 102,* 13–19.

Roizen, J. (1997). Epidemiological issues in alcohol-related violence. In M. Galanter (Ed.), *Recent developments in alcoholism* (Vol. 13). New York: Plenum.

Rooth, G. (1973). Exhibitionism outside Europe and America. *Archives of Sexual Behavior, 2,* 351–363.

Rooth, G. (1974). Exhibitionists around the world. *Human Behavior, 3,* 61.

Rosanoff, A. J., Handy, L. M., & Plesset, I. (1941). The etiology of child behavior difficulties, juvenile delinquency and adult criminality with special reference to their occurrence in twins. *Psychiatric Monographs, 1.* Sacramento Department of Institutions.

Rosanoff, A. J., Handy, L. M., & Rosanoff, F. A. (1934). Criminality and delinquency in twins. *Journal of Criminal Law and Criminology, 24,* 923–934.

Rosecan, J. S., Spitz, H. I., & Gross, B. (1987). Contemporary issues in the treatment of cocaine abuse. In H. I. Spitz & J. S. Rosecan (Eds.), *Cocaine abuse: New directions in treatment and research.* New York: Brunner/Mazel.

Rosenbaum, D. P., Lurigio, A. J., & Davis, R. C. (1998). *The prevention of crime: Social and situational strategies.* Belmont, CA: West/Wadsworth.

Rosenbaum, M. (1989). *Just say what? An alternative view on solving America's drug problem.* San Francisco: National Council of Crime and Delinquency.

Rosenfeld, B., & Ritchie, K. (1998). Competence to stand trial: Clinician reliability and the role of offense severity. *Journal of Forensic Sciences, 43,* 151–157.

Rosenthal, D. (1970). *Genetic theory and abnormal behavior.* New York: McGraw–Hill.

Rosenthal, D. (1971). *Genetics of psychopathology.* New York: McGraw–Hill.

Rosenthal, D. (1975). Heredity in criminality. *Criminal Justice and Behavior, 2,* 3–21.

Rosenzweig, M. R., Leiman, A. L., & Breedlove, S. M. (1999). *Biological psychology: An introduction to behavioral, cognitive, and clinical neuroscience.* Sunderland, MA: Sinauer Associates.

Rosoff, S. M., Pontell, H. N., & Tillman, R. (1998). *Profit without honor: White-collar crime and the looting of America.* Upper Saddle River, NJ: Prentice Hall.

Ross, M. P., & Bachar, K. J. (2002). Rape. In D. Levinson (Ed.), *Encyclopedia of crime and punishment* (Vol. 3). Thousand Oaks, CA: Sage.

Rossmo, D. K. (1997). Geographic profiling. In J. L. Jackson & D. A. Bekerain (Eds.), *Offender profiling: Theory, research, and practice.* Chichester, UK: Wiley.

Rotenberg, M., & Diamond, B. (1971). The biblical conception of psychopathy: The law of the stubborn and rebellious son. *Journal of the History of the Behavioral Sciences, 12,* 29–38.

Roth, J. A. (1996). *Psychoactive substances and violence.* Washington, DC: U.S. Department of Justice. Available: www.ncjrs.org/txtfile/psycho.txt

Rotton, J. (1983). Affective and cognitive consequences of malodorous pollution. *Basic and Applied Psychology, 4,* 171–191.

Rotton, J., & Frey, J. (1985). Air pollution, weather, and violent crimes: Concomitant time-series analysis of archival data. *Journal of Personality and Social Psychology, 49,* 1207–1220.

Rubin, B. (1972). Predictions of dangerousness in mentally ill criminals. *Archives of General Psychiatry, 27,* 397–407.

Rubin, K. H., Bukowski, W., & Parker, J. G. (1998). Peer interactions, relationships, and groups. In W. Damon (Series Ed.) & N. Eisenberg (Vol. Ed.), *Handbook of child psychology: Vol. 3. Social, emotional, and personality development* (5th ed.). New York: Wiley.

Rubinsky, E. W., & Brandt, J. (1986). Amnesia and criminal law: A clinical overview. *Behavioral Sciences and the Law, 4,* 27–46.

Rushton, J. P., & Chrisjohn, R. D. (1981). Extraversion, neuroticism, psychoticism, and self-reported delinquency: Evidence from eight separate samples. *Personality and Individual Differences, 2,* 11–20.

Russell, D. (1973). Emotional aspects of shoplifting. *Psychiatric Annals, 3*, 77–86.

Russell, D. E. H. (1975). *The politics of rape: The victim's perspective*. New York: Stein & Day.

Russell, D. E. H. (1983). The prevalence and incidence of forcible rape and attempted rape of females. *Victimology: An International Journal, 7*, 81–93.

Russell, D. E. H. (1984). *Sexual exploitation*. Beverly Hills, CA: Sage.

Russell, D. E. H., & Finkelhor, D. (1984). The gender gap among perpetrators of child sexual abuse. In D. E. H. Russell (Ed.), *Sexual exploitation*. Beverly Hills, CA: Sage.

Russell, D. E. H., & Howell, N. (1983). The prevalence of rape in the United States revisited. *Signs: Journal of Women in Culture and Society, 8*, 688–695.

Rutter, M., & Giller, H. (1984). *Juvenile delinquency: Trends and perspectives*. New York: Guilford Press.

Salekin, R. T. (2002). Psychopathy and therapeutic pessimism: Clinical lore or clinical reality? *Clinical Psychology Review, 22*, 79–112.

Salekin, R. T., & Rogers, R. (2001). Treating patients found not guilty by reason of insanity. In J. B. Ashford, B. D. Sales, & W. H. Reid (Eds.), *Treating adult and juvenile offenders with special needs*. Washington, DC: American Psychological Association.

Salekin, R. T., Rogers, R., & Sewell, K. W. (1996). A review and meta-analysis of the Psychopathy Checklist and Psychopathy Checklist—Revised: Predictive validity of dangerousness. *Clinical Psychology: Science and Practice, 3*, 203–215.

Salekin, R. T., Rogers, R., & Sewell, K. W. (1997). Construct validity of psychopathy in a female offender sample: A multitrait-multimethod evaluation. *Journal of Abnormal Psychology, 106*, 576–585.

Salekin, R. T., Rogers, R., Ustad, K. L., & Sewell, K. W. (1998). Psychopathy and recidivism among female inmates. *Law and Human Behavior, 22*, 109–128.

Sampson, R. J., & Laub, J. H. (1997). Unraveling the social context of physique and delinquency: A new, long-term look at the Gluecks' classic study. In A. Raine, P. A. Brennan, D. P. Farrington, & S. A. Mednick (Eds.), *Biosocial bases of violence*. New York: Plenum.

Sampson, R. J., & Lauritsen, J. L. (1994). Violent victimization and offending: Individual, situational and community-level risk factors. In A. T. Reiss, Jr., & J. Roth (Eds.), *Understanding and preventing violence: Social Influences* (Vol. 3). Washington, DC: National Academy Press.

Sampson, R. J., & Wilson, W. J. (1993). Toward a theory of race, crime, and urban inequality. In J. Hagan & R. Peterson (Eds.), *Crime and inequality*. Stanford, CA: Stanford University Press.

Santa Clara Criminal Justice Pilot Program. (1972). *Burglary in San Jose*. Springfield, VA: U.S. Department of Commerce.

Santiago, G. B. (2002). Latina battered women: Barriers to service delivery and cultural considerations. In A. R. Roberts (Ed.), *Handbook of domestic violence intervention strategies: Policies, programs, and legal remedies*. New York: Oxford University Press.

Saradjian, A., & Nobus, D. (2003). Cognitive distortion of religious professionals who sexually abuse children. *Journal of Interpersonal Violence, 18*, 905–923.

Sarasalo, E., Bergman, B., & Toth, J. (1996). Personality traits and psychiatric and somatic morbidity among kleptomaniacs. *Acta Psychiatrica Scandinavica, 94*, 358–364.

Sarasalo, E., Bergman, B., & Toth, J. (1997). Kleptomania-like behaviour and psychosocial characteristics among shoplifters. *Legal and Criminological Psychology, 2*, 1–10.

Sarbin, T. R. (1979). The myth of the criminal type. In T. R. Sarbin (Ed.), *Challenges to the criminal justice system: The perspective of community psychology*. New York: Human Services Press.

Satterfield, J. H. (1987). Childhood diagnostic and neurophysiological predictors of teenage arrest rates: An eight-year prospective study. In S. A. Mednick, T. A. Moffitt, & S. A. Stack

(Eds.), *The causes of crime: New biological approaches*. Cambridge: Cambridge University Press.

Satterfield, J. H., Swanson, J., Schell, A., & Lee, F. (1994). Prediction of antisocial behavior in attention-deficit hyperactivity disorder boys from aggression/defiance scores. *Journal of the American Academy of Child and Adolescent Psychiatry, 33,* 185–191.

Saulnier, K., & Perlman, D. (1981). The actor-observer bias is alive and well in prison: A sequel to Wells. *Personality and Social Psychology, 7,* 559–564.

Saunders, D. G., & Azar, S. T. (1989). Treatment programs for family violence. In L. Ohlin & M. Tonry (Eds.), *Family violence* (Vol. 11). Chicago, IL: University of Chicago Press.

Savitz, L. D. (1972). Introduction. In G. Lombroso-Ferrero (Ed.), *Criminal man*. Montclair, NJ: Patterson Smith.

Scaret, D., & Wilgosh, L. (1989). Learning disabilities and juvenile delinquency: A causal relationship? *International Journal for the Advancement of Counselling, 12,* 113–123.

Schacht, T. E. (1985). DSM-III and the politics of truth. *American Psychologist, 40,* 513–521.

Schachter, S. (1971). *Emotion, obesity and crime*. New York: Academic Press.

Schachter, S., & Latane, B. (1964). Crime, cognition, and the autonomic nervous system. In M. R. Jones (Ed.), *Nebraska symposium on motivation*. Lincoln: University of Nebraska Press.

Schacter, D. L. (1986a). Amnesia and crime: How much do we really know? *American Psychologist, 41,* 286–295.

Schacter, D. L. (1986b). On the relation between genuine and simulated amnesia. *Behavioral Sciences & the Law, 4,* 47–64.

Scherer, D. G., Brondino, M. J., Henggeler, S. W., Melton, G. B., & Hanley, J. H. (1994). Multisystemic family preservation therapy: Preliminary findings from a study of rural and minority serious adolescent offenders. *Journal of Emotional and Behavioral Disorders, 2,* 198–206.

Schlosser, E. (2001). *Fast food nation: The dark side of the all-American meal*. Boston: Houghton Mifflin.

Schlossman, S., & Sedlak, M. (1983). The Chicago area project revisited. *Crime and Delinquency, 29,* 398–462.

Schmideberg, M. (1953). Pathological firesetters. *Journal of Criminal Law, Criminology and Police Science, 44,* 30–39.

Schrager, L., & Short, J. (1978). Toward a sociology of organizational crime. *Social Problems, 25,* 407–419.

Schreier, H. (2002). Munchausen by proxy defined. *Pediatrics, 110,* 985–988.

Schubot, D. (2001). Date rape prevalence among female high school students in a rural midwestern state during 1993, 1995, and 1997. *Journal of Interpersonal Violence, 16,* 291–296.

Schuller, R. A., & Vidmar, V. (1992). Battered woman syndrome evidence in the courtroom: A review of the literature. *Law and Human Behavior, 16,* 272–292.

Schulsinger, F. (1972). Psychopathy: Heredity and environment. *International Journal of Mental Health, 1,* 190–206.

Schultz, L. G. (1975). *Rape victimology*. Springfield, IL: Charles C Thomas.

Schuster, M. A., Stein, B. D., Jaycox, L. H., Collins, R. L., Marshall, G. N., & Elliott, M. N. (2001). A national survey of stress reactions after the September 11, 2001, terrorist attacks. *New England Journal of Medicine, 345,* 1507–1512.

Schwartz, I. M. (1989). *(In)Justice for juveniles: Rethinking the best interests of the child*. Lexington, MA: Lexington Books.

Scientific American. (1999). *The Scientific American book of the brain*. New York: Author.

Scully, D., & Marolla, J. (1984). Convicted rapists' vocabulary of motive: Excuses and justifications. *Social Problems, 31,* 530–544.

Scully, D., & Marolla, J. (1985). Rape and vocabularies of motive: Alternative perspectives. In A. W. Burgess (Ed.), *Rape and sexual assault*. New York: Garland.

Seagrave, D., & Grisso, T. (2002). Adolescent development and measurement of juvenile psychopathy. *Law and Human Behavior, 26,* 219–239.

Sears, R., Maccoby, E., & Levin, H. (1957). *Patterns of child rearing*. Evanston, IL: Row, Peterson.

Sebald, H. (1986). Adolescents' shifting orientations toward parents and peers: A curvilinear trend over recent decades. *Journal of Marriage and the Family, 48,* 5–13.

Sechrest, L. (1987). Classification for treatment. In D. M. Gottfredson & M. Tonry (Eds.), *Prediction and classification: Criminal justice decision making* (Vol. 9). Chicago, IL: University of Chicago Press.

Seligman, M. E. (1975). *Helplessness: On depression, development, and death*. San Francisco, CA: W. H. Freeman.

Selkin, J. (1987). *Psychological autopsy in the courtroom*. Denver, CO: Author.

Selkin, J. (1994). Psychological autopsy: Scientific psychohistory or clinical intuition? *American Psychologist, 49,* 74–75.

Sellin, T. (1970). A sociological approach. In M. E. Wolfgang, L. Savitz, & N. Johnson (Eds.), *The sociology of crime and delinquency* (2nd ed.). New York: Wiley.

Serin, R. C., & Amos, N. L. (1995). The role of psychopathy in the assessment of dangerousness. *International Journal of Law & Psychiatry, 18,* 231–238.

Serin, R. C., Peters, R. D., & Barbaree, H. E. (1990). Predictors of psychopathy and release outcome in a criminal population. *Psychological Assessment, 2,* 419–422.

Serin, R. C., & Preston, D. L. (2001). Managing and treating violent offenders. In J. B. Ashford, B. D. Sales, & W. H. Reid (Eds.), *Treating adult and juvenile offenders with special needs*. Washington, DC: American Psychological Association.

Seto, M. C., & Barbaree, H. E. (1999). Psychopathy, treatment behavior, and sex offender recidivism. *Journal of Interpersonal Violence, 14,* 1235–1248.

Seymour, A. (2000). Campus crime and victimization. In G. Coleman, M. Gaboury, M. Murray, & A. Seymour (Eds.), *1999 National Victim Assistance Academy*. Washington, DC: U.S. Department of Justice.

Shafer, S. (1976). *Introduction to criminology*. Reston, VA: Reston.

Shain, R., & Phillips, J. (1991). The stigma of mental illness: Labeling and stereotyping in the news. In L. Wilkins & P. Patterson (Eds.), *Risky business: Communicating issues of science, risk, and public policy*. Westport, CT: Greenwood Press.

Shaw, D. S., Gilliom, M., Ingoldsby, E. M., & Nagin, D. S. (2003). Trajectories leading to school-age conduct problems. *Developmental Psychology, 39,* 189–200.

Sheldon, W. H., Hartl, E. M., & McDermott, E. (1949). *Varieties of delinquent youth: An introduction to constitutional psychiatry*. New York: Harper.

Sheldon, W. H., & Stevens, S. S. (1942). *The varieties of temperament*. New York: Harper.

Sherman, L. W., & Berk, R. A. (1984). The specific deterrent effects of arrest for domestic assault. *American Sociological Review, 49,* 261–272.

Sherman, L. W., Gottfredson, D. C., MacKenzie, D. L., Eck, J., Reuter, P., & Bushway, S. D. (1998). *Preventing crime: What works, what doesn't, what's promising*. Washington, DC: U.S. Department of Justice.

Shields, J. (1962). *Monozygotic twins brought up apart and together*. Oxford: Oxford University Press.

Shiff, A. R., & Wexler, D. (1996). Teen court: A therapeutic jurisprudence perspective. *Criminal Law Bulletin, 12,* 342–357.

Shneidman, E. S. (1994). The psychological autopsy. *American Psychologist, 49,* 75–76.

Short, J. F. (1968). *Gang delinquency and delinquency subcultures*. New York: Harper & Row.

Short, J. F., & Nye, I. (1957). Reported behavior as a criterion of deviant behavior. *Social Problems, 5*, 207–213.

Shover, N. (1972). Structures and careers in burglary. *Journal of Criminal Law, Criminology and Police Science, 63*, 540–548.

Showers, J. (1999). *Never never never shake a baby: The challenges of shaken baby syndrome.* Alexandria, VA: National Association of Children's Hospitals and Related Institutions.

Shuntich, R. J., & Taylor, S. P. (1972). The effects of alcohol on human physical aggressions. *Journal of Experimental Research in Personality, 6*, 34–38.

Siegel, A., & Kohn, L. (1959). Permissiveness, permission, and aggression: The effect of adult presence or absence on aggression in children's play. *Child Development, 30*, 131–141.

Siegel, J. M., Sorenson, S. B., Golding, J. M., Burnam, M. A., & Stein, J. A. (1987). The prevalence of childhood sexual assault: The Los Angeles Epidemiological Catchment Area Project. *American Journal of Epidemiology, 126*, 1141–1153.

Sieh, E. W. (1987). Garment workers: Perceptions of inequity and employee theft. *British Journal of Criminology, 27*, 174–190.

Sigall, H., & Ostrove, N. (1978). Physical attractiveness and jury decisions. In N. Johnson & L. Savitz (Eds.), *Justice and corrections*. New York: Wiley.

Silberman, E. K., & Weingartner, H. (1996). Hemispheric lateralization of functions related to emotion. *Brain and Cognition, 5*, 322–353.

Silva, F., Martorell, C., & Clemente, A. (1986). Socialization and personality: Study through questionnaires in a preadult Spanish population. *Personality and Individual Differences, 7*, 355–372.

Silverman, R. A., & Mukhergee, S. K. (1987). Intimate homicide: An analysis of violent social relationships. *Behavioral Sciences & the Law, 5*, 37–47.

Silvern, L., Karyl, J., Waelde, L., Hodges, W. F., Starek, J., Heidt, E., & Min, K. (1995). Retrospective reports of parental partner abuse: Relationships to depression, trauma symptoms and self-esteem among college students. *Journal of Family Violence, 10*, 177–202.

Simon, R. J. (1983). The defense of insanity. *Journal of Psychiatry and Law, 11*, 183–201.

Simon, R. J., & Aaronson, D. E. (1988). *The insanity defense*. New York: Praeger.

Simon, R. J., & Cockerham, W. (1977). Civil commitment, burden of proof, and dangerous acts: A comparison of the perspectives of judges and psychiatrists. *Journal of Psychiatry and Law, 5*, 571–594.

Simourd, D. J. (1997). The Criminal Sentiments Scale–Modified and Pride in Delinquency scale: Psychometric properties and construct validity of two measures of criminal attitudes. *Criminal Justice and Behavior, 24*, 52–70.

Simourd, D. J., & Hoge, R. D. (2000). Criminal psychopathy: A risk-and-need perspective. *Criminal Justice and Behavior, 27*, 256–272.

Simourd, D. J., & Van De Ven, J. (1999). Assessment of criminal attitudes: Criterion-related validity of the Criminal Sentiments Scale–Modified and Pride in Delinquency scale. *Criminal Justice and Behavior, 26*, 90–106.

Skeem, J. L., & Cauffman, E. (2003). Views of the downward extension: Comparing the youth version of the Psychopathy Checklist with the Youth Psychopathic Traits Inventory. *Behavioral Sciences & the Law, 21*, 737–770.

Skeem, J. L., Edens, J. F., & Colwell, L. H. (2003a, April). *Are there racial differences in levels of psychopathy? A meta-analysis*. Paper presented at the 3rd annual conference of the International Association of Forensic Mental Health Services, Miami, FL.

Skeem, J. L., Edens, J. F., Sanford, G. M., & Colwell, L. H. (2003b). Psychopathic personality and racial/ethnic differences reconsidered: A reply to Lynn (2002). *Personality and Individual Differences, 34*, 1–24.

Skeem, J. L., & Golding, S. (1998). Community examiners' evaluations of competence to stand trial: Common problems and suggestions for improvements. *Professional Psychology: Research and Practice, 29,* 357–367.

Skeem, J. L., Monahan, J., & Mulvey, E. P. (2002). Psychopathy, treatment involvement, and subsequent violence among civil psychiatric patients. *Law and Human Behavior, 26,* 577–603.

Skeem, J. L., Poythress, N., Edens, J., Lilienfeld, S., & Cale, E. (2003). Psychopathic personality or personalities? Exploring potential variants of psychopathy and their implications for risk assessment. *Aggression and Violent Behavior, 8,* 513–546.

Skilling, T. A., Quinsey, V. L., & Craig, W. M. (2001). Evidence of a tax on underlying serious antisocial behavior in boys. *Criminal Justice and Behavior, 28,* 450–470.

Skinner, B. F. (1964). Behaviorism at fifty. In T. W. Wann (Ed.), *Behaviorism and phenomenology.* Chicago, IL: University of Chicago Press.

Skrzpek, G. J. (1969). The effects of perceptual isolation and arousal on anxiety, complexity preference, and novelty preference in psychopathic and neurotic delinquents. *Journal of Abnormal Psychology, 74,* 321–329.

Slobogin, C. (1985). The guilty but mentally ill verdict: An idea whose time should not have come. *George Washington Law Review, 53,* 494–580.

Slobogin, C. (1999). The admissibility of behavioral science information in criminal trials: From primitivism to *Daubert* to voice. *Psychology, Public Policy, and Law, 5,* 100–119.

Slovenko, R. (1989). The multiple personality: A challenge to legal concepts. *The Journal of Psychiatry and Law, 17,* 681–719.

Smart, C. (1976). *Women, crime, and criminology: A feminist critique.* London: Routledge & Kegan Paul.

Smigel, E. O. (1970). Public attitudes toward stealing as related to the size of the victim organization. In E. O. Smigel & H. L. Ross (Eds.), *Crimes against bureaucracy.* New York: Van Nostrand Reinhold.

Smith, D. (2002, June). Helping mentally ill offenders. *Monitor on Psychology, 33,* 64.

Smith, G. A., & Hall, J. A. (1982). Evaluating Michigan's guilty but mentally ill verdict: An empirical study. *Michigan Journal of Law Reform, 16,* 75–112.

Smith, M. D., & Bennett, N. (1985). Poverty, inequality, and theories of forcible rape. *Crime and Delinquency, 31,* 295–305.

Smith, S., & Hudson, R. (1995). A quick screening test of competency to stand trial for defendants with mental retardation. *Psychological Reports, 78,* 234.

Smith, S. S., & Newman, J. P. (1990). Alcohol and drug abuse-dependence disorder in psychopathic and nonpsychopathic criminal offenders. *Journal of Abnormal Psychology, 99,* 430–439.

Smithey, M. (1998). Infant homicide: Victim-offender relationship and causes of death. *Journal of Family Violence, 13,* 285–287.

Snyder, H. N. (2000). *Juvenile arrests 1999.* Washington, DC: U.S. Department of Justice, Office of Juvenile Justice and Delinquency Prevention.

Snyder, H. N. (2002, November). *Juvenile arrests 2000.* Washington, DC: U.S. Department of Justice, Office of Juvenile Justice and Delinquency Prevention.

Snyder, H. N. (2003, December). *Juvenile arrests 2001.* Washington, DC: U.S. Department of Justice, Office of Juvenile Justice and Delinquency Prevention.

Snyder, H. N., Sickmund, M., & Poe-Yamagata, E. (2000). *Juvenile transfer to criminal court in the 1990s: Lessons learned from four studies.* Washington, DC: Office of Juvenile Justice and Delinquency Prevention.

Sobell, M. B., & Sobell, L. C. (1973). Individualized behavior for alcoholics. *Behavior Therapy, 4,* 49–72.

Solomon, J., & King, P. (1993, July 19). Waging war in the workplace. *Newsweek,* 30–34.

Sommer, D. A. (1983). How does menstruation affect cognitive competence and psychophysiological response? *Women and Health, 8,* 53–90.

Sorenson, S. B., Stein, J. A., Siegel, J. M., Golding, J. M., & Burnam, M. A. (1987). The prevalence of adult sexual assault: The Los Angeles Epidemiological Catchment Area Project. *American Journal of Epidemiology, 126,* 1154–1164.

Southerland, M. D., Collins, P. A., & Scarborough, K. E. (1997). *Workplace violence.* Cincinnati, OH: Anderson.

Spaccarelli, S., Coatsworth, J. D., & Bowden, B. S. (1995). Exposure to serious family violence among incarcerated boys: Its association with violent offending and potential mediating variables. *Violence and Victims, 10,* 163–182.

Spain, D. M., Bradess, F. A., & Eggson, A. A. (1951). Alcohol and violent death. *Journal of the American Medical Association, 146,* 334–335.

Spain, S. E., Douglas, K. S., Poythress, N. G., & Epstein, M. (2004). The relationship between psychopathic features, violence and treatment outcomes: The comparison of three youth measures of psychopathic features. *Behavioral Sciences & the Law, 22,* 85–102.

Spencer, C. (1966, September). *A typology of violent offenders.* Administrative Abstract No. 23. California Department of Corrections.

Stadolnik, R. F. (2000). *Drawn to the flame: Assessment and treatment of juvenile firesetting behavior.* Sarasota, FL: Professional Resources Press.

Stagg, V., Wills, G. D., & Howell, M. (1989). Psychopathology in early childhood witnesses of family violence. *Topics in Early Childhood Special Education, 9,* 73–87.

Stahl, A., Sickmund, M., Finnegan, T., Synder, H., Poole, R., & Tierney, N. (1999). *Juvenile court statistics 1996.* Washington, DC: U.S. Department of Justice.

Standards Committee, American Association for Correctional Psychology. (2000). Standards for psychology services in jails, prisons, correctional facilities, and agencies. *Criminal Justice and Behavior, 27,* 433–494.

Stanger, C., Achenbach, T. M., & Verhulst, F. C. (1997). Accelerated longitudinal comparisons of aggressive versus delinquent syndromes. *Development and Psychopathology, 9,* 43–58.

Stanley, B., Molcho, A., Stanley, M., Winchel, R., Gameroff, M. J., Parsons, B., & Mann, J. J. (2000). Association of aggressive behavior with altered sertonergic function in patients who are not suicidal. *American Journal of Psychiatry, 157,* 609–614.

Stark, E. (2002). Preparing for expert testimony in domestic violence cases. In A. R. Roberts (Ed.), *Handbook of domestic violence intervention strategies: Policies, programs, and legal remedies.* New York: Oxford University Press.

Staub, E. (2001). Genocide and mass killing: Their roots and prevention. In D. J. Christie, R. V. Wagner, & D. D. Winter (Eds.), *Peace, conflict, and violence: Peace psychology for the 21st century.* Upper Saddle River, NJ: Prentice Hall.

Staub, E. (2004). Understanding and responding to group violence: Genocide, mass killing, and terrorism. In F. M. Moghaddam & A. J. Marsella (Eds.), *Understanding terrorism: Psychosocial roots, consequences, and interventions.* Washington, DC: American Psychological Association.

Steadman, H. J. (1976). Predicting dangerousness. In D. J. Madden & J. R. Lion (Eds.), *Rage • hate • assault • and other forms of violence.* New York: Spectrum.

Steadman, H. J. (1979). *Beating a rap? Defendants found incompetent to stand trial.* Chicago, IL: University of Chicago Press.

Steadman, H. J., & Cocozza, J. J. (1974). *Careers of the criminally insane.* Lexington, MA: Lexington Books.

Steadman, H. J., Fabisiak, S., Dvoskin, J., & Holobean, E. (1987). A survey of mental disability among state prison inmates. *Hospital and Community Psychiatry, 38,* 1086–1090.

Steadman, H. J., McGreevy, M. A., Morrissey, J. P., Callahan, L. A., Robbins, P. C., & Cirincione, C. (1993). *Before and after Hinckley: Evaluating insanity defense reform*. New York: Guilford Press.

Steadman, H. J., Mulvey, E. P., Monahan, J., Robbins, P. C., Appelbaum, P. S., Grisso, T., Roth, L. H., & Silver, E. (1998). Violence by people discharged from acute psychiatric inpatient facilities and by others in the same neighborhoods. *Archives of General Psychiatry, 55,* 393–401.

Steinmetz, S. K. (1981). A cross-cultural comparison of sibling violence. *International Journal of Family Psychiatry, 2,* 337–351.

Sternberg, R. J. (2003). A duplex theory of hate: Development and application of terrorism, massacres, and genocide. *Review of General Psychology, 7,* 299–328.

Stewart, M. A., & Culver, K. W. (1982). Children who set fires: The clinical picture and a follow-up. *British Journal of Psychiatry, 140,* 357–363.

Stone, A. (1975). *Mental health law: A system in transition*. Washington, DC: U.S. Government Printing Office.

Stone, M. H. (1998). Sadistic personality in murders. In T. Millon, E. Simonsen, M. Burket-Smith, & R. Davis (Eds.), *Psychopathy: Antisocial, criminal, and violent behavior*. New York: Guilford.

Strasser, F. (1989, August 7). One nation, under siege. *The National Law Journal,* S2–S3, S15.

Straus, M. (1991). Discipline and deviance: Physical punishment of children and violence and other crime in adulthood. *Social Problems, 38,* 133–154.

Straus, M. A., & Gelles, R. J. (1990). *Physical violence in American families*. New Brunswick, NJ: Transaction.

Straus, M. A., Gelles, R. J., & Steinmetz, S. K. (1980). *Behind closed doors: Violence in the American family*. New York: Doubleday.

Strentz, T. (1987, November). A hostage psychological survival guide. *FBI Law Enforcement Bulletin,* 1–7.

Stumpfl, F. (1936). *Die Ursprunge des Verbrechens om Lebenshauf von Zwillingen*. Leipzig: Georg Thieme Verlag.

Substance Abuse and Mental Health Services Administration. (2003). *Overview of findings from the 2002 National Survey on Drug Use and Health* (DHHS Publication No. SMA 03-3774). Rockville, MD: Office of Applied Studies.

Surette, R. (1999). *Media, crime, and criminal justice*, 2nd ed. Belmont, CA: West/Wadsworth.

Sutherland, E. H. (1947). *Principles of criminology*, 4th ed. Philadelphia: Lippincott.

Sutherland, E. H. (1949). *White-collar crime*. New York: Holt, Rinehart & Winston.

Sutherland, E. H. (1983). *White-collar crime: The uncut version*. New Haven, CT: Yale University Press.

Sutherland, E. H., & Cressey, D. R. (1974). *Criminology* (9th ed.). Philadelphia: Lippincott.

Sutherland, E. H., & Cressey, D. R. (1978). *Criminology* (10th ed.). Philadelphia: Lippincott.

Sutherland, E. H., Cressey, D. R., & Luckenbill, D. F. (1992). *Principles of criminology* (11th ed.). Dix Hills, NY: General Hall.

Sutker, P. B., & Allain, A. N. (1983). Behavior and personality assessment in men labeled adaptive sociopaths. *Journal of Behavioral Assessment, 5,* 65–79.

Sutker, P. B., Uddo-Crane, M., & Allain, A. N. (1991). Clinical and research assessment of posttraumatic stress disorder: A conceptual overview. *Psychological Assessment: A Journal of Consulting and Clinical Psychology, 3,* 520–530.

Sutton, S. K., Vitale, J. E., & Newman, J. P. (2002). Emotion among women with psychopathy during picture perception. *Journal of Abnormal Psychology, 111,* 610–619.

Svalastoga, K. (1956). Homicide and social contact in Denmark. *American Journal of Sociology, 62,* 37–41.

Swanson, D. W. (1968). Adult sexual abuse of children: The man and circumstances. *Diseases of the Nervous System, 29*, 677–683.

Swanson, J., & Holzer, C. (1991). Violence and the ECA data. *Hospital and Community Psychiatry, 42*, 79–80.

Swanson, J., Holzer, C., Ganju, V., & Jono, R. (1990). Violence and psychiatric disorder in the community: Evidence from the Epidemiologic Catchment Area surveys. *Hospital and Community Psychiatry, 41*, 761–770.

Sykes, G. M. (1956). *Crime and society*. New York: Random House.

Symons, D. (1979). *The evolution of human sexuality*. New York: Oxford University Press.

Tappan, P. W. (1947). Who is the criminal? *American Sociological Review, 12*, 100–110.

Tappan, P. W. (1949). *Juvenile delinquency*. New York: McGraw–Hill.

Tasto, D., & Insel, P. (1977). The premenstrual and menstrual syndromes. In S. Rachman (Ed.), *Contributions to medical psychology* (Vol. 1). Oxford, UK: Pergamon Press.

Taylor, D. M., & Louis, W. (2004). Terrorism and the quest for identity. In F. M. Moghaddam & A. J. Marsella (Eds.), *Understanding terrorism: Psychosocial roots, consequences, and interventions*. Washington, DC: American Psychological Association.

Taylor, M., & Nee, C. (1988). The role of cues in simulated residential burglary. *British Journal of Criminology, 28*, 396–401.

Taylor, S. P. (1967). Aggressive behavior and physiological arousal as a function of provocation and the tendency to inhibit aggression. *Journal of Personality, 35*, 297–310.

Taylor, S. P., & Gammon, C. B. (1975). Effects of type and dose of alcohol on human physical aggression. *Journal of Personality and Social Psychology, 32*, 169–175.

Taylor, S. P., Gammon, C. B., & Capasso, D. R. (1976). Aggression as a function of the interaction of alcohol and threat. *Journal of Personality and Social Psychology, 34*, 938–941.

Taylor, S. P., & Leonard, K. E. (1983). Alcohol and human physical aggression. In R. G. Geen & E. I. Donnerstein (Eds.), *Aggression: Theoretical and empirical reviews* (Vol. 2). New York: Academic Press.

Taylor, S. P., Schmutte, G. T., Leonard, K. E., & Cranston, J. W. (1979). The effects of alcohol and extreme provocation on the use of highly noxious shock. *Motivation and Emotion, 3*, 73–81.

Taylor, S. P., & Sears, J. D. (1988). The effects of alcohol and persuasive social pressure on human physical aggression. *Aggressive Behavior, 14*, 237–244.

Taylor, S. P., Vardaris, R. M., Ravitch, A. B., Gammon, C. B., Cranston, J. W., & Lubetkin, A. E. (1976). The effects of alcohol and delta-9-tetrahydrocannabinol on human physical aggression. *Aggressive Behavior, 2*, 153–161.

Teplin, L. (1984). Criminalizing mental disorder. *American Psychologist, 39*, 794–803.

Teplin, L. (1990). The prevalence of severe mental disorder among male urban jail detainees: Comparisons with the epidemiologic catchment area program. *American Journal of Public Health, 80*, 663–669.

Teplin, L. (2000, October). Psychiatric disorders in youthful offenders. *National Institute of Justice Journal*, 30–32.

Terrorism Research Center. (1997). *The basics: Combating terrorism*. Alexandria, VA: Author.

The informant. (2003). Newsletter of National White Collar Crime Center (Richmond, VA), *August*.

Thompson, K. M. (1990). Refacing inmates: A critical appraisal of plastic surgery programs in prison. *Criminal Justice and Behavior, 17*, 448–466.

Thorley, G. (1984). Review of follow-up and follow-back studies of childhood hyperactivity. *Psychological Bulletin, 96*, 116–132.

Thornberry, T. P., & Jacoby, J. E. (1979). *The criminally insane: A community follow-up of mentally ill offenders*. Chicago, IL: University of Chicago Press.

Tinklenberg, J. R., & Stillman, R. C. (1970). Drug use and violence. In D. Daniels, M. Gilula, & F. Ochberg (Eds.), *Violence and the struggle for existence*. Boston, MA: Little, Brown.

Tinklenberg, J. R., & Woodrow, K. M. (1974). Drug use among youthful assaultive and sexual offenders. In S. H. Frazier (Ed.), *Aggression*. Baltimore, MD: Williams & Wilkins.

Tittle, C. R. (1980). *Sanctions and social deviance: The question of deterrence*. New York: Praeger.

Tittle, C. R. (1983). Social class and criminal behavior: A critique of the theoretical foundation. *Social Forces, 62*, 334–358.

Tittle, C. R., & Villemez, W. J. (1977). Social class and criminality. *Social Forces, 56*, 474–502.

Tjaden, P. (1997, November). *The crime of stalking: How big is the problem?* NIJ Research Preview. Washington, DC: U.S. Department of Justice.

Tjaden, P., & Thoennes, N. (1997). *Stalking in America: Findings from the national violence against women survey*. Denver, CO: Center for Policy Research.

Tjaden, P., & Thoennes, N. (1998a). *Stalking in America: Findings from the national violence against women survey*. Washington, DC: U.S. Department of Justice.

Tjaden, P., & Thoennes, N. (1998b). Prevalence, incidence, and consequences of violence against women: Findings from the National Violence Against Women Survey. *Research in Brief*. Washington, DC: U.S. Department of Justice.

Toch, H. (1969). *Violent men: An inquiry into the psychology of violence*. Chicago, IL: Aldine.

Toch, H. (1977). *Police, prisons, and the problems of violence*. National Institute of Mental Health. Washington, DC: U.S. Government Printing Office.

Toch, H. (1992). *Mosaic of despair: Human breakdowns in prison*. Washington, DC: American Psychological Association.

Toch, H., & Adams, K. (1989). *The disturbed violent offender*. New Haven, CT: Yale University Press.

Toch, H., & Adams, K., with Grant, J. D. (1989). *Coping: Maladaptation in prisons*. New Brunswick, NJ: Transaction.

Tolan, P. H., Gorman-Smith, D., & Henry, D. B. (2003). On developmental ecology of urban males' youth violence. *Developmental Psychology, 39*, 274–279.

Tolan, P. H., & Thomas, P. (1995). The implications of age of onset for delinquency II: Longitudinal data. *Journal of Abnormal Child Psychology, 23*, 157–169.

Tomarken, A. J., Davidson, R. J., Wheeler, R. E., & Doss, R. C. (1992). Individual differences in anterior brain asymmetry and fundamental dimensions of emotion. *Journal of Personality and Social Psychology, 62*, 676–687.

Tonry, M., & Petersilia, J. (1999). (Eds.). *Prisons. Crime and justice. A review of the research* (Vol. 26). Chicago: University of Chicago Press.

Trasler, G. (1987). Some cautions for the biological approach to crime causation. In S. A. Mednick, E. Moffitt, & S. A. Stack (Eds.), *The causes of crime: New biological approach*. Cambridge: Cambridge University Press.

Tsang, J. (2002). Moral rationalizaiton and the integration of situational factors and psychological processes in immoral behavior. *Review of General Psychology, 6*, 25–50.

Tucker, D. M. (1981). Lateral brain function, emotion and conceptualization. *Psychological Bulletin, 89*, 19–46.

Tupin, J. P., Mahar, D., & Smith, D. (1973). Two types of violent offenders with psychosocial descriptors. *Diseases of the Nervous System, 34*, 356–363.

Turrell, S. C. (2000). A descriptive analysis of same-sex relationship violence for a diverse sample. *Journal of Family Violence, 15*, 281–293.

Turvey, B. (2002). *Criminal profiling: An introduction to behavioral evidence analysis* (2nd ed.). San Diego, CA: Academic Press.

Ullman, S. E., & Knight, R. A. (1993). The efficacy of women's resistance strategies in rape situations. *Psychology of Women Quarterly, 17,* 23–38.

University of Michigan. (1999, December). *National survey results on drug use from the Monitoring the Future Study.* Ann Arbor, MI: Institute for Social Research. Available: www.isr.umich.edu/src/mft

University of Michigan. (2002, December). *Monitoring the future: 2002 data from in-school surveys of 8th, 10th, and 12th grade students.* Ann Arbor, MI: Institute for Social Research. Available: http://.monitoringthefuture.org/data/0sdata. html#2002data-drugs

University of Michigan. (2003, September). *Monitoring the future: National survey results on drug use, 1975–2002, Volume II: College students and adults ages 19–40.* Ann Arbor, MI: Institute for Social Research. Available: http://monitoringthefuture.org/pubs/monographs/vol2_2002.pdf

U.S. Advisory Board on Child Abuse and Neglect. (1995). *A nation's shame: Fatal child abuse and neglect in the United States.* Washington, DC: U.S. Department of Health and Human Services.

U.S. Bureau of the Census. (2001). *2000 census of population and housing.* Washington, DC: U.S. Government Printing Office.

U.S. Conference of Mayors. (1998). *A status report on hunger and homelessness in America's cities: 1998.* Washington, DC: Author.

U.S. Department of Health and Human Services. (2003, April 1). *Child abuse prevention: An overview.* Washington, DC: Author.

U.S. Department of Justice. (1976). *Bomb summary—1975.* Washington, DC: U.S. Government Printing Office.

U.S. Department of Justice. (1988). *Report to the nation on crime and justice: The data* (2nd ed.). Washington, DC: U.S. Government Printing Office.

U.S. Department of Justice. (1989a). *Uniform crime reports.* Washington, DC: U.S. Government Printing Office.

U.S. Department of Justice. (1989b). *Criminal victimization in the United States, 1987.* Washington, DC: U.S. Government Printing Office.

U.S. Department of Justice. (1998). *Inhalants.* Washington, DC: Author.

U.S. Department of Justice. (1999). *Cyberstalking: A new challenge for law enforcement and industry.* Washington, DC: Author. Available: www.usdoj.gov/criminal/cybercrime/cyber-stalking.htm

U.S. Department of Justice. (2000a). *Terrorism in the United States—1998.* Washington, DC: Author.

U.S. Department of Justice. (2000b). *The structure of family violence: An analysis of selected incidents.* Washington, DC: Author.

U.S. Department of Justice. (2002a, October). *Highlights from the NISMART Bulletin.* Washington, DC: U.S. Department of Justice, Office of Juvenile Justice and Delinquency Prevention.

U.S. Department of Justice. (2002b, October). *Nonfamily abducted children: National estimates and characteristics.* Washington, DC: U.S. Department of Justice, Office of Juvenile Justice and Delinquency Prevention.

U.S. Fire Administration. (1997). *Arson in the United States.* Washington, DC: Federal Emergency Management Agency, National Fire Data Center.

U.S. Fire Administration. (2000). *Arson and juveniles: Responding to the violence.* Washington, DC: Federal Emergency Management Agency, U.S. Fire Administration.

U.S. Fire Administration. (2002, May). *United States Fire administration Announces Arson Awareness Week.* Washington, DC: Federal Emergency Management Agency, U.S. Fire Administration.

Valenstein, E. S. (1973). *Brain control*. New York: Wiley.

Verkko, V. (1951). *Homicides and suicides in Finland and their dependence on national character*. Copenhagen, Denmark: C. E. R. Gad.

Vetter, H. J., & Silverman, I. J. (1978). *The nature of crime*. Philadelphia, PA: W. B. Saunders.

Vincent, K. R. (1991). Black/white IQ difference? *Journal of Clinical Psychology, 47*, 266–270.

Virkkunen, M. (1975). Victim-precipitated pedophilia offenses. *British Journal of Criminology, 15*, 175–180.

Virrkunen, M., & Linnoila, M. (1993). Brain serotonin, Type II alcoholism and impulsive violence. *Journal of Studies on Alcohol* (Supplement), *11*, 163–169.

Vitale, J. E., & Newman, J. P. (2001). Response perseveration in psychopathic women. *Journal of Abnormal Psychology, 110*, 644–647.

Vitale, J. E., Smith, S. S., Brinkley, C. A., & Newman, J. P. (2002). The reliability and validity of the Psychopathy Checklist—Revised in a sample of female offenders. *Criminal Justice and Behavior, 29*, 202–231.

Volavka, J. (1987). Electroencephalogram among criminals. In S. A. Mednick, T. E. Moffitt, & S. Stack (Eds.), *The causes of crime: New biological approaches*. Cambridge: Cambridge University Press.

Vold, G. B. (1958). *Theoretical criminology*. New York: Oxford University Press.

Vreeland, R. G., & Levin, B. M. (1980). Psychological aspects of firesetting. In D. Canter (Ed.), *Fires and human behaviour*. Chichester, UK: Wiley.

Wadsworth, M. E. J. (1979). *Roots of delinquency: Infancy, adolescence and crime*. Oxford, UK: Martin Robinson.

Wagner, R. V., & Long, K. R. (2004). Terrorism from a peace psychology prspective. In F. M. Moghaddam & A. J. Marsella (Eds.), *Understanding terrorism: Psychosocial roots, consequences, and interventions*. Washington, DC: American Psychological Association.

Wakefield, J. C. (1992). Disorder as harmful dysfunction: A conceptual critique of DSM-III-R's definition of mental disorder. *Psychological Review, 99*, 232–247.

Waldrop, M. F., & Halverson, C. F. (1971). Minor physical anomalies and hyperactive behavior in children. In I. J. Helmuth (Ed.), *Exceptional infant: Studies in abnormality*. New York: Brunner/Mazel.

Waldrop, M. F., Halverson, C. F., & Shetterly, K. (1989). *Manual for assessing minor physical anomalies* (rev. ed.). Unpublished manuscript. University of Georgia, Athens.

Walker, K. L., & Chestnut, D. (2003). The role of ethnocultural variables in response to terrorism. *Cultural Diversity and Ethnic Minority Psychology, 9*, 251–262.

Walker, L. E. (1979). *The battered woman*. New York: Harper Colophon Books.

Walker, S. (2001). *Sense and nonsense about crime and drugs* (5th ed.). Belmont, CA: Wadsworth/Thomson Learning.

Wallace, H., & Seymour, A. (2001). Domestic violence. In G. Coleman, M. Gaboury, M. Murray, & A. Seymour (Eds.), *1999 National Victim Assistance Academy*. Washington, DC: U.S. Department of Justice.

Wallerstein, J. S., & Wyle, J. (1947). *Our law-abiding law breakers. Probation, 25*, 107–112.

Walsh, D. (1980). *Break-ins: Burglary from private houses*. London: Constable.

Walster, E. (1966). Assignment of responsibility for an accident. *Journal of Personality and Social Psychology, 3*, 73–79.

Walters, G. C., & Grusec, J. E. (1977). *Punishment*. San Francisco, CA: W. H. Freeman.

Walters, G. D. (2003). Predicting institutional adjustment and recidivism with the Psychopathy Checklist factor scores: A meta-analysis. *Law and Human Behavior, 27*, 541–558.

Walters, H. F., & Malamud, P. (1975, March 10). Drop that gun, Captain Video. *Newsweek*, 81–82.

Ward, T., & Keenan, T. (1999). Child molesters' implicit theories. *Journal of Interpersonal Violence, 14,* 821–838.

Warren, J. I., Rosenfeld, B., Fitch, W. L., & Hawk, G. (1997). Forensic mental health clinical evaluation: An analysis of interstate and intersystemic differences. *Law and Human Behavior, 21,* 377–390.

Warren, M. Q. (1983). Application of interpersonal-maturity theory of offender populations. In W. S. Laufer & J. M. Day (Eds.), *Personality theory, moral development, and criminal behavior.* Lexington, MA: Lexington Books.

Washington Post. (1993, October 12). Guns at home. *Washington Post Health Section,* pp. 12–15.

Watson, J. B. (1913). Psychology as a behaviorist views it. *Psychological Review, 20,* 158–177.

Watson, R. I. (1973). Investigation into deindividuation using a cross-cultural survey technique. *Journal of Personality and Social Psychology, 25,* 342–345.

Webster, C. D., Douglas, K. S., Eaves, D., & Hart, S. D. (1997). Assessing risk to violence to others. In C. D. Webster & M. A. Jackson (Eds.), *Impulsivity: Theory, assessment and treatment.* New York: Guilford.

Webster, C. D., Harris, G. T., Rice, M. E., Cormier, C., & Quinsey, V. L. (1994). *The violence prediction scheme: Assessing dangerousness in high-risk men.* Toronto, ON: University of Toronto Press.

Webster, C. D., & Menzies, R. J. (1993). Supervision in the deinstitutionalized community. In S. Hodgins (Ed.), *Mental disorder and crime.* Newbury Park, CA: Sage.

Weis, J. G. (1989). Family violence methodology and design. In L. Ohlin & M. Tonry (Eds.), *Family violence* (Vol. 11). Chicago, IL: University of Chicago Press.

Weiss, J., Lamberti, J., & Blackburn, N. (1960). The sudden murderers. *Archives of General Psychiatry, 2,* 670–678.

Weiss, R. D., & Mirin, S. M. (1987). *Cocaine.* Washington, DC: American Psychiatric Press.

Welte, J. W., & Abel, E. L. (1989). Homicide: Drinking by the victim. *Journal of Studies on Alcohol, 50,* 197–201.

Wenk, E. A., Robison, J. O., & Smith, G. W. (1972). Can violence be predicted? *Crime and Delinquency, 18,* 393–402.

Wessler, S., & Moss, M. (2001, October). *Hate crimes on campus: The problem and efforts to confront it.* Washington, DC: U.S. Department of Justice, Office of Justice Programs.

West, D. J., & Farrington, D. P. (1973). *Who becomes delinquent?* London: Heinemann Educational.

Wettstein, R. M. (1984). The prediction of violent behavior and the duty to protect third parties. *Behavioral Sciences & the Law, 2,* 291–316.

Wetzel, R. D., McClure, J. N., & Reich, T. (1971). Premenstrual symptoms in self-referrals to a suicide prevention service. *British Journal of Psychiatry, 119,* 525–526.

Wheatman, S. R., & Shaffer, D. R. (2001). On finding for defendants who plead insanity: The crucial impact of dispositional instructions and opportunity to deliberate. *Law and Human Behavior, 25,* 167–183.

Wheeler, R. W., Davidson, R. J., & Tomarken, A. J. (1993). Frontal brain asymmetry and emotional reactivity: A biological substrate of affective style. *Psychophysiology, 30,* 82–89.

White, J. L., Moffitt, T. E., & Silva, P. A. (1989). A prospective replication of the protective effects of IQ in subjects at high risk for juvenile delinquency. *Journal of Consulting and Clinical Psychology, 57,* 719–724.

White, J. W., & Smith, P. H. (2004). Sexual assault perpetration and reperpetration: From adolescence to young adulthood. *Criminal Justice and Behavior, 31,* 182–202.

Whitcomb, D. (2001). Child victimization. In G. Coleman, M. Gaboury, M. Murray, & A. Seymour (Eds.), 1999 *National Victim Assistance Academy*. Washington, DC: U.S. Department of Justice.

Whitehill, M., DeMyer-Gapin, S., & Scott, T. G. (1976). Stimulation seeking in antisocial preadolescent children. *Journal of Abnormal Psychology, 85*, 101–104.

Wicker, T. (1976). *Time to die*. New York: Ballantine.

Widiger, T. A., Frances, A. J., Pincus, H. A., Davis, W. W., & First, M. B. (1991). Toward an empirical classification of the DSM-IV. *Journal of Abnormal Psychology, 100*, 280–288.

Widom, C. S. (1978). A methodology for studying non-institutionalized psychopaths. In R. D. Hare & D. Schalling (Eds.), *Psychopathic behavior: Approaches to research*. Chichester, UK: Wiley.

Widom, C. S. (2000, January). Childhood victimization: Early adversity, later psychopathology. *The National Institute of Justice Journal*, 3–9.

Widom, C. S., & Newman, J. P. (1985). Characteristics of noninstituionalized psychopaths. In J. Gunn & D. Farrington (Eds.), *Current research in forensic psychiatry and psychology* (Vol. 2). New York: Wiley.

Wiesen, A. E. (1965). *Differential reinforcing effects of onset and offset of stimulation on the operant behavior of normals, neurotics, and psychopaths* (Doctoral dissertation, University of Florida). University Microfilms No. 65–9625.

Wilczynski, A. (1991). Images of women who kill their infants: The mad and the bad. *Women & Criminal Justice, 2*, 71–88.

Wilczynski, A. (1997). Mad or bad? Child-killers, gender, and the courts. *British Journal of Criminology, 37*, 419–436.

Wilentz, W. C. (1953). The alcohol factor in violent deaths. American Practitioner: *Digest of Treatment, 4*, 21–24.

Williams, F. P., & McShane, M. D. (2004). *Criminological theory* (4th ed.). Upper Saddle River, NJ: Prentice Hall.

Williams, J. E., & Holmes, K. A. (1981). *The second assault: Rape and public attitudes*. Westport, CT: Greenwood Press.

Williams, K. (1984). Economic sources of homicides: Re-estimating the effects of poverty and inequality. *American Sociological Review, 49*, 283–289.

Williams, W., & Miller, K. S. (1981). The processing and disposition of incompetent mentally ill offenders. *Law and Human Behavior, 5*, 245–261.

Williamson, S., Hare, R. D., & Wong, S. (1987). Violence: Criminal psychopaths and their victims. *Canadian Journal of Behavioral Science, 19*, 454–462.

Wilson, D. J. (2000). *Drug use, testing, and treatment in jails*. Washington, DC: Bureau of Justice Statistics.

Wilson, J. Q., & Herrnstein, R. J. (1985). *Crime and human nature*. New York: Simon & Schuster.

Wincze, J. P. (1977). Sexual deviance and dysfunction. In D. Rimm & J. Somervill (Eds.), *Abnormal psychology*. New York: Academic Press.

Wolfe, D. A. (1985). Child-abusive parents: An empirical review and analysis. *Psychological Bulletin, 97*, 462–582.

Wolfe, D. A., Jaffe, P. G., Wilson, S. K., & Zak, L. (1985). Children of battered women: The relation of child behavior to family violence and maternal stress. *Journal of Consulting and Clinical Psychology, 53*, 657–665.

Wolfgang, M. E. (1958). *Patterns in criminal homicide*. Philadelphia: University of Pennsylvania Press.

Wolfgang, M. E. (1961). A sociological analysis of criminal homicide. *Federal Probation, 25*, 48–55.

Wolfgang, M. E. (1972). Cesare Lombroso (1835–1909). In H. Mannheim (Ed.), *Pioneers in criminality*. Montclair, NJ: Patterson Smith.

Wolfgang, M. E., & Ferracuti, F. (1967). *The subculture of violence*. London: Tavistock.

Wolford, M. R. (1972). Some attitudinal, psychological and sociological characteristics of incarcerated arsonists. *Fire and Arson Investigator, 16*, 8–13.

Wong, M., & Singer, K. (1973). Abnormal homicide in Hong Kong. *British Journal of Psychiatry, 123*, 37–46.

Wong, M. T. H., Lumsden, J., Fenton, G. W., & Fenwick, P. B. C. (1994). Epilepsy and violence in mentally abnormal offenders in a maximum security mental hospital. *Journal of Epilepsy, 7*, 253–258.

Wong, S. (2000). Psychopathic offenders. In S. Hodgins & R. Muller-Isberner (Eds.), *Violence, crime and mentally disordered offenders: Concepts and methods for effective treatment and prevention*. New York: Wiley.

Wood, J. J., Cowan, P. A., & Baker, B. L. (2002). Behavior problems and peer rejection in preschool boys and girls. *Journal of Genetic Psychology, 163*, 72–89.

Wood, W., Wong, F. Y., & Chachere, J. G. (1991). The effects of media violence on viewers' aggression in unconstrained social interaction. *Psychological Bulletin, 109*, 371–383.

Woodworth, M., & Porter, S. (2001). Historical foundations and current applications of criminal profiling in violent crime investigations. *Expert Evidence, 7*, 241–264.

Woodworth, M., & Porter, S. (2002). In cold blood: Characteristics of criminal homicides as a function of psychopathy. *Journal of Abnormal Psychology, 111*, 436–445.

Wright, R. (1980). Rape and physical violence. In D. J. West (Ed.), *Sex offenders in the criminal justice system*. Cambridge: Cambridge University Institute of Criminology.

Wright, R. T., & Decker, S. (1997). *Armed robbers in action: Stickup and street culture*. Boston, MA: Northeastern University Press.

Xie, H., Farmer, T. W., & Cairns, B. D. (2003). Different forms of aggression among inner-city African-American children: Gender, configurations, and school social networks. *Journal of School Psychology, 41*, 355–375.

Yates, E. (1986). The influence of psychosocial factors on nonsensical shoplifting. *International Journal of Offender Therapy and Comparative Criminology, 30*, 203–211.

Yegidis, B. L. (1986). Date rape and other forced sexual encounters among college students. *Journal of Sex Education and Therapy, 12*, 51–54.

Yeo, R. A., & Gangestad, S. W. (1993). Developmental origins of variation in human hand preference. *Genetica, 89*, 281–296.

Yeo, R. A., Gangestad, S. W., Thoma, R., Shaw, P., & Repa, K. (1997). Developmental instability and cerebral lateralization. *Neuropsychology, 11*, 552–561.

Yesavage, J. A., Benezech, M., Ceccaldi, P., Bourgeois, M., & Addad, M. (1983). Arson in mentally ill and criminal populations. *Journal of Clinical Psychiatry, 44*, 128–130.

Yochelson, S., & Samenow, S. E. (1976). *The criminal personality* (Vol. 1). New York: Jason Aronson.

Yoshimasu, S. (1961). The criminological significance of the family in the light of the studies of criminal twins. *Acta Criminologiae et Medicinae Legalis Japanica, 27*, 117–141.

Yoshimasu, S. (1965). Criminal life curves of monozygotic twin-pairs. *Acta Criminologiae et Medicinae Legalis Japanica, 31*, 9–20.

Zager, L. D. (1988). The MMPI-based criminal classification system. *Criminal Justice and Behavior, 15*, 39–57.

Zamble, E., & Porporino, F. G. (1988). *Coping, behavior, and adaptation in prison inmates*. New York: Springer-Verlag.

Zawitz, M. W., & Strom, K. J. (2000, October). *Firearm injury and death from crime, 1993–1997.* Washington, DC: U.S. Department of Justice.

Zebrowitz, L. A., Andreoletti, C., Collins, M. A., Lee, S. Y., & Blumenthal, J. (1998). Bright, bad, babyfaced boys: Appearance stereotypes do not always yield self-fulfilling prophecy effects. *Journal of Personality and Social Psychology, 75,* 1300–1320.

Zebrowitz, L. A., Collins, M. A., & Dutta, R. (1998). The relationship between appearance and personality across the lifespan. *Personality and Social Psychology Bulletin, 24,* 736–749.

Zeichner, A., & Pihl, R. O. (1979). Effects of alcohol and behavior contingencies on human aggression. *Journal of Abnormal Psychology, 88,* 152–160.

Zeichner, A., & Pihl, R. O. (1980). Effects of alcohol and instigator intent on human aggression. *Journal of Studies on Alcohol, 41,* 265–276.

Zigler, E. (1994). Reshaping early childhood interventions to be a more effective weapon against poverty. *American Journal of Community Psychology, 22,* 37–47.

Zillmann, D. (1971). Excitation transfer in communication-mediated aggressive behavior. *Journal of Experimental Social Psychology, 7,* 419–434.

Zillmann, D. (1979). Hostility and aggression. Hillsdale, NJ: Erlbaum.

Zillmann, D. (1983). Arousal and aggression. In R. G. Geen & E. I. Donnerstein (Eds.), *Aggression: Theoretical and empirical reviews* (Vol. 1). New York: Academic Press.

Zillmann, D. (1988). Cognitive-excitation interdependencies in aggressive behavior. *Aggressive Behavior, 14,* 51–64.

Zillmann, D., Baron, R., & Tamborini, R. (1981). Social costs of smoking: Effects of tobacco smoke on hostile behavior. *Journal of Applied Social Psychology, 11,* 548–561.

Zimbardo, P. G. (1970). The human choice. Individuation, reason, and order versus deindividuation, impulse, and chaos. In W. J. Arnold & D. Levine (Eds.), *Nebraska symposium on motivation 1969.* Lincoln: University of Nebraska Press.

Zimbardo, P. G. (1973). The psychological power and pathology of imprisonment. In E. Aronson & R. Helmreich (Eds.), *Social psychology.* New York: Van Nostrand.

Zoccoulillo, M. (1993). Gender and the development of conduct disorder. *Development and Psychopathology, 5,* 65–78.

Zolondek, S. C., Abel, G. G., Northey, W. F., Jr., & Jordan, A. D. (2001). The self-reported behaviors of juvenile sexual offenders. *Journal of Interpersonal Violence, 16,* 73–85.

Zorza, J. (1991). Woman battering: A major cause of homelessness. *Clearinghouse Review 25*(4).

INDEX